THE
ONE
YEAR™
BIBLE

NEW TESTAMENT

Arranged in 365 Daily Readings

New International Version

D0920734

Tyndale House Publishers, Inc.

WHEATON, ILLINOIS

First printing, March 1988

The One Year New Testament
New International Version

Copyright © 1988 by Tyndale
House Publishers, Inc., Wheaton,
Illinois. All rights reserved.

The One Year New Testament is a
trademark of Tyndale House
Publishers, Inc.

The Holy Bible, New International
Version
Copyright © 1973, 1978, 1984 by
International Bible Society.
Used by permission of
Zondervan Bible Publishers.

"Thoughts" adapted from *Life
Application Bible, New Testament*

Life Application Notes and Bible
Helps copyright © 1986 by Youth
for Christ/USA.

*The Life Application Bible, New
Testament* is a trademark of
Tyndale House Publishers, Inc.

Library of Congress Catalog Card
Number 87–051316
Printed in the United States of
America

ISBN 0–8423–2639–1 Cloth
ISBN 0–8423–2638–3 Kivar

CONTENTS

NOTE *(to be read!)*

The One Year New Testament has been prepared especially for regular Bible readers who wish to read through the entire New Testament in one year.

There are three readings for each day: (1) a passage from the Gospels, Acts, or Revelation; (2) a passage from the Epistles; and (3) a selection from Proverbs. *A Thought*—following each of the first two readings—provides fresh insight on applying that day's reading to daily life. This gives variety and freshness to your daily reading.

Instead of following a Bible reading chart and experiencing the delay of turning from place to place, you will find the text here in sequence, ready for your quiet reading and meditation.

Many Bible scholars have emphasized the importance of reading the Scriptures on a daily basis in order to experience anew the goodness and power of God's Word.

The Publishers

P.S. Although these daily readings begin January 1, you can as easily begin with today's date. Whenever you begin, you will finish the entire New Testament in one year. And it takes only ten minutes a day!

PREFACE

THIS New Testament of the *New International Version* of the Holy Bible is a completely new translation made by over a hundred scholars working directly from the best available Greek texts. It had its beginning in 1965 when, after several years of exploratory study by committees from the Christian Reformed Church and the National Association of Evangelicals, a group of scholars met at Palos Heights, Illinois, and concurred in the need for a new translation of the Bible in contemporary English. This group, though not made up of official church representatives, was transdenominational. Its conclusion was endorsed by a large number of leaders from many denominations who met in Chicago in 1966.

Responsibility for the new version was delegated by the Palos Heights group to a self-governing body of fifteen, the Committee on Bible Translation, composed for the most part of biblical scholars from colleges, universities and seminaries. In 1967 the New York Bible Society (now the International Bible Society) generously undertook the financial sponsorship of the project—a sponsorship that made it possible to enlist the help of many distinguished scholars. The fact that participants from the United States, Great Britain, Canada, Australia and New Zealand worked together gave the project its international scope. That they were from many denominations—including Anglican, Assemblies of God, Baptist, Brethren, Christian Reformed, Church of Christ, Evangelical Free, Lutheran, Mennonite, Methodist, Nazarene, Presbyterian, Wesleyan and other churches—helped to safeguard the translation from sectarian bias.

How it was made helps to give the New International Version its distinctiveness. The translation of each book was assigned to a team of scholars. Next, one of the Intermediate Editorial Committees revised the initial translation, with constant reference to the Hebrew, Aramaic or Greek. Their work then went to one of the General Editorial Committees, which checked it in detail and made another thorough revision. This revision in turn was carefully reviewed by the Committee on Bible Translation, which made further changes and then released the final version for publication. In this way the entire Bible underwent three revisions, during each of which the translation was examined for its faithfulness to the original languages and for its English style.

All this involved many thousands of hours of research and discussion regarding the meaning of the texts and the precise way of putting them into English. It may well be that no other translation has been made by a more thorough process of review and revision from committee to committee than this one.

From the beginning of the project, the Committee on Bible Translation held to certain goals for the New International Version: that it would be an accurate translation and one that would have clarity and literary quality and so prove suitable for public and private reading, teaching, preaching, memorizing and liturgical use. The Committee also sought to preserve some measure of continuity with the long tradition of translating the Scriptures into English.

In working toward these goals, the translators were united in their commitment to the authority and infallibility of the Bible as God's Word in written form. They believe that it contains the divine answer to the deepest needs of humanity, that it sheds unique light on our path in a dark world, and that it sets forth the way to our eternal well-being.

The first concern of the translators has been the accuracy of the translation and its fidelity to the thought of the biblical writers. They have striven for more than a word-for-word translation. Because thought patterns and syntax differ from language to language, faithful communication of the meaning of the writers of the Bible demands frequent modifications in sentence structure and constant regard for the contextual meanings of words.

The Committee on Bible Translation submitted the developing version to a number of stylistic consultants. Samples of the translation were tested for clarity and ease of reading by various kinds of people—young and old, highly educated and less well educated, ministers and laymen. Concern for clear and natural English motivated the translators and consultants. In view of the international use of English, the translators sought to avoid obvious Americanisms on the one hand and obvious Anglicisms on the other. A British edition reflects the comparatively few differences of significant idiom and of spelling.

As for the traditional pronouns "thou," "thee" and "thine" in reference to the Deity, the translators judged that to use these archaisms (along with the old verb forms such as "doest," "wouldest" and "hadst") would violate accuracy in translation. Greek does not use special pronouns for the persons of the Godhead. A present-day translation is not enhanced by forms that in the time of the King James Version were used in everyday speech, whether referring to God or man.

The Greek text used in translating the New Testament was an eclectic one. No other piece of ancient literature has such an abundance of manuscript witnesses as does the New Testament. Where existing manuscripts differ, the translators made their choice of readings according to accepted principles of New Testament textual criticism. Footnotes call attention to places where there was uncertainty about what the original text was. The best current printed texts of the Greek New Testament were used.

There is a sense in which the work of translation is never wholly finished. This applies to all great literature and uniquely so to the Bible. In 1973 the New Testament in the New International Version was published. Since then, suggestions for corrections and revisions have been received from various sources. The Committee on Bible Translation carefully considered the suggestions and adopted a number of them. These were incorporated in the first printing of the entire Bible in 1978. Additional revisions were made by the Committee on Bible Translation in 1983 and appear in printings after that date.

To achieve clarity the translators sometimes supplied words not in the original texts but required by the context. If there was uncertainty about such material, it is enclosed in brackets. Also for the sake of clarity or style, nouns, including some proper nouns, are sometimes substituted for pronouns, and vice versa.

In the New Testament, footnotes that refer to uncertainty regarding the original text are introduced by "Some manuscripts" or similar expressions.

It should be noted that minerals, flora and fauna, architectural details, articles of clothing and jewelry, musical instruments and other articles cannot always be identified with precision. Also measures of capacity in the biblical period are particularly uncertain.

Like all translations of the Bible, made as they are by imperfect man, this one undoubtedly falls short of its goals. Yet we are grateful to God for the extent to which he has enabled us to realize these goals and for the strength he has given us and our colleagues to complete our task. We offer this version of the Bible to him in whose name and for whose glory it has been made. We pray that it will lead many into a better understanding of the Holy Scriptures and a fuller knowledge of Jesus Christ the incarnate Word, of whom the Scriptures so faithfully testify.

The Committee on Bible Translation

June 1978
(Revised August 1983)

Names of the translators and editors may be secured
from the International Bible Society,
translation sponsors of the New International Version,
144 Tices Lane, East Brunswick, New Jersey 08816 U.S.A.

The Genealogy of Jesus/ Matthew 1:1-17

A record of the genealogy of Jesus Christ the son of David, the son of Abraham:

2Abraham was the father of Isaac,
  Isaac the father of Jacob,
  Jacob the father of Judah and his brothers,
    3Judah the father of Perez and Zerah, whose mother was Tamar,
  Perez the father of Hezron,
  Hezron the father of Ram,
    4Ram the father of Amminadab,
  Amminadab the father of Nahshon,
  Nahshon the father of Salmon,
    5Salmon the father of Boaz, whose mother was Rahab,
  Boaz the father of Obed, whose mother was Ruth,
  Obed the father of Jesse,
    6and Jesse the father of King David.

David was the father of Solomon, whose mother had been Uriah's wife,
    7Solomon the father of Rehoboam,
  Rehoboam the father of Abijah,
  Abijah the father of Asa,
    8Asa the father of Jehoshaphat,
  Jehoshaphat the father of Jehoram,
  Jehoram the father of Uzziah,
    9Uzziah the father of Jotham,
  Jotham the father of Ahaz,

Ahaz the father of Hezekiah,
10Hezekiah the father of Manasseh,
Manasseh the father of Amon,
Amon the father of Josiah,
11and Josiah the father of Jeconiah and his brothers at
the time of the exile to Babylon.

12After the exile to Babylon:
Jeconiah was the father of Shealtiel,
Shealtiel the father of Zerubbabel,
13Zerubbabel the father of Abiud,
Abiud the father of Eliakim,
Eliakim the father of Azor,
14Azor the father of Zadok,
Zadok the father of Akim,
Akim the father of Eliud,
15Eliud the father of Eleazar,
Eleazar the father of Matthan,
Matthan the father of Jacob,
16and Jacob the father of Joseph, the husband of Mary,
of whom was born Jesus, who is called Christ.

17Thus there were fourteen generations in all from Abraham to David, fourteen from David to the exile to Babylon, and fourteen from the exile to the Christ.

A THOUGHT: *In these first 17 verses we meet 46 people whose lives span 2,000 years. All were ancestors of Jesus, but they varied considerably in personality, spirituality, and experience. Some were heroes of faith—like Abraham, Isaac, Ruth, and David. Some had shady reputations—like Rahab and Tamar. Many were very ordinary—like Hezron, Ram, Nahshon, and Akim. And others were evil—like Manasseh and Abijah. God's work in history is not limited by human failures or sins, and he works through ordinary people. Just as God used all kinds of people to bring his Son into the world, he uses all kinds today to accomplish his will.*

The Good News about Jesus Christ/ Romans 1:1–7

Paul, a servant of Christ Jesus, called to be an apostle and set apart for the gospel of God— 2the gospel he promised beforehand through his prophets in the Holy Scriptures 3regarding his Son, who as to his human nature was a descendant of David, 4and who through the Spirit of holiness was declared with power to be the Son of God by his resurrection from the dead: Jesus Christ our Lord.

⁵Through him and for his name's sake, we received grace and apostleship to call people from among all the Gentiles to the obedience that comes from faith. ⁶And you also are among those who are called to belong to Jesus Christ.

⁷To all in Rome who are loved by God and called to be saints:

Grace and peace to you from God our Father and from the Lord Jesus Christ.

A THOUGHT: *Paul and the apostles received God's forgiveness as an undeserved privilege. But they also received the responsibility to share the message of God's forgiveness with others. God graciously forgives the sins of those who, by faith, believe in him as Lord. When we believe, we receive his forgiveness. In doing this, however, we are committing ourselves to live a new life. Paul's new life, a gift from God, also involved a call from God—a God-given responsibility—to witness to the world. God may or may not call you to be an overseas missionary, but he does call you (and all believers) to be a witness to Jesus Christ and his redemptive work.*

Proverbs for Today/ 1:1–6

The proverbs of Solomon son of David, king of Israel: for attaining wisdom and discipline; for understanding words of insight; for acquiring a disciplined and prudent life, doing what is right and just and fair; for giving prudence to the simple, knowledge and discretion to the young—let the wise listen and add to their learning, and let the discerning get guidance—for understanding proverbs and parables, the sayings and riddles of the wise.

JANUARY 2

Jesus Is Born in Bethlehem/ Matthew 1:18–25

This is how the birth of Jesus Christ came about: His mother Mary was pledged to be married to Joseph, but before they came together, she was found to be with child through the Holy Spirit. ¹⁹Because Joseph her husband was a righteous man and did not want to expose her to public disgrace, he had in mind to divorce her quietly.

²⁰But after he had considered this, an angel of the Lord

appeared to him in a dream and said, "Joseph son of David, do not be afraid to take Mary home as your wife, because what is conceived in her is from the Holy Spirit. 21She will give birth to a son, and you are to give him the name Jesus, because he will save his people from their sins."

22All this took place to fulfill what the Lord had said through the prophet: 23"The virgin will be with child and will give birth to a son, and they will call him Immanuel"—which means, "God with us."

24When Joseph woke up, he did what the angel of the Lord had commanded him and took Mary home as his wife. 25But he had no union with her until she gave birth to a son. And he gave him the name Jesus.

A THOUGHT: *Why is the Virgin Birth so important to the Christian faith? In order to be the perfect sacrifice for sin, Jesus Christ had to be free from the sinful nature passed on from Adam to all other human beings. Because he was born of a woman, he was a human being; but because he was the Son of God, he was born without any trace of human sin. He was both fully human and fully divine.*

Because Jesus lived as a man, we know that he fully understands our experiences and struggles. Because he is God, he has the power and authority to deliver us from sin. We can tell him all our thoughts, feelings, and needs. He has been where we are now, and he has the ability to help.

Paul's Desire to Visit Rome/ Romans 1:8–15

First, I thank my God through Jesus Christ for all of you, because your faith is being reported all over the world. 9God, whom I serve with my whole heart in preaching the gospel of his Son, is my witness how constantly I remember you 10in my prayers at all times; and I pray that now at last by God's will the way may be opened for me to come to you.

11I long to see you so that I may impart to you some spiritual gift to make you strong— 12that is, that you and I may be mutually encouraged by each other's faith. 13I do not want you to be unaware, brothers, that I planned many times to come to you (but have been prevented from doing so until now) in order that I might have a harvest among you, just as I have had among the other Gentiles.

14I am obligated both to Greeks and non-Greeks, both to the wise and the foolish. 15That is why I am so eager to preach the gospel also to you who are at Rome.

A THOUGHT: *When you pray continually about a concern, don't be surprised at how God answers. Paul prayed to visit Rome so he could teach the Christians there. When he finally arrived in Rome, it was as a prisoner. Paul prayed for a safe trip, and he did arrive safely—after being arrested, slapped in the face, shipwrecked, and, among other things, bitten by a poisonous snake. God's ways of answering our prayers are often far from what we expect. When you pray, expect God to answer—although sometimes in ways you do not expect.*

Proverbs for Today/ 1:7–9

The fear of the LORD is the beginning of knowledge, but fools despise wisdom and discipline. □ Listen, my son, to your father's instruction and do not forsake your mother's teaching. They will be a garland to grace your head and a chain to adorn your neck.

JANUARY 3

The Visit of the Magi/ Matthew 2:1–12

After Jesus was born in Bethlehem in Judea, during the time of King Herod, Magi from the east came to Jerusalem 2and asked, "Where is the one who has been born king of the Jews? We saw his star in the east and have come to worship him."

3When King Herod heard this he was disturbed, and all Jerusalem with him. 4When he had called together all the people's chief priests and teachers of the law, he asked them where the Christ was to be born. 5"In Bethlehem in Judea," they replied, "for this is what the prophet has written:

6" 'But you, Bethlehem, in the land of Judah,
    are by no means least among the rulers of Judah;
  for out of you will come a ruler
    who will be the shepherd of my people Israel.'"

7Then Herod called the Magi secretly and found out from them the exact time the star had appeared. 8He sent them to Bethlehem and said, "Go and make a careful search for the child. As soon as you find him, report to me, so that I too may go and worship him."

⁹After they had heard the king, they went on their way, and the star they had seen in the east went ahead of them until it stopped over the place where the child was. ¹⁰When they saw the star, they were overjoyed. ¹¹On coming to the house, they saw the child with his mother Mary, and they bowed down and worshiped him. Then they opened their treasures and presented him with gifts of gold and of incense and of myrrh. ¹²And having been warned in a dream not to go back to Herod, they returned to their country by another route.

A THOUGHT: *The Magi traveled thousands of miles to see the King of the Jews. When they finally found him, they responded with joy, worship, and gifts. The Magi worshiped Jesus for who he was. This is the essence of true worship—honoring Christ for who he is and being willing to give him what is valuable to you. How different from the approach people often take today. We expect God to come looking for us, to explain himself, prove who he is, and give us gifts. But those who are wise still seek and worship Jesus today, not for what they can get, but for who he is. Worship God because he is the perfect, just, and almighty Creator of the universe, worthy of the best you have to give.*

Paul Declares the Power of the Gospel/ Romans 1:16–17

I am not ashamed of the gospel, because it is the power of God for the salvation of everyone who believes: first for the Jew, then for the Gentile. ¹⁷For in the gospel a righteousness from God is revealed, a righteousness that is by faith from first to last, just as it is written: "The righteous will live by faith."

A THOUGHT: *Paul was not ashamed, because his message was Good News. It was powerful, it was for everyone, and it was part of God's revealed plan. When you are tempted to be ashamed, remember what the Good News is all about. If you focus on God and on what God is doing in the world rather than on your own inadequacy, your embarrassment will soon disappear.*

Proverbs for Today/ 1:10–19

My son, if sinners entice you, do not give in to them. If they say, "Come along with us; let's lie in wait for someone's blood, let's waylay some harmless soul; let's swallow them alive, like the grave, and whole, like those who go down to the pit; we will get all sorts of valuable things and fill our houses with plunder; throw in your lot with us, and we will share a common purse"—my son, do not go along with them, do not set foot on their paths; for their feet rush into sin, they are swift to shed blood. How useless to spread a net in full view of all the birds! These men lie in wait for their own blood; they waylay only themselves! Such is the end of all who go after ill-gotten gain; it takes away the lives of those who get it.

JANUARY 4

Mary and Joseph Flee to Egypt/ Matthew 2:13–23

When they [the Magi] had gone, an angel of the Lord appeared to Joseph in a dream. "Get up," he said, "take the child and his mother and escape to Egypt. Stay there until I tell you, for Herod is going to search for the child to kill him."

14So he got up, took the child and his mother during the night and left for Egypt, 15where he stayed until the death of Herod. And so was fulfilled what the Lord had said through the prophet: "Out of Egypt I called my son."

16When Herod realized that he had been outwitted by the Magi, he was furious, and he gave orders to kill all the boys in Bethlehem and its vicinity who were two years old and under, in accordance with the time he had learned from the Magi. 17Then what was said through the prophet Jeremiah was fulfilled:

18"A voice is heard in Ramah,
    weeping and great mourning,
Rachel weeping for her children
    and refusing to be comforted,
because they are no more."

19After Herod died, an angel of the Lord appeared in a dream to Joseph in Egypt 20and said, "Get up, take the child and his mother and go to the land of Israel, for those who were trying to take the child's life are dead."

²¹So he got up, took the child and his mother and went to the land of Israel. ²²But when he heard that Archelaus was reigning in Judea in place of his father Herod, he was afraid to go there. Having been warned in a dream, he withdrew to the district of Galilee, ²³and he went and lived in a town called Nazareth. So was fulfilled what was said through the prophets: "He will be called a Nazarene."

A THOUGHT: *Herod was afraid that this newborn king would one day take his throne. He completely misunderstood the reason for Christ's coming. Jesus didn't want Herod's throne, he wanted to be king of Herod's life. He wanted to give him eternal life, not take away his present life. Today people are often afraid that Christ wants to take things away when, in reality, he wants to give them real freedom, peace, and joy.*

God's Wrath and Man's Depravity/ Romans 1:18–32

The wrath of God is being revealed from heaven against all the godlessness and wickedness of men who suppress the truth by their wickedness, ¹⁹since what may be known about God is plain to them, because God has made it plain to them. ²⁰For since the creation of the world God's invisible qualities—his eternal power and divine nature—have been clearly seen, being understood from what has been made, so that men are without excuse.

²¹For although they knew God, they neither glorified him as God nor gave thanks to him, but their thinking became futile and their foolish hearts were darkened. ²²Although they claimed to be wise, they became fools ²³and exchanged the glory of the immortal God for images made to look like mortal man and birds and animals and reptiles.

²⁴Therefore God gave them over in the sinful desires of their hearts to sexual impurity for the degrading of their bodies with one another. ²⁵They exchanged the truth of God for a lie, and worshiped and served created things rather than the Creator—who is forever praised. Amen.

²⁶Because of this, God gave them over to shameful lusts. Even their women exchanged natural relations for unnatural ones. ²⁷In the same way the men also abandoned natural relations with women and were inflamed with lust for one another. Men committed indecent acts with other men, and received in themselves the due penalty for their perversion.

²⁸Furthermore, since they did not think it worthwhile to

retain the knowledge of God, he gave them over to a depraved mind, to do what ought not to be done. 29They have become filled with every kind of wickedness, evil, greed and depravity. They are full of envy, murder, strife, deceit and malice. They are gossips, 30slanderers, God-haters, insolent, arrogant and boastful; they invent ways of doing evil; they disobey their parents; 31they are sense-less, faithless, heartless, ruthless. 32Although they know God's righteous decree that those who do such things deserve death, they not only continue to do these very things but also approve of those who practice them.

A THOUGHT: *Paul clearly portrays the inevitable downward spiral into sin. First people reject God; next they make up their own ideas of what a god should be and do; then they fall into sin—sexual sin, greed, hatred, envy, murder, fighting, lying, bitterness, gossip. Finally they grow to hate God and encourage others to do so. God does not cause this steady progression toward evil. Rather, when people reject him, he allows them to live as they choose. Once caught in the downward spiral, no one can get out by oneself. Sinners must trust Christ alone to put them on the path of escape.*

Proverbs for Today/ 1:20–23

Wisdom calls aloud in the street, she raises her voice in the public squares; at the head of the noisy streets she cries out, in the gateways of the city she makes her speech: "How long will you simple ones love your simple ways? How long will mockers delight in mockery and fools hate knowledge? If you had responded to my rebuke, I would have poured out my heart to you and made my thoughts known to you."

JANUARY 5

John the Baptist Preaches Repentance/ Matthew 3:1–12

In those days John the Baptist came, preaching in the Desert of Judea 2and saying, "Repent, for the kingdom of heaven is near." 3This is he who was spoken of through the prophet Isaiah:

> "A voice of one calling in the desert,
> 'Prepare the way for the Lord,
> make straight paths for him.'"

4John's clothes were made of camel's hair, and he had a leather belt around his waist. His food was locusts and wild honey. 5People went out to him from Jerusalem and all Judea and the whole region of the Jordan. 6Confessing their sins, they were baptized by him in the Jordan River.

7But when he saw many of the Pharisees and Sadducees coming to where he was baptizing, he said to them: "You brood of vipers! Who warned you to flee from the coming wrath? 8Produce fruit in keeping with repentance. 9And do not think you can say to yourselves, 'We have Abraham as our father.' I tell you that out of these stones God can raise up children for Abraham. 10The ax is already at the root of the trees, and every tree that does not produce good fruit will be cut down and thrown into the fire.

11"I baptize you with water for repentance. But after me will come one who is more powerful than I, whose sandals I am not fit to carry. He will baptize you with the Holy Spirit and with fire. 12His winnowing fork is in his hand, and he will clear his threshing floor, gathering his wheat into the barn and burning up the chaff with unquenchable fire."

A THOUGHT: *John the Baptist suddenly bursts onto the scene here in Matthew's Gospel (an event chronologically about 30 years after the birth narratives in chapter two). His theme was "Repent, for the kingdom of heaven is near." He meant that we must do an about-face—a 180-degree turn—from the kind of self-centeredness that leads to wrong actions such as lying, cheating, stealing, gossiping, revenge, abuse, and sexual immorality. Instead, we must follow God's prescribed way of living found in his Word. The first step in turning to God is to admit your sin, as John urged. Then God will receive you and help you live the way he wants you to. Remember that only God can get rid of sin. He doesn't expect us to clean up our lives before we come to him.*

God's Judgment on Sin / Romans 2:1–16

You, therefore, have no excuse, you who pass judgment on someone else, for at whatever point you judge the other, you are condemning yourself, because you who pass judgment do the same things. 2Now we know that God's judgment against those who do such things is based on truth. 3So when you, a mere man, pass judgment on them and yet do the same things, do you think you will escape God's judgment? 4Or do you show contempt for the riches of his kindness, tolerance and patience, not realizing that God's kindness leads you toward repentance?

5But because of your stubbornness and your unrepentant heart, you are storing up wrath against yourself for the day of God's wrath, when his righteous judgment will be revealed. 6God "will give to each person according to what he has done." 7To those who by persistence in doing good seek glory, honor and immortality, he will give eternal life. 8But for those who are self-seeking and who reject the truth and follow evil, there will be wrath and anger. 9There will be trouble and distress for every human being who does evil: first for the Jew, then for the Gentile; 10but glory, honor and peace for everyone who does good: first for the Jew, then for the Gentile. 11For God does not show favoritism.

12All who sin apart from the law will also perish apart from the law, and all who sin under the law will be judged by the law. 13For it is not those who hear the law who are righteous in God's sight, but it is those who obey the law who will be declared righteous. 14(Indeed, when Gentiles, who do not have the law, do by nature things required by the law, they are a law for themselves, even though they do not have the law, 15since they show that the requirements of the law are written on their hearts, their consciences also bearing witness, and their thoughts now accusing, now even defending them.) 16This will take place on the day when God will judge men's secrets through Jesus Christ, as my gospel declares.

A THOUGHT: *Whenever we find ourselves feeling justifiably angry about some sin we have observed in our community, we should be careful. We need to speak out against sin, but we must do so in a spirit of humility. Often the sins we see most clearly in others are the ones that have taken root in us. If we look closely at ourselves, we may find that we are committing the same sin in more socially acceptable forms.*

Proverbs for Today/ 1:24–28

But since you rejected me when I [wisdom] called and no one gave heed when I stretched out my hand, since you ignored all my advice and would not accept my rebuke, I in turn will laugh at your disaster; I will mock when calamity overtakes you—when calamity overtakes you like a storm, when distress and trouble overwhelm you. "Then they will call to me but I will not answer; they will look for me but will not find me."

JANUARY 6

John Baptizes Jesus/ Matthew 3:13–17

Then Jesus came from Galilee to the Jordan to be baptized by John. 14But John tried to deter him, saying, "I need to be baptized by you, and do you come to me?"

15Jesus replied, "Let it be so now; it is proper for us to do this to fulfill all righteousness." Then John consented.

16As soon as Jesus was baptized, he went up out of the water. At that moment heaven was opened, and he saw the Spirit of God descending like a dove and lighting on him. 17And a voice from heaven said, "This is my Son, whom I love; with him I am well pleased."

A THOUGHT: *Put yourself in John's shoes. Your work is going well, people are taking notice, everything is growing. But you know that the purpose of your work is to prepare the hearts of the people for Jesus. Now Jesus has arrived, and with him, the real test of your integrity. Will you be able to turn your followers over to him? John passed the test by publicly baptizing Jesus. Soon he would say, "He must become greater; I must become less" (John 3:30). Can we, like John, put our egos and profitable work aside in order to point others to Jesus? Are we willing to lose some of our status so that others will benefit?*

Paul's Warning to Jews/ Romans 2:17–29

Now you, if you call yourself a Jew; if you rely on the law and brag about your relationship to God; 18if you know his will and approve of what is superior because you are instructed by the law; 19if you are convinced that you are a guide for the blind, a light for those who are in the dark, 20an instructor of the foolish, a teacher of infants, because you have in the law the embodiment of knowledge and truth— 21you, then, who teach others, do you not teach yourself? You who preach against stealing, do you steal?

22You who say that people should not commit adultery, do you commit adultery? You who abhor idols, do you rob temples? 23You who brag about the law, do you dishonor God by breaking the law? 24As it is written: "God's name is blasphemed among the Gentiles because of you."

25Circumcision has value if you observe the law, but if you break the law, you have become as though you had not been circumcised. 26If those who are not circumcised keep the law's requirements, will they not be regarded as though they were circumcised? 27The one who is not circumcised physically and yet obeys the law will condemn you who, even though you have the written code and circumcision, are a lawbreaker.

28A man is not a Jew if he is only one outwardly, nor is circumcision merely outward and physical. 29No, a man is a Jew if he is one inwardly; and circumcision is circumcision of the heart, by the Spirit, not by the written code. Such a man's praise is not from men, but from God.

A THOUGHT: *Paul explained to the Jews that they needed to judge themselves, not others, by their law. They knew the law so well that they had learned how to excuse their own actions while criticizing others. But the law is more than the "letter"—it is a guideline for living according to God's will, and it is also a reminder that we cannot live righteously without a relationship with God. As Jesus pointed out, even withholding what rightfully belongs to someone else is stealing, and looking on another person with lustful, adulterous intent is adultery. Before we accuse others, we must look at ourselves and see if that sin, in any form, exists within us.*

Proverbs for Today/ 1:29–33

"Since they hated knowledge and did not choose to fear the LORD, since they would not accept my advice and spurned my rebuke, they will eat the fruit of their ways and be filled with the fruit of their schemes. For the way-wardness of the simple will kill them, and the complacency of fools will destroy them; but whoever listens to me will live in safety and be at ease, without fear of harm."

JANUARY 7

The Temptation of Jesus/ Matthew 4:1–11

Then Jesus was led by the Spirit into the desert to be tempted by the devil. 2After fasting forty days and forty nights, he was hungry. 3The tempter came to him and said, "If you are the Son of God, tell these stones to become bread."

4Jesus answered, "It is written: 'Man does not live on bread alone, but on every word that comes from the mouth of God.'"

5Then the devil took him to the holy city and had him stand on the highest point of the temple. 6"If you are the Son of God," he said, "throw yourself down. For it is written:

> " 'He will command his angels concerning you,
>   and they will lift you up in their hands,
>   so that you will not strike your foot against a
>   stone.'"

7Jesus answered him, "It is also written: 'Do not put the Lord your God to the test.'"

8Again, the devil took him to a very high mountain and showed him all the kingdoms of the world and their splendor. 9"All this I will give you," he said, "if you will bow down and worship me."

10Jesus said to him, "Away from me, Satan! For it is written: 'Worship the Lord your God, and serve him only.'"

11Then the devil left him, and angels came and attended him.

A THOUGHT: *Satan's temptations focused on three areas: (1) physical desires, (2) possessions and power, and (3) pride. Jesus was tempted just like we are, but he never once gave in and sinned. He knows firsthand what we are experiencing, and he is willing and able to help us in our struggles. When tempted, turn to him for strength.*

God's Faithfulness to the Jews/ Romans 3:1–8

What advantage, then, is there in being a Jew, or what value is there in circumcision? 2Much in every way! First of all, they have been entrusted with the very words of God.

³What if some did not have faith? Will their lack of faith nullify God's faithfulness? ⁴Not at all! Let God be true, and every man a liar. As it is written:

> "So that you may be proved right when you speak
>   and prevail when you judge."

⁵But if our unrighteousness brings out God's righteousness more clearly, what shall we say? That God is unjust in bringing his wrath on us? (I am using a human argument.) ⁶Certainly not! If that were so, how could God judge the world? ⁷Someone might argue, "If my falsehood enhances God's truthfulness and so increases his glory, why am I still condemned as a sinner?" ⁸Why not say—as we are being slanderously reported as saying and as some claim that we say—"Let us do evil that good may result"? Their condemnation is deserved.

A THOUGHT: *What a depressing picture Paul painted! All of us—pagan Gentiles, pious Jews, humanitarians, and religious people—are condemned by our own actions. The law, which God gave to show the way to live, holds up our evil deeds to public view. Is there any hope for us? Yes, says Paul. The law condemns us, it is true, but the law is not the basis of our hope. God himself is our hope. He, in his righteousness and wonderful love, offers us eternal life. We receive our salvation not through law, but through faith in Jesus Christ. We do not—cannot—earn salvation, but we accept it as a gift from our loving heavenly Father.*

Proverbs for Today/ 2:1–5

My son, if you accept my words and store up my commands within you, turning your ear to wisdom and applying your heart to understanding, and if you call out for insight and cry aloud for understanding, and if you look for it as for silver and search for it as for hidden treasure, then you will understand the fear of the LORD and find the knowledge of God.

JANUARY 8

Jesus Preaches of the Kingdom/ Matthew 4:12–25

When Jesus heard that John had been put in prison, he returned to Galilee. 13Leaving Nazareth, he went and lived in Capernaum, which was by the lake in the area of Zebulun and Naphtali— 14to fulfill what was said through the prophet Isaiah:

15"Land of Zebulun and land of Naphtali,
the way to the sea, along the Jordan,
Galilee of the Gentiles—
16the people living in darkness
have seen a great light;
on those living in the land of the shadow of death
a light has dawned."

17From that time on Jesus began to preach, "Repent, for the kingdom of heaven is near."

18As Jesus was walking beside the Sea of Galilee, he saw two brothers, Simon called Peter and his brother Andrew. They were casting a net into the lake, for they were fishermen. 19"Come, follow me," Jesus said, "and I will make you fishers of men." 20At once they left their nets and followed him.

21Going on from there, he saw two other brothers, James son of Zebedee and his brother John. They were in a boat with their father Zebedee, preparing their nets. Jesus called them, 22and immediately they left the boat and their father and followed him.

23Jesus went throughout Galilee, teaching in their synagogues, preaching the good news of the kingdom, and healing every disease and sickness among the people. 24News about him spread all over Syria, and people brought to him all who were ill with various diseases, those suffering severe pain, the demon-possessed, those having seizures, and the paralyzed, and he healed them. 25Large crowds from Galilee, the Decapolis, Jerusalem, Judea and the region across the Jordan followed him.

A THOUGHT: *Jesus started his ministry with the very words people had heard John the Baptist say, "Repent, for the kingdom of heaven is near." The message is the same today as when Jesus and John gave it. Becoming a follower of Christ means turning away from our self-centeredness and turning our lives over to Christ's direction and control.*

No One is Righteous/ Romans 3:9–20

What shall we conclude then? Are we any better? Not at all! We have already made the charge that Jews and Gentiles alike are all under sin. ¹⁰As it is written:

"There is no one righteous, not even one;
¹¹ there is no one who understands,
   no one who seeks God.
¹²All have turned away,
   they have together become worthless;
 there is no one who does good,
   not even one."
¹³"Their throats are open graves;
   their tongues practice deceit."

"The poison of vipers is on their lips."
¹⁴ "Their mouths are full of cursing and bitterness."
¹⁵"Their feet are swift to shed blood;
¹⁶ ruin and misery mark their ways,
¹⁷and the way of peace they do not know."
¹⁸ "There is no fear of God before their eyes."

¹⁹Now we know that whatever the law says, it says to those who are under the law, so that every mouth may be silenced and the whole world held accountable to God. ²⁰Therefore no one will be declared righteous in his sight by observing the law; rather, through the law we become conscious of sin.

A THOUGHT: *Paul uses these Old Testament references to show that humanity in general, in its present sinful condition, is unacceptable before God. Have you ever thought to yourself, "Well, I'm not too bad. I'm a pretty good person"? Look at these verses and see if any of them apply to you. Have you ever lied? Have you ever hurt someone's feelings by your words or tone of voice? Are you bitter toward anyone? Do you become angry with those who strongly disagree with you? In thought, word, and deed, we all stand guilty before God apart from the redemption of Jesus Christ. We must remember that apart from Jesus Christ we are alienated sinners in God's sight. Don't deny that you are a sinner. Instead, allow that knowledge to point you toward Christ.*

Proverbs for Today/ 2:6–15

For the LORD gives wisdom, and from his mouth come knowledge and understanding. He holds victory in store for the upright, he is a shield to those whose walk is blameless, for he guards the course of the just and protects the way of his faithful ones. Then you will understand what is right and just and fair—every good path. For wisdom will enter your heart, and knowledge will be pleasant to your soul. Discretion will protect you, and understanding will guard you. Wisdom will save you from the ways of wicked men, from men whose words are perverse, who leave the straight paths to walk in dark ways, who delight in doing wrong and rejoice in the perverseness of evil, whose paths are crooked and who are devious in their ways.

JANUARY 9

The Sermon on the Mount—the Beatitudes/ Matthew 5:1–16

Now when he [Jesus] saw the crowds, he went up on a mountainside and sat down. His disciples came to him, 2and he began to teach them, saying:

3"Blessed are the poor in spirit,
   for theirs is the kingdom of heaven.
4Blessed are those who mourn,
   for they will be comforted.
5Blessed are the meek,
   for they will inherit the earth.
6Blessed are those who hunger and thirst for
         righteousness,
   for they will be filled.
7Blessed are the merciful,
   for they will be shown mercy.
8Blessed are the pure in heart,
   for they will see God.
9Blessed are the peacemakers,
   for they will be called sons of God.

¹⁰Blessed are those who are persecuted because of
righteousness,
for theirs is the kingdom of heaven.

¹¹"Blessed are you when people insult you, persecute
you and falsely say all kinds of evil against you because of
me. ¹²Rejoice and be glad, because great is your reward in
heaven, for in the same way they persecuted the prophets
who were before you.

¹³"You are the salt of the earth. But if the salt loses its
saltiness, how can it be made salty again? It is no longer
good for anything, except to be thrown out and trampled
by men.

¹⁴"You are the light of the world. A city on a hill cannot
be hidden. ¹⁵Neither do people light a lamp and put it under
a bowl. Instead they put it on its stand, and it gives light
to everyone in the house. ¹⁶In the same way, let your light
shine before men, that they may see your good deeds and
praise your Father in heaven."

A THOUGHT: *Matthew 5—7 is called the "Sermon on the Mount"
because Jesus gave it on a hillside near Capernaum. This "sermon"
probably covered several days of preaching. In it, Jesus proclaimed
his attitude toward the law. Position, authority, and money are not
important in his kingdom—what matters is faithful obedience from
the heart.*

*Jesus begins his sermon with a series of beatitudes which tell us
how to be blessed. This word doesn't mean laughter, pleasure, or
earthly prosperity. Jesus turns the world's idea of blessedness (or,
happiness) upside down. To Jesus, happiness means hope and joy,
independent of outward circumstances. To find true hope and joy,
get closer to God by serving and obeying him.*

Salvation through Faith/ Romans 3:21–31

But now a righteousness from God, apart from law, has
been made known, to which the Law and the Prophets
testify. ²²This righteousness from God comes through faith
in Jesus Christ to all who believe. There is no difference,
²³for all have sinned and fall short of the glory of God, ²⁴and
are justified freely by his grace through the redemption that
came by Christ Jesus. ²⁵God presented him as a sacrifice
of atonement, through faith in his blood. He did this to
demonstrate his justice, because in his forbearance he had
left the sins committed beforehand unpunished— ²⁶he did
it to demonstrate his justice at the present time, so as to

be just and the one who justifies those who have faith in Jesus.

27Where, then, is boasting? It is excluded. On what principle? On that of observing the law? No, but on that of faith. 28For we maintain that a man is justified by faith apart from observing the law. 29Is God the God of Jews only? Is he not the God of Gentiles too? Yes, of Gentiles too, 30since there is only one God, who will justify the circumcised by faith and the uncircumcised through that same faith. 31Do we, then, nullify the law by this faith? Not at all! Rather, we uphold the law.

A THOUGHT: *After all this bad news about our sinfulness and God's condemnation, Paul now gives the wonderful news. There is a way to be declared not guilty—by trusting Jesus Christ to take away our sins. Trusting means putting our confidence in him to forgive our sins, to make us right with God, and to empower us to live the way he wants us to live. This is God's solution, and it is available to all of us regardless of our background or past behavior.*

Proverbs for Today/ 2:16–22

It [wisdom] will save you also from the adulteress, from the wayward wife with her seductive words, who has left the partner of her youth and ignored the covenant she made before God. For her house leads down to death and her paths to the spirits of the dead. None who go to her return or attain the paths of life. Thus you will walk in the ways of good men and keep to the paths of the righteous. For the upright will live in the land, and the blameless will remain in it; but the wicked will be cut off from the land, and the unfaithful will be torn from it.

JANUARY 10

The Sermon on the Mount—Jesus Fulfills the Law/ Matthew 5:17–48

"Do not think that I have come to abolish the Law or the Prophets; I have not come to abolish them but to fulfill them. 18I tell you the truth, until heaven and earth disappear, not the smallest letter, not the least stroke of a pen, will by any means disappear from the Law until everything is accomplished. 19Anyone who breaks one of the least of these commandments and teaches others to do the same will be called least in the kingdom of heaven, but whoever practices and teaches these commands will be called great in the kingdom of heaven. 20For I tell you that unless your righteousness surpasses that of the Pharisees and the teachers of the law, you will certainly not enter the kingdom of heaven.

21"You have heard that it was said to the people long ago, 'Do not murder, and anyone who murders will be subject to judgment.' 22But I tell you that anyone who is angry with his brother will be subject to judgment. Again, anyone who says to his brother, 'Raca,' is answerable to the Sanhedrin. But anyone who says, 'You fool!' will be in danger of the fire of hell.

23"Therefore, if you are offering your gift at the altar and there remember that your brother has something against you, 24leave your gift there in front of the altar. First go and be reconciled to your brother; then come and offer your gift.

25"Settle matters quickly with your adversary who is taking you to court. Do it while you are still with him on the way, or he may hand you over to the judge, and the judge may hand you over to the officer, and you may be thrown into prison. 26I tell you the truth, you will not get out until you have paid the last penny.

27"You have heard that it was said, 'Do not commit adultery.' 28But I tell you that anyone who looks at a woman lustfully has already committed adultery with her in his heart. 29If your right eye causes you to sin, gouge it out and throw it away. It is better for you to lose one part of your body than for your whole body to be thrown into hell. 30And if your right hand causes you to sin, cut it off and throw it away. It is better for you to lose one part of your body than for your whole body to go into hell.

31"It has been said, 'Anyone who divorces his wife must give her a certificate of divorce.' 32But I tell you that anyone who divorces his wife, except for marital unfaithfulness, causes her to become an adulteress, and anyone who marries the divorced woman commits adultery.

33"Again, you have heard that it was said to the people

long ago, 'Do not break your oath, but keep the oaths you have made to the Lord.' 34But I tell you, Do not swear at all: either by heaven, for it is God's throne; 35or by the earth, for it is his footstool; or by Jerusalem, for it is the city of the Great King. 36And do not swear by your head, for you cannot make even one hair white or black. 37Simply let your 'Yes' be 'Yes,' and your 'No,' 'No'; anything beyond this comes from the evil one.

38"You have heard that it was said, 'Eye for eye, and tooth for tooth.' 39But I tell you, Do not resist an evil person. If someone strikes you on the right cheek, turn to him the other also. 40And if someone wants to sue you and take your tunic, let him have your cloak as well. 41If someone forces you to go one mile, go with him two miles. 42Give to the one who asks you, and do not turn away from the one who wants to borrow from you.

43"You have heard that it was said, 'Love your neighbor and hate your enemy.' 44But I tell you: Love your enemies and pray for those who persecute you, 45that you may be sons of your Father in heaven. He causes his sun to rise on the evil and the good, and sends rain on the righteous and the unrighteous. 46If you love those who love you, what reward will you get? Are not even the tax collectors doing that? 47And if you greet only your brothers, what are you doing more than others? Do not even pagans do that? 48Be perfect, therefore, as your heavenly Father is perfect."

A THOUGHT: *The Pharisees were exacting and scrupulous in their attempts to follow the Law. So how could Jesus reasonably call us to a greater righteousness than theirs? The Pharisees' weakness was that they were content to obey the Law outwardly without allowing it to change their hearts (or attitudes). Jesus was saying that his listeners needed a different kind of goodness altogether, not just a more intense version of the Pharisees' goodness. Our goodness must (1) come from what God does in us, not what we can do by ourselves, (2) be God-centered, not self-centered, (3) be based on reverence for God, not the approval of people, and (4) go beyond merely keeping the Law to a loving obedience of the principles behind the Law. We can look pious and still be far from the kingdom of God. God judges our hearts as well as our deeds, for it is in the heart where our real allegiance lies. Be just as concerned about your attitudes, which people don't see, as your actions, which are seen by all.*

Abraham Justified by Faith/ Romans 4:1–12

What then shall we say that Abraham, our forefather, discovered in this matter? 2If, in fact, Abraham was justified by works, he had something to boast about—but not before God. 3What does the Scripture say? "Abraham believed God, and it was credited to him as righteousness."

4Now when a man works, his wages are not credited to him as a gift, but as an obligation. 5However, to the man who does not work but trusts God who justifies the wicked, his faith is credited as righteousness. 6David says the same thing when he speaks of the blessedness of the man to whom God credits righteousness apart from works:

7"Blessed are they
whose transgressions are forgiven,
whose sins are covered.
8Blessed is the man
whose sin the Lord will never count against him."

9Is this blessedness only for the circumcised, or also for the uncircumcised? We have been saying that Abraham's faith was credited to him as righteousness. 10Under what circumstances was it credited? Was it after he was circumcised, or before? It was not after, but before! 11And he received the sign of circumcision, a seal of the righteousness that he had by faith while he was still uncircumcised. So then, he is the father of all who believe but have not been circumcised, in order that righteousness might be credited to them. 12And he is also the father of the circumcised who not only are circumcised but who also walk in the footsteps of the faith that our father Abraham had before he was circumcised.

A THOUGHT: *Some people, when they learn that we are saved through faith, start to worry. "Do I have enough faith?" they wonder, "Is my faith strong enough to save me?" These people miss the point. It is Jesus Christ who saves us, not our feelings or actions, and he is strong enough to save us no matter how weak our faith is. Jesus offers us salvation as a gift, because he loves us, not because we have earned it through our powerful faith. What, then, is the role of faith? Faith is believing and trusting in Jesus Christ, reaching out to accept his wonderful gift of salvation. Faith is effective whether it is great or small, timid or bold—because God loves us.*

Proverbs for Today/ 3:1–6

My son, do not forget my teaching, but keep my commands in your heart, for they will prolong your life many years and bring you prosperity. □ Let love and faithfulness never leave you; bind them around your neck, write them on the tablet of your heart. Then you will win favor and a good name in the sight of God and man. □ Trust in the Lord with all your heart and lean not on your own understanding; in all your ways acknowledge him, and he will make your paths straight.

JANUARY 11

The Sermon on the Mount—Religious Hypocrisy/ Matthew 6:1–18

"Be careful not to do your 'acts of righteousness' before men, to be seen by them. If you do, you will have no reward from your Father in heaven.

²"So when you give to the needy, do not announce it with trumpets, as the hypocrites do in the synagogues and on the streets, to be honored by men. I tell you the truth, they have received their reward in full. ³But when you give to the needy, do not let your left hand know what your right hand is doing, ⁴so that your giving may be in secret. Then your Father, who sees what is done in secret, will reward you.

⁵"And when you pray, do not be like the hypocrites, for they love to pray standing in the synagogues and on the street corners to be seen by men. I tell you the truth, they have received their reward in full. ⁶But when you pray, go into your room, close the door and pray to your Father, who is unseen. Then your Father, who sees what is done in secret, will reward you. ⁷And when you pray, do not keep on babbling like pagans, for they think they will be heard because of their many words. ⁸Do not be like them, for your Father knows what you need before you ask him.

⁹"This, then, is how you should pray:

" 'Our Father in heaven,
hallowed be your name,

10your kingdom come,
  your will be done
    on earth as it is in heaven.
11Give us today our daily bread.
12Forgive us our debts,
  as we also have forgiven our debtors.
13And lead us not into temptation,
  but deliver us from the evil one.'

14For if you forgive men when they sin against you, your heavenly Father will also forgive you. 15But if you do not forgive men their sins, your Father will not forgive your sins.

16"When you fast, do not look somber as the hypocrites do, for they disfigure their faces to show men they are fasting. I tell you the truth, they have received their reward in full. 17But when you fast, put oil on your head and wash your face, 18so that it will not be obvious to men that you are fasting, but only to your Father, who is unseen; and your Father, who sees what is done in secret, will reward you."

A THOUGHT: *It's easy to do right for recognition and praise. To insure that our motives are not selfish, we should do our good deeds quietly or in secret, with no thought of reward. Jesus says we should check our motives in three areas: generosity, prayer, and fasting. Those acts should not be self-centered, but God-centered. The reward God promises is not material, and it is never given to those who seek only the reward. Doing something only for ourselves is not a loving sacrifice. With your next good deed, ask, "Would I still do this if no one would ever know I did it?"*

Salvation the Free Gift of God/ Romans 4:13–17

It was not through law that Abraham and his offspring received the promise that he would be heir of the world, but through the righteousness that comes by faith. 14For if those who live by law are heirs, faith has no value and the promise is worthless, 15because law brings wrath. And where there is no law there is no transgression.

16Therefore, the promise comes by faith, so that it may be by grace and may be guaranteed to all Abraham's offspring—not only to those who are of the law but also to those who are of the faith of Abraham. He is the father of us all. 17As it is written: "I have made you a father of many nations." He is our father in the sight of God, in whom he believed—the God who gives life to the dead and calls things that are not as though they were.

A THOUGHT: *Paul explains that Abraham was blessed through his faith alone, before he ever heard about the rituals that would become so important to the Jewish people. We too are saved by faith alone. It is not by loving God and doing good that we are saved; neither is it by faith plus love or faith plus good works. Salvation is not a gift that we in any way coerce God into giving us—it is the free gift of his grace. We are saved only through faith in Christ, trusting him to forgive all our sins.*

Proverbs for Today/ 3:7–8

Do not be wise in your own eyes; fear the LORD and shun evil. This will bring health to your body and nourishment to your bones.

JANUARY 12

The Sermon on the Mount—Treasures in Heaven/ Matthew 6:19–34

"Do not store up for yourselves treasures on earth, where moth and rust destroy, and where thieves break in and steal. 20But store up for yourselves treasures in heaven, where moth and rust do not destroy, and where thieves do not break in and steal. 21For where your treasure is, there your heart will be also.

22"The eye is the lamp of the body. If your eyes are good, your whole body will be full of light. 23But if your eyes are bad, your whole body will be full of darkness. If then the light within you is darkness, how great is that darkness!

24"No one can serve two masters. Either he will hate the one and love the other, or he will be devoted to the one and despise the other. You cannot serve both God and Money.

25"Therefore I tell you, do not worry about your life, what you will eat or drink; or about your body, what you will wear. Is not life more important than food, and the body more important than clothes? 26Look at the birds of the air;

they do not sow or reap or store away in barns, and yet your heavenly Father feeds them. Are you not much more valuable than they? 27Who of you by worrying can add a single hour to his life?

28"And why do you worry about clothes? See how the lilies of the field grow. They do not labor or spin. 29Yet I tell you that not even Solomon in all his splendor was dressed like one of these. 30If that is how God clothes the grass of the field, which is here today and tomorrow is thrown into the fire, will he not much more clothe you, O you of little faith? 31So do not worry, saying, 'What shall we eat?' or 'What shall we drink?' or 'What shall we wear?' 32For the pagans run after all these things, and your heavenly Father knows that you need them. 33But seek first his kingdom and his righteousness, and all these things will be given to you as well. 34Therefore do not worry about tomorrow, for tomorrow will worry about itself. Each day has enough trouble of its own."

A THOUGHT: *Jesus says we can have only one master. We live in a materialistic society where many people serve money. People spend their whole lives collecting and storing it, only to die and leave it behind. Their desire for money and what it can buy far outweighs their commitment to God and spiritual matters. Whatever you store up, you will spend all your time and energy thinking about. Don't fall into the materialistic trap, because "the love of money is a root of all kinds of evil" (1 Timothy 6:10). Can you honestly say that God is your Master, and not money? One test is to ask which one occupies more of your thoughts, time, and effort.*

Abraham Believed God's Promise/ Romans 4:18–25

Against all hope, Abraham in hope believed and so became the father of many nations, just as it had been said to him, "So shall your offspring be." 19Without weakening in his faith, he faced the fact that his body was as good as dead—since he was about a hundred years old—and that Sarah's womb was also dead. 20Yet he did not waver through unbelief regarding the promise of God, but was strengthened in his faith and gave glory to God, 21being fully persuaded that God had power to do what he had promised. 22This is why "it was credited to him as righteousness." 23The words "it was credited to him" were written not for him alone, 24but also for us, to whom God will credit righteousness—for us who believe in him who raised Jesus our Lord from the dead. 25He was delivered over to death for our sins and was raised to life for our justification.

A THOUGHT: *Abraham never doubted that God would fulfill his promise. His life was marked by mistakes, sins, and failures as well as by wisdom and goodness, but he consistently trusted God. His life is an example of faith in action. If he had looked only at his own resources for subduing Canaan and founding a nation, he would have given up in despair. But he looked to God, obeyed him, and waited for God to fulfill his word to him. Abraham died without having seen descendants which were as numerous as the sands of the sea, and yet Abraham died believing in God's promise to him. This is genuine faith—a sincere trust in God in spite of all the circumstances.*

Proverbs for Today/ 3:9–10

Honor the LORD with your wealth, with the firstfruits of all your crops; then your barns will be filled to overflowing, and your vats will brim over with new wine.

JANUARY 13

The Sermon on the Mount—Judging Others/ Matthew 7:1–6

"Do not judge, or you too will be judged. 2For in the same way you judge others, you will be judged, and with the measure you use, it will be measured to you.

3"Why do you look at the speck of sawdust in your brother's eye and pay no attention to the plank in your own eye? 4How can you say to your brother, 'Let me take the speck out of your eye,' when all the time there is a plank in your own eye? 5You hypocrite, first take the plank out of your own eye, and then you will see clearly to remove the speck from your brother's eye.

6"Do not give dogs what is sacred; do not throw your pearls to pigs. If you do, they may trample them under their feet, and then turn and tear you to pieces."

A THOUGHT: *Jesus tells us to examine our own lives instead of criticizing others. The traits that bother us in others are often the habits we dislike in ourselves. Our unbroken bad habits and behavior patterns are the very ones we most want to change in others. Do you find it easy to magnify others' faults while ignoring your own? If you are ready to criticize someone, check to see if you deserve the same criticism. Judge yourself first, and then lovingly forgive and help your neighbor.*

Bearing Trials with Peace and Joy/ Romans 5:1–5

Therefore, since we have been justified through faith, we have peace with God through our Lord Jesus Christ, 2through whom we have gained access by faith into this grace in which we now stand. And we rejoice in the hope of the glory of God. 3Not only so, but we also rejoice in our sufferings, because we know that suffering produces perseverance; 4perseverance, character; and character, hope. 5And hope does not disappoint us, because God has poured out his love into our hearts by the Holy Spirit, whom he has given us.

A THOUGHT: *There are two sides to our Christian life this side of heaven. On the one hand, we are complete in Christ (our acceptance with him is secure); on the other hand, we are growing in Christ (we are becoming more and more like him). At the same time we have the status of kings and the duties of slaves. We feel both the presence of Christ and the pressure of sin. We enjoy the peace that comes from being made right with God, but we still face daily problems that help us grow. If we remember these two sides of the Christian life, we will not grow discouraged as we face temptations and problems. Instead, we will learn to depend on the power available to us from Christ, through the Holy Spirit who lives in us.*

Proverbs for Today/ 3:11–12

My son, do not despise the LORD's discipline and do not resent his rebuke, because the LORD disciplines those he loves, as a father the son he delights in.

JANUARY 14

The Sermon on the Mount—Ask, Seek, Knock/ Matthew 7:7–12

"Ask and it will be given to you; seek and you will find; knock and the door will be opened to you. 8For everyone who asks receives; he who seeks finds; and to him who knocks, the door will be opened.

9"Which of you, if his son asks for bread, will give him a stone? 10Or if he asks for a fish, will give him a snake? 11If you, then, though you are evil, know how to give good gifts to your children, how much more will your Father in heaven give good gifts to those who ask him! 12So in everything, do to others what you would have them do to you, for this sums up the Law and the Prophets."

A THOUGHT: *Jesus tells us to persist in pursuing God. People often give up after a few halfhearted efforts and conclude that God cannot be found. But knowing God takes effort, and Jesus assures us that our efforts will be rewarded. Don't give up in your efforts to seek God. Continue to ask him for more knowledge, patience, wisdom, love, and understanding. He will give them to you.*

God's Mercy toward Sinners/ Romans 5:6–11

You see, at just the right time, when we were still power-less, Christ died for the ungodly. 7Very rarely will anyone die for a righteous man, though for a good man someone might possibly dare to die. 8But God demonstrates his own love for us in this: While we were still sinners, Christ died for us.

9Since we have now been justified by his blood, how much more shall we be saved from God's wrath through him! 10For if, when we were God's enemies, we were reconciled to him through the death of his Son, how much more, having been reconciled, shall we be saved through his life! 11Not only is this so, but we also rejoice in God through our Lord Jesus Christ, through whom we have now received reconciliation.

A THOUGHT: *How does Christ's death make us friends with God? God is holy, and he will not be associated with sin. All people are sinful, and all sin deserves punishment. Instead of punishing us with the death we deserve, however, Christ took our sins upon himself and paid the price for them with his own death—while we were still sinners. Now the way to friendship with God has been opened. Through faith in Christ's work, we become his friends rather than enemies and outcasts.*

Proverbs for Today/ 3:13–15

Blessed is the man who finds wisdom, the man who gains understanding, for she is more profitable than silver and yields better returns than gold. She is more precious than rubies; nothing you desire can compare with her.

The Sermon on the Mount—
The Narrow and Wide Gates/ Matthew 7:13–29

"Enter through the narrow gate. For wide is the gate and broad is the road that leads to destruction, and many enter through it. 14But small is the gate and narrow the road that leads to life, and only a few find it.

15"Watch out for false prophets. They come to you in sheep's clothing, but inwardly they are ferocious wolves. 16By their fruit you will recognize them. Do people pick grapes from thornbushes, or figs from thistles? 17Likewise every good tree bears good fruit, but a bad tree bears bad fruit. 18A good tree cannot bear bad fruit, and a bad tree cannot bear good fruit. 19Every tree that does not bear good fruit is cut down and thrown into the fire. 20Thus, by their fruit you will recognize them.

21"Not everyone who says to me, 'Lord, Lord,' will enter the kingdom of heaven, but only he who does the will of my Father who is in heaven. 22Many will say to me on that day, 'Lord, Lord, did we not prophesy in your name, and in your name drive out demons and perform many miracles?' 23Then I will tell them plainly, 'I never knew you. Away from me, you evildoers!'

24"Therefore everyone who hears these words of mine and puts them into practice is like a wise man who built his house on the rock. 25The rain came down, the streams rose, and the winds blew and beat against that house; yet it did not fall, because it had its foundation on the rock. 26But everyone who hears these words of mine and does not put them into practice is like a foolish man who built his house on sand. 27The rain came down, the streams rose, and the winds blew and beat against that house, and it fell with a great crash."

28When Jesus had finished saying these things, the crowds were amazed at his teaching, 29because he taught as one who had authority, and not as their teachers of the law.

A THOUGHT: *The gateway to heaven is indeed a narrow one. This means there are many ways to live your life, but only one way to live*

eternally with God. Believing in Jesus is the only way to eternal life,
because he alone died for our sins and made us right before God.
At the Day of Judgment, only our relationship with Christ—our
acceptance of him as Savior and our obedience to him—will matter.
Many people think that if they are "good" and sound religious, they
will be rewarded with eternal life. In reality, faith in Christ is what
will count at the Judgment.

Death through Adam, Life through Christ/
Romans 5:12–21

Therefore, just as sin entered the world through one man,
and death through sin, and in this way death came to all
men, because all sinned— 13for before the law was given,
sin was in the world. But sin is not taken into account when
there is no law. 14Nevertheless, death reigned from the
time of Adam to the time of Moses, even over those who
did not sin by breaking a command, as did Adam, who was
a pattern of the one to come.

15But the gift is not like the trespass. For if the many died
by the trespass of the one man, how much more did God's
grace and the gift that came by the grace of the one man,
Jesus Christ, overflow to the many! 16Again, the gift of God
is not like the result of the one man's sin: The judgment
followed one sin and brought condemnation, but the gift
followed many trespasses and brought justification. 17For
if, by the trespass of the one man, death reigned through
that one man, how much more will those who receive God's
abundant provision of grace and of the gift of righteousness
reign in life through the one man, Jesus Christ.

18Consequently, just as the result of one trespass was
condemnation for all men, so also the result of one act of
righteousness was justification that brings life for all men.
19For just as through the disobedience of the one man the
many were made sinners, so also through the obedience of
the one man the many will be made righteous.

20The law was added so that the trespass might increase.
But where sin increased, grace increased all the more, 21so
that, just as sin reigned in death, so also grace might reign
through righteousness to bring eternal life through Jesus
Christ our Lord.

A THOUGHT: *Paul has abundantly shown that keeping the law does not*
bring salvation. Now he adds that death is the result of Adam's sin
and of the sins we all commit, even if they don't resemble Adam's.
For thousands of years, Paul reminds his readers, the law had not

yet been explicitly given, and yet people died. The law was added to help people see their sinfulness, to show them the seriousness of their offenses, and to drive them to God for mercy and pardon. This was true in Moses' day, and it is still true today. Sin is a profound disparity between who we are and who we were created to be. The law points out our sin and places the responsibility for it squarely on our shoulders, but the law offers no remedy for it. When we're convicted of sin, we must turn to Jesus Christ for deliverance from sin.

Proverbs for Today/ 3:16–18

Long life is in her [wisdom's] right hand; in her left hand are riches and honor. Her ways are pleasant ways, and all her paths are peace. She is a tree of life to those who embrace her; those who lay hold of her will be blessed.

JANUARY 16

Miracles of Healing/ Matthew 8:1–17

When he [Jesus] came down from the mountainside, large crowds followed him. 2A man with leprosy came and knelt before him and said, "Lord, if you are willing, you can make me clean."

3Jesus reached out his hand and touched the man. "I am willing," he said. "Be clean!" Immediately he was cured of his leprosy. 4Then Jesus said to him, "See that you don't tell anyone. But go, show yourself to the priest and offer the gift Moses commanded, as a testimony to them."

5When Jesus had entered Capernaum, a centurion came to him, asking for help. 6"Lord," he said, "my servant lies at home paralyzed and in terrible suffering."

7Jesus said to him, "I will go and heal him."

8The centurion replied, "Lord, I do not deserve to have you come under my roof. But just say the word, and my servant will be healed. 9For I myself am a man under authority, with soldiers under me. I tell this one, 'Go,' and he goes; and that one, 'Come,' and he comes. I say to my servant, 'Do this,' and he does it."

10When Jesus heard this, he was astonished and said to those following him, "I tell you the truth, I have not found anyone in Israel with such great faith. [11]I say to you that many will come from the east and the west, and will take their places at the feast with Abraham, Isaac and Jacob in the kingdom of heaven. [12]But the subjects of the kingdom will be thrown outside, into the darkness, where there will be weeping and gnashing of teeth."

[13]Then Jesus said to the centurion, "Go! It will be done just as you believed it would." And his servant was healed at that very hour.

[14]When Jesus came into Peter's house, he saw Peter's mother-in-law lying in bed with a fever. [15]He touched her hand and the fever left her, and she got up and began to wait on him.

[16]When evening came, many who were demon-possessed were brought to him, and he drove out the spirits with a word and healed all the sick. [17]This was to fulfill what was spoken through the prophet Isaiah:

> "He took up our infirmities
>   and carried our diseases."

A THOUGHT: *Leprosy was a feared disease because there was no known cure. In Jesus' day, the word "leprosy" was used for a variety of similar diseases, and some forms were contagious. If a person contracted the contagious type, a priest declared him a leper and banished him from his home and city. He was sent to live in a community with other lepers until he either got better or died. Yet when the leper begged Jesus to heal him, Jesus reached out and touched him, even though his skin was covered with the dread disease.*

Through a single touch, Jesus heals; when he speaks a single word, demons flee his presence. Jesus has authority over all evil powers and all earthly disease. He also has power and authority to conquer sin. Sickness and evil are consequences of living in a fallen world. But in the future, when God cleanses the earth from sin, there will be no more sickness and death. Jesus' healing miracles were a taste of what will one day be common experience in the kingdom of God.

Dead to Sin, Alive in Christ/ Romans 6:1–14

What shall we say, then? Shall we go on sinning so that grace may increase? [2]By no means! We died to sin; how can we live in it any longer? [3]Or don't you know that all of us who were baptized into Christ Jesus were baptized into his death? [4]We were therefore buried with him through baptism into death in order that, just as Christ was raised from the dead through the glory of the Father, we too may live a new life.

⁵If we have been united with him like this in his death, we will certainly also be united with him in his resurrection. ⁶For we know that our old self was crucified with him so that the body of sin might be done away with, that we should no longer be slaves to sin— ⁷because anyone who has died has been freed from sin.

⁸Now if we died with Christ, we believe that we will also live with him. ⁹For we know that since Christ was raised from the dead, he cannot die again; death no longer has mastery over him. ¹⁰The death he died, he died to sin once for all; but the life he lives, he lives to God.

¹¹In the same way, count yourselves dead to sin but alive to God in Christ Jesus. ¹²Therefore do not let sin reign in your mortal body so that you obey its evil desires. ¹³Do not offer the parts of your body to sin, as instruments of wickedness, but rather offer yourselves to God, as those who have been brought from death to life; and offer the parts of your body to him as instruments of righteousness. ¹⁴For sin shall not be your master, because you are not under law, but under grace.

A THOUGHT: *The penalty of sin and its power over our lives died with Christ on the cross. Paul has already stated that through faith in Christ we stand acquitted, "not guilty" before God. Here Paul emphasizes that we need no longer live under sin's power. God does not take us out of the world or make us robots—we will still feel like sinning, and sometimes we will sin. The difference is that before we were saved, we were slaves to our sinful nature, but now we can choose to live for Christ.*

Proverbs for Today/ 3:19–20

By wisdom the LORD laid the earth's foundations, by understanding he set the heavens in place; by his knowledge the deeps were divided, and the clouds let drop the dew.

JANUARY 17

The Cost of Following Jesus/ Matthew 8:18–22

When Jesus saw the crowd around him, he gave orders to cross to the other side of the lake. 19Then a teacher of the law came to him and said, "Teacher, I will follow you wherever you go."

20Jesus replied, "Foxes have holes and birds of the air have nests, but the Son of Man has no place to lay his head."

21Another disciple said to him, "Lord, first let me go and bury my father."

22But Jesus told him, "Follow me, and let the dead bury their own dead."

A THOUGHT: *Following Jesus is not always an easy or comfortable road. It means great cost and sacrifice, without necessarily receiving earthly rewards or having security. Jesus didn't have a place to call home. You may find that following Christ costs you popularity, friendships, leisure time, or treasured habits. But while the costs of following Christ may be high, the value of being Christ's disciple is an investment which lasts for eternity.*

Slaves to Righteousness/ Romans 6:15–23

What then? Shall we sin because we are not under law but under grace? By no means! 16Don't you know that when you offer yourselves to someone to obey him as slaves, you are slaves to the one whom you obey—whether you are slaves to sin, which leads to death, or to obedience, which leads to righteousness? 17But thanks be to God that, though you used to be slaves to sin, you wholeheartedly obeyed the form of teaching to which you were entrusted. 18You have been set free from sin and have become slaves to righteousness.

19I put this in human terms because you are weak in your natural selves. Just as you used to offer the parts of your body in slavery to impurity and to ever-increasing wickedness, so now offer them in slavery to righteousness leading to holiness. 20When you were slaves to sin, you were free from the control of righteousness. 21What benefit did you reap at that time from the things you are now ashamed of? Those things result in death! 22But now that you have been set free from sin and have become slaves to God, the benefit you reap leads to holiness, and the result is eternal life. 23For the wages of sin is death, but the gift of God is eternal life in Christ Jesus our Lord.

A THOUGHT: *In certain skilled crafts, an apprentice trains under a "master," who shapes and molds his apprentice in the finer points of his craft. As spiritual people, we choose a master and pattern ourselves after him. Without Jesus, we would have no choice—we would have to apprentice ourselves to sin, and the results would be guilt, suffering, and separation from God. Thanks to Jesus, however, we can now choose God as our master. Following him, we can enjoy new life and learn the ways of the kingdom. We are either following Christ or we are following sin—it is impossible to be neutral. A Christian is not someone who cannot sin or who never sins, but someone who is no longer a slave to sin. He belongs to God, not to sin. Have you apprenticed yourself to God?*

Proverbs for Today/ 3:21–26

My son, preserve sound judgment and discernment, do not let them out of your sight; they will be life for you, an ornament to grace your neck. Then you will go on your way in safety, and your foot will not stumble; when you lie down, you will not be afraid; when you lie down, your sleep will be sweet. Have no fear of sudden disaster or of the ruin that overtakes the wicked, for the LORD will be your confidence and will keep your foot from being snared.

JANUARY 18

Jesus' Power over Nature and Demons/ Matthew 8:23–34

Then he [Jesus] got into the boat and his disciples followed him. 24Without warning, a furious storm came up on the lake, so that the waves swept over the boat. But Jesus was sleeping. 25The disciples went and woke him, saying, "Lord, save us! We're going to drown!"

26He replied, "You of little faith, why are you so afraid?" Then he got up and rebuked the winds and the waves, and it was completely calm.

²⁷The men were amazed and asked, "What kind of man is this? Even the winds and the waves obey him!"

²⁸When he arrived at the other side in the region of the Gadarenes, two demon-possessed men coming from the tombs met him. They were so violent that no one could pass that way. ²⁹"What do you want with us, Son of God?" they shouted. "Have you come here to torture us before the appointed time?"

³⁰Some distance from them a large herd of pigs was feeding. ³¹The demons begged Jesus, "If you drive us out, send us into the herd of pigs."

³²He said to them, "Go!" So they came out and went into the pigs, and the whole herd rushed down the steep bank into the lake and died in the water. ³³Those tending the pigs ran off, went into the town and reported all this, including what had happened to the demon-possessed men. ³⁴Then the whole town went out to meet Jesus. And when they saw him, they pleaded with him to leave their region.

A THOUGHT: *Although the disciples had witnessed many miracles, they panicked in this storm. As experienced sailors, they knew the danger of storms; what they did not know was that Christ could control the forces of nature. The expectations of the disciples had blinded them. They did not realize that Jesus was more than a mere earthly conqueror—he was God in human flesh. Jesus demonstrates his power as Creator by calming this storm. With a word, God brought order to the universe, bringing it into being, and with a word, Jesus brings order to the chaos of this storm. There is nothing beyond his power. Let us worship Jesus as Creator and let us trust him as the sovereign King over all the affairs in the universe, including the situations in our life. We do not need to exclude him from any area of our lives.*

An Illustration from Marriage/ Romans 7:1–6

Do you not know, brothers—for I am speaking to men who know the law—that the law has authority over a man only as long as he lives? ²For example, by law a married woman is bound to her husband as long as he is alive, but if her husband dies, she is released from the law of marriage. ³So then, if she marries another man while her husband is still alive, she is called an adulteress. But if her husband dies, she is released from that law and is not an adulteress, even though she marries another man.

⁴So, my brothers, you also died to the law through the body of Christ, that you might belong to another, to him

who was raised from the dead, in order that we might bear fruit to God. 5For when we were controlled by the sinful nature, the sinful passions aroused by the law were at work in our bodies, so that we bore fruit for death. 6But now, by dying to what once bound us, we have been released from the law so that we serve in the new way of the Spirit, and not in the old way of the written code.

A THOUGHT: *Paul uses marriage to illustrate our relationship to the law. When a spouse dies, the law of marriage no longer applies. Because we have died with Christ, the law can no longer condemn us. The law gave us no power to live a righteous life, but the Spirit enables us to produce good fruit for God. As new people living new lives in the power of the Spirit, we are bound to Christ and will serve him with our hearts and minds.*

Proverbs for Today/ 3:27–32

Do not withhold good from those who deserve it, when it is in your power to act. Do not say to your neighbor, "Come back later; I'll give it tomorrow"—when you now have it with you. □ Do not plot harm against your neighbor, who lives trustfully near you. Do not accuse a man for no reason—when he has done you no harm. □ Do not envy a violent man or choose any of his ways, for the LORD detests a perverse man but takes the upright into his confidence.

JANUARY 19

Jesus Heals a Paralytic/ Matthew 9:1–8

Jesus stepped into a boat, crossed over and came to his own town. 2Some men brought to him a paralytic, lying on a mat. When Jesus saw their faith, he said to the paralytic, "Take heart, son; your sins are forgiven."

3At this, some of the teachers of the law said to themselves, "This fellow is blaspheming!"

4Knowing their thoughts, Jesus said, "Why do you entertain evil thoughts in your hearts? 5Which is easier: to say, 'Your sins are forgiven,' or to say, 'Get up and walk'? 6But so that you may know that the Son of Man has authority on earth to forgive sins. . . . " Then he said to the paralytic,

"Get up, take your mat and go home." [7]And the man got up and went home. [8]When the crowd saw this, they were filled with awe; and they praised God, who had given such authority to men.

A THOUGHT: *The first words Jesus said to the paralyzed man were, "your sins are forgiven." Then he healed the man. We must be careful not to concentrate on God's power to heal physical sickness more than on his power to forgive spiritual sickness in the form of sin. Jesus saw that in addition to needing physical health, this man needed spiritual health. Spiritual health comes only from Jesus' healing touch.*

God's Law Reveals Sin/ Romans 7:7–13

What shall we say, then? Is the law sin? Certainly not! Indeed I would not have known what sin was except through the law. For I would not have known what coveting really was if the law had not said, "Do not covet." [8]But sin, seizing the opportunity afforded by the commandment, produced in me every kind of covetous desire. For apart from law, sin is dead. [9]Once I was alive apart from law; but when the commandment came, sin sprang to life and I died. [10]I found that the very commandment that was intended to bring life actually brought death. [11]For sin, seizing the opportunity afforded by the commandment, deceived me, and through the commandment put me to death. [12]So then, the law is holy, and the commandment is holy, righteous and good.

[13]Did that which is good, then, become death to me? By no means! But in order that sin might be recognized as sin, it produced death in me through what was good, so that through the commandment sin might become utterly sinful.

A THOUGHT: *Paul gives three lessons he learned in trying to deal with his old sinful desires. (1) Knowledge is not the answer. Paul felt fine as long as he did not understand what the law demanded. When he learned the truth, he knew he was doomed. (2) Self-determination doesn't succeed. Paul found himself sinning in ways that weren't even attractive to him. (3) Even a profound Christian experience does not instantly stamp out all sin from the believer's life. Becoming like Christ is a lifelong process; Paul likens Christian growth to a strenuous race or fight (1 Corinthians 9; 2 Timothy 2). Thus, as Paul has been emphasizing since the beginning of his letter to the Romans, no one in the world is innocent; no one deserves to be saved—not the pagan who doesn't know God's laws, not the Christian or Jew who knows them and tries to keep them. All of us must depend totally on the work of Christ for our salvation. We cannot earn it by our good behavior.*

Proverbs for Today/ 3:33–35

The LORD's curse is on the house of the wicked, but he blesses the home of the righteous. He mocks proud mockers but gives grace to the humble. The wise inherit honor, but fools he holds up to shame.

JANUARY 20

Jesus Calls Matthew/ Matthew 9:9–13

As Jesus went on from there, he saw a man named Matthew sitting at the tax collector's booth. "Follow me," he told him, and Matthew got up and followed him.

10While Jesus was having dinner at Matthew's house, many tax collectors and "sinners" came and ate with him and his disciples. 11When the Pharisees saw this, they asked his disciples, "Why does your teacher eat with tax collectors and 'sinners'?"

12On hearing this, Jesus said, "It is not the healthy who need a doctor, but the sick. 13But go and learn what this means: 'I desire mercy, not sacrifice.' For I have not come to call the righteous, but sinners."

A THOUGHT: *When Jesus called Matthew to be one of his disciples, Matthew jumped up and followed, leaving a lucrative career. When God calls you to follow or obey him, do you do it with as much abandon as Matthew did? Sometimes the decision to follow Christ requires some difficult or painful choices. Like Matthew, we must decide to leave behind those things that would keep us from following Christ.*

The Struggle with Sin/ Romans 7:14–25

We know that the law is spiritual; but I am unspiritual, sold as a slave to sin. 15I do not understand what I do. For what I want to do I do not do, but what I hate I do. 16And if I do what I do not want to do, I agree that the law is good. 17As it is, it is no longer I myself who do it, but it is sin living in me. 18I know that nothing good lives in me, that is, in my sinful nature. For I have the desire to do what is good, but I cannot carry it out. ¹⁹For what I do is not the good I want to do; no, the evil I do not want to do—this I keep on doing. ²⁰Now if I do what I do not want to do, it is no longer I who do it, but it is sin living in me that does it.

²¹So I find this law at work: When I want to do good, evil is right there with me. ²²For in my inner being I delight in God's law; ²³but I see another law at work in the members of my body, waging war against the law of my mind and making me a prisoner of the law of sin at work within my members. ²⁴What a wretched man I am! Who will rescue me from this body of death? ²⁵Thanks be to God—through Jesus Christ our Lord!

So then, I myself in my mind am a slave to God's law, but in the sinful nature a slave to the law of sin.

A THOUGHT: *We sometimes feel that the inward confusion about sin was as real for Paul as it is for us. From Paul we learn what to do about it. Whenever he felt lost, he would return to the beginning of his spiritual life, remembering that he had already been freed by Jesus Christ. When you feel confused, follow his example: thank God he has given you freedom through Jesus Christ. Let the reality of Christ's power lift you up to real victory over sin.*

Proverbs for Today/ 4:1–6

Listen, my sons, to a father's instruction; pay attention and gain understanding. I give you sound learning, so do not forsake my teaching. When I was a boy in my father's house, still tender, and an only child of my mother, he taught me and said, "Lay hold of my words with all your heart; keep my commands and you will live. Get wisdom, get understanding; do not forget my words or swerve from them. Do not forsake wisdom, and she will protect you; love her, and she will watch over you."

The Bridegroom and His Friends/ Matthew 9:14–17

Then John's disciples came and asked him, "How is it that we and the Pharisees fast, but your disciples do not fast?"

15Jesus answered, "How can the guests of the bridegroom mourn while he is with them? The time will come when the bridegroom will be taken from them; then they will fast.

16"No one sews a patch of unshrunk cloth on an old garment, for the patch will pull away from the garment, making the tear worse. 17Neither do men pour new wine into old wineskins. If they do, the skins will burst, the wine will run out and the wineskins will be ruined. No, they pour new wine into new wineskins, and both are preserved."

A THOUGHT: *Jesus did not come to "patch up" the old religious system of Judaism with its rules and traditions. His purpose was to bring in something new, yet something that had been prophesied for centuries. This new message, the gospel, said that Jesus Christ, God's Son, came to earth to offer all people forgiveness of sins and restoration with God. This new message of faith and love did not fit in the old rigid legalistic system of religion. It needed a fresh start. The message will always remain "new" because it must be accepted and applied in every generation. When we follow Christ, we must be prepared for new ways to live, new ways to look at people, and new ways to serve.*

No Condemnation in Christ/ Romans 8:1–8

Therefore, there is now no condemnation for those who are in Christ Jesus, 2because through Christ Jesus the law of the Spirit of life set me free from the law of sin and death. 3For what the law was powerless to do in that it was weakened by the sinful nature, God did by sending his own Son in the likeness of sinful man to be a sin offering. And so he condemned sin in sinful man, 4in order that the righteous requirements of the law might be fully met in us, who do not live according to the sinful nature but according to the Spirit.

5Those who live according to the sinful nature have their minds set on what that nature desires; but those who live in accordance with the Spirit have their minds set on what the Spirit desires. 6The mind of sinful man is death, but the mind controlled by the Spirit is life and peace; [7]the sinful mind is hostile to God. It does not submit to God's law, nor can it do so. [8]Those controlled by the sinful nature cannot please God.

A THOUGHT: *"Not guilty; let him go free"—what would those words mean to you if you were on death row? The fact is, of course, that the whole human race is on death row, justly condemned for repeatedly breaking God's holy law. Without Jesus we would have no hope at all. But thank God! He has declared us not guilty and has offered us freedom from sin and power to do his will.*

Proverbs for Today/ 4:7–10

Wisdom is supreme; therefore get wisdom. Though it cost all you have, get understanding. Esteem her, and she will exalt you; embrace her, and she will honor you. She will set a garland of grace on your head and present you with a crown of splendor." □ Listen, my son, accept what I say, and the years of your life will be many.

JANUARY 22

Jesus Performs Miracles of Healing/ Matthew 9:18–26

While he [Jesus] was saying this, a ruler came and knelt before him and said, "My daughter has just died. But come and put your hand on her, and she will live." [19]Jesus got up and went with him, and so did his disciples.

[20]Just then a woman who had been subject to bleeding for twelve years came up behind him and touched the edge of his cloak. [21]She said to herself, "If I only touch his cloak, I will be healed."

[22]Jesus turned and saw her. "Take heart, daughter," he said, "your faith has healed you." And the woman was healed from that moment.

[23]When Jesus entered the ruler's house and saw the flute players and the noisy crowd, [24]he said, "Go away. The girl is not dead but asleep." But they laughed at him. [25]After

the crowd had been put outside, he went in and took the girl by the hand, and she got up. 26News of this spread through all that region.

A THOUGHT: *Like lepers and those who were demon-possessed, this woman was considered unclean. For twelve years, she too had been one of the "untouchables" and had not been able to live a normal life. But Jesus changed that and restored her. Sometimes we are tempted to give up on people or situations which have not changed for many years. God can change what seems unchangeable, giving new life and hope.*

Life Through the Spirit/ Romans 8:9–17

You, however, are controlled not by the sinful nature but by the Spirit, if the Spirit of God lives in you. And if anyone does not have the Spirit of Christ, he does not belong to Christ. 10But if Christ is in you, your body is dead because of sin, yet your spirit is alive because of righteousness. 11And if the Spirit of him who raised Jesus from the dead is living in you, he who raised Christ from the dead will also give life to your mortal bodies through his Spirit, who lives in you.

12Therefore, brothers, we have an obligation—but it is not to the sinful nature, to live according to it. 13For if you live according to the sinful nature, you will die; but if by the Spirit you put to death the misdeeds of the body, you will live, 14because those who are led by the Spirit of God are sons of God. 15For you did not receive a spirit that makes you a slave again to fear, but you received the Spirit of sonship. And by him we cry, *"Abba,* Father." 16The Spirit himself testifies with our spirit that we are God's children. 17Now if we are children, then we are heirs—heirs of God and co-heirs with Christ, if indeed we share in his sufferings in order that we may also share in his glory.

A THOUGHT: *Paul uses adoption to illustrate the believers' new relationship with God. In Roman culture, the adopted person gained all the rights of a legitimate child in his new family. He became a full heir to his new father's estate. Likewise, when a person becomes a Christian, he or she gains all the privileges and responsibilities of a child in God's family. We are the Master's children; we are no longer cringing and fearful slaves. What a privilege! Because we are God's children, we share in great treasures. God has given great gifts: his Son, forgiveness, the Holy Spirit, and eternal life.*

Proverbs for Today/ 4:11–13

I guide you in the way of wisdom and lead you along straight paths. When you walk, your steps will not be hampered; when you run, you will not stumble. Hold on to instruction, do not let it go; guard it well, for it is your life.

JANUARY 23

Jesus Heals the Blind and Casts Out Demons/ Matthew 9:27–38

As Jesus went on from there, two blind men followed him, calling out, "Have mercy on us, Son of David!"

28When he had gone indoors, the blind men came to him, and he asked them, "Do you believe that I am able to do this?"

"Yes, Lord," they replied.

29Then he touched their eyes and said, "According to your faith will it be done to you"; 30and their sight was restored. Jesus warned them sternly, "See that no one knows about this." 31But they went out and spread the news about him all over that region.

32While they were going out, a man who was demon-possessed and could not talk was brought to Jesus. 33And when the demon was driven out, the man who had been mute spoke. The crowd was amazed and said, "Nothing like this has ever been seen in Israel."

34But the Pharisees said, "It is by the prince of demons that he drives out demons."

35Jesus went through all the towns and villages, teaching in their synagogues, preaching the good news of the kingdom and healing every disease and sickness. 36When he saw the crowds, he had compassion on them, because they were harassed and helpless, like sheep without a shepherd. 37Then he said to his disciples, "The harvest is plentiful but the workers are few. 38Ask the Lord of the harvest, therefore, to send out workers into his harvest field."

A THOUGHT: *Jesus didn't respond immediately to the pleas of the blind men. He waited to see how earnest they were. Not everyone who says he wants help really wants it badly enough to do something about it. Jesus may have waited and questioned these men to make their desire and faith stronger. If, in your prayers, it seems as if God is too slow in giving his answer, maybe he is testing you as he did the blind men. Do you believe God can help you? Do you really want his help?*

Our Future Glory/ Romans 8:18–27

I consider that our present sufferings are not worth comparing with the glory that will be revealed in us. [19]The creation waits in eager expectation for the sons of God to be revealed. [20]For the creation was subjected to frustration, not by its own choice, but by the will of the one who subjected it, in hope [21]that the creation itself will be liberated from its bondage to decay and brought into the glorious freedom of the children of God.

[22]We know that the whole creation has been groaning as in the pains of childbirth right up to the present time. [23]Not only so, but we ourselves, who have the firstfruits of the Spirit, groan inwardly as we wait eagerly for our adoption as sons, the redemption of our bodies. [24]For in this hope we were saved. But hope that is seen is no hope at all. Who hopes for what he already has? [25]But if we hope for what we do not yet have, we wait for it patiently.

[26]In the same way, the Spirit helps us in our weakness. We do not know what we ought to pray for, but the Spirit himself intercedes for us with groans that words cannot express. [27]And he who searches our hearts knows the mind of the Spirit, because the Spirit intercedes for the saints in accordance with God's will.

A THOUGHT: *Believers are not left to their own resources to cope with problems. Even when you don't have words to pray, the Holy Spirit prays with and for you, and God answers. With God helping you pray, you don't need to be afraid to come before him. Ask the Holy Spirit to plead for you "in harmony with God's own will." Then, when you bring your requests to God, trust that he will always do what is best.*

Proverbs for Today/ 4:14–19

Do not set foot on the path of the wicked or walk in the way of evil men. Avoid it, do not travel on it; turn from it and go on your way. For they cannot sleep till they do evil; they are robbed of slumber till they make someone fall. They eat the bread of wickedness and drink the wine of violence. □ The path of the righteous is like the first gleam of dawn, shining ever brighter till the full light of day. But the way of the wicked is like deep darkness; they do not know what makes them stumble.

JANUARY 24

Jesus Commissions the Twelve/ Matthew 10:1–18

He [Jesus] called his twelve disciples to him and gave them authority to drive out evil spirits and to heal every disease and sickness.

2These are the names of the twelve apostles: first, Simon (who is called Peter) and his brother Andrew; James son of Zebedee, and his brother John; 3Philip and Bartholomew; Thomas and Matthew the tax collector; James son of Alphaeus, and Thaddaeus; 4Simon the Zealot and Judas Iscariot, who betrayed him.

5These twelve Jesus sent out with the following instructions: "Do not go among the Gentiles or enter any town of the Samaritans. 6Go rather to the lost sheep of Israel. 7As you go, preach this message: 'The kingdom of heaven is near.' 8Heal the sick, raise the dead, cleanse those who have leprosy, drive out demons. Freely you have received, freely give. 9Do not take along any gold or silver or copper in your belts; 10take no bag for the journey, or extra tunic, or sandals or a staff; for the worker is worth his keep.

11"Whatever town or village you enter, search for some worthy person there and stay at his house until you leave. 12As you enter the home, give it your greeting. 13If the home is deserving, let your peace rest on it; if it is not, let your peace return to you. 14If anyone will not welcome you or listen to your words, shake the dust off your feet when you leave that home or town. 15I tell you the truth, it will be more bearable for Sodom and Gomorrah on the day of judgment than for that town. 16I am sending you out like sheep among wolves. Therefore be as shrewd as snakes and as innocent as doves.

17"Be on your guard against men; they will hand you over to the local councils and flog you in their synagogues. 18On my account you will be brought before governors and kings as witnesses to them and to the Gentiles."

A THOUGHT: *The list of Jesus' 12 disciples doesn't give us many details about them—probably because there weren't many impressive details to tell. Jesus called people from all walks of life—fishermen, political activists, tax collectors. He called common people and leaders; rich and poor; educated and uneducated. God can use anyone no matter how insignificant he or she feels. He uses ordinary people to do his extraordinary work.*

More Than Conquerors through Christ/ Romans 8:28–39

And we know that in all things God works for the good of those who love him, who have been called according to his purpose. 29For those God foreknew he also predestined to be conformed to the likeness of his Son, that he might be the firstborn among many brothers. 30And those he predestined, he also called; those he called, he also justified; those he justified, he also glorified.

31What, then, shall we say in response to this? If God is for us, who can be against us? 32He who did not spare his own Son, but gave him up for us all—how will he not also, along with him, graciously give us all things? 33Who will bring any charge against those whom God has chosen? It is God who justifies. 34Who is he that condemns? Christ Jesus, who died—more than that, who was raised to life—is at the right hand of God and is also interceding for us. 35Who shall separate us from the love of Christ? Shall trouble or hardship or persecution or famine or nakedness or danger or sword? 36As it is written:

> "For your sake we face death all day long;
> we are considered as sheep to be slaughtered."

37No, in all these things we are more than conquerors through him who loved us. 38For I am convinced that neither death nor life, neither angels nor demons, neither the present nor the future, nor any powers, 39neither height nor depth, nor anything else in all creation, will be able to separate us from the love of God that is in Christ Jesus our Lord.

A THOUGHT: *These verses contain one of the most comforting promises in all of Scripture. Believers have always had to face hardships in many forms: persecution, illness, imprisonment, even death. These*

*might cause them to fear that they have been abandoned by Christ.
But Paul exclaims that it is impossible to be separated from Christ.
His death for us is proof of his unconquerable love. He is constantly
present with us. God tells us how great his love is so that we will feel
totally secure in him. If we believe these overwhelming assurances,
we will not be afraid.*

Proverbs for Today/ 4:20—27

My son, pay attention to what I say; listen closely to my
words. Do not let them out of your sight, keep them within
your heart; for they are life to those who find them and
health to a man's whole body. Above all else, guard your
heart, for it is the wellspring of life. Put away perversity
from your mouth; keep corrupt talk far from your lips. Let
your eyes look straight ahead, fix your gaze directly before
you. Make level paths for your feet and take only ways that
are firm. Do not swerve to the right or the left; keep your
foot from evil.

JANUARY 25

Bearing the Cross of Jesus/ Matthew 10:19—11:1

"But when they arrest you [the disciples], do not worry
about what to say or how to say it. At that time you will
be given what to say, 20for it will not be you speaking, but
the Spirit of your Father speaking through you.

21"Brother will betray brother to death, and a father his
child; children will rebel against their parents and have
them put to death. 22All men will hate you because of me,
but he who stands firm to the end will be saved. 23When
you are persecuted in one place, flee to another. I tell you
the truth, you will not finish going through the cities of
Israel before the Son of Man comes.

24"A student is not above his teacher, nor a servant
above his master. 25It is enough for the student to be like
his teacher, and the servant like his master. If the head of
the house has been called Beelzebub, how much more the
members of his household!

26"So do not be afraid of them. There is nothing concealed that will not be disclosed, or hidden that will not be made known. 27What I tell you in the dark, speak in the daylight; what is whispered in your ear, proclaim from the roofs. 28Do not be afraid of those who kill the body but cannot kill the soul. Rather, be afraid of the One who can destroy both soul and body in hell. 29Are not two sparrows sold for a penny? Yet not one of them will fall to the ground apart from the will of your Father. 30And even the very hairs of your head are all numbered. 31So don't be afraid; you are worth more than many sparrows.

32"Whoever acknowledges me before men, I will also acknowledge him before my Father in heaven. 33But whoever disowns me before men, I will disown him before my Father in heaven.

34"Do not suppose that I have come to bring peace to the earth. I did not come to bring peace, but a sword. 35For I have come to turn

> " 'a man against his father,
>   a daughter against her mother,
>   a daughter-in-law against her mother-in-law—
> 36   a man's enemies will be the members of his own
>   household.'

37"Anyone who loves his father or mother more than me is not worthy of me; anyone who loves his son or daughter more than me is not worthy of me; 38and anyone who does not take his cross and follow me is not worthy of me. 39Whoever finds his life will lose it, and whoever loses his life for my sake will find it.

40"He who receives you receives me, and he who receives me receives the one who sent me. 41Anyone who receives a prophet because he is a prophet will receive a prophet's reward, and anyone who receives a righteous man because he is a righteous man will receive a righteous man's reward. 42And if anyone gives even a cup of cold water to one of these little ones because he is my disciple, I tell you the truth, he will certainly not lose his reward."

11:1After Jesus had finished instructing his twelve disciples, he went on from there to teach and preach in the towns of Galilee.

A THOUGHT: *Christian commitment may separate friends and loved ones. In saying this, Jesus was not encouraging disobedience to parents or conflict at home. Rather, he was showing that his presence demands a decision. Since some will follow him and some won't, inevitable conflict will arise. As we "take up our cross and follow him," our different values, morals, goals, and purposes inevitably will set us apart from others.*

We should be totally committed to God and willing to face anything, even suffering and death, for his sake. Clinging to this life may cause us to forfeit the best from Christ in this world and in the next. The more we love this life's rewards, the more we discover how empty they really are. The best way to enjoy life, therefore, is to loosen our greedy grasp on earthly rewards to be free to follow Christ. In doing so, we will inherit eternal life. Don't neglect your family and other earthly responsibilities, but don't neglect your higher calling either. God should be your first priority.

Paul's Longing for the Salvation of the Jews/ Romans 9:1–5

I speak the truth in Christ—I am not lying, my conscience confirms it in the Holy Spirit— ²I have great sorrow and unceasing anguish in my heart. ³For I could wish that I myself were cursed and cut off from Christ for the sake of my brothers, those of my own race, ⁴the people of Israel. Theirs is the adoption as sons; theirs the divine glory, the covenants, the receiving of the law, the temple worship and the promises. ⁵Theirs are the patriarchs, and from them is traced the human ancestry of Christ, who is God over all, forever praised! Amen.

A THOUGHT: *God's covenant promises were made to Abraham, and Paul wanted his people, Abraham's children, to repent and receive those promises. God's covenant people, the true children of Abraham, are not just his biological descendants—the Jews. They are all those who trust in God and in what Jesus Christ has done for them.*

Paul expressed concern for his people Israel by saying he would willingly take their punishment if that could save them. While the only one who can save us is Christ, Paul showed a rare depth of love. Like Jesus, he was willing to sacrifice for others. How concerned are you for those who don't know Christ? Are you willing to sacrifice your time, money, energy, comfort, and safety to see them come to faith in Jesus?

Proverbs for Today/ 5:1–6

My son, pay attention to my wisdom, listen well to my words of insight, that you may maintain discretion and your lips may preserve knowledge. For the lips of an adulteress drip honey, and her speech is smoother than oil; but in the end she is bitter as gall, sharp as a double-edged sword.

Her feet go down to death; her steps lead straight to the grave. She gives no thought to the way of life; her paths are crooked, but she knows it not.

JANUARY 26

Jesus and John the Baptist/ Matthew 11:2–19

When John heard in prison what Christ was doing, he sent his disciples ³to ask him, "Are you the one who was to come, or should we expect someone else?"

⁴Jesus replied, "Go back and report to John what you hear and see: ⁵The blind receive sight, the lame walk, those who have leprosy are cured, the deaf hear, the dead are raised, and the good news is preached to the poor. ⁶Blessed is the man who does not fall away on account of me."

⁷As John's disciples were leaving, Jesus began to speak to the crowd about John: "What did you go out into the desert to see? A reed swayed by the wind? ⁸If not, what did you go out to see? A man dressed in fine clothes? No, those who wear fine clothes are in kings' palaces. ⁹Then what did you go out to see? A prophet? Yes, I tell you, and more than a prophet. ¹⁰This is the one about whom it is written:

" 'I will send my messenger ahead of you,
who will prepare your way before you.'

¹¹I tell you the truth: Among those born of women there has not risen anyone greater than John the Baptist; yet he who is least in the kingdom of heaven is greater than he. ¹²From the days of John the Baptist until now, the kingdom of heaven has been forcefully advancing, and forceful men lay hold of it. ¹³For all the Prophets and the Law prophesied until John. ¹⁴And if you are willing to accept it, he is the

Elijah who was to come. [15]He who has ears, let him hear.

[16]"To what can I compare this generation? They are like children sitting in the marketplaces and calling out to others:

[17]" 'We played the flute for you,
    and you did not dance;
we sang a dirge,
    and you did not mourn.'

[18]For John came neither eating nor drinking, and they say, 'He has a demon.' [19]The Son of Man came eating and drinking, and they say, 'Here is a glutton and a drunkard, a friend of tax collectors and "sinners." ' But wisdom is proved right by her actions."

A THOUGHT: *As John sat in prison, he began to experience some doubts about whether Jesus really was the Messiah. If John's purpose was to prepare people for the coming Messiah, and if Jesus really was that Messiah, then why was John in prison when he could have been preaching to the crowds, preparing their hearts?*

Jesus answered John's doubts by pointing to his acts of healing the blind, lame, and deaf, curing the lepers, raising the dead, and preaching the Good News about God. With so much evidence, Jesus' identity was obvious. If you sometimes doubt your salvation, the forgiveness of your sins, or God's work in your life, look at the evidence in Scripture and the changes in your life. When you doubt, don't turn away from Christ, turn to him.

God's Sovereign Choice/ Romans 9:6–18

It is not as though God's word had failed. For not all who are descended from Israel are Israel. [7]Nor because they are his descendants are they all Abraham's children. On the contrary, "It is through Isaac that your offspring will be reckoned." [8]In other words, it is not the natural children who are God's children, but it is the children of the promise who are regarded as Abraham's offspring. [9]For this was how the promise was stated: "At the appointed time I will return, and Sarah will have a son."

[10]Not only that, but Rebekah's children had one and the same father, our father Isaac. [11]Yet, before the twins were born or had done anything good or bad—in order that God's purpose in election might stand: [12]not by works but by him who calls—she was told, "The older will serve the younger." [13]Just as it is written: "Jacob I loved, but Esau I hated."

14What then shall we say? Is God unjust? Not at all! 15For he says to Moses,

> "I will have mercy on whom I have mercy,
> and I will have compassion on whom I have
> compassion."

16It does not, therefore, depend on man's desire or effort, but on God's mercy. 17For the Scripture says to Pharaoh: "I raised you up for this very purpose, that I might display my power in you and that my name might be proclaimed in all the earth." 18Therefore God has mercy on whom he wants to have mercy, and he hardens whom he wants to harden.

A THOUGHT: *Was it right for God to choose Jacob, the younger, to be over Esau? Keep in mind the kind of God we worship: he is sovereign; he works for our good in everything; he is trustworthy; he will save all who believe in him. When we understand these qualities of God, we know his choices are good even if we don't understand all his reasons. Besides, if we wanted what was our due, we would deserve death for our sins; it is not "fair" for God to punish Christ in our place. But would you think of asking God to take back his offer of salvation because you don't deserve it?*

Proverbs for Today/ 5:7–14

Now then, my sons, listen to me; do not turn aside from what I say. Keep to a path far from her, do not go near the door of her house, lest you give your best strength to others and your years to one who is cruel, lest strangers feast on your wealth and your toil enrich another man's house. At the end of your life you will groan, when your flesh and body are spent. You will say, "How I hated discipline! How my heart spurned correction! I would not obey my teachers or listen to my instructors. I have come to the brink of utter ruin in the midst of the whole assembly."

JANUARY 27

Jesus Denounces Unrepentant Cities/
Matthew 11:20–30

Then Jesus began to denounce the cities in which most of his miracles had been performed, because they did not repent. 21"Woe to you, Korazin! Woe to you, Bethsaida! If the miracles that were performed in you had been performed in Tyre and Sidon, they would have repented long ago in sackcloth and ashes. 22But I tell you, it will be more bearable for Tyre and Sidon on the day of judgment than for you. 23And you, Capernaum, will you be lifted up to the skies? No, you will go down to the depths. If the miracles that were performed in you had been performed in Sodom, it would have remained to this day. 24But I tell you that it will be more bearable for Sodom on the day of judgment than for you."

25At that time Jesus said, "I praise you, Father, Lord of heaven and earth, because you have hidden these things from the wise and learned, and revealed them to little children. 26Yes, Father, for this was your good pleasure.

27"All things have been committed to me by my Father. No one knows the Son except the Father, and no one knows the Father except the Son and those to whom the Son chooses to reveal him.

28"Come to me, all you who are weary and burdened, and I will give you rest. 29Take my yoke upon you and learn from me, for I am gentle and humble in heart, and you will find rest for your souls. 30For my yoke is easy and my burden is light."

A THOUGHT: *A yoke is a heavy wooden harness that fits onto one or more oxen. It is attached to a piece of equipment the oxen are to pull. When an ox wears a yoke, it means that the animal is going to have a long day of hard work. The "heavy yoke" Jesus mentioned here can mean (1) the burden of sin, (2) the burden of the law (the excessive demands of the religious leaders), (3) government oppression, or (4) weariness in the search for God.*

Jesus frees people from all these burdens. The rest Jesus promises is love, healing, and peace with God, not the end of all effort. A relationship with God changes our meaningless toil into spiritual productivity and purpose.

God's Decisions Are Just and Merciful/
Romans 9:19–26

One of you will say to me: "Then why does God still blame us? For who resists his will?" 20But who are you, O man, to talk back to God? "Shall what is formed say to him who formed it, 'Why did you make me like this?' " 21Does not the potter have the right to make out of the same lump of clay some pottery for noble purposes and some for common use?

22What if God, choosing to show his wrath and make his power known, bore with great patience the objects of his wrath—prepared for destruction? 23What if he did this to make the riches of his glory known to the objects of his mercy, whom he prepared in advance for glory— 24even us, whom he also called, not only from the Jews but also from the Gentiles? 25As he says in Hosea:

> "I will call them 'my people' who are not my
>   people;
>   and I will call her 'my loved one' who is not my
>   loved one,"

26and,

> "It will happen that in the very place where it was
>   said to them,
>   'You are not my people,'
> they will be called 'sons of the living God.' "

A THOUGHT: *Paul is not saying that some of us are worth more than others, but simply that the Creator has control over the created object. The created object, therefore, has no right to demand anything from its Creator—its very existence depends on him. Keeping this perspective in mind removes any temptation to have pride in personal achievement.*

Proverbs for Today/ 5:15–21

Drink water from your own cistern, running water from your own well. Should your springs overflow in the streets, your streams of water in the public squares? Let them be yours alone, never to be shared with strangers. May your fountain be blessed, and may you rejoice in the wife of your youth. A loving doe, a graceful deer—may her breasts satisfy you always, may you ever be captivated by her love. Why be captivated, my son, by an adulteress? Why embrace the bosom of another man's wife? For a man's ways are in full view of the LORD, and he examines all his paths.

JANUARY 28

Lord of the Sabbath/ Matthew 12:1–21

At that time Jesus went through the grainfields on the Sabbath. His disciples were hungry and began to pick some heads of grain and eat them. 2When the Pharisees saw this, they said to him, "Look! Your disciples are doing what is unlawful on the Sabbath."

3He answered, "Haven't you read what David did when he and his companions were hungry? 4He entered the house of God, and he and his companions ate the consecrated bread—which was not lawful for them to do, but only for the priests. 5Or haven't you read in the Law that on the Sabbath the priests in the temple desecrate the day and yet are innocent? 6I tell you that one greater than the temple is here. 7If you had known what these words mean, 'I desire mercy, not sacrifice,' you would not have condemned the innocent. 8For the Son of Man is Lord of the Sabbath."

9Going on from that place, he went into their synagogue, 10and a man with a shriveled hand was there. Looking for a reason to accuse Jesus, they asked him, "Is it lawful to heal on the Sabbath?"

11He said to them, "If any of you has a sheep and it falls into a pit on the Sabbath, will you not take hold of it and lift it out? 12How much more valuable is a man than a sheep! Therefore it is lawful to do good on the Sabbath."

13Then he said to the man, "Stretch out your hand." So he stretched it out and it was completely restored, just as sound as the other. 14But the Pharisees went out and plotted how they might kill Jesus.

15Aware of this, Jesus withdrew from that place. Many followed him, and he healed all their sick, 16warning them not to tell who he was. 17This was to fulfill what was spoken through the prophet Isaiah:

18"Here is my servant whom I have chosen,
   the one I love, in whom I delight;
I will put my Spirit on him,
   and he will proclaim justice to the nations.
19He will not quarrel or cry out;
   no one will hear his voice in the streets.
20A bruised reed he will not break,
   and a smoldering wick he will not snuff out,
  till he leads justice to victory.
21 In his name the nations will put their hope."

A THOUGHT: *The Ten Commandments prohibit work on the Sabbath. That was the letter of the law. But because the purpose of the Sabbath is to rest and to worship God, the priests were allowed to work by performing sacrifices and conducting worship services. This "Sabbath work" was serving and worshiping God. Jesus always emphasized the intent of the law, the meaning behind the letter. The Pharisees had lost the spirit of the law and rigidly demanded that the letter (and their interpretation of it) be obeyed.*

As they pointed to the man with the deformed hand, the Pharisees tried to trick Jesus by asking him if it was legal to work by healing on the Sabbath. Their Sabbath rules said that people could be helped on the Sabbath only if their lives were in danger. Jesus healed on the Sabbath several times, and none of those healings could be classed as emergencies. If Jesus had waited until another day, he would have been submitting to the Pharisees' authority, showing that their petty rules were equal to God's law. If he healed the man, the Pharisees could claim that because he broke their rules, his power was not from God. But Jesus made it clear to all those watching how ridiculous and petty their rules were. God is a God of people, not rules. The best time to reach out to someone is when they need help.

Israel's Rock of Stumbling/ Romans 9:27–33

Isaiah cries out concerning Israel:

   "Though the number of the Israelites be like the
      sand by the sea,
   only the remnant will be saved.
28For the Lord will carry out
   his sentence on earth with speed and finality."

29It is just as Isaiah said previously:

   "Unless the Lord Almighty
    had left us descendants,
  we would have become like Sodom,
   we would have been like Gomorrah."

30What then shall we say? That the Gentiles, who did not pursue righteousness, have obtained it, a righteousness that is by faith; 31but Israel, who pursued a law of righteousness, has not attained it. 32Why not? Because they pursued it not by faith but as if it were by works. They stumbled over the "stumbling stone." 33As it is written:

> "See, I lay in Zion a stone that causes men to
>   stumble
>   and a rock that makes them fall,
>   and the one who trusts in him will never be put to
>   shame."

A THOUGHT: *Sometimes we are like these people, "who pursued a law of righteousness." We may think church attendance, church work, giving money, and being nice will be enough. But Paul's words sting—this approach never succeeds. Paul explains that God's plan is not for those who try to earn his favor by being good; it is for those who realize they can never be good enough and so must depend on Christ. Only by putting our faith in what Jesus Christ has done will we be saved. If we do that, we will "never be put to shame."*

Proverbs for Today/ 5:22–23

The evil deeds of a wicked man ensnare him; the cords of his sin hold him fast. He will die for lack of discipline, led astray by his own great folly.

JANUARY 29

The Kingdom of God and the Kingdom of Satan/ Matthew 12:22–37

Then they brought him [Jesus] a demon-possessed man who was blind and mute, and Jesus healed him, so that he could both talk and see. 23All the people were astonished and said, "Could this be the Son of David?"

24But when the Pharisees heard this, they said, "It is only by Beelzebub, the prince of demons, that this fellow drives out demons."

25Jesus knew their thoughts and said to them, "Every kingdom divided against itself will be ruined, and every city or household divided against itself will not stand. 26If Satan drives out Satan, he is divided against himself. How then can his kingdom stand? 27And if I drive out demons by Beelzebub, by whom do your people drive them out? So then, they will be your judges. 28But if I drive out demons by the Spirit of God, then the kingdom of God has come upon you.

29"Or again, how can anyone enter a strong man's house and carry off his possessions unless he first ties up the strong man? Then he can rob his house.

30"He who is not with me is against me, and he who does not gather with me scatters. 31And so I tell you, every sin and blasphemy will be forgiven men, but the blasphemy against the Spirit will not be forgiven. 32Anyone who speaks a word against the Son of Man will be forgiven, but anyone who speaks against the Holy Spirit will not be forgiven, either in this age or in the age to come.

33"Make a tree good and its fruit will be good, or make a tree bad and its fruit will be bad, for a tree is recognized by its fruit. 34You brood of vipers, how can you who are evil say anything good? For out of the overflow of the heart the mouth speaks. 35The good man brings good things out of the good stored up in him, and the evil man brings evil things out of the evil stored up in him. 36But I tell you that men will have to give account on the day of judgment for every careless word they have spoken. 37For by your words you will be acquitted, and by your words you will be condemned."

A THOUGHT: *It is impossible to be neutral about Christ. Anyone who is not actively following Jesus has chosen to reject him. Any person who tries to remain neutral in the cosmic struggle of good against evil is choosing to be separated from God, who alone is good. To refuse to follow Christ is to choose to live for Satan.*

Reconciliation to God through Faith/ Romans 10:1–13

Brothers, my heart's desire and prayer to God for the Israelites is that they may be saved. 2For I can testify about them that they are zealous for God, but their zeal is not based on knowledge. 3Since they did not know the righteousness that comes from God and sought to establish their own, they did not submit to God's righteousness.

⁴Christ is the end of the law so that there may be righteous-ness for everyone who believes.

⁵Moses describes in this way the righteousness that is by the law: "The man who does these things will live by them." ⁶But the righteousness that is by faith says: "Do not say in your heart, 'Who will ascend into heaven?'" (that is, to bring Christ down) ⁷"or 'Who will descend into the deep?'" (that is, to bring Christ up from the dead). ⁸But what does it say? "The word is near you; it is in your mouth and in your heart," that is, the word of faith we are pro-claiming: ⁹That if you confess with your mouth, "Jesus is Lord," and believe in your heart that God raised him from the dead, you will be saved. ¹⁰For it is with your heart that you believe and are justified, and it is with your mouth that you confess and are saved. ¹¹As the Scripture says, "Any-one who trusts in him will never be put to shame." ¹²For there is no difference between Jew and Gentile—the same Lord is Lord of all and richly blesses all who call on him, ¹³for, "Everyone who calls on the name of the Lord will be saved."

A THOUGHT: *What will happen to the Jewish people who believe in God but not in Christ? Since they believe in the same God, won't they be saved? If that were true, Paul would not have worked so hard and sacrificed so much to teach them about Christ. Jesus is the most complete revelation of God, and we cannot fully know God apart from him; and since God appointed Jesus to bring God and man together, we cannot come to God by another path. The Jews, like everyone else, can find salvation only through Jesus Christ. Like Paul, we should wish that all Jews might be saved. We should pray for them and lovingly share the Good News with them.*

Proverbs for Today/ 6:1–5

My son, if you have put up security for your neighbor, if you have struck hands in pledge for another, if you have been trapped by what you said, ensnared by the words of your mouth, then do this, my son, to free yourself, since you have fallen into your neighbor's hands: Go and humble yourself; press your plea with your neighbor! Allow no sleep to your eyes, no slumber to your eyelids. Free your-self, like a gazelle from the hand of the hunter, like a bird from the snare of the fowler.

The Sign of Jonah/ Matthew 12:38–50

Then some of the Pharisees and teachers of the law said to him, "Teacher, we want to see a miraculous sign from you."

³⁹He answered, "A wicked and adulterous generation asks for a miraculous sign! But none will be given it except the sign of the prophet Jonah. ⁴⁰For as Jonah was three days and three nights in the belly of a huge fish, so the Son of Man will be three days and three nights in the heart of the earth. ⁴¹The men of Nineveh will stand up at the judgment with this generation and condemn it; for they repented at the preaching of Jonah, and now one greater than Jonah is here. ⁴²The Queen of the South will rise at the judgment with this generation and condemn it; for she came from the ends of the earth to listen to Solomon's wisdom, and now one greater than Solomon is here.

⁴³"When an evil spirit comes out of a man, it goes through arid places seeking rest and does not find it. ⁴⁴Then it says, 'I will return to the house I left.' When it arrives, it finds the house unoccupied, swept clean and put in order. ⁴⁵Then it goes and takes with it seven other spirits more wicked than itself, and they go in and live there. And the final condition of that man is worse than the first. That is how it will be with this wicked generation."

⁴⁶While Jesus was still talking to the crowd, his mother and brothers stood outside, wanting to speak to him. ⁴⁷Someone told him, "Your mother and brothers are standing outside, wanting to speak to you."

⁴⁸He replied to him, "Who is my mother, and who are my brothers?" ⁴⁹Pointing to his disciples, he said, "Here are my mother and my brothers. ⁵⁰For whoever does the will of my Father in heaven is my brother and sister and mother."

A THOUGHT: *Jonah was a prophet sent to the Assyrian city of Nineveh. Because Assyria was such a cruel and warlike nation, Jonah tried to run from his assignment and ended up spending three days in the belly of a great fish. When he got out, he grudgingly went to Nineveh, preached God's message, and saw the city repent. By contrast, when Jesus came to his people, they refused to repent. Here he is clearly saying that his resurrection would prove that he is the Messiah. Three days after his death he would come back to life, just as Jonah was given a new chance at life after three days in the fish.*

Preaching the Good News/ Romans 10:14–21

How, then, can they call on the one [Jesus] they have not believed in? And how can they believe in the one of whom they have not heard? And how can they hear without someone preaching to them? 15And how can they preach unless they are sent? As it is written, "How beautiful are the feet of those who bring good news!"

16But not all the Israelites accepted the good news. For Isaiah says, "Lord, who has believed our message?" 17Consequently, faith comes from hearing the message, and the message is heard through the word of Christ. 18But I ask: Did they not hear? Of course they did:

"Their voice has gone out into all the earth,
    their words to the ends of the world."

19Again I ask: Did Israel not understand? First, Moses says,

"I will make you envious by those who are not a
        nation;
I will make you angry by a nation that has no
        understanding."

20And Isaiah boldly says,

"I was found by those who did not seek me;
I revealed myself to those who did not ask for
        me."

21But concerning Israel he says,

"All day long I have held out my hands
    to a disobedient and obstinate people."

A THOUGHT: *God's great message of salvation must be taken to others, so they can have the chance to respond to the Good News. How will your loved ones and neighbors hear it unless someone tells them? Is God calling you to take a part in making his message known in your community? Think of one person who needs to hear the Good News, and think of something you can do to help him or her hear it. Then bring the Good News to that person.*

Proverbs for Today/ 6:6–11

Go to the ant, you sluggard; consider its ways and be wise! It has no commander, no overseer or ruler, yet it stores its provisions in summer and gathers its food at harvest. □ How long will you lie there, you sluggard? When will you get up from your sleep? A little sleep, a little slumber, a little folding of the hands to rest—and poverty will come on you like a bandit and scarcity like an armed man.

JANUARY 31

The Parable of the Sower/ Matthew 13:1–23

That same day Jesus went out of the house and sat by the lake. 2Such large crowds gathered around him that he got into a boat and sat in it, while all the people stood on the shore. 3Then he told them many things in parables, saying: "A farmer went out to sow his seed. 4As he was scattering the seed, some fell along the path, and the birds came and ate it up. 5Some fell on rocky places, where it did not have much soil. It sprang up quickly, because the soil was shallow. 6But when the sun came up, the plants were scorched, and they withered because they had no root. 7Other seed fell among thorns, which grew up and choked the plants. 8Still other seed fell on good soil, where it produced a crop—a hundred, sixty or thirty times what was sown. 9He who has ears, let him hear."

10The disciples came to him and asked, "Why do you speak to the people in parables?"

11He replied, "The knowledge of the secrets of the kingdom of heaven has been given to you, but not to them. 12Whoever has will be given more, and he will have an abundance. Whoever does not have, even what he has will be taken from him. 13This is why I speak to them in parables:

"Though seeing, they do not see;
   though hearing, they do not hear or understand.

¹⁴In them is fulfilled the prophecy of Isaiah:

> " 'You will be ever hearing but never
>   understanding;
>   you will be ever seeing but never perceiving.
> ¹⁵For this people's heart has become calloused;
>   they hardly hear with their ears,
>   and they have closed their eyes.
> Otherwise they might see with their eyes,
>   hear with their ears,
>   understand with their hearts
>   and turn, and I would heal them.'

¹⁶But blessed are your eyes because they see, and your ears because they hear. ¹⁷For I tell you the truth, many prophets and righteous men longed to see what you see but did not see it, and to hear what you hear but did not hear it.

¹⁸"Listen then to what the parable of the sower means: ¹⁹When anyone hears the message about the kingdom and does not understand it, the evil one comes and snatches away what was sown in his heart. This is the seed sown along the path. ²⁰The one who received the seed that fell on rocky places is the man who hears the word and at once receives it with joy. ²¹But since he has no root, he lasts only a short time. When trouble or persecution comes because of the word, he quickly falls away. ²²The one who received the seed that fell among the thorns is the man who hears the word, but the worries of this life and the deceitfulness of wealth choke it, making it unfruitful. ²³But the one who received the seed that fell on good soil is the man who hears the word and understands it. He produces a crop, yielding a hundred, sixty or thirty times what was sown."

A THOUGHT: *Jesus used many illustrations, or parables, when speaking to the crowds. A parable compares something familiar to something unfamiliar. It helps us understand spiritual truth by using everyday objects and relationships. Parables compel the listener to discover truth, while at the same time concealing the truth from those too lazy or too stubborn to see it. To those who are honestly searching, the truth becomes clear. We must be careful not to read too much into parables, forcing them to say what they don't mean.*

The four types of soil in this parable represent the different responses we can have to God's message. We respond differently because we are in different states of readiness. Some people are hardened, others are shallow, others are contaminated by distracting cares, and some are receptive. How has God's Word taken root in your life? What kind of soil are you?

The Remnant of Israel/ Romans 11:1–6

I ask then: Did God reject his people? By no means! I am an Israelite myself, a descendant of Abraham, from the tribe of Benjamin. 2God did not reject his people, whom he foreknew. Don't you know what the Scripture says in the passage about Elijah—how he appealed to God against Israel: 3"Lord, they have killed your prophets and torn down your altars; I am the only one left, and they are trying to kill me"? 4And what was God's answer to him? "I have reserved for myself seven thousand who have not bowed the knee to Baal." 5So too, at the present time there is a remnant chosen by grace. 6And if by grace, then it is no longer by works; if it were, grace would no longer be grace.

A THOUGHT: *God chose the Jews to be the people through whom the rest of the world could find salvation. But this did not mean the entire Jewish nation would be saved; only those who were faithful to God were considered true Jews. People are saved through faith in Christ, not because they are part of a nation, religion, or family. On what are you depending for salvation?*

Proverbs for Today/ 6:12–15

A scoundrel and villain, who goes about with a corrupt mouth, who winks with his eye, signals with his feet and motions with his fingers, who plots evil with deceit in his heart—he always stirs up dissension. Therefore disaster will overtake him in an instant; he will suddenly be destroyed—without remedy.

FEBRUARY 1

Parables of the Kingdom/ Matthew 13:24–35

Jesus told them another parable: "The kingdom of heaven is like a man who sowed good seed in his field. 25But while everyone was sleeping, his enemy came and sowed weeds among the wheat, and went away. 26When the wheat sprouted and formed heads, then the weeds also appeared.

27"The owner's servants came to him and said, 'Sir, didn't you sow good seed in your field? Where then did the weeds come from?'

28" 'An enemy did this,' he replied.

"The servants asked him, 'Do you want us to go and pull them up?'

29" 'No,' he answered, 'because while you are pulling the weeds, you may root up the wheat with them. 30Let both grow together until the harvest. At that time I will tell the harvesters: First collect the weeds and tie them in bundles to be burned; then gather the wheat and bring it into my barn.' "

31He told them another parable: "The kingdom of heaven is like a mustard seed, which a man took and planted in his field. 32Though it is the smallest of all your seeds, yet when it grows, it is the largest of garden plants and becomes a tree, so that the birds of the air come and perch in its branches."

33He told them still another parable: "The kingdom of heaven is like yeast that a woman took and mixed into a large amount of flour until it worked all through the dough."

34Jesus spoke all these things to the crowd in parables; he did not say anything to them without using a parable. 35So was fulfilled what was spoken through the prophet:

"I will open my mouth in parables,
    I will utter things hidden since the creation of the world."

A THOUGHT: *The weeds and the young blades of wheat look the same and can't be distinguished until they are grown and ready for harvest. Weeds (unbelievers) and wheat (believers) must live side by side in this world. God is allowing unbelievers to remain for a while just as a farmer allows weeds to remain in his field so the surrounding wheat isn't uprooted with them. At the harvest, however, the weeds will be uprooted and thrown away. God's harvest (judgment) of all mankind is coming. We are to make ourselves ready by making sure our faith is sincere.*

A Stumbling Block to Jews/ Romans 11:7–12

What then? What Israel sought so earnestly it did not obtain, but the elect did. The others were hardened, 8as it is written:

"God gave them a spirit of stupor,
    eyes so that they could not see
    and ears so that they could not hear,
to this very day."

9And David says:

"May their table become a snare and a trap,
    a stumbling block and a retribution for them.
10May their eyes be darkened so they cannot see,
    and their backs be bent forever."

11Again I ask: Did they stumble so as to fall beyond recovery? Not at all! Rather, because of their transgression, salvation has come to the Gentiles to make Israel envious. 12But if their transgression means riches for the world, and their loss means riches for the Gentiles, how much greater riches will their fullness bring!

A THOUGHT: *These verses describe the punishment for hardened hearts predicted by the prophet Isaiah. If people constantly refuse to hear God's Good News, they eventually will be unable to understand it. Paul saw this happening in the synagogues he visited. But Paul had a vision for the church in which all Jews and Gentiles would be united in their love of God and obedience to Christ. While respecting God's law, this ideal church would look to Christ alone for salvation and eternal life. One's ethnic background and social status would be irrelevant—what would matter would be one's faith in Christ.*

Proverbs for Today/ 6:16–19

There are six things the LORD hates, seven that are detestable to him: haughty eyes, a lying tongue, hands that shed innocent blood, a heart that devises wicked schemes, feet that are quick to rush into evil, a false witness who pours out lies and a man who stirs up dissension among brothers.

FEBRUARY 2

The Parable of the Weeds Explained/
Matthew 13:36–43

Then he [Jesus] left the crowd and went into the house. His disciples came to him and said, "Explain to us the parable of the weeds in the field."

37He answered, "The one who sowed the good seed is the Son of Man. 38The field is the world, and the good seed stands for the sons of the kingdom. The weeds are the sons of the evil one, 39and the enemy who sows them is the devil. The harvest is the end of the age, and the harvesters are angels.

40"As the weeds are pulled up and burned in the fire, so it will be at the end of the age. 41The Son of Man will send out his angels, and they will weed out of his kingdom everything that causes sin and all who do evil. 42They will throw them into the fiery furnace, where there will be weeping and gnashing of teeth. 43Then the righteous will shine like the sun in the kingdom of their Father. He who has ears, let him hear."

A THOUGHT: *At the end of the world, angels will separate those who are evil from those who are good. There are true and false believers in our churches today, but we should be cautious in our judgments because the final separation will be made by Christ himself. If you start judging, you may damage some of the good "plants." It's more important to judge our own response to God than to analyze the spiritual condition of others.*

The Ingrafted Branches/ Romans 11:13–21

I am talking to you Gentiles. Inasmuch as I am the apostle to the Gentiles, I make much of my ministry 14in the hope that I may somehow arouse my own people to envy and save some of them. 15For if their rejection is the reconciliation of the world, what will their acceptance be but life from the dead? 16If the part of the dough offered as firstfruits is holy, then the whole batch is holy; if the root is holy, so are the branches.

17If some of the branches have been broken off, and you, though a wild olive shoot, have been grafted in among the others and now share in the nourishing sap from the olive root, 18do not boast over those branches. If you do, consider this: You do not support the root, but the root supports you. 19You will say then, "Branches were broken off so that I could be grafted in." 20Granted. But they were broken off because of unbelief, and you stand by faith. Do not be arrogant, but be afraid. 21For if God did not spare the natural branches, he will not spare you either.

A THOUGHT: *Paul, speaking to Gentile Christians, is warning them not to feel superior because God rejected some Jews. The Jewish religion, he says, is like the root of a tree, and the Jewish people are the tree's natural branches. Gentile believers have been grafted into the tree, and now Jews and Gentiles share its nourishment. Both Jews and Gentiles depend on Christ for life. If there is to be boasting, it should be in the Lord who accomplished the redemption of his people. Our salvation rests upon the grace of God expressed in the giving of his Son for our sins and we can offer nothing from ourselves to bring about or add to this salvation.*

Proverbs for Today/ 6:20–26

My son, keep your father's commands and do not forsake your mother's teaching. Bind them upon your heart forever; fasten them around your neck. When you walk, they will guide you; when you sleep, they will watch over you; when you awake, they will speak to you. For these commands are a lamp, this teaching is a light, and the corrections of discipline are the way to life, keeping you from the immoral woman, from the smooth tongue of the wayward wife. Do not lust in your heart after her beauty or let her captivate you with her eyes, for the prostitute reduces you to a loaf of bread, and the adulteress preys upon your very life.

FEBRUARY 3

Parables of the Kingdom/ Matthew 13:44–58

"The kingdom of heaven is like treasure hidden in a field. When a man found it, he hid it again, and then in his joy went and sold all he had and bought that field.

45"Again, the kingdom of heaven is like a merchant looking for fine pearls. 46When he found one of great value, he went away and sold everything he had and bought it.

47"Once again, the kingdom of heaven is like a net that was let down into the lake and caught all kinds of fish. 48When it was full, the fishermen pulled it up on the shore. Then they sat down and collected the good fish in baskets, but threw the bad away. 49This is how it will be at the end of the age. The angels will come and separate the wicked from the righteous 50and throw them into the fiery furnace, where there will be weeping and gnashing of teeth.

51"Have you understood all these things?" Jesus asked.

"Yes," they replied.

52He said to them, "Therefore every teacher of the law who has been instructed about the kingdom of heaven is like the owner of a house who brings out of his storeroom new treasures as well as old."

53When Jesus had finished these parables, he moved on from there. 54Coming to his hometown, he began teaching the people in their synagogue, and they were amazed. "Where did this man get this wisdom and these miraculous powers?" they asked. 55"Isn't this the carpenter's son? Isn't his mother's name Mary, and aren't his brothers James, Joseph, Simon and Judas? 56Aren't all his sisters with us? Where then did this man get all these things?" 57And they took offense at him.

But Jesus said to them, "Only in his hometown and in his own house is a prophet without honor."

58And he did not do many miracles there because of their lack of faith.

A THOUGHT: *The kingdom of heaven is more valuable than anything else we can have, so a person must be willing to give up everything to obtain it. The man who discovered the treasure in the field stumbled upon it by accident, but he knew its value when he found it. The merchant was earnestly searching for the choice pearl and, when he found it, sold everything he had to purchase it. We too must seek the values of the kingdom above everything else.*

The Kindness and Severity of God/
Romans 11:22–27

Consider therefore the kindness and sternness of God: sternness to those who fell, but kindness to you, provided that you continue in his kindness. Otherwise, you also will be cut off. 23And if they do not persist in unbelief, they will be grafted in, for God is able to graft them in again. 24After all, if you were cut out of an olive tree that is wild by nature, and contrary to nature were grafted into a cultivated olive tree, how much more readily will these, the natural branches, be grafted into their own olive tree!

25I do not want you to be ignorant of this mystery, brothers, so that you may not be conceited: Israel has experienced a hardening in part until the full number of the Gentiles has come in. 26And so all Israel will be saved, as it is written:

"The deliverer will come from Zion;
> he will turn godlessness away from Jacob.
27And this is my covenant with them
> when I take away their sins."

A THOUGHT: *The fact that God has shown his kindness towards us does not mean that we have the freedom to presume upon his grace by disobeying him. God's true children will desire to obey God. Recognize that just as God judged the disobedience of the Jews who constantly refused to turn to God, so he will judge us if we constantly refuse to turn from our wicked ways. But if one who has lived a wicked life turns to God, God is able to graft that one into the family of God.*

Proverbs for Today/ 6:27–35

Can a man scoop fire into his lap without his clothes being burned? Can a man walk on hot coals without his feet being scorched? So is he who sleeps with another man's wife; no one who touches her will go unpunished. □ Men do not despise a thief if he steals to satisfy his hunger when he is starving. Yet if he is caught, he must pay sevenfold, though it costs him all the wealth of his house. But a man who commits adultery lacks judgment; whoever does so destroys himself. Blows and disgrace are his lot, and his shame will never be wiped away; for jealousy arouses a husband's fury, and he will show no mercy when he takes revenge. He will not accept any compensation; he will refuse the bribe, however great it is.

FEBRUARY 4

Herod Beheads John the Baptist/ Matthew 14:1–12

At that time Herod the tetrarch heard the reports about Jesus, 2and he said to his attendants, "This is John the Baptist; he has risen from the dead! That is why miraculous powers are at work in him."

3Now Herod had arrested John and bound him and put him in prison because of Herodias, his brother Philip's wife, 4for John had been saying to him: "It is not lawful for you to have her." 5Herod wanted to kill John, but he was afraid of the people, because they considered him a prophet.

6On Herod's birthday the daughter of Herodias danced for them and pleased Herod so much 7that he promised with an oath to give her whatever she asked. 8Prompted by her mother, she said, "Give me here on a platter the head of John the Baptist." 9The king was distressed, but because of his oaths and his dinner guests, he ordered that her request be granted 10and had John beheaded in the prison. 11His head was brought in on a platter and given to the girl, who carried it to her mother. 12John's disciples came and took his body and buried it. Then they went and told Jesus.

A THOUGHT: *Herod did not want to kill John the Baptist, but he gave the order so he wouldn't be embarrassed in front of his guests. How easy it is to give in to the pressure of the crowd and to let ourselves be coerced into doing wrong. Don't place yourself in a position where it is embarrassing to do what is right; do what is right no matter how embarrassing or painful it may be.*

God's Unchanging Mercy/ Romans 11:28–36

As far as the gospel is concerned, they are enemies on your account; but as far as election is concerned, they are loved on account of the patriarchs, 29for God's gifts and his call are irrevocable. 30Just as you who were at one time disobedient to God have now received mercy as a result of their disobedience, 31so they too have now become disobedient in order that they too may now receive mercy as a result of God's mercy to you. 32For God has bound all men over to disobedience so that he may have mercy on them all.

33Oh, the depth of the riches of the wisdom and
knowledge of God!
How unsearchable his judgments,
and his paths beyond tracing out!
34"Who has known the mind of the Lord?
Or who has been his counselor?"
35"Who has ever given to God,
that God should repay him?"
36For from him and through him and to him are all
things.
To him be the glory forever! Amen.

A THOUGHT: *In this passage Paul shows how the Jews and the Gentiles benefit from each other. Whenever God shows mercy on one group, the other shares the blessing. In God's original plan, the Jews would freely share their blessings with the Gentiles. When the Jews neglected to do this, God blessed the Gentiles anyway through the Jewish Messiah. Now it is the Gentiles' turn to bless the Jews. God's plans will not be thwarted: he will "have mercy on them all."*

Proverbs for Today/ 7:1–5

My son, keep my words and store up my commands within you. Keep my commands and you will live; guard my teachings as the apple of your eye. Bind them on your fingers; write them on the tablet of your heart. Say to wisdom, "You are my sister," and call understanding your kinsman; they will keep you from the adulteress, from the wayward wife with her seductive words.

FEBRUARY 5

Jesus Feeds Five Thousand/ Matthew 14:13–21

When Jesus heard what had happened, he withdrew by boat privately to a solitary place. Hearing of this, the crowds followed him on foot from the towns. [14]When Jesus landed and saw a large crowd, he had compassion on them and healed their sick.

[15]As evening approached, the disciples came to him and said, "This is a remote place, and it's already getting late. Send the crowds away, so they can go to the villages and buy themselves some food."

[16]Jesus replied, "They do not need to go away. You give them something to eat."

[17]"We have here only five loaves of bread and two fish," they answered.

[18]"Bring them here to me," he said. [19]And he directed the people to sit down on the grass. Taking the five loaves and the two fish and looking up to heaven, he gave thanks and broke the loaves. Then he gave them to the disciples, and the disciples gave them to the people. [20]They all ate and were satisfied, and the disciples picked up twelve basketfuls of broken pieces that were left over. [21]The

number of those who ate was about five thousand men, besides women and children.

A THOUGHT: *Jesus multiplied five loaves and two fish to feed over 5,000 people. What he was originally given seemed insufficient, but in his hands it became more than enough. We often feel that our contribution to Jesus is meager, but he can use and multiply whatever we give him, whether it is talent, time, or treasure. It is when we give them to Jesus that our resources are multiplied.*

A Living Sacrifice/ Romans 12:1–5

Therefore, I urge you, brothers, in view of God's mercy, to offer your bodies as living sacrifices, holy and pleasing to God—this is your spiritual act of worship. 2Do not conform any longer to the pattern of this world, but be transformed by the renewing of your mind. Then you will be able to test and approve what God's will is—his good, pleasing and perfect will.

3For by the grace given me I say to every one of you: Do not think of yourself more highly than you ought, but rather think of yourself with sober judgment, in accordance with the measure of faith God has given you. 4Just as each of us has one body with many members, and these members do not all have the same function, 5so in Christ we who are many form one body, and each member belongs to all the others.

A THOUGHT: *When sacrificing an animal according to God's law, a priest killed the animal, cut it in pieces, and placed it on the altar. Sacrifice was important, but even in the Old Testament God made it clear that obedience from the heart was much more important. God wants us to offer ourselves, not animals, as living sacrifices—daily laying aside our own desires to follow him. We do this out of gratitude that our sins have been forgiven. He wants us to be new people with freshness of thought, alive to glorify him. Since he wants only what is best for us, and since he gave his Son to make our new lives possible, we should joyfully offer ourselves as living sacrifices to him.*

Proverbs for Today/ 7:6–23

At the window of my house I looked out through the lattice. I saw among the simple, I noticed among the young men, a youth who lacked judgment. He was going down the street near her corner, walking along in the direction of her house at twilight, as the day was fading, as the dark of night set in. Then out came a woman to meet him, dressed like a prostitute and with crafty intent. (She is loud and defiant, her feet never stay at home; now in the street, now in the squares, at every corner she lurks.) She took hold of him and kissed him and with a brazen face she said: "I have fellowship offerings at home; today I fulfilled my vows. So I came out to meet you; I looked for you and have found you! I have covered my bed with colored linens from Egypt. I have perfumed my bed with myrrh, aloes and cinnamon. Come, let's drink deep of love till morning; let's enjoy ourselves with love! My husband is not at home; he has gone on a long journey. He took his purse filled with money and will not be home till full moon." With persuasive words she led him astray; she seduced him with her smooth talk. All at once he followed her like an ox going to the slaughter, like a deer stepping into a noose till an arrow pierces his liver, like a bird darting into a snare, little knowing it will cost him his life.

FEBRUARY 6

Jesus Walks on the Water/ Matthew 14:22–36

Immediately Jesus made the disciples get into the boat and go on ahead of him to the other side, while he dismissed the crowd. 23After he had dismissed them, he went up on a mountainside by himself to pray. When evening came, he was there alone, 24but the boat was already a considerable distance from land, buffeted by the waves because the wind was against it.

25During the fourth watch of the night Jesus went out to them, walking on the lake. 26When the disciples saw him walking on the lake, they were terrified. "It's a ghost," they said, and cried out in fear.

27But Jesus immediately said to them: "Take courage! It is I. Don't be afraid."

28"Lord, if it's you," Peter replied, "tell me to come to you on the water."

29"Come," he said.

Then Peter got down out of the boat, walked on the water and came toward Jesus. 30But when he saw the wind, he was afraid and, beginning to sink, cried out, "Lord, save me!"

31Immediately Jesus reached out his hand and caught him. "You of little faith," he said, "why did you doubt?"

32And when they climbed into the boat, the wind died down. 33Then those who were in the boat worshiped him, saying, "Truly you are the Son of God."

34When they had crossed over, they landed at Gennesaret. 35And when the men of that place recognized Jesus, they sent word to all the surrounding country. People brought all their sick to him 36and begged him to let the sick just touch the edge of his cloak, and all who touched him were healed.

A THOUGHT: *Although we start out with good intentions, sometimes our faith falters. This doesn't necessarily mean we have failed. When Peter's faith faltered, he reached out to Christ, the only one who could help. He was afraid, but he still looked to Christ. When we are apprehensive about the troubles around us and doubt Christ's presence or ability to help, we must remember that he is the only one who can really help.*

Gifts Are Given to Serve Others/ Romans 12:6–13

We have different gifts, according to the grace given us. If a man's gift is prophesying, let him use it in proportion to his faith. 7If it is serving, let him serve; if it is teaching, let him teach; 8if it is encouraging, let him encourage; if it is contributing to the needs of others, let him give generously; if it is leadership, let him govern diligently; if it is showing mercy, let him do it cheerfully.

9Love must be sincere. Hate what is evil; cling to what is good. 10Be devoted to one another in brotherly love. Honor one another above yourselves. 11Never be lacking in zeal, but keep your spiritual fervor, serving the Lord. 12Be joyful in hope, patient in affliction, faithful in prayer. 13Share with God's people who are in need. Practice hospitality.

A THOUGHT: *Look at this list of gifts and imagine the kinds of people who would have each gift. Prophets are often bold and articulate. Servers are faithful and loyal. Teachers are clear thinkers. Preachers know how to motivate others. Givers are generous and trusting. Administrators are good organizers and managers. Comforters are caring people who are happy to give their time to others. It would be difficult for one person to embody all these gifts. An assertive prophet would not usually make a good counselor, and a generous giver* might fail as an administrator. When you identify your own gifts (and you don't have to stop with this list—it is far from complete), ask how you can use them to glorify God. At the same time, realize that your gifts can't do the work of the church all alone. Be thankful for people whose gifts are completely different from yours. Let your strengths balance their weaknesses, and be grateful that their abilities make up for your deficiencies. Together we can build up the church.

Proverbs for Today/ 7:24–27

Now then, my sons, listen to me; pay attention to what I say. Do not let your heart turn to her [a prostitute's] ways or stray into her paths. Many are the victims she has brought down; her slain are a mighty throng. Her house is a highway to the grave, leading down to the chambers of death.

FEBRUARY 7

Righteousness of the Heart/ Matthew 15:1–20

Then some Pharisees and teachers of the law came to Jesus from Jerusalem and asked, 2"Why do your disciples break the tradition of the elders? They don't wash their hands before they eat!"

3Jesus replied, "And why do you break the command of God for the sake of your tradition? 4For God said, 'Honor your father and mother' and 'Anyone who curses his father or mother must be put to death.' 5But you say that if a man says to his father or mother, 'Whatever help you might otherwise have received from me is a gift devoted to God,' 6he is not to 'honor his father' with it. Thus you nullify the word of God for the sake of your tradition. 7You hypocrites! Isaiah was right when he prophesied about you:

8" 'These people honor me with their lips,
    but their hearts are far from me.
9They worship me in vain;
    their teachings are but rules taught by men.' "

10Jesus called the crowd to him and said, "Listen and understand. 11What goes into a man's mouth does not make him 'unclean,' but what comes out of his mouth, that is what makes him 'unclean.' "

12Then the disciples came to him and asked, "Do you know that the Pharisees were offended when they heard this?"

13He replied, "Every plant that my heavenly Father has not planted will be pulled up by the roots. 14Leave them; they are blind guides. If a blind man leads a blind man, both will fall into a pit."

15Peter said, "Explain the parable to us."

16"Are you still so dull?" Jesus asked them. 17"Don't you see that whatever enters the mouth goes into the stomach and then out of the body? 18But the things that come out of the mouth come from the heart, and these make a man 'unclean.' 19For out of the heart come evil thoughts, murder, adultery, sexual immorality, theft, false testimony, slander. 20These are what make a man 'unclean'; but eating with unwashed hands does not make him 'unclean.' "

A THOUGHT: *We work hard to keep our outward appearance attractive, but what is in our hearts is even more important. The way we are deep down (where others can't see) matters much to God. What are you like inside? When people become Christians, God changes them and actually makes them different on the inside. He will continue to help change them if they only ask. God wants us to seek healthy thoughts and motives, not just healthy food and exercise.*

Conquer Evil with Good/ Romans 12:14–21

Bless those who persecute you; bless and do not curse. 15Rejoice with those who rejoice; mourn with those who mourn. 16Live in harmony with one another. Do not be proud, but be willing to associate with people of low position. Do not be conceited.

17Do not repay anyone evil for evil. Be careful to do what is right in the eyes of everybody. 18If it is possible, as far as it depends on you, live at peace with everyone. 19Do not take revenge, my friends, but leave room for God's wrath, for it is written: "It is mine to avenge; I will repay," says the Lord. 20On the contrary:

"If your enemy is hungry, feed him;
     if he is thirsty, give him something to drink.
In doing this, you will heap burning coals on his
          head."

21Do not be overcome by evil, but overcome evil with good.

A THOUGHT: *In this day of constant lawsuits and incessant demands for legal rights, Paul's command sounds almost impossible. When someone hurts you deeply, instead of giving him what he deserves, Paul says to befriend him. Why does Paul tell us to forgive our enemies? (1) Forgiveness may break a cycle of retaliation and lead to mutual reconciliation. (2) It may make the enemy feel ashamed and change his ways. (3) Returning evil for evil hurts you just as much as it hurts your enemy. Even if your enemy never repents, forgiving him will free you of a heavy load of bitterness. For in loving our enemies in this way, we will be like our Lord Jesus Christ, who died for us while we were in a state of rebellion against him.*

Proverbs for Today/ 8:1–10

Does not wisdom call out? Does not understanding raise her voice? On the heights along the way, where the paths meet, she takes her stand; beside the gates leading into the city, at the entrances, she cries aloud: "To you, O men, I call out; I raise my voice to all mankind. You who are simple, gain prudence; you who are foolish, gain understanding. Listen, for I have worthy things to say; I open my lips to speak what is right. My mouth speaks what is true, for my lips detest wickedness. All the words of my mouth are just; none of them is crooked or perverse. To the discerning all of them are right; they are faultless to those who have knowledge. Choose my instruction instead of silver, knowledge rather than choice gold."

FEBRUARY 8

The Faith of the Canaanite Woman/ Matthew 15:21–28

Leaving that place, Jesus withdrew to the region of Tyre and Sidon. 22A Canaanite woman from that vicinity came to him, crying out, "Lord, Son of David, have mercy on me! My daughter is suffering terribly from demon-possession."

23Jesus did not answer a word. So his disciples came to him and urged him, "Send her away, for she keeps crying out after us."

24He answered, "I was sent only to the lost sheep of Israel."

25The woman came and knelt before him. "Lord, help me!" she said.

26He replied, "It is not right to take the children's bread and toss it to their dogs."

27"Yes, Lord," she said, "but even the dogs eat the crumbs that fall from their masters' table."

28Then Jesus answered, "Woman, you have great faith! Your request is granted." And her daughter was healed from that very hour.

A THOUGHT: *The disciples asked Jesus to get rid of this Canaanite woman because she was bothering them with her begging. They showed no compassion for her or sensitivity to her needs. It is possible to become so occupied with spiritual matters that we miss real spiritual needs right around us, whether out of prejudice or simply the inconvenience they cause. Instead of being bothered, be aware of the opportunities that surround you. Be open to sharing God's message with all people, and do not shut out those who are different from you.*

Obedience to the Authorities/ Romans 13:1–7

Everyone must submit himself to the governing authorities, for there is no authority except that which God has established. The authorities that exist have been established by God. 2Consequently, he who rebels against the authority is rebelling against what God has instituted, and those who do so will bring judgment on themselves. 3For rulers hold no terror for those who do right, but for those who do wrong. Do you want to be free from fear of the one in authority? Then do what is right and he will commend you. 4For he is God's servant to do you good. But if you do wrong, be afraid, for he does not bear the sword for nothing. He is God's servant, an agent of wrath to bring punishment on the wrongdoer. 5Therefore, it is necessary to submit to the authorities, not only because of possible punishment but also because of conscience.

6This is also why you pay taxes, for the authorities are God's servants, who give their full time to governing. 7Give everyone what you owe him: If you owe taxes, pay taxes; if revenue, then revenue; if respect, then respect; if honor, then honor.

A THOUGHT: *Are there times when we should not obey the government? We can never allow the government to force us to disobey God. Jesus and his apostles never disobeyed the government for personal reasons; when they disobeyed, it was in order to follow their higher loyalty to God. Their disobedience was not cheap: they were threatened, beaten, thrown into jail, tortured, and executed for their convictions. Like them, if we are compelled to disobey, we must disobey for the right reasons and we must be ready to accept the consequences.*

Proverbs for Today/ 8:11–13

For wisdom is more precious than rubies, and nothing you desire can compare with her. "I, wisdom, dwell together with prudence; I possess knowledge and discretion. To fear the LORD is to hate evil; I hate pride and arrogance, evil behavior and perverse speech."

FEBRUARY 9

Jesus Feeds Four Thousand/ Matthew 15:29–39

Jesus left there and went along the Sea of Galilee. Then he went up on a mountainside and sat down. 30Great crowds came to him, bringing the lame, the blind, the crippled, the mute and many others, and laid them at his feet; and he healed them. 31The people were amazed when they saw the mute speaking, the crippled made well, the lame walking and the blind seeing. And they praised the God of Israel.

32Jesus called his disciples to him and said, "I have compassion for these people; they have already been with me three days and have nothing to eat. I do not want to send them away hungry, or they may collapse on the way."

33His disciples answered, "Where could we get enough bread in this remote place to feed such a crowd?"

34"How many loaves do you have?" Jesus asked.

"Seven," they replied, "and a few small fish."

35He told the crowd to sit down on the ground. 36Then he took the seven loaves and the fish, and when he had given thanks, he broke them and gave them to the disciples, and they in turn to the people. 37They all ate and were satisfied. Afterward the disciples picked up seven basketfuls of broken pieces that were left over. [38]The number of those who ate was four thousand, besides women and children. [39]After Jesus had sent the crowd away, he got into the boat and went to the vicinity of Magadan.

A THOUGHT: *Jesus had already fed more than 5,000 people with five loaves and two fish. Now, in a similar situation, the disciples were again perplexed. How easily we throw up our hands in despair when faced with tough situations. Like the disciples, we often forget that if God has cared for us in the past, he will do the same now. If you are facing a difficult situation, remember when God cared for you and trust him to work faithfully again.*

Loving Others Is Obedience to God/
Romans 13:8–14

Let no debt remain outstanding, except the continuing debt to love one another, for he who loves his fellowman has fulfilled the law. [9]The commandments, "Do not commit adultery," "Do not murder," "Do not steal," "Do not covet," and whatever other commandment there may be, are summed up in this one rule: "Love your neighbor as yourself." [10]Love does no harm to its neighbor. Therefore love is the fulfillment of the law.

[11]And do this, understanding the present time. The hour has come for you to wake up from your slumber, because our salvation is nearer now than when we first believed. [12]The night is nearly over; the day is almost here. So let us put aside the deeds of darkness and put on the armor of light. [13]Let us behave decently, as in the daytime, not in orgies and drunkenness, not in sexual immorality and debauchery, not in dissension and jealousy. [14]Rather, clothe yourselves with the Lord Jesus Christ, and do not think about how to gratify the desires of the sinful nature.

A THOUGHT: *Somehow many of us have gotten the idea that self-love is wrong. But if this were the case, it would be pointless to love our neighbors as ourselves. But Paul explains what he means by self-love. Even if you have low self-esteem, you probably don't willingly let yourself go hungry. You clothe yourself reasonably well. You make sure there's a roof over your head if you can. You try not to let yourself be cheated or injured. And you get angry if someone tries to ruin your marriage. This is the kind of love we need to have for our neighbors. Do we see that others are fed, clothed, and housed as well as they can be? Are we concerned about issues of social justice? Are our morals above reproach? Loving others as ourselves means to be actively working to see that their needs are met. Interestingly,*

*people who focus on others rather than on themselves rarely suffer
from low self-esteem.*

Proverbs for Today/ 8:14–26

Counsel and sound judgment are mine; I have understanding and power. By me kings reign and rulers make laws that
are just; by me princes govern, and all nobles who rule on
earth. I love those who love me, and those who seek me
find me. With me are riches and honor, enduring wealth and
prosperity. My fruit is better than fine gold; what I yield
surpasses choice silver. I walk in the way of righteousness,
along the paths of justice, bestowing wealth on those who
love me and making their treasuries full. □ "The LORD
brought me forth as the first of his works, before his deeds
of old; I was appointed from eternity, from the beginning,
before the world began. When there were no oceans, I was
given birth, when there were no springs abounding with
water; before the mountains were settled in place, before
the hills, I was given birth, before he made the earth or its
fields or any of the dust of the world."

FEBRUARY 10

The Teachings of the Pharisees and Sadducees/
Matthew 16:1–12

The Pharisees and Sadducees came to Jesus and tested him
by asking him to show them a sign from heaven.

2He replied, "When evening comes, you say, 'It will be
fair weather, for the sky is red,' 3and in the morning,
'Today it will be stormy, for the sky is red and overcast.'
You know how to interpret the appearance of the sky, but
you cannot interpret the signs of the times. 4A wicked and
adulterous generation looks for a miraculous sign, but none
will be given it except the sign of Jonah." Jesus then left
them and went away.

5When they went across the lake, the disciples forgot to
take bread. 6"Be careful," Jesus said to them. "Be on your
guard against the yeast of the Pharisees and Sadducees."

⁷They discussed this among themselves and said, "It is because we didn't bring any bread."

⁸Aware of their discussion, Jesus asked, "You of little faith, why are you talking among yourselves about having no bread? ⁹Do you still not understand? Don't you remember the five loaves for the five thousand, and how many basketfuls you gathered? ¹⁰Or the seven loaves for the four thousand, and how many basketfuls you gathered? ¹¹How is it you don't understand that I was not talking to you about bread? But be on your guard against the yeast of the Pharisees and Sadducees." ¹²Then they understood that he was not telling them to guard against the yeast used in bread, but against the teaching of the Pharisees and Sadducees.

A THOUGHT: *The Pharisees and Sadducees were two different Jewish sects, and their views were diametrically opposed on many issues. The Pharisees carefully followed their religious rules and traditions, believing that this was the way to God. They also believed in the authority of all Scripture and in the resurrection of the dead. The Sadducees accepted only the books of Moses as Scripture and did not believe in life after death.*

Many people, like these Jewish leaders, want a miracle so they can believe. But Jesus knew that miracles would never convince them. Jesus had been healing, raising people from the dead, and feeding thousands, and still people wanted him to prove himself. Do you doubt Christ because you haven't seen a miracle? Do you expect God to prove himself to you personally before you believe? Jesus says, "Blessed are those who have not seen and yet have believed" (John 20:29). We have all the miracles recorded in the Old and New Testaments, 2,000 years of church history, and the witness of thousands. With all this evidence, those who don't believe are proud or stubborn. If you simply step forward in faith and believe, then you will begin to notice God at work in your own life!

The Weak and the Strong/ Romans 14:1–4

Accept him whose faith is weak, without passing judgment on disputable matters. ²One man's faith allows him to eat everything, but another man, whose faith is weak, eats only vegetables. ³The man who eats everything must not look down on him who does not, and the man who does not eat everything must not condemn the man who does, for God has accepted him. ⁴Who are you to judge someone else's servant? To his own master he stands or falls. And he will stand, for the Lord is able to make him stand.

A THOUGHT: *Each person is ultimately accountable to Christ, not to others. While the church must be uncompromising in its stand against activities expressly forbidden by Scripture (adultery, homosexuality, murder, theft), it should not create additional rules and regulations and give them equal standing with God's law. Many times Christians base their moral judgments on opinion, personal dislikes, or cultural bias rather than on the Word of God. When they do this, they show that their own faith is weak. They do not think God is powerful enough to guide his children without having to protect his "interests" by making additional requirements for the Christian life. Let us not become entangled in man-made rules. Instead, let us demonstrate our liberty in Christ by being sensitive to others and loving others unselfishly.*

Proverbs for Today/ 8:27–32

I was there when he set the heavens in place, when he marked out the horizon on the face of the deep, when he established the clouds above and fixed securely the fountains of the deep, when he gave the sea its boundary so the waters would not overstep his command, and when he marked out the foundations of the earth. Then I was the craftsman at his side. I was filled with delight day after day, rejoicing always in his presence, rejoicing in his whole world and delighting in mankind. "Now then, my sons, listen to me; blessed are those who keep my ways."

FEBRUARY 11

Jesus Predicts His Own Death/ Matthew 16:13–28

When Jesus came to the region of Caesarea Philippi, he asked his disciples, "Who do people say the Son of Man is?"

14They replied, "Some say John the Baptist; others say Elijah; and still others, Jeremiah or one of the prophets."

15"But what about you?" he asked. "Who do you say I am?"

16Simon Peter answered, "You are the Christ, the Son of the living God."

17Jesus replied, "Blessed are you, Simon son of Jonah, for this was not revealed to you by man, but by my Father in heaven. 18And I tell you that you are Peter, and on this rock I will build my church, and the gates of Hades will not overcome it. 19I will give you the keys of the kingdom of heaven; whatever you bind on earth will be bound in heaven, and whatever you loose on earth will be loosed in heaven." 20Then he warned his disciples not to tell anyone that he was the Christ.

21From that time on Jesus began to explain to his disciples that he must go to Jerusalem and suffer many things at the hands of the elders, chief priests and teachers of the law, and that he must be killed and on the third day be raised to life.

22Peter took him aside and began to rebuke him. "Never, Lord!" he said. "This shall never happen to you!"

23Jesus turned and said to Peter, "Get behind me, Satan! You are a stumbling block to me; you do not have in mind the things of God, but the things of men."

24Then Jesus said to his disciples, "If anyone would come after me, he must deny himself and take up his cross and follow me. 25For whoever wants to save his life will lose it, but whoever loses his life for me will find it. 26What good will it be for a man if he gains the whole world, yet forfeits his soul? Or what can a man give in exchange for his soul? 27For the Son of Man is going to come in his Father's glory with his angels, and then he will reward each person according to what he has done. 28I tell you the truth, some who are standing here will not taste death before they see the Son of Man coming in his kingdom."

A THOUGHT: *The disciples answered Jesus' question with the view that most people held—that Jesus was one of the great prophets who had come back to life. Peter, however, confesses that Jesus is the promised and long-awaited Messiah. If Jesus asked you this question, how would you answer? Is he your Lord and Messiah? Following Jesus means to be completely committed to him—to take up your cross and follow him—to risk even death, with no turning back.*

Jesus Lord of Both Dead and Living/ Romans 14:5–9

One man considers one day more sacred than another; another man considers every day alike. Each one should be fully convinced in his own mind. 6He who regards one day as special, does so to the Lord. He who eats meat, eats to the Lord, for he gives thanks to God; and he who abstains, does so to the Lord and gives thanks to God. 7For none of us lives to himself alone and none of us dies to himself alone. [8]If we live, we live to the Lord; and if we die, we die to the Lord. So, whether we live or die, we belong to the Lord.

[9]For this very reason, Christ died and returned to life so that he might be the Lord of both the dead and the living.

A THOUGHT: *In all that we do we must remember that we live to obey Jesus Christ. We should see every part of our lives in relationship to God. This gives life meaning. When God is the central focus of all of life, all of life's goals, desires, wants, and activities can be seen in relation to taking joy in God's good gifts, obeying him, and working with the values of his kingdom in mind.*

Proverbs for Today/ 8:33–36

"Listen to my instruction and be wise; do not ignore it. Blessed is the man who listens to me, watching daily at my doors, waiting at my doorway. For whoever finds me finds life and receives favor from the LORD. But whoever fails to find me harms himself; all who hate me love death."

FEBRUARY 12

The Transfiguration of Jesus/ Matthew 17:1–13

After six days Jesus took with him Peter, James and John the brother of James, and led them up a high mountain by themselves. [2]There he was transfigured before them. His face shone like the sun, and his clothes became as white as the light. [3]Just then there appeared before them Moses and Elijah, talking with Jesus.

[4]Peter said to Jesus, "Lord, it is good for us to be here. If you wish, I will put up three shelters—one for you, one for Moses and one for Elijah."

[5]While he was still speaking, a bright cloud enveloped them, and a voice from the cloud said, "This is my Son, whom I love; with him I am well pleased. Listen to him!"

[6]When the disciples heard this, they fell facedown to the ground, terrified. [7]But Jesus came and touched them. "Get up," he said. "Don't be afraid." [8]When they looked up, they saw no one except Jesus.

[9]As they were coming down the mountain, Jesus

instructed them, "Don't tell anyone what you have seen, until the Son of Man has been raised from the dead."

10The disciples asked him, "Why then do the teachers of the law say that Elijah must come first?"

11Jesus replied, "To be sure, Elijah comes and will restore all things. 12But I tell you, Elijah has already come, and they did not recognize him, but have done to him everything they wished. In the same way the Son of Man is going to suffer at their hands." 13Then the disciples understood that he was talking to them about John the Baptist.

A THOUGHT: *Moses and Elijah were two of the greatest prophets in the Old Testament. Moses represents the Law. He wrote the Pentateuch (the first five books of the Bible). Elijah represents the prophets who foretold the coming of the Messiah. Their presence with Jesus confirms his messianic mission—to fulfill God's Law and the words of God's prophets. Just as God's voice in the cloud over Mount Sinai confirmed the authority of the Mosaic law, God's voice at the transfiguration confirmed Jesus' authority as the Son of God.*

Be Sensitive to Others/ Romans 14:10–16

You, then, why do you judge your brother? Or why do you look down on your brother? For we will all stand before God's judgment seat. 11It is written:

" 'As surely as I live,' says the Lord,
'every knee will bow before me;
    every tongue will confess to God.' "

12So then, each of us will give an account of himself to God.

13Therefore let us stop passing judgment on one another. Instead, make up your mind not to put any stumbling block or obstacle in your brother's way. 14As one who is in the Lord Jesus, I am fully convinced that no food is unclean in itself. But if anyone regards something as unclean, then for him it is unclean. 15If your brother is distressed because of what you eat, you are no longer acting in love. Do not by your eating destroy your brother for whom Christ died. 16Do not allow what you consider good to be spoken of as evil.

A THOUGHT: *Both "strong" and "weak" Christians can cause their brothers to stumble. The strong but insensitive Christian may flaunt his freedom and intentionally offend others' consciences. The scrupulous but weak Christian may fence in others with petty rules and regulations until they can't take it any longer. Paul wants his readers* to be both strong in the faith and sensitive to the needs of others. Since we are all strong in some areas and weak in others, we need constantly to monitor the effect of our behavior on others.

Proverbs for Today/ 9:1–6

Wisdom has built her house; she has hewn out its seven pillars. She has prepared her meat and mixed her wine; she has also set her table. She has sent out her maids, and she calls from the highest point of the city. "Let all who are simple come in here!" she says to those who lack judgment. "Come, eat my food and drink the wine I have mixed. Leave your simple ways and you will live; walk in the way of understanding."

FEBRUARY 13

Jesus Heals an Epileptic Boy/ Matthew 17:14–21

When they came to the crowd, a man approached Jesus and knelt before him. 15"Lord, have mercy on my son," he said. "He has seizures and is suffering greatly. He often falls into the fire or into the water. 16I brought him to your disciples, but they could not heal him."

17"O unbelieving and perverse generation," Jesus replied, "how long shall I stay with you? How long shall I put up with you? Bring the boy here to me." 18Jesus rebuked the demon, and it came out of the boy, and he was healed from that moment.

19Then the disciples came to Jesus in private and asked, "Why couldn't we drive it out?"

20He replied, "Because you have so little faith. I tell you the truth, if you have faith as small as a mustard seed, you can say to this mountain, 'Move from here to there' and it will move. Nothing will be impossible for you.*"

A THOUGHT: *The disciples were unable to heal this boy, so they asked Jesus why. He pointed to their little faith which was small even in comparison with a mustard seed. The mustard seed produced a great plant, but their faith produced little. Perhaps they had tried to heal the boy with their own ability rather than relying upon God's power.*

*20 Some manuscripts you. 21But this kind does not go out except by prayer and fasting.

There is great power in even a little faith when God is with us. If we feel weak or powerless as Christians, we should examine our faith, making sure we are trusting not in our own abilities to produce results, but in God's power.

Build Each Other Up/ Romans 14:17–23

For the kingdom of God is not a matter of eating and drinking, but of righteousness, peace and joy in the Holy Spirit, 18because anyone who serves Christ in this way is pleasing to God and approved by men.

19Let us therefore make every effort to do what leads to peace and to mutual edification. 20Do not destroy the work of God for the sake of food. All food is clean, but it is wrong for a man to eat anything that causes someone else to stumble. 21It is better not to eat meat or drink wine or to do anything else that will cause your brother to fall.

22So whatever you believe about these things keep between yourself and God. Blessed is the man who does not condemn himself by what he approves. 23But the man who has doubts is condemned if he eats, because his eating is not from faith; and everything that does not come from faith is sin.

A THOUGHT: *Sin is not just a private matter. Everything we do affects others, and we have to think of others constantly. God created us to be interdependent, not independent. Let us seek to do all things out of love for God and out of a genuine desire to meet the needs of others. If we do this we will be building up the unity of the church.*

Proverbs for Today/ 9:7–8

"Whoever corrects a mocker invites insult; whoever rebukes a wicked man incurs abuse. Do not rebuke a mocker or he will hate you; rebuke a wise man and he will love you."

FEBRUARY 14

A Coin to Pay Taxes/ Matthew 17:22–27

When they came together in Galilee, he said to them, "The Son of Man is going to be betrayed into the hands of men.

23They will kill him, and on the third day he will be raised to life." And the disciples were filled with grief.

24After Jesus and his disciples arrived in Capernaum, the collectors of the two-drachma tax came to Peter and asked, "Doesn't your teacher pay the temple tax?"

25"Yes, he does," he replied.

When Peter came into the house, Jesus was the first to speak. "What do you think, Simon?" he asked. "From whom do the kings of the earth collect duty and taxes—from their own sons or from others?"

26"From others," Peter answered.

"Then the sons are exempt," Jesus said to him. 27"But so that we may not offend them, go to the lake and throw out your line. Take the first fish you catch; open its mouth and you will find a four-drachma coin. Take it and give it to them for my tax and yours."

A THOUGHT: *The disciples didn't understand why Jesus kept talking about his death, because they expected him to set up a political, earthly kingdom—his death would dash their hopes. They didn't know that Jesus' death and resurrection would establish his kingdom.*

As God's people, we are foreigners on earth because our loyalty is always to Jesus—whose kingdom is not of this world. Still we have to cooperate with the governmental authorities and be responsible citizens. Ambassadors to another country keep the local laws in order to represent well the one who sent them. We are Christ's ambassadors. Are you being a good foreign ambassador for him to this world?

Adopt the Attitude of Christ/ Romans 15:1–6

We who are strong ought to bear with the failings of the weak and not to please ourselves. 2Each of us should please his neighbor for his good, to build him up. 3For even Christ did not please himself but, as it is written: "The insults of those who insult you have fallen on me." 4For everything that was written in the past was written to teach us, so that through endurance and the encouragement of the Scriptures we might have hope.

5May the God who gives endurance and encouragement give you a spirit of unity among yourselves as you follow Christ Jesus, 6so that with one heart and mouth you may glorify the God and Father of our Lord Jesus Christ.

A THOUGHT: *To accept Jesus' lordship in all areas of life means to share his values and his perspective. Just as we take Jesus' view on the authority of Scripture, the nature of heaven, and the resurrection,* we are to have his attitude of love toward others as well. As we grow in faith and come to know Jesus better, we become more capable of maintaining this attitude throughout each day.

Proverbs for Today/ 9:9–10

Instruct a wise man and he will be wiser still; teach a righteous man and he will add to his learning. "The fear of the LORD is the beginning of wisdom, and knowledge of the Holy One is understanding."

FEBRUARY 15

Greatness in the Kingdom of Heaven/ Matthew 18:1–20

At that time the disciples came to Jesus and asked, "Who is the greatest in the kingdom of heaven?"

2He called a little child and had him stand among them. 3And he said: "I tell you the truth, unless you change and become like little children, you will never enter the kingdom of heaven. 4Therefore, whoever humbles himself like this child is the greatest in the kingdom of heaven.

5"And whoever welcomes a little child like this in my name welcomes me. 6But if anyone causes one of these little ones who believe in me to sin, it would be better for him to have a large millstone hung around his neck and to be drowned in the depths of the sea.

7"Woe to the world because of the things that cause people to sin! Such things must come, but woe to the man through whom they come! 8If your hand or your foot causes you to sin cut it off and throw it away. It is better for you to enter life maimed or crippled than to have two hands or two feet and be thrown into eternal fire. 9And if your eye causes you to sin, gouge it out and throw it away. It is better for you to enter life with one eye than to have two eyes and be thrown into the fire of hell.

10"See that you do not look down on one of these little ones. For I tell you that their angels in heaven always see the face of my Father in heaven.*

*10 Some manuscripts heaven. 11The Son of Man came to save what was lost.

12"What do you think? If a man owns a hundred sheep, and one of them wanders away, will he not leave the ninety-nine on the hills and go to look for the one that wandered off? 13And if he finds it, I tell you the truth, he is happier about that one sheep than about the ninety-nine that did not wander off. 14In the same way your Father in heaven is not willing that any of these little ones should be lost.

15"If your brother sins against you, go and show him his fault, just between the two of you. If he listens to you, you have won your brother over. 16But if he will not listen, take one or two others along, so that 'every matter may be established by the testimony of two or three witnesses.' 17If he refuses to listen to them, tell it to the church; and if he refuses to listen even to the church, treat him as you would a pagan or a tax collector.

18"I tell you the truth, whatever you bind on earth will be bound in heaven, and whatever you loose on earth will be loosed in heaven.

19"Again, I tell you that if two of you on earth agree about anything you ask for, it will be done for you by my Father in heaven. 20For where two or three come together in my name, there am I with them."

A THOUGHT: *Jesus points to the characteristics of a child to help his self-centered disciples get the message. We are not to be childish (like the disciples, arguing over petty issues), but rather, childlike, with humble and sincere hearts. The disciples were so preoccupied with the organization of Jesus' earthly kingdom that they lost sight of its divine purpose. Instead of seeking a place of service, they sought positions of advantage. How easy it is to lose our eternal perspective and to seek to fulfill our own ambitions. How hard it is to identify with the "little children"—weak and dependent people with no status or influence. Are you being childlike or childish?*

Gentiles Should Rejoice in God's Grace/ Romans 15:7–17

Accept one another, then, just as Christ accepted you, in order to bring praise to God. 8For I tell you that Christ has become a servant of the Jews on behalf of God's truth, to confirm the promises made to the patriarchs 9so that the Gentiles may glorify God for his mercy, as it is written:

> "Therefore I will praise you among the Gentiles;
> I will sing hymns to your name."

¹⁰Again, it says,

"Rejoice, O Gentiles, with his people."

¹¹And again,

"Praise the Lord, all you Gentiles,
    and sing praises to him, all you peoples."

¹²And again, Isaiah says,

"The Root of Jesse will spring up,
    one who will arise to rule over the nations;
the Gentiles will hope in him."

¹³May the God of hope fill you with all joy and peace as you trust in him, so that you may overflow with hope by the power of the Holy Spirit.

¹⁴I myself am convinced, my brothers, that you yourselves are full of goodness, complete in knowledge and competent to instruct one another. ¹⁵I have written you quite boldly on some points, as if to remind you of them again, because of the grace God gave me ¹⁶to be a minister of Christ Jesus to the Gentiles with the priestly duty of proclaiming the gospel of God, so that the Gentiles might become an offering acceptable to God, sanctified by the Holy Spirit.

¹⁷Therefore I glory in Christ Jesus in my service to God.

A THOUGHT: *Paul was not proud of what he had done, but of what God had done through him. Being proud of God's work is not a sin—it is worship. If you are not sure whether your pride is selfish or holy, ask yourself this question: Are you just as proud of what God is doing through other people as of what he is doing through you?*

Proverbs for Today/ 9:11–12

"For through me your days will be many, and years will be added to your life. If you are wise, your wisdom will reward you; if you are a mocker, you alone will suffer."

The Parable of the Unforgiving Servant/
Matthew 18:21–35

Then Peter came to Jesus and asked, "Lord, how many times shall I forgive my brother when he sins against me? Up to seven times?"

22Jesus answered, "I tell you, not seven times, but seventy-seven times.

23"Therefore, the kingdom of heaven is like a king who wanted to settle accounts with his servants. 24As he began the settlement, a man who owed him ten thousand talents was brought to him. 25Since he was not able to pay, the master ordered that he and his wife and his children and all that he had be sold to repay the debt.

26"The servant fell on his knees before him. 'Be patient with me,' he begged, 'and I will pay back everything.' 27The servant's master took pity on him, canceled the debt and let him go.

28"But when that servant went out, he found one of his fellow servants who owed him a hundred denarii. He grabbed him and began to choke him. 'Pay back what you owe me!' he demanded.

29"His fellow servant fell to his knees and begged him, 'Be patient with me, and I will pay you back.'

30"But he refused. Instead, he went off and had the man thrown into prison until he could pay the debt. 31When the other servants saw what had happened, they were greatly distressed and went and told their master everything that had happened.

32"Then the master called the servant in. 'You wicked servant,' he said, 'I canceled all that debt of yours because you begged me to. 33Shouldn't you have had mercy on your fellow servant just as I had on you?' 34In anger his master turned him over to the jailers to be tortured, until he should pay back all he owed.

35"This is how my heavenly Father will treat each of you unless you forgive your brother from your heart."

A THOUGHT: *The rabbis taught that Jews should forgive those who offend them three times. Peter, in trying to be especially generous, asked Jesus if seven (the "perfect" number) was enough times to forgive someone. But Jesus answered, "seventy-seven times," meaning that we shouldn't even keep track of how many times we forgive someone.*

Realizing how completely Christ has forgiven us should produce a free and generous attitude of forgiveness toward others. When we don't forgive others, we are setting ourselves outside and above Christ's law of love.

Paul, Apostle to the Gentiles/ Romans 15:18–22

I will not venture to speak of anything except what Christ has accomplished through me in leading the Gentiles to obey God by what I have said and done— 19by the power of signs and miracles, through the power of the Spirit. So from Jerusalem all the way around to Illyricum, I have fully proclaimed the gospel of Christ. 20It has always been my ambition to preach the gospel where Christ was not known, so that I would not be building on someone else's foundation. 21Rather, as it is written:

> "Those who were not told about him will see,
>   and those who have not heard will understand."

22This is why I have often been hindered from coming to you.

A THOUGHT: *Paul won people to Christ by: (1) boldly preaching the Good News, (2) living a life in accordance with the Good News, and (3) relying on the power of the Holy Spirit. This is a basic pattern that ought to be followed by all Christians in their evangelizing. All three elements are essential to effective Christian missions.*

Proverbs for Today/ 9:13–18

The woman Folly is loud; she is undisciplined and without knowledge. She sits at the door of her house, on a seat at the highest point of the city, calling out to those who pass by, who go straight on their way. "Let all who are simple come in here!" she says to those who lack judgment. "Stolen water is sweet; food eaten in secret is delicious!" But little do they know that the dead are there, that her guests are in the depths of the grave.

Jesus Teaches about Divorce/ Matthew 19:1–12

When Jesus had finished saying these things, he left Galilee and went into the region of Judea to the other side of the Jordan. 2Large crowds followed him, and he healed them there.

3Some Pharisees came to him to test him. They asked, "Is it lawful for a man to divorce his wife for any and every reason?"

4"Haven't you read," he replied, "that at the beginning the Creator 'made them male and female,' 5and said, 'For this reason a man will leave his father and mother and be united to his wife, and the two will become one flesh'? 6So they are no longer two, but one. Therefore what God has joined together, let man not separate."

7"Why then," they asked, "did Moses command that a man give his wife a certificate of divorce and send her away?"

8Jesus replied, "Moses permitted you to divorce your wives because your hearts were hard. But it was not this way from the beginning. 9I tell you that anyone who divorces his wife, except for marital unfaithfulness, and marries another woman commits adultery."

10The disciples said to him, "If this is the situation between a husband and wife, it is better not to marry."

11Jesus replied, "Not everyone can accept this word, but only those to whom it has been given. 12For some are eunuchs because they were born that way; others were made that way by men; and others have renounced marriage because of the kingdom of heaven. The one who can accept this should accept it."

A THOUGHT: *John was put in prison and killed for his public opinions on marriage and divorce, and the Pharisees hoped to trap Jesus too. They were trying to trick Jesus by having him choose sides in a theological controversy. Two main groups had two opposing views on the issue of divorce. One group supported divorce for almost any reason. The other believed divorce could be allowed only for marital unfaithfulness. But in his answer, Jesus focused on marriage rather than on divorce. He pointed out that Scripture intended marriage to be permanent.*

Couples must decide against divorce from the start and build their marriage on mutual commitment. There are also many good reasons for not marrying, one of them being to have more time to work for God's kingdom. Don't assume God wants everyone to marry. For many it may be better if they don't. But be sure you prayerfully seek God's will before you plunge into the lifelong commitment of marriage.

The Collection for the Jerusalem Church/ Romans 15:23–33

But now that there is no more place for me to work in these regions, and since I have been longing for many years to see you, 24I plan to do so when I go to Spain. I hope to visit you while passing through and to have you assist me on my journey there, after I have enjoyed your company for a while. 25Now, however, I am on my way to Jerusalem in the service of the saints there. 26For Macedonia and Achaia were pleased to make a contribution for the poor among the saints in Jerusalem. 27They were pleased to do it, and indeed they owe it to them. For if the Gentiles have shared in the Jews' spiritual blessings, they owe it to the Jews to share with them their material blessings. 28So after I have completed this task and have made sure that they have received this fruit, I will go to Spain and visit you on the way. 29I know that when I come to you, I will come in the full measure of the blessing of Christ.

30I urge you, brothers, by our Lord Jesus Christ and by the love of the Spirit, to join me in my struggle by praying to God for me. 31Pray that I may be rescued from the unbelievers in Judea and that my service in Jerusalem may be acceptable to the saints there, 32so that by God's will I may come to you with joy and together with you be refreshed. 33The God of peace be with you all. Amen.

A THOUGHT: *The Christians in Jerusalem at this time had experienced a severe drought so that many of them were struggling to keep food on the table. Paul had made a point of mentioning this to the Gentile congregations that he evangelized. The Gentile Christians responded in love by sending the necessary financial resources for the Jerusalem church to distribute goods to those in need. It was right that they meet the needs of the Jerusalem Christians because the Jerusalem church had been the source of missionaries who shared the Good News of salvation with the Gentiles. Our concern should also be to share what we have with those in need. God has called us to demonstrate his love in very practical everyday sorts of ways—such as feeding the hungry, clothing the naked, and caring for the sick. Let the love which God has put in our hearts become a reality in sacrificial sharing with those in need.*

Proverbs for Today/ 10:1–2

The proverbs of Solomon: A wise son brings joy to his father, but a foolish son grief to his mother. □ Ill-gotten treasures are of no value, but righteousness delivers from death.

FEBRUARY 18

Jesus Blesses the Little Children/ Matthew 19:13–15

Then little children were brought to Jesus for him to place his hands on them and pray for them. But the disciples rebuked those who brought them.

14Jesus said, "Let the little children come to me, and do not hinder them, for the kingdom of heaven belongs to such as these." 15When he had placed his hands on them, he went on from there.

A THOUGHT: *The disciples must have forgotten what Jesus had said about children. Jesus wanted little children to come because he loves them and because they have the kind of attitude needed to approach God. He didn't mean that the kingdom of heaven is only for children, but that people need childlike attitudes of trust in God. The receptiveness of little children was a great contrast to the stubbornness of the religious leaders who let their religious education and sophistication stand in the way of the simple faith needed to believe in Jesus.*

Paul Greets His Friends at Rome/ Romans 16:1–16

I commend to you our sister Phoebe, a servant of the church in Cenchrea. 2I ask you to receive her in the Lord in a way worthy of the saints and to give her any help she may need from you, for she has been a great help to many people, including me.

3Greet Priscilla and Aquila, my fellow workers in Christ Jesus. 4They risked their lives for me. Not only I but all the churches of the Gentiles are grateful to them. 5Greet also the church that meets at their house.

Greet my dear friend Epenetus, who was the first convert to Christ in the province of Asia.

6Greet Mary, who worked very hard for you.

7Greet Andronicus and Junias, my relatives who have been in prison with me. They are outstanding among the apostles, and they were in Christ before I was.

8Greet Ampliatus, whom I love in the Lord.

9Greet Urbanus, our fellow worker in Christ, and my dear friend Stachys.

10Greet Apelles, tested and approved in Christ.

Greet those who belong to the household of Aristobulus.

11Greet Herodion, my relative.

Greet those in the household of Narcissus who are in the Lord.

12Greet Tryphena and Tryphosa, those women who work hard in the Lord.

Greet my dear friend Persis, another woman who has worked very hard in the Lord.

13Greet Rufus, chosen in the Lord, and his mother, who has been a mother to me, too.

14Greet Asyncritus, Phlegon, Hermes, Patrobas, Hermas and the brothers with them.

15Greet Philologus, Julia, Nereus and his sister, and Olympas and all the saints with them.

16Greet one another with a holy kiss.

All the churches of Christ send greetings.

A THOUGHT: *Paul's personal greetings went to Romans and Greeks, Jews and Gentiles, men and women, prisoners and prominent citizens. The church's base was broad: it crossed cultural, social, and economic lines. From this list we learn that the Christian community was an incredibly diverse group. This is as it ought to be. The oneness we have in Christ should supercede all cultural barriers. The Good News is a great equalizer—it places us all on the same footing before the cross!*

Proverbs for Today/ 10:3–4

The LORD does not let the righteous go hungry but he thwarts the craving of the wicked. □ Lazy hands make a man poor, but diligent hands bring wealth.

Jesus and the Rich Man/ Matthew 19:16–30

Now a man came up to Jesus and asked, "Teacher, what good thing must I do to get eternal life?"

17"Why do you ask me about what is good?" Jesus replied. "There is only One who is good. If you want to enter life, obey the commandments."

18"Which ones?" the man inquired.

Jesus replied, " 'Do not murder, do not commit adultery, do not steal, do not give false testimony, 19honor your father and mother,' and 'love your neighbor as yourself.' "

20"All these I have kept," the young man said. "What do I still lack?"

21Jesus answered, "If you want to be perfect, go, sell your possessions and give to the poor, and you will have treasure in heaven. Then come, follow me."

22When the young man heard this, he went away sad, because he had great wealth.

23Then Jesus said to his disciples, "I tell you the truth, it is hard for a rich man to enter the kingdom of heaven. 24Again I tell you, it is easier for a camel to go through the eye of a needle than for a rich man to enter the kingdom of God."

25When the disciples heard this, they were greatly astonished and asked, "Who then can be saved?"

26Jesus looked at them and said, "With man this is impossible, but with God all things are possible."

27Peter answered him, "We have left everything to follow you! What then will there be for us?"

28Jesus said to them, "I tell you the truth, at the renewal of all things, when the Son of Man sits on his glorious throne, you who have followed me will also sit on twelve thrones, judging the twelve tribes of Israel. 29And everyone who has left houses or brothers or sisters or father or mother or children or fields for my sake will receive a hundred times as much and will inherit eternal life. 30But many who are first will be last, and many who are last will be first."

A THOUGHT: *In response to the young man's question about how to have eternal life, Jesus told him to keep God's Ten Commandments. Jesus then listed six of them, all referring to relationships with others. When the young man replied that he had kept all of these laws, Jesus told him he must do something more—sell everything and give the money to the poor. This request showed the man's weakness. In reality, his wealth was his god, his "graven image," and he would not give it up. We cannot love God with all our hearts and keep our money to ourselves. We must use what God has given us to serve others.*

Avoid Divisive People/ Romans 16:17–27

I urge you, brothers, to watch out for those who cause divisions and put obstacles in your way that are contrary to the teaching you have learned. Keep away from them. 18For such people are not serving our Lord Christ, but their own appetites. By smooth talk and flattery they deceive the minds of naive people. 19Everyone has heard about your obedience, so I am full of joy over you; but I want you to be wise about what is good, and innocent about what is evil.

20The God of peace will soon crush Satan under your feet.

The grace of our Lord Jesus be with you.

21Timothy, my fellow worker, sends his greetings to you, as do Lucius, Jason and Sosipater, my relatives.

22I, Tertius, who wrote down this letter, greet you in the Lord.

23Gaius, whose hospitality I and the whole church here enjoy, sends you his greetings.

Erastus, who is the city's director of public works, and our brother Quartus send you their greetings. '

25Now to him who is able to establish you by my gospel and the proclamation of Jesus Christ, according to the revelation of the mystery hidden for long ages past, 26but now revealed and made known through the prophetic writings by the command of the eternal God, so that all nations might believe and obey him— 27to the only wise God be glory forever through Jesus Christ! Amen.

A THOUGHT: *The unity of the church was very important to Paul. He fought hard against those who wanted to bring division within the church. We also must be careful with those who want to split churches. The church should never be split over minor points of doctrine—as is too often the case. Let us be careful that we do not*

*'23 Some manuscripts *their greetings.* 24May the grace of our Lord Jesus Christ be with all of you. Amen.

divide Christians from Christians—for in Christ we belong to one another. We should avoid those who wish to make such divisions between Christians.

Proverbs for Today/ 10:5

He who gathers crops in summer is a wise son, but he who sleeps during harvest is a disgraceful son.

FEBRUARY 20

The Parable of the Vineyard Workers/ Matthew 20:1–19

"For the kingdom of heaven is like a landowner who went out early in the morning to hire men to work in his vineyard. 2He agreed to pay them a denarius for the day and sent them into his vineyard.

3"About the third hour he went out and saw others standing in the marketplace doing nothing. 4He told them, 'You also go and work in my vineyard, and I will pay you whatever is right.' 5So they went.

"He went out again about the sixth hour and the ninth hour and did the same thing. 6About the eleventh hour he went out and found still others standing around. He asked them, 'Why have you been standing here all day long doing nothing?'

7" 'Because no one has hired us,' they answered.

"He said to them, 'You also go and work in my vineyard.'

8"When evening came, the owner of the vineyard said to his foreman, 'Call the workers and pay them their wages, beginning with the last ones hired and going on to the first.'

9"The workers who were hired about the eleventh hour came and each received a denarius. 10So when those came who were hired first, they expected to receive more. But each one of them also received a denarius. 11When they received it, they began to grumble against the landowner. 12'These men who were hired last worked only one hour,' they said, 'and you have made them equal to us who have borne the burden of the work and the heat of the day.'

13"But he answered one of them, 'Friend, I am not being

unfair to you. Didn't you agree to work for a denarius? 14Take your pay and go. I want to give the man who was hired last the same as I gave you. 15Don't I have the right to do what I want with my own money? Or are you envious because I am generous?'

16"So the last will be first, and the first will be last."

17Now as Jesus was going up to Jerusalem, he took the twelve disciples aside and said to them, 18"We are going up to Jerusalem, and the Son of Man will be betrayed to the chief priests and the teachers of the law. They will condemn him to death 19and will turn him over to the Gentiles to be mocked and flogged and crucified. On the third day he will be raised to life!"

A THOUGHT: *In this parable, God is the estate owner and believers are those who work for him. This parable was for those who felt superior because of heritage or favored position. This parable is not about rewards, but about salvation. It clarifies the membership rules of the kingdom of heaven—entrance is by God's grace alone. Do you resent God's gracious acceptance of the despised, the outcast, and the sinners who have turned to him for forgiveness? Are you ever jealous of what God has given to another person? Instead, focus on God's gracious benefits to you, and be thankful for what you have.*

God's Gifts to the Corinthian Church/ 1 Corinthians 1:1–9

Paul, called to be an apostle of Christ Jesus by the will of God, and our brother Sosthenes,

2To the church of God in Corinth, to those sanctified in Christ Jesus and called to be holy, together with all those everywhere who call on the name of our Lord Jesus Christ—their Lord and ours:

3Grace and peace to you from God our Father and the Lord Jesus Christ.

4I always thank God for you because of his grace given you in Christ Jesus. 5For in him you have been enriched in every way—in all your speaking and in all your knowledge— 6because our testimony about Christ was confirmed in you. 7Therefore you do not lack any spiritual gift as you eagerly wait for our Lord Jesus Christ to be revealed. 8He will keep you strong to the end, so that you will be blameless on the day of our Lord Jesus Christ. 9God, who has called you into fellowship with his Son Jesus Christ our Lord, is faithful.

A THOUGHT: *The Corinthian church members had all the spiritual gifts they needed to live the Christian life, to witness for Christ, and to stand against the paganism and immorality of Corinth. But instead of using what God had given them, they were arguing over which gifts were more important. God has not given us gifts to raise our status, but to give us the spiritual capacity to serve others. Let us not take pride in what has been given to us; rather, let us sacrifice ourselves in service to others.*

Proverbs for Today/ 10:6–7

Blessings crown the head of the righteous, but violence overwhelms the mouth of the wicked. □ The memory of the righteous will be a blessing, but the name of the wicked will rot.

FEBRUARY 21

The True Leader Is a Servant/ Matthew 20:20–28

Then the mother of Zebedee's sons came to Jesus with her sons [James and John] and, kneeling down, asked a favor of him.

21"What is it you want?" he asked.

She said, "Grant that one of these two sons of mine may sit at your right and the other at your left in your kingdom."

22"You don't know what you are asking," Jesus said to them. "Can you drink the cup I am going to drink?"

"We can," they answered.

23Jesus said to them, "You will indeed drink from my cup, but to sit at my right or left is not for me to grant. These places belong to those for whom they have been prepared by my Father."

24When the ten heard about this, they were indignant with the two brothers. 25Jesus called them together and said, "You know that the rulers of the Gentiles lord it over them, and their high officials exercise authority over them. 26Not so with you. Instead, whoever wants to become great among you must be your servant, 27and whoever wants to be first must be your slave— 28just as the Son of Man did not come to be served, but to serve, and to give his life as a ransom for many."

A THOUGHT: *The disciples were upset because James and John were trying to grab the top positions. All the disciples wanted positions of greatness, but Jesus taught them that the greatest person in God's kingdom is the servant of all. Jesus' purpose in life was to serve others and to give his life away. A real leader has a servant's heart. He appreciates the worth of others and realizes he's not above any job. If you see something that needs to be done, don't wait to be asked. Take the initiative and do it like a faithful servant.*

Divisions within the Corinthian Church/
1 Corinthians 1:10–17

I appeal to you, brothers, in the name of our Lord Jesus Christ, that all of you agree with one another so that there may be no divisions among you and that you may be perfectly united in mind and thought. 11My brothers, some from Chloe's household have informed me that there are quarrels among you. 12What I mean is this: One of you says, "I follow Paul"; another, "I follow Apollos"; another, "I follow Cephas"; still another, "I follow Christ."

13Is Christ divided? Was Paul crucified for you? Were you baptized into the name of Paul? 14I am thankful that I did not baptize any of you except Crispus and Gaius, 15so no one can say that you were baptized into my name. 16(Yes, I also baptized the household of Stephanas; beyond that, I don't remember if I baptized anyone else.) 17For Christ did not send me to baptize, but to preach the gospel—not with words of human wisdom, lest the cross of Christ be emptied of its power.

A THOUGHT: *In this large and diverse Corinthian church, the believers favored different preachers. Because there was as yet no written New Testament, the believers depended heavily on preaching and teaching for spiritual insight into the meaning of the Old Testament. Some followed Paul, who had founded their church; some who had heard Peter in Jerusalem followed him; while others listened only to Apollos, an eloquent and popular preacher who had a dynamic ministry in Corinth. Although these three preachers were united in their message, their personalities attracted different people. Now the church was in danger of dividing. By mentioning Jesus Christ ten times in the first ten verses, Paul makes it clear what all preachers and teachers should emphasize—the Person and work of Jesus Christ. The message is more important than the messenger.*

Proverbs for Today/ 10:8–9

The wise in heart accept commands, but a chattering fool comes to ruin. □ The man of integrity walks securely, but he who takes crooked paths will be found out.

FEBRUARY 22

Jesus Heals Two Blind Men/ Matthew 20:29–34

As Jesus and his disciples were leaving Jericho, a large crowd followed him. 30Two blind men were sitting by the roadside, and when they heard that Jesus was going by, they shouted, "Lord, Son of David, have mercy on us!"

31The crowd rebuked them and told them to be quiet, but they shouted all the louder, "Lord, Son of David, have mercy on us!"

32Jesus stopped and called them. "What do you want me to do for you?" he asked.

33"Lord," they answered, "we want our sight."

34Jesus had compassion on them and touched their eyes. Immediately they received their sight and followed him.

A THOUGHT: *The blind men called Jesus "Lord, Son of David" because the Jews knew that the Messiah would be a descendant of King David. This poor blind beggar could see that Jesus was the long-awaited Messiah, while the religious leaders who witnessed Jesus' miracles were blind to his identity, refusing to open their eyes to the truth. Seeing with your eyes doesn't guarantee seeing with your heart.*

The Power of God/ 1 Corinthians 1:18–25

For the message of the cross is foolishness to those who are perishing, but to us who are being saved it is the power of God. 19For it is written:

"I will destroy the wisdom of the wise;
the intelligence of the intelligent I will frustrate."

20Where is the wise man? Where is the scholar? Where is the philosopher of this age? Has not God made foolish the wisdom of the world? 21For since in the wisdom of God the world through its wisdom did not know him, God was pleased through the foolishness of what was preached to save those who believe. 22Jews demand miraculous signs and Greeks look for wisdom, 23but we preach Christ crucified: a stumbling block to Jews and foolishness to Gentiles, 24but to those whom God has called, both Jews and Greeks, Christ the power of God and the wisdom of God. 25For the foolishness of God is wiser than man's wisdom, and the weakness of God is stronger than man's strength.

A THOUGHT: *The message of Christ's death for sins sounds foolish to those who don't believe. Death seems to be the end of the road, the ultimate weakness. But Jesus did not remain dead. His resurrection shows his power even over death, and he will save us from eternal death and give us everlasting life if we trust him as Savior and Lord. This sounds so simple that many people won't accept it. They try other ways to obtain eternal life (being good, being wise, etc.). But their attempts will not work. The "foolish" people who simply accept Christ's offer are actually the wisest of all, because they alone will live eternally with God.*

Proverbs for Today/ 10:10

He who winks maliciously causes grief, and a chattering fool comes to ruin.

FEBRUARY 23

Jesus' Triumphal Entry into Jerusalem/ Matthew 21:1–17

As they approached Jerusalem and came to Bethphage on the Mount of Olives, Jesus sent two disciples, 2saying to them, "Go to the village ahead of you, and at once you will find a donkey tied there, with her colt by her. Untie them and bring them to me. 3If anyone says anything to you, tell him that the Lord needs them, and he will send them right away."

4This took place to fulfill what was spoken through the prophet:

5"Say to the Daughter of Zion,
    'See, your king comes to you,
gentle and riding on a donkey,
    on a colt, the foal of a donkey.'"

⁶The disciples went and did as Jesus had instructed them. ⁷They brought the donkey and the colt, placed their cloaks on them, and Jesus sat on them. ⁸A very large crowd spread their cloaks on the road, while others cut branches from the trees and spread them on the road. ⁹The crowds that went ahead of him and those that followed shouted,

"Hosanna to the Son of David!"

"Blessed is he who comes in the name of the Lord!"

"Hosanna in the highest!"

¹⁰When Jesus entered Jerusalem, the whole city was stirred and asked, "Who is this?"

¹¹The crowds answered, "This is Jesus, the prophet from Nazareth in Galilee."

¹²Jesus entered the temple area and drove out all who were buying and selling there. He overturned the tables of the money changers and the benches of those selling doves. ¹³"It is written," he said to them, " 'My house will be called a house of prayer,' but you are making it a 'den of robbers.' "

¹⁴The blind and the lame came to him at the temple, and he healed them. ¹⁵But when the chief priests and the teachers of the law saw the wonderful things he did and the children shouting in the temple area, "Hosanna to the Son of David," they were indignant.

¹⁶"Do you hear what these children are saying?" they asked him.

"Yes," replied Jesus, "have you never read,

" 'From the lips of children and infants
    you have ordained praise'?"

¹⁷And he left them and went out of the city to Bethany, where he spent the night.

A THOUGHT: *This event is celebrated by Christians on Palm Sunday, one week before Easter. It celebrates Jesus' entry into Jerusalem in fulfillment of messianic prophecy. People lined the highway, praising God, waving palm branches, and throwing their cloaks in front of the colt as it passed before them. They were proclaiming that Jesus was the Messiah. Yet they believed that Jesus would be a political ruler who would throw off the yoke of Roman authority and restore Israel to its former glory (as in David's time). But the people were disappointed when their expectations were not fulfilled. A few days later these same people would bow to political pressure and demand that Jesus be crucified. How easy it is to change our loyalties when our expectations are not met.*

The Foolish Will Shame the Wise/
1 Corinthians 1:26–31

Brothers, think of what you were when you were called. Not many of you were wise by human standards; not many were influential; not many were of noble birth. 27But God chose the foolish things of the world to shame the wise; God chose the weak things of the world to shame the strong. 28He chose the lowly things of this world and the despised things—and the things that are not—to nullify the things that are, 29so that no one may boast before him. 30It is because of him that you are in Christ Jesus, who has become for us wisdom from God—that is, our righteousness, holiness and redemption. 31Therefore, as it is written: "Let him who boasts boast in the Lord."

A THOUGHT: *Paul continues to emphasize that the way to receive salvation is so ordinary and simple that any person who wants to can understand it. Skill does not get you into God's kingdom—simple faith does. God planned it this way so no one could boast that his achievements helped him secure eternal life. Salvation is completely the work of God. Through Jesus' death, we become perfect in God's eyes. There is nothing we can do to become acceptable to God; we need only accept what Jesus has already done for us. He has done the work; we acknowledge that work, recognizing his position as God.*

Proverbs for Today/ 10:11–12

The mouth of the righteous is a fountain of life, but violence overwhelms the mouth of the wicked. □ Hatred stirs up dissension, but love covers over all wrongs.

FEBRUARY 24

The Cursing of the Fig Tree/ Matthew 21:18–22

Early in the morning, as he [Jesus] was on his way back to the city, he was hungry. 19Seeing a fig tree by the road, he went up to it but found nothing on it except leaves. Then he said to it, "May you never bear fruit again!" Immediately the tree withered.

20When the disciples saw this, they were amazed. "How did the fig tree wither so quickly?" they asked.

21Jesus replied, "I tell you the truth, if you have faith and do not doubt, not only can you do what was done to the fig tree, but also you can say to this mountain, 'Go, throw yourself into the sea,' and it will be done. 22If you believe, you will receive whatever you ask for in prayer."

A THOUGHT: *Why did Jesus curse the fig tree? This was not a thoughtless, angry act, but an acted-out parable. Jesus was showing his anger at religion without substance. Just as the fig tree looked good from a distance but was fruitless upon close examination, so the Temple looked impressive at first glance, but its sacrifices and other activities were meaningless because they were not done to worship God sincerely. Genuine faith produces fruit for God's kingdom.*

Preaching Christ Crucified/ 1 Corinthians 2:1–10

When I came to you, brothers, I did not come with eloquence or superior wisdom as I proclaimed to you the testimony about God. 2For I resolved to know nothing while I was with you except Jesus Christ and him crucified. 3I came to you in weakness and fear, and with much trembling. 4My message and my preaching were not with wise and persuasive words, but with a demonstration of the Spirit's power, 5so that your faith might not rest on men's wisdom, but on God's power.

6We do, however, speak a message of wisdom among the mature, but not the wisdom of this age or of the rulers of this age, who are coming to nothing. 7No, we speak of God's secret wisdom, a wisdom that has been hidden and that God destined for our glory before time began. 8None of the rulers of this age understood it, for if they had, they would not have crucified the Lord of glory. 9However, as it is written:

"No eye has seen,
    no ear has heard,
no mind has conceived
    what God has prepared for those who love
        him"—

10but God has revealed it to us by his Spirit.

The Spirit searches all things, even the deep things of God.

A THOUGHT: *As a brilliant scholar, Paul could have overwhelmed his listeners with intellectual arguments and persuasive oratory. Instead he shared the simple message of Jesus Christ by allowing the Holy Spirit to guide his words. In sharing the gospel with others, we should follow Paul's example and keep our message simple and basic. The Holy Spirit will give power to our words and use them to bring glory to Jesus.*

Proverbs for Today/ 10:13–14

Wisdom is found on the lips of the discerning, but a rod is for the back of him who lacks judgment. □ Wise men store up knowledge, but the mouth of a fool invites ruin.

FEBRUARY 25

The Parable of the Disloyal Tenants/ Matthew 21:23–46

Jesus entered the temple courts, and, while he was teaching, the chief priests and the elders of the people came to him. "By what authority are you doing these things?" they asked. "And who gave you this authority?"

24Jesus replied, "I will also ask you one question. If you answer me, I will tell you by what authority I am doing these things. 25John's baptism—where did it come from? Was it from heaven, or from men?"

They discussed it among themselves and said, "If we say, 'From heaven,' he will ask, 'Then why didn't you believe him?' 26But if we say, 'From men'—we are afraid of the people, for they all hold that John was a prophet."

27So they answered Jesus, "We don't know."

Then he said, "Neither will I tell you by what authority I am doing these things.

28"What do you think? There was a man who had two sons. He went to the first and said, 'Son, go and work today in the vineyard.'

29" 'I will not,' he answered, but later he changed his mind and went.

³⁰"Then the father went to the other son and said the same thing. He answered, 'I will, sir,' but he did not go.

³¹"Which of the two did what his father wanted?"

"The first," they answered.

Jesus said to them, "I tell you the truth, the tax collectors and the prostitutes are entering the kingdom of God ahead of you. ³²For John came to you to show you the way of righteousness, and you did not believe him, but the tax collectors and the prostitutes did. And even after you saw this, you did not repent and believe him.

³³"Listen to another parable: There was a landowner who planted a vineyard. He put a wall around it, dug a winepress in it and built a watchtower. Then he rented the vineyard to some farmers and went away on a journey. ³⁴When the harvest time approached, he sent his servants to the tenants to collect his fruit.

³⁵"The tenants seized his servants; they beat one, killed another, and stoned a third. ³⁶Then he sent other servants to them, more than the first time, and the tenants treated them the same way. ³⁷Last of all, he sent his son to them. 'They will respect my son,' he said.

³⁸"But when the tenants saw the son, they said to each other, 'This is the heir. Come, let's kill him and take his inheritance.' ³⁹So they took him and threw him out of the vineyard and killed him.

⁴⁰"Therefore, when the owner of the vineyard comes, what will he do to those tenants?"

⁴¹"He will bring those wretches to a wretched end," they replied, "and he will rent the vineyard to other tenants, who will give him his share of the crop at harvest time."

⁴²Jesus said to them, "Have you never read in the Scriptures:

" 'The stone the builders rejected
　has become the capstone;
the Lord has done this,
　and it is marvelous in our eyes'?

⁴³"Therefore I tell you that the kingdom of God will be taken away from you and given to a people who will produce its fruit. ⁴⁴He who falls on this stone will be broken to pieces, but he on whom it falls will be crushed."

⁴⁵When the chief priests and the Pharisees heard Jesus'

parables, they knew he was talking about them. 46They looked for a way to arrest him, but they were afraid of the crowd because the people held that he was a prophet.

A THOUGHT: *The Pharisees demanded to know where Jesus got his authority. They didn't really want an answer to their question; they only wanted to trap him. Jesus answered them by asking a question concerning the source of John the Baptist's authority. Jesus' question forced the Pharisees into a dilemma. Whatever answer they would give would have negative consequences for their position. So they gave no answer. Since the Pharisees were unwilling to openly answer Jesus' question, Jesus gives his answer in the form of a parable. The main characters in this parable are (1) the landowner—God, (2) the vineyard—Israel, (3) the farmers—the Jewish religious leaders, (4) the landowner's men—the prophets and priests who remained faithful to God and preached to Israel, (5) the son—Jesus, and (6) the others—Gentiles. Jesus tells the parable to expose the religious leaders' hypocrisy and their plot to murder him.*

The Spirit Gives Wisdom/ 1 Corinthians 2:11–16

For who among men knows the thoughts of a man except the man's spirit within him? In the same way no one knows the thoughts of God except the Spirit of God. 12We have not received the spirit of the world but the Spirit who is from God, that we may understand what God has freely given us. 13This is what we speak, not in words taught us by human wisdom but in words taught by the Spirit, expressing spiritual truths in spiritual words. 14The man without the Spirit does not accept the things that come from the Spirit of God, for they are foolishness to him, and he cannot understand them, because they are spiritually discerned. 15The spiritual man makes judgments about all things, but he himself is not subject to any man's judgment:

16"For who has known the mind of the Lord
    that he may instruct him?"

But we have the mind of Christ.

A THOUGHT: *No one can comprehend God by human effort, but by his Spirit many of his thoughts are revealed to us. Believers are spiritual people having insight into some of God's plans, thoughts, and actions. By his Holy Spirit we can begin to know his thoughts, discuss them with him, and expect his answers to our prayers. Are you spending enough time with Christ to have his very mind in you? An intimate relationship with Christ comes only from consistent time spent in his presence and in his Word.*

Proverbs for Today/ 10:15–16

The wealth of the rich is their fortified city, but poverty is the ruin of the poor. □ The wages of the righteous bring them life, but the income of the wicked brings them punishment.

FEBRUARY 26

The Parable of the Wedding Banquet/ Matthew 22:1–14

Jesus spoke to them again in parables, saying: 2"The kingdom of heaven is like a king who prepared a wedding banquet for his son. 3He sent his servants to those who had been invited to the banquet to tell them to come, but they refused to come.

4"Then he sent some more servants and said, 'Tell those who have been invited that I have prepared my dinner: My oxen and fattened cattle have been butchered, and everything is ready. Come to the wedding banquet.'

5"But they paid no attention and went off—one to his field, another to his business. 6The rest seized his servants, mistreated them and killed them. 7The king was enraged. He sent his army and destroyed those murderers and burned their city.

8"Then he said to his servants, 'The wedding banquet is ready, but those I invited did not deserve to come. 9Go to the street corners and invite to the banquet anyone you find.' 10So the servants went out into the streets and gathered all the people they could find, both good and bad, and the wedding hall was filled with guests.

11"But when the king came in to see the guests, he noticed a man there who was not wearing wedding clothes. 12'Friend,' he asked, 'how did you get in here without wedding clothes?' The man was speechless.

13"Then the king told the attendants, 'Tie him hand and foot, and throw him outside, into the darkness, where there will be weeping and gnashing of teeth.'

14"For many are invited, but few are chosen."

A THOUGHT: *In first-century Jewish culture, two invitations were expected when banquets were given. The first asked the guests to attend; the second announced that all was ready. Here the king, God, invited his guests three times—and each time they rejected his invitations. God wants us to join him at his banquet, which will last for eternity. That's why he sends us invitations again and again. Have you accepted his invitation?*

Paul Rebukes Divisive Church Members/ 1 Corinthians 3:1–9

Brothers, I could not address you as spiritual but as worldly—mere infants in Christ. 2I gave you milk, not solid food, for you were not yet ready for it. Indeed, you are still not ready. 3You are still worldly. For since there is jealousy and quarreling among you, are you not worldly? Are you not acting like mere men? 4For when one says, "I follow Paul," and another, "I follow Apollos," are you not mere men?

5What, after all, is Apollos? And what is Paul? Only servants, through whom you came to believe—as the Lord has assigned to each his task. 6I planted the seed, Apollos watered it, but God made it grow. 7So neither he who plants nor he who waters is anything, but only God, who makes things grow. 8The man who plants and the man who waters have one purpose, and each will be rewarded according to his own labor. 9For we are God's fellow workers; you are God's field, God's building.

A THOUGHT: *Paul's work was to plant the seed of God's Word in people's hearts. He was a pioneer missionary, one who brought the message of salvation. Apollos' role was to water—to help the believers grow stronger in the faith Paul had helped them discover. Paul founded the church in Corinth, and Apollos built on that foundation. Tragically, the believers in Corinth had split into factions, pledging loyalty to different teachers. Paul wanted them to see that the preachers were merely their guides to point them to God.*

God's work in the world involves many different individuals with a variety of gifts and abilities. There are no superstars in this task, only team members performing their own special roles. We become useful members of God's team by setting aside the desire to receive glory for what we do. The praise that comes from people is comparatively worthless; invaluable approval comes from God.

Proverbs for Today/ 10:17

He who heeds discipline shows the way to life, but whoever ignores correction leads others astray.

Jesus Answers the Pharisees and the Sadducees/
Matthew 22:15–46

Then the Pharisees went out and laid plans to trap him in his words. 16They sent their disciples to him along with the Herodians. "Teacher," they said, "we know you are a man of integrity and that you teach the way of God in accordance with the truth. You aren't swayed by men, because you pay no attention to who they are. 17Tell us then, what is your opinion? Is it right to pay taxes to Caesar or not?"

18But Jesus, knowing their evil intent, said, "You hypocrites, why are you trying to trap me? 19Show me the coin used for paying the tax." They brought him a denarius, 20and he asked them, "Whose portrait is this? And whose inscription?"

21"Caesar's," they replied.

Then he said to them, "Give to Caesar what is Caesar's, and to God what is God's."

22When they heard this, they were amazed. So they left him and went away.

23That same day the Sadducees, who say there is no resurrection, came to him with a question. 24"Teacher," they said, "Moses told us that if a man dies without having children, his brother must marry the widow and have children for him. 25Now there were seven brothers among us. The first one married and died, and since he had no children, he left his wife to his brother. 26The same thing happened to the second and third brother, right on down to the seventh. 27Finally, the woman died. 28Now then, at the resurrection, whose wife will she be of the seven, since all of them were married to her?"

29Jesus replied, "You are in error because you do not know the Scriptures or the power of God. 30At the resurrection people will neither marry nor be given in marriage; they will be like the angels in heaven. 31But about the resurrection of the dead—have you not read what God said to you, 32'I am the God of Abraham, the God of Isaac, and the God of Jacob'? He is not the God of the dead but of the living."

33When the crowds heard this, they were astonished at his teaching.

34Hearing that Jesus had silenced the Sadducees, the Pharisees got together. 35One of them, an expert in the law, tested him with this question: 36"Teacher, which is the greatest commandment in the Law?"

37Jesus replied: " 'Love the Lord your God with all your heart and with all your soul and with all your mind.' 38This is the first and greatest commandment. 39And the second is like it: 'Love your neighbor as yourself.' 40All the Law and the Prophets hang on these two commandments."

41While the Pharisees were gathered together, Jesus asked them, 42"What do you think about the Christ? Whose son is he?"

"The son of David," they replied.

43He said to them, "How is it then that David, speaking by the Spirit, calls him 'Lord'? For he says,

44" 'The Lord said to my Lord:
  "Sit at my right hand
until I put your enemies
  under your feet." ' '

45If then David calls him 'Lord,' how can he be his son?" 46No one could say a word in reply, and from that day on no one dared to ask him any more questions.

A THOUGHT: *The Pharisees were a religious group opposed to the Roman occupation of Palestine. The Herodians were a Jewish political party who supported Herod Antipas and the policies instituted by Rome. Normally, these two groups were bitter enemies, but here they united against Jesus. Together, men from these two groups asked Jesus a question about paying Roman taxes, thinking they had a foolproof plan to corner him. If Jesus agreed that it was right to pay taxes to Caesar, the Pharisees would say he was opposed to God, the only king they recognized. If Jesus said the taxes should not be paid, the Herodians would hand him over to Rome for tax evasion. Jesus avoided this trap by showing that we have a dual citizenship. Our citizenship in the state requires that we pay money for the services and benefits we receive. Our citizenship in the kingdom of heaven requires that we pledge to God the obedience and commitment of our entire lives.*

After the Pharisees and Herodians failed to trap Jesus, the Sadducees stepped in to try. They did not believe in the resurrection because the Pentateuch (Genesis—Deuteronomy) has no direct teaching on it. The Sadducees thought they had trapped Jesus for sure with their question on marriage. But Jesus answered that there wouldn't be marriage in the resurrection. In each of Jesus' answers, he exposed the evil motives of the questioners and demonstrated his great wisdom.

Everyone's Work Will Be Judged by God/
1 Corinthians 3:10–17

By the grace God has given me, I laid a foundation as an expert builder, and someone else is building on it. But each one should be careful how he builds. [11]For no one can lay any foundation other than the one already laid, which is Jesus Christ. [12]If any man builds on this foundation using gold, silver, costly stones, wood, hay or straw, [13]his work will be shown for what it is, because the Day will bring it to light. It will be revealed with fire, and the fire will test the quality of each man's work. [14]If what he has built survives, he will receive his reward. [15]If it is burned up, he will suffer loss; he himself will be saved, but only as one escaping through the flames.

[16]Don't you know that you yourselves are God's temple and that God's Spirit lives in you? [17]If anyone destroys God's temple, God will destroy him; for God's temple is sacred, and you are that temple.

A THOUGHT: *A building is only as solid as its foundation. The foundation of our lives is Jesus Christ; he is our base, our reason for being. Everything we are and do must fit into the pattern provided by Jesus Christ. Are you building your life on the only real and lasting foundation, or are you building on another foundation such as wealth, security, or success? What is your reason for living?*

Proverbs for Today/ 10:18

He who conceals his hatred has lying lips, and whoever spreads slander is a fool.

FEBRUARY 28

Jesus Condemns the Religious Leaders/
Matthew 23:1–12

Then Jesus said to the crowds and to his disciples: [2]"The teachers of the law and the Pharisees sit in Moses' seat. [3]So you must obey them and do everything they tell you.

But do not do what they do, for they do not practice what they preach. 4They tie up heavy loads and put them on men's shoulders, but they themselves are not willing to lift a finger to move them.

5"Everything they do is done for men to see: They make their phylacteries wide and the tassels on their garments long; 6they love the place of honor at banquets and the most important seats in the synagogues; 7they love to be greeted in the marketplaces and to have men call them 'Rabbi.'

8"But you are not to be called 'Rabbi,' for you have only one Master and you are all brothers. 9And do not call anyone on earth 'father,' for you have one Father, and he is in heaven. 10Nor are you to be called 'teacher,' for you have one Teacher, the Christ. 11The greatest among you will be your servant. 12For whoever exalts himself will be humbled, and whoever humbles himself will be exalted.

A THOUGHT: *Jesus again exposed the hypocritical attitudes of the religious leaders. They knew the Scriptures, but did not live by them. They didn't care about being holy—just looking holy in order to receive the people's admiration and praise. Today, like the Pharisees, many people who know the Bible do not let it change their lives. They say they follow Jesus but don't live by his standards of love. People who live this way are hypocrites. We must make sure our actions match our beliefs.*

Foolishness in God's Sight/
1 Corinthians 3:18–23

Do not deceive yourselves. If any one of you thinks he is wise by the standards of this age, he should become a "fool" so that he may become wise. 19For the wisdom of this world is foolishness in God's sight. As it is written: "He catches the wise in their craftiness"; 20and again, "The Lord knows that the thoughts of the wise are futile." 21So then, no more boasting about men! All things are yours, 22whether Paul or Apollos or Cephas or the world or life or death or the present or the future—all are yours, 23and you are of Christ, and Christ is of God.

A THOUGHT: *Paul is not telling the Corinthian believers to neglect the pursuit of knowledge, but if one has to choose between earthly knowledge and heavenly wisdom, choose heavenly wisdom even though you may look foolish to the world. Worldly wisdom, if it holds you back from God, is no wisdom at all. The Corinthians were using so-called worldly wisdom to evaluate their leaders and teachers. Their pride made them value the presentation of the message more than its content.*

Proverbs for Today/ 10:19

When words are many, sin is not absent, but he who holds his tongue is wise.

MARCH 1

Jesus Denounces the Pharisees/ Matthew 23:13–39

"Woe to you, teachers of the law and Pharisees, you hypocrites! You shut the kingdom of heaven in men's faces. You yourselves do not enter, nor will you let those enter who are trying to. *

15"Woe to you, teachers of the law and Pharisees, you hypocrites! You travel over land and sea to win a single convert, and when he becomes one, you make him twice as much a son of hell as you are.

16"Woe to you, blind guides! You say, 'If anyone swears by the temple, it means nothing; but if anyone swears by the gold of the temple, he is bound by his oath.' 17You blind fools! Which is greater: the gold, or the temple that makes the gold sacred? 18You also say, 'If anyone swears by the altar, it means nothing; but if anyone swears by the gift on it, he is bound by his oath.' 19You blind men! Which is greater: the gift, or the altar that makes the gift sacred? 20Therefore, he who swears by the altar swears by it and by everything on it. 21And he who swears by the temple swears by it and by the one who dwells in it. 22And he who swears by heaven swears by God's throne and by the one who sits on it.

23"Woe to you, teachers of the law and Pharisees, you hypocrites! You give a tenth of your spices—mint, dill and cummin. But you have neglected the more important matters of the law—justice, mercy and faithfulness. You should have practiced the latter, without neglecting the former.

---

*13 Some manuscripts *to.* 14Woe to you, teachers of the law and Pharisees, you hypocrites! You devour widows' houses and for a show make lengthy prayers. Therefore you will be punished more severely.*

24You blind guides! You strain out a gnat but swallow a camel.

25"Woe to you, teachers of the law and Pharisees, you hypocrites! You clean the outside of the cup and dish, but inside they are full of greed and self-indulgence. 26Blind Pharisee! First clean the inside of the cup and dish, and then the outside also will be clean.

27"Woe to you, teachers of the law and Pharisees, you hypocrites! You are like whitewashed tombs, which look beautiful on the outside but on the inside are full of dead men's bones and everything unclean. 28In the same way, on the outside you appear to people as righteous but on the inside you are full of hypocrisy and wickedness.

29"Woe to you, teachers of the law and Pharisees, you hypocrites! You build tombs for the prophets and decorate the graves of the righteous. 30And you say, 'If we had lived in the days of our forefathers, we would not have taken part with them in shedding the blood of the prophets.' 31So you testify against yourselves that you are the descendants of those who murdered the prophets. 32Fill up, then, the measure of the sin of your forefathers!

33"You snakes! You brood of vipers! How will you escape being condemned to hell? 34Therefore I am sending you prophets and wise men and teachers. Some of them you will kill and crucify; others you will flog in your synagogues and pursue from town to town. 35And so upon you will come all the righteous blood that has been shed on earth, from the blood of righteous Abel to the blood of Zechariah son of Berekiah, whom you murdered between the temple and the altar. 36I tell you the truth, all this will come upon this generation.

37"O Jerusalem, Jerusalem, you who kill the prophets and stone those sent to you, how often I have longed to gather your children together, as a hen gathers her chicks under her wings, but you were not willing. 38Look, your house is left to you desolate. 39For I tell you, you will not see me again until you say, 'Blessed is he who comes in the name of the Lord.'"

A THOUGHT: *Jesus condemned the Pharisees and religious leaders for appearing saintly and holy outwardly, but inwardly remaining full of corruption and greed. Likewise, a Christianity which is merely for show is like washing a cup on the outside only. When we are clean on the inside, our cleanliness on the outside won't be a sham.*

Paul and Apollos—Servants of Christ/
1 Corinthians 4:1–7

So then, men ought to regard us as servants of Christ and as those entrusted with the secret things of God. 2Now it is required that those who have been given a trust must prove faithful. 3I care very little if I am judged by you or by any human court; indeed, I do not even judge myself. 4My conscience is clear, but that does not make me innocent. It is the Lord who judges me. 5Therefore judge nothing before the appointed time; wait till the Lord comes. He will bring to light what is hidden in darkness and will expose the motives of men's hearts. At that time each will receive his praise from God.

6Now, brothers, I have applied these things to myself and Apollos for your benefit, so that you may learn from us the meaning of the saying, "Do not go beyond what is written." Then you will not take pride in one man over against another. 7For who makes you different from anyone else? What do you have that you did not receive? And if you did receive it, why do you boast as though you did not?

A THOUGHT: *It is tempting to judge a fellow Christian, evaluating whether or not he or she is a good follower of Christ. But only God knows a person's heart, and he is the only one with the right to judge. Paul's warning to the Corinthians should also warn us. We are to help those who are sinning, but we must not judge who is a better servant for Christ. When you judge someone, you automatically consider yourself better, and this is pride.*

Proverbs for Today/ 10:20–21

The tongue of the righteous is choice silver, but the heart of the wicked is of little value. □ The lips of the righteous nourish many, but fools die for lack of judgment.

MARCH 2

The End of the Age/ Matthew 24:1–31

Jesus left the temple and was walking away when his disciples came up to him to call his attention to its buildings.
²"Do you see all these things?" he asked. "I tell you the truth, not one stone here will be left on another; every one will be thrown down."

³As Jesus was sitting on the Mount of Olives, the disciples came to him privately. "Tell us," they said, "when will this happen, and what will be the sign of your coming and of the end of the age?"

⁴Jesus answered: "Watch out that no one deceives you. ⁵For many will come in my name, claiming, 'I am the Christ,' and will deceive many. ⁶You will hear of wars and rumors of wars, but see to it that you are not alarmed. Such things must happen, but the end is still to come. ⁷Nation will rise against nation, and kingdom against kingdom. There will be famines and earthquakes in various places. ⁸All these are the beginning of birth pains.

⁹"Then you will be handed over to be persecuted and put to death, and you will be hated by all nations because of me. ¹⁰At that time many will turn away from the faith and will betray and hate each other, ¹¹and many false prophets will appear and deceive many people. ¹²Because of the increase of wickedness, the love of most will grow cold, ¹³but he who stands firm to the end will be saved. ¹⁴And this gospel of the kingdom will be preached in the whole world as a testimony to all nations, and then the end will come.

¹⁵"So when you see standing in the holy place 'the abomination that causes desolation,' spoken of through the prophet Daniel—let the reader understand— ¹⁶then let those who are in Judea flee to the mountains. ¹⁷Let no one on the roof of his house go down to take anything out of the house. ¹⁸Let no one in the field go back to get his cloak. ¹⁹How dreadful it will be in those days for pregnant women and nursing mothers! ²⁰Pray that your flight will not take place in winter or on the Sabbath. ²¹For then there will be great distress, unequaled from the beginning of the world until now—and never to be equaled again. ²²If those days

had not been cut short, no one would survive, but for the sake of the elect those days will be shortened. 23At that time if anyone says to you, 'Look, here is the Christ!' or, 'There he is!' do not believe it. 24For false Christs and false prophets will appear and perform great signs and miracles to deceive even the elect—if that were possible. 25See, I have told you ahead of time.

26"So if anyone tells you, 'There he is, out in the desert,' do not go out; or, 'Here he is, in the inner rooms,' do not believe it. 27For as lightning that comes from the east is visible even in the west, so will be the coming of the Son of Man. 28Wherever there is a carcass, there the vultures will gather.

29"Immediately after the distress of those days

" 'the sun will be darkened,
    and the moon will not give its light;
the stars will fall from the sky,
    and the heavenly bodies will be shaken.'

30"At that time the sign of the Son of Man will appear in the sky, and all the nations of the earth will mourn. They will see the Son of Man coming on the clouds of the sky, with power and great glory. 31And he will send his angels with a loud trumpet call, and they will gather his elect from the four winds, from one end of the heavens to the other."

A THOUGHT: *The Old Testament frequently mentions false prophets. They were people who claimed to receive messages from God, but who preached a "health and wealth" message. They told the people only what they wanted to hear, even when the nation was not following God as it should. There were false prophets in Jesus' day, and we have them today. They are the popular leaders who preach a false gospel, telling people what they want to hear—such as, "God wants you to be rich," "Do whatever your desires tell you," or "There is no such thing as sin or hell." Jesus said false teachers would come, and he warned his disciples, as he warns us, not to listen to their dangerous words.*

The Corinthians' Pride and the Apostles' Humility/ 1 Corinthians 4:8–13

Already you have all you want! Already you have become rich! You have become kings—and that without us! How I wish that you really had become kings so that we might be kings with you! 9For it seems to me that God has put us apostles on display at the end of the procession, like men condemned to die in the arena. We have been made a spectacle to the whole universe, to angels as well as to men. 10We are fools for Christ, but you are so wise in Christ! We are weak, but you are strong! You are honored, we are dishonored! 11To this very hour we go hungry and thirsty, we are in rags, we are brutally treated, we are homeless. 12We work hard with our own hands. When we are cursed, we bless; when we are persecuted, we endure it; 13when we are slandered, we answer kindly. Up to this moment we have become the scum of the earth, the refuse of the world.

A THOUGHT: *The Corinthians had split into various cliques, each following its own superstar preacher (Paul, Apollos, Peter, etc.). Each clique really believed it was the only one who had the whole truth, and thus felt spiritually proud. But Paul told the groups not to boast about being tied to a particular preacher because even the superstars were simply humble servants who had each suffered many things for the same message of salvation in Jesus Christ. No preacher of God has more authority than another. The authority resides in the message and the Author of the message, not in the messenger.*

Proverbs for Today/ 10:22

The blessing of the LORD brings wealth, and he adds no trouble to it.

MARCH 3

Prepare for the Lord's Coming/ Matthew 24:32–51

"Now learn this lesson from the fig tree: As soon as its twigs get tender and its leaves come out, you know that summer is near. 33Even so, when you see all these things, you know that it is near, right at the door. 34I tell you the truth, this generation will certainly not pass away until all these things have happened. 35Heaven and earth will pass away, but my words will never pass away.

36"No one knows about that day or hour, not even the angels in heaven, nor the Son, but only the Father. 37As it was in the days of Noah, so it will be at the coming of the Son of Man. 38For in the days before the flood, people were eating and drinking, marrying and giving in marriage, up to the day Noah entered the ark; 39and they knew nothing about what would happen until the flood came and took them all away. That is how it will be at the coming of the Son of Man. 40Two men will be in the field; one will be taken and the other left. 41Two women will be grinding with a hand mill; one will be taken and the other left.

42"Therefore keep watch, because you do not know on what day your Lord will come. 43But understand this: If the owner of the house had known at what time of night the thief was coming, he would have kept watch and would not have let his house be broken into. 44So you also must be ready, because the Son of Man will come at an hour when you do not expect him.

45"Who then is the faithful and wise servant, whom the master has put in charge of the servants in his household to give them their food at the proper time? 46It will be good for that servant whose master finds him doing so when he returns. 47I tell you the truth, he will put him in charge of all his possessions. 48But suppose that servant is wicked and says to himself, 'My master is staying away a long time,' 49and he then begins to beat his fellow servants and to eat and drink with drunkards. 50The master of that servant will come on a day when he does not expect him and at an hour he is not aware of. 51He will cut him to pieces and assign him a place with the hypocrites, where there will be weeping and gnashing of teeth."

A THOUGHT: *Knowing that Christ's return will be sudden should motivate us always to be prepared. We are not to live irresponsibly—(1) sitting and waiting, doing nothing; (2) seeking self-serving pleasure; (3) using his tarrying as an excuse not to do God's work of building his kingdom; (4) developing a false security based on precise calculations of events; or (5) letting our curiosity about the end times divert us from doing God's work.*

Paul Counsels His Beloved Children/
1 Corinthians 4:14–21

I am not writing this to shame you, but to warn you, as my dear children. 15Even though you have ten thousand guardians in Christ, you do not have many fathers, for in Christ Jesus I became your father through the gospel. 16Therefore I urge you to imitate me. 17For this reason I am sending to you Timothy, my son whom I love, who is faithful in the Lord. He will remind you of my way of life in Christ Jesus, which agrees with what I teach everywhere in every church.

18Some of you have become arrogant, as if I were not coming to you. 19But I will come to you very soon, if the Lord is willing, and then I will find out not only how these arrogant people are talking, but what power they have. 20For the kingdom of God is not a matter of talk but of power. 21What do you prefer? Shall I come to you with a whip, or in love and with a gentle spirit?

A THOUGHT: *Some people talk a lot about faith, but that's all it is—talk. They may know all the right words to say, but their lives are not examples of Christian living. Paul says the kingdom of God is to be lived, not just discussed. There is a big difference between knowing the right words and living them out. Don't be content to have the right answers about Christ. Let your life put flesh on your words.*

Proverbs for Today/ 10:23

A fool finds pleasure in evil conduct, but a man of understanding delights in wisdom.

MARCH 4

The Parable of the Ten Virgins/ Matthew 25:1–13

"At that time the kingdom of heaven will be like ten virgins who took their lamps and went out to meet the bridegroom. 2Five of them were foolish and five were wise. 3The foolish ones took their lamps but did not take any oil with them. 4The wise, however, took oil in jars along with their lamps. 5The bridegroom was a long time in coming, and they all became drowsy and fell asleep.

6"At midnight the cry rang out: 'Here's the bridegroom! Come out to meet him!'

7"Then all the virgins woke up and trimmed their lamps. 8The foolish ones said to the wise, 'Give us some of your oil; our lamps are going out.'

9" 'No,' they replied, 'there may not be enough for both us and you. Instead, go to those who sell oil and buy some for yourselves.'

¹⁰"But while they were on their way to buy the oil, the bridegroom arrived. The virgins who were ready went in with him to the wedding banquet. And the door was shut.

¹¹"Later the others also came. 'Sir! Sir!' they said. 'Open the door for us!'

¹²"But he replied, 'I tell you the truth, I don't know you.'

¹³"Therefore keep watch, because you do not know the day or the hour."

A THOUGHT: *This parable is about a wedding. In Jewish culture, a couple was engaged for a long time before the actual marriage, and the engagement promise was just as binding as the marriage vows. On the wedding day the bridegroom went to the bride's house for the ceremony; then the bride and groom, along with a great parade, returned to the groom's house where a feast took place, often lasting a full week.*

The ten virgins were waiting to join the parade, hoping to take part in the wedding banquet. But when the groom didn't come when they expected, five of them let their lamps run out of oil. By the time they had purchased extra oil, it was too late to join the feast.

When Jesus returns to take his people to heaven, we must be ready. Spiritual preparation cannot be bought or borrowed at the last minute. Our relationship with God must be our own.

Paul Condemns Immorality in the Church/
1 Corinthians 5:1–8

It is actually reported that there is sexual immorality among you, and of a kind that does not occur even among pagans: A man has his father's wife. ²And you are proud! Shouldn't you rather have been filled with grief and have put out of your fellowship the man who did this? ³Even though I am not physically present, I am with you in spirit. And I have already passed judgment on the one who did this, just as if I were present. ⁴When you are assembled in the name of our Lord Jesus and I am with you in spirit, and the power of our Lord Jesus is present, ⁵hand this man over to Satan, so that the sinful nature may be destroyed and his spirit saved on the day of the Lord.

⁶Your boasting is not good. Don't you know that a little yeast works through the whole batch of dough? ⁷Get rid of the old yeast that you may be a new batch without yeast—as you really are. For Christ, our Passover lamb, has been sacrificed. ⁸Therefore let us keep the Festival,

not with the old yeast, the yeast of malice and wickedness, but with bread without yeast, the bread of sincerity and truth.

A THOUGHT: *The church must discipline flagrant sin among its members—such actions, left unchecked, can polarize and paralyze a church. The correction, however, is never to be vengeful. Instead, it is intended to bring about a cure. The Corinthian church had a specific sin in their midst, but they had refused to deal with it. In this case, a man was having an affair with his mother (or step-mother), and the church members were trying to ignore the situation. Paul was telling the church that they had a responsibility to maintain the standards of morality found in God's Word. God tells us not to judge others, but he also tells us not to tolerate flagrant sin that opposes his holiness and has a dangerous influence on the lives of other believers.*

Proverbs for Today/ 10:24–25

What the wicked dreads will overtake him; what the righteous desire will be granted. □When the storm has swept by, the wicked are gone, but the righteous stand firm forever.

MARCH 5

The Parable of the Talents/ Matthew 25:14–30

"Again, it will be like a man going on a journey, who called his servants and entrusted his property to them. 15To one he gave five talents of money, to another two talents, and to another one talent, each according to his ability. Then he went on his journey. 16The man who had received the five talents went at once and put his money to work and gained five more. 17So also, the one with the two talents gained two more. 18But the man who had received the one talent went off, dug a hole in the ground and hid his master's money.

19"After a long time the master of those servants returned and settled accounts with them. 20The man who had received the five talents brought the other five. 'Master,' he said, 'you entrusted me with five talents. See, I have gained five more.'

21"His master replied, 'Well done, good and faithful servant! You have been faithful with a few things; I will put you in charge of many things. Come and share your master's happiness!'

22"The man with the two talents also came. 'Master,' he said, 'you entrusted me with two talents; see, I have gained two more.'

23"His master replied, 'Well done, good and faithful servant! You have been faithful with a few things; I will put you in charge of many things. Come and share your master's happiness!'

24"Then the man who had received the one talent came. 'Master,' he said, 'I knew that you are a hard man, harvesting where you have not sown and gathering where you have not scattered seed. 25So I was afraid and went out and hid your talent in the ground. See, here is what belongs to you.'

26"His master replied, 'You wicked, lazy servant! So you knew that I harvest where I have not sown and gather where I have not scattered seed? 27Well then, you should have put my money on deposit with the bankers, so that when I returned I would have received it back with interest.

28" 'Take the talent from him and give it to the one who has the ten talents. 29For everyone who has will be given more, and he will have an abundance. Whoever does not have, even what he has will be taken from him. 30And throw that worthless servant outside, into the darkness, where there will be weeping and gnashing of teeth.' "

A THOUGHT: *The master divided the money up among his servants according to their abilities—no one received more or less money than he could handle. If he failed in his master's assignment, his excuse could not be that he was overwhelmed. Failure could come only from laziness or hatred for the master. Money, as used here, represents any kind of resource we are given. God gives us time, abilities, gifts, and other resources, and he expects us to invest them wisely until he returns. We are responsible to use well what God has given us. The issue is not how much we have, but what we do with what we have.*

In the World, Not of the World/
1 Corinthians 5:9–13

I have written you in my letter not to associate with sexually immoral people— 10not at all meaning the people of this world who are immoral, or the greedy and swindlers, or idolaters. In that case you would have to leave this world. [11]But now I am writing you that you must not associate with anyone who calls himself a brother but is sexually immoral or greedy, an idolater or a slanderer, a drunkard or a swindler. With such a man do not even eat.

[12]What business is it of mine to judge those outside the church? Are you not to judge those inside? [13]God will judge those outside. "Expel the wicked man from among you."

A THOUGHT: *Paul makes it clear that we should not dissociate ourselves from unbelievers—otherwise, we could not carry out Christ's command to tell them about salvation. But we are to distance ourselves from the person who claims to be a Christian, yet indulges in sins explicitly forbidden in Scripture and then rationalizes his or her actions. Those who continue in sin harm others for whom Christ died and dim the image of God in themselves. A church that includes greedy people and sexual sinners is hardly fit to be the light of the world. It is distorting the picture of Christ it presents to the world. Instead of joining Christ's kingdom with its constant fight to replace darkness with light, it is adding to the darkness.*

Proverbs for Today/ 10:26

As vinegar to the teeth and smoke to the eyes, so is a sluggard to those who send him.

MARCH 6

Separation of the Sheep from the Goats/ Matthew 25:31–46

"When the Son of Man comes in his glory, and all the angels with him, he will sit on his throne in heavenly glory. [32]All the nations will be gathered before him, and he will separate the people one from another as a shepherd separates the sheep from the goats. [33]He will put the sheep on his right and the goats on his left.

[34]"Then the King will say to those on his right, 'Come, you who are blessed by my Father; take your inheritance, the kingdom prepared for you since the creation of the world. [35]For I was hungry and you gave me something to eat, I was thirsty and you gave me something to drink, I was a stranger and you invited me in, [36]I needed clothes

and you clothed me, I was sick and you looked after me, I was in prison and you came to visit me.'

37"Then the righteous will answer him, 'Lord, when did we see you hungry and feed you, or thirsty and give you something to drink? 38When did we see you a stranger and invite you in, or needing clothes and clothe you? 39When did we see you sick or in prison and go to visit you?'

40"The King will reply, 'I tell you the truth, whatever you did for one of the least of these brothers of mine, you did for me.'

41"Then he will say to those on his left, 'Depart from me, you who are cursed, into the eternal fire prepared for the devil and his angels. 42For I was hungry and you gave me nothing to eat, I was thirsty and you gave me nothing to drink, 43I was a stranger and you did not invite me in, I needed clothes and you did not clothe me, I was sick and in prison and you did not look after me.'

44"They also will answer, 'Lord, when did we see you hungry or thirsty or a stranger or needing clothes or sick or in prison, and did not help you?'

45"He will reply, 'I tell you the truth, whatever you did not do for one of the least of these, you did not do for me.'

46"Then they will go away to eternal punishment, but the righteous to eternal life."

A THOUGHT: *This parable describes acts of mercy we all can do every day. These acts are not dependent on wealth, ability, or intelligence; they are simple acts freely given and freely received. We have no legitimate excuse for neglecting those who have deep needs, and we cannot hand over this responsibility to the church or the government. Jesus demands personal involvement in caring for the needs of others.*

Lawsuits among Believers/ 1 Corinthians 6:1–9a

If any of you has a dispute with another, dare he take it before the ungodly for judgment instead of before the saints? 2Do you not know that the saints will judge the world? And if you are to judge the world, are you not competent to judge trivial cases? 3Do you not know that we will judge angels? How much more the things of this life! 4Therefore, if you have disputes about such matters, appoint as judges even men of little account in the church! 5I say this to shame you. Is it possible that there is nobody among you wise enough to judge a dispute between believers? 6But instead, one brother goes to law against another—and this in front of unbelievers!

7The very fact that you have lawsuits among you means you have been completely defeated already. Why not rather be wronged? Why not rather be cheated? 8Instead, you yourselves cheat and do wrong, and you do this to your brothers.

9Do you not know that the wicked will not inherit the kingdom of God?

A THOUGHT: *Why does Paul say it isn't good to sue another Christian? (1) If the judge and jury are not Christians, they are unlikely to be sensitive to Christian values. (2) The basis for going to court is often revenge; this should never be a Christian's motive. (3) Lawsuits make the church look bad, causing unbelievers to focus on its problems rather than its purpose. Paul says that disagreeing Christians should not have to go to a secular court to resolve their differences. As Christians we have the Holy Spirit and the mind of Christ, so why should we turn to those who lack God's wisdom? With all that we have been given as believers, and the power that we will have in the future to judge the world and the angels, we should be able to deal with the disputes between ourselves.*

Proverbs for Today/ 10:27–28

The fear of the Lord adds length to life, but the years of the wicked are cut short. □ The prospect of the righteous is joy, but the hopes of the wicked come to nothing.

MARCH 7

The Priests Plot Jesus' Death/ Matthew 26:1–16

When Jesus had finished saying all these things, he said to his disciples, 2"As you know, the Passover is two days away—and the Son of Man will be handed over to be crucified."

3Then the chief priests and the elders of the people assembled in the palace of the high priest, whose name was Caiaphas, 4and they plotted to arrest Jesus in some sly way and kill him. 5"But not during the Feast," they said, "or there may be a riot among the people."

6While Jesus was in Bethany in the home of a man known

as Simon the Leper, 7a woman came to him with an alabaster jar of very expensive perfume, which she poured on his head as he was reclining at the table.

8When the disciples saw this, they were indignant. "Why this waste?" they asked. 9"This perfume could have been sold at a high price and the money given to the poor."

10Aware of this, Jesus said to them, "Why are you bothering this woman? She has done a beautiful thing to me. 11The poor you will always have with you, but you will not always have me. 12When she poured this perfume on my body, she did it to prepare me for burial. 13I tell you the truth, wherever this gospel is preached throughout the world, what she has done will also be told, in memory of her."

14Then one of the Twelve—the one called Judas Iscariot—went to the chief priests 15and asked, "What are you willing to give me if I hand him over to you?" So they counted out for him thirty silver coins. 16From then on Judas watched for an opportunity to hand him over.

A THOUGHT: *In the midst of the murderous plots of the Jewish religious leadership and Judas' betrayal, we find this woman who pours perfume over Jesus' head. It was this act of humble sacrifice, by an oppressed member of first-century Jewish society that Jesus accepted as the preparation for his burial. God has indeed chosen the humble of this world to shame the proud. Let us be numbered among the humble and the poor—true greatness is not found in the honor we find among others, but rather in the obedient and humble service to others where the servant seeks no reward.*

Washed in Christ's Blood/ 1 Corinthians 6:9b–13a

Do not be deceived: Neither the sexually immoral nor idolaters nor adulterers nor male prostitutes nor homosexual offenders 10nor thieves nor the greedy nor drunkards nor slanderers nor swindlers will inherit the kingdom of God. 11And that is what some of you were. But you were washed, you were sanctified, you were justified in the name of the Lord Jesus Christ and by the Spirit of our God.

12"Everything is permissible for me"—but not everything is beneficial. "Everything is permissible for me"—but I will not be mastered by anything. 13"Food for the stomach and the stomach for food"—but God will destroy them both.

In a permissive society it is easy for Christians to overlook or accept immoral behavior (sexual sins, greed, drunkenness, gossip, etc.) because it is so widespread. Although it surrounds us, we cannot take part in it or condone it in any way. Staying away from generally accepted sin is difficult, but it is no harder for us than it was for the Corinthians. God expects his followers in any age to have high moral standards.

Proverbs for Today/ 10:29–30

The way of the LORD is a refuge for the righteous, but it is the ruin of those who do evil. □ The righteous will never be uprooted, but the wicked will not remain in the land.

MARCH 8

The Last Supper/ Matthew 26:17–35

On the first day of the Feast of Unleavened Bread, the disciples came to Jesus and asked, "Where do you want us to make preparations for you to eat the Passover?"

18He replied, "Go into the city to a certain man and tell him, 'The Teacher says: My appointed time is near. I am going to celebrate the Passover with my disciples at your house.'" 19So the disciples did as Jesus had directed them and prepared the Passover.

20When evening came, Jesus was reclining at the table with the Twelve. 21And while they were eating, he said, "I tell you the truth, one of you will betray me."

22They were very sad and began to say to him one after the other, "Surely not I, Lord?"

23Jesus replied, "The one who has dipped his hand into the bowl with me will betray me. 24The Son of Man will go just as it is written about him. But woe to that man who betrays the Son of Man! It would be better for him if he had not been born."

25Then Judas, the one who would betray him, said, "Surely not I, Rabbi?"

Jesus answered, "Yes, it is you."

26While they were eating, Jesus took bread, gave thanks and broke it, and gave it to his disciples, saying, "Take and eat; this is my body."

27Then he took the cup, gave thanks and offered it to them, saying, "Drink from it, all of you. 28This is my blood of the covenant, which is poured out for many for the forgiveness of sins. 29I tell you, I will not drink of this fruit of the vine from now on until that day when I drink it anew with you in my Father's kingdom."

30When they had sung a hymn, they went out to the Mount of Olives.

31Then Jesus told them, "This very night you will all fall away on account of me, for it is written:

" 'I will strike the shepherd,
    and the sheep of the flock will be scattered.'

32But after I have risen, I will go ahead of you into Galilee."

33Peter replied, "Even if all fall away on account of you, I never will."

34"I tell you the truth," Jesus answered, "this very night, before the rooster crows, you will disown me three times."

35But Peter declared, "Even if I have to die with you, I will never disown you." And all the other disciples said the same.

A THOUGHT: *This supper, which Jesus and his disciples observed to commemorate the Passover, is celebrated by the church as one of its most holy sacraments. Each name we use for this sacrament brings out a different dimension of it. It is the Lord's Supper because it commemorates the Passover meal Jesus ate with his disciples; it is the Eucharist (thanksgiving) because in it we thank God for Christ's work for us; it is Communion because through it we commune with God and with other believers. As we eat the bread and drink the wine, we should reflect upon Jesus' suffering and death for the church, express our gratefulness to God for his wonderful grace towards us, and manifest in our actions towards others the grace of God which we have experienced.*

The Body, Temple of the Holy Spirit/
1 Corinthians 6:13b–20

The body is not meant for sexual immorality, but for the Lord, and the Lord for the body. 14By his power God raised the Lord from the dead, and he will raise us also. 15Do you not know that your bodies are members of Christ himself? Shall I then take the members of Christ and unite them with a prostitute? Never! 16Do you not know that he who unites himself with a prostitute is one with her in body? For it is said, "The two will become one flesh." [17]But he who unites himself with the Lord is one with him in spirit.

[18]Flee from sexual immorality. All other sins a man commits are outside his body, but he who sins sexually sins against his own body. [19]Do you not know that your body is a temple of the Holy Spirit, who is in you, whom you have received from God? You are not your own; [20]you were bought at a price. Therefore honor God with your body.

A THOUGHT: *Many of the world's religions think the soul is important and the body is not, and Christianity has sometimes been influenced by them. In truth, however, Christianity is a very physical religion. We worship a God who created a physical world and pronounced it good. He promises us a new earth where real people continue to live physical lives—not a pink cloud where disembodied souls listen to harp music. At the heart of Christianity is the story of God himself taking on flesh and blood and coming to live with us.*

We humans, like Adam, are a combination of dust and spirit. Just as our spiritual lives affect our bodies, so our physical lives affect our souls. We cannot commit sin with our bodies without damaging our souls, because our bodies and souls are inseparably joined. In the new earth we will have resurrection bodies that are not corrupted by sin. Then we will enjoy the fullness of our salvation.

Proverbs for Today/ 10:31–32

The mouth of the righteous brings forth wisdom, but a perverse tongue will be cut out. The lips of the righteous know what is fitting, but the mouth of the wicked only what is perverse.

MARCH 9

Jesus Betrayed at Gethsemane/ Matthew 26:36–56

Then Jesus went with his disciples to a place called Gethsemane, and he said to them, "Sit here while I go over there and pray." [37]He took Peter and the two sons of Zebedee along with him, and he began to be sorrowful and troubled. [38]Then he said to them, "My soul is overwhelmed with sorrow to the point of death. Stay here and keep watch with me."

[39]Going a little farther, he fell with his face to the ground

and prayed, "My Father, if it is possible, may this cup be taken from me. Yet not as I will, but as you will."

40Then he returned to his disciples and found them sleeping. "Could you men not keep watch with me for one hour?" he asked Peter. 41"Watch and pray so that you will not fall into temptation. The spirit is willing, but the body is weak."

42He went away a second time and prayed, "My Father, if it is not possible for this cup to be taken away unless I drink it, may your will be done."

43When he came back, he again found them sleeping, because their eyes were heavy. 44So he left them and went away once more and prayed the third time, saying the same thing.

45Then he returned to the disciples and said to them, "Are you still sleeping and resting? Look, the hour is near, and the Son of Man is betrayed into the hands of sinners. 46Rise, let us go! Here comes my betrayer!"

47While he [Jesus] was still speaking, Judas, one of the Twelve, arrived. With him was a large crowd armed with swords and clubs, sent from the chief priests and the elders of the people. 48Now the betrayer had arranged a signal with them: "The one I kiss is the man; arrest him." 49Going at once to Jesus, Judas said, "Greetings, Rabbi!" and kissed him.

50Jesus replied, "Friend, do what you came for."

Then the men stepped forward, seized Jesus and arrested him. 51With that, one of Jesus' companions reached for his sword, drew it out and struck the servant of the high priest, cutting off his ear.

52"Put your sword back in its place," Jesus said to him, "for all who draw the sword will die by the sword. 53Do you think I cannot call on my Father, and he will at once put at my disposal more than twelve legions of angels? 54But how then would the Scriptures be fulfilled that say it must happen in this way?"

55At that time Jesus said to the crowd, "Am I leading a rebellion, that you have come out with swords and clubs to capture me? Every day I sat in the temple courts teaching, and you did not arrest me. 56But this has all taken place that the writings of the prophets might be fulfilled." Then all the disciples deserted him and fled.

A THOUGHT: *Jesus was in great anguish over his coming physical pain, separation from the Father, and death for the sins of the world. The divine course was set; but he, in his human nature, still struggled. Because of the anguish he faced, he can relate to our suffering. His strength to obey came from his relationship with God the Father, who is also the source of our strength.*

Paul's Advice to Married Couples/ 1 Corinthians 7:1–9

Now for the matters you wrote about: It is good for a man not to marry. 2But since there is so much immorality, each man should have his own wife, and each woman her own husband. 3The husband should fulfill his marital duty to his wife, and likewise the wife to her husband. 4The wife's body does not belong to her alone but also to her husband. In the same way, the husband's body does not belong to him alone but also to his wife. 5Do not deprive each other except by mutual consent and for a time, so that you may devote yourselves to prayer. Then come together again so that Satan will not tempt you because of your lack of self-control. 6I say this as a concession, not as a command. 7I wish that all men were as I am. But each man has his own gift from God; one has this gift, another has that.

8Now to the unmarried and the widows I say: It is good for them to stay unmarried, as I am. 9But if they cannot control themselves, they should marry, for it is better to marry than to burn with passion.

A THOUGHT: *Sexual temptations are difficult to withstand because they appeal to the normal and natural desires God has given us. Marriage is meant, in part, to satisfy these natural sexual desires and to strengthen the partners against temptation. Married couples have the responsibility to care for each other. Therefore, husbands and wives should not withhold themselves from one another, but should fulfill each other's needs and desires.*

Proverbs for Today/ 11:1–3

The LORD abhors dishonest scales, but accurate weights are his delight. □ When pride comes, then comes disgrace, but with humility comes wisdom. □ The integrity of the upright guides them, but the unfaithful are destroyed by their duplicity.

Jesus Appears Before the Sanhedrin/
Matthew 26:57-75

Those who had arrested Jesus took him to Caiaphas, the high priest, where the teachers of the law and the elders had assembled. 58But Peter followed him at a distance, right up to the courtyard of the high priest. He entered and sat down with the guards to see the outcome.

59The chief priests and the whole Sanhedrin were looking for false evidence against Jesus so that they could put him to death. 60But they did not find any, though many false witnesses came forward.

Finally two came forward 61and declared, "This fellow said, 'I am able to destroy the temple of God and rebuild it in three days.'"

62Then the high priest stood up and said to Jesus, "Are you not going to answer? What is this testimony that these men are bringing against you?" 63But Jesus remained silent.

The high priest said to him, "I charge you under oath by the living God: Tell us if you are the Christ, the Son of God."

64"Yes, it is as you say," Jesus replied. "But I say to all of you: In the future you will see the Son of Man sitting at the right hand of the Mighty One and coming on the clouds of heaven."

65Then the high priest tore his clothes and said, "He has spoken blasphemy! Why do we need any more witnesses? Look, now you have heard the blasphemy. 66What do you think?"

"He is worthy of death," they answered.

67Then they spit in his face and struck him with their fists. Others slapped him 68and said, "Prophesy to us, Christ. Who hit you?"

69Now Peter was sitting out in the courtyard, and a servant girl came to him. "You also were with Jesus of Galilee," she said.

70But he denied it before them all. "I don't know what you're talking about," he said.

⁷¹Then he went out to the gateway, where another girl saw him and said to the people there, "This fellow was with Jesus of Nazareth."

⁷²He denied it again, with an oath: "I don't know the man!"

⁷³After a little while, those standing there went up to Peter and said, "Surely you are one of them, for your accent gives you away."

⁷⁴Then he began to call down curses on himself and he swore to them, "I don't know the man!"

Immediately a rooster crowed. ⁷⁵Then Peter remembered the word Jesus had spoken: "Before the rooster crows, you will disown me three times." And he went outside and wept bitterly.

A THOUGHT: *After Judas singled out Jesus for arrest, the mob took Jesus to Caiaphas, the High Priest. The Sanhedrin found two witnesses who distorted Jesus' teaching concerning the Temple. They claimed that Jesus had said he would destroy the Temple—a blasphemous boast. Actually, Jesus had said, "[You] destroy this temple, and I will raise it up . . ."(John 2:19). Jesus, of course, was talking about his body, not a building. Ironically, the religious leaders were about to destroy Jesus' body just as he had said, and three days later he would rise from the dead.*

Jesus' trial, a mockery of justice, ended at daybreak with the decision of the court—to kill him. They needed Rome's permission for the death sentence, so Jesus was taken to Pilate who legally sentenced Jesus to die.

Paul's Advice on Divorce/ 1 Corinthians 7:10–17

To the married I give this command (not I, but the Lord): A wife must not separate from her husband. ¹¹But if she does, she must remain unmarried or else be reconciled to her husband. And a husband must not divorce his wife.

¹²To the rest I say this (I, not the Lord): If any brother has a wife who is not a believer and she is willing to live with him, he must not divorce her. ¹³And if a woman has a husband who is not a believer and he is willing to live with her, she must not divorce him. ¹⁴For the unbelieving husband has been sanctified through his wife, and the unbelieving wife has been sanctified through her believing husband. Otherwise your children would be unclean, but as it is, they are holy.

¹⁵But if the unbeliever leaves, let him do so. A believing man or woman is not bound in such circumstances; God has

called us to live in peace. 16How do you know, wife, whether you will save your husband? Or, how do you know, husband, whether you will save your wife?

17Nevertheless, each one should retain the place in life that the Lord assigned to him and to which God has called him. This is the rule I lay down in all the churches.

A THOUGHT: *Because of their desire to serve Christ, some people in the Corinthian church thought they ought to divorce their pagan spouses and marry Christians. But Paul affirmed the marriage commitment. God's ideal is for marriages to stay together—even when one spouse is not a believer. The Christian spouse should try to win the other to Christ. It would be easy to rationalize leaving; however, Paul makes a strong case for staying with the unbelieving spouse and being a positive influence on the marriage. Paul, like Jesus, taught that marriage is to be a permanent relationship.*

Proverbs for Today/ 11:4

Wealth is worthless in the day of wrath, but righteousness delivers from death.

MARCH 11

The Religious Leaders Plot against Jesus/ Matthew 27:1–10

Early in the morning, all the chief priests and the elders of the people came to the decision to put Jesus to death. 2They bound him, led him away and handed him over to Pilate, the governor.

3When Judas, who had betrayed him, saw that Jesus was condemned, he was seized with remorse and returned the thirty silver coins to the chief priests and the elders. 4"I have sinned," he said, "for I have betrayed innocent blood."

"What is that to us?" they replied. "That's your responsibility."

5So Judas threw the money into the temple and left. Then he went away and hanged himself.

6The chief priests picked up the coins and said, "It is against the law to put this into the treasury, since it is blood money." 7So they decided to use the money to buy the potter's field as a burial place for foreigners. [8]That is why it has been called the Field of Blood to this day. [9]Then what was spoken by Jeremiah the prophet was fulfilled: "They took the thirty silver coins, the price set on him by the people of Israel, [10]and they used them to buy the potter's field, as the Lord commanded me."

A THOUGHT: *The religious leaders had to induce the Roman government to sentence Jesus to death because they did not have the authority to do it themselves. The Romans had taken away the religious leaders' authority to inflict capital punishment. Politically, it looked better for the religious leaders if someone else was responsible for killing Jesus. They wanted the death to appear to be the responsibility of the Romans so that the crowds couldn't blame them. They had arrested Jesus on theological grounds—blasphemy; but since this charge would be thrown out of a Roman court, they had to come up with a political reason for Jesus' death. Their strategy was to show Jesus as a rebel who claimed to be God and thus higher than Caesar.*

Bought at a Price/ 1 Corinthians 7:18–24

Was a man already circumcised when he was called? He should not become uncircumcised. Was a man uncircumcised when he was called? He should not be circumcised. [19]Circumcision is nothing and uncircumcision is nothing. Keeping God's commands is what counts. [20]Each one should remain in the situation which he was in when God called him. [21]Were you a slave when you were called? Don't let it trouble you—although if you can gain your freedom, do so. [22]For he who was a slave when he was called by the Lord is the Lord's freedman; similarly, he who was a free man when he was called is Christ's slave. [23]You were bought at a price; do not become slaves of men. [24]Brothers, each man, as responsible to God, should remain in the situation God called him to.

A THOUGHT: *Slavery was common throughout the Roman Empire. Some Christians in the Corinthian church were slaves. Paul said that although they were slaves to men, they were free from the power of sin in their lives. People today are slaves to sin until they commit their lives to Christ, who alone can conquer sin's power. Sin, pride, and fear no longer have claim over us, just as a slaveowner no longer has power over slaves he has sold. The Bible says we become Christ's slaves when we become Christians, but this actually means we gain our freedom, because sin no longer controls us. We have been bought with a high price—the shed blood of Jesus Christ. Our new status in Christ gives us the freedom to walk in righteousness through the power of the Holy Spirit. Therefore, let us walk in the Spirit and live in righteousness.*

Proverbs for Today/ 11:5–6

The righteousness of the blameless makes a straight way for them, but the wicked are brought down by their own wickedness. □ The righteousness of the upright delivers them, but the unfaithful are trapped by evil desires.

MARCH 12

Jesus Appears Before Pilate/ Matthew 27:11–30

Meanwhile Jesus stood before the governor, and the governor asked him, "Are you the king of the Jews?"

"Yes, it is as you say," Jesus replied.

12When he was accused by the chief priests and the elders, he gave no answer. 13Then Pilate asked him, "Don't you hear the testimony they are bringing against you?" 14But Jesus made no reply, not even to a single charge—to the great amazement of the governor.

15Now it was the governor's custom at the Feast to release a prisoner chosen by the crowd. 16At that time they had a notorious prisoner, called Barabbas. 17So when the crowd had gathered, Pilate asked them, "Which one do you want me to release to you: Barabbas, or Jesus who is called Christ?" 18For he knew it was out of envy that they had handed Jesus over to him.

19While Pilate was sitting on the judge's seat, his wife sent him this message: "Don't have anything to do with that innocent man, for I have suffered a great deal today in a dream because of him."

20But the chief priests and the elders persuaded the crowd to ask for Barabbas and to have Jesus executed.

21"Which of the two do you want me to release to you?" asked the governor.

"Barabbas," they answered.

22"What shall I do, then, with Jesus who is called Christ?" Pilate asked.

They all answered, "Crucify him!"

23"Why? What crime has he committed?" asked Pilate.

But they shouted all the louder, "Crucify him!"

24When Pilate saw that he was getting nowhere, but that instead an uproar was starting, he took water and washed his hands in front of the crowd. "I am innocent of this man's blood," he said. "It is your responsibility!"

25All the people answered, "Let his blood be on us and on our children!"

26Then he released Barabbas to them. But he had Jesus flogged, and handed him over to be crucified.

27Then the governor's soldiers took Jesus into the Praetorium and gathered the whole company of soldiers around him. 28They stripped him and put a scarlet robe on him, 29and then twisted together a crown of thorns and set it on his head. They put a staff in his right hand and knelt in front of him and mocked him. "Hail, king of the Jews!" they said. 30They spit on him, and took the staff and struck him on the head again and again.

A THOUGHT: *Before Pilate, the religious leaders accused Jesus of different crimes from the ones for which they had arrested him. They arrested him for blasphemy (claiming to be God), but that charge would mean nothing to the Romans. So the religious leaders had to accuse Jesus of crimes that would have concerned the Roman government, such as encouraging the people not to pay taxes, claiming to be a king, and causing riots. These accusations were not true, but they were determined to kill Jesus; and they broke several commandments in order to carry out their murderous plot.*

At first Pilate hesitated to give the religious leaders permission to crucify Jesus. He thought they were simply jealous of a teacher who was more popular with the people than they were. But when the Jews threatened to report Pilate to Caesar, he became afraid. Historical records indicate that the Jews had already threatened to lodge a formal complaint against Pilate for his stubborn flouting of their traditions—and such a complaint would most likely have led to his recall by Rome. His job was in jeopardy. The Roman government could not afford to put large numbers of troops in all the regions under their control, so one of Pilate's main duties was to do whatever was necessary to maintain peace—in this case, to allow the murder of an innocent man—the Son of God.

Paul's Advice to Unmarried Women/
1 Corinthians 7:25–31

Now about virgins: I have no command from the Lord, but I give a judgment as one who by the Lord's mercy is trustworthy. 26Because of the present crisis, I think that it is good for you to remain as you are. 27Are you married? Do not seek a divorce. Are you unmarried? Do not look for a wife. 28But if you do marry, you have not sinned; and if a virgin marries, she has not sinned. But those who marry will face many troubles in this life, and I want to spare you this.

29What I mean, brothers, is that the time is short. From now on those who have wives should live as if they had none; 30those who mourn, as if they did not; those who are happy, as if they were not; those who buy something, as if it were not theirs to keep; 31those who use the things of the world, as if not engrossed in them. For this world in its present form is passing away.

A THOUGHT: *Many people naively think that marriage will solve all their problems. Here are some problems marriage won't solve: (1) loneliness, (2) sexual temptation, (3) satisfaction of one's deepest emotional needs, (4) elimination of life's difficulties. Marriage alone does not hold two people together, but commitment does—commitment to Christ and to each other despite conflicts and problems. As wonderful as it is, marriage does not solve problems. Whether married or single, we must be content with our situation and focus on Christ, not other people, to solve our problems.*

Proverbs for Today/ 11:7

When a wicked man dies, his hope perishes; all he expected from his power comes to nothing.

MARCH 13

The Crucifixion of Jesus/ Matthew 27:31–56

After they [the soldiers] had mocked him [Jesus], they took off the robe and put his own clothes on him. Then they led him away to crucify him.

32As they were going out, they met a man from Cyrene, named Simon, and they forced him to carry the cross. 33They came to a place called Golgotha (which means The Place of the Skull). 34There they offered Jesus wine to drink, mixed with gall; but after tasting it, he refused to drink it. 35When they had crucified him, they divided up his clothes by casting lots. 36And sitting down, they kept watch over him there. 37Above his head they placed the written charge against him: THIS IS JESUS, THE KING OF THE JEWS. 38Two robbers were crucified with him, one on his right and one on his left. 39Those who passed by hurled insults at him, shaking their heads 40and saying, "You who are going to destroy the temple and build it in three days, save yourself! Come down from the cross, if you are the Son of God!"

41In the same way the chief priests, the teachers of the law and the elders mocked him. 42"He saved others," they said, "but he can't save himself! He's the King of Israel! Let him come down now from the cross, and we will believe in him. 43He trusts in God. Let God rescue him now if he wants him, for he said, 'I am the Son of God.'" 44In the same way the robbers who were crucified with him also heaped insults on him.

45From the sixth hour until the ninth hour darkness came over all the land. 46About the ninth hour Jesus cried out in a loud voice, *"Eloi, Eloi, lama sabachthani?"*—which means, "My God, my God, why have you forsaken me?"

47When some of those standing there heard this, they said, "He's calling Elijah."

48Immediately one of them ran and got a sponge. He filled it with wine vinegar, put it on a stick, and offered it to Jesus to drink. 49The rest said, "Now leave him alone. Let's see if Elijah comes to save him."

50And when Jesus had cried out again in a loud voice, he gave up his spirit.

51At that moment the curtain of the temple was torn in two from top to bottom. The earth shook and the rocks split. 52The tombs broke open and the bodies of many holy people who had died were raised to life. 53They came out of the tombs, and after Jesus' resurrection they went into the holy city and appeared to many people.

54When the centurion and those with him who were guarding Jesus saw the earthquake and all that had happened, they were terrified, and exclaimed, "Surely he was the Son of God!"

55Many women were there, watching from a distance. They had followed Jesus from Galilee to care for his needs. 56Among them were Mary Magdalene, Mary the mother of James and Joses, and the mother of Zebedee's sons.

A THOUGHT: *The Roman soldiers took Jesus to the armory, a part of the Praetorium, and mocked him, dressing him with a scarlet robe and a crown of thorns. They then led him to the crucifixion site*

*outside the city. He was so weakened by his beatings that he could
not carry his cross. So a man from Cyrene was forced to carry it to
Golgotha.*

*Christ's death was accompanied by at least four miraculous
events: darkness, the splitting of the curtain in the Temple, an
earthquake, and dead people rising from their tombs. The curtain
in the Temple separated the Holy Place from the Most Holy Place.
The fact that it was torn in two symbolized that the barrier between
God and people was removed by Christ's death. Now all people are
free to approach God because of Christ's sacrifice for our sins.*

Paul's Advice to Unmarried Men/
1 Corinthians 7:32–40

I would like you to be free from concern. An unmarried man
is concerned about the Lord's affairs—how he can please
the Lord. 33But a married man is concerned about the
affairs of this world—how he can please his wife— 34and
his interests are divided. An unmarried woman or virgin is
concerned about the Lord's affairs: Her aim is to be devoted to the Lord in both body and spirit. But a married
woman is concerned about the affairs of this world—how
she can please her husband. 35I am saying this for your own
good, not to restrict you, but that you may live in a right
way in undivided devotion to the Lord.

36If anyone thinks he is acting improperly toward the
virgin he is engaged to, and if she is getting along in years
and he feels he ought to marry, he should do as he wants.
He is not sinning. They should get married. 37But the man
who has settled the matter in his own mind, who is under
no compulsion but has control over his own will, and who
has made up his mind not to marry the virgin—this man also
does the right thing. 38So then, he who marries the virgin
does right, but he who does not marry her does even
better.

39A woman is bound to her husband as long as he lives.
But if her husband dies, she is free to marry anyone she
wishes, but he must belong to the Lord. 40In my judgment,
she is happier if she stays as she is—and I think that I too
have the Spirit of God.

A THOUGHT: *Some single people feel tremendous pressure to be married. They think their lives can be complete only with a spouse. But
Paul underlines one advantage of being single—the potential of a
greater focus on Christ and his work. If you are unmarried, use your
special opportunity to serve Christ wholeheartedly.*

Proverbs for Today/ 11:8

The righteous man is rescued from trouble, and it comes on the wicked instead.

MARCH 14

Jesus' Burial/ Matthew 27:57–66

As evening approached, there came a rich man from Arimathea, named Joseph, who had himself become a disciple of Jesus. 58Going to Pilate, he asked for Jesus' body, and Pilate ordered that it be given to him. 59Joseph took the body, wrapped it in a clean linen cloth, 60and placed it in his own new tomb that he had cut out of the rock. He rolled a big stone in front of the entrance to the tomb and went away. 61Mary Magdalene and the other Mary were sitting there opposite the tomb.

62The next day, the one after Preparation Day, the chief priests and the Pharisees went to Pilate. 63"Sir," they said, "we remember that while he was still alive that deceiver said, 'After three days I will rise again.' 64So give the order for the tomb to be made secure until the third day. Otherwise, his disciples may come and steal the body and tell the people that he has been raised from the dead. This last deception will be worse than the first."

65"Take a guard," Pilate answered. "Go, make the tomb as secure as you know how." 66So they went and made the tomb secure by putting a seal on the stone and posting the guard.

A THOUGHT: *Joseph of Arimathea was a secret follower of Jesus. He was a religious leader, an honored member of the Sanhedrin. In the past, Joseph had been afraid to speak against the religious leaders who opposed Jesus; now he was bold, courageously asking to take Jesus' body from the cross and bury it. The disciples who publicly followed Jesus had fled, but this Jewish leader, who followed Jesus in secret, came forward and did what was right.*

Food Sacrificed to Idols/ 1 Corinthians 8:1–13

Now about food sacrificed to idols: We know that we all possess knowledge. Knowledge puffs up, but love builds up. ²The man who thinks he knows something does not yet know as he ought to know. ³But the man who loves God is known by God.

⁴So then, about eating food sacrificed to idols: We know that an idol is nothing at all in the world and that there is no God but one. ⁵For even if there are so-called gods, whether in heaven or on earth (as indeed there are many "gods" and many "lords"), ⁶yet for us there is but one God, the Father, from whom all things came and for whom we live; and there is but one Lord, Jesus Christ, through whom all things came and through whom we live.

⁷But not everyone knows this. Some people are still so accustomed to idols that when they eat such food they think of it as having been sacrificed to an idol, and since their conscience is weak, it is defiled. ⁸But food does not bring us near to God; we are no worse if we do not eat, and no better if we do.

⁹Be careful, however, that the exercise of your freedom does not become a stumbling block to the weak. ¹⁰For if anyone with a weak conscience sees you who have this knowledge eating in an idol's temple, won't he be emboldened to eat what has been sacrificed to idols? ¹¹So this weak brother, for whom Christ died, is destroyed by your knowledge. ¹²When you sin against your brothers in this way and wound their weak conscience, you sin against Christ. ¹³Therefore, if what I eat causes my brother to fall into sin, I will never eat meat again, so that I will not cause him to fall.

A THOUGHT: *Christian freedom does not mean "anything goes." It means that our salvation is not determined by legalism, good works, or rules, but by the free gift of God. Christian freedom, then, is inseparably tied to Christian responsibility. New believers are often very sensitive to what is right or wrong, what they should or shouldn't do. Some actions may be perfectly all right for us to do, but may harm a Christian brother or sister who is still young in the faith and learning what the Christian life is all about. We must be careful not to offend or lead into sin, a sensitive or younger Christian. When we love others, our freedom to do certain things won't be as important to us as strengthening the faith of a brother or sister in Christ.*

Proverbs for Today/ 11:9–11

With his mouth the godless destroys his neighbor, but through knowledge the righteous escape. □ When the righteous prosper, the city rejoices; when the wicked perish, there are shouts of joy. □Through the blessing of the upright a city is exalted, but by the mouth of the wicked it is destroyed.

MARCH 15

Jesus Rises from the Grave/ Matthew 28:1–15

After the Sabbath, at dawn on the first day of the week, Mary Magdalene and the other Mary went to look at the tomb.

2There was a violent earthquake, for an angel of the Lord came down from heaven and, going to the tomb, rolled back the stone and sat on it. 3His appearance was like lightning, and his clothes were white as snow. 4The guards were so afraid of him that they shook and became like dead men.

5The angel said to the women, "Do not be afraid, for I know that you are looking for Jesus, who was crucified. 6He is not here; he has risen, just as he said. Come and see the place where he lay. 7Then go quickly and tell his disciples: 'He has risen from the dead and is going ahead of you into Galilee. There you will see him.' Now I have told you."

8So the women hurried away from the tomb, afraid yet filled with joy, and ran to tell his disciples. 9Suddenly Jesus met them. "Greetings," he said. They came to him, clasped his feet and worshiped him. 10Then Jesus said to them, "Do not be afraid. Go and tell my brothers to go to Galilee; there they will see me."

11While the women were on their way, some of the guards went into the city and reported to the chief priests everything that had happened. 12When the chief priests had met with the elders and devised a plan, they gave the soldiers a large sum of money, 13telling them, "You are to say, 'His disciples came during the night and stole him away while we were asleep.' 14If this report gets to the governor, we will satisfy him and keep you out of trouble." 15So the soldiers took the money and did as they were instructed. And this story has been widely circulated among the Jews to this very day.

A THOUGHT: *The angel who announced the Good News of the resurrection to the women gave them four messages: (1) Don't be frightened. The reality of the resurrection brings joy, not fear. When you are afraid, remember the empty tomb. (2) He isn't here. Jesus is not dead and is not to be looked for among the dead. He is alive, with his people. (3) Come in and see. The women could check the evidence themselves. The tomb was empty then, and is empty today. The resurrection is a historical fact. (4) Go quickly and tell. They were to spread the joy of the resurrection. We too are to spread the Good News about Jesus' resurrection.*

The Rights of an Apostle/ 1 Corinthians 9:1–10

Am I not free? Am I not an apostle? Have I not seen Jesus our Lord? Are you not the result of my work in the Lord? 2Even though I may not be an apostle to others, surely I am to you! For you are the seal of my apostleship in the Lord.

3This is my defense to those who sit in judgment on me. 4Don't we have the right to food and drink? 5Don't we have the right to take a believing wife along with us, as do the other apostles and the Lord's brothers and Cephas? 6Or is it only I and Barnabas who must work for a living?

7Who serves as a soldier at his own expense? Who plants a vineyard and does not eat of its grapes? Who tends a flock and does not drink of the milk? 8Do I say this merely from a human point of view? Doesn't the Law say the same thing? 9For it is written in the Law of Moses: "Do not muzzle an ox while it is treading out the grain." Is it about oxen that God is concerned? 10Surely he says this for us, doesn't he? Yes, this was written for us, because when the plowman plows and the thresher threshes, they ought to do so in the hope of sharing in the harvest.

A THOUGHT: *Paul uses himself as an illustration of giving up personal rights. Paul had the right to hospitality, to be married, to bring guests, to be paid for his work; but he willingly gave up these rights to win people to Christ. When your focus is on living for Christ, your rights become comparatively unimportant. Obedience to God is far more important than maintaining our "rights."*

Proverbs for Today/ 11:12–13

A man who lacks judgment derides his neighbor, but a man of understanding holds his tongue. □ A gossip betrays a confidence, but a trustworthy man keeps a secret.

MARCH 16

Jesus Commissions His Disciples/
Matthew 28:16–20

Then the eleven disciples went to Galilee, to the mountain where Jesus had told them to go. 17When they saw him, they worshiped him; but some doubted. 18Then Jesus came to them and said, "All authority in heaven and on earth has been given to me. 19Therefore go and make disciples of all nations, baptizing them in the name of the Father and of the Son and of the Holy Spirit, 20and teaching them to obey everything I have commanded you. And surely I am with you always, to the very end of the age."

A THOUGHT: *When someone is dying or leaving us, the last words spoken by that person are very important. Jesus left the disciples with these last words of instruction: they were under his authority; they were to make more disciples; they were to baptize and teach new disciples to obey Jesus; he would be with them always. Whereas in previous missions Jesus had sent his disciples only to the Jews, their mission from now on would be worldwide. Jesus is Lord of the earth, and he died for the sins of all people.*

We are to go—whether it is next door or to another country—and make disciples. It is not an option, but a command to all who call Jesus Lord. We are not all evangelists, but we have all received gifts that we can use in helping to fulfill the Great Commission. As we obey, we have comfort in the knowledge that Jesus is always with us.

The Gospel Preached without Compensation/
1 Corinthians 9:11–18

If we have sown spiritual seed among you, is it too much if we reap a material harvest from you? 12If others have this right of support from you, shouldn't we have it all the more?

But we did not use this right. On the contrary, we put up with anything rather than hinder the gospel of Christ. 13Don't you know that those who work in the temple get their food from the temple, and those who serve at the altar share in what is offered on the altar? 14In the same way, the Lord has commanded that those who preach the gospel should receive their living from the gospel.

15But I have not used any of these rights. And I am not writing this in the hope that you will do such things for me. I would rather die than have anyone deprive me of this boast. 16Yet when I preach the gospel, I cannot boast, for I am compelled to preach. Woe to me if I do not preach the gospel! 17If I preach voluntarily, I have a reward; if not voluntarily, I am simply discharging the trust committed to me. 18What then is my reward? Just this: that in preaching the gospel I may offer it free of charge, and so not make use of my rights in preaching it.

A THOUGHT: *Preaching the gospel was Paul's gift and calling, and he said he couldn't stop preaching if he wanted to. He was driven by the desire to do what God wanted, using his gifts for God's glory. He did not seek money or fame, rather he sought to know Christ and to bring him glory. This is true discipleship. What special gifts has God given you? Are you motivated, like Paul, to glorify God with your gifts?*

Proverbs for Today/ 11:14

For lack of guidance a nation falls, but many advisers make victory sure.

MARCH 17

John the Baptist Prepares the Way/ Mark 1:1–8

The beginning of the gospel about Jesus Christ, the Son of God.

2It is written in Isaiah the prophet:

"I will send my messenger ahead of you,
who will prepare your way"—
3"a voice of one calling in the desert,
'Prepare the way for the Lord,
make straight paths for him.'"

4And so John came, baptizing in the desert region and preaching a baptism of repentance for the forgiveness of sins. 5The whole Judean countryside and all the people of Jerusalem went out to him. Confessing their sins, they were baptized by him in the Jordan River. 6John wore clothing made of camel's hair, with a leather belt around his waist, and he ate locusts and wild honey. 7And this was his message: "After me will come one more powerful than I, the thongs of whose sandals I am not worthy to stoop down and untie. [8]I baptize you with water, but he will baptize you with the Holy Spirit."

A THOUGHT: *The purpose of John's preaching was to prepare people to accept Jesus as God's Son. When John challenged the people to confess sin individually, he signaled the start of a new approach to having a relationship with God.*

Is change needed in your life before you can hear and understand Jesus' message? People have to admit that they need forgiveness before they can accept forgiveness; thus true repentance must come before a person can have true faith in Jesus Christ. To prepare to receive Christ, we must repent, denouncing the world's dead-end attractions, sinful temptations, and harmful attitudes.

All Things to All Men/ 1 Corinthians 9:19–27

Though I am free and belong to no man, I make myself a slave to everyone, to win as many as possible. [20]To the Jews I became like a Jew, to win the Jews. To those under the law I became like one under the law (though I myself am not under the law), so as to win those under the law. [21]To those not having the law I became like one not having the law (though I am not free from God's law but am under Christ's law), so as to win those not having the law. [22]To the weak I became weak, to win the weak. I have become all things to all men so that by all possible means I might save some. [23]I do all this for the sake of the gospel, that I may share in its blessings.

[24]Do you not know that in a race all the runners run, but only one gets the prize? Run in such a way as to get the prize. [25]Everyone who competes in the games goes into strict training. They do it to get a crown that will not last; but we do it to get a crown that will last forever. [26]Therefore I do not run like a man running aimlessly; I do not fight like a man beating the air. [27]No, I beat my body and make it my slave so that after I have preached to others, I myself will not be disqualified for the prize.

A THOUGHT: *Paul gives several important principles for ministry: (1) find common ground with those you contact; (2) avoid a know-it-all attitude; (3) make others feel accepted; (4) be sensitive to their needs and concerns; and (5) look for opportunities to tell them about Christ. These principles are just as valid for us today as they were for Paul.*

Proverbs for Today/ 11:15

He who puts up security for another will surely suffer, but whoever refuses to strike hands in pledge is safe.

MARCH 18

Jesus' Baptism and Temptation/ Mark 1:9–13

At that time Jesus came from Nazareth in Galilee and was baptized by John in the Jordan. 10As Jesus was coming up out of the water, he saw heaven being torn open and the Spirit descending on him like a dove. 11And a voice came from heaven: "You are my Son, whom I love; with you I am well pleased."

12At once the Spirit sent him out into the desert, 13and he was in the desert forty days, being tempted by Satan. He was with the wild animals, and angels attended him.

A THOUGHT: *Jesus left the crowds and went into the desert where he was tempted by Satan. Temptation is bad for us only when we give in. Times of inner testing should not be hated and resented, because through them our character can be strengthened and God can teach us valuable lessons. When you face Satan and must deal with his temptations and the turmoil he brings, remember Jesus. He used God's Word against Satan and won. You can do the same.*

Examples From Israel's History/ 1 Corinthians 10:1–14

For I do not want you to be ignorant of the fact, brothers, that our forefathers were all under the cloud and that they all passed through the sea. 2They were all baptized into Moses in the cloud and in the sea. 3They all ate the same spiritual food 4and drank the same spiritual drink; for they drank from the spiritual rock that accompanied them, and that rock was Christ. 5Nevertheless, God was not pleased with most of them; their bodies were scattered over the desert.

6Now these things occurred as examples to keep us from setting our hearts on evil things as they did. 7Do not be idolaters, as some of them were; as it is written: "The people sat down to eat and drink and got up to indulge in pagan revelry." [8]We should not commit sexual immorality, as some of them did—and in one day twenty-three thousand of them died. [9]We should not test the Lord, as some of them did—and were killed by snakes. [10]And do not grumble, as some of them did—and were killed by the destroying angel.

[11]These things happened to them as examples and were written down as warnings for us, on whom the fulfillment of the ages has come. [12]So, if you think you are standing firm, be careful that you don't fall! [13]No temptation has seized you except what is common to man. And God is faithful; he will not let you be tempted beyond what you can bear. But when you are tempted, he will also provide a way out so that you can stand up under it.

[14]Therefore, my dear friends, flee from idolatry.

A THOUGHT: *In a culture filled with moral depravity and pressures, Paul gave strong encouragement to the Corinthians about temptation. He said: wrong desires and temptations happen to everyone, so don't feel you've been singled out; others have resisted temptation, and so can you; any temptation can be resisted, because God will help you resist it. God helps you resist temptation by helping you (1) recognize those people and situations that give you trouble, (2) run from anything you know is wrong, (3) choose to do only what is right, (4) pray for God's help, and (5) seek friends who love God and can offer help in times of temptation. Running from a tempting situation is often the first step to victory.*

Proverbs for Today/ 11:16–17

A kindhearted woman gains respect, but ruthless men gain only wealth. □ A kind man benefits himself, but a cruel man brings trouble on himself.

MARCH 19

Jesus Calls His First Disciples/ Mark 1:14–20

After John was put in prison, Jesus went into Galilee, proclaiming the good news of God. [15]"The time has come," he said. "The kingdom of God is near. Repent and believe the good news!"

[16]As Jesus walked beside the Sea of Galilee, he saw

Simon and his brother Andrew casting a net into the lake, for they were fishermen. 17"Come, follow me," Jesus said, "and I will make you fishers of men." 18At once they left their nets and followed him.

19When he had gone a little farther, he saw James son of Zebedee and his brother John in a boat, preparing their nets. 20Without delay he called them, and they left their father Zebedee in the boat with the hired men and followed him.

A THOUGHT: *What is God's Good News? These first words spoken by Jesus in Mark's Gospel give the core of his teaching: that the long-awaited Messiah has come to begin God's personal reign on earth. Most of the people who heard this message were oppressed, poor, and without hope. Jesus' words were good news because they offered freedom, blessings, and promise.*

Sharing in the Lord's Death/
1 Corinthians 10:15–22

I speak to sensible people; judge for yourselves what I say. 16Is not the cup of thanksgiving for which we give thanks a participation in the blood of Christ? And is not the bread that we break a participation in the body of Christ? 17Because there is one loaf, we, who are many, are one body, for we all partake of the one loaf.

18Consider the people of Israel: Do not those who eat the sacrifices participate in the altar? 19Do I mean then that a sacrifice offered to an idol is anything, or that an idol is anything? 20No, but the sacrifices of pagans are offered to demons, not to God, and I do not want you to be participants with demons. 21You cannot drink the cup of the Lord and the cup of demons too; you cannot have a part in both the Lord's table and the table of demons. 22Are we trying to arouse the Lord's jealousy? Are we stronger than he?

A THOUGHT: *As followers of Christ we must give him our total allegiance. We cannot, as Paul explains, eat at "both the Lord's table and the table of demons." Eating at the Lord's table means communing with Christ and identifying with his death. Eating at the table of demons means identifying with Satan by participating in evil actions. Are you trying to lead two lives, following the desires of both Christ and the crowd? The Bible says you can't do both at the same time. We must choose whom we will serve.*

Proverbs for Today/ 11:18–19

The wicked man earns deceptive wages, but he who sows righteousness reaps a sure reward. □ The truly righteous man attains life, but he who pursues evil goes to his death.

MARCH 20

Jesus Demonstrates His Authority/ Mark 1:21–28

They went to Capernaum, and when the Sabbath came, Jesus went into the synagogue and began to teach. 22The people were amazed at his teaching, because he taught them as one who had authority, not as the teachers of the law. 23Just then a man in their synagogue who was possessed by an evil spirit cried out, 24"What do you want with us, Jesus of Nazareth? Have you come to destroy us? I know who you are—the Holy One of God!"

25"Be quiet!" said Jesus sternly. "Come out of him!" 26The evil spirit shook the man violently and came out of him with a shriek.

27The people were all so amazed that they asked each other, "What is this? A new teaching—and with authority! He even gives orders to evil spirits and they obey him." 28News about him spread quickly over the whole region of Galilee.

A THOUGHT: *The Jewish teachers often quoted from well-known rabbis to give their words more authority. But Jesus didn't need to do that. Jesus' authority was not derived from the wisdom of others; his authority was bound up with the fact that he is God's Son. He is the ultimate authority. Jesus demonstrated his power and authority by casting out demons and healing the sick. Jesus didn't have to conduct elaborate exorcism rituals. His word was enough to send out the demons.*

Do All to the Glory of God/ 1 Corinthians 10:23—11:1

"Everything is permissible"—but not everything is beneficial. "Everything is permissible"—but not everything is constructive. 24Nobody should seek his own good, but the good of others.

25Eat anything sold in the meat market without raising

questions of conscience, ²⁶for, "The earth is the Lord's, and everything in it."

²⁷If some unbeliever invites you to a meal and you want to go, eat whatever is put before you without raising questions of conscience. ²⁸But if anyone says to you, "This has been offered in sacrifice," then do not eat it, both for the sake of the man who told you and for conscience' sake— ²⁹the other man's conscience, I mean, not yours. For why should my freedom be judged by another's conscience? ³⁰If I take part in the meal with thankfulness, why am I denounced because of something I thank God for?

³¹So whether you eat or drink or whatever you do, do it all for the glory of God. ³²Do not cause anyone to stumble, whether Jews, Greeks or the church of God— ³³even as I try to please everybody in every way. For I am not seeking my own good but the good of many, so that they may be saved. ^{11:1}Follow my example, as I follow the example of Christ.

A THOUGHT: *Sometimes it's hard to know when to defer to the weaker brother. Paul gives a simple rule of thumb to help in making the decision—we should be sensitive and gracious. While we have freedom in Christ, we shouldn't exercise our freedom at the cost of hurting a Christian brother or sister. In all that we do, we must seek to obey God. Obedience to God is most clearly seen in our love for one another (which involves sacrificing our own desires for the desires of others).*

Proverbs for Today/ 11:20–21

The LORD detests men of perverse heart but he delights in those whose ways are blameless. □ Be sure of this: The wicked will not go unpunished, but those who are righteous will go free.

MARCH 21

Jesus Casts Out Demons and Heals Many/ Mark 1:29–39

As soon as they [Jesus and his disciples] left the synagogue, they went with James and John to the home of

Simon and Andrew. 30Simon's mother-in-law was in bed with a fever, and they told Jesus about her. 31So he went to her, took her hand and helped her up. The fever left her and she began to wait on them.

32That evening after sunset the people brought to Jesus all the sick and demon-possessed. 33The whole town gathered at the door, 34and Jesus healed many who had various diseases. He also drove out many demons, but he would not let the demons speak because they knew who he was.

35Very early in the morning, while it was still dark, Jesus got up, left the house and went off to a solitary place, where he prayed. 36Simon and his companions went to look for him, 37and when they found him, they exclaimed: "Everyone is looking for you!"

38Jesus replied, "Let us go somewhere else—to the nearby villages—so I can preach there also. That is why I have come." 39So he traveled throughout Galilee, preaching in their synagogues and driving out demons.

A THOUGHT: *Jesus announced the presence of the kingdom of God. He did this in both word and deed. In his words he announced God's Good News. In his deeds he demonstrated the power of God's rule through casting out demons and healing many. Ultimately, he established the entrance into the kingdom of God by his death and resurrection.*

Women in the Church/ 1 Corinthians 11:2–16

I praise you for remembering me in everything and for holding to the teachings, just as I passed them on to you.

3Now I want you to realize that the head of every man is Christ, and the head of the woman is man, and the head of Christ is God. 4Every man who prays or prophesies with his head covered dishonors his head. 5And every woman who prays or prophesies with her head uncovered dishonors her head—it is just as though her head were shaved. 6If a woman does not cover her head, she should have her hair cut off; and if it is a disgrace for a woman to have her hair cut or shaved off, she should cover her head. 7A man ought not to cover his head, since he is the image and glory of God; but the woman is the glory of man. 8For man did not come from woman, but woman from man; 9neither was man created for woman, but woman for man. 10For this reason, and because of the angels, the woman ought to have a sign of authority on her head.

11In the Lord, however, woman is not independent of man, nor is man independent of woman. 12For as woman came from man, so also man is born of woman. But everything comes from God. 13Judge for yourselves: Is it proper for a woman to pray to God with her head uncovered? 14Does not the very nature of things teach you that if a man has long hair, it is a disgrace to him, 15but that if a woman has long hair, it is her glory? For long hair is given to her as a covering. 16If anyone wants to be contentious about this, we have no other practice—nor do the churches of God.

A THOUGHT: *This section focuses on attitudes toward worship, not on marriage or the role of women in the church. While Paul's specific instructions may be cultural (women wearing head coverings in worship), the principles behind his specific instructions are timeless, including respect for spouse, reverence and appropriateness in worship, and focusing all of life on God. If anything you do easily offends members and divides the church, then change your ways to promote church unity. Thus Paul told the women who were not wearing head coverings to wear them; not because it was a scriptural command, but because it kept the congregation from dividing over a petty issue that served only to take people's minds off Christ.*

Proverbs for Today/ 11:22

Like a gold ring in a pig's snout is a beautiful woman who shows no discretion.

MARCH 22

Jesus Heals a Leper/ Mark 1:40–45

A man with leprosy came to him [Jesus] and begged him on his knees, "If you are willing, you can make me clean."
41Filled with compassion, Jesus reached out his hand and touched the man. "I am willing," he said. "Be clean!" 42Immediately the leprosy left him and he was cured.
43Jesus sent him away at once with a strong warning: 44"See that you don't tell this to anyone. But go, show yourself to the priest and offer the sacrifices that Moses commanded for your cleansing, as a testimony to them." 45Instead he went out and began to talk freely, spreading

the news. As a result, Jesus could no longer enter a town openly but stayed outside in lonely places. Yet the people still came to him from everywhere.

A THOUGHT: *Jewish leaders declared lepers unclean. This meant they were unfit to participate in any religious or social activity. Because their law said that contact with any unclean person made them unclean too, some even threw rocks at lepers to keep them at a safe distance. But Jesus reached out in compassion and touched this leper.*

The real value of a person is on the inside, not what appears on the outside. Although a person's body may be diseased or deformed, the person inside is no less valuable to God than a physically healthy person. God's compassion reaches out to all without any such distinctions. In a sense, we are all lepers, because we have all been deformed by the ugliness of sin. But God, by sending his Son Jesus, has touched us, giving us the opportunity to be healed. When you feel repulsed by someone, stop and remember how God feels about that person—and about you.

Extremes at Communion Services/
1 Corinthians 11:17–22

In the following directives I have no praise for you, for your meetings do more harm than good. 18In the first place, I hear that when you come together as a church, there are divisions among you, and to some extent I believe it. 19No doubt there have to be differences among you to show which of you have God's approval. 20When you come together, it is not the Lord's Supper you eat, 21for as you eat, each of you goes ahead without waiting for anybody else. One remains hungry, another gets drunk. 22Don't you have homes to eat and drink in? Or do you despise the church of God and humiliate those who have nothing? What shall I say to you? Shall I praise you for this? Certainly not!

A THOUGHT: *When the Lord's Supper was celebrated in the early church, it included a feast or fellowship meal followed by communion. In Corinth the fellowship meal had become a time of gluttony and excessive drinking rather than a time of preparation for communion. Although the feast was similar to a potluck, there was little sharing and caring. This certainly did not demonstrate the unity and love that should characterize the church, nor was it a preparation for communion. Paul condemned these actions and reminded the church of the real purpose of the Lord's Supper—participation in the Lord's death. Christ should be the central focus of the communion service.*

Proverbs for Today/ 11:23

The desire of the righteous ends only in good, but the hope of the wicked only in wrath.

MARCH 23

Jesus Heals a Paralytic/ Mark 2:1–12

A few days later, when Jesus again entered Capernaum, the people heard that he had come home. 2So many gathered that there was no room left, not even outside the door, and he preached the word to them. 3Some men came, bringing to him a paralytic, carried by four of them. 4Since they could not get him to Jesus because of the crowd, they made an opening in the roof above Jesus and, after digging through it, lowered the mat the paralyzed man was lying on. 5When Jesus saw their faith, he said to the paralytic, "Son, your sins are forgiven."

6Now some teachers of the law were sitting there, thinking to themselves, 7"Why does this fellow talk like that? He's blaspheming! Who can forgive sins but God alone?"

8Immediately Jesus knew in his spirit that this was what they were thinking in their hearts, and he said to them, "Why are you thinking these things? 9Which is easier: to say to the paralytic, 'Your sins are forgiven,' or to say, 'Get up, take your mat and walk'? 10But that you may know that the Son of Man has authority on earth to forgive sins . . . ." He said to the paralytic, 11"I tell you, get up, take your mat and go home." 12He got up, took his mat and walked out in full view of them all. This amazed everyone and they praised God, saying, "We have never seen anything like this!"

A THOUGHT: *Instead of saying to the paralyzed man, "You are healed," Jesus said, "Your sins are forgiven." To the Jewish leaders this was blasphemy, claiming to do something only God could do. According to Jewish law, this sin deserved death.*

The religious leaders understood correctly that Jesus was claiming to be the Messiah, but their judgment of him was wrong. Jesus was not blaspheming, because his claim was true. As God's Son, Jesus has the authority to forgive sin, and he proved his claim by healing the paralyzed man.

Sharing at the Lord's Table/ 1 Corinthians 11:23–34

For I received from the Lord what I also passed on to you: The Lord Jesus, on the night he was betrayed, took bread, 24and when he had given thanks, he broke it and said, "This is my body, which is for you; do this in remembrance of me." 25In the same way, after supper he took the cup, saying, "This cup is the new covenant in my blood; do this, whenever you drink it, in remembrance of me." 26For whenever you eat this bread and drink this cup, you proclaim the Lord's death until he comes.

27Therefore, whoever eats the bread or drinks the cup of the Lord in an unworthy manner will be guilty of sinning against the body and blood of the Lord. 28A man ought to examine himself before he eats of the bread and drinks of the cup. 29For anyone who eats and drinks without recognizing the body of the Lord eats and drinks judgment on himself. 30That is why many among you are weak and sick, and a number of you have fallen asleep. 31But if we judged ourselves, we would not come under judgment. 32When we are judged by the Lord, we are being disciplined so that we will not be condemned with the world.

33So then, my brothers, when you come together to eat, wait for each other. 34If anyone is hungry, he should eat at home, so that when you meet together it may not result in judgment.

And when I come I will give further directions.

A THOUGHT: *Paul gives specific instructions on how the Lord's Supper should be observed. (1) We should take the Lord's Supper with a repentant attitude because we are remembering that Christ died for our sins. (2) We should take it after self-examination. We are to be prepared and ready, doing it only through our belief in and love for Christ. (3) We should take it in recognition of Jesus' act of love in taking away the punishment we deserve for our sins. (4) We should take it with mutual consideration, waiting until everyone is present and eating in an orderly and unified manner.*

Proverbs for Today/ 11:24–26

One man gives freely, yet gains even more; another withholds unduly, but comes to poverty. □ A generous man will prosper; he who refreshes others will himself be refreshed. □ People curse the man who hoards grain, but blessing crowns him who is willing to sell.

MARCH 24

Jesus Calls Levi/ Mark 2:13–17

Once again Jesus went out beside the lake. A large crowd came to him, and he began to teach them. 14As he walked along, he saw Levi son of Alphaeus sitting at the tax collector's booth. "Follow me," Jesus told him, and Levi got up and followed him.

15While Jesus was having dinner at Levi's house, many tax collectors and "sinners" were eating with him and his disciples, for there were many who followed him. 16When the teachers of the law who were Pharisees saw him eating with the "sinners" and tax collectors, they asked his disciples: "Why does he eat with tax collectors and 'sinners'?"

17On hearing this, Jesus said to them, "It is not the healthy who need a doctor, but the sick. I have not come to call the righteous, but sinners."

A THOUGHT: *"Such scum," the self-righteous Pharisees said, describing the people with whom Jesus ate. But Jesus associated with sinners because he loved them and because he knew they needed to hear what he had to say. He spent time with whoever needed or wanted to hear his message—poor, rich, evil, and good. We, too, must befriend those who need Christ, even if they do not seem to be ideal companions. Are there people you have been neglecting because of their reputation? They may be the ones who most need to see and hear the message of Christ's love from you.*

Judging the Truthfulness of a Message/ 1 Corinthians 12:1–3

Now about spiritual gifts, brothers, I do not want you to be ignorant. 2You know that when you were pagans, somehow or other you were influenced and led astray to mute idols. 3Therefore I tell you that no one who is speaking by the Spirit of God says, "Jesus be cursed," and no one can say, "Jesus is Lord," except by the Holy Spirit.

A THOUGHT: *Anyone can claim to speak for God, and the world is full of false teachers. Paul gives us a test to help us discern whether or not a messenger is really from God: does he or she confess Christ as Lord? Don't naively accept the words of all who claim to speak for God; test their credentials by finding out what they teach about Christ.*

Proverbs for Today/ 11:27

He who seeks good finds goodwill, but evil comes to him who searches for it.

MARCH 25

The Bridegroom and His Friends/ Mark 2:18–22

Now John's disciples and the Pharisees were fasting. Some people came and asked Jesus, "How is it that John's disciples and the disciples of the Pharisees are fasting, but yours are not?"

19Jesus answered, "How can the guests of the bridegroom fast while he is with them? They cannot, so long as they have him with them. 20But the time will come when the bridegroom will be taken from them, and on that day they will fast.

21"No one sews a patch of unshrunk cloth on an old garment. If he does, the new piece will pull away from the old, making the tear worse. 22And no one pours new wine into old wineskins. If he does, the wine will burst the skins, and both the wine and the wineskins will be ruined. No, he pours new wine into new wineskins."

A THOUGHT: *John the Baptist's ministry had two purposes: to announce to people that they needed to repent of their sin, and to prepare them for Christ's coming. This was a time of sober reflection, and so it included fasting, an outward sign of humility and regret for sin. Fasting is a turning away from food; repentance is a turning away from sin. Jesus' disciples did not need to fast to prepare for his coming, because he was with them. Jesus did not condemn fasting. He himself fasted for 40 days. Nevertheless, he emphasized fasting with the right motives. The Pharisees fasted twice a week to show how holy they were. Jesus explained that if people fast only to impress others, they have missed the purpose of fasting. Christian fasting should be a turning away from meeting our own needs—the time we normally set aside for eating—to pray, to worship God, or to serve God by serving others.*

Spiritual Gifts in the Church/ 1 Corinthians 12:4–11

There are different kinds of gifts, but the same Spirit. 5There are different kinds of service, but the same Lord.

6There are different kinds of working, but the same God works all of them in all men.

7Now to each one the manifestation of the Spirit is given for the common good. 8To one there is given through the Spirit the message of wisdom, to another the message of knowledge by means of the same Spirit, 9to another faith by the same Spirit, to another gifts of healing by that one Spirit, 10to another miraculous powers, to another prophecy, to another distinguishing between spirits, to another speaking in different kinds of tongues, and to still another the interpretation of tongues. 11All these are the work of one and the same Spirit, and he gives them to each one, just as he determines.

A THOUGHT: *There is both unity and diversity in the body of Christ. There is unity in the fact that we all belong to the same Lord, we are all empowered by the same Spirit, and we all belong to the same community (the church). Within this great unity is a great diversity of gifts. Each of these gifts is given by the Holy Spirit to individuals for the building up of the whole body of Christ. Spiritual gifts should not be a source of contention over who has the "greater" gifts. God did not give the gifts to improve our status, but to allow us the opportunity to participate in the building up of the church. Therefore, let us employ our spiritual gifts as God intended them to be used—to build up the church.*

Proverbs for Today/ 11:28

Whoever trusts in his riches will fall, but the righteous will thrive like a green leaf.

MARCH 26

Lord of the Sabbath/ Mark 2:23—3:6

One Sabbath Jesus was going through the grainfields, and as his disciples walked along, they began to pick some heads of grain. 24The Pharisees said to him, "Look, why are they doing what is unlawful on the Sabbath?"

25He answered, "Have you never read what David did when he and his companions were hungry and in need? 26In the days of Abiathar the high priest, he entered the house of God and ate the consecrated bread, which is lawful only for priests to eat. And he also gave some to his companions."

27Then he said to them, "The Sabbath was made for man, not man for the Sabbath. 28So the Son of Man is Lord even of the Sabbath."

3:1Another time he went into the synagogue, and a man with a shriveled hand was there. 2Some of them were looking for a reason to accuse Jesus, so they watched him closely to see if he would heal him on the Sabbath. 3Jesus said to the man with the shriveled hand, "Stand up in front of everyone."

4Then Jesus asked them, "Which is lawful on the Sabbath: to do good or to do evil, to save life or to kill?" But they remained silent.

5He looked around at them in anger and, deeply distressed at their stubborn hearts, said to the man, "Stretch out your hand." He stretched it out, and his hand was completely restored. 6Then the Pharisees went out and began to plot with the Herodians how they might kill Jesus.

A THOUGHT: *Jesus used the example of King David to point out how ridiculous the Pharisees' accusations were. Jesus said that God created the Sabbath for our benefit, not his own. God derives no benefit from having us rest on the Sabbath, but we are restored both physically and spiritually when we take time to rest and focus on God. For the Pharisees, Sabbath laws had become more important than the reason for the Sabbath. Both David and Jesus understood that the true intent of God's Law is to promote love for God and for others. Don't blindly keep a law without looking carefully at the reasons for the law. Keeping the spirit of the law is more important than merely following the letter of the law.*

The Body of Christ Has Many Parts/
1 Corinthians 12:12–18

The body is a unit, though it is made up of many parts; and though all its parts are many, they form one body. So it is with Christ. 13For we were all baptized by one Spirit into one body—whether Jews or Greeks, slave or free—and we were all given the one Spirit to drink.

14Now the body is not made up of one part but of many. 15If the foot should say, "Because I am not a hand, I do not belong to the body," it would not for that reason cease to be part of the body. 16And if the ear should say, "Because I am not an eye, I do not belong to the body," it would not for that reason cease to be part of the body. 17If the whole body were an eye, where would the sense of hearing be? If the whole body were an ear, where would the sense of smell be? 18But in fact God has arranged the parts in the body, every one of them, just as he wanted them to be.

A THOUGHT: *Using the analogy of the body, Paul emphasizes the importance of each church member. If a seemingly insignificant part is taken away, the whole body becomes less effective. Thinking that your gift is more important than someone else's is spiritual pride. We should not look down on those who seem unimportant, and we should not be jealous of others who have impressive gifts. Instead, we must use the gifts we have been given and encourage others to use theirs. If we don't, the body of believers will be less effective.*

Proverbs for Today/ 11:29–31

He who brings trouble on his family will inherit only wind, and the fool will be servant to the wise. □ The fruit of the righteous is a tree of life, and he who wins souls is wise. □ If the righteous receive their due on earth, how much more the ungodly and the sinner!

MARCH 27

Jesus Chooses His Twelve Disciples/ Mark 3:7–19

Jesus withdrew with his disciples to the lake, and a large crowd from Galilee followed. 8When they heard all he was doing, many people came to him from Judea, Jerusalem, Idumea, and the regions across the Jordan and around Tyre and Sidon. 9Because of the crowd he told his disciples to have a small boat ready for him, to keep the people from crowding him. 10For he had healed many, so that those with diseases were pushing forward to touch him. 11Whenever the evil spirits saw him, they fell down before him and cried out, "You are the Son of God." 12But he gave them strict orders not to tell who he was.

13Jesus went up on a mountainside and called to him those he wanted, and they came to him. 14He appointed twelve—designating them apostles—that they might be with him and that he might send them out to preach 15and to have authority to drive out demons. 16These are the twelve he appointed: Simon (to whom he gave the name Peter); [17]James son of Zebedee and his brother John (to them he gave the name Boanerges, which means Sons of Thunder); [18]Andrew, Philip, Bartholomew, Matthew, Thomas, James son of Alphaeus, Thaddaeus, Simon the Zealot [19]and Judas Iscariot, who betrayed him.

A THOUGHT: *Jesus was surrounded by followers, from whom he chose twelve to be his regular companions. He did not choose these twelve because of their faith, because their faith faltered. He didn't choose them because of their talent and ability, because no one stood out with unusual ability. The disciples represented a wide range of backgrounds and life experiences, but apparently they had no more leadership potential than those who were not chosen. The one characteristic they all shared was their willingness to obey and follow Jesus. After Jesus' ascension, they were filled with the Holy Spirit and carried out special roles in the early church. We should not disqualify ourselves from service to Christ because we do not have the right credentials. Being a good disciple is not a matter of credentials, but of following Jesus with a willing heart.*

All Parts of the Body Necessary/
1 Corinthians 12:19–27

If they were all one part, where would the body be? [20]As it is, there are many parts, but one body.

[21]The eye cannot say to the hand, "I don't need you!" And the head cannot say to the feet, "I don't need you!" [22]On the contrary, those parts of the body that seem to be weaker are indispensable, [23]and the parts that we think are less honorable we treat with special honor. And the parts that are unpresentable are treated with special modesty, [24]while our presentable parts need no special treatment. But God has combined the members of the body and has given greater honor to the parts that lacked it, [25]so that there should be no division in the body, but that its parts should have equal concern for each other. [26]If one part suffers, every part suffers with it; if one part is honored, every part rejoices with it.

[27]Now you are the body of Christ, and each one of you is a part of it.

A THOUGHT: *What is your response when a fellow Christian is honored? When someone is suffering? We are called to rejoice with those who rejoice and weep with those who weep. Too often, unfortunately, we are jealous of those who rejoice and separate ourselves from those who weep. Believers are in the world together—there is no room in the church for an individualistic Christianity. We can't concern ourselves solely with our own relationship with God; we need to be concerned for the needs of others.*

Proverbs for Today/ 12:1

Whoever loves discipline loves knowledge, but he who hates correction is stupid.

MARCH 28

The Kingdom of God and the Kingdom of Satan/ Mark 3:20–35

Then Jesus entered a house, and again a crowd gathered, so that he and his disciples were not even able to eat. 21When his family heard about this, they went to take charge of him, for they said, "He is out of his mind."

22And the teachers of the law who came down from Jerusalem said, "He is possessed by Beelzebub! By the prince of demons he is driving out demons."

23So Jesus called them and spoke to them in parables: "How can Satan drive out Satan? 24If a kingdom is divided against itself, that kingdom cannot stand. 25If a house is divided against itself, that house cannot stand. 26And if Satan opposes himself and is divided, he cannot stand; his end has come. 27In fact, no one can enter a strong man's house and carry off his possessions unless he first ties up the strong man. Then he can rob his house. 28I tell you the truth, all the sins and blasphemies of men will be forgiven them. 29But whoever blasphemes against the Holy Spirit will never be forgiven; he is guilty of an eternal sin."

30He said this because they were saying, "He has an evil spirit."

31Then Jesus' mother and brothers arrived. Standing outside, they sent someone in to call him. 32A crowd was sitting around him, and they told him, "Your mother and brothers are outside looking for you."

33"Who are my mother and my brothers?" he asked.

34Then he looked at those seated in a circle around him and said, "Here are my mother and my brothers! 35Whoever does God's will is my brother and sister and mother."

A THOUGHT: *God's family is open and doesn't exclude anyone. Although Jesus cared for his mother and brothers, he also cared for all those who loved him. Jesus did not show partiality; he allowed everyone the privilege of obeying God and becoming part of his family. He shows us how to relate to other believers in a new way. In our increasingly computerized, impersonal world, warm relationships among members of God's family take on major importance. The church can give loving, personalized care that many people find nowhere else.*

The Gifts of the Spirit/ 1 Corinthians 12:28–31

And in the church God has appointed first of all apostles, second prophets, third teachers, then workers of miracles, also those having gifts of healing, those able to help others, those with gifts of administration, and those speaking in different kinds of tongues. 29Are all apostles? Are all prophets? Are all teachers? Do all work miracles? 30Do all have gifts of healing? Do all speak in tongues? Do all interpret? 31But eagerly desire the greater gifts.

And now I will show you the most excellent way.

A THOUGHT: *The more important gifts are those that are more beneficial to the body of Christ. Paul has already made it clear that one gift is not superior to another, but he urges the believers to discover how they can serve Christ's body best with the gifts God has given them. Your spiritual gifts are not for your own self-advancement. They were given for serving God and enhancing the spiritual growth of the body.*

Proverbs for Today/ 12:2–3

A good man obtains favor from the LORD, but the LORD condemns a crafty man. □ A man cannot be established through wickedness, but the righteous cannot be uprooted.

MARCH 29

The Parable of the Sower/ Mark 4:1–20

Again Jesus began to teach by the lake. The crowd that gathered around him was so large that he got into a boat and sat in it out on the lake, while all the people were along the shore at the water's edge. 2He taught them many things by parables, and in his teaching said: 3"Listen! A farmer went out to sow his seed. 4As he was scattering the seed, some fell along the path, and the birds came and ate it up. 5Some fell on rocky places, where it did not have much soil. It sprang up quickly, because the soil was shallow. 6But when the sun came up, the plants were scorched, and they withered because they had no root. 7Other seed fell among thorns, which grew up and choked the plants, so that they did not bear grain. 8Still other seed fell on good soil. It came up, grew and produced a crop, multiplying thirty, sixty, or even a hundred times."

9Then Jesus said, "He who has ears to hear, let him hear."

10When he was alone, the Twelve and the others around him asked him about the parables. 11He told them, "The secret of the kingdom of God has been given to you. But to those on the outside everything is said in parables 12so that,

" 'they may be ever seeing but never perceiving,
    and ever hearing but never understanding;
otherwise they might turn and be forgiven!' "

13Then Jesus said to them, "Don't you understand this parable? How then will you understand any parable? 14The farmer sows the word. 15Some people are like seed along the path, where the word is sown. As soon as they hear it, Satan comes and takes away the word that was sown in them. 16Others, like seed sown on rocky places, hear the word and at once receive it with joy. 17But since they have no root, they last only a short time. When trouble or persecution comes because of the word, they quickly fall away. 18Still others, like seed sown among thorns, hear the word; 19but the worries of this life, the deceitfulness of wealth and the desires for other things come in and choke the word, making it unfruitful. 20Others, like seed sown on good soil, hear the word, accept it, and produce a crop—thirty, sixty or even a hundred times what was sown."

A THOUGHT: *Jesus taught the people by telling stories, often called parables. A parable uses familiar scenes to explain deeper spiritual truth. This method of teaching compels the listener to think. It conceals the truth from those who are too stubborn or prejudiced to hear what is being taught. We hear with our ears, but there is a deeper kind of listening with the mind and heart that is necessary in order to gain spiritual understanding from Jesus' words. We must allow ourselves to be impacted by the truth of the story in order to hear with this deeper kind of listening. All of God's Word should impact us at this deeper level—where God's Word transforms our lives.*

The Characteristics of Love/ 1 Corinthians 13:1–7

If I speak in the tongues of men and of angels, but have not love, I am only a resounding gong or a clanging cymbal. 2If I have the gift of prophecy and can fathom all mysteries and all knowledge, and if I have a faith that can move mountains, but have not love, I am nothing. 3If I give all I possess to the poor and surrender my body to the flames, but have not love, I gain nothing.

4Love is patient, love is kind. It does not envy, it does not boast, it is not proud. 5It is not rude, it is not self-seeking, it is not easily angered, it keeps no record of wrongs. 6Love does not delight in evil but rejoices with the truth. 7It always protects, always trusts, always hopes, always perseveres.

A THOUGHT: *After discussing spiritual gifts in some detail, Paul comes to the core of spirituality—love. No matter what gift a person has, if he or she does not express love in using that gift, then whatever is done is empty. The greatest measure of spirituality is how much our lives are filled with Christlike love. This is not love that we can muster up within ourselves; it is a supernatural love that is produced by the Holy Spirit. Love is to be central to all that we do, for it is the most important part of spirituality. The more intimately we know Christ, the more we will unselfishly love others.*

Proverbs for Today/ 12:4

A wife of noble character is her husband's crown, but a disgraceful wife is like decay in his bones.

MARCH 30

Parables of the Kingdom/ Mark 4:21–34

He [Jesus] said to them, "Do you bring in a lamp to put it under a bowl or a bed? Instead, don't you put it on its stand? 22For whatever is hidden is meant to be disclosed, and whatever is concealed is meant to be brought out into the open. 23If anyone has ears to hear, let him hear."

24"Consider carefully what you hear," he continued. "With the measure you use, it will be measured to you—and even more. 25Whoever has will be given more; whoever does not have, even what he has will be taken from him."

26He also said, "This is what the kingdom of God is like. A man scatters seed on the ground. 27Night and day, whether he sleeps or gets up, the seed sprouts and grows, though he does not know how. 28All by itself the soil produces grain—first the stalk, then the head, then the full kernel in the head. 29As soon as the grain is ripe, he puts the sickle to it, because the harvest has come."

30Again he said, "What shall we say the kingdom of God is like, or what parable shall we use to describe it? 31It is like a mustard seed, which is the smallest seed you plant in the ground. 32Yet when planted, it grows and becomes the largest of all garden plants, with such big branches that the birds of the air can perch in its shade."

33With many similar parables Jesus spoke the word to them, as much as they could understand. 34He did not say anything to them without using a parable. But when he was alone with his own disciples, he explained everything.

A THOUGHT: *Jesus adapted his methods to his audience's ability and desire to understand. He didn't speak in parables to confuse people, but to challenge sincere seekers to discover the true meaning of his words. These parables are about the kingdom of God. They point to the fact that the kingdom cannot be hidden; though it is small now, it will continue to grow and become a full harvest (or a very large plant). When you feel alone in your stand for Christ, realize that God is building a worldwide kingdom. He has faithful followers in every part of the world, and your faith, no matter how small, can join with that of others to accomplish great things.*

Love Is the Greatest Gift/ 1 Corinthians 13:8–13

Love never fails. But where there are prophecies, they will cease; where there are tongues, they will be stilled; where there is knowledge, it will pass away. 9For we know in part and we prophesy in part, 10but when perfection comes, the imperfect disappears. 11When I was a child, I talked like a child, I thought like a child, I reasoned like a child. When I became a man, I put childish ways behind me. 12Now we see but a poor reflection as in a mirror; then we shall see face to face. Now I know in part; then I shall know fully, even as I am fully known.

13And now these three remain: faith, hope and love. But the greatest of these is love.

A THOUGHT: *In the morally corrupt society of Corinth, love had become a mixed-up term with little meaning. Today people are still confused about love. Love is the greatest of all human qualities. It involves unselfish service to others; therefore, it should permeate all that we do or think. We should constantly be called back to a recommitment to love as Christ loved.*

Proverbs for Today/ 12:5–7

The plans of the righteous are just, but the advice of the wicked is deceitful. □ The words of the wicked lie in wait for blood, but the speech of the upright rescues them. □ Wicked men are overthrown and are no more, but the house of the righteous stands firm.

MARCH 31

Jesus Calms the Storm/ Mark 4:35–41

That day when evening came, he said to his disciples, "Let us go over to the other side." 36Leaving the crowd behind, they took him along, just as he was, in the boat. There were also other boats with him. 37A furious squall came up, and the waves broke over the boat, so that it was nearly swamped. 38Jesus was in the stern, sleeping on a cushion. The disciples woke him and said to him, "Teacher, don't you care if we drown?"

39He got up, rebuked the wind and said to the waves, "Quiet! Be still!" Then the wind died down and it was completely calm.

40He said to his disciples, "Why are you so afraid? Do you still have no faith?"

41They were terrified and asked each other, "Who is this? Even the wind and the waves obey him!"

A THOUGHT: *The disciples lived with Jesus, but they did not understand who he really was. They were expecting a political messiah who would deliver Israel from the power of Roman domination. They failed to see that Jesus was the divine Son of God. We should respond to Jesus' demonstrations of power with awe and worship. We should also be careful not to allow our cultural expectations to blind us to the truth of God's Word before us.*

Prophecy and Tongues/ 1 Corinthians 14:1–5

Follow the way of love and eagerly desire spiritual gifts, especially the gift of prophecy. 2For anyone who speaks in a tongue does not speak to men but to God. Indeed, no one understands him; he utters mysteries with his spirit. 3But everyone who prophesies speaks to men for their strengthening, encouragement and comfort. 4He who speaks in a tongue edifies himself, but he who prophesies edifies the church. 5I would like every one of you to speak in tongues, but I would rather have you prophesy. He who prophesies is greater than one who speaks in tongues, unless he interprets, so that the church may be edified.

A THOUGHT: *Paul makes several points about speaking in tongues: (1) it is a spiritual gift from God; (2) it is a desirable gift even though it isn't a requirement of faith; (3) it is less important than prophecy and teaching. Although Paul himself spoke in tongues, he stresses prophecy (preaching) because it benefits the whole church, while speaking in tongues primarily benefits the speaker. Public worship must be understandable and beneficial to the whole church.*

Proverbs for Today/ 12:8–9

A man is praised according to his wisdom, but men with warped minds are despised. □ Better to be a nobody and yet have a servant than pretend to be somebody and have no food.

APRIL 1

Jesus Casts Out Demons/ Mark 5:1–20

They [Jesus and his disciples] went across the lake to the region of the Gerasenes. 2When Jesus got out of the boat, a man with an evil spirit came from the tombs to meet him. 3This man lived in the tombs, and no one could bind him any more, not even with a chain. 4For he had often been chained hand and foot, but he tore the chains apart and broke the irons on his feet. No one was strong enough to subdue him. 5Night and day among the tombs and in the hills he would cry out and cut himself with stones.

6When he saw Jesus from a distance, he ran and fell on his knees in front of him. 7He shouted at the top of his voice, "What do you want with me, Jesus, Son of the Most High God? Swear to God that you won't torture me!" 8For Jesus had said to him, "Come out of this man, you evil spirit!"

9Then Jesus asked him, "What is your name?"

"My name is Legion," he replied, "for we are many." 10And he begged Jesus again and again not to send them out of the area.

11A large herd of pigs was feeding on the nearby hillside. 12The demons begged Jesus, "Send us among the pigs; allow us to go into them." 13He gave them permission, and the evil spirits came out and went into the pigs. The herd, about two thousand in number, rushed down the steep bank into the lake and were drowned.

14Those tending the pigs ran off and reported this in the town and countryside, and the people went out to see what had happened. 15When they came to Jesus, they saw the man who had been possessed by the legion of demons, sitting there, dressed and in his right mind; and they were afraid. 16Those who had seen it told the people what had happened to the demon-possessed man—and told about the pigs as well. 17Then the people began to plead with Jesus to leave their region.

18As Jesus was getting into the boat, the man who had been demon-possessed begged to go with him. 19Jesus did not let him, but said, "Go home to your family and tell them how much the Lord has done for you, and how he has had mercy on you." 20So the man went away and began to tell in the Decapolis how much Jesus had done for him. And all the people were amazed.

A THOUGHT: *Jesus brings about the restoration of this demon-possessed man by commanding the legion of demons to come out. Jesus is demonstrating by this action the presence of the kingdom of God in his own person. His work on the cross defeated Satan and his evil angels; although the ultimate consummation of this defeat is yet to come, Satan's defeat is sure. While it is important to recognize situations or activities in which demons might be involved, so that we can stay away from them, we must avoid any curiosity about or involvement with demonic forces or the occult. If we resist the devil and his influences, he will flee from us, for the Lord Jesus Christ has overcome the Evil One.*

The Need for Understanding/ 1 Corinthians 14:6–12

Now, brothers, if I come to you and speak in tongues, what good will I be to you, unless I bring you some revelation or knowledge or prophecy or word of instruction? 7Even in the case of lifeless things that make sounds, such as the flute or harp, how will anyone know what tune is being played unless there is a distinction in the notes? 8Again, if the trumpet does not sound a clear call, who will get ready for battle? 9So it is with you. Unless you speak intelligible words with your tongue, how will anyone know what you are saying? You will just be speaking into the air. 10Undoubtedly there are all sorts of languages in the world, yet none of them is without meaning. 11If then I do not grasp the meaning of what someone is saying, I am a foreigner to the speaker, and he is a foreigner to me. 12So it is with you. Since you are eager to have spiritual gifts, try to excel in gifts that build up the church.

A THOUGHT: *Since spiritual gifts are to be used to build up the body of Christ, all that we do should lead to the benefit of others. Gifts of speaking should always seek to edify the other person through helping them to understand. If a person cannot understand what we are attempting to communicate, they cannot be served. Let us seek to bring spiritual understanding in the use of speaking gifts in the church and not serve ourselves.*

Proverbs for Today/ 12:10

A righteous man cares for the needs of his animal, but the kindest acts of the wicked are cruel.

APRIL 2

Miracles of Healing/ Mark 5:21–43

When Jesus had again crossed over by boat to the other side of the lake, a large crowd gathered around him while he was by the lake. 22Then one of the synagogue rulers, named Jairus, came there. Seeing Jesus, he fell at his feet 23and pleaded earnestly with him, "My little daughter is dying. Please come and put your hands on her so that she will be healed and live." 24So Jesus went with him.

A large crowd followed and pressed around him. 25And a woman was there who had been subject to bleeding for twelve years. 26She had suffered a great deal under the care of many doctors and had spent all she had, yet instead of getting better she grew worse. 27When she heard about Jesus, she came up behind him in the crowd and touched his cloak, 28because she thought, "If I just touch his clothes, I will be healed." 29Immediately her bleeding stopped and she felt in her body that she was freed from her suffering.

30At once Jesus realized that power had gone out from him. He turned around in the crowd and asked, "Who touched my clothes?"

31"You see the people crowding against you," his disciples answered, "and yet you can ask, 'Who touched me?' "

32But Jesus kept looking around to see who had done it. 33Then the woman, knowing what had happened to her, came and fell at his feet and, trembling with fear, told him the whole truth. 34He said to her, "Daughter, your faith has healed you. Go in peace and be freed from your suffering."

35While Jesus was still speaking, some men came from the house of Jairus, the synagogue ruler. "Your daughter is dead," they said. "Why bother the teacher any more?"

36Ignoring what they said, Jesus told the synagogue ruler, "Don't be afraid; just believe."

37He did not let anyone follow him except Peter, James and John the brother of James. 38When they came to the home of the synagogue ruler, Jesus saw a commotion, with people crying and wailing loudly. 39He went in and said to them, "Why all this commotion and wailing? The child is not dead but asleep." 40But they laughed at him.

After he put them all out, he took the child's father and mother and the disciples who were with him, and went in where the child was. 41He took her by the hand and said to her, *"Talitha koum!"* (which means, "Little girl, I say to you, get up!"). 42Immediately the girl stood up and walked around (she was twelve years old). At this they were completely astonished. 43He gave strict orders not to let anyone know about this, and told them to give her something to eat.

A THOUGHT: *Jesus not only demonstrated great power; he also showed tremendous compassion. Jesus' power over nature, demons, and death was motivated by compassion—for a demonic man who lived among tombs, for a diseased woman, and for the family of a dead girl. The rabbis of the day considered such people unclean. Polite society avoided them. But Jesus reached out and helped anyone in need.*

Pray for the Ability to Interpret/
1 Corinthians 14:13–17

For this reason anyone who speaks in a tongue should pray that he may interpret what he says. 14For if I pray in a tongue, my spirit prays, but my mind is unfruitful. 15So what shall I do? I will pray with my spirit, but I will also pray with my mind; I will sing with my spirit, but I will also sing with my mind. 16If you are praising God with your spirit, how can one who finds himself among those who do not understand say "Amen" to your thanksgiving, since he does not know what you are saying? 17You may be giving thanks well enough, but the other man is not edified.

A THOUGHT: *In order to promote unity and understanding in the church, if someone speaks in tongues there should always be someone to interpret the utterance. If there is no one to interpret the utterance, one should keep silent. For the purpose of employing a spiritual gift in the assembly is the upbuilding of all believers. In order for others to participate in what is being shared, people must understand. Therefore, when someone employs one of the speaking gifts, let there be interpreters to give understanding to the rest of the body.*

Proverbs for Today/ 12:11

He who works his land will have abundant food, but he who chases fantasies lacks judgment.

APRIL 3

A Prophet Without Honor/ Mark 6:1–6

Jesus left there and went to his hometown, accompanied by his disciples. 2When the Sabbath came, he began to teach in the synagogue, and many who heard him were amazed.

"Where did this man get these things?" they asked. "What's this wisdom that has been given him, that he even does miracles! 3Isn't this the carpenter? Isn't this Mary's son and the brother of James, Joseph, Judas and Simon? Aren't his sisters here with us?" And they took offense at him.

4Jesus said to them, "Only in his hometown, among his relatives and in his own house is a prophet without honor." 5He could not do any miracles there, except lay his hands on a few sick people and heal them. 6And he was amazed at their lack of faith.

Then Jesus went around teaching from village to village.

A THOUGHT: *Jesus was teaching effectively and wisely, but the people of his hometown saw him as only a carpenter. "Isn't this the carpenter? Isn't this Mary's son and the brother of James, Joses, Judas and Simon?" they asked. They were offended that others could be impressed by him and follow him. They rejected his authority because he was one of their peers. They thought they knew him, but their preconceived notions about who he was made it impossible for them to accept his message. Don't let prejudice blind you to truth. As you learn more about Jesus, try to see him for who he really is.*

Tongues a Sign to Unbelievers/ 1 Corinthians 14:18–25

I thank God that I speak in tongues more than all of you. 19But in the church I would rather speak five intelligible words to instruct others than ten thousand words in a tongue.

20Brothers, stop thinking like children. In regard to evil be infants, but in your thinking be adults. 21In the Law it is written:

"Through men of strange tongues
    and through the lips of foreigners

I will speak to this people,
> but even then they will not listen to me,"

says the Lord.

22Tongues, then, are a sign, not for believers but for unbelievers; prophecy, however, is for believers, not for unbelievers. 23So if the whole church comes together and everyone speaks in tongues, and some who do not understand or some unbelievers come in, will they not say that you are out of your mind? 24But if an unbeliever or someone who does not understand comes in while everybody is prophesying, he will be convinced by all that he is a sinner and will be judged by all, 25and the secrets of his heart will be laid bare. So he will fall down and worship God, exclaiming, "God is really among you!"

A THOUGHT: *The way the Corinthians were speaking in tongues wasn't helpful because believers did not understand what was being said and unbelievers thought the people speaking in tongues were crazy. Speaking in tongues was supposed to be a sign to unbelievers. After speaking in tongues, believers were supposed to explain what was said and give the credit to God. The unsaved people would then be convinced of a spiritual reality and motivated to search the Christian faith further. While this is one way to reach unbelievers, Paul says that clear preaching is usually better.*

Proverbs for Today/ 12:12–14

The wicked desire the plunder of evil men, but the root of the righteous flourishes. □ An evil man is trapped by his sinful talk, but a righteous man escapes trouble. □ From the fruit of his lips a man is filled with good things as surely as the work of his hands rewards him.

APRIL 4

Jesus Commissions the Twelve Disciples/ Mark 6:7–13

Calling the Twelve to him, he [Jesus] sent them out two by two and gave them authority over evil spirits.

8These were his instructions: "Take nothing for the journey except a staff—no bread, no bag, no money in your belts. 9Wear sandals but not an extra tunic. 10Whenever you enter a house, stay there until you leave that town. [11]And if any place will not welcome you or listen to you, shake the dust off your feet when you leave, as a testimony against them."

[12]They went out and preached that people should repent. [13]They drove out many demons and anointed many sick people with oil and healed them.

A THOUGHT: *The disciples were sent out in pairs. Individually they could have reached more areas of the country, but this was not Christ's plan. One advantage in going out by twos was that they could strengthen and encourage each other, especially when they faced rejection. Our strength comes from God, but he meets many of our needs through our teamwork with others. As you serve him, don't try to go it alone.*

Gifts to Build the Church/ 1 Corinthians 14:26–32

What then shall we say, brothers? When you come together, everyone has a hymn, or a word of instruction, a revelation, a tongue or an interpretation. All of these must be done for the strengthening of the church. [27]If anyone speaks in a tongue, two—or at the most three—should speak, one at a time, and someone must interpret. [28]If there is no interpreter, the speaker should keep quiet in the church and speak to himself and God.

[29]Two or three prophets should speak, and the others should weigh carefully what is said. [30]And if a revelation comes to someone who is sitting down, the first speaker should stop. [31]For you can all prophesy in turn so that everyone may be instructed and encouraged. [32]The spirits of prophets are subject to the control of prophets.

A THOUGHT: *Everything done in worship services must be beneficial to the worshipers. This principle touches every aspect—singing, preaching, and the exercise of spiritual gifts. Those contributing to the service (singers, speakers, readers) must have love as their chief motivation, giving useful words or help that will strengthen the faith of other believers.*

Proverbs for Today/ 12:15–17

The way of a fool seems right to him, but a wise man listens to advice. □ A fool shows his annoyance at once, but a prudent man overlooks an insult. □ A truthful witness gives honest testimony, but a false witness tells lies.

John the Baptist's Death/ Mark 6:14–29

King Herod heard about this, for Jesus' name had become well known. Some were saying, "John the Baptist has been raised from the dead, and that is why miraculous powers are at work in him."

15Others said, "He is Elijah."

And still others claimed, "He is a prophet, like one of the prophets of long ago."

16But when Herod heard this, he said, "John, the man I beheaded, has been raised from the dead!"

17For Herod himself had given orders to have John arrested, and he had him bound and put in prison. He did this because of Herodias, his brother Philip's wife, whom he had married. 18For John had been saying to Herod, "It is not lawful for you to have your brother's wife." 19So Herodias nursed a grudge against John and wanted to kill him. But she was not able to, 20because Herod feared John and protected him, knowing him to be a righteous and holy man. When Herod heard John, he was greatly puzzled; yet he liked to listen to him.

21Finally the opportune time came. On his birthday Herod gave a banquet for his high officials and military commanders and the leading men of Galilee. 22When the daughter of Herodias came in and danced, she pleased Herod and his dinner guests.

The king said to the girl, "Ask me for anything you want, and I'll give it to you." 23And he promised her with an oath, "Whatever you ask I will give you, up to half my kingdom."

24She went out and said to her mother, "What shall I ask for?"

"The head of John the Baptist," she answered.

25At once the girl hurried in to the king with the request: "I want you to give me right now the head of John the Baptist on a platter."

26The king was greatly distressed, but because of his oaths and his dinner guests, he did not want to refuse her. 27So he immediately sent an executioner with orders to bring John's head. The man went, beheaded John in the prison, 28and brought back his head on a platter. He presented it to the girl, and she gave it to her mother. 29On hearing of this, John's disciples came and took his body and laid it in a tomb.

A THOUGHT: *Herod, along with many others, wondered who Jesus really was. Unable to accept Jesus' claim to be God's Son, many people made up their own explanations for his power and authority. Herod thought Jesus was John the Baptist come back to life; some who were familiar with the Old Testament thought he was Elijah. Still others believed he was a teaching prophet in the tradition of Moses, Isaiah, or Jeremiah. Today people still have to make up their minds about Jesus. Some think that if they can name what he is—prophet, teacher, good man—they can weaken the power of his claim on their lives. But what they think does not change who Jesus is.*

Order in Christian Worship/ 1 Corinthians 14:33–40

For God is not a God of disorder but of peace.

As in all the congregations of the saints, 34women should remain silent in the churches. They are not allowed to speak, but must be in submission, as the Law says. 35If they want to inquire about something, they should ask their own husbands at home; for it is disgraceful for a woman to speak in the church.

36Did the word of God originate with you? Or are you the only people it has reached? 37If anybody thinks he is a prophet or spiritually gifted, let him acknowledge that what I am writing to you is the Lord's command. 38If he ignores this, he himself will be ignored.

39Therefore, my brothers, be eager to prophesy, and do not forbid speaking in tongues. 40But everything should be done in a fitting and orderly way.

A THOUGHT: *Does this passage mean that women should not speak in church services today? It is clear from an earlier passage in this epistle that women can pray and prophesy in the church, apparently in public meetings. It is also clear in chapters 12—14 that women have spiritual gifts, and they are encouraged to exercise them in the body of Christ. Women have much to contribute and can participate in worship services.*

In the Corinthian culture, women were not allowed to confront men in public. Apparently some of the women who had become Christians thought their Christian freedom gave them the right to speak up in public worship and question the men. This was causing division in the church. In addition, women of that day did not receive formal religious education as did the men. Women may have been raising questions in the worship service which could have more easily been answered at home without disrupting the church service. To promote unity, Paul was asking the women not to flaunt their Christian freedom during the worship service. The purpose of Paul's words here was to promote unity, not to teach about the women's role in the church.

Proverbs for Today/ 12:18

Reckless words pierce like a sword, but the tongue of the wise brings healing.

APRIL 6

Jesus Feeds Five Thousand/ Mark 6:30–44

The apostles gathered around Jesus and reported to him all they had done and taught. 31Then, because so many people were coming and going that they did not even have a chance to eat, he said to them, "Come with me by yourselves to a quiet place and get some rest."

32So they went away by themselves in a boat to a solitary place. 33But many who saw them leaving recognized them and ran on foot from all the towns and got there ahead of them. 34When Jesus landed and saw a large crowd, he had compassion on them, because they were like sheep without a shepherd. So he began teaching them many things.

35By this time it was late in the day, so his disciples came to him. "This is a remote place," they said, "and it's already very late. 36Send the people away so they can go to the surrounding countryside and villages and buy themselves something to eat."

37But he answered, "You give them something to eat."

They said to him, "That would take eight months of a man's wages! Are we to go and spend that much on bread and give it to them to eat?"

38"How many loaves do you have?" he asked. "Go and see."

When they found out, they said, "Five—and two fish."

39Then Jesus directed them to have all the people sit down in groups on the green grass. 40So they sat down in groups of hundreds and fifties. 41Taking the five loaves and the two fish and looking up to heaven, he gave thanks and broke the loaves. Then he gave them to his disciples to set before the people. He also divided the two fish among them all. 42They all ate and were satisfied, 43and the disciples picked up twelve basketfuls of broken pieces of bread and fish. 44The number of the men who had eaten was five thousand.

A THOUGHT: *Jesus asked the disciples to provide food for over 5,000 people. They responded, "That would take eight months of a man's wages!" How do you react when you are given an impossible task? A situation that seems impossible with human means is simply an opportunity for God. The disciples did everything they could—they gathered the available food and organized the people into groups. Then, in answer to prayer, God did the impossible. When facing a seemingly impossible task, do what you can and ask God to do the rest. He may see fit to make the impossible happen.*

Christ's Resurrection Appearances/ 1 Corinthians 15:1–11

Now, brothers, I want to remind you of the gospel I preached to you, which you received and on which you have taken your stand. 2By this gospel you are saved, if you hold firmly to the word I preached to you. Otherwise, you have believed in vain.

3For what I received I passed on to you as of first importance: that Christ died for our sins according to the Scriptures, 4that he was buried, that he was raised on the third day according to the Scriptures, 5and that he appeared to Peter, and then to the Twelve. 6After that, he appeared to more than five hundred of the brothers at the same time, most of whom are still living, though some have fallen asleep. 7Then he appeared to James, then to all the apostles, 8and last of all he appeared to me also, as to one abnormally born.

9For I am the least of the apostles and do not even deserve to be called an apostle, because I persecuted the church of God. 10But by the grace of God I am what I am, and his grace to me was not without effect. No, I worked harder than all of them—yet not I, but the grace of God that was with me. 11Whether, then, it was I or they, this is what we preach, and this is what you believed.

A THOUGHT: *There will always be people who say Jesus didn't rise from the dead. Paul assures us that many people saw Jesus after his* resurrection, *including more than 500 Christian believers. The resurrection is a historical fact. Don't be discouraged by doubters who deny the resurrection. Be filled with hope by the knowledge that one day everyone will stand before the living Christ. We who are believers in Christ can take comfort in his promise of eternal life—an eternal life with a resurrected body like Christ's. For those who do not know Christ, judgment awaits them.*

Proverbs for Today/ 12:19–20

Truthful lips endure forever, but a lying tongue lasts only a moment. □ There is deceit in the hearts of those who plot evil, but joy for those who promote peace.

APRIL 7

Jesus Walks on the Water/ Mark 6:45–56

Immediately Jesus made his disciples get into the boat and go on ahead of him to Bethsaida, while he dismissed the crowd. 46After leaving them, he went up on a mountainside to pray.

47When evening came, the boat was in the middle of the lake, and he was alone on land. 48He saw the disciples straining at the oars, because the wind was against them. About the fourth watch of the night he went out to them, walking on the lake. He was about to pass by them, 49but when they saw him walking on the lake, they thought he was a ghost. They cried out, 50because they all saw him and were terrified.

Immediately he spoke to them and said, "Take courage! It is I. Don't be afraid." 51Then he climbed into the boat with them, and the wind died down. They were completely amazed, 52for they had not understood about the loaves; their hearts were hardened.

53When they had crossed over, they landed at Gennesaret and anchored there. 54As soon as they got out of the boat, people recognized Jesus. 55They ran throughout that whole region and carried the sick on mats to wherever they heard he was. 56And wherever he went—into villages, towns or countryside—they placed the sick in the marketplaces. They begged him to let them touch even the edge of his cloak, and all who touched him were healed.

A THOUGHT: *The disciples were utterly amazed at Jesus walking on the water and his ability to calm the storm. Their conception of Messiah did not include such demonstrations of power. They did not transfer the truth they had already experienced about Jesus to new situations because they were blinded by their own expectations of what Messiah was supposed to be like. We worship Jesus whose power, compassion, and wisdom far exceed our expectations or wildest dreams. Let us worship the Lord Jesus Christ for who he is and remember that this same Jesus is present with us.*

The Resurrection—the Foundation of Faith/ 1 Corinthians 15:12–20

But if it is preached that Christ has been raised from the dead, how can some of you say that there is no resurrection of the dead? 13If there is no resurrection of the dead, then not even Christ has been raised. 14And if Christ has not been raised, our preaching is useless and so is your faith. 15More than that, we are then found to be false witnesses about God, for we have testified about God that he raised Christ from the dead. But he did not raise him if in fact the dead are not raised. 16For if the dead are not raised, then Christ has not been raised either. 17And if Christ has not been raised, your faith is futile; you are still in your sins. 18Then those also who have fallen asleep in Christ are lost. 19If only for this life we have hope in Christ, we are to be pitied more than all men.

20But Christ has indeed been raised from the dead, the firstfruits of those who have fallen asleep.

A THOUGHT: *Most Greeks did not believe that people's bodies would be resurrected after death. They saw the afterlife as something that happened only to the soul. According to Platonic Greek philosophers, the soul was the real person, imprisoned in a physical body, and at death the soul was released. There was no immortality for the body, but the soul entered an eternal state. In Scripture, by contrast, the body and soul will be united after resurrection. The church at Corinth was in the heart of Greek culture. Thus many believers had a difficult time believing in a bodily resurrection. Paul wrote this part of his letter to solve this confusion about the resurrection.*

The resurrection of Christ is the center of the Christian faith. Because Christ rose from the dead, we know that what he said is true—he is God. Because he rose, his death for our sins was validated and we can be forgiven. Because he rose, he lives and makes intercession for us. Because he rose and defeated death, we know we will also rise.

Proverbs for Today/ 12:21–23

No harm befalls the righteous, but the wicked have their fill of trouble. □ The LORD detests lying lips, but he delights in men who are truthful. □ A prudent man keeps his knowledge to himself, but the heart of fools blurts out folly.

APRIL 8

Inner Purity/ Mark 7:1–23

The Pharisees and some of the teachers of the law who had come from Jerusalem gathered around Jesus and 2saw some of his disciples eating food with hands that were "unclean," that is, unwashed. 3(The Pharisees and all the Jews do not eat unless they give their hands a ceremonial washing, holding to the tradition of the elders. 4When they come from the marketplace they do not eat unless they wash. And they observe many other traditions, such as the washing of cups, pitchers and kettles.)

5So the Pharisees and teachers of the law asked Jesus, "Why don't your disciples live according to the tradition of the elders instead of eating their food with 'unclean' hands?"

6He replied, "Isaiah was right when he prophesied about you hypocrites; as it is written:

" 'These people honor me with their lips,
    but their hearts are far from me.
7They worship me in vain;
    their teachings are but rules taught by men.'

8You have let go of the commands of God and are holding on to the traditions of men."

9And he said to them: "You have a fine way of setting aside the commands of God in order to observe your own traditions! 10For Moses said, 'Honor your father and your mother,' and, 'Anyone who curses his father or mother must be put to death.' 11But you say that if a man says to his father or mother: 'Whatever help you might otherwise have received from me is Corban' (that is, a gift devoted to God), 12then you no longer let him do anything for his father or mother. 13Thus you nullify the word of God by your tradition that you have handed down. And you do many things like that."

14Again Jesus called the crowd to him and said, "Listen to me, everyone, and understand this. 15Nothing outside a man can make him 'unclean' by going into him. Rather, it is what comes out of a man that makes him 'unclean.'* "

17After he had left the crowd and entered the house, his disciples asked him about this parable. 18"Are you so dull?" he asked. "Don't you see that nothing that enters a man from the outside can make him 'unclean'? 19For it doesn't go into his heart but into his stomach, and then out of his body." (In saying this, Jesus declared all foods "clean.")

20He went on: "What comes out of a man is what makes him 'unclean.' 21For from within, out of men's hearts, come evil thoughts, sexual immorality, theft, murder, adultery, 22greed, malice, deceit, lewdness, envy, slander, arrogance and folly. 23All these evils come from inside and make a man 'unclean.' "

A THOUGHT: *Hypocrisy is pretending to be something you are not. Jesus called the Pharisees hypocrites because they did not worship God out of love for him, but because it made them look holy, and it increased their status in the community. We become hypocrites when we (1) pay more attention to reputation than to character, (2) carefully follow certain religious practices while allowing our hearts to remain distant from God, and (3) emphasize our virtues (overlooking our own sins), but (4) constantly point out sins in others.*

Death Will Be Defeated/ 1 Corinthians 15:21–28

For since death came through a man, the resurrection of the dead comes also through a man. 22For as in Adam all die, so in Christ all will be made alive. 23But each in his own turn: Christ, the firstfruits; then, when he comes, those who belong to him. 24Then the end will come, when he hands over the kingdom to God the Father after he has destroyed all dominion, authority and power. 25For he must reign until he has put all his enemies under his feet. 26The last enemy to be destroyed is death. 27For he "has put everything under his feet." Now when it says that "everything" has been put under him, it is clear that this does not include God himself, who put everything under Christ.

*15 Some early manuscripts *'unclean.'* 16*If anyone has ears to hear, let him hear.*

28When he has done this, then the Son himself will be made subject to him who put everything under him, so that God may be all in all.

A THOUGHT: *The redemption which Christ accomplished on the cross has reversed the consequences of the Fall. Adam brought death; Christ brings eternal life through the resurrection of the body. Adam brought sin; Christ brings forgiveness and righteousness. The final enemy to be defeated in this great reversal is death. The fullness of salvation will be experienced when death is ultimately defeated, to appear no more. In bringing about this great defeat, Christ will demonstrate that his authority is supreme in heaven and earth. Let us worship Christ for who he is—the Great Redeemer and King.*

Proverbs for Today/ 12:24

Diligent hands will rule, but laziness ends in slave labor.

APRIL 9

Jesus Demonstrates His Redemptive Power/ Mark 7:24–37

Jesus left that place and went to the vicinity of Tyre. He entered a house and did not want anyone to know it; yet he could not keep his presence secret. 25In fact, as soon as she heard about him, a woman whose little daughter was possessed by an evil spirit came and fell at his feet. 26The woman was a Greek, born in Syrian Phoenicia. She begged Jesus to drive the demon out of her daughter.

27"First let the children eat all they want," he told her, "for it is not right to take the children's bread and toss it to their dogs."

28"Yes, Lord," she replied, "but even the dogs under the table eat the children's crumbs."

29Then he told her, "For such a reply, you may go; the demon has left your daughter."

30She went home and found her child lying on the bed, and the demon gone.

31Then Jesus left the vicinity of Tyre and went through Sidon, down to the Sea of Galilee and into the region of the Decapolis. 32There some people brought to him a man who was deaf and could hardly talk, and they begged him to place his hand on the man.

33After he took him aside, away from the crowd, Jesus put his fingers into the man's ears. Then he spit and touched the man's tongue. 34He looked up to heaven and with a deep sigh said to him, *"Ephphatha!"* (which means, "Be opened!"). 35At this, the man's ears were opened, his tongue was loosened and he began to speak plainly.

36Jesus commanded them not to tell anyone. But the more he did so, the more they kept talking about it. 37People were overwhelmed with amazement. "He has done everything well," they said. "He even makes the deaf hear and the mute speak."

A THOUGHT: *In this passage, Jesus demonstrates his compassion. In the setting of the Jewish culture of that day, this Syrophoenician woman had two strikes against her: (1) she was a woman (women were considered to be property to be bought and sold like cattle); and (2) she was a Gentile (Gentiles were generally considered to be beyond the grace of God). Here Jesus shows compassion to this woman, granting her request, and even commends her faith.*

True Meaning in Life/ 1 Corinthians 15:29–34

Now if there is no resurrection, what will those do who are baptized for the dead? If the dead are not raised at all, why are people baptized for them? 30And as for us, why do we endanger ourselves every hour? 31I die every day—I mean that, brothers—just as surely as I glory over you in Christ Jesus our Lord. 32If I fought wild beasts in Ephesus for merely human reasons, what have I gained? If the dead are not raised,

> "Let us eat and drink,
>   for tomorrow we die."

33Do not be misled: "Bad company corrupts good character." 34Come back to your senses as you ought, and stop sinning; for there are some who are ignorant of God—I say this to your shame.

A THOUGHT: *If death ended it all, enjoying the moment would be all that mattered. But Christians know that there is life beyond the grave and that our life on earth is only a preparation for our life that will never end. What you do today matters for eternity. In light of eternity, sin is a foolish gamble.*

Proverbs for Today/ 12:25

An anxious heart weighs a man down, but a kind word cheers him up.

APRIL 10

Jesus Feeds Four Thousand/ Mark 8:1–10

During those days another large crowd gathered. Since they had nothing to eat, Jesus called his disciples to him and said, ²"I have compassion for these people; they have already been with me three days and have nothing to eat. ³If I send them home hungry, they will collapse on the way, because some of them have come a long distance."

⁴His disciples answered, "But where in this remote place can anyone get enough bread to feed them?"

⁵"How many loaves do you have?" Jesus asked.

"Seven," they replied.

⁶He told the crowd to sit down on the ground. When he had taken the seven loaves and given thanks, he broke them and gave them to his disciples to set before the people, and they did so. ⁷They had a few small fish as well; he gave thanks for them also and told the disciples to distribute them. ⁸The people ate and were satisfied. Afterward the disciples picked up seven basketfuls of broken pieces that were left over. ⁹About four thousand men were present. And having sent them away, ¹⁰he got into the boat with his disciples and went to the region of Dalmanutha.

A THOUGHT: *Do you ever feel God is so busy with important concerns that he can't possibly be aware of your needs? Just as Jesus was concerned about these who needed food, he is concerned about our daily needs. At another time Jesus said, "So do not worry, saying, 'What shall we eat?' or 'What shall we drink?' or 'What shall we wear?' For the pagans run after these things, and your heavenly Father knows that you need them" (Matthew 6:31–32). Do you have concerns that you think would not interest God? There is no concern too large for him to handle and no need too small to escape his interest.*

The Resurrection Body/ 1 Corinthians 15:35–44

But someone may ask, "How are the dead raised? With what kind of body will they come?" 36How foolish! What you sow does not come to life unless it dies. 37When you sow, you do not plant the body that will be, but just a seed, perhaps of wheat or of something else. 38But God gives it a body as he has determined, and to each kind of seed he gives its own body. 39All flesh is not the same: Men have one kind of flesh, animals have another, birds another and fish another. 40There are also heavenly bodies and there are earthly bodies; but the splendor of the heavenly bodies is one kind, and the splendor of the earthly bodies is another. 41The sun has one kind of splendor, the moon another and the stars another; and star differs from star in splendor.

42So will it be with the resurrection of the dead. The body that is sown is perishable, it is raised imperishable; 43it is sown in dishonor, it is raised in glory; it is sown in weakness, it is raised in power; 44it is sown a natural body, it is raised a spiritual body.

If there is a natural body, there is also a spiritual body.

A THOUGHT: *Paul launches into a discussion here about what our resurrected bodies will be like. If you could select your own body, what kind would you choose—strong, athletic, beautiful? Paul explains that we will be recognized in our resurrected bodies, yet they will be better than we can imagine, for they will be made to live forever. We will still have our own personalities and individualities, but these will be perfected through Christ's work. Scripture does not say what our resurrected bodies will be able to do, but we know they will be perfect, without sickness or disease.*

Proverbs for Today/ 12:26

A righteous man is cautious in friendship, but the way of the wicked leads them astray.

Beware of the Teaching of Herod and the Pharisees/ Mark 8:11–21

The Pharisees came and began to question Jesus. To test him, they asked him for a sign from heaven. 12He sighed deeply and said, "Why does this generation ask for a miraculous sign? I tell you the truth, no sign will be given to it." 13Then he left them, got back into the boat and crossed to the other side.

14The disciples had forgotten to bring bread, except for one loaf they had with them in the boat. 15"Be careful," Jesus warned them. "Watch out for the yeast of the Pharisees and that of Herod."

16They discussed this with one another and said, "It is because we have no bread."

17Aware of their discussion, Jesus asked them: "Why are you talking about having no bread? Do you still not see or understand? Are your hearts hardened? 18Do you have eyes but fail to see, and ears but fail to hear? And don't you remember? 19When I broke the five loaves for the five thousand, how many basketfuls of pieces did you pick up?"

"Twelve," they replied.

20"And when I broke the seven loaves for the four thousand, how many basketfuls of pieces did you pick up?"

They answered, "Seven."

21He said to them, "Do you still not understand?"

A THOUGHT: *How could the disciples experience so many of Jesus' miracles and yet be so slow to comprehend his true identity? They had already seen Jesus feed over 5,000 people with five loaves and two fish, yet now they doubted whether he could feed another large group.*

Sometimes we are also slow to catch on. Although Christ has brought us through trials and temptations in the past, we are slow to believe he will do it in the future. Is your heart too closed to take in all that God can do for you? Don't be like the disciples. Remember what Christ has done, and have faith that he will do it again.

Adam and Christ/ 1 Corinthians 15:45–49

So it is written: "The first man Adam became a living being"; the last Adam, a life-giving spirit. 46The spiritual did not come first, but the natural, and after that the spiritual. 47The first man was of the dust of the earth, the second man from heaven. 48As was the earthly man, so are those who are of the earth; and as is the man from heaven, so also are those who are of heaven. 49And just as we have borne the likeness of the earthly man, so shall we bear the likeness of the man from heaven.

A THOUGHT: *When Christ rose from the dead, he became "life-giving Spirit." This means he entered into a new form of existence. Christ's new glorified human body now suits his new glorified life—just as Adam's human body was suitable to his natural life. When we are resurrected, God will give us a glorified body suited to our new eternal life.*

Proverbs for Today/ 12:27–28

The lazy man does not roast his game, but the diligent man prizes his possessions. □ In the way of righteousness there is life; along that path is immortality.

APRIL 12

Jesus Heals a Blind Man/ Mark 8:22–26

They [Jesus and his disciples] came to Bethsaida, and some people brought a blind man and begged Jesus to touch him. 23He took the blind man by the hand and led him outside the village. When he had spit on the man's eyes and put his hands on him, Jesus asked, "Do you see anything?"

24He looked up and said, "I see people; they look like trees walking around."

25Once more Jesus put his hands on the man's eyes. Then his eyes were opened, his sight was restored, and he saw everything clearly. 26Jesus sent him home, saying, "Don't go into the village."

A THOUGHT: *Why did Jesus touch the man a second time before he could see? This miracle was not too difficult for Jesus, but he chose to do it in stages, possibly to show the disciples that some healing would be gradual rather than instantaneous or to demonstrate that spiritual truth is not always perceived clearly at first. Before Jesus left, however, the man was healed completely.*

Transformation in the Twinkling of an Eye/
1 Corinthians 15:50–58

I declare to you, brothers, that flesh and blood cannot inherit the kingdom of God, nor does the perishable inherit the imperishable. 51Listen, I tell you a mystery: We will not all sleep, but we will all be changed— 52in a flash, in the twinkling of an eye, at the last trumpet. For the trumpet will sound, the dead will be raised imperishable, and we will be changed. 53For the perishable must clothe itself with the imperishable, and the mortal with immortality. 54When the perishable has been clothed with the imperishable, and the mortal with immortality, then the saying that is written will come true: "Death has been swallowed up in victory."

55"Where, O death, is your victory?
Where, O death, is your sting?"

56The sting of death is sin, and the power of sin is the law. 57But thanks be to God! He gives us the victory through our Lord Jesus Christ.

58Therefore, my dear brothers, stand firm. Let nothing move you. Always give yourselves fully to the work of the Lord, because you know that your labor in the Lord is not in vain.

A THOUGHT: *Paul said that because of the resurrection, nothing we do is wasted. Sometimes we hesitate to do good because we don't see any results. But if we can maintain a heavenly perspective, we understand that we don't often see the good that results from our efforts. If we truly believe that Christ has won the ultimate victory, it must affect the way we live right now. Don't let discouragement over an apparent lack of results keep you from working. Do the good that you have opportunity to do, knowing your work will have eternal results.*

Proverbs for Today/ 13:1

A wise son heeds his father's instruction, but a mocker does not listen to rebuke.

APRIL 13

Peter's Confession/ Mark 8:27–38

Jesus and his disciples went on to the villages around Caesarea Philippi. On the way he asked them, "Who do people say I am?"

28They replied, "Some say John the Baptist; others say Elijah; and still others, one of the prophets."

29"But what about you?" he asked. "Who do you say I am?"

Peter answered, "You are the Christ."

30Jesus warned them not to tell anyone about him.

31He then began to teach them that the Son of Man must suffer many things and be rejected by the elders, chief priests and teachers of the law, and that he must be killed and after three days rise again. 32He spoke plainly about this, and Peter took him aside and began to rebuke him.

33But when Jesus turned and looked at his disciples, he rebuked Peter. "Get behind me, Satan!" he said. "You do not have in mind the things of God, but the things of men."

34Then he called the crowd to him along with his disciples and said: "If anyone would come after me, he must deny himself and take up his cross and follow me. 35For whoever wants to save his life will lose it, but whoever loses his life for me and for the gospel will save it. 36What good is it for a man to gain the whole world, yet forfeit his soul? 37Or what can a man give in exchange for his soul? 38If anyone is ashamed of me and my words in this adulterous and sinful generation, the Son of Man will be ashamed of him when he comes in his Father's glory with the holy angels."

A THOUGHT: *Jesus asked the disciples who others thought he was; then he focused on them: "Who do you say I am?" At this point Peter made his famous confession. However, it is clear from the rest of the story that Peter's conception of Messiah and Jesus' conception were very different. Jesus went on to explain that he was going to die soon and that three days later he would be resurrected from the dead. Jesus calls all of his disciples to follow in his footsteps—to take up crosses and follow him. Commitment to Jesus involves sacrificing self-interests to love and serve others in obedience to him. The Christian life is not a paved road to wealth and ease. It often involves hard work, persecution, privation, and suffering.*

The Collection for the Jerusalem Church/
1 Corinthians 16:1–9

Now about the collection for God's people: Do what I told the Galatian churches to do. ²On the first day of every week, each one of you should set aside a sum of money in keeping with his income, saving it up, so that when I come no collections will have to be made. ³Then, when I arrive, I will give letters of introduction to the men you approve and send them with your gift to Jerusalem. ⁴If it seems advisable for me to go also, they will accompany me.

⁵After I go through Macedonia, I will come to you—for I will be going through Macedonia. ⁶Perhaps I will stay with you awhile, or even spend the winter, so that you can help me on my journey, wherever I go. ⁷I do not want to see you now and make only a passing visit; I hope to spend some time with you, if the Lord permits. ⁸But I will stay on at Ephesus until Pentecost, ⁹because a great door for effective work has opened to me, and there are many who oppose me.

A THOUGHT: *The Christians in Jerusalem were suffering from poverty and famine, so Paul was collecting money for them. Paul suggested that believers set aside a certain amount of money each week until he arrived to take it on to Jerusalem. Paul had planned to go straight to Corinth from Ephesus, but he changed his mind. When he finally arrived in Jerusalem, he took the gift and delivered it to the Jerusalem church. Paul's concern for the poor should also motivate us to greater involvement in serving the poor.*

Proverbs for Today/ 13:2–3

From the fruit of his lips a man enjoys good things, but the unfaithful have a craving for violence. □ He who guards his lips guards his life, but he who speaks rashly will come to ruin.

APRIL 14

The Transfiguration of Jesus/ Mark 9:1–13

And he [Jesus] said to them, "I tell you the truth, some who are standing here will not taste death before they see the kingdom of God come with power."

2After six days Jesus took Peter, James and John with him and led them up a high mountain, where they were all alone. There he was transfigured before them. 3His clothes became dazzling white, whiter than anyone in the world could bleach them. 4And there appeared before them Elijah and Moses, who were talking with Jesus.

5Peter said to Jesus, "Rabbi, it is good for us to be here. Let us put up three shelters—one for you, one for Moses and one for Elijah." 6(He did not know what to say, they were so frightened.)

7Then a cloud appeared and enveloped them, and a voice came from the cloud: "This is my Son, whom I love. Listen to him!"

8Suddenly, when they looked around, they no longer saw anyone with them except Jesus.

9As they were coming down the mountain, Jesus gave them orders not to tell anyone what they had seen until the Son of Man had risen from the dead. 10They kept the matter to themselves, discussing what "rising from the dead" meant.

11And they asked him, "Why do the teachers of the law say that Elijah must come first?"

12Jesus replied, "To be sure, Elijah does come first, and restores all things. Why then is it written that the Son of Man must suffer much and be rejected? 13But I tell you, Elijah has come, and they have done to him everything they wished, just as it is written about him."

A THOUGHT: *The transfiguration revealed Christ's true nature as God's Son. God singled Jesus out from Moses and Elijah as the long-awaited Messiah with full divine authority. Moses represented the Law, and Elijah, the Prophets. Jesus was shown as the fulfillment of both the Old Testament Law and the prophetic promises.*

Jesus was not a reincarnation of Elijah or Moses. He was not merely one of the prophets. As God's only Son, he far surpasses their authority and power. Many voices try to tell us how to live and how to know God personally. Some of these are helpful; many are not.

We must first listen to Jesus, and then evaluate all other authorities in light of his revelation.

Paul's Final Instructions/ 1 Corinthians 16:10–18

If Timothy comes, see to it that he has nothing to fear while he is with you, for he is carrying on the work of the Lord, just as I am. 11No one, then, should refuse to accept him. Send him on his way in peace so that he may return to me. I am expecting him along with the brothers.

12Now about our brother Apollos: I strongly urged him to go to you with the brothers. He was quite unwilling to go now, but he will go when he has the opportunity.

13Be on your guard; stand firm in the faith; be men of courage; be strong. 14Do everything in love.

15You know that the household of Stephanas were the first converts in Achaia, and they have devoted themselves to the service of the saints. I urge you, brothers, 16to submit to such as these and to everyone who joins in the work, and labors at it. 17I was glad when Stephanas, Fortunatus and Achaicus arrived, because they have supplied what was lacking from you. 18For they refreshed my spirit and yours also. Such men deserve recognition.

A THOUGHT: *As the Corinthians awaited Paul's next visit, they were directed to (1) be alert to spiritual dangers, (2) stand true to the Lord, (3) behave maturely, (4) be strong, and (5) do all things with kindness and love. Today, as we await the return of Christ, we should follow the same instructions.*

Proverbs for Today/ 13:4

The sluggard craves and gets nothing, but the desires of the diligent are fully satisfied.

APRIL 15

Jesus Casts Out a Demon/ Mark 9:14–29

When they [Jesus, Peter, James and John] came to the other disciples, they saw a large crowd around them and the teachers of the law arguing with them. 15As soon as all the people saw Jesus, they were overwhelmed with wonder and ran to greet him.

¹⁶"What are you arguing with them about?" he asked.

¹⁷A man in the crowd answered, "Teacher, I brought you my son, who is possessed by a spirit that has robbed him of speech. ¹⁸Whenever it seizes him, it throws him to the ground. He foams at the mouth, gnashes his teeth and becomes rigid. I asked your disciples to drive out the spirit, but they could not."

¹⁹"O unbelieving generation," Jesus replied, "how long shall I stay with you? How long shall I put up with you? Bring the boy to me."

²⁰So they brought him. When the spirit saw Jesus, it immediately threw the boy into a convulsion. He fell to the ground and rolled around, foaming at the mouth.

²¹Jesus asked the boy's father, "How long has he been like this?"

"From childhood," he answered. ²²"It has often thrown him into fire or water to kill him. But if you can do anything, take pity on us and help us."

²³" 'If you can'?" said Jesus. "Everything is possible for him who believes."

²⁴Immediately the boy's father exclaimed, "I do believe; help me overcome my unbelief!"

²⁵When Jesus saw that a crowd was running to the scene, he rebuked the evil spirit. "You deaf and mute spirit," he said, "I command you, come out of him and never enter him again."

²⁶The spirit shrieked, convulsed him violently and came out. The boy looked so much like a corpse that many said, "He's dead." ²⁷But Jesus took him by the hand and lifted him to his feet, and he stood up.

²⁸After Jesus had gone indoors, his disciples asked him privately, "Why couldn't we drive it out?"

²⁹He replied, "This kind can come out only by prayer."

A THOUGHT: *Faith is not something tangible to be taken like medicine. It is an attitude of trusting and believing. But even our ability to believe is a gift from God. No matter how much faith we have, we never reach the point of being self-sufficient. Faith is not stored away like money in the bank. Growing in faith is a constant process of daily renewing our trust in Jesus. Jesus was telling the disciples that they would face difficult situations that could be resolved only through prayer. Prayer is the key that unlocks faith in our lives. Effective prayer needs both an attitude—complete dependence—and an action—asking. Prayer demonstrates our reliance on God as we humbly invite God to fill us with faith and power. There is no substitute for prayer, especially in circumstances that seem unconquerable.*

Greetings from Other Believers/
1 Corinthians 16:19–24

The churches in the province of Asia send you greetings. Aquila and Priscilla greet you warmly in the Lord, and so does the church that meets at their house. 20All the brothers here send you greetings. Greet one another with a holy kiss.

21I, Paul, write this greeting in my own hand.

22If anyone does not love the Lord—a curse be on him. Come, O Lord!

23The grace of the Lord Jesus be with you.

24My love to all of you in Christ Jesus. Amen.

A THOUGHT: *The Lord Jesus Christ is coming back to earth again. To Paul, this was a glad hope, the best he could look forward to. He was not afraid of seeing Christ—he could hardly wait! Do you share Paul's eager anticipation? Those who love Christ are looking forward to that wonderful time of his return.*

Proverbs for Today/ 13:5–6

The righteous hate what is false, but the wicked bring shame and disgrace. □ Righteousness guards the man of integrity, but wickedness overthrows the sinner.

APRIL 16

The Greatest Must Be the Servant of All/
Mark 9:30–37

They [Jesus and his disciples] left that place and passed through Galilee. Jesus did not want anyone to know where they were, 31because he was teaching his disciples. He said to them, "The Son of Man is going to be betrayed into the hands of men. They will kill him, and after three days he will rise." 32But they did not understand what he meant and were afraid to ask him about it.

33They came to Capernaum. When he was in the house, he asked them, "What were you arguing about on the road?" 34But they kept quiet because on the way they had argued about who was the greatest.

35Sitting down, Jesus called the Twelve and said, "If anyone wants to be first, he must be the very last, and the servant of all."

36He took a little child and had him stand among them. Taking him in his arms, he said to them, 37"Whoever welcomes one of these little children in my name welcomes me; and whoever welcomes me does not welcome me but the one who sent me."

A THOUGHT: *The disciples had been caught up in a constant struggle for personal success, and they were embarrassed to answer Jesus' question. It is always painful to compare our motives with Christ's. It is not wrong for believers to be industrious or ambitious, but inappropriate ambition is sin. Pride or insecurity can cause us to value position and prestige more than service. In God's kingdom, such motives are destructive. Our ambition should be for Christ's kingdom, not for our own advancement. What do you use as your measure of greatness—personal achievement or unselfish service?*

The God of Comfort/ 2 Corinthians 1:1–7

Paul, an apostle of Christ Jesus by the will of God, and Timothy our brother,

To the church of God in Corinth, together with all the saints throughout Achaia:

2Grace and peace to you from God our Father and the Lord Jesus Christ.

3Praise be to the God and Father of our Lord Jesus Christ, the Father of compassion and the God of all comfort, 4who comforts us in all our troubles, so that we can comfort those in any trouble with the comfort we ourselves have received from God. 5For just as the sufferings of Christ flow over into our lives, so also through Christ our comfort overflows. 6If we are distressed, it is for your comfort and salvation; if we are comforted, it is for your comfort, which produces in you patient endurance of the same sufferings we suffer. 7And our hope for you is firm, because we know that just as you share in our sufferings, so also you share in our comfort.

A THOUGHT: *Many think that when God comforts us, our hardships should go away. But if that were always so, people would turn to God only to be relieved of pain and not out of love for him. We must understand that comfort can also mean receiving strength, encouragement, and hope to deal with our hardships. The more we suffer, the more comfort God gives us. If you are feeling overwhelmed, allow God to comfort you. Remember that every trial you endure will later become an opportunity to minister to other people suffering similar hardships.*

Proverbs for Today/ 13:7–8

One man pretends to be rich, yet has nothing; another pretends to be poor, yet has great wealth. □ A man's riches may ransom his life, but a poor man hears no threat.

APRIL 17

God's Righteous Kingdom/ Mark 9:38–50

"Teacher," said John, "we saw a man driving out demons in your name and we told him to stop, because he was not one of us."

³⁹"Do not stop him," Jesus said. "No one who does a miracle in my name can in the next moment say anything bad about me, ⁴⁰for whoever is not against us is for us. ⁴¹I tell you the truth, anyone who gives you a cup of water in my name because you belong to Christ will certainly not lose his reward.

⁴²"And if anyone causes one of these little ones who believe in me to sin, it would be better for him to be thrown into the sea with a large millstone tied around his neck. ⁴³If your hand causes you to sin, cut it off. It is better for you to enter life maimed than with two hands to go into hell, where the fire never goes out. * ⁴⁵And if your foot causes you to sin, cut it off. It is better for you to enter life crippled than to have two feet and be thrown into hell. * ⁴⁷And if your eye causes you to sin, pluck it out. It is better for you

---

*43 Some manuscripts *out,* ⁴⁴*where* / "'*their worm does not die,* / *and the fire is not quenched.'* *45 Some manuscripts *hell,* ⁴⁶*where* / "'*their worm does not die,* / *and the fire is not quenched.'*

to enter the kingdom of God with one eye than to have two eyes and be thrown into hell, 48where

"'their worm does not die,
and the fire is not quenched.'

49Everyone will be salted with fire.

50"Salt is good, but if it loses its saltiness, how can you make it salty again? Have salt in yourselves, and be at peace with each other."

A THOUGHT: *Jesus used startling language to stress the importance of cutting sin out of our lives. Painful discipline is required of his true followers. Giving up a relationship, job, or habit that is against God's will may seem just as painful as cutting off a hand. Our high goal, however, is worth any sacrifice; Christ is worth any possible loss. Nothing should stand in the way of faith. We must be ruthless in removing sins from our lives. Make your choices from an eternal perspective.*

Hardships and Triumphs in Paul's Ministry/ 2 Corinthians 1:8–14

We do not want you to be uninformed, brothers, about the hardships we suffered in the province of Asia. We were under great pressure, far beyond our ability to endure, so that we despaired even of life. 9Indeed, in our hearts we felt the sentence of death. But this happened that we might not rely on ourselves but on God, who raises the dead. 10He has delivered us from such a deadly peril, and he will deliver us. On him we have set our hope that he will continue to deliver us, 11as you help us by your prayers. Then many will give thanks on our behalf for the gracious favor granted us in answer to the prayers of many.

12Now this is our boast: Our conscience testifies that we have conducted ourselves in the world, and especially in our relations with you, in the holiness and sincerity that are from God. We have done so not according to worldly wisdom but according to God's grace. 13For we do not write you anything you cannot read or understand. And I hope that, 14as you have understood us in part, you will come to understand fully that you can boast of us just as we will boast of you in the day of the Lord Jesus.

A THOUGHT: *We often depend on our own skills and abilities when life seems easy, but when we feel powerless to help ourselves, we turn to God. We must recognize that even when life seems easy we are dependent upon God, for he upholds the universe with his power. Dependence is not defeat, but the realization that our source of truth and power is God. With this attitude, problems drive us to God rather than away from him. Learn how to depend on God daily.*

Proverbs for Today/ 13:9–10

The light of the righteous shines brightly, but the lamp of the wicked is snuffed out. □ Pride only breeds quarrels, but wisdom is found in those who take advice.

APRIL 18

Jesus' Teachings on Divorce/ Mark 10:1–12

Jesus then left that place and went into the region of Judea and across the Jordan. Again crowds of people came to him, and as was his custom, he taught them.

²Some Pharisees came and tested him by asking, "Is it lawful for a man to divorce his wife?"

³"What did Moses command you?" he replied.

⁴They said, "Moses permitted a man to write a certificate of divorce and send her away."

⁵"It was because your hearts were hard that Moses wrote you this law," Jesus replied. ⁶"But at the beginning of creation God 'made them male and female.' ⁷For this reason a man will leave his father and mother and be united to his wife, ⁸and the two will become one flesh.' So they are no longer two, but one. ⁹Therefore what God has joined together, let man not separate."

¹⁰When they were in the house again, the disciples asked Jesus about this. ¹¹He answered, "Anyone who divorces his wife and marries another woman commits adultery against her. ¹²And if she divorces her husband and marries another man, she commits adultery."

A THOUGHT: *God allowed divorce as a concession to people's sinfulness. Divorce was not approved, but it was instituted to protect the injured party in the midst of a bad situation. Unfortunately, many Pharisees had set up legal traditions to allow for divorce for almost any reason (the cause for divorce being left up to the discretion of the husband). Jesus explained that this was not God's intent; instead, God wants married people to consider their marriage permanent.*

Don't enter marriage with the option of getting out, but be committed to the permanence of the relationship. You'll stand a much better chance of making your marriage work. Don't be hard-hearted like these Pharisees, but be hard-headed in your determination, with God's help, to stay together.

Paul's Plan to Visit the Corinthians/ 2 Corinthians 1:15–24

Because I was confident of this, I planned to visit you first so that you might benefit twice. 16I planned to visit you on my way to Macedonia and to come back to you from Macedonia, and then to have you send me on my way to Judea. 17When I planned this, did I do it lightly? Or do I make my plans in a worldly manner so that in the same breath I say, "Yes, yes" and "No, no"?

18But as surely as God is faithful, our message to you is not "Yes" and "No." 19For the Son of God, Jesus Christ, who was preached among you by me and Silas and Timothy, was not "Yes" and "No," but in him it has always been "Yes." 20For no matter how many promises God has made, they are "Yes" in Christ. And so through him the "Amen" is spoken by us to the glory of God. 21Now it is God who makes both us and you stand firm in Christ. He anointed us, 22set his seal of ownership on us, and put his Spirit in our hearts as a deposit, guaranteeing what is to come.

23I call God as my witness that it was in order to spare you that I did not return to Corinth. 24Not that we lord it over your faith, but we work with you for your joy, because it is by faith you stand firm.

A THOUGHT: *Paul mentions two gifts God gives when we become believers: a "mark of ownership" to show who our master is, and the Holy Spirit as a guarantee that we belong to him. With the privilege of belonging to God comes the responsibility of identifying ourselves as faithful representatives and servants of our master. Don't be ashamed to let others know you are his.*

Proverbs for Today/ 13:11

Dishonest money dwindles away, but he who gathers money little by little makes it grow.

Jesus and the Little Children/ Mark 10:13–16

People were bringing little children to Jesus to have him touch them, but the disciples rebuked them. 14When Jesus saw this, he was indignant. He said to them, "Let the little children come to me, and do not hinder them, for the kingdom of God belongs to such as these. 15I tell you the truth, anyone who will not receive the kingdom of God like a little child will never enter it." 16And he took the children in his arms, put his hands on them and blessed them.

A THOUGHT: *Jesus was often criticized for spending too much time with the wrong people—children, sinners, tax collectors. Some, including the disciples, thought Jesus should be spending more time with important leaders and the devout, because this was the way to improve his position and avoid criticism. But Jesus reverses this whole conception of position and greatness by showing that the kingdom of God belongs to those who have a childlike trust in God, not a confident trust in their own greatness. To become great in the kingdom of God, one must become the servant of all.*

Paul's Sorrowful Letter/ 2 Corinthians 2:1–4

So I made up my mind that I would not make another painful visit to you. 2For if I grieve you, who is left to make me glad but you whom I have grieved? 3I wrote as I did so that when I came I should not be distressed by those who ought to make me rejoice. I had confidence in all of you, that you would all share my joy. 4For I wrote you out of great distress and anguish of heart and with many tears, not to grieve you but to let you know the depth of my love for you.

A THOUGHT: *Paul did not enjoy reprimanding his friends and fellow believers, but he cared enough for the Corinthians to confront them about their wrongdoing. Proverbs 27:6 says that "The kisses of an enemy may be profuse, but faithful are the wounds of a friend." Sometimes our friends make choices that we know are wrong. If we ignore their behavior and let them continue, we aren't showing love to them. Love means honestly sharing our concerns with those we love. When we don't move to help, we show that we are more concerned about what will happen to us than what will happen to them.*

Proverbs for Today/ 13:12–14

Hope deferred makes the heart sick, but a longing fulfilled is a tree of life. □ He who scorns instruction will pay for it, but he who respects a command is rewarded. □ The teaching of the wise is a fountain of life, turning a man from the snares of death.

APRIL 20

Jesus and the Rich Man/ Mark 10:17–31

As Jesus started on his way, a man ran up to him and fell on his knees before him. "Good teacher," he asked, "what must I do to inherit eternal life?"

18"Why do you call me good?" Jesus answered. "No one is good—except God alone. 19You know the commandments: 'Do not murder, do not commit adultery, do not steal, do not give false testimony, do not defraud, honor your father and mother.'"

20"Teacher," he declared, "all these I have kept since I was a boy."

21Jesus looked at him and loved him. "One thing you lack," he said. "Go, sell everything you have and give to the poor, and you will have treasure in heaven. Then come, follow me."

22At this the man's face fell. He went away sad, because he had great wealth.

23Jesus looked around and said to his disciples, "How hard it is for the rich to enter the kingdom of God!"

24The disciples were amazed at his words. But Jesus said again, "Children, how hard it is to enter the kingdom of God! 25It is easier for a camel to go through the eye of a needle than for a rich man to enter the kingdom of God."

26The disciples were even more amazed, and said to each other, "Who then can be saved?"

27Jesus looked at them and said, "With man this is impossible, but not with God; all things are possible with God."

28Peter said to him, "We have left everything to follow you!"

29"I tell you the truth," Jesus replied, "no one who has left home or brothers or sisters or mother or father or children or fields for me and the gospel 30will fail to receive a hundred times as much in this present age (homes, brothers, sisters, mothers, children and fields—and with them, persecutions) and in the age to come, eternal life. 31But many who are first will be last, and the last first."

A THOUGHT: *There was a barrier keeping this young man out of the kingdom: his love of money. Money represented his pride of accomplishment and self-effort. Ironically, his attitude made him unable to keep the first commandment, to let nothing be more important than God. This man came to Jesus wondering what he could do; he left seeing what he was unable to do. Jesus said it was very difficult for the rich to get into the kingdom of God because the rich have most of their basic physical needs met and thus often become self-reliant. When they feel empty, they can buy something new to dull the pain that was meant to drive them toward God. Their abundance becomes their deficiency. Jesus explained that in the world to come, the values of this world will be reversed. Those who seek status and importance here will have none in heaven. The person who has everything on earth can still lack what is most important—eternal life. What barriers are keeping you from turning your life over to Christ?*

Forgive the Repentant Sinner/ 2 Corinthians 2:5–11

If anyone has caused grief, he has not so much grieved me as he has grieved all of you, to some extent—not to put it too severely. 6The punishment inflicted on him by the majority is sufficient for him. 7Now instead, you ought to forgive and comfort him, so that he will not be overwhelmed by excessive sorrow. 8I urge you, therefore, to reaffirm your love for him. 9The reason I wrote you was to see if you would stand the test and be obedient in everything. 10If you forgive anyone, I also forgive him. And what I have forgiven—if there was anything to forgive—I have forgiven in the sight of Christ for your sake, 11in order that Satan might not outwit us. For we are not unaware of his schemes.

A THOUGHT: *It was time to forgive the man who had been punished by the church and had subsequently repented. He now needed friendship and comfort. Church discipline should always allow for restoration. Two mistakes can be made in church discipline—being too lenient with sin and not correcting mistakes, or being too harsh and unforgiving. There is a time to confront and a time to comfort. We must remember that our purpose in discipline is to restore a person to the fellowship, not to destroy him or her. We must be cautious that personal anger is not vented under the guise of church discipline.*

Proverbs for Today/ 13:15–16

Good understanding wins favor, but the way of the unfaithful is hard. □ Every prudent man acts out of knowledge, but a fool exposes his folly.

APRIL 21

The Greatest Must Be the Servant of All/ Mark 10:32–45

They were on their way up to Jerusalem, with Jesus leading the way, and the disciples were astonished, while those who followed were afraid. Again he took the Twelve aside and told them what was going to happen to him. 33"We are going up to Jerusalem," he said, "and the Son of Man will be betrayed to the chief priests and teachers of the law. They will condemn him to death and will hand him over to the Gentiles, 34who will mock him and spit on him, flog him and kill him. Three days later he will rise."

35Then James and John, the sons of Zebedee, came to him. "Teacher," they said, "we want you to do for us whatever we ask."

36"What do you want me to do for you?" he asked.

37They replied, "Let one of us sit at your right and the other at your left in your glory."

38"You don't know what you are asking," Jesus said. "Can you drink the cup I drink or be baptized with the baptism I am baptized with?"

39"We can," they answered.

Jesus said to them, "You will drink the cup I drink and be baptized with the baptism I am baptized with, 40but to sit at my right or left is not for me to grant. These places belong to those for whom they have been prepared."

41When the ten heard about this, they became indignant with James and John. 42Jesus called them together and said, "You know that those who are regarded as rulers of the Gentiles lord it over them, and their high officials exercise authority over them. 43Not so with you. Instead, whoever wants to become great among you must be your servant,

44and whoever wants to be first must be slave of all. 45For even the Son of Man did not come to be served, but to serve, and to give his life as a ransom for many."

A THOUGHT: *James and John wanted the highest positions in Jesus' kingdom. But Jesus told them that true greatness comes in serving others. Most businesses, organizations, and institutions in our world measure greatness by high personal achievement. In Christ's kingdom, however, service is the measure of greatness. The desire to be on top isn't a help but a hindrance to the kingdom of God.*

The Fragrance of the Gospel/ 2 Corinthians 2:12–17

Now when I went to Troas to preach the gospel of Christ and found that the Lord had opened a door for me, 13I still had no peace of mind, because I did not find my brother Titus there. So I said good-by to them and went on to Macedonia.

14But thanks be to God, who always leads us in triumphal procession in Christ and through us spreads everywhere the fragrance of the knowledge of him. 15For we are to God the aroma of Christ among those who are being saved and those who are perishing. 16To the one we are the smell of death; to the other, the fragrance of life. And who is equal to such a task? 17Unlike so many, we do not peddle the word of God for profit. On the contrary, in Christ we speak before God with sincerity, like men sent from God.

A THOUGHT: *Believers are to be like a sweet perfume whose fragrance others can't help but notice. Just as we cannot control a person's opinion about a perfume's fragrance, we cannot control a person's reaction to our Christian message and actions. But if we remain true to Christ, his Spirit working in us will attract others.*

Proverbs for Today/ 13:17–19

A wicked messenger falls into trouble, but a trustworthy envoy brings healing. □ He who ignores discipline comes to poverty and shame, but whoever heeds correction is honored. □ A longing fulfilled is sweet to the soul, but fools detest turning from evil.

APRIL 22

Jesus Heals Blind Bartimaeus/ Mark 10:46–52

Then they came to Jericho. As Jesus and his disciples, together with a large crowd, were leaving the city, a blind man, Bartimaeus (that is, the Son of Timaeus), was sitting by the roadside begging. 47When he heard that it was Jesus of Nazareth, he began to shout, "Jesus, Son of David, have mercy on me!"

48Many rebuked him and told him to be quiet, but he shouted all the more, "Son of David, have mercy on me!"

49Jesus stopped and said, "Call him."

So they called to the blind man, "Cheer up! On your feet! He's calling you." 50Throwing his cloak aside, he jumped to his feet and came to Jesus.

51"What do you want me to do for you?" Jesus asked him.

The blind man said, "Rabbi, I want to see."

52"Go," said Jesus, "your faith has healed you." Immediately he received his sight and followed Jesus along the road.

A THOUGHT: *Beggars were a common sight in most towns in first-century Israel. Since most occupations of that day required physical labor, anyone with a crippling disease or handicap was at a severe disadvantage and was usually forced to beg, even though God's laws commanded care for such needy people. Blindness was considered a curse from God for sin; but Jesus refuted this idea when he reached out to heal those who were blind. It was to the ignored, oppressed, and despised of society that Jesus went to proclaim—in both word and deed—the Good News of the Kingdom. Our task is to reach out with God's love to the ignored, oppressed, and despised of our society.*

Law Brings Death, Spirit Gives Life/ 2 Corinthians 3:1–6

Are we beginning to commend ourselves again? Or do we need, like some people, letters of recommendation to you or from you? 2You yourselves are our letter, written on our hearts, known and read by everybody. 3You show that you are a letter from Christ, the result of our ministry, written not with ink but with the Spirit of the living God, not on tablets of stone but on tablets of human hearts.

4Such confidence as this is ours through Christ before God. 5Not that we are competent in ourselves to claim anything for ourselves, but our competence comes from God. 6He has made us competent as ministers of a new covenant—not of the letter but of the Spirit; for the letter kills, but the Spirit gives life.

A THOUGHT: *The last sentence of verse six says, "the letter kills, but the Spirit gives life." No one but Jesus has ever fulfilled the written law perfectly, and thus the whole world is condemned to death. The law makes people realize their sin, but it cannot give life. Eternal life comes from the Holy Spirit, who gives new life to all who believe in Christ. The moral law is still helpful to point out sin and show us how to live a life pleasing to God, but forgiveness comes only through the grace and mercy of Christ.*

Proverbs for Today/ 13:20–23

He who walks with the wise grows wise, but a companion of fools suffers harm. □ Misfortune pursues the sinner, but prosperity is the reward of the righteous. □ A good man leaves an inheritance for his children's children, but a sinner's wealth is stored up for the righteous. □ A poor man's field may produce abundant food, but injustice sweeps it away.

APRIL 23

Jesus' Triumphal Entry/ Mark 11:1–11

As they approached Jerusalem and came to Bethphage and Bethany at the Mount of Olives, Jesus sent two of his disciples, 2saying to them, "Go to the village ahead of you, and just as you enter it, you will find a colt tied there, which no one has ever ridden. Untie it and bring it here. 3If anyone asks you, 'Why are you doing this?' tell him, 'The Lord needs it and will send it back here shortly.' "

4They went and found a colt outside in the street, tied at a doorway. As they untied it, 5some people standing there asked, "What are you doing, untying that colt?" 6They answered as Jesus had told them to, and the people let them go. 7When they brought the colt to Jesus and threw their cloaks over it, he sat on it. 8Many people spread their cloaks on the road, while others spread branches they had cut in the fields. 9Those who went ahead and those who followed shouted,

> "Hosanna!"

> "Blessed is he who comes in the name of the Lord!"

> 10"Blessed is the coming kingdom of our father David!"

> "Hosanna in the highest!"

11Jesus entered Jerusalem and went to the temple. He looked around at everything, but since it was already late, he went out to Bethany with the Twelve.

A THOUGHT: *This was Sunday of the week Jesus would be crucified, and the great Passover festival was about to begin. Jews came to Jerusalem from all over the Roman world during this week-long celebration to remember the great exodus from Egypt. Many in the crowds had heard of or seen Jesus and were hoping he would come to the Temple.*

Jesus did come, not as a conquering king on a white horse (symbolizing victory), but on a donkey's colt that had never been ridden (symbolizing humility). The people were anticipating that Jesus would become a great political Messiah who would overthrow Roman domination. A few days later some of these people who were shouting, "Hosanna!" would cry out, "Crucify him!"

The Old and New Covenants Compared/ 2 Corinthians 3:7–18

Now if the ministry that brought death, which was engraved in letters on stone, came with glory, so that the Israelites could not look steadily at the face of Moses because of its glory, fading though it was, 8will not the ministry of the Spirit be even more glorious? 9If the ministry that condemns men is glorious, how much more glorious is the ministry that brings righteousness! 10For what was glorious has no glory now in comparison with the surpassing glory. 11And if what was fading away came with glory, how much greater is the glory of that which lasts!

12Therefore, since we have such a hope, we are very bold. 13We are not like Moses, who would put a veil over his face to keep the Israelites from gazing at it while the radiance was fading away. 14But their minds were made dull, for to this day the same veil remains when the old covenant is read. It has not been removed, because only in Christ is it taken away. 15Even to this day when Moses is read, a veil covers their hearts. 16But whenever anyone turns to the Lord, the veil is taken away. 17Now the Lord is the Spirit, and where the Spirit of the Lord is, there is freedom. 18And we, who with unveiled faces all reflect the Lord's glory, are being transformed into his likeness with ever-increasing glory, which comes from the Lord, who is the Spirit.

A THOUGHT: *When Moses came down Mount Sinai with the Ten Commandments, his face glowed from being in God's presence. He put on a veil to keep the people from being terrified by the brightness of his face. Paul adds that his veil kept them from seeing the glory fade away. The glory that the Spirit imparts to the believer is greater both in quality and longevity than that which Moses experienced. The glory experienced in the new covenant gradually transforms the believer into Christlikeness. Becoming Christlike is a progressive experience. The more closely we relate to him, the more we will be like him.*

Proverbs for Today/ 13:24–25

He who spares the rod hates his son, but he who loves him is careful to discipline him. □ The righteous eat to their hearts' content, but the stomach of the wicked goes hungry.

APRIL 24

Jesus Clears the Temple/ Mark 11:12–25

The next day as they were leaving Bethany, Jesus was hungry. 13Seeing in the distance a fig tree in leaf, he went to find out if it had any fruit. When he reached it, he found nothing but leaves, because it was not the season for figs. 14Then he said to the tree, "May no one ever eat fruit from you again." And his disciples heard him say it.

15On reaching Jerusalem, Jesus entered the temple area and began driving out those who were buying and selling there. He overturned the tables of the money changers and the benches of those selling doves, 16and would not allow anyone to carry merchandise through the temple courts. [17]And as he taught them, he said, "Is it not written:

" 'My house will be called
    a house of prayer for all nations'?

But you have made it 'a den of robbers.' "

[18]The chief priests and the teachers of the law heard this and began looking for a way to kill him, for they feared him, because the whole crowd was amazed at his teaching.

[19]When evening came, they went out of the city.

[20]In the morning, as they went along, they saw the fig tree withered from the roots. [21]Peter remembered and said to Jesus, "Rabbi, look! The fig tree you cursed has withered!"

[22]"Have faith in God," Jesus answered. [23]"I tell you the truth, if anyone says to this mountain, 'Go, throw yourself into the sea,' and does not doubt in his heart but believes that what he says will happen, it will be done for him. [24]Therefore I tell you, whatever you ask for in prayer, believe that you have received it, and it will be yours. [25]And when you stand praying, if you hold anything against anyone, forgive him, so that your Father in heaven may forgive you your sins. *"

A THOUGHT: *There are two parts to this unusual incident: the cursing of the fig tree and the cleansing of the Temple. The cursing of the fig tree was an acted-out parable related to the cleansing of the Temple. The Temple was supposed to be a place of worship, but true worship of God had virtually disappeared. The fig tree showed promise of fruit, but it produced none. Jesus was showing his anger at religious life without substance. If you "go through the motions" of faith without putting it to work in your life, you are like the fig tree that withered and died. Genuine faith has great potential; ask God to help you bear fruit for his kingdom.*

Treasure in Jars of Clay/ 2 Corinthians 4:1–7

Therefore, since through God's mercy we have this ministry, we do not lose heart. [2]Rather, we have renounced secret and shameful ways; we do not use deception, nor do we distort the word of God. On the contrary, by setting forth the truth plainly we commend ourselves to every man's conscience in the sight of God. [3]And even if our gospel is veiled, it is veiled to those who are perishing.

*25 Some manuscripts sins. [26]But if you do not forgive, neither will your Father who is in heaven forgive your sins.

4The god of this age has blinded the minds of unbelievers, so that they cannot see the light of the gospel of the glory of Christ, who is the image of God. 5For we do not preach ourselves, but Jesus Christ as Lord, and ourselves as your servants for Jesus' sake. 6For God, who said, "Let light shine out of darkness," made his light shine in our hearts to give us the light of the knowledge of the glory of God in the face of Christ.

7But we have this treasure in jars of clay to show that this all-surpassing power is from God and not from us.

A THOUGHT: *The supremely valuable message of salvation in Jesus Christ has been entrusted by God to frail and fallible human beings. Paul's focus, however, is not on the perishable container but on its priceless contents—God's power dwelling in us. Though we are weak, God uses us to spread his Good News and gives us power to do his work. Knowing that the power is his, not ours, keeps us from pride and motivates us to keep daily contact with God, our power source. Our responsibility is to let people see God through us.*

Proverbs for Today/ 14:1–2

The wise woman builds her house, but with her own hands the foolish one tears hers down. □ He whose walk is upright fears the LORD, but he whose ways are devious despises him.

APRIL 25

The Parable of the Disloyal Tenants/
Mark 11:27—12:12

They [Jesus and his disciples] arrived again in Jerusalem, and while Jesus was walking in the temple courts, the chief priests, the teachers of the law and the elders came to him. 28"By what authority are you doing these things?" they asked. "And who gave you authority to do this?"

29Jesus replied, "I will ask you one question. Answer me, and I will tell you by what authority I am doing these things. 30John's baptism—was it from heaven, or from men? Tell me!"

31They discussed it among themselves and said, "If we

say, 'From heaven,' he will ask, 'Then why didn't you believe him?' 32But if we say, 'From men' . . . ." (They feared the people, for everyone held that John really was a prophet.)

33So they answered Jesus, "We don't know."

Jesus said, "Neither will I tell you by what authority I am doing these things."

12:1He then began to speak to them in parables: "A man planted a vineyard. He put a wall around it, dug a pit for the winepress and built a watchtower. Then he rented the vineyard to some farmers and went away on a journey. 2At harvest time he sent a servant to the tenants to collect from them some of the fruit of the vineyard. 3But they seized him, beat him and sent him away empty-handed. 4Then he sent another servant to them; they struck this man on the head and treated him shamefully. 5He sent still another, and that one they killed. He sent many others; some of them they beat, others they killed.

6"He had one left to send, a son, whom he loved. He sent him last of all, saying, 'They will respect my son.'

7"But the tenants said to one another, 'This is the heir. Come, let's kill him, and the inheritance will be ours.' 8So they took him and killed him, and threw him out of the vineyard.

9"What then will the owner of the vineyard do? He will come and kill those tenants and give the vineyard to others. 10Haven't you read this scripture:

" 'The stone the builders rejected
    has become the capstone;
11the Lord has done this,
    and it is marvelous in our eyes'?"

12Then they looked for a way to arrest him because they knew he had spoken the parable against them. But they were afraid of the crowd; so they left him and went away.

A THOUGHT: *The Pharisees asked Jesus, who gave him the authority to chase away the merchants and moneychangers. Their request, however, was a trap. If Jesus said his authority was from God, they would accuse him of blasphemy; if he said his authority was his own, they would overrule him and dismiss him as a fanatic. To expose their real motives, Jesus countered their question with a question about John the Baptist. The Pharisees' silence proved they were not interested in the truth. In response to the silence of the Pharisees,*

Jesus tells this parable of the disloyal tenants to indicate: (1) that his source of authority is God (he is pictured as the son in the parable), and (2) that the Pharisees were really at odds with the landowner (God) when they should have been cultivating the vineyard.

Triumph in Suffering/ 2 Corinthians 4:8–17

We are hard pressed on every side, but not crushed; perplexed, but not in despair; 9persecuted, but not abandoned; struck down, but not destroyed. 10We always carry around in our body the death of Jesus, so that the life of Jesus may also be revealed in our body. 11For we who are alive are always being given over to death for Jesus' sake, so that his life may be revealed in our mortal body. 12So then, death is at work in us, but life is at work in you.

13It is written: "I believed; therefore I have spoken." With that same spirit of faith we also believe and therefore speak, 14because we know that the one who raised the Lord Jesus from the dead will also raise us with Jesus and present us with you in his presence. 15All this is for your benefit, so that the grace that is reaching more and more people may cause thanksgiving to overflow to the glory of God.

16Therefore we do not lose heart. Though outwardly we are wasting away, yet inwardly we are being renewed day by day. 17For our light and momentary troubles are achieving for us an eternal glory that far outweighs them all.

A THOUGHT: *Paul suffered many trials as he preached the Good News, but he knew that they would one day be over and he would obtain God's great blessings. As we face great troubles, it's easy to focus on the pain rather than on our ultimate goal. Just as athletes concentrate on the finish line and ignore their discomfort, we too must focus on the reward for our faith and the joy that lasts forever. No matter what happens to us in this life, we have the assurance of eternal life where all suffering will end.*

Proverbs for Today/ 14:3–4

A fool's talk brings a rod to his back, but the lips of the wise protect them. □ Where there are no oxen, the manger is empty, but from the strength of an ox comes an abundant harvest.

APRIL 26

Jesus Answers the Pharisees and the Sadducees/ Mark 12:13–34

Later they [the Jewish leaders] sent some of the Pharisees and Herodians to Jesus to catch him in his words. 14They came to him and said, "Teacher, we know you are a man of integrity. You aren't swayed by men, because you pay no attention to who they are; but you teach the way of God in accordance with the truth. Is it right to pay taxes to Caesar or not? 15Should we pay or shouldn't we?"

But Jesus knew their hypocrisy. "Why are you trying to trap me?" he asked. "Bring me a denarius and let me look at it." 16They brought the coin, and he asked them, "Whose portrait is this? And whose inscription?"

"Caesar's," they replied.

17Then Jesus said to them, "Give to Caesar what is Caesar's and to God what is God's."

And they were amazed at him.

18Then the Sadducees, who say there is no resurrection, came to him with a question. 19"Teacher," they said, "Moses wrote for us that if a man's brother dies and leaves a wife but no children, the man must marry the widow and have children for his brother. 20Now there were seven brothers. The first one married and died without leaving any children. 21The second one married the widow, but he also died, leaving no child. It was the same with the third. 22In fact, none of the seven left any children. Last of all, the woman died too. 23At the resurrection whose wife will she be, since the seven were married to her?"

24Jesus replied, "Are you not in error because you do not know the Scriptures or the power of God? 25When the dead rise, they will neither marry nor be given in marriage; they will be like the angels in heaven. 26Now about the dead rising—have you not read in the book of Moses, in the account of the bush, how God said to him, 'I am the God of Abraham, the God of Isaac, and the God of Jacob'? 27He is not the God of the dead, but of the living. You are badly mistaken!"

28One of the teachers of the law came and heard them

debating. Noticing that Jesus had given them a good answer, he asked him, "Of all the commandments, which is the most important?"

29"The most important one," answered Jesus, "is this: 'Hear, O Israel, the Lord our God, the Lord is one. 30Love the Lord your God with all your heart and with all your soul and with all your mind and with all your strength.' 31The second is this: 'Love your neighbor as yourself.' There is no commandment greater than these."

32"Well said, teacher," the man replied. "You are right in saying that God is one and there is no other but him. 33To love him with all your heart, with all your understanding and with all your strength, and to love your neighbor as yourself is more important than all burnt offerings and sacrifices."

34When Jesus saw that he had answered wisely, he said to him, "You are not far from the kingdom of God." And from then on no one dared ask him any more questions.

A THOUGHT: *The Pharisees and Herodians thought they had the perfect question to trap Jesus. But Jesus answered wisely, once again exposing their self-interest and wrong motives. Jesus said that since the coin had the impression of the emperor's image, it should be given to the emperor. But whatever belongs to God—the earth and everyone who lives on the earth—should be offered up to God. Are you giving God all that is rightfully his? Make sure your life is wholly given to God.*

The Hope of the Resurrection/
2 Corinthians 4:18—5:10

So we fix our eyes not on what is seen, but on what is unseen. For what is seen is temporary, but what is unseen is eternal.

5:1Now we know that if the earthly tent we live in is destroyed, we have a building from God, an eternal house in heaven, not built by human hands. 2Meanwhile we groan, longing to be clothed with our heavenly dwelling, 3because when we are clothed, we will not be found naked. 4For while we are in this tent, we groan and are burdened, because we do not wish to be unclothed but to be clothed with our heavenly dwelling, so that what is mortal may be swallowed up by life. 5Now it is God who has made us for this very purpose and has given us the Spirit as a deposit, guaranteeing what is to come.

6Therefore we are always confident and know that as

long as we are at home in the body we are away from the Lord. 7We live by faith, not by sight. 8We are confident, I say, and would prefer to be away from the body and at home with the Lord. 9So we make it our goal to please him, whether we are at home in the body or away from it. 10For we must all appear before the judgment seat of Christ, that each one may receive what is due him for the things done while in the body, whether good or bad.

A THOUGHT: *The ultimate hope in terrible illness, persecution, or pain is realizing that this life is not all there is—there is life after death! Death is frightening for many people because it is mysterious and unknown. Paul was not afraid to die because he was confident of spending eternity with Christ. Of course, facing the unknown is cause for anxiety and leaving loved ones hurts deeply, but if we believe in Jesus Christ, we can share Paul's hope and confidence in the resurrection of the body and eternal life with Christ. Knowing that we will live forever with God in a place without sin and suffering helps us live above the pain we must face in this life.*

Proverbs for Today/ 14:5–6

A truthful witness does not deceive, but a false witness pours out lies. □ The mocker seeks wisdom and finds none, but knowledge comes easily to the discerning.

APRIL 27

Proud Teachers and a Humble Widow/ Mark 12:35–44

While Jesus was teaching in the temple courts, he asked, "How is it that the teachers of the law say that the Christ is the son of David? 36David himself, speaking by the Holy Spirit, declared:

" 'The Lord said to my Lord:
"Sit at my right hand
until I put your enemies
under your feet." '

37David himself calls him 'Lord.' How then can he be his son?"

The large crowd listened to him with delight.

^{38}As he taught, Jesus said, "Watch out for the teachers of the law. They like to walk around in flowing robes and be greeted in the marketplaces, ^{39}and have the most important seats in the synagogues and the places of honor at banquets. ^{40}They devour widows' houses and for a show make lengthy prayers. Such men will be punished most severely."

^{41}Jesus sat down opposite the place where the offerings were put and watched the crowd putting their money into the temple treasury. Many rich people threw in large amounts. ^{42}But a poor widow came and put in two very small copper coins, worth only a fraction of a penny.

^{43}Calling his disciples to him, Jesus said, "I tell you the truth, this poor widow has put more into the treasury than all the others. ^{44}They all gave out of their wealth; but she, out of her poverty, put in everything—all she had to live on."

A THOUGHT: *Jesus warned against the teachers of religion who loved to appear holy and receive honor when, in reality, they were phonies. Greatness is not measured by appearance, but by genuine obedience to God from a humble heart. In the Lord's eyes, the poor widow gave more than all the others put together, although her gift was by far the smallest. The value of a gift is not determined by its amount, but by the spirit in which it is given. In the same way, the value of acts of kindness or service should not be measured by quantity, nor by their value in the eyes of men, but by their value in the eyes of God.*

New Creations in Christ/ 2 Corinthians 5:11–21

Since, then, we know what it is to fear the Lord, we try to persuade men. What we are is plain to God, and I hope it is also plain to your conscience. ^{12}We are not trying to commend ourselves to you again, but are giving you an opportunity to take pride in us, so that you can answer those who take pride in what is seen rather than in what is in the heart. ^{13}If we are out of our mind, it is for the sake of God; if we are in our right mind, it is for you. ^{14}For Christ's love compels us, because we are convinced that one died for all, and therefore all died. ^{15}And he died for all, that those who live should no longer live for themselves but for him who died for them and was raised again.

^{16}So from now on we regard no one from a worldly point of view. Though we once regarded Christ in this way, we do so no longer. ^{17}Therefore, if anyone is in Christ, he is a new creation; the old has gone, the new has come! 18All this is from God, who reconciled us to himself through Christ and gave us the ministry of reconciliation: 19that God was reconciling the world to himself in Christ, not counting men's sins against them. And he has committed to us the message of reconciliation. 20We are therefore Christ's ambassadors, as though God were making his appeal through us. We implore you on Christ's behalf: Be reconciled to God. 21God made him who had no sin to be sin for us, so that in him we might become the righteousness of God.

A THOUGHT: *Christians are brand new people on the inside. The Holy Spirit gives them new life, and they are not the same any more. We are not reformed, rehabilitated, or reeducated—we are new creations, living in vital union with Christ. We are not merely turning over a new leaf; we are beginning a new life under a new master. The Christian life involves this continual process of transformation by the power of the Holy Spirit. Gradually we become more and more like Jesus Christ in our thoughts, attitudes, and actions.*

Proverbs for Today/ 14:7–8

Stay away from a foolish man, for you will not find knowledge on his lips. □ The wisdom of the prudent is to give thought to their ways, but the folly of fools is deception.

APRIL 28

Jesus Preaches about the End Times/ Mark 13:1–13

As he [Jesus] was leaving the temple, one of his disciples said to him, "Look, Teacher! What massive stones! What magnificent buildings!"

2"Do you see all these great buildings?" replied Jesus. "Not one stone here will be left on another; every one will be thrown down."

3As Jesus was sitting on the Mount of Olives opposite the temple, Peter, James, John and Andrew asked him privately, 4"Tell us, when will these things happen? And what will be the sign that they are all about to be fulfilled?"

5Jesus said to them: "Watch out that no one deceives you. 6Many will come in my name, claiming, 'I am he,' and will deceive many. [7]When you hear of wars and rumors of wars, do not be alarmed. Such things must happen, but the end is still to come. [8]Nation will rise against nation, and kingdom against kingdom. There will be earthquakes in various places, and famines. These are the beginning of birth pains.

[9]"You must be on your guard. You will be handed over to the local councils and flogged in the synagogues. On account of me you will stand before governors and kings as witnesses to them. [10]And the gospel must first be preached to all nations. [11]Whenever you are arrested and brought to trial, do not worry beforehand about what to say. Just say whatever is given you at the time, for it is not you speaking, but the Holy Spirit.

[12]"Brother will betray brother to death, and a father his child. Children will rebel against their parents and have them put to death. [13]All men will hate you because of me, but he who stands firm to the end will be saved.

A THOUGHT: *What are the signs of the end times? There have been people in every generation since Christ's resurrection claiming to know exactly when Jesus would return. No one has yet been right. Christ will return on God's timetable, not man's. Jesus predicted that many would be misled before his return by false teachers claiming to have revelations from God.*

In Scripture, the one clear sign of Christ's return is that all mankind will see him coming in the clouds. In other words, you do not have to wonder whether a certain person is the Messiah or whether these are the "end times." When Jesus returns, you will know beyond a doubt that it is he. Beware of groups that claim special knowledge of the last days, because no one knows when this time will be. Be cautious about saying, "This is it!" but be bold in your commitment to have your heart and life ready for his return.

Suffering for the Gospel/ 2 Corinthians 6:1–7

As God's fellow workers we urge you not to receive God's grace in vain. [2]For he says,

> "In the time of my favor I heard you,
>   and in the day of salvation I helped you."

I tell you, now is the time of God's favor, now is the day of salvation.

[3]We put no stumbling block in anyone's path, so that our ministry will not be discredited. [4]Rather, as servants of God we commend ourselves in every way: in great

endurance; in troubles, hardships and distresses; [5]in beatings, imprisonments and riots; in hard work, sleepless nights and hunger; [6]in purity, understanding, patience and kindness; in the Holy Spirit and in sincere love; [7]in truthful speech and in the power of God; with weapons of righteousness in the right hand and in the left.

A THOUGHT: *In everything he did, Paul always considered what his actions communicated about Jesus Christ. If you are a believer, you are a minister for God. In the course of each day, non-Christians observe you. Consider whether your actions will keep anyone from God. Don't let your careless or undisciplined actions be another's excuse for rejecting God.*

Proverbs for Today/ 14:9–10

Fools mock at making amends for sin, but goodwill is found among the upright. □ Each heart knows its own bitterness, and no one else can share its joy.

APRIL 29

Prepare for the End/ Mark 13:14–37

"When you see 'the abomination that causes desolation' standing where it does not belong—let the reader understand—then let those who are in Judea flee to the mountains. [15]Let no one on the roof of his house go down or enter the house to take anything out. [16]Let no one in the field go back to get his cloak. [17]How dreadful it will be in those days for pregnant women and nursing mothers! [18]Pray that this will not take place in winter, [19]because those will be days of distress unequaled from the beginning, when God created the world, until now—and never to be equaled again. [20]If the Lord had not cut short those days, no one would survive. But for the sake of the elect, whom he has chosen, he has shortened them. [21]At that time if anyone says to you, 'Look, here is the Christ!' or, 'Look, there he is!' do not believe it. [22]For false Christs and false prophets will appear and perform signs and miracles to deceive the elect—if that were possible. [23]So be on your guard; I have told you everything ahead of time.

24"But in those days, following that distress,

" 'the sun will be darkened,
and the moon will not give its light;
25the stars will fall from the sky,
and the heavenly bodies will be shaken.'

26"At that time men will see the Son of Man coming in clouds with great power and glory. 27And he will send his angels and gather his elect from the four winds, from the ends of the earth to the ends of the heavens.

28"Now learn this lesson from the fig tree: As soon as its twigs get tender and its leaves come out, you know that summer is near. 29Even so, when you see these things happening, you know that it is near, right at the door. 30I tell you the truth, this generation will certainly not pass away until all these things have happened. 31Heaven and earth will pass away, but my words will never pass away.

32"No one knows about that day or hour, not even the angels in heaven, nor the Son, but only the Father. 33Be on guard! Be alert! You do not know when that time will come. 34It's like a man going away: He leaves his house and puts his servants in charge, each with his assigned task, and tells the one at the door to keep watch.

35"Therefore keep watch because you do not know when the owner of the house will come back—whether in the evening, or at midnight, or when the rooster crows, or at dawn. 36If he comes suddenly, do not let him find you sleeping. 37What I say to you, I say to everyone: 'Watch!' "

A THOUGHT: *Is it possible for Christians to be deceived? Yes. So convincing will be the arguments and proofs from deceivers in the end times that it will be difficult not to fall away from Christ. If we are prepared, Jesus says, we can remain faithful, but if we are not prepared we will not endure. To penetrate the disguises of false teachers, we can ask: (1) Have their predictions come true, or do they have to revise them to fit what's already happened? (2) Does any teaching utilize a small section of the Bible to the neglect of the whole? (3) Does the teaching go against what is known in the Bible about God? (4) Are the practices meant to glorify the teacher or Christ? (5) Do the teachings promote hostility toward other Christians?*

Paul's Love for the Corinthians/ 2 Corinthians 6:8–13

Through glory and dishonor, bad report and good report; genuine, yet regarded as impostors; 9known, yet regarded as unknown; dying, and yet we live on; beaten, and yet not killed; [10]sorrowful, yet always rejoicing; poor, yet making many rich; having nothing, and yet possessing everything.

[11]We have spoken freely to you, Corinthians, and opened wide our hearts to you. [12]We are not withholding our affection from you, but you are withholding yours from us. [13]As a fair exchange—I speak as to my children—open wide your hearts also.

A THOUGHT: *What a difference knowing Jesus can make! He turns everything around, caring for us in spite of what the world thinks. Christians don't have to give in to public opinion and pressure. Paul stood true to God whether people praised him or condemned him. He remained active, joyous, and content in the most difficult conditions. Don't let circumstances or people's expectations control you. Be firm as you stand true to God, and refuse to compromise on his standards for living.*

Proverbs for Today/ 14:11–12

The house of the wicked will be destroyed, but the tent of the upright will flourish. □ There is a way that seems right to a man, but in the end it leads to death.

APRIL 30

Judas Betrays Jesus/ Mark 14:1–11

Now the Passover and the Feast of Unleavened Bread were only two days away, and the chief priests and the teachers of the law were looking for some sly way to arrest Jesus and kill him. [2]"But not during the Feast," they said, "or the people may riot."

[3]While he was in Bethany, reclining at the table in the home of a man known as Simon the Leper, a woman came with an alabaster jar of very expensive perfume, made of pure nard. She broke the jar and poured the perfume on his head.

[4]Some of those present were saying indignantly to one another, "Why this waste of perfume? [5]It could have been sold for more than a year's wages and the money given to the poor." And they rebuked her harshly.

⁶"Leave her alone," said Jesus. "Why are you bothering her? She has done a beautiful thing to me. ⁷The poor you will always have with you, and you can help them any time you want. But you will not always have me. ⁸She did what she could. She poured perfume on my body beforehand to prepare for my burial. ⁹I tell you the truth, wherever the gospel is preached throughout the world, what she has done will also be told, in memory of her."

¹⁰Then Judas Iscariot, one of the Twelve, went to the chief priests to betray Jesus to them. ¹¹They were delighted to hear this and promised to give him money. So he watched for an opportunity to hand him over.

A THOUGHT: *Why would Judas want to betray Jesus? Judas, like the other disciples, may have expected Jesus to start a political rebellion and overthrow Rome. As treasurer, Judas certainly assumed (as did the other disciples) that he would be given an important position in Jesus' new government. But when Jesus praised Mary for pouring out the perfume, thought to be worth half a year's salary, Judas may have realized that Jesus' kingdom was not physical or political, but spiritual. Judas' greedy desire for money and status could not be realized if he followed Jesus, so he betrayed him in exchange for money and favor from the religious leaders. We must be careful not to allow our expectations to be a barrier to hearing God's truth.*

Don't Become One with Unbelievers/ 2 Corinthians 6:14—7:4

Do not be yoked together with unbelievers. For what do righteousness and wickedness have in common? Or what fellowship can light have with darkness? ¹⁵What harmony is there between Christ and Belial? What does a believer have in common with an unbeliever? ¹⁶What agreement is there between the temple of God and idols? For we are the temple of the living God. As God has said: "I will live with them and walk among them, and I will be their God, and they will be my people."

¹⁷"Therefore come out from them
　　and be separate,

　　　　　　　　　　　　says the Lord.

　Touch no unclean thing,
　　and I will receive you."
¹⁸"I will be a Father to you,
　　and you will be my sons and daughters,
　　　　　　　　　　　says the Lord Almighty."

7:1Since we have these promises, dear friends, let us purify ourselves from everything that contaminates body and spirit, perfecting holiness out of reverence for God.

2Make room for us in your hearts. We have wronged no one, we have corrupted no one, we have exploited no one. 3I do not say this to condemn you; I have said before that you have such a place in our hearts that we would live or die with you. 4I have great confidence in you; I take great pride in you. I am greatly encouraged; in all our troubles my joy knows no bounds.

A THOUGHT: *Paul urged believers not to form binding relationships with nonbelievers, because this might weaken their Christian commitment, integrity, or standards. Earlier, Paul had explained that this did not mean isolating themselves from nonbelievers, for we have been called to evangelize those who are not Christians. Paul wanted believers to be active in their witness for Christ to nonbelievers, but they should not lock themselves into personal or business relationships which could cause them to compromise their faith. Just as those in business should avoid conflicts of interest, all believers should avoid situations that would force them to divide their loyalties.*

Proverbs for Today/ 14:13–14

Even in laughter the heart may ache, and joy may end in grief. □ The faithless will be fully repaid for their ways, and the good man rewarded for his.

MAY 1

The Last Supper/ Mark 14:12–31

On the first day of the Feast of Unleavened Bread, when it was customary to sacrifice the Passover lamb, Jesus' disciples asked him, "Where do you want us to go and make preparations for you to eat the Passover?"

13So he sent two of his disciples, telling them, "Go into the city, and a man carrying a jar of water will meet you. Follow him. 14Say to the owner of the house he enters, 'The Teacher asks: Where is my guest room, where I may eat the Passover with my disciples?' 15He will show you a large upper room, furnished and ready. Make preparations for us there."

¹⁶The disciples left, went into the city and found things just as Jesus had told them. So they prepared the Passover.

¹⁷When evening came, Jesus arrived with the Twelve. ¹⁸While they were reclining at the table eating, he said, "I tell you the truth, one of you will betray me—one who is eating with me."

¹⁹They were saddened, and one by one they said to him, "Surely not I?"

²⁰"It is one of the Twelve," he replied, "one who dips bread into the bowl with me. ²¹The Son of Man will go just as it is written about him. But woe to that man who betrays the Son of Man! It would be better for him if he had not been born."

²²While they were eating, Jesus took bread, gave thanks and broke it, and gave it to his disciples, saying, "Take it; this is my body."

²³Then he took the cup, gave thanks and offered it to them, and they all drank from it.

²⁴"This is my blood of the covenant, which is poured out for many," he said to them. ²⁵"I tell you the truth, I will not drink again of the fruit of the vine until that day when I drink it anew in the kingdom of God."

²⁶When they had sung a hymn, they went out to the Mount of Olives.

²⁷"You will all fall away," Jesus told them, "for it is written:

" 'I will strike the shepherd,
    and the sheep will be scattered.'

²⁸But after I have risen, I will go ahead of you into Galilee."

²⁹Peter declared, "Even if all fall away, I will not."

³⁰"I tell you the truth," Jesus answered, "today—yes, tonight—before the rooster crows twice you yourself will disown me three times."

³¹But Peter insisted emphatically, "Even if I have to die with you, I will never disown you." And all the others said the same.

A THOUGHT: *Jesus' death for us on the cross seals a new agreement between God and mankind. The old agreement involved forgiveness of sins through the blood of an animal sacrifice. But, instead of a spotless lamb on the altar, Jesus came as the Lamb of God to sacrifice himself to bring forgiveness for sin once and for all. Jesus was the final sacrifice for sins, and his blood sealed the new agreement between God and us (also called the "new covenant" or "new testament"). Now all of us can come to God through Jesus, in full confidence that he will hear us and save us from our sins.*

The Good Report from Titus/ 2 Corinthians 7:5–10

For when we came into Macedonia, this body of ours had no rest, but we were harassed at every turn—conflicts on the outside, fears within. 6But God, who comforts the downcast, comforted us by the coming of Titus, 7and not only by his coming but also by the comfort you had given him. He told us about your longing for me, your deep sorrow, your ardent concern for me, so that my joy was greater than ever.

8Even if I caused you sorrow by my letter, I do not regret it. Though I did regret it—I see that my letter hurt you, but only for a little while— 9yet now I am happy, not because you were made sorry, but because your sorrow led you to repentance. For you became sorrowful as God intended and so were not harmed in any way by us. 10Godly sorrow brings repentance that leads to salvation and leaves no regret, but worldly sorrow brings death.

A THOUGHT: *True repentance means being sorry for our sins and changing our behavior. Many people are sorry only for the effects of their sins or for being caught. Compare Peter's remorse and repentance with Judas' bitterness and suicide. Both denied Christ. One repented and was restored to faith and service; the other took his own life. True repentance should lead us into deeper relationship with God.*

Proverbs for Today/ 14:15–16

A simple man believes anything, but a prudent man gives thought to his steps. □ A wise man fears the LORD and shuns evil, but a fool is hotheaded and reckless.

MAY 2

Jesus Arrested in Gethsemane/ Mark 14:32–52

They went to a place called Gethsemane, and Jesus said to his disciples, "Sit here while I pray." 33He took Peter, James and John along with him, and he began to be deeply distressed and troubled. 34"My soul is overwhelmed with sorrow to the point of death," he said to them. "Stay here and keep watch."

35Going a little farther, he fell to the ground and prayed that if possible the hour might pass from him. 36"*Abba*, Father," he said, "everything is possible for you. Take this cup from me. Yet not what I will, but what you will."

37Then he returned to his disciples and found them sleeping. "Simon," he said to Peter, "are you asleep? Could you not keep watch for one hour? 38Watch and pray so that you will not fall into temptation. The spirit is willing, but the body is weak."

39Once more he went away and prayed the same thing. 40When he came back, he again found them sleeping, because their eyes were heavy. They did not know what to say to him.

41Returning the third time, he said to them, "Are you still sleeping and resting? Enough! The hour has come. Look, the Son of Man is betrayed into the hands of sinners. 42Rise! Let us go! Here comes my betrayer!"

43Just as he was speaking, Judas, one of the Twelve, appeared. With him was a crowd armed with swords and clubs, sent from the chief priests, the teachers of the law, and the elders.

44Now the betrayer had arranged a signal with them: "The one I kiss is the man; arrest him and lead him away under guard." 45Going at once to Jesus, Judas said, "Rabbi!" and kissed him. 46The men seized Jesus and arrested him. 47Then one of those standing near drew his sword and struck the servant of the high priest, cutting off his ear.

48"Am I leading a rebellion," said Jesus, "that you have come out with swords and clubs to capture me? 49Every day I was with you, teaching in the temple courts, and you did not arrest me. But the Scriptures must be fulfilled." 50Then everyone deserted him and fled.

51A young man, wearing nothing but a linen garment, was following Jesus. When they seized him, 52he fled naked, leaving his garment behind.

A THOUGHT: *Was Jesus trying to get out of his task by praying "Take this cup from me"? Jesus expressed his true feelings, but he did not deny or rebel against God's will. He reaffirmed his desire to do what God wanted—"Yet not what I will, but what you will." His prayer highlights the terrible suffering he had to endure—an agony worse than dying, because he had to take on the sins of the whole world. This "cup" was the alienation Jesus knew would occur when he was separated from God, his Father, at the cross. The sinless Son of God took on our sins and was separated in that moment from God in order that we could be saved.*

Paul's Sorrowful Letter/ 2 Corinthians 7:11–16

See what this godly sorrow has produced in you: what earnestness, what eagerness to clear yourselves, what indignation, what alarm, what longing, what concern, what readiness to see justice done. At every point you have proved yourselves to be innocent in this matter. 12So even though I wrote to you, it was not on account of the one who did the wrong or of the injured party, but rather that before God you could see for yourselves how devoted to us you are. 13By all this we are encouraged.

In addition to our own encouragement, we were especially delighted to see how happy Titus was, because his spirit has been refreshed by all of you. 14I had boasted to him about you, and you have not embarrassed me. But just as everything we said to you was true, so our boasting about you to Titus has proved to be true as well. 15And his affection for you is all the greater when he remembers that you were all obedient, receiving him with fear and trembling. 16I am glad I can have complete confidence in you.

A THOUGHT: *It is difficult to hear that we have sinned, and even more difficult to get rid of sin. Paul praised the Corinthians for clearing up an especially troublesome situation. Do you tend to be defensive when confronted? Don't let pride keep you from admitting your sins. Accept confrontation as a tool for growth, and do all you can to correct problems that are pointed out to you.*

Proverbs for Today/ 14:17–19

A quick-tempered man does foolish things, and a crafty man is hated. □ The simple inherit folly, but the prudent are crowned with knowledge. □ Evil men will bow down in the presence of the good, and the wicked at the gates of the righteous.

MAY 3

Jesus Before the Sanhedrin/ Mark 14:53–72

They took Jesus to the high priest, and all the chief priests, elders and teachers of the law came together. 54Peter followed him at a distance, right into the courtyard of the high priest. There he sat with the guards and warmed himself at the fire.

55The chief priests and the whole Sanhedrin were looking for evidence against Jesus so that they could put him to death, but they did not find any. 56Many testified falsely against him, but their statements did not agree.

57Then some stood up and gave this false testimony against him: 58"We heard him say, 'I will destroy this man-made temple and in three days will build another, not made by man.' " 59Yet even then their testimony did not agree.

60Then the high priest stood up before them and asked Jesus, "Are you not going to answer? What is this testimony that these men are bringing against you?" 61But Jesus remained silent and gave no answer.

Again the high priest asked him, "Are you the Christ, the Son of the Blessed One?"

62"I am," said Jesus. "And you will see the Son of Man sitting at the right hand of the Mighty One and coming on the clouds of heaven."

63The high priest tore his clothes. "Why do we need any more witnesses?" he asked. 64"You have heard the blasphemy. What do you think?"

They all condemned him as worthy of death. 65Then some began to spit at him; they blindfolded him, struck him with their fists, and said, "Prophesy!" And the guards took him and beat him.

66While Peter was below in the courtyard, one of the servant girls of the high priest came by. 67When she saw Peter warming himself, she looked closely at him.

"You also were with that Nazarene, Jesus," she said.

68But he denied it. "I don't know or understand what you're talking about," he said, and went out into the entryway.

69When the servant girl saw him there, she said again to those standing around, "This fellow is one of them."

70Again he denied it.

After a little while, those standing near said to Peter, "Surely you are one of them, for you are a Galilean."

71He began to call down curses on himself, and he swore to them, "I don't know this man you're talking about."

72Immediately the rooster crowed the second time. Then Peter remembered the word Jesus had spoken to him: "Before the rooster crows twice you will disown me three times." And he broke down and wept.

A THOUGHT: *This trial by the Sanhedrin had two phases. A small group met at night, and then the full council met at daybreak. They tried Jesus for religious offenses such as calling himself the Son of God, which, according to the Law, was blasphemy. The trial was obviously "fixed," because these religious leaders had already decided to kill Jesus.*

To the first question of the Sanhedrin, Jesus made no reply because the evidence itself was confusing and erroneous. In his response to the second question, Jesus predicted a powerful role reversal. That they would see Jesus sitting at the right hand of God implied that on Judgment Day Jesus would judge them and they would be answering his questions.

Generous Giving Glorifies the Lord/ 2 Corinthians 8:1–8

And now, brothers, we want you to know about the grace that God has given the Macedonian churches. 2Out of the most severe trial, their overflowing joy and their extreme poverty welled up in rich generosity. 3For I testify that they gave as much as they were able, and even beyond their ability. Entirely on their own, 4they urgently pleaded with us for the privilege of sharing in this service to the saints. 5And they did not do as we expected, but they gave themselves first to the Lord and then to us in keeping with God's will. 6So we urged Titus, since he had earlier made a beginning, to bring also to completion this act of grace on your part. 7But just as you excel in everything—in faith, in speech, in knowledge, in complete earnestness and in your love for us—see that you also excel in this grace of giving.

8I am not commanding you, but I want to test the sincerity of your love by comparing it with the earnestness of others.

A THOUGHT: *While making his third missionary journey, Paul was collecting money for the impoverished believers in Jerusalem. The churches in Macedonia—Philippi, Thessalonica, and Beroea—gave money even though they were poor, and they gave more than Paul expected. This was sacrificial giving—they were poor themselves, but they wanted to help. The point of giving is not so much the amount we give, but why and how we give. God does not want gifts given grudgingly. Instead, he wants us to give as these churches did—out of dedication to him, love for fellow believers, the joy of helping those in need, and because it is right to do so. How well does your giving measure up to the standards set by the Macedonian churches?*

Proverbs for Today/ 14:20–21

The poor are shunned even by their neighbors, but the rich have many friends. □ He who despises his neighbor sins, but blessed is he who is kind to the needy.

MAY 4

Jesus on Trial Before Pilate/ Mark 15:1–20

Very early in the morning, the chief priests, with the elders, the teachers of the law and the whole Sanhedrin, reached a decision. They bound Jesus, led him away and handed him over to Pilate.

2"Are you the king of the Jews?" asked Pilate.

"Yes, it is as you say," Jesus replied.

3The chief priests accused him of many things. 4So again Pilate asked him, "Aren't you going to answer? See how many things they are accusing you of."

5But Jesus still made no reply, and Pilate was amazed.

6Now it was the custom at the Feast to release a

prisoner whom the people requested. 7A man called Barabbas was in prison with the insurrectionists who had committed murder in the uprising. 8The crowd came up and asked Pilate to do for them what he usually did.

9"Do you want me to release to you the king of the Jews?" asked Pilate, 10knowing it was out of envy that the chief priests had handed Jesus over to him. 11But the chief priests stirred up the crowd to have Pilate release Barabbas instead.

12"What shall I do, then, with the one you call the king of the Jews?" Pilate asked them.

13"Crucify him!" they shouted.

14"Why? What crime has he committed?" asked Pilate. But they shouted all the louder, "Crucify him!"

15Wanting to satisfy the crowd, Pilate released Barabbas to them. He had Jesus flogged, and handed him over to be crucified.

16The soldiers led Jesus away into the palace (that is, the Praetorium) and called together the whole company of soldiers. 17They put a purple robe on him, then twisted together a crown of thorns and set it on him. 18And they began to call out to him, "Hail, king of the Jews!" 19Again and again they struck him on the head with a staff and spit on him. Falling on their knees, they paid homage to him. 20And when they had mocked him, they took off the purple robe and put his own clothes on him. Then they led him out to crucify him.

A THOUGHT: *Although Pilate knew that Jesus was innocent according to Roman law, Pilate caved in under political pressure. He abandoned what he knew was right. He tried to second-guess the Jewish leaders and give a decision that would please everyone while keeping himself safe. When we lay aside God's clear statements of right and wrong and make decisions based on our audience, we fall into compromise and lawlessness. God promises to honor those who do right, not those who make everyone happy.*

Christ Became Poor for Our Benefit/ 2 Corinthians 8:9–15

For you know the grace of our Lord Jesus Christ, that though he was rich, yet for your sakes he became poor, so that you through his poverty might become rich.

10And here is my advice about what is best for you in this matter: Last year you were the first not only to give but also to have the desire to do so. [11]Now finish the work, so that your eager willingness to do it may be matched by your completion of it, according to your means. [12]For if the willingness is there, the gift is acceptable according to what one has, not according to what he does not have.

[13]Our desire is not that others might be relieved while you are hard pressed, but that there might be equality. [14]At the present time your plenty will supply what they need, so that in turn their plenty will supply what you need. Then there will be equality, [15]as it is written: "He who gathered much did not have too much, and he who gathered little did not have too little."

A THOUGHT: *The Corinthian church had money, and Paul challenged them to share with the Jerusalem Christians just as the Macedonian churches had done. Four principles of giving emerge here: (1) your willingness to give cheerfully is more important than the amount you give; (2) you should strive to fulfill your financial commitments; (3) if you give to others in need, they will in turn help you when you are in need; (4) you should give as a response to Christ, not for anything you can get out of it. How you give reflects your devotion to Christ. These principles apply regardless of your financial condition.*

Proverbs for Today/ 14:22–24

Do not those who plot evil go astray? But those who plan what is good find love and faithfulness. □ All hard work brings a profit, but mere talk leads only to poverty. □ The wealth of the wise is their crown, but the folly of fools yields folly.

MAY 5

Jesus' Crucifixion/ Mark 15:21–32

A certain man from Cyrene, Simon, the father of Alexander and Rufus, was passing by on his way in from the country, and they [the Roman soldiers] forced him to carry the cross. [22]They brought Jesus to the place called Golgotha (which means The Place of the Skull). [23]Then they offered him wine mixed with myrrh, but he did not take it. [24]And they crucified him. Dividing up his clothes, they cast lots to see what each would get.

25It was the third hour when they crucified him. 26The written notice of the charge against him read: THE KING OF THE JEWS. 27They crucified two robbers with him, one on his right and one on his left. * 29Those who passed by hurled insults at him, shaking their heads and saying, "So! You who are going to destroy the temple and build it in three days, 30come down from the cross and save yourself!"

31In the same way the chief priests and the teachers of the law mocked him among themselves. "He saved others," they said, "but he can't save himself! 32Let this Christ, this King of Israel, come down now from the cross, that we may see and believe." Those crucified with him also heaped insults on him.

A THOUGHT: *Jesus could have saved himself, but he endured this suffering because of his love for us. He could have chosen not to take the pain and humiliation; he could have killed those who mocked him—but he suffered through it all because he loved even his enemies. We had a significant part in the drama that afternoon because our sin was on the cross too. Jesus died on that cross for us, and the penalty for our sin was paid by his death. The only adequate response we can make is to confess our sin and freely accept the fact that Jesus paid for it so we wouldn't have to. Don't insult God with indifference toward the greatest act of genuine love in history.*

The Ministry of Titus/ 2 Corinthians 8:16–24

I thank God, who put into the heart of Titus the same concern I have for you. 17For Titus not only welcomed our appeal, but he is coming to you with much enthusiasm and on his own initiative. 18And we are sending along with him the brother who is praised by all the churches for his service to the gospel. 19What is more, he was chosen by the churches to accompany us as we carry the offering, which we administer in order to honor the Lord himself and to show our eagerness to help. 20We want to avoid any criticism of the way we administer this liberal gift. 21For we are taking pains to do what is right, not only in the eyes of the Lord but also in the eyes of men.

22In addition, we are sending with them our brother who has often proved to us in many ways that he is zealous, and now even more so because of his great confidence in you.

*27 Some manuscripts *left,* 28*and the scripture was fulfilled which says, "He was counted with the lawless ones"* (Isaiah 53:12)

23As for Titus, he is my partner and fellow worker among you; as for our brothers, they are representatives of the churches and an honor to Christ. 24Therefore show these men the proof of your love and the reason for our pride in you, so that the churches can see it.

A THOUGHT: *Titus was a true disciple of Christ. He was eager to serve, he took joy in the growth of others, he had integrity, he was a servant, and he was concerned for the needs of others. Let us imitate Titus in his Christlikeness—this kind of character is what true Christian leadership is made of.*

Proverbs for Today/ 14:25

A truthful witness saves lives, but a false witness is deceitful.

MAY 6

The Death and Burial of Jesus/ Mark 15:33–47

At the sixth hour darkness came over the whole land until the ninth hour. 34And at the ninth hour Jesus cried out in a loud voice, *"Eloi, Eloi, lama sabachthani?"*—which means, "My God, my God, why have you forsaken me?"

35When some of those standing near heard this, they said, "Listen, he's calling Elijah."

36One man ran, filled a sponge with wine vinegar, put it on a stick, and offered it to Jesus to drink. "Now leave him alone. Let's see if Elijah comes to take him down," he said.

37With a loud cry, Jesus breathed his last.

38The curtain of the temple was torn in two from top to bottom. 39And when the centurion, who stood there in front of Jesus, heard his cry and saw how he died, he said, "Surely this man was the Son of God!"

40Some women were watching from a distance. Among them were Mary Magdalene, Mary the mother of James the younger and of Joses, and Salome. 41In Galilee these women had followed him and cared for his needs. Many other women who had come up with him to Jerusalem were also there.

42It was Preparation Day (that is, the day before the

Sabbath). So as evening approached, 43Joseph of Arimathea, a prominent member of the Council, who was himself waiting for the kingdom of God, went boldly to Pilate and asked for Jesus' body. 44Pilate was surprised to hear that he was already dead. Summoning the centurion, he asked him if Jesus had already died. 45When he learned from the centurion that it was so, he gave the body to Joseph. 46So Joseph bought some linen cloth, took down the body, wrapped it in the linen, and placed it in a tomb cut out of rock. Then he rolled a stone against the entrance of the tomb. 47Mary Magdalene and Mary the mother of Joses saw where he was laid.

A THOUGHT: *After Jesus died on the cross, Joseph of Arimathea asked for his body and then sealed it in a new tomb. Although an honored member of the Sanhedrin, Joseph was a secret disciple of Jesus. Not all the religious leaders hated Jesus. Joseph risked his reputation as a religious leader to give a proper burial to the One he followed. It is frightening to risk one's reputation even for what is right. If your Christian witness endangers your reputation, consider Joseph. Today he is well known in the Christian church. How many of the other members of the Sanhedrin can you name?*

Paul's Confidence in the Corinthians/ 2 Corinthians 9:1–5

There is no need for me to write to you about this service to the saints. 2For I know your eagerness to help, and I have been boasting about it to the Macedonians, telling them that since last year you in Achaia were ready to give; and your enthusiasm has stirred most of them to action. 3But I am sending the brothers in order that our boasting about you in this matter should not prove hollow, but that you may be ready, as I said you would be. 4For if any Macedonians come with me and find you unprepared, we—not to say anything about you—would be ashamed of having been so confident. 5So I thought it necessary to urge the brothers to visit you in advance and finish the arrangements for the generous gift you had promised. Then it will be ready as a generous gift, not as one grudgingly given.

A THOUGHT: *The example of giving here was at the heart of Jewish piety, for they showed their godliness by sharing with the poor. Christians today have forgotten this central idea of true godly living, largely because it is not tax-deductible! Of course, giving to organizations is still important, but we are urged to fulfill this biblical mandate by helping the poor, whether or not it is tax-deductible.*

Proverbs for Today/ 14:26–27

He who fears the LORD has a secure fortress, and for his children it will be a refuge. The fear of the LORD is a fountain of life, turning a man from the snares of death.

MAY 7

The Resurrection of Jesus/ Mark 16:1–20

When the Sabbath was over, Mary Magdalene, Mary the mother of James, and Salome bought spices so that they might go to anoint Jesus' body. 2Very early on the first day of the week, just after sunrise, they were on their way to the tomb 3and they asked each other, "Who will roll the stone away from the entrance of the tomb?"

4But when they looked up, they saw that the stone, which was very large, had been rolled away. 5As they entered the tomb, they saw a young man dressed in a white robe sitting on the right side, and they were alarmed.

6"Don't be alarmed," he said. "You are looking for Jesus the Nazarene, who was crucified. He has risen! He is not here. See the place where they laid him. 7But go, tell his disciples and Peter, 'He is going ahead of you into Galilee. There you will see him, just as he told you.' "

8Trembling and bewildered, the women went out and fled from the tomb. They said nothing to anyone, because they were afraid.

[The most reliable early manuscripts and other ancient witnesses do not have Mark 16:9–20.]

9When Jesus rose early on the first day of the week, he appeared first to Mary Magdalene, out of whom he had driven seven demons. 10She went and told those who had been with him and who were mourning and weeping. 11When they heard that Jesus was alive and that she had seen him, they did not believe it.

¹²Afterward Jesus appeared in a different form to two of them while they were walking in the country. ¹³These returned and reported it to the rest; but they did not believe them either.

¹⁴Later Jesus appeared to the Eleven as they were eating; he rebuked them for their lack of faith and their stubborn refusal to believe those who had seen him after he had risen.

¹⁵He said to them, "Go into all the world and preach the good news to all creation. ¹⁶Whoever believes and is baptized will be saved, but whoever does not believe will be condemned. ¹⁷And these signs will accompany those who believe: In my name they will drive out demons; they will speak in new tongues; ¹⁸they will pick up snakes with their hands; and when they drink deadly poison, it will not hurt them at all; they will place their hands on sick people, and they will get well."

¹⁹After the Lord Jesus had spoken to them, he was taken up into heaven and he sat at the right hand of God. ²⁰Then the disciples went out and preached everywhere, and the Lord worked with them and confirmed his word by the signs that accompanied it.

A THOUGHT: *The resurrection is vitally important for many reasons: (1) Jesus kept his promise to rise from the dead, so we can believe he will keep all his other promises. (2) The resurrection ensures that the ruler of God's eternal kingdom will be the living Christ, not just an idea, hope, or dream. (3) Christ rose from the dead, giving us the assurance that we also will be resurrected. (4) The power of God that brought Christ's body back from the dead is available to us to bring our morally and spiritually dead selves back to life so we can change and grow. (5) The resurrection provides the substance of the church's witness to the world. We do not merely tell lessons from the life of a good teacher; we proclaim the reality of the resurrection of Jesus Christ.*

God Loves a Cheerful Giver/ 2 Corinthians 9:6–15

Remember this: Whoever sows sparingly will also reap sparingly, and whoever sows generously will also reap generously. ⁷Each man should give what he has decided in his heart to give, not reluctantly or under compulsion, for God loves a cheerful giver. ⁸And God is able to make all grace abound to you, so that in all things at all times, having all that you need, you will abound in every good work. ⁹As it is written:

"He has scattered abroad his gifts to the poor;
    his righteousness endures forever."

10Now he who supplies seed to the sower and bread for food will also supply and increase your store of seed and will enlarge the harvest of your righteousness. 11You will be made rich in every way so that you can be generous on every occasion, and through us your generosity will result in thanksgiving to God.

12This service that you perform is not only supplying the needs of God's people but is also overflowing in many expressions of thanks to God. 13Because of the service by which you have proved yourselves, men will praise God for the obedience that accompanies your confession of the gospel of Christ, and for your generosity in sharing with them and with everyone else. 14And in their prayers for you their hearts will go out to you, because of the surpassing grace God has given you. 15Thanks be to God for his indescribable gift!

A THOUGHT: *People may hesitate to give generously to God if they worry about having enough money left over to meet their own needs. Paul assured the Corinthians that God is able to meet their needs. The person who gives only a little will receive only a little in return. Don't let a lack of faith keep you from giving freely and generously out of a love and concern for others and a desire to further the work of God's kingdom.*

Proverbs for Today/ 14:28–29

A large population is a king's glory, but without subjects a prince is ruined. □ A patient man has great understanding, but a quick-tempered man displays folly.

MAY 8

John the Baptist's Birth Foretold/ Luke 1:1–25

Many have undertaken to draw up an account of the things that have been fulfilled among us, 2just as they were handed down to us by those who from the first were eyewitnesses and servants of the word. 3Therefore, since I myself have carefully investigated everything from the beginning, it seemed good also to me to write an orderly account for you, most excellent Theophilus, 4so that you may know the certainty of the things you have been taught.

5In the time of Herod king of Judea there was a priest named Zechariah, who belonged to the priestly division of Abijah; his wife Elizabeth was also a descendant of Aaron. 6Both of them were upright in the sight of God, observing all the Lord's commandments and regulations blamelessly. 7But they had no children, because Elizabeth was barren; and they were both well along in years.

8Once when Zechariah's division was on duty and he was serving as priest before God, 9he was chosen by lot, according to the custom of the priesthood, to go into the temple of the Lord and burn incense. 10And when the time for the burning of incense came, all the assembled worshipers were praying outside.

11Then an angel of the Lord appeared to him, standing at the right side of the altar of incense. 12When Zechariah saw him, he was startled and was gripped with fear. 13But the angel said to him: "Do not be afraid, Zechariah; your prayer has been heard. Your wife Elizabeth will bear you a son, and you are to give him the name John. 14He will be a joy and delight to you, and many will rejoice because of his birth, 15for he will be great in the sight of the Lord. He is never to take wine or other fermented drink, and he will be filled with the Holy Spirit even from birth. 16Many of the people of Israel will he bring back to the Lord their God. 17And he will go on before the Lord, in the spirit and power of Elijah, to turn the hearts of the fathers to their children and the disobedient to the wisdom of the righteous—to make ready a people prepared for the Lord."

18Zechariah asked the angel, "How can I be sure of this? I am an old man and my wife is well along in years."

19The angel answered, "I am Gabriel. I stand in the presence of God, and I have been sent to speak to you and to tell you this good news. 20And now you will be silent and not able to speak until the day this happens, because you did not believe my words, which will come true at their proper time."

21Meanwhile, the people were waiting for Zechariah and wondering why he stayed so long in the temple. 22When he came out, he could not speak to them. They realized he had seen a vision in the temple, for he kept making signs to them but remained unable to speak.

23When his time of service was completed, he returned home. 24After this his wife Elizabeth became pregnant and for five months remained in seclusion. 25"The Lord has done this for me," she said. "In these days he has shown his favor and taken away my disgrace among the people."

A THOUGHT: *Zacharias, while offering incense on the altar, was also praying, perhaps for a son or for the coming of the Messiah. In either case, his prayer was answered. He would soon have a son who would prepare the way for the Messiah. God answers prayer in his own way and in his own time. He worked in an "impossible" situation—Zacharias' wife was barren—to bring about the fulfillment of all the prophecies concerning the coming of the Messiah. If we want to have our prayers answered, we must be open to what God can do in impossible situations. And we must wait for him to work in his way, in his time.*

God's Mighty Weapons/ 2 Corinthians 10:1–6

By the meekness and gentleness of Christ, I appeal to you—I, Paul, who am "timid" when face to face with you, but "bold" when away! 2I beg you that when I come I may not have to be as bold as I expect to be toward some people who think that we live by the standards of this world. 3For though we live in the world, we do not wage war as the world does. 4The weapons we fight with are not the weapons of the world. On the contrary, they have divine power to demolish strongholds. 5We demolish arguments and every pretension that sets itself up against the knowledge of God, and we take captive every thought to make it obedient to Christ. 6And we will be ready to punish every act of disobedience, once your obedience is complete.

A THOUGHT: *The Christian must choose whose methods to use, God's or man's. Paul assures us that God's mighty weapons—prayer, faith, hope, love, God's Word—are powerful and effective! When dealing with the pride that keeps people from a relationship with Christ, we may be tempted to use our own methods. But nothing can break down these barriers like God's weapons.*

Proverbs for Today/ 14:30–31

A heart at peace gives life to the body, but envy rots the bones. □ He who oppresses the poor shows contempt for their Maker, but whoever is kind to the needy honors God.

MAY 9

Jesus' Birth Foretold/ Luke 1:26–56

In the sixth month, God sent the angel Gabriel to Nazareth, a town in Galilee, 27to a virgin pledged to be married to a man named Joseph, a descendant of David. The virgin's name was Mary. 28The angel went to her and said, "Greetings, you who are highly favored! The Lord is with you."

29Mary was greatly troubled at his words and wondered what kind of greeting this might be. 30But the angel said to her, "Do not be afraid, Mary, you have found favor with God. 31You will be with child and give birth to a son, and you are to give him the name Jesus. 32He will be great and will be called the Son of the Most High. The Lord God will give him the throne of his father David, 33and he will reign over the house of Jacob forever; his kingdom will never end."

34"How will this be," Mary asked the angel, "since I am a virgin?"

35The angel answered, "The Holy Spirit will come upon you, and the power of the Most High will overshadow you. So the holy one to be born will be called the Son of God. 36Even Elizabeth your relative is going to have a child in her old age, and she who was said to be barren is in her sixth month. 37For nothing is impossible with God."

38"I am the Lord's servant," Mary answered. "May it be to me as you have said." Then the angel left her.

39At that time Mary got ready and hurried to a town in the hill country of Judea, 40where she entered Zechariah's home and greeted Elizabeth. 41When Elizabeth heard Mary's greeting, the baby leaped in her womb, and Elizabeth was filled with the Holy Spirit. 42In a loud voice she exclaimed: "Blessed are you among women, and blessed is the child you will bear! 43But why am I so favored, that the mother of my Lord should come to me? 44As soon as the sound of your greeting reached my ears, the baby in my womb leaped for joy. 45Blessed is she who has believed that what the Lord has said to her will be accomplished!"

46And Mary said:

"My soul glorifies the Lord
47 and my spirit rejoices in God my Savior,

⁴⁸for he has been mindful
　　of the humble state of his servant.
　From now on all generations will call me blessed,
⁴⁹ for the Mighty One has done great things for
　　　me—
　　holy is his name.
⁵⁰His mercy extends to those who fear him,
　　from generation to generation.
⁵¹He has performed mighty deeds with his arm;
　　he has scattered those who are proud in their
　　　inmost thoughts.
⁵²He has brought down rulers from their thrones
　　but has lifted up the humble.
⁵³He has filled the hungry with good things
　　but has sent the rich away empty.
⁵⁴He has helped his servant Israel,
　　remembering to be merciful
⁵⁵to Abraham and his descendants forever,
　　even as he said to our fathers."

⁵⁶Mary stayed with Elizabeth for about three months and
then returned home.

A THOUGHT: *A young unmarried girl who became pregnant risked
disaster. Unless the father of the child agreed to marry her, she would
probably remain unmarried for life. If her own father rejected her,
she could be forced into begging or prostitution in order to earn her
living. And Mary, with her story about being made pregnant by the
Holy Spirit, risked being considered crazy as well. Still she said,
despite the possible costs, "May it be to me as you have said." When
Mary said that, she didn't know about the tremendous blessing she
would receive. She only knew God was asking her to serve him, and
she willingly obeyed. Don't wait to see the bottom line before offering
your life to God. Offer yourself willingly, even when the results of
doing so look disastrous.*

The Shallow Vision of the Corinthians/
2 Corinthians 10:7–12

You are looking only on the surface of things. If anyone is
confident that he belongs to Christ, he should consider
again that we belong to Christ just as much as he. ⁸For even
if I boast somewhat freely about the authority the Lord
gave us for building you up rather than pulling you down,
I will not be ashamed of it. ⁹I do not want to seem to be

trying to frighten you with my letters. 10For some say, "His letters are weighty and forceful, but in person he is unimpressive and his speaking amounts to nothing." 11Such people should realize that what we are in our letters when we are absent, we will be in our actions when we are present.

12We do not dare to classify or compare ourselves with some who commend themselves. When they measure themselves by themselves and compare themselves with themselves, they are not wise.

A THOUGHT: *Paul criticized the false teachers who tried to prove their goodness by comparing themselves with others rather than with God. When we compare ourselves with others, we may feel proud because we think we're better. But when we measure ourselves against God's standards, it becomes obvious that we're not nearly good enough. Don't worry about how other people live. Instead, continually ask how your life measures up to what God wants you to be and how your life compares to that of Jesus Christ.*

Proverbs for Today/ 14:32–33

When calamity comes, the wicked are brought down, but even in death the righteous have a refuge. □ Wisdom reposes in the heart of the discerning and even among fools she lets herself be known.

MAY 10

The Birth of John the Baptist/ Luke 1:57–80

When it was time for Elizabeth to have her baby, she gave birth to a son. 58Her neighbors and relatives heard that the Lord had shown her great mercy, and they shared her joy.

59On the eighth day they came to circumcise the child, and they were going to name him after his father Zechariah, 60but his mother spoke up and said, "No! He is to be called John."

61They said to her, "There is no one among your relatives who has that name."

62Then they made signs to his father, to find out what he would like to name the child. 63He asked for a writing tablet, and to everyone's astonishment he wrote, "His name is John." 64Immediately his mouth was opened and his tongue was loosed, and he began to speak, praising God. 65The neighbors were all filled with awe, and throughout the hill country of Judea people were talking about all these things. 66Everyone who heard this wondered about it, asking, "What then is this child going to be?" For the Lord's hand was with him.

67His father Zechariah was filled with the Holy Spirit and prophesied:

68"Praise be to the Lord, the God of Israel,
   because he has come and has redeemed his
      people.
69He has raised up a horn of salvation for us
   in the house of his servant David
70(as he said through his holy prophets of long ago),
71salvation from our enemies
   and from the hand of all who hate us—
72to show mercy to our fathers
   and to remember his holy covenant,
73 the oath he swore to our father Abraham:
74to rescue us from the hand of our enemies,
   and to enable us to serve him without fear
75 in holiness and righteousness before him all our
      days.

76And you, my child, will be called a prophet of the
      Most High;
   for you will go on before the Lord to prepare the
      way for him,
77to give his people the knowledge of salvation
   through the forgiveness of their sins,
78because of the tender mercy of our God,
   by which the rising sun will come to us from
      heaven
79to shine on those living in darkness
   and in the shadow of death,
   to guide our feet into the path of peace."

80And the child grew and became strong in spirit; and he lived in the desert until he appeared publicly to Israel.

A THOUGHT: *Zacharias praised God with his first words after months of silence. In a song that is often called the Benedictus (named after its first words in the Latin translation of this passage), Zacharias prophesied the coming of a Savior who would redeem his people, and he predicted that his son John would prepare the Messiah's way. All the Old Testament prophecies were coming true—no wonder Zacharias praised God! The Messiah would come in his lifetime, and his son had been chosen to pave the way.*

Boast in the Lord/ 2 Corinthians 10:13–18

We, however, will not boast beyond proper limits, but will confine our boasting to the field God has assigned to us, a field that reaches even to you. 14We are not going too far in our boasting, as would be the case if we had not come to you, for we did get as far as you with the gospel of Christ. 15Neither do we go beyond our limits by boasting of work done by others. Our hope is that, as your faith continues to grow, our area of activity among you will greatly expand, 16so that we can preach the gospel in the regions beyond you. For we do not want to boast about work already done in another man's territory. 17But, "Let him who boasts boast in the Lord." 18For it is not the one who commends himself who is approved, but the one whom the Lord commends.

A THOUGHT: *When we do something well, we want to tell others and be recognized. But recognition is dangerous—it can lead to inflated pride. How much better to seek the praise of God rather than people. Interestingly, these two are usually opposites. To earn God's praise means giving up the praise of others. How should you live differently to receive God's commendation?*

Proverbs for Today/ 14:34–35

Righteousness exalts a nation, but sin is a disgrace to any people. □ A king delights in a wise servant, but a shameful servant incurs his wrath.

Jesus Born in Bethlehem/ Luke 2:1–20

In those days Caesar Augustus issued a decree that a census should be taken of the entire Roman world. 2(This was the first census that took place while Quirinius was governor of Syria.) 3And everyone went to his own town to register.

4So Joseph also went up from the town of Nazareth in Galilee to Judea, to Bethlehem the town of David, because he belonged to the house and line of David. 5He went there to register with Mary, who was pledged to be married to him and was expecting a child. 6While they were there, the time came for the baby to be born, 7and she gave birth to her firstborn, a son. She wrapped him in cloths and placed him in a manger, because there was no room for them in the inn.

8And there were shepherds living out in the fields nearby, keeping watch over their flocks at night. 9An angel of the Lord appeared to them, and the glory of the Lord shone around them, and they were terrified. 10But the angel said to them, "Do not be afraid. I bring you good news of great joy that will be for all the people. 11Today in the town of David a Savior has been born to you; he is Christ the Lord. 12This will be a sign to you: You will find a baby wrapped in cloths and lying in a manger."

13Suddenly a great company of the heavenly host appeared with the angel, praising God and saying,

14"Glory to God in the highest,
and on earth peace to men on whom his favor rests."

15When the angels had left them and gone into heaven, the shepherds said to one another, "Let's go to Bethlehem and see this thing that has happened, which the Lord has told us about."

16So they hurried off and found Mary and Joseph, and the baby, who was lying in the manger. 17When they had seen him, they spread the word concerning what had been told them about this child, 18and all who heard it were amazed at what the shepherds said to them. ¹⁹But Mary treasured up all these things and pondered them in her heart. ²⁰The shepherds returned, glorifying and praising God for all the things they had heard and seen, which were just as they had been told.

A THOUGHT: *The greatest event in history had just happened! The Messiah was born! For ages the Jews had waited for this, and when it finally happened, the announcement came to humble shepherds. The good news about Jesus is that he comes to all, including the plain and the ordinary. He comes to anyone with a heart humble enough to accept him. Whoever you are, whatever you do, you can have Jesus in your life. Don't think you need extraordinary qualifications—he accepts you as you are.*

Paul's Concern for the Corinthians/ 2 Corinthians 11:1–6

I hope you will put up with a little of my foolishness; but you are already doing that. ²I am jealous for you with a godly jealousy. I promised you to one husband, to Christ, so that I might present you as a pure virgin to him. ³But I am afraid that just as Eve was deceived by the serpent's cunning, your minds may somehow be led astray from your sincere and pure devotion to Christ. ⁴For if someone comes to you and preaches a Jesus other than the Jesus we preached, or if you receive a different spirit from the one you received, or a different gospel from the one you accepted, you put up with it easily enough. ⁵But I do not think I am in the least inferior to those "super-apostles." ⁶I may not be a trained speaker, but I do have knowledge. We have made this perfectly clear to you in every way.

A THOUGHT: *The Corinthians' pure and simple devotion to Christ was being threatened by false teaching. Paul did not want the believers to lose their single-minded love for Christ. Keeping Christ first in our lives can be very difficult when we have so many distractions threatening to sidetrack our faith. As Eve lost her focus by listening to the serpent, we too can lose our focus by letting our lives become overcrowded and confused. Is there anything that threatens your ability to keep Christ first in your life? How can you minimize the distractions that threaten your devotion to Christ?*

Proverbs for Today/ 15:1–3

A gentle answer turns away wrath, but a harsh word stirs up anger. The tongue of the wise commends knowledge, but the mouth of the fool gushes folly. □ The eyes of the Lord are everywhere, keeping watch on the wicked and the good.

MAY 12

Simeon and Anna Recognize the Messiah/ Luke 2:21–40

On the eighth day, when it was time to circumcise him, he was named Jesus, the name the angel had given him before he had been conceived.

22When the time of their purification according to the Law of Moses had been completed, Joseph and Mary took him to Jerusalem to present him to the Lord 23(as it is written in the Law of the Lord, "Every firstborn male is to be consecrated to the Lord"), 24and to offer a sacrifice in keeping with what is said in the Law of the Lord: "a pair of doves or two young pigeons."

25Now there was a man in Jerusalem called Simeon, who was righteous and devout. He was waiting for the consolation of Israel, and the Holy Spirit was upon him. 26It had been revealed to him by the Holy Spirit that he would not die before he had seen the Lord's Christ. 27Moved by the Spirit, he went into the temple courts. When the parents brought in the child Jesus to do for him what the custom of the Law required, 28Simeon took him in his arms and praised God, saying:

29"Sovereign Lord, as you have promised,
　　you now dismiss your servant in peace.
30For my eyes have seen your salvation,
31　which you have prepared in the sight of all
　　　　people,
32a light for revelation to the Gentiles
　　and for glory to your people Israel."

33The child's father and mother marveled at what was said about him. 34Then Simeon blessed them and said to Mary, his mother: "This child is destined to cause the falling and rising of many in Israel, and to be a sign that will be spoken against, 35so that the thoughts of many hearts will be revealed. And a sword will pierce your own soul too."

36There was also a prophetess, Anna, the daughter of Phanuel, of the tribe of Asher. She was very old; she had lived with her husband seven years after her marriage, 37and then was a widow until she was eighty-four. She never left the temple but worshiped night and day, fasting and praying. 38Coming up to them at that very moment, she gave thanks to God and spoke about the child to all who were looking forward to the redemption of Jerusalem.

39When Joseph and Mary had done everything required by the Law of the Lord, they returned to Galilee to their own town of Nazareth. 40And the child grew and became strong; he was filled with wisdom, and the grace of God was upon him.

A THOUGHT: *Although Simeon and Anna were very old, they still hoped to see the Messiah. Led by the Holy Spirit, they were among the first to bear witness to Jesus. In the Jewish culture, elders were respected, and Simeon's and Anna's prophecies carried extra weight because they were not young. Our society, however, values youthfulness over wisdom, and potential contributions by the elderly are often ignored. As Christians, we should reverse those values wherever we can. Encourage older people to share their wisdom and experience. Listen carefully when they speak. Offer them your friendship and help them find ways to continue to serve God.*

True and False Apostleship/ 2 Corinthians 11:7–15

Was it a sin for me to lower myself in order to elevate you by preaching the gospel of God to you free of charge? 8I robbed other churches by receiving support from them so as to serve you. 9And when I was with you and needed something, I was not a burden to anyone, for the brothers who came from Macedonia supplied what I needed. I have kept myself from being a burden to you in any way, and will continue to do so. 10As surely as the truth of Christ is in me, nobody in the regions of Achaia will stop this boasting of mine. 11Why? Because I do not love you? God knows I do! 12And I will keep on doing what I am doing in order to cut the ground from under those who want an opportunity to be considered equal with us in the things they boast about.

13For such men are false apostles, deceitful workmen,

masquerading as apostles of Christ. [14]And no wonder, for Satan himself masquerades as an angel of light. [15]It is not surprising, then, if his servants masquerade as servants of righteousness. Their end will be what their actions deserve.

A THOUGHT: *The Corinthians may have thought that preachers could be judged by how much money they demanded. A good speaker would charge a large sum, a fair speaker would be a little cheaper, and a poor speaker would speak for free. The false teachers may have argued that because Paul asked no fee for his preaching, he must be an amateur, with little authority. Believers today must be careful not to assume that every speaker who is well known and receives large sums of money has something valuable to say. Don't be fooled by external appearances. Our impressions alone are not an accurate indicator of who is or isn't a true follower of Christ. It helps to ask these questions: (1) Do their teachings confirm Scripture? (2) Do the teachers affirm and proclaim that Jesus Christ is God who came into the world as a man to save people from their sins? (3) Is their lifestyle consistent with biblical morality?*

Proverbs for Today/ 15:4

The tongue that brings healing is a tree of life, but a deceitful tongue crushes the spirit.

MAY 13

Jesus with the Teachers of the Law/ Luke 2:41–52

Every year his parents [Mary and Joseph] went to Jerusalem for the Feast of the Passover. [42]When he [Jesus] was twelve years old, they went up to the Feast, according to the custom. [43]After the Feast was over, while his parents were returning home, the boy Jesus stayed behind in Jerusalem, but they were unaware of it. [44]Thinking he was in their company, they traveled on for a day. Then they began looking for him among their relatives and friends. [45]When they did not find him, they went back to Jerusalem to look for him. [46]After three days they found him in the temple courts, sitting among the teachers, listening to them and asking them questions. [47]Everyone who heard him was amazed at his understanding and his answers. [48]When his parents saw him, they were astonished. His mother said to him, "Son, why have you treated us like this? Your father and I have been anxiously searching for you."

⁴⁹"Why were you searching for me?" he asked. "Didn't you know I had to be in my Father's house?" ⁵⁰But they did not understand what he was saying to them.

⁵¹Then he went down to Nazareth with them and was obedient to them. But his mother treasured all these things in her heart. ⁵²And Jesus grew in wisdom and stature, and in favor with God and men.

A THOUGHT: *At age 12, Jesus was considered almost an adult, so he didn't spend a lot of time with his parents during the festival. Those who attended these festivals often traveled in caravans for protection from robbers along the roads throughout Israel. It was customary for the women and children to travel at the front of the caravan, with the men bringing up the rear. A 12-year-old boy could have been in either group, and Mary and Joseph assumed Jesus was with the others. But when the caravan left Jerusalem, Jesus stayed behind, absorbed in his discussion with the religious leaders, amazing them with his wisdom.*

Paul's Apostleship Validated Through Suffering/ 2 Corinthians 11:16–33

I repeat: Let no one take me for a fool. But if you do, then receive me just as you would a fool, so that I may do a little boasting. ¹⁷In this self-confident boasting I am not talking as the Lord would, but as a fool. ¹⁸Since many are boasting in the way the world does, I too will boast. ¹⁹You gladly put up with fools since you are so wise! ²⁰In fact, you even put up with anyone who enslaves you or exploits you or takes advantage of you or pushes himself forward or slaps you in the face. ²¹To my shame I admit that we were too weak for that!

What anyone else dares to boast about—I am speaking as a fool—I also dare to boast about. ²²Are they Hebrews? So am I. Are they Israelites? So am I. Are they Abraham's descendants? So am I. ²³Are they servants of Christ? (I am out of my mind to talk like this.) I am more. I have worked much harder, been in prison more frequently, been flogged more severely, and been exposed to death again and again. ²⁴Five times I received from the Jews the forty lashes minus one. ²⁵Three times I was beaten with rods, once I was stoned, three times I was shipwrecked, I spent a night and a day in the open sea, ²⁶I have been constantly on the move. I have been in danger from rivers, in danger from bandits, in danger from my own countrymen, in danger from Gentiles; in danger in the city, in danger in the country, in danger at sea; and in danger from false brothers. 27I have labored and toiled and have often gone without sleep; I have known hunger and thirst and have often gone without food; I have been cold and naked. 28Besides everything else, I face daily the pressure of my concern for all the churches. 29Who is weak, and I do not feel weak? Who is led into sin, and I do not inwardly burn?

30If I must boast, I will boast of the things that show my weakness. 31The God and Father of the Lord Jesus, who is to be praised forever, knows that I am not lying. 32In Damascus the governor under King Aretas had the city of the Damascenes guarded in order to arrest me. 33But I was lowered in a basket from a window in the wall and slipped through his hands.

A THOUGHT: *Paul was angry that the false teachers had impressed and deceived the Corinthians. He had to reestablish his credibility and authority by listing the trials he had endured in his service for Christ. These trials showed that he was sacrificing his life for the gospel, something the false teachers would never do. The trials and hurts you have experienced for Christ's sake have built your character, demonstrated your faith, and prepared you to work for the Lord.*

Proverbs for Today/ 15:5–7

A fool spurns his father's discipline, but whoever heeds correction shows prudence. □ The house of the righteous contains great treasure, but the income of the wicked brings them trouble. □ The lips of the wise spread knowledge; not so the hearts of fools.

MAY 14

John the Baptist Warns of Coming Judgment/ Luke 3:1–18

In the fifteenth year of the reign of Tiberius Caesar—when Pontius Pilate was governor of Judea, Herod tetrarch of Galilee, his brother Philip tetrarch of Iturea and Traconitis, and Lysanias tetrarch of Abilene— ²during the high priest-hood of Annas and Caiaphas, the word of God came to John son of Zechariah in the desert. ³He went into all the country around the Jordan, preaching a baptism of repentance for the forgiveness of sins. ⁴As is written in the book of the words of Isaiah the prophet:

"A voice of one calling in the desert,
'Prepare the way for the Lord,
    make straight paths for him.
⁵Every valley shall be filled in,
    every mountain and hill made low.
The crooked roads shall become straight,
    the rough ways smooth.
⁶And all mankind will see God's salvation.' "

⁷John said to the crowds coming out to be baptized by him, "You brood of vipers! Who warned you to flee from the coming wrath? ⁸Produce fruit in keeping with repen-tance. And do not begin to say to yourselves, 'We have Abraham as our father.' For I tell you that out of these stones God can raise up children for Abraham. ⁹The ax is already at the root of the trees, and every tree that does not produce good fruit will be cut down and thrown into the fire."

¹⁰"What should we do then?" the crowd asked.

¹¹John answered, "The man with two tunics should share with him who has none, and the one who has food should do the same."

¹²Tax collectors also came to be baptized. "Teacher," they asked, "what should we do?"

¹³"Don't collect any more than you are required to," he told them.

¹⁴Then some soldiers asked him, "And what should we do?"

He replied, "Don't extort money and don't accuse people falsely—be content with your pay."

¹⁵The people were waiting expectantly and were all won-dering in their hearts if John might possibly be the Christ. ¹⁶John answered them all, "I baptize you with water. But one more powerful than I will come, the thongs of whose sandals I am not worthy to untie. He will baptize you with the Holy Spirit and with fire. ¹⁷His winnowing fork is in his

hand to clear his threshing floor and to gather the wheat into his barn, but he will burn up the chaff with unquenchable fire." 18And with many other words John exhorted the people and preached the good news to them.

A THOUGHT: *Repentance has two sides—turning away from sins, and turning toward God. To be forgiven, we must do both. We can't just say we believe and then live any way we want to, neither can we simply live a morally correct life without reference to God, because that alone cannot bring forgiveness from sin. Faith and works are inseparable. Faith without works is a lifeless faith. Jesus' harshest words were to the respectable religious leaders who lacked true faith. Repentance must be tied to action, or it isn't real. Is the fruit of your faith ripening as your faith grows, or is it rotting as you fail to act upon what God shows you?*

God's Grace Is Sufficient/ 2 Corinthians 12:1–10

I must go on boasting. Although there is nothing to be gained, I will go on to visions and revelations from the Lord. 2I know a man in Christ who fourteen years ago was caught up to the third heaven. Whether it was in the body or out of the body I do not know—God knows. 3And I know that this man—whether in the body or apart from the body I do not know, but God knows— 4was caught up to paradise. He heard inexpressible things, things that man is not permitted to tell. 5I will boast about a man like that, but I will not boast about myself, except about my weaknesses. 6Even if I should choose to boast, I would not be a fool, because I would be speaking the truth. But I refrain, so no one will think more of me than is warranted by what I do or say.

7To keep me from becoming conceited because of these surpassingly great revelations, there was given me a thorn in my flesh, a messenger of Satan, to torment me. 8Three times I pleaded with the Lord to take it away from me. 9But he said to me, "My grace is sufficient for you, for my power is made perfect in weakness." Therefore I will boast all the more gladly about my weaknesses, so that Christ's power may rest on me. 10That is why, for Christ's sake, I delight in weaknesses, in insults, in hardships, in persecutions, in difficulties. For when I am weak, then I am strong.

A THOUGHT: *Although God did not remove Paul's physical affliction, he promised to demonstrate his power in Paul. The fact that God's power shows up in weak people should give us courage. When we are strong in abilities or resources, we are tempted to do God's work on our own, and that leads to pride. We must rely on God for our effectiveness rather than on our own energy, effort, or talent. Our weakness not only helps develop Christian character, it also deepens our worship; in admitting our weakness, we affirm God's strength. When we are weak, and when we allow God to fill us with his power, then we are stronger than we could ever be on our own. We must depend on God—only his power makes us effective for him and does work that has lasting value.*

Proverbs for Today/ 15:8–10

The LORD detests the sacrifice of the wicked, but the prayer of the upright pleases him. The LORD detests the way of the wicked but he loves those who pursue righteousness. Stern discipline awaits him who leaves the path; he who hates correction will die.

MAY 15

The Baptism of Jesus/ Luke 3:19–23a

But when John rebuked Herod the tetrarch because of Herodias, his brother's wife, and all the other evil things he had done, 20Herod added this to them all: He locked John up in prison.

21When all the people were being baptized, Jesus was baptized too. And as he was praying, heaven was opened 22and the Holy Spirit descended on him in bodily form like a dove. And a voice came from heaven: "You are my Son, whom I love; with you I am well pleased."

23Now Jesus himself was about thirty years old when he began his ministry.

A THOUGHT: *Luke emphasizes Jesus' humanness. He came to humble parents, unannounced except to shepherds and foreigners. This baptism was the first public declaration of his ministry. Instead of going to Jerusalem and identifying with the established religious leaders, Jesus went to a river and identified himself with those who were repenting of sin. When Jesus, at age twelve, visited the Temple, he understood his mission. Eighteen years later, at his baptism, he began carrying it out. And as he prayed, God spoke to him and confirmed his decision to act. God broke into human history in Jesus Christ.*

Paul's Sacrifice for His Children/
2 Corinthians 12:11–15

I have made a fool of myself, but you drove me to it. I ought to have been commended by you, for I am not in the least inferior to the "super-apostles," even though I am nothing. 12The things that mark an apostle—signs, wonders and miracles—were done among you with great perseverance. 13How were you inferior to the other churches, except that I was never a burden to you? Forgive me this wrong!

14Now I am ready to visit you for the third time, and I will not be a burden to you, because what I want is not your possessions but you. After all, children should not have to save up for their parents, but parents for their children. 15So I will very gladly spend for you everything I have and expend myself as well. If I love you more, will you love me less?

A THOUGHT: *Paul is not merely revealing his feelings; he is defending his authority as an apostle of Jesus Christ. He was hurt that the church in Corinth was doubting and questioning him, but he was defending himself for the cause of the gospel, not to satisfy his ego. When you are "put on trial," do you think only about saving your reputation or are you more concerned about what people will think about Christ?*

Proverbs for Today/ 15:11

Death and Destruction lie open before the LORD— how much more the hearts of men!

MAY 16

The Genealogy of Jesus/ Luke 3:23b–38

He [Jesus] was the son, so it was thought, of Joseph,

the son of Heli, 24the son of Matthat,
the son of Levi, the son of Melki,
the son of Jannai, the son of Joseph,
25the son of Mattathias, the son of Amos,
the son of Nahum, the son of Esli,
the son of Naggai, 26the son of Maath,
the son of Mattathias, the son of Semein,

the son of Josech, the son of Joda,
27the son of Joanan, the son of Rhesa,
the son of Zerubbabel, the son of Shealtiel,
the son of Neri, 28the son of Melki,
the son of Addi, the son of Cosam,
the son of Elmadam, the son of Er,
29the son of Joshua, the son of Eliezer,
the son of Jorim, the son of Matthat,
the son of Levi, 30the son of Simeon,
the son of Judah, the son of Joseph,
the son of Jonam, the son of Eliakim,
31the son of Melea, the son of Menna,
the son of Mattatha, the son of Nathan,
the son of David, 32the son of Jesse,
the son of Obed, the son of Boaz,
the son of Salmon, the son of Nahshon,
33the son of Amminadab, the son of Ram,
the son of Hezron, the son of Perez,
the son of Judah, 34the son of Jacob,
the son of Isaac, the son of Abraham,
the son of Terah, the son of Nahor,
35the son of Serug, the son of Reu,
the son of Peleg, the son of Eber,
the son of Shelah, 36the son of Cainan,
the son of Arphaxad, the son of Shem,
the son of Noah, the son of Lamech,
37the son of Methuselah, the son of Enoch,
the son of Jared, the son of Mahalalel,
the son of Kenan, 38the son of Enosh,
the son of Seth, the son of Adam,
the son of God.

A THOUGHT: *Here Jesus' genealogy seems to be traced back through Mary. The genealogy recorded in Matthew 1:1–17 traces his line through Joseph, his legal, but not biological father. Matthew's genealogy goes back to Abraham and shows that Jesus was related to all Jews. Luke's goes back to Adam, showing he is related to all human beings. This is consistent with Luke's picture of Jesus as the Savior of the whole world.*

Paul Fears Another Sorrowful Visit/ 2 Corinthians 12:16–21

Be that as it may, I have not been a burden to you. Yet, crafty fellow that I am, I caught you by trickery! 17Did I exploit you through any of the men I sent you? 18I urged Titus to go to you and I sent our brother with him. Titus did not exploit you, did he? Did we not act in the same spirit and follow the same course?

19Have you been thinking all along that we have been defending ourselves to you? We have been speaking in the sight of God as those in Christ; and everything we do, dear friends, is for your strengthening. 20For I am afraid that when I come I may not find you as I want you to be, and you may not find me as you want me to be. I fear that there may be quarreling, jealousy, outbursts of anger, factions, slander, gossip, arrogance and disorder. 21I am afraid that when I come again my God will humble me before you, and I will be grieved over many who have sinned earlier and have not repented of the impurity, sexual sin and debauchery in which they have indulged.

A THOUGHT: *After reading this catalog of sins, it is hard to believe that Paul is referring to the same group of people which he described as not lacking "any spiritual gift" (1 Corinthians 1:7). Paul feared that the practices of wicked Corinth had invaded the congregation, and he wrote sternly in hope that they would straighten up their lives before he arrived. We must live differently than unbelievers, not letting secular society dictate how we are to live.*

Proverbs for Today/ 15:12–14

A mocker resents correction; he will not consult the wise. □ A happy heart makes the face cheerful, but heartache crushes the spirit. □ The discerning heart seeks knowledge, but the mouth of a fool feeds on folly.

MAY 17

Jesus Tempted by Satan/ Luke 4:1–13

Jesus, full of the Holy Spirit, returned from the Jordan and was led by the Spirit in the desert, 2where for forty days he was tempted by the devil. He ate nothing during those days, and at the end of them he was hungry.

3The devil said to him, "If you are the Son of God, tell this stone to become bread."

⁴Jesus answered, "It is written: 'Man does not live on bread alone.'"

⁵The devil led him up to a high place and showed him in an instant all the kingdoms of the world. ⁶And he said to him, "I will give you all their authority and splendor, for it has been given to me, and I can give it to anyone I want to. ⁷So if you worship me, it will all be yours."

⁸Jesus answered, "It is written: 'Worship the Lord your God and serve him only.'"

⁹The devil led him to Jerusalem and had him stand on the highest point of the temple. "If you are the Son of God," he said, "throw yourself down from here. ¹⁰For it is written:

" 'He will command his angels concerning you
    to guard you carefully;
¹¹they will lift you up in their hands,
    so that you will not strike your foot against a
        stone.'"

¹²Jesus answered, "It says: 'Do not put the Lord your God to the test.'"

¹³When the devil had finished all this tempting, he left him until an opportune time.

A THOUGHT: *Knowing and obeying God's Word is an effective weapon against temptation. Jesus used Scripture to counter Satan's attacks, and you can too. But to use it effectively you must have faith in God's promises, because Satan also knows Scripture and is adept at twisting it to suit his purpose. Obeying the Scriptures is more important than simply having a verse to quote, so read them daily and apply them to your life. Then your "sword" will always be sharp.*

Paul's Warnings/ 2 Corinthians 13:1–6

This will be my third visit to you. "Every matter must be established by the testimony of two or three witnesses." ²I already gave you a warning when I was with you the second time. I now repeat it while absent: On my return I will not spare those who sinned earlier or any of the others, ³since you are demanding proof that Christ is speaking through me. He is not weak in dealing with you, but is powerful among you. ⁴For to be sure, he was crucified in weakness, yet he lives by God's power. Likewise, we are weak in him, yet by God's power we will live with him to serve you.

⁵Examine yourselves to see whether you are in the faith; test yourselves. Do you not realize that Christ Jesus is in you—unless, of course, you fail the test? ⁶And I trust that you will discover that we have not failed the test.

A THOUGHT: *Just as we get physical check-ups, Paul urges us to give ourselves spiritual check-ups. We should look for a growing awareness of Christ's presence and power in our lives. Only then will we know if we are true Christians or imposters. If we're not taking active steps to grow closer to God, we are growing farther away from him.*

Proverbs for Today/ 15:15–17

All the days of the oppressed are wretched, but the cheerful heart has a continual feast. □ Better a little with the fear of the LORD than great wealth with turmoil. Better a meal of vegetables where there is love than a fattened calf with hatred.

MAY 18

Jesus Teaches in the Synagogues/ Luke 4:14–30

Jesus returned to Galilee in the power of the Spirit, and news about him spread through the whole countryside. ¹⁵He taught in their synagogues, and everyone praised him.

¹⁶He went to Nazareth, where he had been brought up, and on the Sabbath day he went into the synagogue, as was his custom. And he stood up to read. ¹⁷The scroll of the prophet Isaiah was handed to him. Unrolling it, he found the place where it is written:

¹⁸"The Spirit of the Lord is on me,
    because he has anointed me
    to preach good news to the poor.
He has sent me to proclaim freedom for the
        prisoners
    and recovery of sight for the blind,
    to release the oppressed,
¹⁹ to proclaim the year of the Lord's favor."

²⁰Then he rolled up the scroll, gave it back to the

attendant and sat down. The eyes of everyone in the synagogue were fastened on him, 21and he began by saying to them, "Today this scripture is fulfilled in your hearing."

22All spoke well of him and were amazed at the gracious words that came from his lips. "Isn't this Joseph's son?" they asked.

23Jesus said to them, "Surely you will quote this proverb to me: 'Physician, heal yourself! Do here in your hometown what we have heard that you did in Capernaum.' "

24"I tell you the truth," he continued, "no prophet is accepted in his hometown. 25I assure you that there were many widows in Israel in Elijah's time, when the sky was shut for three and a half years and there was a severe famine throughout the land. 26Yet Elijah was not sent to any of them, but to a widow in Zarephath in the region of Sidon. 27And there were many in Israel with leprosy in the time of Elisha the prophet, yet not one of them was cleansed— only Naaman the Syrian."

28All the people in the synagogue were furious when they heard this. 29They got up, drove him out of the town, and took him to the brow of the hill on which the town was built, in order to throw him down the cliff. 30But he walked right through the crowd and went on his way.

A THOUGHT: *Jesus quoted from Isaiah 61:1–2, stopping in the middle of verse two, just before "and the day of vengeance of our God." He did this because the time of God's blessings is fulfilled in Jesus' first coming, but the time of God's wrath awaits his Second Coming. His hearers were expecting just the opposite of the Messiah: they thought he would crush their enemies first, and then usher in God's blessings. Jesus was demonstrating from the Scriptures that he was the fulfillment of all that the prophets had spoken concerning Messiah. Two advents comprise Jesus' messiahship—one as suffering servant (Jesus' earthly ministry accomplishing mankind's redemption), and one at the end, as conquering King (bringing to fulfillment all the blessings of salvation for God's people).*

Paul's Final Advice and Greetings/ 2 Corinthians 13:7–14

Now we pray to God that you will not do anything wrong. Not that people will see that we have stood the test but that you will do what is right even though we may seem to have failed. 8For we cannot do anything against the truth, but only for the truth. 9We are glad whenever we are weak but you are strong; and our prayer is for your perfection.

10This is why I write these things when I am absent, that when I come I may not have to be harsh in my use of authority—the authority the Lord gave me for building you up, not for tearing you down.

11Finally, brothers, good-by. Aim for perfection, listen to my appeal, be of one mind, live in peace. And the God of love and peace will be with you.

12Greet one another with a holy kiss. 13All the saints send their greetings.

14May the grace of the Lord Jesus Christ, and the love of God, and the fellowship of the Holy Spirit be with you all.

A THOUGHT: *Paul's closing words—what he wanted the Corinthians to remember about the qualities the church should possess—are still fitting for the church today. But even when these qualities are present, there are problems to be dealt with in the church. These traits do not come to a church by glossing over problems, conflicts, and difficulties; they are not produced by neglect, denial, withdrawal, or bitterness. They are traits which are the natural by-product of the difficult work of problem solving. Just as Paul and the Corinthians had to hammer out difficulties to bring peace, so we must do the same. We must receive and obey the principles of God's Word and not just hear them.*

Proverbs for Today/ 15:18–19

A hot-tempered man stirs up dissension, but a patient man calms a quarrel. □ The way of the sluggard is blocked with thorns, but the path of the upright is a highway.

MAY 19

Jesus Casts Out Demons and Heals Many/ Luke 4:31–44

Then he [Jesus] went down to Capernaum, a town in Galilee, and on the Sabbath began to teach the people. 32They were amazed at his teaching, because his message had authority.

33In the synagogue there was a man possessed by a demon, an evil spirit. He cried out at the top of his voice, 34"Ha! What do you want with us, Jesus of Nazareth? Have you come to destroy us? I know who you are—the Holy One of God!"

35"Be quiet!" Jesus said sternly. "Come out of him!" Then the demon threw the man down before them all and came out without injuring him.

36All the people were amazed and said to each other, "What is this teaching? With authority and power he gives orders to evil spirits and they come out!" 37And the news about him spread throughout the surrounding area.

38Jesus left the synagogue and went to the home of Simon. Now Simon's mother-in-law was suffering from a high fever, and they asked Jesus to help her. 39So he bent over her and rebuked the fever, and it left her. She got up at once and began to wait on them.

40When the sun was setting, the people brought to Jesus all who had various kinds of sickness, and laying his hands on each one, he healed them. 41Moreover, demons came out of many people, shouting, "You are the Son of God!" But he rebuked them and would not allow them to speak, because they knew he was the Christ.

42At daybreak Jesus went out to a solitary place. The people were looking for him and when they came to where he was, they tried to keep him from leaving them. 43But he said, "I must preach the good news of the kingdom of God to the other towns also, because that is why I was sent." 44And he kept on preaching in the synagogues of Judea.

A THOUGHT: *The people were amazed at Jesus' authority to cast out demons—evil spirits ruled by Satan and sent to tempt people to sin. Like their leader, demons are fallen angels who have joined him in rebellion against God. Demons can cause a person to become mute, deaf, blind, or insane. Jesus faced many demons during his time on earth, and he always exerted authority over them. Not only did the demon leave this man, the man was not even hurt. By casting out this demon, Jesus was demonstrating the presence of the kingdom of God in his own person. Jesus carries God's authority because he is God.*

Paul's Greeting and Prayer/ Galatians 1:1–5

Paul, an apostle—sent not from men nor by man, but by Jesus Christ and God the Father, who raised him from the dead— 2and all the brothers with me,

To the churches in Galatia:

³Grace and peace to you from God our Father and the Lord Jesus Christ, ⁴who gave himself for our sins to rescue us from the present evil age, according to the will of our God and Father, ⁵to whom be glory for ever and ever. Amen.

A THOUGHT: *God's plan all along was to save us by Jesus' death. We have been rescued from the power of this evil world—a world ruled by Satan, full of cruelty, tragedy, temptation, and deception. Being rescued from this evil world doesn't mean we are taken out of it, but that we are no longer enslaved to it. We have been saved to live righteous lives for God, and we have been promised eternity with him.*

Proverbs for Today/ 15:20–21

A wise son brings joy to his father, but a foolish man despises his mother. □ Folly delights a man who lacks judgment, but a man of understanding keeps a straight course.

MAY 20

The Great Catch of Fish/ Luke 5:1–11

One day as Jesus was standing by the Lake of Gennesaret, with the people crowding around him and listening to the word of God, ²he saw at the water's edge two boats, left there by the fishermen, who were washing their nets. ³He got into one of the boats, the one belonging to Simon, and asked him to put out a little from shore. Then he sat down and taught the people from the boat.

⁴When he had finished speaking, he said to Simon, "Put out into deep water, and let down the nets for a catch."

⁵Simon answered, "Master, we've worked hard all night and haven't caught anything. But because you say so, I will let down the nets."

⁶When they had done so, they caught such a large number of fish that their nets began to break. ⁷So they signaled their partners in the other boat to come and help them, and they came and filled both boats so full that they began to sink.

⁸When Simon Peter saw this, he fell at Jesus' knees and

said, "Go away from me, Lord; I am a sinful man!" 9For he and all his companions were astonished at the catch of fish they had taken, 10and so were James and John, the sons of Zebedee, Simon's partners.

Then Jesus said to Simon, "Don't be afraid; from now on you will catch men." 11So they pulled their boats up on shore, left everything and followed him.

A THOUGHT: *Peter was awestruck at this miracle, and his first response was to feel his own insignificance in comparison to Jesus' greatness. Peter knew Jesus had healed the sick and cast out demons, but he was amazed that Jesus cared about his day-to-day routine and understood his needs. God's power reaches into every dimension of our lives. As we come to recognize the greatness of God's power expressed in the life of the church, we will find ourselves humbled at the reality of who he is and at the magnitude of his grace towards us.*

There Is No Other Gospel/ Galatians 1:6–12

I am astonished that you are so quickly deserting the one who called you by the grace of Christ and are turning to a different gospel— 7which is really no gospel at all. Evidently some people are throwing you into confusion and are trying to pervert the gospel of Christ. 8But even if we or an angel from heaven should preach a gospel other than the one we preached to you, let him be eternally condemned! 9As we have already said, so now I say again: If anybody is preaching to you a gospel other than what you accepted, let him be eternally condemned!

10Am I now trying to win the approval of men, or of God? Or am I trying to please men? If I were still trying to please men, I would not be a servant of Christ.

11I want you to know, brothers, that the gospel I preached is not something that man made up. 12I did not receive it from any man, nor was I taught it; rather, I received it by revelation from Jesus Christ.

A THOUGHT: *The "different gospel" was preached by people who wanted Gentile believers to follow Jewish laws in order to obtain salvation. Those proclaiming this different way believed that faith in Christ was not enough; a Christian must also follow the Jewish laws and customs, especially the rite of circumcision, in order to be saved. This message undermined the truth of the Good News that salvation is a gift, not a reward. Jesus Christ has made this gift available to all people, not just to those who are Jewish in orientation. Beware of people who say that more is needed for salvation than faith in Christ.*

When people set up additional requirements for salvation, they deny the power of Christ's redemptive work on the cross.

Proverbs for Today/ 15:22–23

Plans fail for lack of counsel, but with many advisers they succeed. □ A man finds joy in giving an apt reply—and how good is a timely word!

MAY 21

Jesus Heals a Leper/ Luke 5:12–16

While Jesus was in one of the towns, a man came along who was covered with leprosy. When he saw Jesus, he fell with his face to the ground and begged him, "Lord, if you are willing, you can make me clean."

13Jesus reached out his hand and touched the man. "I am willing," he said. "Be clean!" And immediately the leprosy left him.

14Then Jesus ordered him, "Don't tell anyone, but go, show yourself to the priest and offer the sacrifices that Moses commanded for your cleansing, as a testimony to them."

15Yet the news about him spread all the more, so that crowds of people came to hear him and to be healed of their sicknesses. 16But Jesus often withdrew to lonely places and prayed.

A THOUGHT: *Leprosy was a feared disease because it was often highly contagious and there was no known cure for it. (Sometimes called Hansen's disease, leprosy still exists today in a less contagious form that can be treated.) The priests monitored the disease—banishing from the community those persons whose leprosy was active, to prevent the spread of infection, and readmitting lepers whose disease was in remission. Since leprosy destroyed the nerve endings, lepers often unknowingly damaged their fingers, toes, and noses.*

Lepers were considered untouchable because people feared contracting their disease. Yet Jesus reached out and touched this leper to heal him. We may consider certain people untouchable or repulsive. We must not be afraid to reach out and touch them with God's love. Who do you know that needs God's touch of love?

Paul Reviews His Conversion/ Galatians 1:13–24

For you have heard of my previous way of life in Judaism, how intensely I persecuted the church of God and tried to destroy it. 14I was advancing in Judaism beyond many Jews of my own age and was extremely zealous for the traditions of my fathers. 15But when God, who set me apart from birth and called me by his grace, was pleased 16to reveal his Son in me so that I might preach him among the Gentiles, I did not consult any man, 17nor did I go up to Jerusalem to see those who were apostles before I was, but I went immediately into Arabia and later returned to Damascus.

18Then after three years, I went up to Jerusalem to get acquainted with Peter and stayed with him fifteen days. 19I saw none of the other apostles—only James, the Lord's brother. 20I assure you before God that what I am writing you is no lie. 21Later I went to Syria and Cilicia. 22I was personally unknown to the churches of Judea that are in Christ. 23They only heard the report: "The man who formerly persecuted us is now preaching the faith he once tried to destroy." 24And they praised God because of me.

A THOUGHT: *Paul tells of his conversion to show that his message came directly from God. God commissioned him to preach the Good News to the Gentiles. After his call, Paul did not consult with the apostles until he had spent three years in the desert. Then he spoke with Peter and James, but he had no other contact with Jewish Christians for several more years. During those years, he was preaching to the Gentiles the message God gave him. His Good News did not ultimately come from man; it came from God.*

Proverbs for Today/ 15:24–26

The path of life leads upward for the wise to keep him from going down to the grave. □ The LORD tears down the proud man's house but he keeps the widow's boundaries intact. □ The LORD detests the thoughts of the wicked, but those of the pure are pleasing to him.

Jesus Heals a Paralytic/ Luke 5:17–26

One day as he [Jesus] was teaching, Pharisees and teachers of the law, who had come from every village of Galilee and from Judea and Jerusalem, were sitting there. And the power of the Lord was present for him to heal the sick. 18Some men came carrying a paralytic on a mat and tried to take him into the house to lay him before Jesus. 19When they could not find a way to do this because of the crowd, they went up on the roof and lowered him on his mat through the tiles into the middle of the crowd, right in front of Jesus.

20When Jesus saw their faith, he said, "Friend, your sins are forgiven."

21The Pharisees and the teachers of the law began thinking to themselves, "Who is this fellow who speaks blasphemy? Who can forgive sins but God alone?"

22Jesus knew what they were thinking and asked, "Why are you thinking these things in your hearts? 23Which is easier: to say, 'Your sins are forgiven,' or to say, 'Get up and walk'? 24But that you may know that the Son of Man has authority on earth to forgive sins. . . ." He said to the paralyzed man, "I tell you, get up, take your mat and go home." 25Immediately he stood up in front of them, took what he had been lying on and went home praising God. 26Everyone was amazed and gave praise to God. They were filled with awe and said, "We have seen remarkable things today."

A THOUGHT: *When Jesus told the paralyzed man his sins were forgiven, the Jewish leaders accused him of blasphemy—claiming to be God or to do what only God can do. In Jewish law, blasphemy was punishable by death. In labeling Jesus' claim to forgive sins blasphemous, the religious leaders did not understand that he is God, and he has God's power to heal both the body and the soul. Forgiveness of sins was a sign that the Messianic Age had come.*

Paul Stood Firm for the Gospel/ Galatians 2:1–5

Fourteen years later I went up again to Jerusalem, this time with Barnabas. I took Titus along also. 2I went in response to a revelation and set before them the gospel that I preach among the Gentiles. But I did this privately to those who seemed to be leaders, for fear that I was running or had run my race in vain. ³Yet not even Titus, who was with me, was compelled to be circumcised, even though he was a Greek. ⁴This matter arose, because some false brothers had infiltrated our ranks to spy on the freedom we have in Christ Jesus and to make us slaves. ⁵We did not give in to them for a moment, so that the truth of the gospel might remain with you.

A THOUGHT: *Even though God had specifically sent Paul to the Gentiles, Paul was willing to discuss his gospel message with the leaders of the Jerusalem church. This meeting prevented a major split in the church, and it formally acknowledged the apostles' approval of Paul's preaching. Sometimes we avoid conferring with others because we fear that problems or arguments may develop. Instead, we should openly discuss our plans and actions with others. This helps everyone understand the situation better, it reduces gossip, and builds unity in the church.*

Proverbs for Today/ 15:27–28

A greedy man brings trouble to his family, but he who hates bribes will live. □ The heart of the righteous weighs its answers, but the mouth of the wicked gushes evil.

MAY 23

Jesus Came to Save Sinners/ Luke 5:27–39

After this, Jesus went out and saw a tax collector by the name of Levi sitting at his tax booth. "Follow me," Jesus said to him, ²⁸and Levi got up, left everything and followed him.

²⁹Then Levi held a great banquet for Jesus at his house, and a large crowd of tax collectors and others were eating with them. ³⁰But the Pharisees and the teachers of the law who belonged to their sect complained to his disciples, "Why do you eat and drink with tax collectors and 'sinners'?"

³¹Jesus answered them, "It is not the healthy who need a doctor, but the sick. ³²I have not come to call the righteous, but sinners to repentance."

33They said to him, "John's disciples often fast and pray, and so do the disciples of the Pharisees, but yours go on eating and drinking."

34Jesus answered, "Can you make the guests of the bridegroom fast while he is with them? 35But the time will come when the bridegroom will be taken from them; in those days they will fast."

36He told them this parable: "No one tears a patch from a new garment and sews it on an old one. If he does, he will have torn the new garment, and the patch from the new will not match the old. 37And no one pours new wine into old wineskins. If he does, the new wine will burst the skins, the wine will run out and the wineskins will be ruined. 38No, new wine must be poured into new wineskins. 39And no one after drinking old wine wants the new, for he says, 'The old is better.' "

A THOUGHT: *The Pharisees wrapped their sin in respectability. They made themselves appear good by publicly doing good deeds and pointing out the sins of others. Jesus chose to spend time, not with these self-righteous religious leaders, but with people who sensed their own sin and knew they were not good enough for God. In order to come to God, you must repent; in order to repent, you must recognize your sin. As sinners, we can have hope because Jesus came to save sinners, not those who considered themselves righteous.*

The Apostles Accept Paul's Gospel/
Galatians 2:6–10

As for those who seemed to be important—whatever they were makes no difference to me; God does not judge by external appearance—those men added nothing to my message. 7On the contrary, they saw that I had been entrusted with the task of preaching the gospel to the Gentiles, just as Peter had been to the Jews. 8For God, who was at work in the ministry of Peter as an apostle to the Jews, was also at work in my ministry as an apostle to the Gentiles. 9James, Peter and John, those reputed to be pillars, gave me and Barnabas the right hand of fellowship when they recognized the grace given to me. They agreed that we should go to the Gentiles, and they to the Jews. 10All they asked was that we should continue to remember the poor, the very thing I was eager to do.

A THOUGHT: *Here the apostles were expressing their concern for the poor of Jerusalem. While many Gentile converts were financially* comfortable, the Jerusalem church was suffering from a severe famine. Much of Paul's time was spent gathering funds for the Jewish Christians. The need for believers to care for the poor is a constant theme of Scripture, but often we do nothing about it. We get caught up in meeting our own needs and desires, or we just don't see enough poor people to remember their needs. Both in your own city and across the oceans there are people who need help. What can you do to show them tangible evidence of God's love?

Proverbs for Today/ 15:29–30

The LORD is far from the wicked but he hears the prayer of the righteous. □ A cheerful look brings joy to the heart, and good news gives health to the bones.

MAY 24

Lord of the Sabbath/ Luke 6:1–11

One Sabbath Jesus was going through the grainfields, and his disciples began to pick some heads of grain, rub them in their hands and eat the kernels. 2Some of the Pharisees asked, "Why are you doing what is unlawful on the Sabbath?"

3Jesus answered them, "Have you never read what David did when he and his companions were hungry? 4He entered the house of God, and taking the consecrated bread, he ate what is lawful only for priests to eat. And he also gave some to his companions." 5Then Jesus said to them, "The Son of Man is Lord of the Sabbath."

6On another Sabbath he went into the synagogue and was teaching, and a man was there whose right hand was shriveled. 7The Pharisees and the teachers of the law were looking for a reason to accuse Jesus, so they watched him closely to see if he would heal on the Sabbath. 8But Jesus knew what they were thinking and said to the man with the shriveled hand, "Get up and stand in front of everyone." So he got up and stood there.

9Then Jesus said to them, "I ask you, which is lawful on the Sabbath: to do good or to do evil, to save life or to destroy it?"

10He looked around at them all, and then said to the man,

"Stretch out your hand." He did so, and his hand was completely restored. 11But they were furious and began to discuss with one another what they might do to Jesus.

A THOUGHT: *The Pharisees had written in the Mishnah, their hand-book of rabbinic law, 39 categories of activities that were forbidden on the Sabbath—and harvesting was one of them. The rabbinic religious leaders had also invented a law that said no healing could be done on the Sabbath. It was more important for the religious leaders to protect their laws than to free a person from painful suffering. For Jesus, practicing mercy towards another was to truly fulfill the purpose of the Sabbath command—which was to relieve people from their toil and suffering throughout the week.*

When Jesus said he was master of the Sabbath, he revealed to the Pharisees that he had the authority to overrule their traditions and regulations because he had created the Sabbath. The creator is always greater than the creation.

Paul Confronts Peter in Antioch/ Galatians 2:11–16

When Peter came to Antioch, I opposed him to his face, because he was clearly in the wrong. 12Before certain men came from James, he used to eat with the Gentiles. But when they arrived, he began to draw back and separate himself from the Gentiles because he was afraid of those who belonged to the circumcision group. 13The other Jews joined him in his hypocrisy, so that by their hypocrisy even Barnabas was led astray.

14When I saw that they were not acting in line with the truth of the gospel, I said to Peter in front of them all, "You are a Jew, yet you live like a Gentile and not like a Jew. How is it, then, that you force Gentiles to follow Jewish customs?

15"We who are Jews by birth and not 'Gentile sinners' 16know that a man is not justified by observing the law, but by faith in Jesus Christ. So we, too, have put our faith in Christ Jesus that we may be justified by faith in Christ and not by observing the law, because by observing the law no one will be justified."

A THOUGHT: *The Judaizers accused Paul of watering down the gospel to make it easier for Gentiles to accept, while Paul accused the Judaizers of nullifying the truth of the gospel by adding conditions to it. The basis of salvation was the issue—is salvation through Christ alone, or does it come through Christ and adherence to the law? The argument came to a head when Peter, Paul, some Judaizers, and some Gentile Christians all gathered together in Antioch to share a meal. Peter probably thought that by staying aloof from the Gentiles, he was promoting harmony—he did not want to offend the friends of James. But Paul charged that Peter's action violated the gospel. By joining the Judaizers, Peter implicitly supported their claim that Christ was not sufficient for salvation. Compromise is an important element in getting along with others, but we should never compromise the truth of God's Word. If we feel we have to change our Christian beliefs to match those of our companions, we are on dangerous ground.*

Proverbs for Today/ 15:31–32

He who listens to a life-giving rebuke will be at home among the wise. □ He who ignores discipline despises himself, but whoever heeds correction gains understanding.

MAY 25

Jesus Chooses His Twelve Disciples/ Luke 6:12–16

One of those days Jesus went out to a mountainside to pray, and spent the night praying to God. 13When morning came, he called his disciples to him and chose twelve of them, whom he also designated apostles: 14Simon (whom he named Peter), his brother Andrew, James, John, Philip, Bartholomew, 15Matthew, Thomas, James son of Alphaeus, Simon who was called the Zealot, 16Judas son of James, and Judas Iscariot, who became a traitor.

A THOUGHT: *Jesus selected ordinary people to be his disciples, and they exhibited a real mixture of backgrounds and personalities. They were "ordinary" people with a high calling. Today, God calls "ordinary" people together to build his church, teach salvation's message, and serve others out of love. Alone we may feel unqualified to serve Christ effectively, but together we make up a group strong enough to serve God in any way. Ask for patience to accept the differences in people in your church, and build on the variety of strengths represented in your group.*

The Law Cannot Bring Salvation/ Galatians 2:17–21

"If, while we seek to be justified in Christ, it becomes evident that we ourselves are sinners, does that mean that Christ promotes sin? Absolutely not! 18If I rebuild what I destroyed, I prove that I am a lawbreaker. 19For through the law I died to the law so that I might live for God. 20I have been crucified with Christ and I no longer live, but Christ lives in me. The life I live in the body, I live by faith in the Son of God, who loved me and gave himself for me. 21I do not set aside the grace of God, for if righteousness could be gained through the law, Christ died for nothing!"

A THOUGHT: *Through studying the Old Testament Scripture, Paul realized that he could not be saved by obeying God's laws. The prophets knew that God's plan of salvation did not rest upon keeping the Law. Because we have all been infected by sin, we cannot keep God's laws perfectly. Fortunately, God has provided a way of salvation that depends on Jesus Christ, not on our own efforts. We ignore God's system and try to earn our salvation whenever we think God accepts us because we do good things or because we are better than other people. In truth, only by trusting in Christ to take away our sin will we be acceptable to God.*

Proverbs for Today/ 15:33

The fear of the LORD teaches a man wisdom, and humility comes before honor.

MAY 26

The Sermon on the Plain/ Luke 6:17–38

He [Jesus] went down with them [the twelve disciples] and stood on a level place. A large crowd of his disciples was there and a great number of people from all over Judea, from Jerusalem, and from the coast of Tyre and Sidon, 18who had come to hear him and to be healed of their diseases. Those troubled by evil spirits were cured, 19and the people all tried to touch him, because power was coming from him and healing them all.

20Looking at his disciples, he said:

"Blessed are you who are poor,
for yours is the kingdom of God.
21Blessed are you who hunger now,
for you will be satisfied.
Blessed are you who weep now,
for you will laugh.

22Blessed are you when men hate you,
     when they exclude you and insult you
     and reject your name as evil,
          because of the Son of Man.

23"Rejoice in that day and leap for joy, because great is your reward in heaven. For that is how their fathers treated the prophets.

24"But woe to you who are rich,
     for you have already received your comfort.
25Woe to you who are well fed now,
     for you will go hungry.
  Woe to you who laugh now,
     for you will mourn and weep.
26Woe to you when all men speak well of you,
     for that is how their fathers treated the false
          prophets.

27"But I tell you who hear me: Love your enemies, do good to those who hate you, 28bless those who curse you, pray for those who mistreat you. 29If someone strikes you on one cheek, turn to him the other also. If someone takes your cloak, do not stop him from taking your tunic. 30Give to everyone who asks you, and if anyone takes what belongs to you, do not demand it back. 31Do to others as you would have them do to you.

32"If you love those who love you, what credit is that to you? Even 'sinners' love those who love them. 33And if you do good to those who are good to you, what credit is that to you? Even 'sinners' do that. 34And if you lend to those from whom you expect repayment, what credit is that to you? Even 'sinners' lend to 'sinners,' expecting to be repaid in full. 35But love your enemies, do good to them, and lend to them without expecting to get anything back. Then your reward will be great, and you will be sons of the Most High, because he is kind to the ungrateful and wicked. 36Be merciful, just as your Father is merciful.

37"Do not judge, and you will not be judged. Do not condemn, and you will not be condemned. Forgive, and you will be forgiven. 38Give, and it will be given to you. A good measure, pressed down, shaken together and running over, will be poured into your lap. For with the measure you use, it will be measured to you."

A THOUGHT: *These "Blessed are you . . ." verses are called the Beatitudes, from the Latin word meaning "blessing." They describe what it means to be Christ's follower. They are a standard of conduct. They contrast kingdom values with worldly values, showing what Christ's followers can expect from the world and what God will give them. They contrast fake piety with true humility. And finally, they show how the Old Testament expectations will be fulfilled in God's kingdom.*

True Children of Abraham/ Galatians 3:1–9

You foolish Galatians! Who has bewitched you? Before your very eyes Jesus Christ was clearly portrayed as crucified. 2I would like to learn just one thing from you: Did you receive the Spirit by observing the law, or by believing what you heard? 3Are you so foolish? After beginning with the Spirit, are you now trying to attain your goal by human effort? 4Have you suffered so much for nothing—if it really was for nothing? 5Does God give you his Spirit and work miracles among you because you observe the law, or because you believe what you heard?

6Consider Abraham: "He believed God, and it was credited to him as righteousness." 7Understand, then, that those who believe are children of Abraham. 8The Scripture foresaw that God would justify the Gentiles by faith, and announced the gospel in advance to Abraham: "All nations will be blessed through you." 9So those who have faith are blessed along with Abraham, the man of faith.

A THOUGHT: *The main argument of the Judaizers was that Gentiles had to become Jews in order to become Christians. Paul exposed the flaw in this argument by showing that real children of Abraham are those who have faith, not those who keep the Law. Abraham himself was saved by his faith. All believers of all time and from every nation share Abraham's blessing. This is a comforting promise, a great heritage, and a solid foundation for living.*

Proverbs for Today/ 16:1–3

To man belong the plans of the heart, but from the LORD comes the reply of the tongue. □ All a man's ways seem innocent to him, but motives are weighed by the LORD. □ Commit to the LORD whatever you do, and your plans will succeed.

MAY 27

A Collection of Jesus' Parables/ Luke 6:39–49

He [Jesus] also told them this parable: "Can a blind man lead a blind man? Will they not both fall into a pit? ⁴⁰A student is not above his teacher, but everyone who is fully trained will be like his teacher.

⁴¹"Why do you look at the speck of sawdust in your brother's eye and pay no attention to the plank in your own eye? ⁴²How can you say to your brother, 'Brother, let me take the speck out of your eye,' when you yourself fail to see the plank in your own eye? You hypocrite, first take the plank out of your eye, and then you will see clearly to remove the speck from your brother's eye.

⁴³"No good tree bears bad fruit, nor does a bad tree bear good fruit. ⁴⁴Each tree is recognized by its own fruit. People do not pick figs from thornbushes, or grapes from briers. ⁴⁵The good man brings good things out of the good stored up in his heart, and the evil man brings evil things out of the evil stored up in his heart. For out of the overflow of his heart his mouth speaks.

⁴⁶"Why do you call me, 'Lord, Lord,' and do not do what I say? ⁴⁷I will show you what he is like who comes to me and hears my words and puts them into practice. ⁴⁸He is like a man building a house, who dug down deep and laid the foundation on rock. When a flood came, the torrent struck that house but could not shake it, because it was well built. ⁴⁹But the one who hears my words and does not put them into practice is like a man who built a house on the ground without a foundation. The moment the torrent struck that house, it collapsed and its destruction was complete."

A THOUGHT: *This collection of parables centers upon the appropriate basis for judging the ethical character of oneself and others. We must be very aware of our own shortcomings when we approach another with the intent to "set them straight." We must recognize that we too have areas that need correcting. We should also take care that we are not attempting to correct the small faults in others when in reality we are the ones in greatest need of correction. Genuine humility is always appropriate when evaluating others.*

True spirituality must be from the heart and must be evidenced by good deeds ("good fruit"). If our words do not match the true quality of our lives, it is time for self-examination.

Christ Became a Curse for Us/ Galatians 3:10–14

All who rely on observing the law are under a curse, for it is written: "Cursed is everyone who does not continue to do everything written in the Book of the Law." [11]Clearly no one is justified before God by the law, because, "The righteous will live by faith." [12]The law is not based on faith; on the contrary, "The man who does these things will live by them." [13]Christ redeemed us from the curse of the law by becoming a curse for us, for it is written: "Cursed is everyone who is hung on a tree." [14]He redeemed us in order that the blessing given to Abraham might come to the Gentiles through Christ Jesus, so that by faith we might receive the promise of the Spirit.

A THOUGHT: *Paul quotes Deuteronomy 27:26 to prove that, contrary to what the Judaizers claimed, the law cannot justify and save—it can only condemn. Breaking even one commandment brings a person under condemnation. Because everyone has broken the commandments, everyone is condemned, and the Law can do nothing to reverse the condemnation. But Christ took the curse of the Law upon himself when he hung on the cross. He did this so we wouldn't have to bear our own punishment and so we could be saved through him. The only condition is that we accept Christ's work on the cross.*

Proverbs for Today/ 16:4–5

The LORD works out everything for his own ends—even the wicked for a day of disaster. □ The LORD detests all the proud of heart. Be sure of this: They will not go unpunished.

MAY 28

The Faith of a Roman Centurion/ Luke 7:1–10

When Jesus had finished saying all this in the hearing of the people, he entered Capernaum. [2]There a centurion's servant, whom his master valued highly, was sick and about to die. [3]The centurion heard of Jesus and sent some elders of the Jews to him, asking him to come and heal his servant. [4]When they came to Jesus, they pleaded earnestly with him, "This man deserves to have you do this, [5]because he loves our nation and has built our synagogue." [6]So Jesus went with them.

He was not far from the house when the centurion sent friends to say to him: "Lord, don't trouble yourself, for I do not deserve to have you come under my roof. [7]That is why I did not even consider myself worthy to come to you. But say the word, and my servant will be healed. [8]For I myself am a man under authority, with soldiers under me. I tell this one, 'Go,' and he goes; and that one, 'Come,' and he comes. I say to my servant, 'Do this,' and he does it."

[9]When Jesus heard this, he was amazed at him, and turning to the crowd following him, he said, "I tell you, I have not found such great faith even in Israel." [10]Then the men who had been sent returned to the house and found the servant well.

A THOUGHT: *This Roman centurion recognized the authority of Jesus in a way that many of the religious leaders had not. When the centurion spoke a word, his soldiers and servants immediately responded with action. He recognized that Jesus' authority was far greater than his, so he was confident that Jesus could heal by just saying the word. Faith in Jesus must be this kind of implicit trust in his great power and ability, not only to deliver from physical ailment, but much more for his ability to transform our lives.*

God's Promise to Abraham Fulfilled/ Galatians 3:15–20

Brothers, let me take an example from everyday life. Just as no one can set aside or add to a human covenant that has been duly established, so it is in this case. [16]The promises were spoken to Abraham and to his seed. The Scripture does not say "and to seeds," meaning many people, but "and to your seed," meaning one person, who is Christ. [17]What I mean is this: The law, introduced 430 years later, does not set aside the covenant previously established by God and thus do away with the promise. [18]For if the inheritance depends on the law, then it no longer depends on a promise; but God in his grace gave it to Abraham through a promise.

[19]What, then, was the purpose of the law? It was added because of transgressions until the Seed to whom the

promise referred had come. The law was put into effect through angels by a mediator. ²⁰A mediator, however, does not represent just one party; but God is one.

A THOUGHT: *Paul says that Jesus was the fulfillment of the Law. Jesus inaugurated a new order—the kingdom of God. The Judaizers had misunderstood the nature of forgiveness and the Law, they saw the Law as a way to earn God's favor. But the Law was to be seen as a response to relationship with God (the covenant), not as an isolated code to be followed in order to gain God's favor. The Law was intended to flow from faith; it was not to be a prerequisite for faith. Similarly, right living is not the condition for faith, but the result of it. When we understand the transforming power of faith we will want to live in a way that demonstrates this transformation.*

Proverbs for Today/ 16:6–7

Through love and faithfulness sin is atoned for; through the fear of the LORD a man avoids evil. □ When a man's ways are pleasing to the LORD, he makes even his enemies live at peace with him.

MAY 29

Jesus Resurrects a Widow's Son/ Luke 7:11–17

Soon afterward, Jesus went to a town called Nain, and his disciples and a large crowd went along with him. ¹²As he approached the town gate, a dead person was being carried out—the only son of his mother, and she was a widow. And a large crowd from the town was with her. ¹³When the Lord saw her, his heart went out to her and he said, "Don't cry."

¹⁴Then he went up and touched the coffin, and those carrying it stood still. He said, "Young man, I say to you, get up!" ¹⁵The dead man sat up and began to talk, and Jesus gave him back to his mother.

¹⁶They were all filled with awe and praised God. "A great prophet has appeared among us," they said. "God has come to help his people." ¹⁷This news about Jesus spread throughout Judea and the surrounding country.

A THOUGHT: *The widow's situation was serious. She had lost her husband, and now her only son was dead—her last means of support. The crowd of mourners would go home, and she would be left penniless and friendless. She was probably past the age of childbearing and would not marry again. Unless a relative came to her aid, her future was bleak. She would be an easy prey for swindlers, and she would likely be reduced to begging for food. In fact, as Luke repeatedly emphasizes, she was just the kind of person Jesus came to help—and help her he did. Jesus has the power to bring hope out of any tragedy.*

Unity in Christ/ Galatians 3:21–29

Is the law, therefore, opposed to the promises of God? Absolutely not! For if a law had been given that could impart life, then righteousness would certainly have come by the law. 22But the Scripture declares that the whole world is a prisoner of sin, so that what was promised, being given through faith in Jesus Christ, might be given to those who believe.

23Before this faith came, we were held prisoners by the law, locked up until faith should be revealed. 24So the law was put in charge to lead us to Christ that we might be justified by faith. 25Now that faith has come, we are no longer under the supervision of the law.

26You are all sons of God through faith in Christ Jesus, 27for all of you who were baptized into Christ have clothed yourselves with Christ. 28There is neither Jew nor Greek, slave nor free, male nor female, for you are all one in Christ Jesus. 29If you belong to Christ, then you are Abraham's seed, and heirs according to the promise.

A THOUGHT: *It's our natural inclination to feel uncomfortable around those who are different from us and to gravitate toward those who resemble us. But when we allow our differences to separate us from our fellow believers, we are disregarding clear biblical teaching. We must remember that in Christ we have all been put on equal footing before the cross. No one has any greater value than anyone else. Make a point of seeking out and appreciating people who are not just like you and your friends. You may find that you and they have a lot in common.*

Proverbs for Today/ 16:8–9

Better a little with righteousness than much gain with injustice. □ In his heart a man plans his course, but the LORD determines his steps.

MAY 30

Jesus Commends John the Baptist/ Luke 7:18–35

John's disciples told him about all these things. Calling two of them, ¹⁹he sent them to the Lord to ask, "Are you the one who was to come, or should we expect someone else?"

²⁰When the men came to Jesus, they said, "John the Baptist sent us to you to ask, 'Are you the one who was to come, or should we expect someone else?'"

²¹At that very time Jesus cured many who had diseases, sicknesses and evil spirits, and gave sight to many who were blind. ²²So he replied to the messengers, "Go back and report to John what you have seen and heard: The blind receive sight, the lame walk, those who have leprosy are cured, the deaf hear, the dead are raised, and the good news is preached to the poor. ²³Blessed is the man who does not fall away on account of me."

²⁴After John's messengers left, Jesus began to speak to the crowd about John: "What did you go out into the desert to see? A reed swayed by the wind? ²⁵If not, what did you go out to see? A man dressed in fine clothes? No, those who wear expensive clothes and indulge in luxury are in palaces. ²⁶But what did you go out to see? A prophet? Yes, I tell you, and more than a prophet. ²⁷This is the one about whom it is written:

" 'I will send my messenger ahead of you,
who will prepare your way before you.'

²⁸I tell you, among those born of women there is no one greater than John; yet the one who is least in the kingdom of God is greater than he."

²⁹(All the people, even the tax collectors, when they heard Jesus' words, acknowledged that God's way was right, because they had been baptized by John. ³⁰But the Pharisees and experts in the law rejected God's purpose for themselves, because they had not been baptized by John.)

³¹"To what, then, can I compare the people of this generation? What are they like? ³²They are like children sitting in the marketplace and calling out to each other:

" 'We played the flute for you,
   and you did not dance;
we sang a dirge,
   and you did not cry.'

33For John the Baptist came neither eating bread nor drinking wine, and you say, 'He has a demon.' 34The Son of Man came eating and drinking, and you say, 'Here is a glutton and a drunkard, a friend of tax collectors and "sinners." ' 35But wisdom is proved right by all her children."

A THOUGHT: *John was confused because the reports he received about Jesus were unexpected and incomplete. His doubts were natural, and Jesus didn't rebuke him for them. Instead, he responded in a way that John would understand—expaining that he had in fact accomplished those things that the Messiah was supposed to accomplish. God also can handle our doubts, and he welcomes our questions. Do you have questions about Jesus—about who he is or what he expects of you? Admit them to yourself and to God, and begin looking for answers. Only as you admit your doubts can you begin to resolve them.*

Adopted as God's Children/ Galatians 4:1–7

What I am saying is that as long as the heir is a child, he is no different from a slave, although he owns the whole estate. 2He is subject to guardians and trustees until the time set by his father. 3So also, when we were children, we were in slavery under the basic principles of the world. 4But when the time had fully come, God sent his Son, born of a woman, born under law, 5to redeem those under law, that we might receive the full rights of sons. 6Because you are sons, God sent the Spirit of his Son into our hearts, the Spirit who calls out, *"Abba,* Father." 7So you are no longer a slave, but a son; and since you are a son, God has made you also an heir.

A THOUGHT: *Under Roman law, an adopted male child was guaranteed all legal rights to his father's property. He was not a second-class son; he was equal to all other sons, biological or adopted, in his father's family. As adopted children of God, we share with Jesus all rights to God's resources. As God's heirs, we can claim what he has provided for us—our full identity as his children.*

Proverbs for Today/ 16:10–11

The lips of a king speak as an oracle, and his mouth should not betray justice. □ Honest scales and balances are from the LORD; all the weights in the bag are of his making.

A Sinful Woman Anoints Jesus' Feet/ Luke 7:36–50

Now one of the Pharisees invited Jesus to have dinner with him, so he went to the Pharisee's house and reclined at the table. 37When a woman who had lived a sinful life in that town learned that Jesus was eating at the Pharisee's house, she brought an alabaster jar of perfume, 38and as she stood behind him at his feet weeping, she began to wet his feet with her tears. Then she wiped them with her hair, kissed them and poured perfume on them.

39When the Pharisee who had invited him saw this, he said to himself, "If this man were a prophet, he would know who is touching him and what kind of woman she is—that she is a sinner."

40Jesus answered him, "Simon, I have something to tell you."

"Tell me, teacher," he said.

41"Two men owed money to a certain moneylender. One owed him five hundred denarii, and the other fifty. 42Neither of them had the money to pay him back, so he canceled the debts of both. Now which of them will love him more?"

43Simon replied, "I suppose the one who had the bigger debt canceled."

"You have judged correctly," Jesus said.

44Then he turned toward the woman and said to Simon, "Do you see this woman? I came into your house. You did not give me any water for my feet, but she wet my feet with her tears and wiped them with her hair. 45You did not give me a kiss, but this woman, from the time I entered, has not stopped kissing my feet. 46You did not put oil on my head, but she has poured perfume on my feet. 47Therefore, I tell you, her many sins have been forgiven—for she loved much. But he who has been forgiven little loves little."

48Then Jesus said to her, "Your sins are forgiven."

49The other guests began to say among themselves, "Who is this who even forgives sins?"

50Jesus said to the woman, "Your faith has saved you; go in peace."

A THOUGHT: *Again the Pharisees are contrasted with sinners—and again the sinners come out ahead. Simon had committed a social error in neglecting to wash Jesus' feet (a courtesy that was extended to guests, because sandaled feet got very dirty), anoint his head with oil, and offer him the kiss of greeting. Did he perhaps feel he was too good to treat Jesus as an equal? The sinful woman, by contrast, lavished tears, expensive perfume, and kisses on her Savior. In this story it is the generous prostitute, not the stingy religious leader, whose sins are forgiven. Sinners who seek forgiveness will be accepted into God's kingdom, while those who think they're too good to sin will not be accepted.*

Do Not Become Enslaved Again/ Galatians 4:8–11

Formerly, when you did not know God, you were slaves to those who by nature are not gods. ⁹But now that you know God—or rather are known by God—how is it that you are turning back to those weak and miserable principles? Do you wish to be enslaved by them all over again? ¹⁰You are observing special days and months and seasons and years! ¹¹I fear for you, that somehow I have wasted my efforts on you.

A THOUGHT: *The legal traditions that had been handed down to the Jews by the rabbis had become oppressive to the people. They had become legalistic and were missing the real heart of the Law which was to love God and your neighbor. Paul is concerned for the Galatians. They were once again placing themselves under the oppressive legal system. Paul reminds them that perfection cannot be gained by keeping the Law. Perfection comes from the Perfect One—Jesus Christ. It is on the basis of Christ's sacrifice for sins that we will be acceptable to God. And it is the work of the Spirit, not our own good work, that transforms us into Christlikeness. To reject these two truths is to deny the very heart of Christianity.*

Proverbs for Today/ 16:12–13

Kings detest wrongdoing, for a throne is established through righteousness. Kings take pleasure in honest lips; they value a man who speaks the truth.

JUNE 1

Some Disciples of Jesus/ Luke 8:1–3

After this, Jesus traveled about from one town and village to another, proclaiming the good news of the kingdom of God. The Twelve were with him, ²and also some women who had been cured of evil spirits and diseases: Mary (called Magdalene) from whom seven demons had come out; ³Joanna the wife of Cuza, the manager of Herod's household; Susanna; and many others. These women were helping to support them out of their own means.

A THOUGHT: *Jesus raised women from the degradation and servitude imposed upon them by their male-dominated society, to fellowship and service. In Jewish culture, women were not supposed to learn from rabbis. By allowing these women to travel with him, Jesus was showing that all people are equal under God. These women supported Jesus' ministry with their own money. They owed a great debt to him, for he had cast demons out of some and healed others.*

Paul's Longing for Fellowship/ Galatians 4:12–20

I plead with you, brothers, become like me, for I became like you. You have done me no wrong. ¹³As you know, it was because of an illness that I first preached the gospel to you. ¹⁴Even though my illness was a trial to you, you did not treat me with contempt or scorn. Instead, you welcomed me as if I were an angel of God, as if I were Christ Jesus himself. ¹⁵What has happened to all your joy? I can testify that, if you could have done so, you would have torn out your eyes and given them to me. ¹⁶Have I now become your enemy by telling you the truth?

¹⁷Those people are zealous to win you over, but for no good. What they want is to alienate you ‚from us‚, so that you may be zealous for them. ¹⁸It is fine to be zealous, provided the purpose is good, and to be so always and not just when I am with you. ¹⁹My dear children, for whom I am again in the pains of childbirth until Christ is formed in you, ²⁰how I wish I could be with you now and change my tone, because I am perplexed about you!

A THOUGHT: *Paul led many people to Christ and helped them mature spiritually. Perhaps one reason for his success as a spiritual father was the deep concern he felt for his spiritual children; he compared his pain over their faithlessness to the pain of childbirth. We should* have the same intense care for those to whom we are spiritual parents. When you lead people to Christ, remember to stay by to help them grow.

Proverbs for Today/ 16:14–15

A king's wrath is a messenger of death, but a wise man will appease it. □ When a king's face brightens, it means life; his favor is like a rain cloud in spring.

JUNE 2

The Parable of the Sower/ Luke 8:4–15

While a large crowd was gathering and people were coming to Jesus from town after town, he told this parable: 5"A farmer went out to sow his seed. As he was scattering the seed, some fell along the path; it was trampled on, and the birds of the air ate it up. 6Some fell on rock, and when it came up, the plants withered because they had no moisture. 7Other seed fell among thorns, which grew up with it and choked the plants. 8Still other seed fell on good soil. It came up and yielded a crop, a hundred times more than was sown."

When he said this, he called out, "He who has ears to hear, let him hear."

9His disciples asked him what this parable meant. 10He said, "The knowledge of the secrets of the kingdom of God has been given to you, but to others I speak in parables, so that,

" 'though seeing, they may not see;
though hearing, they may not understand.'

11"This is the meaning of the parable: The seed is the word of God. 12Those along the path are the ones who hear, and then the devil comes and takes away the word from their hearts, so that they may not believe and be saved. 13Those on the rock are the ones who receive the word with joy when they hear it, but they have no root. They believe for a while, but in the time of testing they fall away. 14The seed that fell among thorns stands for those who hear, but as they go on their way they are choked by life's worries, riches and pleasures, and they do not mature. ¹⁵But the seed on good soil stands for those with a noble and good heart, who hear the word, retain it, and by persevering produce a crop."

A THOUGHT: *Hard-rock people, like the religious leaders, refused to believe God's message. Stony-ground people, like the crowds who followed Jesus, trusted God but never got around to doing anything about it. Thistle-patch people, overcome by materialism, left no room in their lives for God. Good-soil people, by contrast to all the other groups, followed God's Word no matter what the cost. Which type of soil do you represent?*

Sarah and Hagar/ Galatians 4:21–31

Tell me, you who want to be under the law, are you not aware of what the law says? ²²For it is written that Abraham had two sons, one by the slave woman and the other by the free woman. ²³His son by the slave woman was born in the ordinary way; but his son by the free woman was born as the result of a promise.

²⁴These things may be taken figuratively, for the women represent two covenants. One covenant is from Mount Sinai and bears children who are to be slaves: This is Hagar. ²⁵Now Hagar stands for Mount Sinai in Arabia and corresponds to the present city of Jerusalem, because she is in slavery with her children. ²⁶But the Jerusalem that is above is free, and she is our mother. ²⁷For it is written:

"Be glad, O barren woman,
    who bears no children;
break forth and cry aloud,
    you who have no labor pains;
because more are the children of the desolate
        woman
    than of her who has a husband."

²⁸Now you, brothers, like Isaac, are children of promise. ²⁹At that time the son born in the ordinary way persecuted the son born by the power of the Spirit. It is the same now. ³⁰But what does the Scripture say? "Get rid of the slave woman and her son, for the slave woman's son will never share in the inheritance with the free woman's son." ³¹Therefore, brothers, we are not children of the slave woman, but of the free woman.

A THOUGHT: *People are saved because of their faith in Christ, not because of what they do. Paul contrasts those who are enslaved to the Law (represented by Hagar, the slave woman) with those who are free from the Law (represented by Sarah, the free woman). Since we are joint-heirs with Christ, God's Son (the fulfillment of the Abrahamic promise), we are children of the promise. Our acceptance before God is the same as Abraham's—faith in the promise; but we have faith in the promise fulfilled (our faith is in Christ himself who has already come and accomplished our redemption).*

Proverbs for Today/ 16:16–17

How much better to get wisdom than gold, to choose understanding rather than silver! □ The highway of the upright avoids evil; he who guards his way guards his life.

JUNE 3

The Lamp on a Stand/ Luke 8:16–18

"No one lights a lamp and hides it in a jar or puts it under a bed. Instead, he puts it on a stand, so that those who come in can see the light. 17For there is nothing hidden that will not be disclosed, and nothing concealed that will not be known or brought out into the open. 18Therefore consider carefully how you listen. Whoever has will be given more; whoever does not have, even what he thinks he has will be taken from him."

A THOUGHT: *In God's eyes, people's hearts—their thoughts and motives—are as visible as a lamp mounted in the open. No matter how hard we try to cover up bad attitudes, deeds, or words, we cannot deceive God. Instead of hiding our faults, we should ask God to change our lives so we no longer have to be ashamed. If you are trying to hide anything from God it won't work. Only when you confess your hidden sins and seek God's forgiveness will you have the help you need to do right.*

Freedom from Slavery/ Galatians 5:1–6

It is for freedom that Christ has set us free. Stand firm, then, and do not let yourselves be burdened again by a yoke of slavery.

2Mark my words! I, Paul, tell you that if you let your-selves be circumcised, Christ will be of no value to you at all. 3Again I declare to every man who lets himself be circumcised that he is obligated to obey the whole law. 4You who are trying to be justified by law have been alienated from Christ; you have fallen away from grace. 5But by faith we eagerly await through the Spirit the righteousness for which we hope. 6For in Christ Jesus neither circumcision nor uncircumcision has any value. The only thing that counts is faith expressing itself through love.

A THOUGHT: *Christ died to set us free from the bondage to sin and from a long list of laws and regulations. Christ came to set us free—not free to do whatever we want, for that would lead back into slavery to our selfish desires. Rather, thanks to Christ, we are now free and able to do what was impossible before—to live unselfishly. Those who appeal to their freedom in order to get their own way or indulge in selfish pursuits are falling back into sin. Do you use your freedom to serve yourself or others?*

Proverbs for Today/ 16:18

Pride goes before destruction, a haughty spirit before a fall.

JUNE 4

The Family of God/ Luke 8:19–21

Now Jesus' mother and brothers came to see him, but they were not able to get near him because of the crowd. 20Someone told him, "Your mother and brothers are standing outside, wanting to see you."

21He replied, "My mother and brothers are those who hear God's word and put it into practice."

A THOUGHT: *Jesus' true relatives are those who hear and obey his words. Hearing without obeying is not enough. As Jesus loved his mother, so he loves us. He offers us an intimate family relationship with him.*

Freedom to Serve/ Galatians 5:7–15

You were running a good race. Who cut in on you and kept you from obeying the truth? 8That kind of persuasion does not come from the one who calls you. 9"A little yeast works through the whole batch of dough." 10I am confident in the Lord that you will take no other view. The one who is throwing you into confusion will pay the penalty, whoever he may be. ¹¹Brothers, if I am still preaching circumcision, why am I still being persecuted? In that case the offense of the cross has been abolished. ¹²As for those agitators, I wish they would go the whole way and emasculate themselves!

¹³You, my brothers, were called to be free. But do not use your freedom to indulge the sinful nature; rather, serve one another in love. ¹⁴The entire law is summed up in a single command: "Love your neighbor as yourself." ¹⁵If you keep on biting and devouring each other, watch out or you will be destroyed by each other.

A THOUGHT: *Paul distinguished between freedom to sin and freedom to serve. Freedom to sin is no freedom at all, because it enslaves us to Satan, others, or our own evil desires. People who are slaves to sin are not free to live a righteous life. Christians, by contrast, should not be slaves to sin because they are free to do right and glorify God through their actions by the power of the Holy Spirit.*

Proverbs for Today/ 16:19–20

Better to be lowly in spirit and among the oppressed than to share plunder with the proud. □ Whoever gives heed to instruction prospers, and blessed is he who trusts in the LORD.

JUNE 5

Jesus Calms the Storm/ Luke 8:22–25

One day Jesus said to his disciples, "Let's go over to the other side of the lake." So they got into a boat and set out. ²³As they sailed, he fell asleep. A squall came down on the lake, so that the boat was being swamped, and they were in great danger.

²⁴The disciples went and woke him, saying, "Master, Master, we're going to drown!"

He got up and rebuked the wind and the raging waters; the storm subsided, and all was calm. ²⁵"Where is your faith?" he asked his disciples.

In fear and amazement they asked one another, "Who is this? He commands even the winds and the water, and they obey him."

A THOUGHT: *The Sea of Galilee is still the scene of fierce storms, sometimes with waves as high as 20 feet. Jesus' disciples were not frightened without cause. Even though several of them were expert fishermen and knew how to handle a boat, their peril was real. We, like the disciples, should be awestruck at the immense power of Jesus—he can even calm fierce storms with a word. Jesus demonstrates his power over creation in a way that only the Creator could. Throughout this story we recognize that Jesus the Messiah is the Creator of the universe.*

The Spirit and Our Sinful Nature/ Galatians 5:16–21

So I say, live by the Spirit, and you will not gratify the desires of the sinful nature. 17For the sinful nature desires what is contrary to the Spirit, and the Spirit what is contrary to the sinful nature. They are in conflict with each other, so that you do not do what you want. 18But if you are led by the Spirit, you are not under law.

19The acts of the sinful nature are obvious: sexual immorality, impurity and debauchery; 20idolatry and witchcraft; hatred, discord, jealousy, fits of rage, selfish ambition, dissensions, factions 21and envy; drunkenness, orgies, and the like. I warn you, as I did before, that those who live like this will not inherit the kingdom of God.

A THOUGHT: *Paul describes the two forces at work within us—the Holy Spirit and our evil inclinations. Paul is not saying that these forces are equal. The Holy Spirit is infinitely stronger, but we are weak. Left to our own sinful ways, we will make wrong choices. Our only way to freedom from our natural evil desires is through the redemption of Christ and the empowering of the Holy Spirit.*

Proverbs for Today/ 16:21–23

The wise in heart are called discerning, and pleasant words promote instruction. □ Understanding is a fountain of life to those who have it, but folly brings punishment to fools. □ A wise man's heart guides his mouth, and his lips promote instruction.

JUNE 6

Jesus Casts Out a Legion of Demons/ Luke 8:26–40

They [Jesus and his disciples] sailed to the region of the Gerasenes, which is across the lake from Galilee. 27When Jesus stepped ashore, he was met by a demon-possessed man from the town. For a long time this man had not worn clothes or lived in a house, but had lived in the tombs. 28When he saw Jesus, he cried out and fell at his feet, shouting at the top of his voice, "What do you want with me, Jesus, Son of the Most High God? I beg you, don't torture me!" 29For Jesus had commanded the evil spirit to come out of the man. Many times it had seized him, and though he was chained hand and foot and kept under guard, he had broken his chains and had been driven by the demon into solitary places.

30Jesus asked him, "What is your name?"

"Legion," he replied, because many demons had gone into him. 31And they begged him repeatedly not to order them to go into the Abyss.

32A large herd of pigs was feeding there on the hillside. The demons begged Jesus to let them go into them, and he gave them permission. 33When the demons came out of the man, they went into the pigs, and the herd rushed down the steep bank into the lake and was drowned.

34When those tending the pigs saw what had happened, they ran off and reported this in the town and countryside, 35and the people went out to see what had happened. When they came to Jesus, they found the man from whom the demons had gone out, sitting at Jesus' feet, dressed and in his right mind; and they were afraid. 36Those who had seen it told the people how the demon-possessed man had been cured. 37Then all the people of the region of the Gerasenes asked Jesus to leave them, because they were overcome with fear. So he got into the boat and left.

38The man from whom the demons had gone out begged to go with him, but Jesus sent him away, saying, 39"Return home and tell how much God has done for you." So the man went away and told all over town how much Jesus had done for him.

40Now when Jesus returned, a crowd welcomed him, for they were all expecting him.

A THOUGHT: *Why didn't Jesus just destroy these demons—or send them to the Bottomless Pit? Because his time for such work had not yet come. He healed many people of the destructive work of demon-possession, but he did not yet destroy demons. The same question could be asked today—why doesn't Jesus destroy or stop the evil in the world? His time for that has not yet come. But it will come. The book of Revelation records the future victory of Jesus over Satan, his demons, and all evil.*

The Fruit of the Spirit/ Galatians 5:22–26

But the fruit of the Spirit is love, joy, peace, patience, kindness, goodness, faithfulness, 23gentleness and self-control. Against such things there is no law. 24Those who belong to Christ Jesus have crucified the sinful nature with its passions and desires. 25Since we live by the Spirit, let us keep in step with the Spirit. 26Let us not become conceited, provoking and envying each other.

A THOUGHT: *The Spirit produces character traits, not specific actions. We can't go out and do these things in our own power, and we can't obtain them by working to get them. If we want the fruit of the Spirit to develop in our lives, we must recognize that all of these characteristics are found in Christ. Thus the way to grow in them is to join our lives to his. We must know him, love him, remember him, imitate him. The result will be that we will fulfill the intended purpose of the Law—to love God and man. Which of these qualities needs further development in your life?*

Proverbs for Today/ 16:24

Pleasant words are a honeycomb, sweet to the soul and healing to the bones.

JUNE 7

Jesus' Power over Sickness and Death/ Luke 8:41–56

Then a man named Jairus, a ruler of the synagogue, came and fell at Jesus' feet, pleading with him to come to his house 42because his only daughter, a girl of about twelve, was dying.

As Jesus was on his way, the crowds almost crushed him. ⁴³And a woman was there who had been subject to bleeding for twelve years, but no one could heal her. ⁴⁴She came up behind him and touched the edge of his cloak, and immediately her bleeding stopped.

⁴⁵"Who touched me?" Jesus asked.

When they all denied it, Peter said, "Master, the people are crowding and pressing against you."

⁴⁶But Jesus said, "Someone touched me; I know that power has gone out from me."

⁴⁷Then the woman, seeing that she could not go unnoticed, came trembling and fell at his feet. In the presence of all the people, she told why she had touched him and how she had been instantly healed. ⁴⁸Then he said to her, "Daughter, your faith has healed you. Go in peace."

⁴⁹While Jesus was still speaking, someone came from the house of Jairus, the synagogue ruler. "Your daughter is dead," he said. "Don't bother the teacher any more."

⁵⁰Hearing this, Jesus said to Jairus, "Don't be afraid; just believe, and she will be healed."

⁵¹When he arrived at the house of Jairus, he did not let anyone go in with him except Peter, John and James, and the child's father and mother. ⁵²Meanwhile, all the people were wailing and mourning for her. "Stop wailing," Jesus said. "She is not dead but asleep."

⁵³They laughed at him, knowing that she was dead. ⁵⁴But he took her by the hand and said, "My child, get up!" ⁵⁵Her spirit returned, and at once she stood up. Then Jesus told them to give her something to eat. ⁵⁶Her parents were astonished, but he ordered them not to tell anyone what had happened.

A THOUGHT: *The bleeding woman acted upon her faith by reaching out to touch Jesus. When she did touch him, she was immediately healed. In the same way, Jairus came to Jesus asking him to heal his daughter. Jesus once again demonstrated his great power by raising Jairus' daughter from the dead. In both of these cases, God's compassion for the powerless of society is evident. God's grace reached down to a woman, who was considered unclean by her community, and to a little girl, who had little or no status in society, and restored them both to full health.*

You Reap What You Sow/ Galatians 6:1–10

Brothers, if someone is caught in a sin, you who are spiritual should restore him gently. But watch yourself, or you also may be tempted. 2Carry each other's burdens, and in this way you will fulfill the law of Christ. 3If anyone thinks he is something when he is nothing, he deceives himself. 4Each one should test his own actions. Then he can take pride in himself, without comparing himself to somebody else, 5for each one should carry his own load.

6Anyone who receives instruction in the word must share all good things with his instructor.

7Do not be deceived: God cannot be mocked. A man reaps what he sows. 8The one who sows to please his sinful nature, from that nature will reap destruction; the one who sows to please the Spirit, from the Spirit will reap eternal life. 9Let us not become weary in doing good, for at the proper time we will reap a harvest if we do not give up. 10Therefore, as we have opportunity, let us do good to all people, especially to those who belong to the family of believers.

A THOUGHT: *It would certainly be a surprise if you planted corn in the ground and pumpkins came up. But it probably would not be a surprise if you gossiped about your friends and soon found that you had no friends. It's a law of life—both physical and spiritual—that you reap what you sow. Every action has results. If you plant to please your own desires, you'll reap a crop of sorrow and evil; if you plant to please God, you'll reap joy and everlasting life. What kind of seeds are you sowing in the soil of your life?*

Proverbs for Today/ 16:25

There is a way that seems right to a man, but in the end it leads to death.

JUNE 8

Jesus Sends Out the Twelve/ Luke 9:1–9

When Jesus had called the Twelve together, he gave them power and authority to drive out all demons and to cure diseases, 2and he sent them out to preach the kingdom of

God and to heal the sick. ³He told them: "Take nothing for the journey—no staff, no bag, no bread, no money, no extra tunic. ⁴Whatever house you enter, stay there until you leave that town. ⁵If people do not welcome you, shake the dust off your feet when you leave their town, as a testimony against them." ⁶So they set out and went from village to village, preaching the gospel and healing people everywhere.

⁷Now Herod the tetrarch heard about all that was going on. And he was perplexed, because some were saying that John had been raised from the dead, ⁸others that Elijah had appeared, and still others that one of the prophets of long ago had come back to life. ⁹But Herod said, "I beheaded John. Who, then, is this I hear such things about?" And he tried to see him.

A THOUGHT: *Why did Jesus announce his kingdom with preaching and healing? If he had limited himself to preaching, people might have seen his kingdom as spiritual only. On the other hand, if he had healed without preaching, people might have not realized the spiritual importance of his mission. Most of his listeners expected a Messiah who would bring wealth and power to their nation; they preferred material blessings to spiritual discernment. The truth about Jesus is that he is both God and man, both spiritual and physical; and the salvation he offers is both for the soul and the body. Any group or teaching that emphasizes soul at the expense of body or body at the expense of soul is in danger of distorting Jesus' Good News.*

Paul's Closing Words/ Galatians 6:11–18

See what large letters I use as I write to you with my own hand!

¹²Those who want to make a good impression outwardly are trying to compel you to be circumcised. The only reason they do this is to avoid being persecuted for the cross of Christ. ¹³Not even those who are circumcised obey the law, yet they want you to be circumcised that they may boast about your flesh. ¹⁴May I never boast except in the cross of our Lord Jesus Christ, through which the world has been crucified to me, and I to the world. ¹⁵Neither circumcision nor uncircumcision means anything; what counts is a new creation. ¹⁶Peace and mercy to all who follow this rule, even to the Israel of God.

¹⁷Finally, let no one cause me trouble, for I bear on my body the marks of Jesus.

18The grace of our Lord Jesus Christ be with your spirit, brothers. Amen.

A THOUGHT: *Some of the Judaizers emphasized circumcision as proof of holiness, but ignored the other Jewish laws. People often choose a certain principle or prohibition and make it the measuring rod of faith. Some may abhor drunkenness but ignore gluttony. Others despise promiscuity but tolerate prejudice. The Bible in its entirety is our rule of faith and practice. We cannot pick and choose the mandates we will follow.*

Proverbs for Today/ 16:26–27

The laborer's appetite works for him; his hunger drives him on. □ A scoundrel plots evil, and his speech is like a scorching fire.

JUNE 9

Jesus Feeds Five Thousand/ Luke 9:10–17

When the apostles returned, they reported to Jesus what they had done. Then he took them with him and they withdrew by themselves to a town called Bethsaida, 11but the crowds learned about it and followed him. He welcomed them and spoke to them about the kingdom of God, and healed those who needed healing.

12Late in the afternoon the Twelve came to him and said, "Send the crowd away so they can go to the surrounding villages and countryside and find food and lodging, because we are in a remote place here."

13He replied, "You give them something to eat."

They answered, "We have only five loaves of bread and two fish—unless we go and buy food for all this crowd." 14(About five thousand men were there.)

But he said to his disciples, "Have them sit down in groups of about fifty each." 15The disciples did so, and everybody sat down. 16Taking the five loaves and the two fish and looking up to heaven, he gave thanks and broke them. Then he gave them to the disciples to set before the people. 17They all ate and were satisfied, and the disciples picked up twelve basketfuls of broken pieces that were left over.

A THOUGHT: *The kingdom of God was a focal point of Jesus' teaching. He explained that it was not just a future kingdom; it was among them, embodied in him, the Messiah. Even though the kingdom will not be complete until Jesus comes again in glory, we do not have to wait to taste it. The kingdom of God begins in the hearts of those who believe in Jesus. It is as present with us today as it was with the Judeans two thousand years ago.*

Jesus demonstrated the presence of the kingdom of God through feeding all these people. Just as God had provided manna for Moses and the people of Israel in the wilderness so that they had more than they needed to eat, so Jesus provides food for these people to the point that they suffered no lack. Our sufficiency for all of life can be found in Jesus.

God's Overflowing Kindness/ Ephesians 1:1–8

Paul, an apostle of Christ Jesus by the will of God,

To the saints in Ephesus, the faithful in Christ Jesus:

2Grace and peace to you from God our Father and the Lord Jesus Christ.

3Praise be to the God and Father of our Lord Jesus Christ, who has blessed us in the heavenly realms with every spiritual blessing in Christ. 4For he chose us in him before the creation of the world to be holy and blameless in his sight. In love 5he predestined us to be adopted as his sons through Jesus Christ, in accordance with his pleasure and will— 6to the praise of his glorious grace, which he has freely given us in the One he loves. 7In him we have redemption through his blood, the forgiveness of sins, in accordance with the riches of God's grace 8that he lavished on us with all wisdom and understanding.

A THOUGHT: *To speak of Jesus' blood was an important first-century way of speaking of Christ's death. His death points to two wonderful truths—redemption and forgiveness. Redemption was the price paid to gain freedom for a slave. Through his death, Jesus paid the price to release us from slavery to sin. Forgiveness was granted in Old Testament times on the basis of the shedding of animals' blood. Now we are forgiven on the basis of God's grace in the shedding of Jesus' blood, because he died as the perfect and final sacrifice for our sins. Grace is God's voluntary and loving favor given to those he saves. We can't earn it, nor do we deserve it. No religious or moral effort can gain it, for it comes only from God's mercy and love expressed in the death and resurrection of his Son for our redemption.*

Proverbs for Today/ 16:28–30

A perverse man stirs up dissension, and a gossip separates close friends. □ A violent man entices his neighbor and leads him down a path that is not good. □ He who winks with his eye is plotting perversity; he who purses his lips is bent on evil.

JUNE 10

Peter's Confession/ Luke 9:18–22

Once when Jesus was praying in private and his disciples were with him, he asked them, "Who do the crowds say I am?"

19They replied, "Some say John the Baptist; others say Elijah; and still others, that one of the prophets of long ago has come back to life."

20"But what about you?" he asked. "Who do you say I am?"

Peter answered, "The Christ of God."

21Jesus strictly warned them not to tell this to anyone. 22And he said, "The Son of Man must suffer many things and be rejected by the elders, chief priests and teachers of the law, and he must be killed and on the third day be raised to life."

A THOUGHT: *Jesus told his disciples not to tell anyone he was the Messiah because, at this point, they didn't fully understand the significance of that statement—nor did anyone else. God had revealed to Peter that Jesus was in fact the Messiah, but Peter, along with everyone else, still expected a messiah who would be a conquering king. But Jesus, as the Messiah, still had to suffer, be rejected by the leaders, be killed, and rise from the dead. Christians must confess with Peter that Jesus is indeed the Messiah, but the Suffering-Servant Messiah who accomplished the redemption of mankind and who will soon come to establish his kingdom on earth. The ultimate question for us as hearers of the Good News is the one that Jesus asked Peter, "Who do you think I am?"*

God's Plan of Redemption/ Ephesians 1:9–14

And he [God the Father] made known to us the mystery of his will according to his good pleasure, which he purposed in Christ, ¹⁰to be put into effect when the times will have reached their fulfillment—to bring all things in heaven and on earth together under one head, even Christ.

¹¹In him we were also chosen, having been predestined according to the plan of him who works out everything in conformity with the purpose of his will, ¹²in order that we, who were the first to hope in Christ, might be for the praise of his glory. ¹³And you also were included in Christ when you heard the word of truth, the gospel of your salvation. Having believed, you were marked in him with a seal, the promised Holy Spirit, ¹⁴who is a deposit guaranteeing our inheritance until the redemption of those who are God's possession—to the praise of his glory.

A THOUGHT: *The Holy Spirit is God's guarantee to us that he will do what he has promised. He is like a down payment, a deposit, a validating signature on the contract. The presence of the Holy Spirit in our lives is our assurance of eternal life with all its blessings. His power at work in us now is transforming our lives, and is a taste of the total change we will experience in eternity.*

Proverbs for Today/ 16:31–33

Gray hair is a crown of splendor; it is attained by a righteous life. □ Better a patient man than a warrior, a man who controls his temper than one who takes a city. □ The lot is cast into the lap, but its every decision is from the LORD.

JUNE 11

Take Up Your Cross and Follow Jesus/
Luke 9:23–27

Then he [Jesus] said to them all: "If anyone would come after me, he must deny himself and take up his cross daily and follow me. ²⁴For whoever wants to save his life will lose it, but whoever loses his life for me will save it. ²⁵What good is it for a man to gain the whole world, and yet lose or forfeit his very self? ²⁶If anyone is ashamed of me and my words, the Son of Man will be ashamed of him when he comes in his glory and in the glory of the Father and of the holy angels. ²⁷I tell you the truth, some who are standing here will not taste death before they see the kingdom of God."

A THOUGHT: *People are willing to pay a high price for something they value. Is it any surprise that Jesus should demand this much commitment from those who would follow him? There are at least three conditions that must be met by people who want to follow Jesus. They must be willing to deny self, to carry their crosses, and to give up control over their lives. Anything less is superficial lip service.*

Paul's Prayer for the Ephesians/ Ephesians 1:15–23

For this reason, ever since I heard about your faith in the Lord Jesus and your love for all the saints, 16I have not stopped giving thanks for you, remembering you in my prayers. 17I keep asking that the God of our Lord Jesus Christ, the glorious Father, may give you the Spirit of wisdom and revelation, so that you may know him better. 18I pray also that the eyes of your heart may be enlightened in order that you may know the hope to which he has called you, the riches of his glorious inheritance in the saints, 19and his incomparably great power for us who believe. That power is like the working of his mighty strength, 20which he exerted in Christ when he raised him from the dead and seated him at his right hand in the heavenly realms, 21far above all rule and authority, power and dominion, and every title that can be given, not only in the present age but also in the one to come. 22And God placed all things under his feet and appointed him to be head over everything for the church, 23which is his body, the fullness of him who fills everything in every way.

A THOUGHT: *Paul's prayer for the Ephesians was that they might really understand who Christ is. Christ is our goal and our model, and the more we know of him, the more we will be like him. Study Jesus' life in the Bible to see what he was like on earth 2,000 years ago, and get to know him in prayer now. Personal knowledge of Christ is life-changing!*

Proverbs for Today/ 17:1

Better a dry crust with peace and quiet than a house full of feasting, with strife.

JUNE 12

The Transfiguration of Jesus/ Luke 9:28–36

About eight days after Jesus said this, he took Peter, John and James with him and went up onto a mountain to pray. 29As he was praying, the appearance of his face changed, and his clothes became as bright as a flash of lightning. 30Two men, Moses and Elijah, 31appeared in glorious splendor, talking with Jesus. They spoke about his departure, which he was about to bring to fulfillment at Jerusalem. 32Peter and his companions were very sleepy, but when they became fully awake, they saw his glory and the two men standing with him. 33As the men were leaving Jesus, Peter said to him, "Master, it is good for us to be here. Let us put up three shelters—one for you, one for Moses and one for Elijah." (He did not know what he was saying.)

34While he was speaking, a cloud appeared and enveloped them, and they were afraid as they entered the cloud. 35A voice came from the cloud, saying, "This is my Son, whom I have chosen; listen to him." 36When the voice had spoken, they found that Jesus was alone. The disciples kept this to themselves, and told no one at that time what they had seen.

A THOUGHT: *Jesus took Peter, James, and John to the top of a mountain to show them who he really was—not just a great prophet, but God's own Son. Moses, representing the Law, and Elijah, representing the Prophets, appeared with Jesus. God's voice singled out Jesus as the long-awaited Messiah who possessed divine authority. The authority of Jesus superceded that of the Law and the Prophets represented by Moses and Elijah, for Jesus is the fulfillment of both the Law and the Prophets.*

As God's Son, Jesus has ultimate power and authority; thus, his words should be our final authority. If a person's teaching is true, it will go along with Jesus' teachings. Test everything you hear against Jesus' words, and you will not be led astray.

Dead in Sin, Alive in Christ/ Ephesians 2:1–7

As for you, you were dead in your transgressions and sins, 2in which you used to live when you followed the ways of this world and of the ruler of the kingdom of the air, the spirit who is now at work in those who are disobedient. 3All of us also lived among them at one time, gratifying the cravings of our sinful nature and following its desires and thoughts. Like the rest, we were by nature objects of wrath. 4But because of his great love for us, God, who is rich in mercy, 5made us alive with Christ even when we were dead in transgressions—it is by grace you have been saved. 6And God raised us up with Christ and seated us with him in the heavenly realms in Christ Jesus, 7in order that in the coming ages he might show the incomparable riches of his grace, expressed in his kindness to us in Christ Jesus.

A THOUGHT: *The fact that all people, without exception, commit sin proves that they share in the sinful nature. Does this mean there are no good people who are not Christians? Of course not. Many people do good to others. On a relative scale, many are moral, kind, keep the laws, and so on. Comparing these people to criminals, we would say they are very good indeed. But on God's absolute scale, no one is good. Only through uniting our lives to Christ's perfect life can we become good in God's sight.*

Proverbs for Today/ 17:2–3

A wise servant will rule over a disgraceful son, and will share the inheritance as one of the brothers. □ The crucible for silver and the furnace for gold, but the LORD tests the heart.

JUNE 13

Jesus Heals a Demon-Possesed Boy/ Luke 9:37–43a

The next day, when they [Jesus and his disciples] came down from the mountain, a large crowd met him. 38A man in the crowd called out, "Teacher, I beg you to look at my son, for he is my only child. 39A spirit seizes him and he suddenly screams; it throws him into convulsions so that he foams at the mouth. It scarcely ever leaves him and is destroying him. 40I begged your disciples to drive it out, but they could not."

41"O unbelieving and perverse generation," Jesus

replied, "how long shall I stay with you and put up with you? Bring your son here."

42Even while the boy was coming, the demon threw him to the ground in a convulsion. But Jesus rebuked the evil spirit, healed the boy and gave him back to his father. 43And they were all amazed at the greatness of God.

A THOUGHT: *This account is set in contrast to the transfiguration of Jesus which Peter, James, and John had just seen. The disciples were unable to cast out the demon from this boy because they lacked the faith. They did not recognize that the One who had commissioned them to preach the Good News, to heal, and to cast out demons, was the divine Son of God. Jesus demonstrated that he possessed the authority of God through casting out the demon from the boy—a sign that the kingdom of God was present in the person of Jesus Christ himself. Recognizing God's great power should move us to worship him and live in humble obedience before him.*

Saved by Grace through Faith/ Ephesians 2:8–13

For it is by grace you have been saved, through faith—and this not from yourselves, it is the gift of God— 9not by works, so that no one can boast. 10For we are God's workmanship, created in Christ Jesus to do good works, which God prepared in advance for us to do.

11Therefore, remember that formerly you who are Gentiles by birth and called "uncircumcised" by those who call themselves "the circumcision" (that done in the body by the hands of men)— 12remember that at that time you were separate from Christ, excluded from citizenship in Israel and foreigners to the covenants of the promise, without hope and without God in the world. 13But now in Christ Jesus you who once were far away have been brought near through the blood of Christ.

A THOUGHT: *We become Christians through God's unmerited gift to us, not as the result of any effort, ability, intelligent choice, or act of service to others on our part. However, out of gratitude for this free gift, we will seek to help and serve others with kindness, charity, and goodness, and not merely please ourselves. While no action or "work" we do can help us obtain salvation, God's intention is that our salvation will result in works of service. We are not saved merely for our own benefit. We are saved to glorify him and build up the church.*

Proverbs for Today/ 17:4–5

A wicked man listens to evil lips; a liar pays attention to a malicious tongue. □ He who mocks the poor shows contempt for their Maker; whoever gloats over disaster will not go unpunished.

JUNE 14

Servanthood Is the Measure of Greatness/ Luke 9:43b–50

While everyone was marveling at all that Jesus did, he said to his disciples, 44"Listen carefully to what I am about to tell you: The Son of Man is going to be betrayed into the hands of men." 45But they did not understand what this meant. It was hidden from them, so that they did not grasp it, and they were afraid to ask him about it.

46An argument started among the disciples as to which of them would be the greatest. 47Jesus, knowing their thoughts, took a little child and had him stand beside him. 48Then he said to them, "Whoever welcomes this little child in my name welcomes me; and whoever welcomes me welcomes the one who sent me. For he who is least among you all—he is the greatest."

49"Master," said John, "we saw a man driving out demons in your name and we tried to stop him, because he is not one of us."

50"Do not stop him," Jesus said, "for whoever is not against you is for you."

A THOUGHT: *The disciples didn't understand Jesus' words about his death. They still thought of Jesus as an earthly king, and they were concerned about securing high places for themselves in his kingdom. So they ignored his words about his death and began arguing about who would be greatest. It is ironic that, immediately following Jesus' explanation of his betrayal and suffering, the disciples should be arguing about greatness. When we seek honor and glory for ourselves, we can be assured that it is not true greatness that we will find, for true greatness is marked by genuine self-sacrifice and obedience to God—true greatness is in Christlikeness.*

Unity in Christ/ Ephesians 2:14–22

For he himself is our peace, who has made the two one and has destroyed the barrier, the dividing wall of hostility, 15by abolishing in his flesh the law with its commandments and regulations. His purpose was to create in himself one new man out of the two, thus making peace, [16]and in this one body to reconcile both of them to God through the cross, by which he put to death their hostility. [17]He came and preached peace to you who were far away and peace to those who were near. [18]For through him we both have access to the Father by one Spirit.

[19]Consequently, you are no longer foreigners and aliens, but fellow citizens with God's people and members of God's household, [20]built on the foundation of the apostles and prophets, with Christ Jesus himself as the chief cornerstone. [21]In him the whole building is joined together and rises to become a holy temple in the Lord. [22]And in him you too are being built together to become a dwelling in which God lives by his Spirit.

A THOUGHT: *There are many barriers that can divide us from other Christians: age, appearance, intelligence, political persuasion, economic status, race, theological perspective. One of the best ways to stifle Christ's love is to cater only to those for whom we have natural affinity. Fortunately, Christ has knocked down the barriers and unified all believers in one family. His cross should be the focus of our unity. The Holy Spirit helps us look beyond the barriers to the unity we are called to enjoy.*

Proverbs for Today/ 17:6

Children's children are a crown to the aged, and parents are the pride of their children.

JUNE 15

Would-Be Disciples/ Luke 9:51–62

As the time approached for him to be taken up to heaven, Jesus resolutely set out for Jerusalem. [52]And he sent messengers on ahead, who went into a Samaritan village to get things ready for him; [53]but the people there did not welcome him, because he was heading for Jerusalem. [54]When the disciples James and John saw this, they asked, "Lord, do you want us to call fire down from heaven to destroy them?" 55But Jesus turned and rebuked them, 56and they went to another village.

57As they were walking along the road, a man said to him, "I will follow you wherever you go."

58Jesus replied, "Foxes have holes and birds of the air have nests, but the Son of Man has no place to lay his head."

59He said to another man, "Follow me."

But the man replied, "Lord, first let me go and bury my father."

60Jesus said to him, "Let the dead bury their own dead, but you go and proclaim the kingdom of God."

61Still another said, "I will follow you, Lord; but first let me go back and say good-by to my family."

62Jesus replied, "No one who puts his hand to the plow and looks back is fit for service in the kingdom of God."

A THOUGHT: *What does Jesus want from us? He wants total dedication, not halfhearted commitment. We can't pick and choose among Jesus' ideas and follow him selectively; we have to accept the cross along with the crown, judgment as well as mercy. We must count the cost and be willing to abandon everything else that has given us security. With our focus on Jesus, we should allow nothing to distract us from the manner of living he calls us to live out.*

Paul's Special Mission to Gentiles/ Ephesians 3:1–7

For this reason I, Paul, the prisoner of Christ Jesus for the sake of you Gentiles—

2Surely you have heard about the administration of God's grace that was given to me for you, 3that is, the mystery made known to me by revelation, as I have already written briefly. 4In reading this, then, you will be able to understand my insight into the mystery of Christ, 5which was not made known to men in other generations as it has now been revealed by the Spirit to God's holy apostles and prophets. 6This mystery is that through the gospel the Gentiles are heirs together with Israel, members together of one body, and sharers together in the promise in Christ Jesus.

7I became a servant of this gospel by the gift of God's grace given me through the working of his power.

A THOUGHT: *God gave the apostle Paul the ability to share effectively the gospel of Christ. You may not be an apostle or even an evangelist, but God will also give you opportunities to tell others about Christ—and with the opportunity he will provide the ability, courage, and power. Whenever an opportunity presents itself, make yourself available to God. As you focus on the other person and his or her needs, God will communicate your caring attitude, and your words will be natural, loving, and compelling.*

Proverbs for Today/ 17:7–8

Arrogant lips are unsuited to a fool—how much worse lying lips to a ruler! □ A bribe is a charm to the one who gives it; wherever he turns, he succeeds.

JUNE 16

Jesus Sends out Seventy-two Disciples/ Luke 10:1–24

After this the Lord appointed seventy-two others and sent them two by two ahead of him to every town and place where he was about to go. 2He told them, "The harvest is plentiful, but the workers are few. Ask the Lord of the harvest, therefore, to send out workers into his harvest field. 3Go! I am sending you out like lambs among wolves. 4Do not take a purse or bag or sandals; and do not greet anyone on the road.

5"When you enter a house, first say, 'Peace to this house.' 6If a man of peace is there, your peace will rest on him; if not, it will return to you. 7Stay in that house, eating and drinking whatever they give you, for the worker deserves his wages. Do not move around from house to house.

8"When you enter a town and are welcomed, eat what is set before you. 9Heal the sick who are there and tell them, 'The kingdom of God is near you.' 10But when you enter a town and are not welcomed, go into its streets and say, 11'Even the dust of your town that sticks to our feet we wipe off against you. Yet be sure of this: The kingdom of God is near.' 12I tell you, it will be more bearable on that day for Sodom than for that town.

13"Woe to you, Korazin! Woe to you, Bethsaida! For if the miracles that were performed in you had been performed in Tyre and Sidon, they would have repented long ago, sitting in sackcloth and ashes. 14But it will be more bearable for Tyre and Sidon at the judgment than for you. 15And you, Capernaum, will you be lifted up to the skies? No, you will go down to the depths.

16"He who listens to you listens to me; he who rejects you rejects me; but he who rejects me rejects him who sent me."

17The seventy-two returned with joy and said, "Lord, even the demons submit to us in your name."

18He replied, "I saw Satan fall like lightning from heaven. 19I have given you authority to trample on snakes and scorpions and to overcome all the power of the enemy; nothing will harm you. 20However, do not rejoice that the spirits submit to you, but rejoice that your names are written in heaven."

21At that time Jesus, full of joy through the Holy Spirit, said, "I praise you, Father, Lord of heaven and earth, because you have hidden these things from the wise and learned, and revealed them to little children. Yes, Father, for this was your good pleasure.

22"All things have been committed to me by my Father. No one knows who the Son is except the Father, and no one knows who the Father is except the Son and those to whom the Son chooses to reveal him."

23Then he turned to his disciples and said privately, "Blessed are the eyes that see what you see. 24For I tell you that many prophets and kings wanted to see what you see but did not see it, and to hear what you hear but did not hear it."

A THOUGHT: *The disciples had seen tremendous results as they ministered in Jesus' name and with his authority. They were elated by the victories they had witnessed, and Jesus shared their enthusiasm. He brought them down to earth, however, by reminding them of their most important victory—that their names were registered among the citizens of heaven. This honor was more important than any of their accomplishments. As we see God's wonders at work in us and through us, we should not lose sight of the greatest wonder of all—the grace of God expressed in our heavenly citizenship.*

Confidence Before God/ Ephesians 3:8–13

Although I am less than the least of all God's people, this grace was given me: to preach to the Gentiles the unsearchable riches of Christ, 9and to make plain to everyone the administration of this mystery, which for ages past was kept hidden in God, who created all things. 10His intent was that now, through the church, the manifold wisdom of God should be made known to the rulers and authorities in the heavenly realms, 11according to his eternal purpose which he accomplished in Christ Jesus our Lord. 12In him and through faith in him we may approach God with freedom and confidence. 13I ask you, therefore, not to be discouraged because of my sufferings for you, which are your glory.

A THOUGHT: *When Paul describes himself as a useless Christian, he is saying that without God's help, he would never be able to do God's work. Yet God chose him to share the gospel with the Gentiles and gave him the power to do this. If we feel useless, we may be right—except that we have forgotten what a difference God makes. How does God want to use you? Do your part and faithfully perform the special role you play in God's plan.*

Proverbs for Today/ 17:9–11

He who covers over an offense promotes love, but whoever repeats the matter separates close friends. □ A rebuke impresses a man of discernment more than a hundred lashes a fool. □ An evil man is bent only on rebellion; a merciless official will be sent against him.

JUNE 17

The Parable of the Good Samaritan/ Luke 10:25–37

On one occasion an expert in the law stood up to test Jesus. "Teacher," he asked, "what must I do to inherit eternal life?"

26"What is written in the Law?" he replied. "How do you read it?"

27He answered: " 'Love the Lord your God with all your heart and with all your soul and with all your strength and with all your mind'; and, 'Love your neighbor as yourself.'"

28"You have answered correctly," Jesus replied. "Do this and you will live."

²⁹But he wanted to justify himself, so he asked Jesus, "And who is my neighbor?"

³⁰In reply Jesus said: "A man was going down from Jerusalem to Jericho, when he fell into the hands of robbers. They stripped him of his clothes, beat him and went away, leaving him half dead. ³¹A priest happened to be going down the same road, and when he saw the man, he passed by on the other side. ³²So too, a Levite, when he came to the place and saw him, passed by on the other side. ³³But a Samaritan, as he traveled, came where the man was; and when he saw him, he took pity on him. ³⁴He went to him and bandaged his wounds, pouring on oil and wine. Then he put the man on his own donkey, took him to an inn and took care of him. ³⁵The next day he took out two silver coins and gave them to the innkeeper. 'Look after him,' he said, 'and when I return, I will reimburse you for any extra expense you may have.'

³⁶"Which of these three do you think was a neighbor to the man who fell into the hands of robbers?"

³⁷The expert in the law replied, "The one who had mercy on him."

Jesus told him, "Go and do likewise."

A THOUGHT: *The legal experts treated the wounded man as a topic for discussion; the thieves, as an object to exploit; the priest, as a problem to avoid; and the temple assistant, as an object of curiosity. Only the Samaritan treated him as a person to love. From the parable we learn three principles about loving our neighbor: (1) lack of love is often easy to justify; (2) our neighbor is anyone of any race or creed or social background who is in need; and (3) love means acting to meet the need. Wherever you live, there are needy people close by. There is no good rationale for refusing to help.*

Paul Prays for the Ephesians/ Ephesians 3:14–21

For this reason I kneel before the Father, ¹⁵from whom his whole family in heaven and on earth derives its name. ¹⁶I pray that out of his glorious riches he may strengthen you with power through his Spirit in your inner being, ¹⁷so that Christ may dwell in your hearts through faith. And I pray that you, being rooted and established in love, ¹⁸may have power, together with all the saints, to grasp how wide and long and high and deep is the love of Christ, ¹⁹and to know this love that surpasses knowledge—that you may be filled to the measure of all the fullness of God.

20Now to him who is able to do immeasurably more than all we ask or imagine, according to his power that is at work within us, 21to him be glory in the church and in Christ Jesus throughout all generations, for ever and ever! Amen.

A THOUGHT: *The great family of God includes all who have believed in him in the past, all who believe in the present, and all who will believe in the future. We are all a family because we have the same Father. He is the source of all creation, the rightful owner of everything. God promises his love and power to his family, the church; if we want to receive his blessings, it is important that we stay in living contact with other believers in the body of Christ. Those who isolate themselves from God's family and try to go it alone are cutting themselves off from the primary avenue through which God has chosen to work.*

Proverbs for Today/ 17:12–13

Better to meet a bear robbed of her cubs than a fool in his folly. □ If a man pays back evil for good, evil will never leave his house.

JUNE 18

Mary and Martha/ Luke 10:38–42

As Jesus and his disciples were on their way, he came to a village where a woman named Martha opened her home to him. 39She had a sister called Mary, who sat at the Lord's feet listening to what he said. 40But Martha was distracted by all the preparations that had to be made. She came to him and asked, "Lord, don't you care that my sister has left me to do the work by myself? Tell her to help me!"

41"Martha, Martha," the Lord answered, "you are worried and upset about many things, 42but only one thing is needed. Mary has chosen what is better, and it will not be taken away from her."

A THOUGHT: *Mary and Martha both loved Jesus. On this occasion they were both serving him. But Martha implied that Mary's style of serving was inferior to hers. She didn't realize that in her desire to serve, she was actually neglecting Jesus. Are you so busy doing things for Jesus that you're not spending any time with him? Don't let your service become self-serving. It is important to know whom you are serving.*

One Body in Christ/ Ephesians 4:1–10

As a prisoner for the Lord, then, I urge you to live a life worthy of the calling you have received. ²Be completely humble and gentle; be patient, bearing with one another in love. ³Make every effort to keep the unity of the Spirit through the bond of peace. ⁴There is one body and one Spirit— just as you were called to one hope when you were called— ⁵one Lord, one faith, one baptism; ⁶one God and Father of all, who is over all and through all and in all.

⁷But to each one of us grace has been given as Christ apportioned it. ⁸This is why it says:

"When he ascended on high,
he led captives in his train
and gave gifts to men."

⁹(What does "he ascended" mean except that he also descended to the lower, earthly regions? ¹⁰He who descended is the very one who ascended higher than all the heavens, in order to fill the whole universe.)

A THOUGHT: *"There is one body," says Paul, and we have been given many gifts and abilities to use within it. Unity does not just happen; we have to work at it. Often differences among people can lead to division, but this should not be true in the church. Instead of concentrating on what divides us, we should remember what unites us: one body, one Spirit, one future, one Lord, one faith, one baptism, one God! Have you learned to appreciate people who are different from you? Can you see how their differing gifts and viewpoints can help the church as it does God's work? Learn to enjoy the way the members of Christ's body compliment one another.*

Proverbs for Today/ 17:14–15

Starting a quarrel is like breaching a dam; so drop the matter before a dispute breaks out. □ Acquitting the guilty and condemning the innocent—the LORD detests them both.

JUNE 19

Jesus Teaches about Prayer/ Luke 11:1–13

One day Jesus was praying in a certain place. When he finished, one of his disciples said to him, "Lord, teach us to pray, just as John taught his disciples."

2He said to them, "When you pray, say:

> " 'Father,
> hallowed be your name,
> your kingdom come.
> 3Give us each day our daily bread.
> 4Forgive us our sins,
>   for we also forgive everyone who sins against us.
>   And lead us not into temptation.' "

5Then he said to them, "Suppose one of you has a friend, and he goes to him at midnight and says, 'Friend, lend me three loaves of bread, 6because a friend of mine on a journey has come to me, and I have nothing to set before him.'

7"Then the one inside answers, 'Don't bother me. The door is already locked, and my children are with me in bed. I can't get up and give you anything.' 8I tell you, though he will not get up and give him the bread because he is his friend, yet because of the man's boldness he will get up and give him as much as he needs.

9"So I say to you: Ask and it will be given to you; seek and you will find; knock and the door will be opened to you. 10For everyone who asks receives; he who seeks finds; and to him who knocks, the door will be opened.

11"Which of you fathers, if your son asks for a fish, will give him a snake instead? 12Or if he asks for an egg, will give him a scorpion? 13If you then, though you are evil, know how to give good gifts to your children, how much more will your Father in heaven give the Holy Spirit to those who ask him!"

A THOUGHT: *When Jesus begins to teach his disciples about prayer, he gives them a pattern to follow—a model prayer. Notice the order in this prayer. First Jesus praises God; then he makes his requests. Praising God first puts us in the right frame of mind to tell him about our needs. Too often our prayers are more like shopping lists than conversations.*

Jesus also made forgiving others a central part of our relationship with God. God has forgiven our sins; we must forgive those who have wronged us. To remain unforgiving shows we have not understood that we, along with all other human beings, deeply need to be forgiven. Think of some people who have wronged you. Have you truly forgiven them, or do you still carry a grudge against them? Our communion with God in prayer is directly affected by our relationship with those around us.

God's Gifts to the Church/ Ephesians 4:11–16

It was he who gave some to be apostles, some to be prophets, some to be evangelists, and some to be pastors and teachers, 12to prepare God's people for works of service, so that the body of Christ may be built up 13until we all reach unity in the faith and in the knowledge of the Son of God and become mature, attaining to the whole measure of the fullness of Christ.

14Then we will no longer be infants, tossed back and forth by the waves, and blown here and there by every wind of teaching and by the cunning and craftiness of men in their deceitful scheming. 15Instead, speaking the truth in love, we will in all things grow up into him who is the Head, that is, Christ. 16From him the whole body, joined and held together by every supporting ligament, grows and builds itself up in love, as each part does its work.

A THOUGHT: *All believers in Christ belong to one body; all are united under one Head, who is Christ himself. Each believer has God-given abilities that can strengthen the whole body. Our oneness in Christ does not destroy our individuality. The Holy Spirit has given each Christian special gifts for building up the church. Now that we have these gifts, it is crucial to use them. Are you spiritually mature, exercising the gifts God has given you? If you know what your gifts are, look for opportunities to serve. If you don't know, ask God to show you what your gifts are. Then, as you begin to recognize your special area of service, use your gifts to strengthen and encourage the church.*

Proverbs for Today/ 17:16

Of what use is money in the hand of a fool, since he has no desire to get wisdom?

JUNE 20

The Kingdom of God and the Kingdom of Satan/ Luke 11:14–28

Jesus was driving out a demon that was mute. When the demon left, the man who had been mute spoke, and the crowd was amazed. 15But some of them said, "By Beelzebub, the prince of demons, he is driving out demons." 16Others tested him by asking for a sign from heaven.

17Jesus knew their thoughts and said to them: "Any kingdom divided against itself will be ruined, and a house divided against itself will fall. 18If Satan is divided against himself, how can his kingdom stand? I say this because you claim that I drive out demons by Beelzebub. 19Now if I drive out demons by Beelzebub, by whom do your followers drive them out? So then, they will be your judges. 20But if I drive out demons by the finger of God, then the kingdom of God has come to you.

21"When a strong man, fully armed, guards his own house, his possessions are safe. 22But when someone stronger attacks and overpowers him, he takes away the armor in which the man trusted and divides up the spoils.

23"He who is not with me is against me, and he who does not gather with me, scatters.

24"When an evil spirit comes out of a man, it goes through arid places seeking rest and does not find it. Then it says, 'I will return to the house I left.' 25When it arrives, it finds the house swept clean and put in order. 26Then it goes and takes seven other spirits more wicked than itself, and they go in and live there. And the final condition of that man is worse than the first."

27As Jesus was saying these things, a woman in the crowd called out, "Blessed is the mother who gave you birth and nursed you."

28He replied, "Blessed rather are those who hear the word of God and obey it."

A THOUGHT: *Jesus proved to his listeners that the kingdom of God had arrived in his person. Jesus was casting out the demons who belonged to the kingdom of darkness. This account, along with the many other accounts of casting out demons, pointed to Satan's defeat and the establishment of the kingdom of God. God will bring about his ultimate victory over Satan in the end when he casts Satan and all of his followers into the Lake of Fire. Are we among those who recognize the power of God in Jesus Christ?*

Throw off the Old, Put on the New/ Ephesians 4:17–24

So I tell you this, and insist on it in the Lord, that you must no longer live as the Gentiles do, in the futility of their thinking. 18They are darkened in their understanding and separated from the life of God because of the ignorance that is in them due to the hardening of their hearts. 19Having lost all sensitivity, they have given themselves over to sensuality so as to indulge in every kind of impurity, with a continual lust for more.

20You, however, did not come to know Christ that way. 21Surely you heard of him and were taught in him in accordance with the truth that is in Jesus. 22You were taught, with regard to your former way of life, to put off your old self, which is being corrupted by its deceitful desires; 23to be made new in the attitude of your minds; 24and to put on the new self, created to be like God in true righteousness and holiness.

A THOUGHT: *People should be able to see a difference between Christians and non-Christians because of the way Christians live. Paul tells the Ephesians to leave behind the old life of sin now that they are followers of Christ. The Christian life is a process. We don't automatically have good thoughts and attitudes when we become new people in Christ. But if we keep listening to God, we will be changing all the time. As you look over the last year, do you see a process of change for the better in your thoughts, attitudes, and actions? Although change may be slow, it comes about if you trust God to change you.*

Proverbs for Today/ 17:17–18

A friend loves at all times, and a brother is born for adversity. □ A man lacking in judgment strikes hands in pledge and puts up security for his neighbor.

JUNE 21

The Sign of Jonah/ Luke 11:29–36

As the crowds increased, Jesus said, "This is a wicked generation. It asks for a miraculous sign, but none will be given it except the sign of Jonah. 30For as Jonah was a sign to the Ninevites, so also will the Son of Man be to this generation. 31The Queen of the South will rise at the judgment with the men of this generation and condemn them; for she came from the ends of the earth to listen to Solomon's wisdom, and now one greater than Solomon is here. 32The men of Nineveh will stand up at the judgment with this generation and condemn it; for they repented at the preaching of Jonah, and now one greater than Jonah is here.

33"No one lights a lamp and puts it in a place where it will be hidden, or under a bowl. Instead he puts it on its stand, so that those who come in may see the light. 34Your eye is the lamp of your body. When your eyes are good, your whole body also is full of light. But when they are bad, your body also is full of darkness. 35See to it, then, that the light within you is not darkness. 36Therefore, if your whole body is full of light, and no part of it dark, it will be completely lighted, as when the light of a lamp shines on you."

A THOUGHT: *The cruel, warlike men of Assyria repented when Jonah preached to them—and Jonah did not really care about them. The heathen Queen of Sheba praised the God of Israel when she heard Solomon's wisdom, and Solomon was full of faults. By contrast, Jesus, the perfect Son of God, came to people whom he loved dearly—and they rejected him. Thus God's chosen people made themselves more liable to judgment than either a notoriously wicked nation or a powerful pagan queen. The people of Nineveh and the Queen of Sheba had turned to God with far less evidence than Jesus was giving his listeners—and far less than we have today. We have eyewitness reports of the risen Jesus, the continuing power of the Holy Spirit, easy access to the Bible, and 2,000 years of church history recording Christ's redemptive activity. Do you take full advantage of your opportunities to know God?*

Christian Living/ Ephesians 4:25–32

Therefore each of you must put off falsehood and speak truthfully to his neighbor, for we are all members of one body. 26"In your anger do not sin": Do not let the sun go down while you are still angry, 27and do not give the devil a foothold. 28He who has been stealing must steal no longer, but must work, doing something useful with his own hands, that he may have something to share with those in need.

29Do not let any unwholesome talk come out of your mouths, but only what is helpful for building others up according to their needs, that it may benefit those who listen. 30And do not grieve the Holy Spirit of God, with whom you were sealed for the day of redemption. 31Get rid of all bitterness, rage and anger, brawling and slander, along with every form of malice. 32Be kind and compassionate to one another, forgiving each other, just as in Christ God forgave you.

A THOUGHT: *We can cause the Holy Spirit sorrow by the way we live. Paul warns us against bad language, meanness, improper use of anger, quarrels, harsh words, and bad attitudes toward others. Instead of acting that way, we should be forgiving, just as God has forgiven us. Are you grieving or pleasing God with your attitudes and actions? Act in love toward your brothers and sisters in Christ, just as God acted in love by sending his Son to die for your sins.*

Proverbs for Today/ 17:19–21

He who loves a quarrel loves sin; he who builds a high gate invites destruction. □ A man of perverse heart does not prosper; he whose tongue is deceitful falls into trouble. □ To have a fool for a son brings grief; there is no joy for the father of a fool.

JUNE 22

Jesus Denounces the Pharisees/ Luke 11:37–54

When Jesus had finished speaking, a Pharisee invited him to eat with him; so he went in and reclined at the table. 38But the Pharisee, noticing that Jesus did not first wash before the meal, was surprised.

39Then the Lord said to him, "Now then, you Pharisees clean the outside of the cup and dish, but inside you are full of greed and wickedness. 40You foolish people! Did not the one who made the outside make the inside also? 41But give what is inside ⌊the dish⌋ to the poor, and everything will be clean for you.

42"Woe to you Pharisees, because you give God a tenth of your mint, rue and all other kinds of garden herbs, but you neglect justice and the love of God. You should have practiced the latter without leaving the former undone.

43"Woe to you Pharisees, because you love the most important seats in the synagogues and greetings in the marketplaces.

44"Woe to you, because you are like unmarked graves, which men walk over without knowing it."

45One of the experts in the law answered him, "Teacher, when you say these things, you insult us also."

46Jesus replied, "And you experts in the law, woe to you, because you load people down with burdens they can hardly carry, and you yourselves will not lift one finger to help them.

47"Woe to you, because you build tombs for the prophets, and it was your forefathers who killed them. 48So you testify that you approve of what your forefathers did; they killed the prophets, and you build their tombs. 49Because of this, God in his wisdom said, 'I will send them prophets and apostles, some of whom they will kill and others they will persecute.' 50Therefore this generation will be held responsible for the blood of all the prophets that has been shed since the beginning of the world, 51from the blood of Abel to the blood of Zechariah, who was killed between the altar and the sanctuary. Yes, I tell you, this generation will be held responsible for it all.

52"Woe to you experts in the law, because you have taken away the key to knowledge. You yourselves have not entered, and you have hindered those who were entering."

53When Jesus left there, the Pharisees and the teachers of the law began to oppose him fiercely and to besiege him with questions, 54waiting to catch him in something he might say.

A THOUGHT: *Jesus criticized the Pharisees harshly because they (1) washed their hands but not their hearts, (2) remembered to tithe but forgot justice, (3) loved people's praise, (4) made impossible religious demands, and (5) would not accept the truth about Jesus and prevented others from believing it as well. They went wrong by focusing on outward appearances and ignoring the inner condition of their hearts. We do the same when our service is motivated by a desire to be seen rather than from a pure heart and love for others. Others may be fooled, but God isn't. Don't be a Christian on the outside only. Bring your inner life under God's control, and your outer life will naturally reflect him.*

Imitators of Christ/ Ephesians 5:1–9

Be imitators of God, therefore, as dearly loved children ²and live a life of love, just as Christ loved us and gave himself up for us as a fragrant offering and sacrifice to God.

³But among you there must not be even a hint of sexual immorality, or of any kind of impurity, or of greed, because these are improper for God's holy people. ⁴Nor should there be obscenity, foolish talk or coarse joking, which are out of place, but rather thanksgiving. ⁵For of this you can be sure: No immoral, impure or greedy person—such a man is an idolater—has any inheritance in the kingdom of Christ and of God. ⁶Let no one deceive you with empty words, for because of such things God's wrath comes on those who are disobedient. ⁷Therefore do not be partners with them.

⁸For you were once darkness, but now you are light in the Lord. Live as children of light ⁹(for the fruit of the light consists in all goodness, righteousness and truth).

A THOUGHT: *Just as children imitate their parents, we should imitate Christ. His great love for us led him to sacrifice himself so that we might live. Our love for others should be of the same kind—a love that goes beyond affection to self-sacrificing service.*

Proverbs for Today/ 17:22

A cheerful heart is good medicine, but a crushed spirit dries up the bones.

JUNE 23

Warnings and Encouragement/ Luke 12:1–12

Meanwhile, when a crowd of many thousands had gathered, so that they were trampling on one another, Jesus began to speak first to his disciples, saying: "Be on your guard against the yeast of the Pharisees, which is hypocrisy. ²There is nothing concealed that will not be disclosed, or hidden that will not be made known. ³What you have said in the dark will be heard in the daylight, and what you have whispered in the ear in the inner rooms will be proclaimed from the roofs.

⁴"I tell you, my friends, do not be afraid of those who kill the body and after that can do no more. ⁵But I will show you whom you should fear: Fear him who, after the killing of the body, has power to throw you into hell. Yes, I tell you, fear him. ⁶Are not five sparrows sold for two pennies? Yet not one of them is forgotten by God. ⁷Indeed, the very hairs of your head are all numbered. Don't be afraid; you are worth more than many sparrows.

⁸"I tell you, whoever acknowledges me before men, the Son of Man will also acknowledge him before the angels of God. ⁹But he who disowns me before men will be disowned before the angels of God. ¹⁰And everyone who speaks a word against the Son of Man will be forgiven, but anyone who blasphemes against the Holy Spirit will not be forgiven.

¹¹"When you are brought before synagogues, rulers and authorities, do not worry about how you will defend yourselves or what you will say, ¹²for the Holy Spirit will teach you at that time what you should say."

A THOUGHT: *As Jesus watched the huge crowds approach to hear him, he warned his disciples against hypocrisy—trying to appear good when one's heart is far from God. The Pharisees could not keep their attitudes hidden forever. Their selfishness would grow like yeast, and soon they would expose themselves for what they really were—power-hungry impostors, not devoted religious leaders. We must be sure that we are more concerned with our relationship with God than we are with how we look to others. Our relationship with God will even involve facing opposition and ridicule in order to stand up for Christ.*

Living to Please God/ Ephesians 5:10–20

And find out what pleases the Lord. ¹¹Have nothing to do with the fruitless deeds of darkness, but rather expose them. ¹²For it is shameful even to mention what the disobedient do in secret. ¹³But everything exposed by the light becomes visible, ¹⁴for it is light that makes everything visible. This is why it is said:

"Wake up, O sleeper,
  rise from the dead,
and Christ will shine on you."

15Be very careful, then, how you live—not as unwise but as wise, 16making the most of every opportunity, because the days are evil. 17Therefore do not be foolish, but understand what the Lord's will is. 18Do not get drunk on wine, which leads to debauchery. Instead, be filled with the Spirit. 19Speak to one another with psalms, hymns and spiritual songs. Sing and make music in your heart to the Lord, 20always giving thanks to God the Father for everything, in the name of our Lord Jesus Christ.

A THOUGHT: *It is not enough to know what God wants us to do; we must also do it. We must follow our beliefs with actions. We must seek to please God in all that we do. God is pleased when we obey him. Study God's Word in order to know what pleases God, and then in the power of the Spirit, obey!*

Proverbs for Today/ 17:23

A wicked man accepts a bribe in secret to pervert the course of justice.

JUNE 24

Jesus Teaches in Parables/ Luke 12:13–34

Someone in the crowd said to him, "Teacher, tell my brother to divide the inheritance with me."

14Jesus replied, "Man, who appointed me a judge or an arbiter between you?" 15Then he said to them, "Watch out! Be on your guard against all kinds of greed; a man's life does not consist in the abundance of his possessions."

16And he told them this parable: "The ground of a certain rich man produced a good crop. 17He thought to himself, 'What shall I do? I have no place to store my crops.' 18"Then he said, 'This is what I'll do. I will tear down my barns and build bigger ones, and there I will store all my grain and my goods. 19And I'll say to myself, "You have plenty of good things laid up for many years. Take life easy; eat, drink and be merry." '

20"But God said to him, 'You fool! This very night your life will be demanded from you. Then who will get what you have prepared for yourself?'

21"This is how it will be with anyone who stores up things for himself but is not rich toward God."

22Then Jesus said to his disciples: "Therefore I tell you, do not worry about your life, what you will eat; or about your body, what you will wear. 23Life is more than food, and the body more than clothes. 24Consider the ravens: They do not sow or reap, they have no storeroom or barn; yet God feeds them. And how much more valuable you are than birds! 25Who of you by worrying can add a single hour to his life? 26Since you cannot do this very little thing, why do you worry about the rest?

27"Consider how the lilies grow. They do not labor or spin. Yet I tell you, not even Solomon in all his splendor was dressed like one of these. 28If that is how God clothes the grass of the field, which is here today, and tomorrow is thrown into the fire, how much more will he clothe you, O you of little faith! 29And do not set your heart on what you will eat or drink; do not worry about it. 30For the pagan world runs after all such things, and your Father knows that you need them. 31But seek his kingdom, and these things will be given to you as well.

32"Do not be afraid, little flock, for your Father has been pleased to give you the kingdom. 33Sell your possessions and give to the poor. Provide purses for yourselves that will not wear out, a treasure in heaven that will not be exhausted, where no thief comes near and no moth destroys. 34For where your treasure is, there your heart will be also."

A THOUGHT: *Jesus says that the good life has nothing to do with being wealthy. This is the exact opposite of what our society usually tells us. Advertisers spend millions of dollars to entice us to think that if we buy more and more of their products, we will be happier, more in tune, more comfortable. How do you respond to the constant pressure to buy? Learn to tune out expensive enticements and concentrate on the truly good life—living in a relationship with God and doing his work.*

Submit to One Another/ Ephesians 5:21–33

Submit to one another out of reverence for Christ. 22Wives, submit to your husbands as to the Lord. 23For the husband is the head of the wife as Christ is the head of the church, his body, of which he is the Savior. 24Now as the church submits to Christ, so also wives should submit to their husbands in everything.

25Husbands, love your wives, just as Christ loved the church and gave himself up for her 26to make her holy, cleansing her by the washing with water through the word, 27and to present her to himself as a radiant church, without stain or wrinkle or any other blemish, but holy and blameless. 28In this same way, husbands ought to love their wives as their own bodies. He who loves his wife loves himself. 29After all, no one ever hated his own body, but he feeds and cares for it, just as Christ does the church—30for we are members of his body. 31"For this reason a man will leave his father and mother and be united to his wife, and the two will become one flesh." 32This is a profound mystery—but I am talking about Christ and the church. 33However, each one of you also must love his wife as he loves himself, and the wife must respect her husband.

A THOUGHT: *Submission is an often misunderstood word. It does not mean becoming a doormat. Christ—at whose name "every knee should bow, in heaven and on earth and under the earth" (Philippians 2:10)—submitted his will to the Father, and we honor Christ by following his example. When we submit to God, we become more willing to obey his command to submit to others—that is, to subordinate our rights to theirs. In a marriage relationship both husband and wife are called to submit. For both the husband and the wife this means putting aside self-interests in order to care for the interests of the other. This kind of mutual submission preserves order and harmony in the family while it increases love and respect among family members.*

Proverbs for Today/ 17:24–25

A discerning man keeps wisdom in view, but a fool's eyes wander to the ends of the earth. □ A foolish son brings grief to his father and bitterness to the one who bore him.

JUNE 25

Watchful and Ready/ Luke 12:35–48

"Be dressed ready for service and keep your lamps burning, 36like men waiting for their master to return from a wedding banquet, so that when he comes and knocks they can immediately open the door for him. 37It will be good for those servants whose master finds them watching when he comes. I tell you the truth, he will dress himself to serve, will have them recline at the table and will come and wait on them. 38It will be good for those servants whose master finds them ready, even if he comes in the second or third watch of the night. 39But understand this: If the owner of the house had known at what hour the thief was coming, he would not have let his house be broken into. 40You also must be ready, because the Son of Man will come at an hour when you do not expect him."

41Peter asked, "Lord, are you telling this parable to us, or to everyone?"

42The Lord answered, "Who then is the faithful and wise manager, whom the master puts in charge of his servants to give them their food allowance at the proper time? 43It will be good for that servant whom the master finds doing so when he returns. 44I tell you the truth, he will put him in charge of all his possessions. 45But suppose the servant says to himself, 'My master is taking a long time in coming,' and he then begins to beat the menservants and maidservants and to eat and drink and get drunk. 46The master of that servant will come on a day when he does not expect him and at an hour he is not aware of. He will cut him to pieces and assign him a place with the unbelievers.

47"That servant who knows his master's will and does not get ready or does not do what his master wants will be beaten with many blows. 48But the one who does not know and does things deserving punishment will be beaten with few blows. From everyone who has been given much, much will be demanded; and from the one who has been entrusted with much, much more will be asked."

A THOUGHT: *Christ's return at an unexpected time is not a trap, a trick by which God hopes to catch us off guard. In fact, God is delaying his return so more will have an opportunity to follow Christ. During this time before his return, we have the opportunity to live out our beliefs and to reflect Jesus' love as we relate to others.*

People who are ready for their Lord's return are (1) not hypocritical, but sincere; (2) not fearful, but ready to witness; (3) not anxious, but trusting; (4) not greedy, but generous; (5) not lazy, but diligent. Is your life growing more like Christ's so that when he comes, you will be ready to greet him joyfully?

Instructions to Parents and Children/ Ephesians 6:1–4

Children, obey your parents in the Lord, for this is right. [2]"Honor your father and mother"—which is the first commandment with a promise— [3]"that it may go well with you and that you may enjoy long life on the earth."

[4]Fathers, do not exasperate your children; instead, bring them up in the training and instruction of the Lord.

A THOUGHT: *If our faith in Christ is real, it will usually prove itself at home, in our relationships with those who know us best. Children and parents have a responsibility to each other. Children should honor their parents even if the parents are demanding and unfair. Parents should gently care for their children, even if the children are disobedient and unpleasant. Ideally, of course, Christian parents and Christian children will relate to each other with thoughtfulness and love. This will happen if parents and children put the others' interests above their own.*

Proverbs for Today/ 17:26

It is not good to punish an innocent man, or to flog officials for their integrity.

JUNE 26

Jesus Came to Bring Division/ Luke 12:49–59

"I have come to bring fire on the earth, and how I wish it were already kindled! [50]But I have a baptism to undergo, and how distressed I am until it is completed! [51]Do you think I came to bring peace on earth? No, I tell you, but division. [52]From now on there will be five in one family divided against each other, three against two and two against three. [53]They will be divided, father against son and son against father, mother against daughter and daughter against mother, mother-in-law against daughter-in-law and daughter-in-law against mother-in-law."

54He said to the crowd: "When you see a cloud rising in the west, immediately you say, 'It's going to rain,' and it does. 55And when the south wind blows, you say, 'It's going to be hot,' and it is. 56Hypocrites! You know how to interpret the appearance of the earth and the sky. How is it that you don't know how to interpret this present time?

57"Why don't you judge for yourselves what is right? 58As you are going with your adversary to the magistrate, try hard to be reconciled to him on the way, or he may drag you off to the judge, and the judge turn you over to the officer, and the officer throw you into prison. 59I tell you, you will not get out until you have paid the last penny."

A THOUGHT: *In these strange and unsettling words, Jesus revealed that his coming often results in conflict. He demands a response, and close groups can be torn apart when some choose to follow him and others refuse to do so. There is no middle ground with Jesus. Loyalties must be declared and commitments made, sometimes to the severing of other relationships. Life is easiest when a family is united in its belief in Christ, but this often does not happen. Are you willing to risk your family's approval in order to gain eternal life?*

Instructions to Slaves and Masters/ Ephesians 6:5–9

Slaves, obey your earthly masters with respect and fear, and with sincerity of heart, just as you would obey Christ. 6Obey them not only to win their favor when their eye is on you, but like slaves of Christ, doing the will of God from your heart. 7Serve wholeheartedly, as if you were serving the Lord, not men, 8because you know that the Lord will reward everyone for whatever good he does, whether he is slave or free.

9And masters, treat your slaves in the same way. Do not threaten them, since you know that he who is both their Master and yours is in heaven, and there is no favoritism with him.

A THOUGHT: *Paul's instructions encourage responsibility and integrity on the job. Christian employees should do their jobs as if Jesus Christ were their supervisor, and Christian employers should treat their employees fairly and with respect. Are you trusted in any job to do your best, whether or not the boss is around? Do you work hard and with enthusiasm? Do you treat your employees as people, not ma-*

chines? *Remember that no matter whom you work for, and no matter who works for you, the One you ultimately want to please is your Father in heaven.*

Proverbs for Today/ 17:27–28

A man of knowledge uses words with restraint, and a man of understanding is even-tempered. Even a fool is thought wise if he keeps silent, and discerning if he holds his tongue.

JUNE 27

A Call to Repentance/ Luke 13:1–9

Now there were some present at that time who told Jesus about the Galileans whose blood Pilate had mixed with their sacrifices. 2Jesus answered, "Do you think that these Galileans were worse sinners than all the other Galileans because they suffered this way? 3I tell you, no! But unless you repent, you too will all perish. 4Or those eighteen who died when the tower in Siloam fell on them—do you think they were more guilty than all the others living in Jerusalem? 5I tell you, no! But unless you repent, you too will all perish."

6Then he told this parable: "A man had a fig tree, planted in his vineyard, and he went to look for fruit on it, but did not find any. 7So he said to the man who took care of the vineyard, 'For three years now I've been coming to look for fruit on this fig tree and haven't found any. Cut it down! Why should it use up the soil?'

8"'Sir,' the man replied, 'leave it alone for one more year, and I'll dig around it and fertilize it. 9If it bears fruit next year, fine! If not, then cut it down.'"

A THOUGHT: *In the Old Testament, a fruitful tree was often used as a symbol of godly living. Jesus pointed out what would happen to the other kind of tree—the kind that took up space but produced nothing for the patient gardener. This was one way he warned his listeners that God would not tolerate their lack of productivity forever. Repentance is an essential part of Christian commitment. We must turn from our wicked ways and turn to God. Respond to the gardener's patient care and start preparing to bear fruit by living for God.*

The Whole Armor of God/ Ephesians 6:10–17

Finally, be strong in the Lord and in his mighty power. 11Put on the full armor of God so that you can take your stand against the devil's schemes. 12For our struggle is not against flesh and blood, but against the rulers, against the authorities, against the powers of this dark world and against the spiritual forces of evil in the heavenly realms. 13Therefore put on the full armor of God, so that when the day of evil comes, you may be able to stand your ground, and after you have done everything, to stand. 14Stand firm then, with the belt of truth buckled around your waist, with the breastplate of righteousness in place, 15and with your feet fitted with the readiness that comes from the gospel of peace. 16In addition to all this, take up the shield of faith, with which you can extinguish all the flaming arrows of the evil one. 17Take the helmet of salvation and the sword of the Spirit, which is the word of God.

A THOUGHT: *In the Christian life, we battle against powerful evil forces, headed by Satan, a vicious fighter. To withstand his attacks, we must depend on God's strength and use every piece of his armor. Paul is giving this counsel to all individuals within the church. The whole body needs to be armed. As you do battle against "the powers of this dark world," fight in the strength of the church, whose power comes from the Holy Spirit.*

Proverbs for Today/ 18:1

An unfriendly man pursues selfish ends; he defies all sound judgment.

JUNE 28

A Healing on the Sabbath/ Luke 13:10–17

On a Sabbath Jesus was teaching in one of the synagogues, 11and a woman was there who had been crippled by a spirit for eighteen years. She was bent over and could not straighten up at all. 12When Jesus saw her, he called her forward and said to her, "Woman, you are set free from your infirmity." 13Then he put his hands on her, and immediately she straightened up and praised God.

14Indignant because Jesus had healed on the Sabbath, the synagogue ruler said to the people, "There are six days for work. So come and be healed on those days, not on the Sabbath."

15The Lord answered him, "You hypocrites! Doesn't each of you on the Sabbath untie his ox or donkey from the stall and lead it out to give it water? 16Then should not this woman, a daughter of Abraham, whom Satan has kept bound for eighteen long years, be set free on the Sabbath day from what bound her?"

17When he said this, all his opponents were humiliated, but the people were delighted with all the wonderful things he was doing.

A THOUGHT: *Why was healing considered work? The religious leaders saw healing as part of a doctor's profession, and practicing one's profession on the Sabbath was prohibited. The synagogue leader could not see beyond the law to Jesus' compassion in healing this handicapped woman. Jesus shamed him and the other leaders by pointing out their hypocrisy. The Pharisees hid behind their own set of laws to avoid love's obligations. We too can use the letter of the law to rationalize away our obligation to care for others (for example, tithing regularly then refusing to give help to a needy neighbor). But peoples' needs are more important than laws. Take time to lovingly help others, even if doing so might make you look less spiritual.*

Prayer in the Spirit/ Ephesians 6:18–24

And pray in the Spirit on all occasions with all kinds of prayers and requests. With this in mind, be alert and always keep on praying for all the saints.

19Pray also for me, that whenever I open my mouth, words may be given me so that I will fearlessly make known the mystery of the gospel, 20for which I am an ambassador in chains. Pray that I may declare it fearlessly, as I should.

21Tychicus, the dear brother and faithful servant in the Lord, will tell you everything, so that you also may know how I am and what I am doing. 22I am sending him to you for this very purpose, that you may know how we are, and that he may encourage you.

23Peace to the brothers, and love with faith from God the Father and the Lord Jesus Christ. 24Grace to all who love our Lord Jesus Christ with an undying love.

A THOUGHT: *How can anyone pray all the time? One way to pray constantly is to make quick, brief prayers your habitual response to every situation you meet throughout the day. Another way is to order your life around God's desires and teachings so that your very life becomes a prayer. You don't have to isolate yourself from other people and from daily work in order to pray constantly. You can make prayer your life and your life a prayer while living in a world that needs God's powerful influence.*

Proverbs for Today/ 18:2–3

A fool finds no pleasure in understanding but delights in airing his own opinions. □ When wickedness comes, so does contempt, and with shame comes disgrace.

JUNE 29

Parables of the Kingdom/ Luke 13:18–21

Then Jesus asked, "What is the kingdom of God like? What shall I compare it to? 19It is like a mustard seed, which a man took and planted in his garden. It grew and became a tree, and the birds of the air perched in its branches."

20Again he asked, "What shall I compare the kingdom of God to? 21It is like yeast that a woman took and mixed into a large amount of flour until it worked all through the dough."

A THOUGHT: *The general expectation among Jesus' hearers was that the Messiah would come as a great king and leader, freeing Israel from Roman domination and restoring Israel's former glory. But Jesus said his kingdom was beginning small and quietly. Like the tiny mustard seed that grows into an enormous bush or the spoonful of yeast that doubles the bread dough, the kingdom of God would eventually push outward until the whole world was changed.*

God Will Complete the Work He Began/ Philippians 1:1–6

Paul and Timothy, servants of Christ Jesus,

To all the saints in Christ Jesus at Philippi, together with the overseers and deacons:

2Grace and peace to you from God our Father and the Lord Jesus Christ.

3I thank my God every time I remember you. 4In all my

prayers for all of you, I always pray with joy ⁵because of your partnership in the gospel from the first day until now, ⁶being confident of this, that he who began a good work in you will carry it on to completion until the day of Christ Jesus.

A THOUGHT: *The God who begins his good work in us will continue it throughout our lives and will finish it when we meet him face to face. God's work for us began when Christ died on the cross to forgive our sins. His work in us begins when the Holy Spirit comes into our hearts, enabling us to be more like Christ every day. Paul is describing the process of Christian growth and maturity that begins when we accept Jesus and continues until Christ returns. Do you sometimes feel as if you'll never make progress in your spiritual life? When God starts a project, he finishes it! Trust God to keep his promise.*

Proverbs for Today/ 18:4–5

The words of a man's mouth are deep waters, but the fountain of wisdom is a bubbling brook. □ It is not good to be partial to the wicked or to deprive the innocent of justice.

JUNE 30

The Narrow Way/ Luke 13:22–30

Then Jesus went through the towns and villages, teaching as he made his way to Jerusalem. ²³Someone asked him, "Lord, are only a few people going to be saved?"

He said to them, ²⁴"Make every effort to enter through the narrow door, because many, I tell you, will try to enter and will not be able to. ²⁵Once the owner of the house gets up and closes the door, you will stand outside knocking and pleading, 'Sir, open the door for us.'

"But he will answer, 'I don't know you or where you come from.'

²⁶"Then you will say, 'We ate and drank with you, and you taught in our streets.'

²⁷"But he will reply, 'I don't know you or where you come from. Away from me, all you evildoers!'

²⁸"There will be weeping there, and gnashing of teeth, when you see Abraham, Isaac and Jacob and all the

prophets in the kingdom of God, but you yourselves thrown out. 29People will come from east and west and north and south, and will take their places at the feast in the kingdom of God. 30Indeed there are those who are last who will be first, and first who will be last."

A THOUGHT: *There will be many surprises in God's kingdom. Some who are despised now will be greatly honored then; some influential people here will be left outside the gates. Many "great" people on this earth (in God's eyes) are virtually ignored by the rest of the world. What matters to God is not one's earthly popularity, status, wealth, heritage, or power, but one's commitment to Christ. How do your values and actions match what the Bible tells us to do and to value? Make sure you put God in first place so you will join the people from all over the world who will take their places in the kingdom of Heaven.*

Paul's Love for the Philippians/ Philippians 1:7–11

It is right for me to feel this way about all of you, since I have you in my heart; for whether I am in chains or defending and confirming the gospel, all of you share in God's grace with me. 8God can testify how I long for all of you with the affection of Christ Jesus.

9And this is my prayer: that your love may abound more and more in knowledge and depth of insight, 10so that you may be able to discern what is best and may be pure and blameless until the day of Christ, 11filled with the fruit of righteousness that comes through Jesus Christ—to the glory and praise of God.

A THOUGHT: *Have you ever longed to see a friend with whom you share fond memories? Paul had such a longing to see the Christians at Philippi. His love and affection for them was based, not merely on past experiences, but upon the unity that comes when believers draw upon Christ's love. All Christians are part of God's family and thus share equally in the transforming power of his love. Do you feel a deep love for fellow Christians, friends and strangers alike? Let Christ's love for you motivate you to love other Christians.*

Proverbs for Today/ 18:6–7

A fool's lips bring him strife, and his mouth invites a beating. A fool's mouth is his undoing, and his lips are a snare to his soul.

Jesus Laments over Jerusalem/ Luke 13:31–35

At that time some Pharisees came to Jesus and said to him, "Leave this place and go somewhere else. Herod wants to kill you."

³²He replied, "Go tell that fox, 'I will drive out demons and heal people today and tomorrow, and on the third day I will reach my goal.' ³³In any case, I must keep going today and tomorrow and the next day—for surely no prophet can die outside Jerusalem!

³⁴"O Jerusalem, Jerusalem, you who kill the prophets and stone those sent to you, how often I have longed to gather your children together, as a hen gathers her chicks under her wings, but you were not willing! ³⁵Look, your house is left to you desolate. I tell you, you will not see me again until you say, 'Blessed is he who comes in the name of the Lord.'"

A THOUGHT: *Why was Jesus aiming for Jerusalem? Jerusalem, the city of God, symbolized the entire nation. It was Israel's largest city and the nation's spiritual and political capital, and Jews from around the world visited it frequently. But Jerusalem had a history of rejecting the prophets sent by God, and it would reject the Messiah just as it had rejected his forerunners. God's love and grace have been shown to mankind in the midst of rebellion against him. His supreme act of love can be seen in Jesus Christ, who was rejected by those who followed him and yet died to redeem people from their sins. Truly God's grace is amazing!*

The Gospel Advanced through Paul's Chains/ Philippians 1:12–18a

Now I want you to know, brothers, that what has happened to me has really served to advance the gospel. ¹³As a result, it has become clear throughout the whole palace guard and to everyone else that I am in chains for Christ. ¹⁴Because of my chains, most of the brothers in the Lord have been encouraged to speak the word of God more courageously and fearlessly.

¹⁵It is true that some preach Christ out of envy and rivalry, but others out of goodwill. ¹⁶The latter do so in love, knowing that I am put here for the defense of the gospel. ¹⁷The former preach Christ out of selfish ambition,

not sincerely, supposing that they can stir up trouble for me while I am in chains. 18But what does it matter? The important thing is that in every way, whether from false motives or true, Christ is preached. And because of this I rejoice.

A THOUGHT: *Being imprisoned would cause many people to become bitter or to give up, but Paul saw it as one more opportunity to spread the Good News of Christ. Paul realized that his current circumstances weren't as important as what he did with them. Turning a bad situation into a good one, Paul reached out to the Roman soldiers who were assigned to guard him and encouraged those Christians who were afraid of persecution. We may not be in prison, but we still have plenty of opportunities to be discouraged—times of indecision, financial burdens, family conflict, church conflict, or the loss of our jobs. How we act in such situations reflects what we believe. Like Paul, look for opportunities to demonstrate your faith even in bad situations. Whether or not the situation improves, your faith will grow stronger.*

Proverbs for Today/ 18:8

The words of a gossip are like choice morsels; they go down to a man's inmost parts.

JULY 2

Jesus Heals on the Sabbath/ Luke 14:1–6

One Sabbath, when Jesus went to eat in the house of a prominent Pharisee, he was being carefully watched. 2There in front of him was a man suffering from dropsy. 3Jesus asked the Pharisees and experts in the law, "Is it lawful to heal on the Sabbath or not?" 4But they remained silent. So taking hold of the man, he healed him and sent him away.

5Then he asked them, "If one of you has a son or an ox that falls into a well on the Sabbath day, will you not immediately pull him out?" 6And they had nothing to say.

A THOUGHT: *By healing this man on the Sabbath, Jesus was rejecting the Pharisaic tradition which did not allow for this. The Pharisees were more concerned for their traditions than they were for following the intent of God's Sabbath law. The Sabbath law was intended for restoration, not oppression. Jesus was giving this man rest by restoring him to full health—relieving him from the toil of his disease. Showing mercy should always take precedence over a rigid keeping of rules.*

Life is Christ, Death is Gain/ Philippians 1:18b–30

Yes, and I will continue to rejoice, [19]for I know that through your prayers and the help given by the Spirit of Jesus Christ, what has happened to me will turn out for my deliverance. [20]I eagerly expect and hope that I will in no way be ashamed, but will have sufficient courage so that now as always Christ will be exalted in my body, whether by life or by death. [21]For to me, to live is Christ and to die is gain. [22]If I am to go on living in the body, this will mean fruitful labor for me. Yet what shall I choose? I do not know! [23]I am torn between the two: I desire to depart and be with Christ, which is better by far; [24]but it is more necessary for you that I remain in the body. [25]Convinced of this, I know that I will remain, and I will continue with all of you for your progress and joy in the faith, [26]so that through my being with you again your joy in Christ Jesus will overflow on account of me.

[27]Whatever happens, conduct yourselves in a manner worthy of the gospel of Christ. Then, whether I come and see you or only hear about you in my absence, I will know that you stand firm in one spirit, contending as one man for the faith of the gospel [28]without being frightened in any way by those who oppose you. This is a sign to them that they will be destroyed, but that you will be saved—and that by God. [29]For it has been granted to you on behalf of Christ not only to believe on him, but also to suffer for him, [30]since you are going through the same struggle you saw I had, and now hear that I still have.

A THOUGHT: *To those who don't believe in God, life on earth is all there is, and so it is natural for them to strive for the things that this world values—money, popularity, power, and prestige. For Paul, however, life meant developing eternal values and telling others about Christ, who alone can help us see life from an eternal perspective. Paul's whole purpose in life was to speak out boldly for Christ and to become more like him. Thus Paul could confidently say that dying would be even better than living because in death he would be spared from the troubles of the world and see Christ face to face. If you're not ready to die, then you're not ready to live. Once you know your eternal purpose, then you're free to serve—devoting your life to what really counts without fear of dying.*

Proverbs for Today/ 18:9–10

One who is slack in his work is brother to one who destroys. □ The name of the LORD is a strong tower; the righteous run to it and are safe.

JULY 3

The Privilege of Entering the Kingdom of God/ Luke 14:7–24

When he [Jesus] noticed how the guests picked the places of honor at the table, he told them this parable: 8"When someone invites you to a wedding feast, do not take the place of honor, for a person more distinguished than you may have been invited. 9If so, the host who invited both of you will come and say to you, 'Give this man your seat.' Then, humiliated, you will have to take the least important place. 10But when you are invited, take the lowest place, so that when your host comes, he will say to you, 'Friend, move up to a better place.' Then you will be honored in the presence of all your fellow guests. 11For everyone who exalts himself will be humbled, and he who humbles himself will be exalted."

12Then Jesus said to his host, "When you give a luncheon or dinner, do not invite your friends, your brothers or relatives, or your rich neighbors; if you do, they may invite you back and so you will be repaid. 13But when you give a banquet, invite the poor, the crippled, the lame, the blind, 14and you will be blessed. Although they cannot repay you, you will be repaid at the resurrection of the righteous."

15When one of those at the table with him heard this, he said to Jesus, "Blessed is the man who will eat at the feast in the kingdom of God."

16Jesus replied: "A certain man was preparing a great banquet and invited many guests. 17At the time of the banquet he sent his servant to tell those who had been invited, 'Come, for everything is now ready.'

18"But they all alike began to make excuses. The first

said, 'I have just bought a field, and I must go and see it. Please excuse me.'

19"Another said, 'I have just bought five yoke of oxen, and I'm on my way to try them out. Please excuse me.'

20"Still another said, 'I just got married, so I can't come.'

21"The servant came back and reported this to his master. Then the owner of the house became angry and ordered his servant, 'Go out quickly into the streets and alleys of the town and bring in the poor, the crippled, the blind and the lame.'

22"'Sir,' the servant said, 'what you ordered has been done, but there is still room.'

23"Then the master told his servant, 'Go out to the roads and country lanes and make them come in, so that my house will be full. 24I tell you, not one of those men who were invited will get a taste of my banquet.'"

A THOUGHT: *Jesus taught two lessons here. First he spoke to the guests, telling them not to seek places of honor. Service is more important in God's kingdom than status. Second he told the host not to be exclusive about whom he invites. God opens his kingdom to everyone—especially to those who can never repay his invitation. Entering the kingdom of God comes by God's grace alone. In response to the experience of God's grace in our own lives, we should share the grace of God with others.*

Imitating the Humility of Christ/ Philippians 2:1–11

If you have any encouragement from being united with Christ, if any comfort from his love, if any fellowship with the Spirit, if any tenderness and compassion, 2then make my joy complete by being like-minded, having the same love, being one in spirit and purpose. 3Do nothing out of selfish ambition or vain conceit, but in humility consider others better than yourselves. 4Each of you should look not only to your own interests, but also to the interests of others.

5Your attitude should be the same as that of Christ Jesus:

6Who, being in very nature God,
    did not consider equality with God something to
        be grasped,
7but made himself nothing,
    taking the very nature of a servant,
    being made in human likeness.

8And being found in appearance as a man,
    he humbled himself
    and became obedient to death—
        even death on a cross!
9Therefore God exalted him to the highest place
    and gave him the name that is above every name,
10that at the name of Jesus every knee should bow,
    in heaven and on earth and under the earth,
11and every tongue confess that Jesus Christ is Lord,
    to the glory of God the Father.

A THOUGHT: *Many people—even Christians—live only to make a good impression on others or to please themselves. This is self-centered living. If people are concerned only for themselves, seeds of discord are sown. Paul therefore stresses spiritual unity, asking the Philippians to love one another and to work together with one heart and purpose. When we work together, caring for the problems of others as if they were our own, we are demonstrating Christ's example of putting others first. This brings unity. Don't be concerned about making a good impression or pleasing yourself to the point where you strain your relationship with others in God's family. Let the Spirit of God work through you to attract fellow believers to himself.*

Proverbs for Today/ 18:11–12

The wealth of the rich is their fortified city; they imagine it an unscalable wall. □ Before his downfall a man's heart is proud, but humility comes before honor.

JULY 4

The Cost of Discipleship/ Luke 14:25–35

Large crowds were traveling with Jesus, and turning to them he said: 26"If anyone comes to me and does not hate his father and mother, his wife and children, his brothers and sisters—yes, even his own life—he cannot be my disciple. 27And anyone who does not carry his cross and follow me cannot be my disciple.

28"Suppose one of you wants to build a tower. Will he not first sit down and estimate the cost to see if he has enough money to complete it? 29For if he lays the foundation and is not able to finish it, everyone who sees it will ridicule him, ³⁰saying, 'This fellow began to build and was not able to finish.'

³¹"Or suppose a king is about to go to war against another king. Will he not first sit down and consider whether he is able with ten thousand men to oppose the one coming against him with twenty thousand? ³²If he is not able, he will send a delegation while the other is still a long way off and will ask for terms of peace. ³³In the same way, any of you who does not give up everything he has cannot be my disciple.

³⁴"Salt is good, but if it loses its saltiness, how can it be made salty again? ³⁵It is fit neither for the soil nor for the manure pile; it is thrown out.

"He who has ears to hear, let him hear."

A THOUGHT: *Jesus' audience was well aware of what it meant to carry one's own cross. When the Romans led a criminal to his execution site, he was forced to carry the cross on which he was to be hanged. Following Christ does not mean that we will have a trouble-free life. On the contrary, following Christ costs us a great deal—discipleship demands that we follow Christ with complete commitment. We must carefully count the cost of becoming Christ's disciples so that we know what we are getting into and are not later tempted to turn back. Following Christ means total submission to him—perhaps even to death.*

Lights to the World/ Philippians 2:12–18

Therefore, my dear friends, as you have always obeyed—not only in my presence, but now much more in my absence—continue to work out your salvation with fear and trembling, ¹³for it is God who works in you to will and to act according to his good purpose.

¹⁴Do everything without complaining or arguing, ¹⁵so that you may become blameless and pure, children of God without fault in a crooked and depraved generation, in which you shine like stars in the universe ¹⁶as you hold out the word of life—in order that I may boast on the day of Christ that I did not run or labor for nothing. ¹⁷But even if I am being poured out like a drink offering on the sacrifice and service coming from your faith, I am glad and rejoice with all of you. ¹⁸So you too should be glad and rejoice with me.

A THOUGHT: *Our lives should be characterized by purity, patience, and peacefulness, so that we will shine out "like stars in the universe." A transformed life is an effective witness to the power of God's Word.*

Is your light shining brightly, or is it clouded by complaints and arguing? Be a clean, radiant light shining out for God.

Proverbs for Today/ 18:13

He who answers before listening—that is his folly and his shame.

JULY 5

A Lost Sheep and a Lost Coin/ Luke 15:1–10

Now the tax collectors and "sinners" were all gathering around to hear him. ²But the Pharisees and the teachers of the law muttered, "This man welcomes sinners and eats with them."

³Then Jesus told them this parable: ⁴"Suppose one of you has a hundred sheep and loses one of them. Does he not leave the ninety-nine in the open country and go after the lost sheep until he finds it? ⁵And when he finds it, he joyfully puts it on his shoulders ⁶and goes home. Then he calls his friends and neighbors together and says, 'Rejoice with me; I have found my lost sheep.' ⁷I tell you that in the same way there will be more rejoicing in heaven over one sinner who repents than over ninety-nine righteous persons who do not need to repent.

⁸"Or suppose a woman has ten silver coins and loses one. Does she not light a lamp, sweep the house and search carefully until she finds it? ⁹And when she finds it, she calls her friends and neighbors together and says, 'Rejoice with me; I have found my lost coin.' ¹⁰In the same way, I tell you, there is rejoicing in the presence of the angels of God over one sinner who repents."

A THOUGHT: *It seems foolish for the shepherd to leave the 99 sheep to search for just one which is missing. But God's love for each individual is so great that he seeks each one out and rejoices when he or she is "found." God values the lost one so much that, like the woman searching for the lost coin, he searches diligently until the lost one is found. Jesus associated with sinners—those who were lost and assumed to be beyond the grace of God—in order to bring them the Good News of God's kingdom. The amazing truth is that God, in his great love, searches for sinners and then forgives them. This is the kind of extraordinary love God has for you. If you feel far from God, don't despair. He is searching for you.*

Timothy and Epaphroditus/ Philippians 2:19–30

I hope in the Lord Jesus to send Timothy to you soon, that I also may be cheered when I receive news about you. 20I have no one else like him, who takes a genuine interest in your welfare. 21For everyone looks out for his own interests, not those of Jesus Christ. 22But you know that Timothy has proved himself, because as a son with his father he has served with me in the work of the gospel. 23I hope, therefore, to send him as soon as I see how things go with me. 24And I am confident in the Lord that I myself will come soon.

25But I think it is necessary to send back to you Epaphroditus, my brother, fellow worker and fellow soldier, who is also your messenger, whom you sent to take care of my needs. 26For he longs for all of you and is distressed because you heard he was ill. 27Indeed he was ill, and almost died. But God had mercy on him, and not on him only but also on me, to spare me sorrow upon sorrow. 28Therefore I am all the more eager to send him, so that when you see him again you may be glad and I may have less anxiety. 29Welcome him in the Lord with great joy, and honor men like him, 30because he almost died for the work of Christ, risking his life to make up for the help you could not give me.

A THOUGHT: *Timothy and Epaphroditus serve as examples of Christian living for us. Timothy was faithful in the work of the Lord, with a constant, genuine concern for those he was serving. Epaphroditus was also faithful in the work of the Lord—he risked his life for Christ. True discipleship includes such self-sacrifice. Let us follow in the footsteps of these servants of God in our service to others.*

Proverbs for Today/ 18:14–15

A man's spirit sustains him in sickness, but a crushed spirit who can bear? □ The heart of the discerning acquires knowledge; the ears of the wise seek it out.

JULY 6

The Prodigal Son/ Luke 15:11–32

Jesus continued: "There was a man who had two sons. 12The younger one said to his father, 'Father, give me my share of the estate.' So he divided his property between them.

13"Not long after that, the younger son got together all he had, set off for a distant country and there squandered his wealth in wild living. 14After he had spent everything, there was a severe famine in that whole country, and he began to be in need. 15So he went and hired himself out to a citizen of that country, who sent him to his fields to feed pigs. 16He longed to fill his stomach with the pods that the pigs were eating, but no one gave him anything.

17"When he came to his senses, he said, 'How many of my father's hired men have food to spare, and here I am starving to death! 18I will set out and go back to my father and say to him: Father, I have sinned against heaven and against you. 19I am no longer worthy to be called your son; make me like one of your hired men.' 20So he got up and went to his father.

"But while he was still a long way off, his father saw him and was filled with compassion for him; he ran to his son, threw his arms around him and kissed him.

21"The son said to him, 'Father, I have sinned against heaven and against you. I am no longer worthy to be called your son.'

22"But the father said to his servants, 'Quick! Bring the best robe and put it on him. Put a ring on his finger and sandals on his feet. 23Bring the fattened calf and kill it. Let's have a feast and celebrate. 24For this son of mine was dead and is alive again; he was lost and is found.' So they began to celebrate.

25"Meanwhile, the older son was in the field. When he came near the house, he heard music and dancing. 26So he called one of the servants and asked him what was going on. 27'Your brother has come,' he replied, 'and your father has killed the fattened calf because he has him back safe and sound.'

28"The older brother became angry and refused to go in. So his father went out and pleaded with him. 29But he answered his father, 'Look! All these years I've been slaving for you and never disobeyed your orders. Yet you never gave me even a young goat so I could celebrate with my friends. 30But when this son of yours who has squandered your property with prostitutes comes home, you kill the fattened calf for him!'

31" 'My son,' the father said, 'you are always with me, and everything I have is yours. 32But we had to celebrate and be glad, because this brother of yours was dead and is alive again; he was lost and is found.' "

A THOUGHT: *Some people need to hit bottom in order to come to their senses. The younger son's attitude was based on a desire to be free to live as he pleased. That is not so different from the desires of most people in our society today. It may take great sorrow and tragedy to cause them to look up to the only One who can help them. Are you trying to live life your way, selfishly pushing aside anything that gets in your way? Don't take leave of your senses—stop and look before you hit bottom, and save yourself and your family much grief.*

Paul's Jewish Heritage/ Philippians 3:1-7

Finally, my brothers, rejoice in the Lord! It is no trouble for me to write the same things to you again, and it is a safeguard for you.

2Watch out for those dogs, those men who do evil, those mutilators of the flesh. 3For it is we who are the circumcision, we who worship by the Spirit of God, who glory in Christ Jesus, and who put no confidence in the flesh— 4though I myself have reasons for such confidence.

If anyone else thinks he has reasons to put confidence in the flesh, I have more: 5circumcised on the eighth day, of the people of Israel, of the tribe of Benjamin, a Hebrew of Hebrews; in regard to the law, a Pharisee; 6as for zeal, persecuting the church; as for legalistic righteousness, faultless.

7But whatever was to my profit I now consider loss for the sake of Christ.

A THOUGHT: *At first glance, it seems that Paul is boasting about his achievements. But he is actually doing the opposite, showing that human achievements, no matter how impressive, cannot earn a person salvation and eternal life with God. Paul had impressive credentials: upbringing, nationality, family background, inheritance, orthodoxy, activity, and morality. But when he was converted to faith in Christ, it wasn't based upon his credentials, but upon the grace of Christ. Paul did not depend on his credentials to please God, because even the most impressive credentials fall short of God's holy standards. Are you depending on Christian parents, church affiliation, or just being good to make you right with God? Credentials, accomplishments, or reputation cannot earn salvation. Like Paul, you must realize that salvation comes only through faith in Christ.*

Proverbs for Today/ 18:16–18

A gift opens the way for the giver and ushers him into the presence of the great. □ The first to present his case seems right, till another comes forward and questions him. □ Casting the lot settles disputes and keeps strong opponents apart.

JULY 7

The Parable of the Dishonest Manager/ Luke 16:1–14

Jesus told his disciples: "There was a rich man whose manager was accused of wasting his possessions. 2So he called him in and asked him, 'What is this I hear about you? Give an account of your management, because you cannot be manager any longer.'

3"The manager said to himself, 'What shall I do now? My master is taking away my job. I'm not strong enough to dig, and I'm ashamed to beg— 4I know what I'll do so that, when I lose my job here, people will welcome me into their houses.'

5"So he called in each one of his master's debtors. He asked the first, 'How much do you owe my master?'

6" 'Eight hundred gallons of olive oil,' he replied.

"The manager told him, 'Take your bill, sit down quickly, and make it four hundred.'

7"Then he asked the second, 'And how much do you owe?'

" 'A thousand bushels of wheat,' he replied.

"He told him, 'Take your bill and make it eight hundred.'

8"The master commended the dishonest manager because he had acted shrewdly. For the people of this world are more shrewd in dealing with their own kind than are the people of the light. 9I tell you, use worldly wealth to gain friends for yourselves, so that when it is gone, you will be welcomed into eternal dwellings.

10"Whoever can be trusted with very little can also be trusted with much, and whoever is dishonest with very little will also be dishonest with much. 11So if you have not been trustworthy in handling worldly wealth, who will trust you with true riches? 12And if you have not been trustworthy with someone else's property, who will give you property of your own?

13"No servant can serve two masters. Either he will hate the one and love the other, or he will be devoted to the one and despise the other. You cannot serve both God and Money."

14The Pharisees, who loved money, heard all this and were sneering at Jesus.

A THOUGHT: *Our integrity often meets its match in money matters. God calls us to be honest even in small details we could rationalize away. Heaven's riches are far more valuable than earthly wealth—but if we are untrustworthy with our earthly wealth (no matter how much or little we have), we are unfit to handle the vast riches of God's kingdom. Don't let your integrity slip in small matters, and it will not fail you in crucial decisions either.*

The Value of Knowing Christ/ Philippians 3:8–12

What is more, I consider everything a loss compared to the surpassing greatness of knowing Christ Jesus my Lord, for whose sake I have lost all things. I consider them rubbish, that I may gain Christ 9and be found in him, not having a righteousness of my own that comes from the law, but that which is through faith in Christ—the righteousness that comes from God and is by faith. 10I want to know Christ and the power of his resurrection and the fellowship of sharing in his sufferings, becoming like him in his death, 11and so, somehow, to attain to the resurrection from the dead.

12Not that I have already obtained all this, or have already been made perfect, but I press on to take hold of that for which Christ Jesus took hold of me.

A THOUGHT: *After Paul considered everything he had accomplished in his life, he said that it was all worthless when compared with knowing Christ. This is a profound statement about values; a person's relationship with Christ is more important than anything else. To know Christ should be our ultimate goal. Consider your values. Do you place anything above your relationship with Christ? If your priorities are wrong, how can you reorder them?*

Proverbs for Today/ 18:19

An offended brother is more unyielding than a fortified city, and disputes are like the barred gates of a citadel.

JULY 8

Lazarus and the Rich Man/ Luke 16:15–31

He [Jesus] said to them [the Pharisees], "You are the ones who justify yourselves in the eyes of men, but God knows your hearts. What is highly valued among men is detestable in God's sight.

16"The Law and the Prophets were proclaimed until John. Since that time, the good news of the kingdom of God is being preached, and everyone is forcing his way into it. 17It is easier for heaven and earth to disappear than for the least stroke of a pen to drop out of the Law.

18"Anyone who divorces his wife and marries another woman commits adultery, and the man who marries a divorced woman commits adultery.

19"There was a rich man who was dressed in purple and fine linen and lived in luxury every day. 20At his gate was laid a beggar named Lazarus, covered with sores 21and longing to eat what fell from the rich man's table. Even the dogs came and licked his sores.

22"The time came when the beggar died and the angels carried him to Abraham's side. The rich man also died and was buried. 23In hell, where he was in torment, he looked up and saw Abraham far away, with Lazarus by his side. 24So he called to him, 'Father Abraham, have pity on me and send Lazarus to dip the tip of his finger in water and cool my tongue, because I am in agony in this fire.'

25"But Abraham replied, 'Son, remember that in your lifetime you received your good things, while Lazarus received bad things, but now he is comforted here and you are in agony. 26And besides all this, between us and you a great chasm has been fixed, so that those who want to go from here to you cannot, nor can anyone cross over from there to us.'

27"He answered, 'Then I beg you, father, send Lazarus to my father's house, 28for I have five brothers. Let him warn them, so that they will not also come to this place of torment.'

29"Abraham replied, 'They have Moses and the Prophets; let them listen to them.'

30"'No, father Abraham,' he said, 'but if someone from the dead goes to them, they will repent.'

31"He said to him, 'If they do not listen to Moses and the Prophets, they will not be convinced even if someone rises from the dead.'"

A THOUGHT: *The Pharisees considered wealth evidence of God's blessing. Jesus startled them with this story in which a diseased beggar is rewarded and a rich man is punished. The rich man did not go to hell because of his wealth, but because he was selfish with it. He did not feed Lazarus, take him in, or care for his health. He was hard-hearted in spite of his great blessings. The amount of money we have is not so important as the way we use it. Rich people can be generous or stingy—and so can poor people. What is your attitude toward your possessions? Do you hoard them selfishly, or do you use them to bless others?*

Pressing on Toward the Goal/ Philippians 3:13–16

Brothers, I do not consider myself yet to have taken hold of it. But one thing I do: Forgetting what is behind and straining toward what is ahead, 14I press on toward the goal to win the prize for which God has called me heavenward in Christ Jesus.

15All of us who are mature should take such a view of things. And if on some point you think differently, that too God will make clear to you. 16Only let us live up to what we have already attained.

A THOUGHT: *Paul said his goal was to know Christ, to be like Christ, and to be all Christ has in mind for him. This goal absorbed all his energy. This is an example for us. We should not let anything take our eyes off our goal—Christ. With the singlemindedness of an athlete in training, we must lay aside everything harmful and forsake even the good things that may distract us from being effective Christians.*

Proverbs for Today/ 18:20–21

From the fruit of his mouth a man's stomach is filled; with the harvest from his lips he is satisfied. □ The tongue has the power of life and death, and those who love it will eat its fruit.

JULY 9

Temptation and Forgiveness/ Luke 17:1–4

Jesus said to his disciples: "Things that cause people to sin are bound to come, but woe to that person through whom they come. 2It would be better for him to be thrown into the sea with a millstone tied around his neck than for him to cause one of these little ones to sin. 3So watch yourselves.

"If your brother sins, rebuke him, and if he repents, forgive him. 4If he sins against you seven times in a day, and seven times comes back to you and says, 'I repent,' forgive him."

A THOUGHT: *To rebuke someone does not mean to point out every sin we see; it means to bring sin to a person's attention with the purpose of restoring him or her to God and to fellow believers. When you feel you must rebuke another Christian for a sin, check your own attitudes before opening your mouth. Do you love the person? Are you willing to forgive? Unless rebuke is tied to forgiveness, it will not help the sinning person.*

Citizenship in Heaven/ Philippians 3:17–21

Join with others in following my example, brothers, and take note of those who live according to the pattern we gave you. 18For, as I have often told you before and now say again even with tears, many live as enemies of the cross of Christ. 19Their destiny is destruction, their god is their stomach, and their glory is in their shame. Their mind is on earthly things. 20But our citizenship is in heaven. And we eagerly await a Savior from there, the Lord Jesus Christ, 21who, by the power that enables him to bring everything under his control, will transform our lowly bodies so that they will be like his glorious body.

A THOUGHT: *Citizens of Philippi had the same rights and privileges as the citizens of Rome because Philippi was a Roman colony. Likewise we Christians will one day experience all the special privileges of our heavenly citizenship because we belong to Christ. Knowing that our ultimate home is in heaven with God should shape the way we live today. To be truly heavenly minded, we need to live like Christ on earth.*

Proverbs for Today/ 18:22

He who finds a wife finds what is good and receives favor from the LORD.

JULY 10

Jesus Teaches about Faith/ Luke 17:5–10

The apostles said to the Lord, "Increase our faith!"

⁶He replied, "If you have faith as small as a mustard seed, you can say to this mulberry tree, 'Be uprooted and planted in the sea,' and it will obey you.

⁷"Suppose one of you had a servant plowing or looking after the sheep. Would he say to the servant when he comes in from the field, 'Come along now and sit down to eat'? ⁸Would he not rather say, 'Prepare my supper, get yourself ready and wait on me while I eat and drink; after that you may eat and drink'? ⁹Would he thank the servant because he did what he was told to do? ¹⁰So you also, when you have done everything you were told to do, should say, 'We are unworthy servants; we have only done our duty.' "

A THOUGHT: *A mustard seed is small, but it has great potential for growth. Like this tiny seed, a small amount of genuine faith in God will take root and grow. The amount of faith is not as important as its object and its genuineness. What is faith? It is total dependence on God and a willingness to do his will. It is not something we use to put on a show for others. It is complete and humble obedience to God's will, readiness to do whatever he calls us to do. The amount of faith isn't as important as the right kind of faith—faith in our all-powerful God.*

Joy in the Lord/ Philippians 4:1–7

Therefore, my brothers, you whom I love and long for, my joy and crown, that is how you should stand firm in the Lord, dear friends!

2I plead with Euodia and I plead with Syntyche to agree with each other in the Lord. 3Yes, and I ask you, loyal yokefellow, help these women who have contended at my side in the cause of the gospel, along with Clement and the rest of my fellow workers, whose names are in the book of life.

4Rejoice in the Lord always. I will say it again: Rejoice! 5Let your gentleness be evident to all. The Lord is near. 6Do not be anxious about anything, but in everything, by prayer and petition, with thanksgiving, present your requests to God. 7And the peace of God, which transcends all understanding, will guard your hearts and your minds in Christ Jesus.

A THOUGHT: *It seems strange that a man in prison would be telling a church to be joyful. Paul's attitude serves to teach us an important lesson—our inner attitudes do not have to reflect our outward circumstances. Paul was full of joy because he knew that no matter what happened to him, Jesus Christ was with him. Several times in this letter, Paul urges the Philippians to be joyful, probably because they needed to hear this. It's easy to get discouraged about unpleasant circumstances or to take unimportant events too seriously. If you haven't been joyful lately, you may not be looking at life from the right perspective.*

Proverbs for Today/ 18:23–24

A poor man pleads for mercy, but a rich man answers harshly. □ A man of many companions may come to ruin, but there is a friend who sticks closer than a brother.

JULY 11

Jesus Heals Ten Lepers/ Luke 17:11–19

Now on his way to Jerusalem, Jesus traveled along the border between Samaria and Galilee. 12As he was going into a village, ten men who had leprosy met him. They stood at a distance ¹³and called out in a loud voice, "Jesus, Master, have pity on us!"

¹⁴When he saw them, he said, "Go, show yourselves to the priests." And as they went, they were cleansed.

¹⁵One of them, when he saw he was healed, came back, praising God in a loud voice. ¹⁶He threw himself at Jesus' feet and thanked him—and he was a Samaritan.

¹⁷Jesus asked, "Were not all ten cleansed? Where are the other nine? ¹⁸Was no one found to return and give praise to God except this foreigner?" ¹⁹Then he said to him, "Rise and go; your faith has made you well."

A THOUGHT: *Lepers were required to stay apart from other people and to announce their presence by yelling "Unclean, unclean!" if they had to come near. Sometimes leprosy went into remission; if a leper thought his leprosy had gone away, he was supposed to present himself to a priest who could declare him clean. Jesus sent the ten lepers to the priest before they were healed—and they went! They responded in faith, and Jesus healed them on the way. Is your trust in God so strong that you act on what he says even before it happens?*

Jesus healed all ten lepers, but only one returned to thank him. It is possible to receive God's great gifts with an ungrateful spirit—nine of the lepers did so. Only the thankful leper, however, learned that his faith had played a role in his healing. God does not demand that we thank him, but he is pleased when we do so, and he uses our spirit of thankfulness to teach us more about his kingdom.

Think about Pure and Lovely Things/ Philippians 4:8–14

Finally, brothers, whatever is true, whatever is noble, whatever is right, whatever is pure, whatever is lovely, whatever is admirable—if anything is excellent or praiseworthy—think about such things. ⁹Whatever you have learned or received or heard from me, or seen in me—put it into practice. And the God of peace will be with you.

¹⁰I rejoice greatly in the Lord that at last you have renewed your concern for me. Indeed, you have been concerned, but you had no opportunity to show it. ¹¹I am not saying this because I am in need, for I have learned to be content whatever the circumstances. ¹²I know what it is to be in need, and I know what it is to have plenty. I have learned the secret of being content in any and every situation, whether well fed or hungry, whether living in plenty

or in want. 13I can do everything through him who gives me strength.

14Yet it was good of you to share in my troubles.

A THOUGHT: *What we put into our minds determines what comes out in our words and actions. Paul tells us to fix our thoughts on "whatever is true, whatever is noble, whatever is right, whatever is pure." Do you have problems with impure thoughts and daydreams? Examine what you are putting into your mind through television, books, movies, and magazines. Replace harmful input with wholesome material. Above all, read God's Word and pray. Ask him to help you focus your mind on what is good and pure. It takes practice, but it can be done.*

Proverbs for Today/ 19:1–3

Better a poor man whose walk is blameless than a fool whose lips are perverse. □ It is not good to have zeal without knowledge, nor to be hasty and miss the way. □ A man's own folly ruins his life, yet his heart rages against the LORD.

JULY 12

Instructions about the Last Days/ Luke 17:20–37

Once, having been asked by the Pharisees when the kingdom of God would come, Jesus replied, "The kingdom of God does not come with your careful observation, 21nor will people say, 'Here it is,' or 'There it is,' because the kingdom of God is within you."

22Then he said to his disciples, "The time is coming when you will long to see one of the days of the Son of Man, but you will not see it. 23Men will tell you, 'There he is!' or 'Here he is!' Do not go running off after them. 24For the Son of Man in his day will be like the lightning, which flashes and lights up the sky from one end to the other. 25But first he must suffer many things and be rejected by this generation.

26"Just as it was in the days of Noah, so also will it be in the days of the Son of Man. 27People were eating, drinking, marrying and being given in marriage up to the day Noah entered the ark. Then the flood came and destroyed them all.

28"It was the same in the days of Lot. People were eating and drinking, buying and selling, planting and building. 29But the day Lot left Sodom, fire and sulfur rained down from heaven and destroyed them all.

30"It will be just like this on the day the Son of Man is revealed. 31On that day no one who is on the roof of his house, with his goods inside, should go down to get them. Likewise, no one in the field should go back for anything. 32Remember Lot's wife! 33Whoever tries to keep his life will lose it, and whoever loses his life will preserve it. 34I tell you, on that night two people will be in one bed; one will be taken and the other left. 35Two women will be grinding grain together; one will be taken and the other left. *"

37"Where, Lord?" they asked.

He replied, "Where there is a dead body, there the vultures will gather."

A THOUGHT: *Life will be going on as usual on the day that Christ returns. There will be no prior warning. People will be going about their everyday tasks, indifferent to the things of God. They will be as surprised by Christ's return as the people in Noah's day were by the flood or the people in Lot's day by the destruction of Sodom. We don't know the day or the hour of Christ's return, but we do know he is coming. It may be today, or tomorrow, or centuries in the future. Whenever it is, we must be ready. Live as if Jesus were coming today, and then you will be ready for his return.*

Paul Thanks the Philippians/ Philippians 4:15–23

Moreover, as you Philippians know, in the early days of your acquaintance with the gospel, when I set out from Macedonia, not one church shared with me in the matter of giving and receiving, except you only; 16for even when I was in Thessalonica, you sent me aid again and again when I was in need. 17Not that I am looking for a gift, but I am looking for what may be credited to your account. 18I have received full payment and even more; I am amply supplied, now that I have received from Epaphroditus the gifts you sent. They are a fragrant offering, an acceptable sacrifice,

*35 Some manuscripts *left.* 36*Two men will be in the field; one will be taken and the other left.*

pleasing to God. 19And my God will meet all your needs according to his glorious riches in Christ Jesus.

20To our God and Father be glory for ever and ever. Amen.

21Greet all the saints in Christ Jesus. The brothers who are with me send greetings. 22All the saints send you greetings, especially those who belong to Caesar's household.

23The grace of the Lord Jesus Christ be with your spirit. Amen.

A THOUGHT: *We can trust that God will always meet our needs, but we must remember that he may not supply them all in this life. Christians suffer and die (tradition says Paul himself was beheaded), and God does not always intervene to spare them. We must also be careful not to confuse needs with wants and desires. In our materialistic society we often consider many luxuries necessities. God has promised to meet our needs, but he has not promised that he will meet our evil indulgent desires. Our hope is in having a relationship with God, not in the accumulation of goods! What goods we have we must be willing to share with others sacrificially.*

Proverbs for Today/ 19:4–5

Wealth brings many friends, but a poor man's friend deserts him. □ A false witness will not go unpunished, and he who pours out lies will not go free.

JULY 13

A Parable about Prayer/ Luke 18:1–8

Then Jesus told his disciples a parable to show them that they should always pray and not give up. 2He said: "In a certain town there was a judge who neither feared God nor cared about men. 3And there was a widow in that town who kept coming to him with the plea, 'Grant me justice against my adversary.'

4"For some time he refused. But finally he said to himself, 'Even though I don't fear God or care about men, 5yet because this widow keeps bothering me, I will see that she gets justice, so that she won't eventually wear me out with her coming!' "

6And the Lord said, "Listen to what the unjust judge says. 7And will not God bring about justice for his chosen ones, who cry out to him day and night? Will he keep putting them off? 8I tell you, he will see that they get justice, and quickly. However, when the Son of Man comes, will he find faith on the earth?"

A THOUGHT: *To repeat our prayers until the answer comes does not mean endless repetition or painfully long prayer sessions. Constant prayer means keeping our requests constantly before God as we live for him day by day, always believing he will answer. When we thus live by faith, we are not to give up. God may delay answering, but his delays always have good reasons, and we must not confuse them with neglect. As we persist in prayer we grow in character, faith, and hope.*

Paul Thanks God for the Colossians/ Colossians 1:1–6

Paul, an apostle of Christ Jesus by the will of God, and Timothy our brother,

2To the holy and faithful brothers in Christ at Colosse:

Grace and peace to you from God our Father.

3We always thank God, the Father of our Lord Jesus Christ, when we pray for you, 4because we have heard of your faith in Christ Jesus and of the love you have for all the saints— 5the faith and love that spring from the hope that is stored up for you in heaven and that you have already heard about in the word of truth, the gospel 6that has come to you. All over the world this gospel is bearing fruit and growing, just as it has been doing among you since the day you heard it and understood God's grace in all its truth.

A THOUGHT: *Wherever Paul went, he preached the gospel—to Gentile audiences, to hostile Jewish leaders, and even to his Roman guards. Whenever people believed in the message, they were changed. God's Word is not just for our information, it is for our transformation! Becoming a Christian means beginning a whole new relationship with God, not just turning over a new leaf or determining to do right. New believers have a changed purpose, direction, attitude, and behavior. They no longer seek to serve themselves, but to serve God. Can you point to any areas where hearing God's Word has changed your life, or where it should do so?*

Proverbs for Today/ 19:6–7

Many curry favor with a ruler, and everyone is the friend of a man who gives gifts. □ A poor man is shunned by all his relatives—how much more do his friends avoid him! Though he pursues them with pleading, they are nowhere to be found.

JULY 14

The Pharisee and the Tax Collector/ Luke 18:9–17

To some who were confident of their own righteousness and looked down on everybody else, Jesus told this parable: 10"Two men went up to the temple to pray, one a Pharisee and the other a tax collector. 11The Pharisee stood up and prayed about himself: 'God, I thank you that I am not like other men—robbers, evildoers, adulterers— or even like this tax collector. 12I fast twice a week and give a tenth of all I get.'

13"But the tax collector stood at a distance. He would not even look up to heaven, but beat his breast and said, 'God, have mercy on me, a sinner.'

14"I tell you that this man, rather than the other, went home justified before God. For everyone who exalts himself will be humbled, and he who humbles himself will be exalted."

15People were also bringing babies to Jesus to have him touch them. When the disciples saw this, they rebuked them. 16But Jesus called the children to him and said, "Let the little children come to me, and do not hinder them, for the kingdom of God belongs to such as these. 17I tell you the truth, anyone who will not receive the kingdom of God like a little child will never enter it."

A THOUGHT: *The Pharisee did not go to the Temple to pray to God but to announce to all within earshot how good he was. The tax collector went to the Temple recognizing his sin and begging for mercy. Self-righteousness is sin. It leads to pride, causes a person to despise others, and prevents him or her from learning anything from God. The tax collector's prayer should be our prayer because we all need*

God's mercy every day. Don't let pride get in the way of your relationship with God or with others.

Epaphras' Good Report/ Colossians 1:7–9

You learned it from Epaphras, our dear fellow servant, who is a faithful minister of Christ on our behalf, 8and who also told us of your love in the Spirit.

9For this reason, since the day we heard about you, we have not stopped praying for you and asking God to fill you with the knowledge of his will through all spiritual wisdom and understanding.

A THOUGHT: *The Colossians had a great love for others because the Holy Spirit had transformed their lives. The ability to love others in the same way Christ loved us comes through the working of the Holy Spirit. The Bible speaks of love as an action and attitude, not just an emotion. It is a by-product of our new life in Christ. Christians have no excuse for failing to love others, because Christian love is not a feeling but a decision to act in the best interests of others.*

Proverbs for Today/ 19:8–9

He who gets wisdom loves his own soul; he who cherishes understanding prospers. □ A false witness will not go unpunished, and he who pours out lies will perish.

JULY 15

Jesus and the Rich Man/ Luke 18:18–30

A certain ruler asked him [Jesus], "Good teacher, what must I do to inherit eternal life?"

19"Why do you call me good?" Jesus answered. "No one is good—except God alone. 20You know the commandments: 'Do not commit adultery, do not murder, do not steal, do not give false testimony, honor your father and mother.'"

21"All these I have kept since I was a boy," he said.

22When Jesus heard this, he said to him, "You still lack one thing. Sell everything you have and give to the poor, and you will have treasure in heaven. Then come, follow me."

23When he heard this, he became very sad, because he was a man of great wealth. 24Jesus looked at him and said, "How hard it is for the rich to enter the kingdom of God! 25Indeed, it is easier for a camel to go through the eye of a needle than for a rich man to enter the kingdom of God."

26Those who heard this asked, "Who then can be saved?"

27Jesus replied, "What is impossible with men is possible with God."

28Peter said to him, "We have left all we had to follow you!"

29"I tell you the truth," Jesus said to them, "no one who has left home or wife or brothers or parents or children for the sake of the kingdom of God 30will fail to receive many times as much in this age and, in the age to come, eternal life."

A THOUGHT: *This man's wealth gave him power and prestige. When Jesus told him to sell everything he owned, he was touching this man's very security. Because money represents power, authority, and success, it is often difficult for wealthy people to realize their need for God and their powerlessness to save themselves. Unless God reaches down into their lives, they will not come to him. Jesus surprised some of his hearers by offering salvation to the poor; he may surprise some people today by offering it to the rich. It is difficult for a rich person to realize his need and come to Jesus, but "what is impossible with men is possible with God." Jesus asks us all to get rid of anything that has become more important to us than God. What is the ultimate source of your security?*

Prayerful Response to Epaphras' Report/ Colossians 1:10–14

And we pray this in order that you may live a life worthy of the Lord and may please him in every way: bearing fruit in every good work, growing in the knowledge of God, 11being strengthened with all power according to his glorious might so that you may have great endurance and patience, and joyfully 12giving thanks to the Father, who has qualified you to share in the inheritance of the saints in the kingdom of light. 13For he has rescued us from the dominion of darkness and brought us into the kingdom of the Son he loves, 14in whom we have redemption, the forgiveness of sins.

A THOUGHT: *Sometimes we wonder how to pray for missionaries and other leaders we have never met. Paul had never met the Colossians, but he faithfully prayed for them. His prayers teach us how to pray for others, whether we know them or not. We can request that they (1) understand God's will, (2) gain spiritual wisdom, (3) live lives pleasing and honoring to God, (4) do kind things for others, (5) know God better and better, (6) be filled with God's strength, (7) endure in faith, (8) stay full of Christ's joy, and (9) always be thankful. All believers have these same basic needs. When you don't know how to pray for someone, remember the pattern of Paul's prayer for the Colossians.*

Proverbs for Today/ 19:10–12

It is not fitting for a fool to live in luxury— how much worse for a slave to rule over princes! □ A man's wisdom gives him patience; it is to his glory to overlook an offense. □ A king's rage is like the roar of a lion, but his favor is like dew on the grass.

JULY 16

Jesus Predicts His Death/ Luke 18:31–34

Jesus took the Twelve aside and told them, "We are going up to Jerusalem, and everything that is written by the prophets about the Son of Man will be fulfilled. 32He will be handed over to the Gentiles. They will mock him, insult him, spit on him, flog him and kill him. 33On the third day he will rise again."

34The disciples did not understand any of this. Its meaning was hidden from them, and they did not know what he was talking about.

A THOUGHT: *Although the disciples had spent a great deal of time with Jesus, they did not understand his statements concerning suffering and death. Their expectations for a conquering king were so great that they could not fathom Jesus' words. Despite the fact that no one on earth understood what Jesus was going through—his disciples all abandoned him when he was crucified—Jesus went to Jerusalem this last time fully knowing what was ahead of him. He willingly submitted to the misunderstandings, the mockings, the shame, the crucifixion, and death in order to redeem mankind.*

Christ's Supremacy/ Colossians 1:15–18

He [Christ] is the image of the invisible God, the firstborn over all creation. 16For by him all things were created: things in heaven and on earth, visible and invisible, whether thrones or powers or rulers or authorities; all things were created by him and for him. 17He is before all things, and in him all things hold together. 18And he is the head of the body, the church; he is the beginning and the firstborn from among the dead, so that in everything he might have the supremacy.

A THOUGHT: *This is one of the strongest statements about the divine nature of Christ found anywhere in the Bible. Jesus is not only equal to God, he is God. He not only reflects God, but he reveals God to us. He came from heaven, not from the dust of the ground, and is Lord of all. He is completely holy, and he has authority to judge the world. Therefore, he is supreme over all creation, including the spirit world. We, like the Colossian believers, must believe in the deity of Jesus Christ (that Jesus is God), or our Christian faith is hollow, misdirected, and meaningless. The deity of Christ is a central truth of Christianity.*

Proverbs for Today/ 19:13–14

A foolish son is his father's ruin, and a quarrelsome wife is like a constant dripping. □ Houses and wealth are inherited from parents, but a prudent wife is from the LORD.

JULY 17

Jesus Heals a Blind Man/ Luke 18:35–43

As Jesus approached Jericho, a blind man was sitting by the roadside begging. 36When he heard the crowd going by, he asked what was happening. 37They told him, "Jesus of Nazareth is passing by."

38He called out, "Jesus, Son of David, have mercy on me!"

39Those who led the way rebuked him and told him to be quiet, but he shouted all the more, "Son of David, have mercy on me!"

40Jesus stopped and ordered the man to be brought to

him. When he came near, Jesus asked him, 41"What do you want me to do for you?"

"Lord, I want to see," he replied.

42Jesus said to him, "Receive your sight; your faith has healed you." 43Immediately he received his sight and followed Jesus, praising God. When all the people saw it, they also praised God.

A THOUGHT: *Beggars often waited along the roads near cities because that was where they would be able to contact the most people. Usually handicapped in some way, these beggars were unable to earn a living. Medical help was not available for their problems, and others tended to ignore their obligation to care for the needy. Thus beggars had little hope of escaping their degrading way of life. But this blind beggar took hope in the Messiah. He shamelessly cried out for Jesus' attention, and Jesus said his faith made him see. No matter how desperate your situation may seem, if you call out to Jesus in faith, he will help you.*

Reconciliation Through Christ/ Colossians 1:19–23

For God was pleased to have all his fullness dwell in him [Christ], 20and through him to reconcile to himself all things, whether things on earth or things in heaven, by making peace through his blood, shed on the cross.

21Once you were alienated from God and were enemies in your minds because of your evil behavior. 22But now he has reconciled you by Christ's physical body through death to present you holy in his sight, without blemish and free from accusation— 23if you continue in your faith, established and firm, not moved from the hope held out in the gospel. This is the gospel that you heard and that has been proclaimed to every creature under heaven, and of which I, Paul, have become a servant.

A THOUGHT: *Christ's death provided a way for all people to come to God. It cleared away the sin that keeps us from having a right relationship with our Creator. This does not mean that everyone has been saved, but that the way has been cleared for anyone who will trust Christ to be saved. God gives salvation to all those who by faith accept Christ's death for themselves. Salvation reconciles people to God and to each other, thus the cross of Christ brings peace.*

Proverbs for Today/ 19:15–16

Laziness brings on deep sleep, and the shiftless man goes hungry. □ He who obeys instructions guards his life, but he who is contemptuous of his ways will die.

JULY 18

Salvation Comes to Zacchaeus' Home/
Luke 19:1–10

Jesus entered Jericho and was passing through. ²A man was there by the name of Zacchaeus; he was a chief tax collector and was wealthy. ³He wanted to see who Jesus was, but being a short man he could not, because of the crowd. ⁴So he ran ahead and climbed a sycamore-fig tree to see him, since Jesus was coming that way.

⁵When Jesus reached the spot, he looked up and said to him, "Zacchaeus, come down immediately. I must stay at your house today." ⁶So he came down at once and welcomed him gladly.

⁷All the people saw this and began to mutter, "He has gone to be the guest of a 'sinner.' "

⁸But Zacchaeus stood up and said to the Lord, "Look, Lord! Here and now I give half of my possessions to the poor, and if I have cheated anybody out of anything, I will pay back four times the amount."

⁹Jesus said to him, "Today salvation has come to this house, because this man, too, is a son of Abraham. ¹⁰For the Son of Man came to seek and to save what was lost."

A THOUGHT: *To finance their great world empire, the Romans levied heavy taxes against all nations under their control. The Jews opposed these taxes because they supported a secular government and its pagan gods, but they were still forced to pay. Tax collectors—Jews by birth who chose to work for Rome—were considered traitors among the people of Israel. Besides, it was common knowledge that tax collectors made themselves rich by gouging their fellow Jews of extra tax money which they kept for themselves. No wonder the crowds were displeased when Jesus went home with the tax collector Zacchaeus. But despite the fact that Zacchaeus was both dishonest and a turncoat, Jesus loved him, and in response, the little tax collector was converted. In every society certain groups of people are considered "untouchable" because of their politics, their immoral behavior, or their lifestyle. We should not give in to social pressure to avoid these people. Jesus loves them, and they need to hear his Good News.*

Christ in You/ Colossians 1:24–29

Now I rejoice in what was suffered for you, and I fill up in my flesh what is still lacking in regard to Christ's afflictions, for the sake of his body, which is the church. 25I have become its servant by the commission God gave me to present to you the word of God in its fullness— 26the mystery that has been kept hidden for ages and generations, but is now disclosed to the saints. 27To them God has chosen to make known among the Gentiles the glorious riches of this mystery, which is Christ in you, the hope of glory.

28We proclaim him, admonishing and teaching everyone with all wisdom, so that we may present everyone perfect in Christ. 29To this end I labor, struggling with all his energy, which so powerfully works in me.

A THOUGHT: *The false teachers in the Colossian church believed spiritual perfection was a secret and hidden plan that only a few privileged people would discover. Their secret plan was meant to be exclusive. Paul calls God's plan a secret, not because only a few would understand, but because it was hidden until Christ came. Who could have imagined that God's secret plan was to have his Son, Jesus Christ, live in the hearts of all who believe in him?*

Proverbs for Today/ 19:17

He who is kind to the poor lends to the LORD, and he will reward him for what he has done.

JULY 19

The Nobleman and His Servants/ Luke 19:11–27

While they were listening to this, he went on to tell them a parable, because he was near Jerusalem and the people thought that the kingdom of God was going to appear at once. 12He said: "A man of noble birth went to a distant country to have himself appointed king and then to return. 13So he called ten of his servants and gave them ten minas. 'Put this money to work,' he said, 'until I come back.'

14"But his subjects hated him and sent a delegation after him to say, 'We don't want this man to be our king.'

15"He was made king, however, and returned home. Then he sent for the servants to whom he had given the money, in order to find out what they had gained with it.

16"The first one came and said, 'Sir, your mina has earned ten more.'

17" 'Well done, my good servant!' his master replied. 'Because you have been trustworthy in a very small matter, take charge of ten cities.'

18"The second came and said, 'Sir, your mina has earned five more.'

19"His master answered, 'You take charge of five cities.'

20"Then another servant came and said, 'Sir, here is your mina; I have kept it laid away in a piece of cloth. 21I was afraid of you, because you are a hard man. You take out what you did not put in and reap what you did not sow.'

22"His master replied, 'I will judge you by your own words, you wicked servant! You knew, did you, that I am a hard man, taking out what I did not put in, and reaping what I did not sow? 23Why then didn't you put my money on deposit, so that when I came back, I could have collected it with interest?'

24"Then he said to those standing by, 'Take his mina away from him and give it to the one who has ten minas.'

25" 'Sir,' they said, 'he already has ten!'

26"He replied, 'I tell you that to everyone who has, more will be given, but as for the one who has nothing, even what he has will be taken away. 27But those enemies of mine who did not want me to be king over them—bring them here and kill them in front of me.' "

A THOUGHT: *Why was the king so hard on this man who had not increased the money entrusted to him? He punished the man because (1) he didn't share his master's interest in the kingdom; (2) he didn't trust his master's intentions; and (3) his only loyalty was to himself. Like the king in this story, God has given us gifts to use for the benefit of his kingdom. Jesus expects us to use these talents so that people will be drawn into the kingdom. He asks each of us, "What are you doing with what I have given you?" While awaiting the coming of the kingdom of God in glory, we must do his work.*

Treasures of Wisdom and Knowledge/ Colossians 2:1–10

I want you to know how much I am struggling for you and for those at Laodicea, and for all who have not met me personally. 2My purpose is that they may be encouraged in heart and united in love, so that they may have the full riches of complete understanding, in order that they may know the mystery of God, namely, Christ, ³in whom are hidden all the treasures of wisdom and knowledge. ⁴I tell you this so that no one may deceive you by fine-sounding arguments. ⁵For though I am absent from you in body, I am present with you in spirit and delight to see how orderly you are and how firm your faith in Christ is.

⁶So then, just as you received Christ Jesus as Lord, continue to live in him, ⁷rooted and built up in him, strengthened in the faith as you were taught, and overflowing with thankfulness.

⁸See to it that no one takes you captive through hollow and deceptive philosophy, which depends on human tradition and the basic principles of this world rather than on Christ.

⁹For in Christ all the fullness of the Deity lives in bodily form, ¹⁰and you have been given fullness in Christ, who is the head over every power and authority.

A THOUGHT: *The problem Paul was combatting in the Colossian church was similar to the heresy of Gnosticism (from the Greek word meaning "knowledge"). This heresy (a teaching contrary to biblical doctrine) attacked Christianity in several basic ways: (1) It insisted that important hidden knowledge was a secret kept from most believers; Paul, however, said that in Christ we see all we need to see of God's provision for us. (2) It taught that the body was evil; Paul countered this by saying that God himself dwelt in a body—that is, he was embodied in Jesus Christ. (3) It said that Christ seemed to be human, but was not. Paul insisted that in Jesus we see one who is fully human and fully divine.*

Gnosticism became fashionable in the second century. Even in Paul's day, these ideas sounded attractive to many and could easily seduce a church that didn't know Christian doctrine well. Aspects of this early heresy still pose significant problems for many in the church today. The antidote for heretical ideas is a thorough acquaintance with God's Word through personal study and sound Bible teaching.

Proverbs for Today/ 19:18–19

Discipline your son, for in that there is hope; do not be a willing party to his death. □ A hot-tempered man must pay the penalty; if you rescue him, you will have to do it again.

JULY 20

Jesus' Triumphal Entry/ Luke 19:28–40

After Jesus had said this, he went on ahead, going up to Jerusalem. 29As he approached Bethphage and Bethany at the hill called the Mount of Olives, he sent two of his disciples, saying to them, 30"Go to the village ahead of you, and as you enter it, you will find a colt tied there, which no one has ever ridden. Untie it and bring it here. 31If anyone asks you, 'Why are you untying it?' tell him, 'The Lord needs it.'"

32Those who were sent ahead went and found it just as he had told them. 33As they were untying the colt, its owners asked them, "Why are you untying the colt?"

34They replied, "The Lord needs it."

35They brought it to Jesus, threw their cloaks on the colt and put Jesus on it. 36As he went along, people spread their cloaks on the road.

37When he came near the place where the road goes down the Mount of Olives, the whole crowd of disciples began joyfully to praise God in loud voices for all the miracles they had seen:

38"Blessed is the king who comes in the name of the Lord!"

"Peace in heaven and glory in the highest!"

39Some of the Pharisees in the crowd said to Jesus, "Teacher, rebuke your disciples!"

40"I tell you," he replied, "if they keep quiet, the stones will cry out."

A THOUGHT: *This is the event Christians celebrate on Palm Sunday. The people lined the highway, praising God, waving palm branches, and throwing their cloaks in front of the colt as it passed before them. "Long live the King" was the meaning of their joyful shouts, because they knew Jesus was intentionally fulfilling the prophecy in Zechariah 9:9: "See, your king comes to you, righteous and having salvation, gentle and riding on a donkey, on a colt, the foal of a donkey." To announce that he was indeed the Messiah, Jesus chose a time when all Israel would be gathered at Jerusalem, a place where huge crowds could see him, and a way of proclaiming his mission that was unmistakable. Now the people were sure their liberation was at hand. They were praising God for giving them a king, but they had the wrong idea about Jesus' kingship. They were sure he would be a national leader who would restore their nation to its former glory, and thus they were deaf to the words of their prophets and blind to Jesus' real mission. When it became apparent that Jesus was not going to fulfill their hopes, many people turned against him.*

Alive with Christ/ Colossians 2:11–15

In him you were also circumcised, in the putting off of the sinful nature, not with a circumcision done by the hands of men but with the circumcision done by Christ, 12having been buried with him in baptism and raised with him through your faith in the power of God, who raised him from the dead.

13When you were dead in your sins and in the uncircumcision of your sinful nature, God made you alive with Christ. He forgave us all our sins, 14having canceled the written code, with its regulations, that was against us and that stood opposed to us; he took it away, nailing it to the cross. 15And having disarmed the powers and authorities, he made a public spectacle of them, triumphing over them by the cross.

A THOUGHT: *Before we believed in Christ, our nature was evil. The Christian, however, has a new nature. God has crucified the old rebellious nature and given us a new, loving nature. The penalty of sin died with Christ on the cross. God has declared us not guilty, and we need no longer live under sin's power. God does not take us out of the world or make us robots—we will still feel like sinning, and sometimes we will sin. The difference is that before we were saved, we were slaves to our sinful nature, but now we can choose to live for Christ.*

Proverbs for Today/ 19:20–21

Listen to advice and accept instruction, and in the end you will be wise. □ Many are the plans in a man's heart, but it is the LORD's purpose that prevails.

JULY 21

Jesus Weeps over Jerusalem/ Luke 19:41–48

As he [Jesus] approached Jerusalem and saw the city, he wept over it ⁴²and said, "If you, even you, had only known on this day what would bring you peace—but now it is hidden from your eyes. ⁴³The days will come upon you when your enemies will build an embankment against you and encircle you and hem you in on every side. ⁴⁴They will dash you to the ground, you and the children within your walls. They will not leave one stone on another, because you did not recognize the time of God's coming to you."

⁴⁵Then he entered the temple area and began driving out those who were selling. ⁴⁶"It is written," he said to them, " 'My house will be a house of prayer'; but you have made it 'a den of robbers.' "

⁴⁷Every day he was teaching at the temple. But the chief priests, the teachers of the law and the leaders among the people were trying to kill him. ⁴⁸Yet they could not find any way to do it, because all the people hung on his words.

A THOUGHT: *Why would the business community—which included the leading political, commercial, and judicial men among the people—want to get rid of Jesus? Obviously he had damaged business in the Temple by driving the merchants out. In addition, he preached against injustice, and his teachings often favored the poor over the rich. Further, his great popularity was in danger of attracting Rome's attention, and the leaders of Israel wanted as little as possible to do with Rome. These leaders not only refused God's offer of salvation, they sought to kill the Savior! God continues to offer salvation to the people he loves, both Jews and Gentiles. Eternal peace is within your reach—accept it before it is too late.*

Do Not Be Enslaved by Legalism/ Colossians 2:16–23

Therefore do not let anyone judge you by what you eat or drink, or with regard to a religious festival, a New Moon celebration or a Sabbath day. ¹⁷These are a shadow of the things that were to come; the reality, however, is found in Christ. ¹⁸Do not let anyone who delights in false humility and the worship of angels disqualify you for the prize. Such a person goes into great detail about what he has seen, and his unspiritual mind puffs him up with idle notions. ¹⁹He has lost connection with the Head, from whom the whole body, supported and held together by its ligaments and sinews, grows as God causes it to grow.

20Since you died with Christ to the basic principles of this world, why, as though you still belonged to it, do you submit to its rules: 21"Do not handle! Do not taste! Do not touch!"? 22These are all destined to perish with use, because they are based on human commands and teachings. 23Such regulations indeed have an appearance of wisdom, with their self-imposed worship, their false humility and their harsh treatment of the body, but they lack any value in restraining sensual indulgence.

A THOUGHT: *We cannot reach up to God by following rules and rituals or by practicing religion. Paul isn't saying all rules are bad. But no keeping of laws or rules will earn salvation. The Good News is that God reaches down to man, and we respond. Man-made religions focus on human effort; Christianity focuses on Christ's work. Paul agrees that believers must put aside sinful desires, but that is the by-product of our new life in Christ, not the cause of it. Our salvation does not depend on our own discipline and rule-keeping, but on the power of Christ's death and resurrection.*

We can guard against man-made religions by asking these questions of any religious group: (1) Does it stress man-made rules and taboos rather than God's grace? (2) Does it foster a critical spirit about others, or does it exercise discipline discreetly and lovingly? (3) Does it stress formulas, secret knowledge, or special visions more than the Word of God? (4) Does it elevate self-righteousness, honoring those who keep the rules, rather than elevating Christ? (5) Does it neglect Christ's universal church, claiming to be an elite group? (6) Does it teach humiliation of the body as a means to spiritual growth rather than focusing on the growth of the whole person? (7) Does it disregard the family rather than holding it in high regard as the Bible does?

Proverbs for Today/ 19:22–23

What a man desires is unfailing love; better to be poor than a liar. □ The fear of the LORD leads to life: Then one rests content, untouched by trouble.

JULY 22

The Parable of the Disloyal Tenants/ Luke 20:1–19

One day as he [Jesus] was teaching the people in the temple courts and preaching the gospel, the chief priests and the teachers of the law, together with the elders, came up to him. 2"Tell us by what authority you are doing these things," they said. "Who gave you this authority?"

3He replied, "I will also ask you a question. Tell me, 4John's baptism—was it from heaven, or from men?"

5They discussed it among themselves and said, "If we say, 'From heaven,' he will ask, 'Why didn't you believe him?' 6But if we say, 'From men,' all the people will stone us, because they are persuaded that John was a prophet."

7So they answered, "We don't know where it was from."

8Jesus said, "Neither will I tell you by what authority I am doing these things."

9He went on to tell the people this parable: "A man planted a vineyard, rented it to some farmers and went away for a long time. 10At harvest time he sent a servant to the tenants so they would give him some of the fruit of the vineyard. But the tenants beat him and sent him away empty-handed. 11He sent another servant, but that one also they beat and treated shamefully and sent away empty-handed. 12He sent still a third, and they wounded him and threw him out.

13"Then the owner of the vineyard said, 'What shall I do? I will send my son, whom I love; perhaps they will respect him.'

14"But when the tenants saw him, they talked the matter over. 'This is the heir,' they said. 'Let's kill him, and the inheritance will be ours.' 15So they threw him out of the vineyard and killed him.

"What then will the owner of the vineyard do to them? 16He will come and kill those tenants and give the vineyard to others."

When the people heard this, they said, "May this never be!"

17Jesus looked directly at them and asked, "Then what is the meaning of that which is written:

" 'The stone the builders rejected
has become the capstone'?

18Everyone who falls on that stone will be broken to pieces,
but he on whom it falls will be crushed."

19The teachers of the law and the chief priests looked for
a way to arrest him immediately, because they knew he had
spoken this parable against them. But they were afraid of
the people.

A THOUGHT: *This group of religious leaders wanted to get rid of Jesus,
so they tried to trap him with their question. If Jesus answered that
his authority came from God, then they would accuse him of
blasphemy—claiming to be the Son of God—and bring him to trial.
Jesus did not let himself be caught. Instead, he turned the question
on them. Thus he exposed their motives and avoided their trap by
answering them in a parable.*

*The characters in this parable are easily identified. The religious
leaders understood it. The landowner is God; the vineyard is Israel;
the tenant farmers are the religious leaders; the landowner's men
are the prophets and priests God sent to Israel to denounce their
sins; the son is the Messiah, Jesus; and the others are the Gentiles.
Jesus' parable indirectly answered the religious leaders' question
about his authority; it also showed them that he knew their plan to
kill him.*

Keep Your Heart on Things Above/
Colossians 3:1–8

Since, then, you have been raised with Christ, set your
hearts on things above, where Christ is seated at the right
hand of God. 2Set your minds on things above, not on
earthly things. 3For you died, and your life is now hidden
with Christ in God. 4When Christ, who is your life, appears,
then you also will appear with him in glory.

5Put to death, therefore, whatever belongs to your
earthly nature: sexual immorality, impurity, lust, evil desires and greed, which is idolatry. 6Because of these, the
wrath of God is coming. 7You used to walk in these ways,
in the life you once lived. 8But now you must rid yourselves
of all such things as these: anger, rage, malice, slander, and
filthy language from your lips.

A THOUGHT: *The Christian's real home is where Christ lives. This
gives us a different perspective on our lives here on earth. To let
heaven fill your thoughts means to look at life from God's perspective.
This is the antidote to materialism; we gain the proper perspective
on material goods when we take God's view of them. The more we*

see the life around us as God sees it, the more we live in harmony with him. We must not become too attached to what is only temporary.

Proverbs for Today/ 19:24–25

The sluggard buries his hand in the dish; he will not even bring it back to his mouth! □ Flog a mocker, and the simple will learn prudence; rebuke a discerning man, and he will gain knowledge.

JULY 23

Paying Taxes to Caesar/ Luke 20:20–26

Keeping a close watch on him, they [the religious leaders] sent spies, who pretended to be honest. They hoped to catch Jesus in something he said so that they might hand him over to the power and authority of the governor. 21So the spies questioned him: "Teacher, we know that you speak and teach what is right, and that you do not show partiality but teach the way of God in accordance with the truth. 22Is it right for us to pay taxes to Caesar or not?"

23He saw through their duplicity and said to them, 24"Show me a denarius. Whose portrait and inscription are on it?"

25"Caesar's," they replied.

He said to them, "Then give to Caesar what is Caesar's, and to God what is God's."

26They were unable to trap him in what he had said there in public. And astonished by his answer, they became silent.

A THOUGHT: *This question concerning taxes was indeed a loaded question. The Jews were enraged at having to pay taxes to Rome which supported the pagan government and its gods. They hated the system which allowed tax collectors to charge exorbitant rates and keep the extra for themselves. If Jesus said they should pay taxes, they would call him a traitor to their nation and their religion. But if he said they should not pay taxes, they could report him to Rome as a rebel. Jesus' questioners thought they had him this time, but he outwitted them again. Jesus turned his enemies' attempt to trap him into a powerful lesson: God's followers have legitimate obligations to both God and the government. But what is important is to keep our priorities straight. When the two authorities conflict, our duty to God always comes before our duty to the government.*

Principles for Holy Living/ Colossians 3:9–14

Do not lie to each other, since you have taken off your old self with its practices ¹⁰and have put on the new self, which is being renewed in knowledge in the image of its Creator. ¹¹Here there is no Greek or Jew, circumcised or uncircumcised, barbarian, Scythian, slave or free, but Christ is all, and is in all.

¹²Therefore, as God's chosen people, holy and dearly loved, clothe yourselves with compassion, kindness, humility, gentleness and patience. ¹³Bear with each other and forgive whatever grievances you may have against one another. Forgive as the Lord forgave you. ¹⁴And over all these virtues put on love, which binds them all together in perfect unity.

A THOUGHT: *The Christian is in a continuing education program. The more we know of Christ and his work, the more we are being changed to be like him. Because this process is lifelong, we must never cease learning and obeying. There is no justification for drifting along, but there is an incentive to find the rich treasures of growing in him. It takes practice, review, patience, and concentration to keep in line with God's will.*

Proverbs for Today/ 19:26

He who robs his father and drives out his mother is a son who brings shame and disgrace.

JULY 24

Jesus Answers the Sadducees/ Luke 20:27–47

Some of the Sadducees, who say there is no resurrection, came to Jesus with a question. ²⁸"Teacher," they said, "Moses wrote for us that if a man's brother dies and leaves a wife but no children, the man must marry the widow and have children for his brother. ²⁹Now there were seven brothers. The first one married a woman and died childless.

30The second 31and then the third married her, and in the same way the seven died, leaving no children. 32Finally, the woman died too. 33Now then, at the resurrection whose wife will she be, since the seven were married to her?"

34Jesus replied, "The people of this age marry and are given in marriage. 35But those who are considered worthy of taking part in that age and in the resurrection from the dead will neither marry nor be given in marriage, 36and they can no longer die; for they are like the angels. They are God's children, since they are children of the resurrection. 37But in the account of the bush, even Moses showed that the dead rise, for he calls the Lord 'the God of Abraham, and the God of Isaac, and the God of Jacob.' 38He is not the God of the dead, but of the living, for to him all are alive."

39Some of the teachers of the law responded, "Well said, teacher!" 40And no one dared to ask him any more questions.

41Then Jesus said to them, "How is it that they say the Christ is the Son of David? 42David himself declares in the Book of Psalms:

> " 'The Lord said to my Lord:
> "Sit at my right hand
> 43until I make your enemies
> a footstool for your feet." '

44David calls him 'Lord.' How then can he be his son?"

45While all the people were listening, Jesus said to his disciples, 46"Beware of the teachers of the law. They like to walk around in flowing robes and love to be greeted in the marketplaces and have the most important seats in the synagogues and the places of honor at banquets. 47They devour widows' houses and for a show make lengthy prayers. Such men will be punished most severely."

A THOUGHT: *The Sadducees, a group of conservative religious leaders, honored only the Pentateuch—Genesis through Deuteronomy—as Scripture and did not believe in a resurrection of the dead because they could find no mention of it in these books. They decided to try their hand at tricking Jesus, so they brought him a question that had always stumped the Pharisees. After addressing their question about marriage, Jesus answered their real question about resurrection. Basing his answer on the writings of Moses—an authority they respected—he upheld belief in resurrection.*

The Peace of Christ/ Colossians 3:15–17

Let the peace of Christ rule in your hearts, since as members of one body you were called to peace. And be thankful. 16Let the word of Christ dwell in you richly as you teach and admonish one another with all wisdom, and as you sing psalms, hymns and spiritual songs with gratitude in your hearts to God. 17And whatever you do, whether in word or deed, do it all in the name of the Lord Jesus, giving thanks to God the Father through him.

A THOUGHT: *Christians should live in perfect harmony. This does not mean there cannot be differences in opinion, but loving Christians will work together despite their differences. Such love is not a feeling, but a decision to meet others' needs. It leads to peace between individuals and among the members of the body of believers. Do problems in your relationship with other Christians cause open conflicts or mutual silence? Consider what you can do to heal those relationships with selfless acts of love.*

Proverbs for Today/ 19:27–29

Stop listening to instruction, my son, and you will stray from the words of knowledge. □ A corrupt witness mocks at justice, and the mouth of the wicked gulps down evil. □ Penalties are prepared for mockers, and beatings for the backs of fools.

JULY 25

The Poor Widow's Offering/ Luke 21:1–4

As he looked up, Jesus saw the rich putting their gifts into the temple treasury. 2He also saw a poor widow put in two very small copper coins. 3"I tell you the truth," he said, "this poor widow has put in more than all the others. 4All these people gave their gifts out of their wealth; but she out of her poverty put in all she had to live on."

A THOUGHT: *Jesus was probably in the area of the Temple called the Court of the Women, where it is thought that the treasury was located. In this area were seven boxes in which men could deposit their Temple tax and six boxes for freewill offerings like the one this woman gave. Not only was she poor; as a widow she had few resources for making money. Her small gift was a sacrifice, but she gave it willingly. This widow gave all she had, in stark contrast to the way most of us handle our money. When we consider giving a certain percentage of our income a great accomplishment, we resemble "all the others" who gave only a little of what they didn't need. Here, Jesus is admiring sacrificial giving. As believers, we should increase our giving—whether of money, time, or talents—to a point beyond that which is convenient or safe.*

Principles for the Christian Community/ Colossians 3:18—4:1

Wives, submit to your husbands, as is fitting in the Lord.

19Husbands, love your wives and do not be harsh with them.

20Children, obey your parents in everything, for this pleases the Lord.

21Fathers, do not embitter your children, or they will become discouraged.

22Slaves, obey your earthly masters in everything; and do it, not only when their eye is on you and to win their favor, but with sincerity of heart and reverence for the Lord. 23Whatever you do, work at it with all your heart, as working for the Lord, not for men, 24since you know that you will receive an inheritance from the Lord as a reward. It is the Lord Christ you are serving. 25Anyone who does wrong will be repaid for his wrong, and there is no favoritism.

4:1Masters, provide your slaves with what is right and fair, because you know that you also have a Master in heaven.

A THOUGHT: *Paul describes three relationships: (1) husbands and wives, (2) parents and children, and (3) masters and slaves. In each case there is mutual responsibility to submit and love, to obey and encourage, to work hard and be fair. Examine your family and work relationships. Do you relate to others as God intended?*

Proverbs for Today/ 20:1

Wine is a mocker and beer a brawler; whoever is led astray by them is not wise.

Signs of the Last Days/ Luke 21:5–19

Some of his disciples were remarking about how the temple was adorned with beautiful stones and with gifts dedicated to God. But Jesus said, 6"As for what you see here, the time will come when not one stone will be left on another; every one of them will be thrown down."

7"Teacher," they asked, "when will these things happen? And what will be the sign that they are about to take place?"

8He replied: "Watch out that you are not deceived. For many will come in my name, claiming, 'I am he,' and, 'The time is near.' Do not follow them. 9When you hear of wars and revolutions, do not be frightened. These things must happen first, but the end will not come right away."

10Then he said to them: "Nation will rise against nation, and kingdom against kingdom. 11There will be great earthquakes, famines and pestilences in various places, and fearful events and great signs from heaven.

12"But before all this, they will lay hands on you and persecute you. They will deliver you to synagogues and prisons, and you will be brought before kings and governors, and all on account of my name. 13This will result in your being witnesses to them. 14But make up your mind not to worry beforehand how you will defend yourselves. 15For I will give you words and wisdom that none of your adversaries will be able to resist or contradict. 16You will be betrayed even by parents, brothers, relatives and friends, and they will put some of you to death. 17All men will hate you because of me. 18But not a hair of your head will perish. 19By standing firm you will gain life."

A THOUGHT: *Jesus did not leave his disciples unprepared for the difficult years ahead. He warned them against false messiahs and persecutions, but he assured them he would be with them to protect them and make his kingdom known through them. In the end, he promised, he would return in power and glory to save them. Jesus' warnings and promises to his disciples still apply to us as we look forward to his return.*

Diligence in Prayer/ Colossians 4:2–6

Devote yourselves to prayer, being watchful and thankful. ³And pray for us, too, that God may open a door for our message, so that we may proclaim the mystery of Christ, for which I am in chains. ⁴Pray that I may proclaim it clearly, as I should. ⁵Be wise in the way you act toward outsiders; make the most of every opportunity. ⁶Let your conversation be always full of grace, seasoned with salt, so that you may know how to answer everyone.

A THOUGHT: *Have you ever grown tired of praying for something or someone? Paul emphasizes the need to keep at it. Persistence demonstrates our faith in the fact that God answers our prayers. Faith shouldn't die if the answers don't come immediately, for the delay may be God's way of working his will in your life. When you feel weary in your prayers, know that God is present, always listening, always acting—maybe not in ways you had hoped, but in ways that are best.*

Proverbs for Today/ 20:2–3

A king's wrath is like the roar of a lion; he who angers him forfeits his life. □ It is to a man's honor to avoid strife, but every fool is quick to quarrel.

JULY 27

Ready for Christ's Return/ Luke 21:20–38

"When you see Jerusalem being surrounded by armies, you will know that its desolation is near. ²¹Then let those who are in Judea flee to the mountains, let those in the city get out, and let those in the country not enter the city. ²²For this is the time of punishment in fulfillment of all that has been written. ²³How dreadful it will be in those days for pregnant women and nursing mothers! There will be great distress in the land and wrath against this people. ²⁴They will fall by the sword and will be taken as prisoners to all the nations. Jerusalem will be trampled on by the Gentiles until the times of the Gentiles are fulfilled.

²⁵"There will be signs in the sun, moon and stars. On the earth, nations will be in anguish and perplexity at the roar-

ing and tossing of the sea. 26Men will faint from terror, apprehensive of what is coming on the world, for the heavenly bodies will be shaken. 27At that time they will see the Son of Man coming in a cloud with power and great glory. 28When these things begin to take place, stand up and lift up your heads, because your redemption is drawing near."

29He told them this parable: "Look at the fig tree and all the trees. 30When they sprout leaves, you can see for yourselves and know that summer is near. 31Even so, when you see these things happening, you know that the kingdom of God is near.

32"I tell you the truth, this generation will certainly not pass away until all these things have happened. 33Heaven and earth will pass away, but my words will never pass away.

34"Be careful, or your hearts will be weighed down with dissipation, drunkenness and the anxieties of life, and that day will close on you unexpectedly like a trap. 35For it will come upon all those who live on the face of the whole earth. 36Be always on the watch, and pray that you may be able to escape all that is about to happen, and that you may be able to stand before the Son of Man."

37Each day Jesus was teaching at the temple, and each evening he went out to spend the night on the hill called the Mount of Olives, 38and all the people came early in the morning to hear him at the temple.

A THOUGHT: *Jesus told the disciples to keep a constant watch for his return. Although nearly two thousand years have passed since he spoke these words, their truth remains: he is coming again, and we need to watch and be ready. This means faithfully working at the tasks God has given us. Our attitude toward all we do should be colored with our joyful expectation of Christ's return.*

Greetings from Paul's Christian Friends/ Colossians 4:7–18

Tychicus will tell you all the news about me. He is a dear brother, a faithful minister and fellow servant in the Lord. 8I am sending him to you for the express purpose that you may know about our circumstances and that he may encourage your hearts. 9He is coming with Onesimus, our faithful and dear brother, who is one of you. They will tell you everything that is happening here.

10My fellow prisoner Aristarchus sends you his

greetings, as does Mark, the cousin of Barnabas. (You have received instructions about him; if he comes to you, welcome him.) 11Jesus, who is called Justus, also sends greetings. These are the only Jews among my fellow workers for the kingdom of God, and they have proved a comfort to me. 12Epaphras, who is one of you and a servant of Christ Jesus, sends greetings. He is always wrestling in prayer for you, that you may stand firm in all the will of God, mature and fully assured. 13I vouch for him that he is working hard for you and for those at Laodicea and Hierapolis. 14Our dear friend Luke, the doctor, and Demas send greetings. 15Give my greetings to the brothers at Laodicea, and to Nympha and the church in her house.

16After this letter has been read to you, see that it is also read in the church of the Laodiceans and that you in turn read the letter from Laodicea.

17Tell Archippus: "See to it that you complete the work you have received in the Lord."

18I, Paul, write this greeting in my own hand. Remember my chains. Grace be with you.

A THOUGHT: *Tychicus was one of Paul's personal respresentatives and probably the bearer of the letters to the Colossians and Ephesians. He accompanied Paul to Jerusalem with the collection for the church.*

Mark went with Paul and Barnabas on their first missionary journey, but then left in the middle of the trip for unknown reasons. Barnabas and Mark were relatives, and when Paul refused to take Mark on another journey, Barnabas and Mark journeyed together to preach the Good News. Mark also worked with Peter. Later, Mark and Paul were reconciled. Mark wrote the Gospel which bears his name.

Epaphras founded the Colossian church, and his report to Paul in Rome caused Paul to write this letter. Epaphras was a hero of the Colossian church, one of the believers who helped keep the church together in spite of growing troubles. His earnest prayers for the believers show his deep love and concern for them.

Luke spent much time with Paul, not only accompanying him on most of his third missionary journey, but sitting with him in the prison at Rome. Luke wrote the Gospel which bears his name and the book of Acts. Demas was faithful to Paul for a while, but then left him.

Proverbs for Today/ 20:4–6

A sluggard does not plow in season; so at harvest time he looks but finds nothing. □ The purposes of a man's heart are deep waters, but a man of understanding draws them out. □ Many a man claims to have unfailing love, but a faithful man who can find?

JULY 28

The Last Supper/ Luke 22:1–23

Now the Feast of Unleavened Bread, called the Passover, was approaching, 2and the chief priests and the teachers of the law were looking for some way to get rid of Jesus, for they were afraid of the people. 3Then Satan entered Judas, called Iscariot, one of the Twelve. 4And Judas went to the chief priests and the officers of the temple guard and discussed with them how he might betray Jesus. 5They were delighted and agreed to give him money. 6He consented, and watched for an opportunity to hand Jesus over to them when no crowd was present.

7Then came the day of Unleavened Bread on which the Passover lamb had to be sacrificed. 8Jesus sent Peter and John, saying, "Go and make preparations for us to eat the Passover."

9"Where do you want us to prepare for it?" they asked.

10He replied, "As you enter the city, a man carrying a jar of water will meet you. Follow him to the house that he enters, 11and say to the owner of the house, 'The Teacher asks: Where is the guest room, where I may eat the Passover with my disciples?' 12He will show you a large upper room, all furnished. Make preparations there."

13They left and found things just as Jesus had told them. So they prepared the Passover.

14When the hour came, Jesus and his apostles reclined at the table. 15And he said to them, "I have eagerly desired to eat this Passover with you before I suffer. 16For I tell you, I will not eat it again until it finds fulfillment in the kingdom of God."

17After taking the cup, he gave thanks and said, "Take this and divide it among you. 18For I tell you I will not drink again of the fruit of the vine until the kingdom of God comes."

19And he took bread, gave thanks and broke it, and gave it to them, saying, "This is my body given for you; do this in remembrance of me."

20In the same way, after the supper he took the cup, saying, "This cup is the new covenant in my blood, which is poured out for you. 21But the hand of him who is going to betray me is with mine on the table. 22The Son of Man will go as it has been decreed, but woe to that man who betrays him." 23They began to question among themselves which of them it might be who would do this.

A THOUGHT: *The Passover commemorated Israel's escape from Egypt when the blood of a lamb, painted on their doorposts, saved them from the angel of death who was killing the firstborn in all the homes in Egypt. This event foreshadowed Jesus' work on the cross. As the spotless Lamb of God, his blood would be spilled in order to save his people from the death brought by sin and judgment.*

Jesus asked the disciples to eat the bread and drink the wine "in remembrance of me." He wanted them to remember his sacrifice, which is the basis for forgiveness of sins, and also his friendship, which they could continue to enjoy through the work of the Holy Spirit. Although the exact meaning of communion has been strongly debated almost since the church began, Christians still take bread and wine in remembrance of their Lord, Savior, and friend, Jesus Christ. Do not neglect participating in the Lord's Supper. Let it remind you of what Christ did for you.

Paul Commends the Thessalonians' Faith/ 1 Thessalonians 1:1–10

Paul, Silas and Timothy,

To the church of the Thessalonians in God the Father and the Lord Jesus Christ:

Grace and peace to you.

2We always thank God for all of you, mentioning you in our prayers. 3We continually remember before our God and Father your work produced by faith, your labor prompted by love, and your endurance inspired by hope in our Lord Jesus Christ.

4For we know, brothers loved by God, that he has chosen you, 5because our gospel came to you not simply with words, but also with power, with the Holy Spirit and with deep conviction. You know how we lived among you for your sake. 6You became imitators of us and of the Lord; in spite of severe suffering, you welcomed the message with the joy given by the Holy Spirit. 7And so you became a model to all the believers in Macedonia and Achaia. 8The Lord's message rang out from you not only in Macedonia and Achaia—your faith in God has become known everywhere. Therefore we do not need to say anything about it, 9for they themselves report what kind of reception you gave us. They tell how you turned to God from idols to serve the living and true God, 10and to wait for his Son from heaven, whom he raised from the dead—Jesus, who rescues us from the coming wrath.

A THOUGHT: *The Good News produced a powerful effect upon the Thessalonians. These Christians stood firm when they were persecuted. Paul commends these young believers for their loving deeds, strong faith, and deep commitment to Christ. These characteristics are the marks of an effective Christian. Whenever the Word of God is heard and obeyed, lives are changed! Christianity is more than a collection of interesting facts; it is the power of God for salvation to every one who believes. What has God's power done in your life since you first put your faith in Christ?*

Proverbs for Today/ 20:7

The righteous man leads a blameless life; blessed are his children after him.

JULY 29

Leaders Must Be Servants/ Luke 22:24–30

Also a dispute arose among them [the disciples] as to which of them was considered to be greatest. 25Jesus said to them, "The kings of the Gentiles lord it over them; and those who exercise authority over them call themselves Benefactors. 26But you are not to be like that. Instead, the greatest among you should be like the youngest, and the one who rules like the one who serves. 27For who is greater, the one who is at the table or the one who serves? Is it not the one who is at the table? But I am among you as one who serves. 28You are those who have stood by me in my trials. 29And I confer on you a kingdom, just as my Father conferred one on me, 30so that you may eat and drink at my table in my kingdom and sit on thrones, judging the twelve tribes of Israel.

A THOUGHT: *The world's system of leadership is very different from the kingdom's. Worldly leaders are often selfish and arrogant as they claw their way to the top. But among Christians, the leader is to be the one who serves best. There are different styles of leadership—some lead through public speaking, some through administering, some through relationships—but all leaders need a servant's heart. Ask the people you lead how you can serve them better.*

Paul Reviews His Ministry in Thessalonica/ 1 Thessalonians 2:1–8

You know, brothers, that our visit to you was not a failure. 2We had previously suffered and been insulted in Philippi, as you know, but with the help of our God we dared to tell you his gospel in spite of strong opposition. 3For the appeal we make does not spring from error or impure motives, nor are we trying to trick you. 4On the contrary, we speak as men approved by God to be entrusted with the gospel. We are not trying to please men but God, who tests our hearts. 5You know we never used flattery, nor did we put on a mask to cover up greed—God is our witness. 6We were not looking for praise from men, not from you or anyone else.

As apostles of Christ we could have been a burden to you, 7but we were gentle among you, like a mother caring for her little children. 8We loved you so much that we were delighted to share with you not only the gospel of God but our lives as well, because you had become so dear to us.

A THOUGHT: *When Paul was with the Thessalonians, he didn't flatter them, didn't take their money, didn't seek their praise, and wasn't a burden to them. He and Silas completely focused their efforts on presenting God's message of salvation to the Thessalonians. This was important! The Thessalonian believers had their lives changed by God, not Paul; it was Christ's message they believed, not Paul's. When we witness for Christ, our focus should not be on the impression we make. As true ministers of Christ, we should point to him, not to ourselves. In trying to persuade people, we often alter our position just enough to make our message more palatable. Paul never changed his message to make it more acceptable, but he did tailor his presentation to each audience. Although our presentation must be altered to be appropriate to the situation, the truth of the gospel must never be compromised.*

Proverbs for Today/ 20:8–10

When a king sits on his throne to judge, he winnows out all evil with his eyes. □ Who can say, "I have kept my heart pure; I am clean and without sin"? □ Differing weights and differing measures—the LORD detests them both.

JULY 30

Jesus Predicts Peter's Denial/ Luke 22:31–34

"Simon, Simon, Satan has asked to sift you as wheat. 32But I have prayed for you, Simon, that your faith may not fail. And when you have turned back, strengthen your brothers."

33But he replied, "Lord, I am ready to go with you to prison and to death."

34Jesus answered, "I tell you, Peter, before the rooster crows today, you will deny three times that you know me."

A THOUGHT: *Satan wanted to crush Peter like a grain of wheat. He hoped to find only chaff and blow it away. But Jesus assured Peter that his faith, although it would falter, would not be destroyed. It would be renewed, and he would become a powerful leader. In the same way, we often fall short of what God demands of us. But when we turn to God, he will restore us and deepen our faith.*

Paul's Work among the Thessalonians/ 1 Thessalonians 2:9–13

Surely you remember, brothers, our toil and hardship; we worked night and day in order not to be a burden to anyone while we preached the gospel of God to you.

10You are witnesses, and so is God, of how holy, righteous and blameless we were among you who believed. 11For you know that we dealt with each of you as a father deals with his own children, 12encouraging, comforting and urging you to live lives worthy of God, who calls you into his kingdom and glory.

13And we also thank God continually because, when you received the word of God, which you heard from us, you accepted it not as the word of men, but as it actually is, the word of God, which is at work in you who believe.

A THOUGHT: *No loving father would neglect the safety of his children, allowing them to walk into circumstances that might prove fatal or permanently damaging. In the same way, we must take new believers under our wing until they are mature enough to stand firm in their faith. When new Christians are strong enough to influence others for the gospel, rather than be influenced by others to practices contrary to the gospel, they are ready to be out from under our wings.*

Proverbs for Today/ 20:11

Even a child is known by his actions, by whether his conduct is pure and right.

JULY 31

Jesus Prepares the Disciples for His Death/ Luke 22:35–38

Then Jesus asked them [the disciples], "When I sent you without purse, bag or sandals, did you lack anything?"

"Nothing," they answered.

36He said to them, "But now if you have a purse, take it, and also a bag; and if you don't have a sword, sell your cloak and buy one. 37It is written: 'And he was numbered with the transgressors'; and I tell you that this must be fulfilled in me. Yes, what is written about me is reaching its fulfillment."

38The disciples said, "See, Lord, here are two swords."

"That is enough," he replied.

A THOUGHT: *Now Jesus reverses his earlier advice regarding how to travel. The disciples were to bring a bag, money, and a sword. They would be facing hatred and persecution and would need to be prepared. When Jesus said "Enough," he may have meant that two swords were enough or that they had talked enough. In either case, their need for a sword vividly communicated the trials they were soon to face.*

Persecuted for Spreading the Gospel/ 1 Thessalonians 2:14—3:4

For you, brothers, became imitators of God's churches in Judea, which are in Christ Jesus: You suffered from your own countrymen the same things those churches suffered

from the Jews, 15who killed the Lord Jesus and the prophets and also drove us out. They displease God and are
hostile to all men 16in their effort to keep us from speaking
to the Gentiles so that they may be saved. In this way they
always heap up their sins to the limit. The wrath of God has
come upon them at last.

17But, brothers, when we were torn away from you for
a short time (in person, not in thought), out of our intense
longing we made every effort to see you. 18For we wanted
to come to you—certainly I, Paul, did, again and again—but
Satan stopped us. 19For what is our hope, our joy, or the
crown in which we will glory in the presence of our Lord
Jesus when he comes? Is it not you? 20Indeed, you are our
glory and joy.

3:1So when we could stand it no longer, we thought it
best to be left by ourselves in Athens. 2We sent Timothy,
who is our brother and God's fellow worker in spreading
the gospel of Christ, to strengthen and encourage you in
your faith, 3so that no one would be unsettled by these
trials. You know quite well that we were destined for them.
4In fact, when we were with you, we kept telling you that
we would be persecuted. And it turned out that way, as you
well know.

A THOUGHT: *Just as the Jewish Christians in Jerusalem were persecuted by their own people, so the Gentile Christians in Thessalonica
were persecuted by their fellow Gentiles. It is discouraging to face
persecution, especially when it comes from your own people. But
when we take a stand for Christ, we must face opposition, disap-
proval, ridicule, and persecution from our neighbors, friends, and
even family members.*

Proverbs for Today/ 20:12

Ears that hear and eyes that see— the LORD has made them
both.

AUGUST 1

Judas Betrays Jesus/ Luke 22:39–53

Jesus went out as usual to the Mount of Olives, and his disciples followed him. 40On reaching the place, he said to them, "Pray that you will not fall into temptation." 41He withdrew about a stone's throw beyond them, knelt down and prayed, 42"Father, if you are willing, take this cup from me; yet not my will, but yours be done." 43An angel from heaven appeared to him and strengthened him. 44And being in anguish, he prayed more earnestly, and his sweat was like drops of blood falling to the ground.

45When he rose from prayer and went back to the disciples, he found them asleep, exhausted from sorrow. 46"Why are you sleeping?" he asked them. "Get up and pray so that you will not fall into temptation."

47While he was still speaking a crowd came up, and the man who was called Judas, one of the Twelve, was leading them. He approached Jesus to kiss him, 48but Jesus asked him, "Judas, are you betraying the Son of Man with a kiss?"

49When Jesus' followers saw what was going to happen, they said, "Lord, should we strike with our swords?" 50And one of them struck the servant of the high priest, cutting off his right ear.

51But Jesus answered, "No more of this!" And he touched the man's ear and healed him.

52Then Jesus said to the chief priests, the officers of the temple guard, and the elders, who had come for him, "Am I leading a rebellion, that you have come with swords and clubs? 53Every day I was with you in the temple courts, and you did not lay a hand on me. But this is your hour—when darkness reigns."

A THOUGHT: *Jesus asked the disciples to pray that they would not be overcome by temptation because he knew he would soon be leaving them. He also knew they would need extra strength to face the temptations ahead—temptations to run away, or to deny their relationship with him. Also, they were about to see him die—would they still think he was the Messiah? Their strongest temptation would be to think they had been deceived.*

Timothy's Good Report/ 1 Thessalonians 3:5–8

For this reason, when I could stand it no longer, I sent to find out about your faith. I was afraid that in some way the tempter might have tempted you and our efforts might have been useless.

6But Timothy has just now come to us from you and has brought good news about your faith and love. He has told us that you always have pleasant memories of us and that you long to see us, just as we also long to see you. 7Therefore, brothers, in all our distress and persecution we were encouraged about you because of your faith. 8For now we really live, since you are standing firm in the Lord.

A THOUGHT: *Paul is encouraged by Timothy's report concerning the Thessalonian Christians. These young believers were standing firm in the faith despite fierce persecution. In the midst of persecution or pressure, believers should encourage each other. Compliments, expressions of thanks, and support for those who are wavering in the faith help to build up fellow believers.*

Proverbs for Today/ 20:13–15

Do not love sleep or you will grow poor; stay awake and you will have food to spare. □ "It's no good, it's no good!" says the buyer; then off he goes and boasts about his purchase. □ Gold there is, and rubies in abundance, but lips that speak knowledge are a rare jewel.

AUGUST 2

Peter's Denials/ Luke 22:54–62

Then seizing him [Jesus], they led him away and took him into the house of the high priest. Peter followed at a distance. 55But when they had kindled a fire in the middle of the courtyard and had sat down together, Peter sat down with them. 56A servant girl saw him seated there in the firelight. She looked closely at him and said, "This man was with him."

57But he denied it. "Woman, I don't know him," he said.

58A little later someone else saw him and said, "You also are one of them."

"Man, I am not!" Peter replied.

59About an hour later another asserted, "Certainly this fellow was with him, for he is a Galilean."

60Peter replied, "Man, I don't know what you're talking about!" Just as he was speaking, the rooster crowed. 61The Lord turned and looked straight at Peter. Then Peter remembered the word the Lord had spoken to him: "Before the rooster crows today, you will disown me three times." 62And he went outside and wept bitterly.

A THOUGHT: *Peter wept bitterly, not only because he realized that he had denied his Lord, the Messiah, but also because he had turned away from a very dear friend, a person who had loved and taught him for three years. Peter had said he would never deny Christ—despite Jesus' prediction—but when frightened, he went against all he had boldly promised. Unable to stand up for his Lord for even 12 hours, he had failed as a disciple and as a friend. We need to be aware of our own breaking points and not become overconfident or self-sufficient. If we fail, we must remember that Christ can use those who recognize their failure. From this humiliating experience Peter learned much that would help him in the leadership responsibilities he would soon assume.*

Paul Prays for the Thessalonians/ 1 Thessalonians 3:9–13

How can we thank God enough for you in return for all the joy we have in the presence of our God because of you? 10Night and day we pray most earnestly that we may see you again and supply what is lacking in your faith.

11Now may our God and Father himself and our Lord Jesus clear the way for us to come to you. 12May the Lord make your love increase and overflow for each other and for everyone else, just as ours does for you. 13May he strengthen your hearts so that you will be blameless and holy in the presence of our God and Father when our Lord Jesus comes with all his holy ones.

A THOUGHT: *It is a great joy for Christians to see another person come to faith in Christ and mature in that faith. Paul experienced this joy countless times. He thanked God for those who had come to know Christ and prayed for their continued growth in faith. If there are new Christians who have brought you joy, thank God for them and support them as they continue to grow in their walk with God.*

Proverbs for Today/ 20:16–18

Take the garment of one who puts up security for a stranger; hold it in pledge if he does it for a wayward woman. □ Food gained by fraud tastes sweet to a man, but he ends up with a mouth full of gravel. □ Make plans by seeking advice; if you wage war, obtain guidance.

AUGUST 3

Jesus Before the Jewish Council/ Luke 22:63–71

The men who were guarding Jesus began mocking and beating him. 64They blindfolded him and demanded, "Prophesy! Who hit you?" 65And they said many other insulting things to him.

66At daybreak the council of the elders of the people, both the chief priests and teachers of the law, met together, and Jesus was led before them. 67"If you are the Christ," they said, "tell us."

Jesus answered, "If I tell you, you will not believe me, 68and if I asked you, you would not answer. 69But from now on, the Son of Man will be seated at the right hand of the mighty God."

70They all asked, "Are you then the Son of God?"

He replied, "You are right in saying I am."

71Then they said, "Why do we need any more testimony? We have heard it from his own lips."

A THOUGHT: *Jesus identified himself with God by using a familiar title for God found in the Old Testament: "I Am." The High Priest recognized Jesus' claim and accused him of blasphemy, the sin of claiming to be God. Blasphemy was punishable by death. The Jewish leaders had the evidence they wanted, but they were about to bring about the greatest injustice ever perpetrated on earth. Jesus willingly submitted to this great injustice to make salvation available to all who genuinely want to be reconciled to God.*

Living to Please God/ 1 Thessalonians 4:1–8

Finally, brothers, we instructed you how to live in order to please God, as in fact you are living. Now we ask you and urge you in the Lord Jesus to do this more and more. 2For you know what instructions we gave you by the authority of the Lord Jesus.

3It is God's will that you should be sanctified: that you should avoid sexual immorality; 4that each of you should learn to control his own body in a way that is holy and honorable, 5not in passionate lust like the heathen, who do not know God; 6and that in this matter no one should wrong his brother or take advantage of him. The Lord will punish men for all such sins, as we have already told you and warned you. 7For God did not call us to be impure, but to live a holy life. 8Therefore, he who rejects this instruction does not reject man but God, who gives you his Holy Spirit.

A THOUGHT: *Sexual desires and activities must be placed under Christ's control. God created sex for procreation, pleasure, and as an expression of love between a husband and wife. Sexual experience must be limited to the marriage relationship to avoid hurting ourselves, our relationship with God, and our relationships with others.*

Proverbs for Today/ 20:19

A gossip betrays a confidence; so avoid a man who talks too much.

AUGUST 4

Jesus Before Pilate and Herod/ Luke 23:1–25

Then the whole assembly rose and led him off to Pilate. 2And they began to accuse him, saying, "We have found this man subverting our nation. He opposes payment of taxes to Caesar and claims to be Christ, a king."

3So Pilate asked Jesus, "Are you the king of the Jews?"

"Yes, it is as you say," Jesus replied.

4Then Pilate announced to the chief priests and the crowd, "I find no basis for a charge against this man."

5But they insisted, "He stirs up the people all over Judea by his teaching. He started in Galilee and has come all the way here."

6On hearing this, Pilate asked if the man was a Galilean.

⁷When he learned that Jesus was under Herod's jurisdiction, he sent him to Herod, who was also in Jerusalem at that time.

⁸When Herod saw Jesus, he was greatly pleased, because for a long time he had been wanting to see him. From what he had heard about him, he hoped to see him perform some miracle. ⁹He plied him with many questions, but Jesus gave him no answer. ¹⁰The chief priests and the teachers of the law were standing there, vehemently accusing him. ¹¹Then Herod and his soldiers ridiculed and mocked him. Dressing him in an elegant robe, they sent him back to Pilate. ¹²That day Herod and Pilate became friends—before this they had been enemies.

¹³Pilate called together the chief priests, the rulers and the people, ¹⁴and said to them, "You brought me this man as one who was inciting the people to rebellion. I have examined him in your presence and have found no basis for your charges against him. ¹⁵Neither has Herod, for he sent him back to us; as you can see, he has done nothing to deserve death. ¹⁶Therefore, I will punish him and then release him. ·"

¹⁸With one voice they cried out, "Away with this man! Release Barabbas to us!" ¹⁹(Barabbas had been thrown into prison for an insurrection in the city, and for murder.)

²⁰Wanting to release Jesus, Pilate appealed to them again. ²¹But they kept shouting, "Crucify him! Crucify him!"

²²For the third time he spoke to them: "Why? What crime has this man committed? I have found in him no grounds for the death penalty. Therefore I will have him punished and then release him."

²³But with loud shouts they insistently demanded that he be crucified, and their shouts prevailed. ²⁴So Pilate decided to grant their demand. ²⁵He released the man who had been thrown into prison for insurrection and murder, the one they asked for, and surrendered Jesus to their will.

A THOUGHT: *Pilate wanted to release Jesus, but the crowd loudly demanded his death, so Pilate sentenced Jesus to die. No doubt Pilate did not want to risk losing his position (which may already have been shaky), by allowing a riot to occur in his province. As a career politician, he knew the importance of compromise, and he saw*

---

*16 Some manuscripts *him.*" 17*Now he was obliged to release one man to them at the Feast.*

Jesus more as a political threat than as a human being with rights and dignity.

When the stakes are high, it is hard to stand up for what is right, and it is easy to see our opponents as problems to be solved rather than as people to be respected. Had Pilate been a man of real courage, he would have released Jesus no matter what the consequences. But the crowd roared, and Pilate buckled. When you have a difficult decision to make, don't discount the effects of peer pressure. Realize beforehand that the right decision could have unpleasant consequences: social rejection, career derailment, public ridicule. Then think of Pilate and resolve to stand up for what is right no matter what other people pressure you to do.

Christian Ambition/ 1 Thessalonians 4:9–12

Now about brotherly love we do not need to write to you, for you yourselves have been taught by God to love each other. 10And in fact, you do love all the brothers throughout Macedonia. Yet we urge you, brothers, to do so more and more.

11Make it your ambition to lead a quiet life, to mind your own business and to work with your hands, just as we told you, 12so that your daily life may win the respect of outsiders and so that you will not be dependent on anybody.

A THOUGHT: *Ambition is a characteristic that people in our society value greatly. However, society's view of ambition is "getting ahead;" "grabbing all the gusto," "living for number one." All of these ambitions center on pursuits for the self. The Christian's ambition, however, is to strive for the kingdom of God. Christians do not live to be flashy; instead, they seek to be obedient servants of Jesus Christ who is Lord of the church. Whatever we do, let us do it faithfully, as unto the Lord, and let us be a positive force in society—serving those around us rather than stepping on people to get to the top.*

Proverbs for Today/ 20:20–21

If a man curses his father or mother, his lamp will be snuffed out in pitch darkness. □ An inheritance quickly gained at the beginning will not be blessed at the end.

Jesus' Crucifixion/ Luke 23:26–43

As they led him [Jesus] away, they seized Simon from Cyrene, who was on his way in from the country, and put the cross on him and made him carry it behind Jesus. 27A large number of people followed him, including women who mourned and wailed for him. 28Jesus turned and said to them, "Daughters of Jerusalem, do not weep for me; weep for yourselves and for your children. 29For the time will come when you will say, 'Blessed are the barren women, the wombs that never bore and the breasts that never nursed!' 30Then

> " 'they will say to the mountains, "Fall on us!"
> and to the hills, "Cover us!" ' '

31For if men do these things when the tree is green, what will happen when it is dry?"

32Two other men, both criminals, were also led out with him to be executed. 33When they came to the place called the Skull, there they crucified him, along with the criminals—one on his right, the other on his left. 34Jesus said, "Father, forgive them, for they do not know what they are doing." And they divided up his clothes by casting lots.

35The people stood watching, and the rulers even sneered at him. They said, "He saved others; let him save himself if he is the Christ of God, the Chosen One."

36The soldiers also came up and mocked him. They offered him wine vinegar 37and said, "If you are the king of the Jews, save yourself."

38There was a written notice above him, which read: THIS IS THE KING OF THE JEWS.

39One of the criminals who hung there hurled insults at him: "Aren't you the Christ? Save yourself and us!"

40But the other criminal rebuked him. "Don't you fear God," he said, "since you are under the same sentence? 41We are punished justly, for we are getting what our deeds deserve. But this man has done nothing wrong."

42Then he said, "Jesus, remember me when you come into your kingdom."

43Jesus answered him, "I tell you the truth, today you will be with me in paradise."

A THOUGHT: *As Jesus was led away through the streets of Jerusalem, he could no longer carry his cross, and Simon of Cyrene was given the burden. Jesus was crucified, along with common criminals, on a hill outside Jerusalem. When James and John asked Jesus for the places of honor next to him in his kingdom, he told them they didn't know what they were asking. Now that Jesus was inaugurating his kingdom through his death, the places on his right and on his left were taken by dying men—criminals. As Jesus explained to his two power-hungry disciples, a person who wants to be close to Jesus must be prepared to suffer and die as he himself was doing. The way to greatness in the kingdom is the way of the cross.*

The Hope of the Resurrection/
1 Thessalonians 4:13—5:3

Brothers, we do not want you to be ignorant about those who fall asleep, or to grieve like the rest of men, who have no hope. 14We believe that Jesus died and rose again and so we believe that God will bring with Jesus those who have fallen asleep in him. 15According to the Lord's own word, we tell you that we who are still alive, who are left till the coming of the Lord, will certainly not precede those who have fallen asleep. 16For the Lord himself will come down from heaven, with a loud command, with the voice of the archangel and with the trumpet call of God, and the dead in Christ will rise first. 17After that, we who are still alive and are left will be caught up together with them in the clouds to meet the Lord in the air. And so we will be with the Lord forever. 18Therefore encourage each other with these words.

5:1Now, brothers, about times and dates we do not need to write to you, 2for you know very well that the day of the Lord will come like a thief in the night. 3While people are saying, "Peace and safety," destruction will come on them suddenly, as labor pains on a pregnant woman, and they will not escape.

A THOUGHT: *Because Jesus Christ came back to life, so will all believers. All Christians, including those living when he returns, will live with Jesus forever. Therefore, we need not despair when Christian loved ones die or world events take a tragic turn. For God will turn our tragedies to triumphs, our pain to glory, and our defeat to victory. All believers throughout history will stand reunited in God's very presence, safe and secure. As Paul comforted the Thessalonians with the promise of the resurrection, so we should comfort and reassure one another with this great hope.*

Proverbs for Today/ 20:22–23

Do not say, "I'll pay you back for this wrong!" Wait for the LORD, and he will deliver you. □ The LORD detests differing weights, and dishonest scales do not please him.

AUGUST 6

Jesus' Death and Burial/ Luke 23:44–56

It was now about the sixth hour, and darkness came over the whole land until the ninth hour, 45for the sun stopped shining. And the curtain of the temple was torn in two. 46Jesus called out with a loud voice, "Father, into your hands I commit my spirit." When he had said this, he breathed his last.

47The centurion, seeing what had happened, praised God and said, "Surely this was a righteous man." 48When all the people who had gathered to witness this sight saw what took place, they beat their breasts and went away. 49But all those who knew him, including the women who had followed him from Galilee, stood at a distance, watching these things.

50Now there was a man named Joseph, a member of the Council, a good and upright man, 51who had not consented to their decision and action. He came from the Judean town of Arimathea and he was waiting for the kingdom of God. 52Going to Pilate, he asked for Jesus' body. 53Then he took it down, wrapped it in linen cloth and placed it in a tomb cut in the rock, one in which no one had yet been laid. 54It was Preparation Day, and the Sabbath was about to begin.

55The women who had come with Jesus from Galilee followed Joseph and saw the tomb and how his body was laid in it. 56Then they went home and prepared spices and perfumes. But they rested on the Sabbath in obedience to the commandment.

A THOUGHT: *Darkness covered the entire land for about three hours in the middle of the day. All nature seemed to mourn over the stark tragedy of the death of God's Son. In the midst of this darkness, the curtain separating the Most Holy Place from the Holy Place was torn in two. This significant event symbolized Christ's work on the cross. The Temple had three parts: the courtyard area; the Holy Place, where only priests could enter; and the Most Holy Place, where the High Priest alone could enter once a year to atone for the sins of the people. It was in the Most Holy Place that the Ark of the Covenant (the symbol of God's presence) rested. The curtain that split was the one that closed off the Most Holy Place. At Christ's death, the barrier between God and man was torn apart. Now all people are able to approach God directly through Christ.*

Live in the Light of Jesus' Coming/
1 Thessalonians 5:4–11

But you, brothers, are not in darkness so that this day should surprise you like a thief. 5You are all sons of the light and sons of the day. We do not belong to the night or to the darkness. 6So then, let us not be like others, who are asleep, but let us be alert and self-controlled. 7For those who sleep, sleep at night, and those who get drunk, get drunk at night. 8But since we belong to the day, let us be self-controlled, putting on faith and love as a breastplate, and the hope of salvation as a helmet. 9For God did not appoint us to suffer wrath but to receive salvation through our Lord Jesus Christ. 10He died for us so that, whether we are awake or asleep, we may live together with him. 11Therefore encourage one another and build each other up, just as in fact you are doing.

A THOUGHT: *As you near the end of a foot race, your legs ache, your throat burns, and your whole body cries out for you to stop. This is when supporters are most valuable. Their encouragement helps you push through the pain to the finish. In the same way, Christians are to encourage one another. A word of encouragement offered at the right moment can be the difference between finishing well and collapsing along the way. Look around you. Be sensitive to another's need for encouragement and offer supportive words or actions.*

Proverbs for Today/ 20:24–25

A man's steps are directed by the LORD. How then can anyone understand his own way? ◻ It is a trap for a man to dedicate something rashly and only later to consider his vows.

AUGUST 7

Jesus Rises from the Dead/ Luke 24:1–12

On the first day of the week, very early in the morning, the women took the spices they had prepared and went to the tomb. ²They found the stone rolled away from the tomb, ³but when they entered, they did not find the body of the Lord Jesus. ⁴While they were wondering about this, suddenly two men in clothes that gleamed like lightning stood beside them. ⁵In their fright the women bowed down with their faces to the ground, but the men said to them, "Why do you look for the living among the dead? ⁶He is not here; he has risen! Remember how he told you, while he was still with you in Galilee: ⁷'The Son of Man must be delivered into the hands of sinful men, be crucified and on the third day be raised again.' " ⁸Then they remembered his words.

⁹When they came back from the tomb, they told all these things to the Eleven and to all the others. ¹⁰It was Mary Magdalene, Joanna, Mary the mother of James, and the others with them who told this to the apostles. ¹¹But they did not believe the women, because their words seemed to them like nonsense. ¹²Peter, however, got up and ran to the tomb. Bending over, he saw the strips of linen lying by themselves, and he went away, wondering to himself what had happened.

A THOUGHT: *The resurrection of Jesus from the dead is central to the Christian faith. Why is the resurrection so important? (1) Because Christ was raised from the dead, we know that the kingdom of heaven has broken into earth's history. (2) Because of the resurrection, we know that death has been conquered, and we too will be raised from the dead to live forever with Christ. (3) The resurrection gives meaning to the church's regular feast, the Lord's Supper. Like the disciples on the Emmaus Road, we break bread with our risen Lord, who comes in power to save us. (4) The resurrection helps us find meaning even in the midst of great tragedy. No matter what happens to us as we walk with the Lord, the resurrection gives us hope for the future. (5) God's power that brought Jesus back from the dead is available to us so that we can live for him in an evil world.*

Christians can look very different from one another; they can hold widely varying beliefs about politics, lifestyle, and even some aspects of theology. But one central belief unites all true Christians—Jesus Christ rose from the dead!

Instructions for Holy Living/
1 Thessalonians 5:12–22

Now we ask you, brothers, to respect those who work hard among you, who are over you in the Lord and who admonish you. 13Hold them in the highest regard in love because of their work. Live in peace with each other. 14And we urge you, brothers, warn those who are idle, encourage the timid, help the weak, be patient with everyone. 15Make sure that nobody pays back wrong for wrong, but always try to be kind to each other and to everyone else.

16Be joyful always; 17pray continually; 18give thanks in all circumstances, for this is God's will for you in Christ Jesus.

19Do not put out the Spirit's fire; 20do not treat prophecies with contempt. 21Test everything. Hold on to the good. 22Avoid every kind of evil.

A THOUGHT: *Don't lie down with the lazy; warn them. Don't yell at the frightened; comfort them. At times it's difficult to distinguish between laziness and fear. Two people may be doing nothing—one because he is lazy and the other out of fear of doing something wrong. The key to ministry is sensitivity—sensing the condition of each person and offering the appropriate remedy for each situation. You can't effectively help until you know the problem. You can't apply the right medicine until you know what kind of wound there is that needs to be treated.*

Proverbs for Today/ 20:26–27

A wise king winnows out the wicked; he drives the threshing wheel over them. □ The lamp of the LORD searches the spirit of a man; it searches out his inmost being.

AUGUST 8

Jesus Appears on the Emmaus Road/
Luke 24:13–34

Now that same day two of them were going to a village called Emmaus, about seven miles from Jerusalem. 14They were talking with each other about everything that had happened. 15As they talked and discussed these things with each other, Jesus himself came up and walked along with them; 16but they were kept from recognizing him.

17He asked them, "What are you discussing together as you walk along?"

They stood still, their faces downcast. 18One of them, named Cleopas, asked him, "Are you only a visitor to Jerusalem and do not know the things that have happened there in these days?"

19"What things?" he asked.

"About Jesus of Nazareth," they replied. "He was a prophet, powerful in word and deed before God and all the people. 20The chief priests and our rulers handed him over to be sentenced to death, and they crucified him; 21but we had hoped that he was the one who was going to redeem Israel. And what is more, it is the third day since all this took place. 22In addition, some of our women amazed us. They went to the tomb early this morning 23but didn't find his body. They came and told us that they had seen a vision of angels, who said he was alive. 24Then some of our companions went to the tomb and found it just as the women had said, but him they did not see."

25He said to them, "How foolish you are, and how slow of heart to believe all that the prophets have spoken! 26Did not the Christ have to suffer these things and then enter his glory?" 27And beginning with Moses and all the Prophets, he explained to them what was said in all the Scriptures concerning himself.

28As they approached the village to which they were going, Jesus acted as if he were going farther. 29But they urged him strongly, "Stay with us, for it is nearly evening; the day is almost over." So he went in to stay with them.

30When he was at the table with them, he took bread, gave thanks, broke it and began to give it to them. 31Then their eyes were opened and they recognized him, and he disappeared from their sight. 32They asked each other, "Were not our hearts burning within us while he talked with us on the road and opened the Scriptures to us?"

33They got up and returned at once to Jerusalem. There they found the Eleven and those with them, assembled together 34and saying, "It is true! The Lord has risen and has appeared to Simon."

A THOUGHT: *The two disciples returning to Emmaus missed the significance of history's greatest event because they focused on their disappointments and problems—so much so that they didn't recognize that it was Jesus walking beside them. To compound the problem, they were walking in the wrong direction—away from the fellowship of believers in Jerusalem. We are likely to miss Jesus and withdraw from the strength found in other believers when we become preoccupied with our dashed hopes and frustrated plans. Only when we are looking for Jesus in our midst will we experience the power and help he can bring.*

Paul's Prayer and Final Greetings/ 1 Thessalonians 5:23–28

May God himself, the God of peace, sanctify you through and through. May your whole spirit, soul and body be kept blameless at the coming of our Lord Jesus Christ. 24The one who calls you is faithful and he will do it.

25Brothers, pray for us. 26Greet all the brothers with a holy kiss. 27I charge you before the Lord to have this letter read to all the brothers.

28The grace of our Lord Jesus Christ be with you.

A THOUGHT: *The spirit, soul, and body are integral parts of a person. This expression is Paul's way of saying that God must be involved in every aspect of our lives. It is wrong to think we can separate our spiritual lives from everything else, obeying God only in some ethereal sense or living for him only one day each week. Christ must control all of us, not just a "religious" part.*

Proverbs for Today/ 20:28–30

Love and faithfulness keep a king safe; through love his throne is made secure. □ The glory of young men is their strength, gray hair the splendor of the old. □ Blows and wounds cleanse away evil, and beatings purge the inmost being.

AUGUST 9

The Ascension of Jesus/ Luke 24:35–53

Then the two [from Emmaus] told what had happened on the way, and how Jesus was recognized by them when he broke the bread.

36While they were still talking about this, Jesus himself stood among them and said to them, "Peace be with you."

37They were startled and frightened, thinking they saw a ghost. 38He said to them, "Why are you troubled, and why do doubts rise in your minds? 39Look at my hands and my feet. It is I myself! Touch me and see; a ghost does not have flesh and bones, as you see I have."

40When he had said this, he showed them his hands and feet. 41And while they still did not believe it because of joy and amazement, he asked them, "Do you have anything here to eat?" 42They gave him a piece of broiled fish, 43and he took it and ate it in their presence.

44He said to them, "This is what I told you while I was still with you: Everything must be fulfilled that is written about me in the Law of Moses, the Prophets and the Psalms."

45Then he opened their minds so they could understand the Scriptures. 46He told them, "This is what is written: The Christ will suffer and rise from the dead on the third day, 47and repentance and forgiveness of sins will be preached in his name to all nations, beginning at Jerusalem. 48You are witnesses of these things. 49I am going to send you what my Father has promised; but stay in the city until you have been clothed with power from on high."

50When he had led them out to the vicinity of Bethany, he lifted up his hands and blessed them. 51While he was blessing them, he left them and was taken up into heaven. 52Then they worshiped him and returned to Jerusalem with great joy. 53And they stayed continually at the temple, praising God.

A THOUGHT: *As the disciples stood and watched, Jesus began rising into the air, and soon he disappeared into heaven. Seeing Jesus leave must have been frightening, but they knew he would keep his promise to be with them in the Spirit. This same Jesus who lived with the disciples, who died and rose from the dead, and who loves us, promises to be with us always. We can get to know him better through studying the Scriptures, praying, and allowing the Holy Spirit to make us more like him.*

Paul Encourages the Thessalonians/ 2 Thessalonians 1:1–12

Paul, Silas and Timothy,

To the church of the Thessalonians in God our Father and the Lord Jesus Christ:

2Grace and peace to you from God the Father and the Lord Jesus Christ.

3We ought always to thank God for you, brothers, and rightly so, because your faith is growing more and more, and the love every one of you has for each other is increasing. 4Therefore, among God's churches we boast about your perseverance and faith in all the persecutions and trials you are enduring.

5All this is evidence that God's judgment is right, and as a result you will be counted worthy of the kingdom of God, for which you are suffering. 6God is just: He will pay back trouble to those who trouble you 7and give relief to you who are troubled, and to us as well. This will happen when the Lord Jesus is revealed from heaven in blazing fire with his powerful angels. 8He will punish those who do not know God and do not obey the gospel of our Lord Jesus. 9They will be punished with everlasting destruction and shut out from the presence of the Lord and from the majesty of his power 10on the day he comes to be glorified in his holy people and to be marveled at among all those who have believed. This includes you, because you believed our testimony to you.

11With this in mind, we constantly pray for you, that our God may count you worthy of his calling, and that by his power he may fulfill every good purpose of yours and every act prompted by your faith. 12We pray this so that the name of our Lord Jesus may be glorified in you, and you in him, according to the grace of our God and the Lord Jesus Christ.

A THOUGHT: *As we live for Christ, we will experience troubles and hardships. Some say troubles are a result of sin or lack of faith. But Paul teaches that they may be a part of God's plan for believers. Our problems help us look upward and forward, not inward; they help build strong character; and they help us be sensitive to others who also struggle. Problems are unavoidable for godly people in an ungodly world. Your troubles may well be a sign of effective Christian living.*

Proverbs for Today/ 21:1–2

The king's heart is in the hand of the LORD; he directs it like a watercourse wherever he pleases. □ All a man's ways seem right to him, but the LORD weighs the heart.

AUGUST 10

Christ, the Word Made Flesh/ John 1:1–14

In the beginning was the Word, and the Word was with God, and the Word was God. 2He was with God in the beginning.

3Through him all things were made; without him nothing was made that has been made. 4In him was life, and that life was the light of men. 5The light shines in the darkness, but the darkness has not understood it.

6There came a man who was sent from God; his name was John. 7He came as a witness to testify concerning that light, so that through him all men might believe. 8He himself was not the light; he came only as a witness to the light. 9The true light that gives light to every man was coming into the world.

10He was in the world, and though the world was made through him, the world did not recognize him. 11He came to that which was his own, but his own did not receive him. 12Yet to all who received him, to those who believed in his name, he gave the right to become children of God— 13children born not of natural descent, nor of human decision or a husband's will, but born of God.

14The Word became flesh and made his dwelling among us. We have seen his glory, the glory of the One and Only, who came from the Father, full of grace and truth.

A THOUGHT: *When Jesus Christ was born, God became a man. He was not part man and part God; he was completely human and completely divine. Before Christ came, people could know God* partially. After Christ came, people could know God fully because he became visible and tangible in Christ. Christ is the perfect expression of God in human form. The two most common errors are to minimize Jesus' humanity or to minimize his divinity. Jesus is both God and man. We can be comforted with the knowledge that our great God and Savior has walked among us and experienced the struggles and difficulties we experience. Jesus went far beyond merely sharing our experiences here on earth—he died in our stead to make an intimate relationship with God the Father possible.

Don't Be Deceived/ 2 Thessalonians 2:1–6

Concerning the coming of our Lord Jesus Christ and our being gathered to him, we ask you, brothers, ²not to become easily unsettled or alarmed by some prophecy, report or letter supposed to have come from us, saying that the day of the Lord has already come. ³Don't let anyone deceive you in any way, for that day will not come until the rebellion occurs and the man of lawlessness is revealed, the man doomed to destruction. ⁴He will oppose and will exalt himself over everything that is called God or is worshiped, so that he sets himself up in God's temple, proclaiming himself to be God.

⁵Don't you remember that when I was with you I used to tell you these things? ⁶And now you know what is holding him back, so that he may be revealed at the proper time.

A THOUGHT: *Here Paul launches into a discussion about the end of the world and Christ's Second Coming. He says that great suffering and trouble lie ahead, but evil will not prevail, because Christ will return to judge all people. Although Paul presents a few signs of the end times, his emphasis, like Jesus', is not on specific or current events but on each person's need to prepare for Christ's return by living rightly day by day. If we are ready, we won't have to be concerned about what will happen or when it will happen. Our confidence is that God is in control of all events.*

Proverbs for Today/ 21:3

To do what is right and just is more acceptable to the LORD than sacrifice.

John Proclaims Jesus as the Messiah/ John 1:15–34

John testifies concerning him [Jesus]. He cries out, saying, "This was he of whom I said, 'He who comes after me has surpassed me because he was before me.'" 16From the fullness of his grace we have all received one blessing after another. 17For the law was given through Moses; grace and truth came through Jesus Christ. 18No one has ever seen God, but God the One and Only, who is at the Father's side, has made him known.

19Now this was John's testimony when the Jews of Jerusalem sent priests and Levites to ask him who he was. 20He did not fail to confess, but confessed freely, "I am not the Christ."

21They asked him, "Then who are you? Are you Elijah?"

He said, "I am not."

"Are you the Prophet?"

He answered, "No."

22Finally they said, "Who are you? Give us an answer to take back to those who sent us. What do you say about yourself?"

23John replied in the words of Isaiah the prophet, "I am the voice of one calling in the desert, 'Make straight the way for the Lord.'"

24Now some Pharisees who had been sent 25questioned him, "Why then do you baptize if you are not the Christ, nor Elijah, nor the Prophet?"

26"I baptize with water," John replied, "but among you stands one you do not know. 27He is the one who comes after me, the thongs of whose sandals I am not worthy to untie."

28This all happened at Bethany on the other side of the Jordan, where John was baptizing.

29The next day John saw Jesus coming toward him and said, "Look, the Lamb of God, who takes away the sin of the world! 30This is the one I meant when I said, 'A man who comes after me has surpassed me because he was before me.' 31I myself did not know him, but the reason I came baptizing with water was that he might be revealed to Israel."

32Then John gave this testimony: "I saw the Spirit come down from heaven as a dove and remain on him. 33I would not have known him, except that the one who sent me to baptize with water told me, 'The man on whom you see the Spirit come down and remain is he who will baptize with the Holy Spirit.' 34I have seen and I testify that this is the Son of God."

A THOUGHT: *In the Pharisees' minds, there were four options regarding John the Baptist's identity: he was (1) the Prophet who would speak God's words, (2) Elijah, (3) the Messiah, or (4) a false prophet. John denied being the first three personages, and instead referred to himself, in the words of the Old Testament prophet Isaiah, as the voice shouting in the wilderness. The leaders kept pressing him to say who he was, because people were expecting the Messiah to come. But John emphasized only why he had come—to prepare the way for the Messiah. The Pharisees missed the point. They wanted to know who John was, but John wanted them to know who Jesus was.*

John the Baptist's job was to point people to Jesus, the Messiah for whom they were looking. Today people are looking for someone to give them security in an insecure world. Our job is to point them to Christ and to show that he is the One they seek.

The Man of Lawlessness/ 2 Thessalonians 2:7–17

For the secret power of lawlessness is already at work; but the one who now holds it back will continue to do so till he is taken out of the way. 8And then the lawless one will be revealed, whom the Lord Jesus will overthrow with the breath of his mouth and destroy by the splendor of his coming. 9The coming of the lawless one will be in accordance with the work of Satan displayed in all kinds of counterfeit miracles, signs and wonders, 10and in every sort of evil that deceives those who are perishing. They perish because they refused to love the truth and so be saved. 11For this reason God sends them a powerful delusion so that they will believe the lie 12and so that all will be condemned who have not believed the truth but have delighted in wickedness.

13But we ought always to thank God for you, brothers loved by the Lord, because from the beginning God chose you to be saved through the sanctifying work of the Spirit and through belief in the truth. 14He called you to this through our gospel, that you might share in the glory of our Lord Jesus Christ. 15So then, brothers, stand firm and hold to the teachings we passed on to you, whether by word of mouth or by letter.

16May our Lord Jesus Christ himself and God our Father, who loved us and by his grace gave us eternal encouragement and good hope, 17encourage your hearts and strengthen you in every good deed and word.

A THOUGHT: *Paul knew that the Thessalonians would face persecutions, false teachers, worldliness, apathy, and the temptation to wander from the truth and to leave the faith; so he urged them to hold on to the truth and to stand firm. We are also confronted with temptations to turn away from God. We should hold on to the truth found in Christ's teachings because our lives depend on it. Never forget the reality of his life and love!*

Proverbs for Today/ 21:4

Haughty eyes and a proud heart, the lamp of the wicked, are sin!

AUGUST 12

Jesus Calls His First Disciples/ John 1:35–51

The next day John was there again with two of his disciples. 36When he saw Jesus passing by, he said, "Look, the Lamb of God!"

37When the two disciples heard him say this, they followed Jesus. 38Turning around, Jesus saw them following and asked, "What do you want?"

They said, "Rabbi" (which means Teacher), "where are you staying?"

39"Come," he replied, "and you will see."

So they went and saw where he was staying, and spent that day with him. It was about the tenth hour.

40Andrew, Simon Peter's brother, was one of the two who heard what John had said and who had followed Jesus. 41The first thing Andrew did was to find his brother Simon and tell him, "We have found the Messiah" (that is, the Christ). 42And he brought him to Jesus.

Jesus looked at him and said, "You are Simon son of John. You will be called Cephas" (which, when translated, is Peter).

43The next day Jesus decided to leave for Galilee. Finding Philip, he said to him, "Follow me."

44Philip, like Andrew and Peter, was from the town of Bethsaida. 45Philip found Nathanael and told him, "We have found the one Moses wrote about in the Law, and about whom the prophets also wrote—Jesus of Nazareth, the son of Joseph."

46"Nazareth! Can anything good come from there?" Nathanael asked.

"Come and see," said Philip.

47When Jesus saw Nathanael approaching, he said of him, "Here is a true Israelite, in whom there is nothing false."

48"How do you know me?" Nathanael asked.

Jesus answered, "I saw you while you were still under the fig tree before Philip called you."

49Then Nathanael declared, "Rabbi, you are the Son of God; you are the King of Israel."

50Jesus said, "You believe because I told you I saw you under the fig tree. You shall see greater things than that." 51He then added, "I tell you the truth, you shall see heaven open, and the angels of God ascending and descending on the Son of Man."

A THOUGHT: *These new disciples used several names for Jesus: Lamb of God, Rabbi or Teacher, Messiah, Son of God, King of Israel. As they got to know Jesus, their appreciation for him grew. The more time we spend getting to know Christ, the more we understand and appreciate who he is. We may be drawn to him for his teaching, but we will come to know him as the Son of God. Although these disciples made this verbal shift in a few days, they would not fully understand until three years later. What they so easily professed had to be worked out in experience. We may find that words of faith come easily, but deep appreciation for Christ comes with living by faith.*

Paul Requests Prayer/ 2 Thessalonians 3:1–5

Finally, brothers, pray for us that the message of the Lord may spread rapidly and be honored, just as it was with you. 2And pray that we may be delivered from wicked and evil men, for not everyone has faith. 3But the Lord is faithful, and he will strengthen and protect you from the evil one.

⁴We have confidence in the Lord that you are doing and will continue to do the things we command. ⁵May the Lord direct your hearts into God's love and Christ's perseverance.

A THOUGHT: *Beneath the surface of the routine of daily life, a fierce struggle among invisible spiritual powers is being waged. Like the wind, the power of evil forces can be devastating. Our main defense is prayer that God will protect us and that he will make us strong. The following guidelines can help you prepare for satanic attacks: (1) take the threat of spiritual attack seriously; (2) pray for strength and help from God; (3) study the Bible to recognize Satan's style and tactics; (4) memorize Scripture so it will be a source of help no matter where you are; (5) associate with those who speak the truth; and (6) practice what you are taught by spiritual leaders.*

Proverbs for Today/ 21:5–7

The plans of the diligent lead to profit as surely as haste leads to poverty. □ A fortune made by a lying tongue is a fleeting vapor and a deadly snare. □ The violence of the wicked will drag them away, for they refuse to do what is right.

AUGUST 13

Jesus Turns Water into Wine/ John 2:1–12

On the third day a wedding took place at Cana in Galilee. Jesus' mother was there, ²and Jesus and his disciples had also been invited to the wedding. ³When the wine was gone, Jesus' mother said to him, "They have no more wine."

⁴"Dear woman, why do you involve me?" Jesus replied. "My time has not yet come."

⁵His mother said to the servants, "Do whatever he tells you."

⁶Nearby stood six stone water jars, the kind used by the Jews for ceremonial washing, each holding from twenty to thirty gallons.

⁷Jesus said to the servants, "Fill the jars with water"; so they filled them to the brim.

8Then he told them, "Now draw some out and take it to the master of the banquet."

They did so, 9and the master of the banquet tasted the water that had been turned into wine. He did not realize where it had come from, though the servants who had drawn the water knew. Then he called the bridegroom aside 10and said, "Everyone brings out the choice wine first and then the cheaper wine after the guests have had too much to drink; but you have saved the best till now."

11This, the first of his miraculous signs, Jesus performed at Cana in Galilee. He thus revealed his glory, and his disciples put their faith in him.

12After this he went down to Capernaum with his mother and brothers and his disciples. There they stayed for a few days.

A THOUGHT: *Miracles are not merely superhuman happenings, but happenings that demonstrate God's power. Jesus performed miracles to renew people—restoring sight, making the lame to walk, even restoring life to the dead. Believe in him, not because he is a superman, but because he is God, graciously renewing his creation. Although God does not always choose to bring full restoration this side of heaven, God does have a special concern for the poor, the weak, the crippled, the orphaned, the blind, the lame, and the oppressed. Our concern should be like God's—to care for the powerless in society by bringing Christ's message of redemption in both our words and actions.*

An Admonishment against Idleness/ 2 Thessalonians 3:6–18

In the name of the Lord Jesus Christ, we command you, brothers, to keep away from every brother who is idle and does not live according to the teaching you received from us. 7For you yourselves know how you ought to follow our example. We were not idle when we were with you, 8nor did we eat anyone's food without paying for it. On the contrary, we worked night and day, laboring and toiling so that we would not be a burden to any of you. 9We did this, not because we do not have the right to such help, but in order to make ourselves a model for you to follow. 10For even when we were with you, we gave you this rule: "If a man will not work, he shall not eat."

11We hear that some among you are idle. They are not busy; they are busybodies. 12Such people we command and urge in the Lord Jesus Christ to settle down and earn the bread they eat. 13And as for you, brothers, never tire of doing what is right.

14If anyone does not obey our instruction in this letter, take special note of him. Do not associate with him, in order that he may feel ashamed. 15Yet do not regard him as an enemy, but warn him as a brother.

16Now may the Lord of peace himself give you peace at all times and in every way. The Lord be with all of you.

17I, Paul, write this greeting in my own hand, which is the distinguishing mark in all my letters. This is how I write.

18The grace of our Lord Jesus Christ be with you all.

A THOUGHT: *Some people in the Thessalonian church were falsely teaching that since Christ's Second Coming could happen any day, people should set aside their responsibilities, quit work, do no future planning, and just wait for Christ. But their lack of activity only led them into sin. They became a burden to the church, which was supporting them; they wasted time that could have been used for helping others; and they gossiped. They may have thought they were being more spiritual by not working, but Paul told them to be responsible and get back to work. Being ready for Christ means obeying him in every area of life. Because we know Christ is coming, we must do everything we can to live in a way that will please him when he arrives.*

Proverbs for Today/ 21:8–10

The way of the guilty is devious, but the conduct of the innocent is upright. □ Better to live on a corner of the roof than share a house with a quarrelsome wife. □ The wicked man craves evil; his neighbor gets no mercy from him.

AUGUST 14

Jesus Clears the Temple/ John 2:13–25

When it was almost time for the Jewish Passover, Jesus went up to Jerusalem. 14In the temple courts he found men selling cattle, sheep and doves, and others sitting at tables exchanging money. 15So he made a whip out of cords, and drove all from the temple area, both sheep and cattle; he scattered the coins of the money changers and overturned their tables. 16To those who sold doves he said, "Get these out of here! How dare you turn my Father's house into a market!"

17His disciples remembered that it is written: "Zeal for your house will consume me."

18Then the Jews demanded of him, "What miraculous sign can you show us to prove your authority to do all this?"

19Jesus answered them, "Destroy this temple, and I will raise it again in three days."

20The Jews replied, "It has taken forty-six years to build this temple, and you are going to raise it in three days?" 21But the temple he had spoken of was his body. 22After he was raised from the dead, his disciples recalled what he had said. Then they believed the Scripture and the words that Jesus had spoken.

23Now while he was in Jerusalem at the Passover Feast, many people saw the miraculous signs he was doing and believed in his name. 24But Jesus would not entrust himself to them, for he knew all men. 25He did not need man's testimony about man, for he knew what was in a man.

A THOUGHT: *The Passover celebration took place yearly at the Temple in Jerusalem. Every Jewish male was expected to make a pilgrimage to Jerusalem during this time. This was a week-long festival—the Passover was one day, and the Feast of Unleavened Bread lasted the rest of the week. The entire week commemorated the freeing of the Jews from slavery in Egypt. To Jews, the Passover was the most important celebration of the year. Yet in the midst of this holy celebration merchants were using God's Temple as a marketplace. They forgot, or didn't care, that God's house is a place of worship, not a marketplace for making a profit. Our attitude toward the church is wrong if we see it as a place for personal or business contacts. Make sure your purpose for attending a church meeting is to worship God.*

Paul Warns about False Teachers/ 1 Timothy 1:1–6

Paul, an apostle of Christ Jesus by the command of God our Savior and of Christ Jesus our hope,

2To Timothy my true son in the faith:

Grace, mercy and peace from God the Father and Chrst Jesus our Lord.

3As I urged you when I went into Macedonia, stay there in Ephesus so that you may command certain men not to teach false doctrines any longer 4nor to devote themselves to myths and endless genealogies. These promote controversies rather than God's work—which is by faith. 5The goal of this command is love, which comes from a pure heart and a good conscience and a sincere faith. 6Some have wandered away from these and turned to meaningless talk.

A THOUGHT: *The church at Ephesus was probably plagued by the same heresy that threatened the church at Colosse, the false doctrine that to be acceptable to God one had to find favor with angels. To aid in their salvation, some Ephesians constructed lists and biographies of angels. The false teachers mentioned here were motivated by their own interests rather than Christ's. They embroiled the church in endless and irrelevant disputes. Today we have many opportunities to enter into such worthless and irrelevant discussions. Such disputes crowd out the life-changing message of Christ. Stay away from religious speculation and theological haggling. It may seem harmless at first, but it has a way of sidetracking us from the central message of the gospel—the person and work of Jesus Christ.*

Proverbs for Today/ 21:11–12

When a mocker is punished, the simple gain wisdom; when a wise man is instructed, he gets knowledge. □ The Righteous One takes note of the house of the wicked and brings the wicked to ruin.

AUGUST 15

Nicodemus Visits Jesus/ John 3:1–21

Now there was a man of the Pharisees named Nicodemus, a member of the Jewish ruling council. 2He came to Jesus at night and said, "Rabbi, we know you are a teacher who has come from God. For no one could perform the miraculous signs you are doing if God were not with him."

3In reply Jesus declared, "I tell you the truth, no one can see the kingdom of God unless he is born again."

4"How can a man be born when he is old?" Nicodemus asked. "Surely he cannot enter a second time into his mother's womb to be born!"

5Jesus answered, "I tell you the truth, no one can enter the kingdom of God unless he is born of water and the

Spirit. 6Flesh gives birth to flesh, but the Spirit gives birth to spirit. 7You should not be surprised at my saying, 'You must be born again.' 8The wind blows wherever it pleases. You hear its sound, but you cannot tell where it comes from or where it is going. So it is with everyone born of the Spirit."

9"How can this be?" Nicodemus asked.

10"You are Israel's teacher," said Jesus, "and do you not understand these things? 11I tell you the truth, we speak of what we know, and we testify to what we have seen, but still you people do not accept our testimony. 12I have spoken to you of earthly things and you do not believe; how then will you believe if I speak of heavenly things? 13No one has ever gone into heaven except the one who came from heaven—the Son of Man. 14Just as Moses lifted up the snake in the desert, so the Son of Man must be lifted up, 15that everyone who believes in him may have eternal life.

16"For God so loved the world that he gave his one and only Son, that whoever believes in him shall not perish but have eternal life. 17For God did not send his Son into the world to condemn the world, but to save the world through him. 18Whoever believes in him is not condemned, but whoever does not believe stands condemned already because he has not believed in the name of God's one and only Son. 19This is the verdict: Light has come into the world, but men loved darkness instead of light because their deeds were evil. 20Everyone who does evil hates the light, and will not come into the light for fear that his deeds will be exposed. 21But whoever lives by the truth comes into the light, so that it may be seen plainly that what he has done has been done through God."

A THOUGHT: *What did Nicodemus know about the kingdom? From the Bible he knew it would be ruled by God, it would be restored on earth, and it would incorporate God's people. Jesus revealed to this devout Pharisee that the kingdom would come to the whole world, not just the Jews, and that Nicodemus wouldn't be a part of it unless he was personally born again. This was a revolutionary concept; the kingdom is personal, not national or ethnic, and its entrance requirements are repentance and spiritual rebirth. Jesus later taught that God's kingdom has already begun in the hearts of believers through the presence of the Holy Spirit. It will be fully realized when Jesus returns again to judge the world and abolish evil forever.*

The Purpose of the Law/ 1 Timothy 1:7–11

They want to be teachers of the law, but they do not know what they are talking about or what they so confidently affirm.

8We know that the law is good if one uses it properly. 9We also know that law is made not for the righteous but for lawbreakers and rebels, the ungodly and sinful, the unholy and irreligious; for those who kill their fathers or mothers, for murderers, 10for adulterers and perverts, for slave traders and liars and perjurers—and for whatever else is contrary to the sound doctrine 11that conforms to the glorious gospel of the blessed God, which he entrusted to me.

A THOUGHT: *Theological hairsplitting—arguing about tiny details of Scripture—can take us into interesting, but irrelevant bypaths and cause us to miss the intent of God's message. The false teachers at Ephesus constructed vast speculative systems and then argued about the minor details of their wholly imaginary ideas. We should allow nothing to distract us from the Good News of Jesus Christ, the main point of Scripture. We need to know what the Scriptures say, apply them to our lives daily, and teach them to others. When we do this we will be able to evaluate all teachings in light of the central truth about Jesus. Don't spend so much time on the minute details of Scripture that you miss the main point of what God is trying to teach you.*

Proverbs for Today/ 21:13

If a man shuts his ears to the cry of the poor, he too will cry out and not be answered.

AUGUST 16

John the Baptist Testifies of Jesus/ John 3:22–36

After this, Jesus and his disciples went out into the Judean countryside, where he spent some time with them, and baptized. 23Now John also was baptizing at Aenon near Salim, because there was plenty of water, and people were constantly coming to be baptized. 24(This was before John was put in prison.) 25An argument developed between some of John's disciples and a certain Jew over the matter of ceremonial washing. 26They came to John and said to him, "Rabbi, that man who was with you on the other side of the Jordan—the one you testified about—well, he is baptizing, and everyone is going to him."

27To this John replied, "A man can receive only what is given him from heaven. 28You yourselves can testify that I said, 'I am not the Christ but am sent ahead of him.' 29The bride belongs to the bridegroom. The friend who attends the bridegroom waits and listens for him, and is full of joy when he hears the bridegroom's voice. That joy is mine, and it is now complete. 30He must become greater; I must become less.

31"The one who comes from above is above all; the one who is from the earth belongs to the earth, and speaks as one from the earth. The one who comes from heaven is above all. 32He testifies to what he has seen and heard, but no one accepts his testimony. 33The man who has accepted it has certified that God is truthful. 34For the one whom God has sent speaks the words of God, for God gives the Spirit without limit. 35The Father loves the Son and has placed everything in his hands. 36Whoever believes in the Son has eternal life, but whoever rejects the Son will not see life, for God's wrath remains on him."

A THOUGHT: *John the Baptist's disciples were disturbed because people were following Jesus instead of John. It is easy to grow jealous of the popularity of another person's ministry. But we must remember that our true mission is to win people to follow Christ, not us—Christ must become greater and greater to those we minister to, and we must become less and less. Beware of those leaders who put more emphasis on their own achievements than on God's kingdom.*

The Greatest of Sinners/ 1 Timothy 1:12–17

I thank Christ Jesus our Lord, who has given me strength, that he considered me faithful, appointing me to his service. 13Even though I was once a blasphemer and a persecutor and a violent man, I was shown mercy because I acted in ignorance and unbelief. 14The grace of our Lord was poured out on me abundantly, along with the faith and love that are in Christ Jesus.

15Here is a trustworthy saying that deserves full acceptance: Christ Jesus came into the world to save sinners—of whom I am the worst. 16But for that very reason I was shown mercy so that in me, the worst of sinners, Christ Jesus might display his unlimited patience as an example for those who would believe on him and receive eternal life. 17Now to the King eternal, immortal, invisible, the only God, be honor and glory for ever and ever. Amen.

A THOUGHT: *People can feel so guilt-ridden by their past that they think God could never forgive and accept them. But consider Paul's past. He had hunted down and murdered God's own people before coming to faith in Christ. God forgave Paul and he can forgive you.*

Proverbs for Today/ 21:14–16

A gift given in secret soothes anger, and a bribe concealed in the cloak pacifies great wrath. □ When justice is done, it brings joy to the righteous but terror to evildoers. □ A man who strays from the path of understanding comes to rest in the company of the dead.

AUGUST 17

Jesus Talks to a Samaritan Woman/ John 4:1–30

The Pharisees heard that Jesus was gaining and baptizing more disciples than John, 2although in fact it was not Jesus who baptized, but his disciples. 3When the Lord learned of this, he left Judea and went back once more to Galilee.

4Now he had to go through Samaria. 5So he came to a town in Samaria called Sychar, near the plot of ground Jacob had given to his son Joseph. 6Jacob's well was there, and Jesus, tired as he was from the journey, sat down by the well. It was about the sixth hour.

7When a Samaritan woman came to draw water, Jesus said to her, "Will you give me a drink?" 8(His disciples had gone into the town to buy food.)

9The Samaritan woman said to him, "You are a Jew and I am a Samaritan woman. How can you ask me for a drink?" (For Jews do not associate with Samaritans.)

10Jesus answered her, "If you knew the gift of God and who it is that asks you for a drink, you would have asked him and he would have given you living water."

11"Sir," the woman said, "you have nothing to draw with

and the well is deep. Where can you get this living water? [12]Are you greater than our father Jacob, who gave us the well and drank from it himself, as did also his sons and his flocks and herds?"

[13]Jesus answered, "Everyone who drinks this water will be thirsty again, [14]but whoever drinks the water I give him will never thirst. Indeed, the water I give him will become in him a spring of water welling up to eternal life."

[15]The woman said to him, "Sir, give me this water so that I won't get thirsty and have to keep coming here to draw water."

[16]He told her, "Go, call your husband and come back."

[17]"I have no husband," she replied.

Jesus said to her, "You are right when you say you have no husband. [18]The fact is, you have had five husbands, and the man you now have is not your husband. What you have just said is quite true."

[19]"Sir," the woman said, "I can see that you are a prophet. [20]Our fathers worshiped on this mountain, but you Jews claim that the place where we must worship is in Jerusalem."

[21]Jesus declared, "Believe me, woman, a time is coming when you will worship the Father neither on this mountain nor in Jerusalem. [22]You Samaritans worship what you do not know; we worship what we do know, for salvation is from the Jews. [23]Yet a time is coming and has now come when the true worshipers will worship the Father in spirit and truth, for they are the kind of worshipers the Father seeks. [24]God is spirit, and his worshipers must worship in spirit and in truth."

[25]The woman said, "I know that Messiah" (called Christ) "is coming. When he comes, he will explain everything to us."

[26]Then Jesus declared, "I who speak to you am he."

[27]Just then his disciples returned and were surprised to find him talking with a woman. But no one asked, "What do you want?" or "Why are you talking with her?"

[28]Then, leaving her water jar, the woman went back to the town and said to the people, [29]"Come, see a man who told me everything I ever did. Could this be the Christ?" [30]They came out of the town and made their way toward him.

A THOUGHT: *This woman (1) was a Samaritan, a member of a hated mixed race, (2) had a bad reputation, and (3) was in a public place. No respectable Jewish man would talk to a woman under such circumstances. But Jesus did. The gospel is for every person, no matter what his or her race, social position, or past sins. We must be prepared to share this gospel at any time in any place. Jesus crossed all barriers to share the Good News, and we who follow him must do no less.*

Fight the Good Fight/ 1 Timothy 1:18–20

Timothy, my son, I give you this instruction in keeping with the prophecies once made about you, so that by following them you may fight the good fight, 19holding on to faith and a good conscience. Some have rejected these and so have shipwrecked their faith. 20Among them are Hymenaeus and Alexander, whom I have handed over to Satan to be taught not to blaspheme.

A THOUGHT: *How can you keep your conscience clear? Treasure your faith in Christ more than anything else and do what you know is right. Each time you deliberately ignore your conscience, you are hardening your heart. Soon your capacity to tell right from wrong will disappear. But when you walk with God, he is able to speak to you through your conscience, letting you know the difference between right and wrong. Be sure to act on those inner tugs to do what is right—then your conscience will remain clear.*

Proverbs for Today/ 21:17–18

He who loves pleasure will become poor; whoever loves wine and oil will never be rich. □ The wicked become a ransom for the righteous, and the unfaithful for the upright.

AUGUST 18

The Harvest/ John 4:31–42

Meanwhile his disciples urged him [Jesus], "Rabbi, eat something."

32But he said to them, "I have food to eat that you know nothing about."

33Then his disciples said to each other, "Could someone have brought him food?"

34"My food," said Jesus, "is to do the will of him who sent

me and to finish his work. 35Do you not say, 'Four months more and then the harvest'? I tell you, open your eyes and look at the fields! They are ripe for harvest. 36Even now the reaper draws his wages, even now he harvests the crop for eternal life, so that the sower and the reaper may be glad together. 37Thus the saying 'One sows and another reaps' is true. 38I sent you to reap what you have not worked for. Others have done the hard work, and you have reaped the benefits of their labor."

39Many of the Samaritans from that town believed in him because of the woman's testimony, "He told me everything I ever did." 40So when the Samaritans came to him, they urged him to stay with them, and he stayed two days. 41And because of his words many more became believers.

42They said to the woman, "We no longer believe just because of what you said; now we have heard for ourselves, and we know that this man really is the Savior of the world."

A THOUGHT: *Sometimes Christians excuse themselves from witnessing by saying their family or friends aren't ready to believe. Jesus, however, makes it clear that around us a continual harvest waits to be reaped. Don't let Jesus find you making excuses. Look around. You will find people ready to hear God's Word.*

Instructions for Worship/ 1 Timothy 2:1–8

I urge, then, first of all, that requests, prayers, intercession and thanksgiving be made for everyone— 2for kings and all those in authority, that we may live peaceful and quiet lives in all godliness and holiness. 3This is good, and pleases God our Savior, 4who wants all men to be saved and to come to a knowledge of the truth. 5For there is one God and one mediator between God and men, the man Christ Jesus, 6who gave himself as a ransom for all men—the testimony given in its proper time. 7And for this purpose I was appointed a herald and an apostle—I am telling the truth, I am not lying—and a teacher of the true faith to the Gentiles.

8I want men everywhere to lift up holy hands in prayer, without anger or disputing.

A THOUGHT: *Although God is all-powerful and all-knowing, he has chosen to let us help him change the world through our prayers. How this works is a mystery to us because of our limited understanding, but it is a reality. Paul urges us to pray for each other and for our leaders in government. Our earnest prayers will have powerful results.*

Proverbs for Today/ 21:19–20

Better to live in a desert than with a quarrelsome and ill-tempered wife. □ In the house of the wise are stores of choice food and oil, but a foolish man devours all he has.

AUGUST 19

Jesus Heals an Official's Son/ John 4:43–54

After the two days he [Jesus] left for Galilee. 44(Now Jesus himself had pointed out that a prophet has no honor in his own country.) 45When he arrived in Galilee, the Galileans welcomed him. They had seen all that he had done in Jerusalem at the Passover Feast, for they also had been there.

46Once more he visited Cana in Galilee, where he had turned the water into wine. And there was a certain royal official whose son lay sick at Capernaum. 47When this man heard that Jesus had arrived in Galilee from Judea, he went to him and begged him to come and heal his son, who was close to death.

48"Unless you people see miraculous signs and wonders," Jesus told him, "you will never believe."

49The royal official said, "Sir, come down before my child dies."

50Jesus replied, "You may go. Your son will live."

The man took Jesus at his word and departed. 51While he was still on the way, his servants met him with the news that his boy was living. 52When he inquired as to the time when his son got better, they said to him, "The fever left him yesterday at the seventh hour."

53Then the father realized that this was the exact time at which Jesus had said to him, "Your son will live." So he and all his household believed.

54This was the second miraculous sign that Jesus performed, having come from Judea to Galilee.

A THOUGHT: *This government official not only believed Jesus could heal; he also obeyed Jesus by returning home, thus demonstrating his faith. It isn't enough for us to say we believe Jesus can take care of our problems. We need to act as if he can. When you pray about a need or problem, live as though you believe Jesus can do what he says.*

Women in the Church/ 1 Timothy 2:9–15

I also want women to dress modestly, with decency and propriety, not with braided hair or gold or pearls or expensive clothes, 10but with good deeds, appropriate for women who profess to worship God.

11A woman should learn in quietness and full submission. 12I do not permit a woman to teach or to have authority over a man; she must be silent. 13For Adam was formed first, then Eve. 14And Adam was not the one deceived; it was the woman who was deceived and became a sinner. 15But women will be saved through childbearing—if they continue in faith, love and holiness with propriety.

A THOUGHT: *To understand this passage, we must understand the situation in which Paul and Timothy worked. In first-century Jewish culture, women were not allowed to study. When Paul said women should learn quietly and humbly, he was offering them new opportunities. Paul did not want the Ephesian women to teach because they didn't yet have enough knowledge or experience. The Ephesian church had a particular problem with false teachers. Evidently the women were especially susceptible to their teaching, because they did not yet have enough biblical knowledge to see through the false claims. In addition, some of the women were apparently flaunting their new-found Christian freedom by wearing inappropriate clothing. Paul was telling Timothy not to put anyone (in this case, women) into positions of leadership who were not yet mature in the faith. The same principle applies to churches today.*

Proverbs for Today/ 21:21–22

He who pursues righteousness and love finds life, prosperity and honor. □ A wise man attacks the city of the mighty and pulls down the stronghold in which they trust.

A Healing at Bethesda Pool/ John 5:1–24

Some time later, Jesus went up to Jerusalem for a feast of the Jews. 2Now there is in Jerusalem near the Sheep Gate a pool, which in Aramaic is called Bethesda and which is surrounded by five covered colonnades. 3Here a great number of disabled people used to lie—the blind, the lame, the paralyzed. * 5One who was there had been an invalid for thirty-eight years. 6When Jesus saw him lying there and learned that he had been in this condition for a long time, he asked him, "Do you want to get well?"

7"Sir," the invalid replied, "I have no one to help me into the pool when the water is stirred. While I am trying to get in, someone else goes down ahead of me."

8Then Jesus said to him, "Get up! Pick up your mat and walk." 9At once the man was cured; he picked up his mat and walked.

The day on which this took place was a Sabbath, 10and so the Jews said to the man who had been healed, "It is the Sabbath; the law forbids you to carry your mat."

11But he replied, "The man who made me well said to me, 'Pick up your mat and walk.' "

12So they asked him, "Who is this fellow who told you to pick it up and walk?"

13The man who was healed had no idea who it was, for Jesus had slipped away into the crowd that was there.

14Later Jesus found him at the temple and said to him, "See, you are well again. Stop sinning or something worse may happen to you." 15The man went away and told the Jews that it was Jesus who had made him well.

16So, because Jesus was doing these things on the Sabbath, the Jews persecuted him. 17Jesus said to them, "My Father is always at his work to this very day, and I, too, am working." 18For this reason the Jews tried all the harder to kill him; not only was he breaking the Sabbath, but he

---

*3 Some less important manuscripts *paralyzed—and they waited for the moving of the waters.* 4*From time to time an angel of the Lord would come down and stir up the waters. The first one into the pool after each such disturbance would be cured of whatever disease he had.*

was even calling God his own Father, making himself equal with God.

19Jesus gave them this answer: "I tell you the truth, the Son can do nothing by himself; he can do only what he sees his Father doing, because whatever the Father does the Son also does. 20For the Father loves the Son and shows him all he does. Yes, to your amazement he will show him even greater things than these. 21For just as the Father raises the dead and gives them life, even so the Son gives life to whom he is pleased to give it. 22Moreover, the Father judges no one, but has entrusted all judgment to the Son, 23that all may honor the Son just as they honor the Father. He who does not honor the Son does not honor the Father, who sent him.

24"I tell you the truth, whoever hears my word and believes him who sent me has eternal life and will not be condemned; he has crossed over from death to life."

A THOUGHT: *A man who hadn't walked for 38 years was healed, but the Pharisees were more concerned about their petty rules than the life and health of a human being. It is easy to get so caught up in our man-made structures and rules that we forget the people involved. Are your guidelines for living God-made or man-made? Are they helping people, or have they become needless stumbling blocks?*

Requirements for Overseers/ 1 Timothy 3:1–7

Here is a trustworthy saying: If anyone sets his heart on being an overseer, he desires a noble task. 2Now the overseer must be above reproach, the husband of but one wife, temperate, self-controlled, respectable, hospitable, able to teach, 3not given to drunkenness, not violent but gentle, not quarrelsome, not a lover of money. 4He must manage his own family well and see that his children obey him with proper respect. 5(If anyone does not know how to manage his own family, how can he take care of God's church?) 6He must not be a recent convert, or he may become conceited and fall under the same judgment as the devil. 7He must also have a good reputation with outsiders, so that he will not fall into disgrace and into the devil's trap.

A THOUGHT: *It is good to want to be a spiritual leader, but the standards are high. Paul enumerates some of the qualifications here. Do you hold a position of spiritual leadership, or would you like to be a leader some day? Check yourself against Paul's standard of excellence. Those with great responsibility must meet high expectations.*

Proverbs for Today/ 21:23–24

He who guards his mouth and his tongue keeps himself from calamity. □ The proud and arrogant man—"Mocker" is his name; he behaves with overweening pride.

AUGUST 21

Jesus the Son of God/ John 5:25–47

"I tell you the truth, a time is coming and has now come when the dead will hear the voice of the Son of God and those who hear will live. 26For as the Father has life in himself, so he has granted the Son to have life in himself. 27And he has given him authority to judge because he is the Son of Man.

28"Do not be amazed at this, for a time is coming when all who are in their graves will hear his voice 29and come out—those who have done good will rise to live, and those who have done evil will rise to be condemned. 30By myself I can do nothing; I judge only as I hear, and my judgment is just, for I seek not to please myself but him who sent me.

31"If I testify about myself, my testimony is not valid. 32There is another who testifies in my favor, and I know that his testimony about me is valid.

33"You have sent to John and he has testified to the truth. 34Not that I accept human testimony; but I mention it that you may be saved. 35John was a lamp that burned and gave light, and you chose for a time to enjoy his light.

36"I have testimony weightier than that of John. For the very work that the Father has given me to finish, and which I am doing, testifies that the Father has sent me. 37And the Father who sent me has himself testified concerning me. You have never heard his voice nor seen his form, 38nor does his word dwell in you, for you do not believe the one he sent. 39You diligently study the Scriptures because you think that by them you possess eternal life. These are the

Scriptures that testify about me, [40]yet you refuse to come to me to have life.

[41]"I do not accept praise from men, [42]but I know you. I know that you do not have the love of God in your hearts. [43]I have come in my Father's name, and you do not accept me; but if someone else comes in his own name, you will accept him. [44]How can you believe if you accept praise from one another, yet make no effort to obtain the praise that comes from the only God?

[45]"But do not think I will accuse you before the Father. Your accuser is Moses, on whom your hopes are set. [46]If you believed Moses, you would believe me, for he wrote about me. [47]But since you do not believe what he wrote, how are you going to believe what I say?"

A THOUGHT: *Whose approval do you seek? The religious leaders enjoyed great prestige in Israel, but their stamp of approval meant nothing to Jesus. He was concerned about God's approval. This is a good principle for us. If even the highest officials in the world approve of our actions and God does not, we should be greatly concerned. But if God approves, even though others don't, we should be content.*

Requirements for Deacons/ 1 Timothy 3:8–15

Deacons, likewise, are to be men worthy of respect, sincere, not indulging in much wine, and not pursuing dishonest gain. [9]They must keep hold of the deep truths of the faith with a clear conscience. [10]They must first be tested; and then if there is nothing against them, let them serve as deacons.

[11]In the same way, their wives are to be women worthy of respect, not malicious talkers but temperate and trustworthy in everything.

[12]A deacon must be the husband of but one wife and must manage his children and his household well. [13]Those who have served well gain an excellent standing and great assurance in their faith in Christ Jesus.

[14]Although I hope to come to you soon, I am writing you these instructions so that, [15]if I am delayed, you will know how people ought to conduct themselves in God's household, which is the church of the living God, the pillar and foundation of the truth.

A THOUGHT: *Deacon means "one who serves." This position was begun by the apostles in the Jerusalem church to care for the physical needs of the congregation, especially the needs of the Greek-speaking widows. Deacons were leaders in the church and their qualifications resemble those of elders. In some churches today, the office of deacon has become a catch-all position in which new and young Christians are often asked to serve. That is not the New Testament pattern. Paul says people are to be tested with lesser responsibilities before being made deacons.*

Proverbs for Today/ 21:25–26

The sluggard's craving will be the death of him, because his hands refuse to work. All day long he craves for more, but the righteous give without sparing.

AUGUST 22

Jesus Feeds Five Thousand/ John 6:1–15

Some time after this, Jesus crossed to the far shore of the Sea of Galilee (that is, the Sea of Tiberias), 2and a great crowd of people followed him because they saw the miraculous signs he had performed on the sick. 3Then Jesus went up on a mountainside and sat down with his disciples. 4The Jewish Passover Feast was near.

5When Jesus looked up and saw a great crowd coming toward him, he said to Philip, "Where shall we buy bread for these people to eat?" 6He asked this only to test him, for he already had in mind what he was going to do.

7Philip answered him, "Eight months' wages would not buy enough bread for each one to have a bite!"

8Another of his disciples, Andrew, Simon Peter's brother, spoke up, 9"Here is a boy with five small barley loaves and two small fish, but how far will they go among so many?"

10Jesus said, "Have the people sit down." There was plenty of grass in that place, and the men sat down, about five thousand of them. 11Jesus then took the loaves, gave thanks, and distributed to those who were seated as much as they wanted. He did the same with the fish.

12When they had all had enough to eat, he said to his disciples, "Gather the pieces that are left over. Let nothing be wasted." 13So they gathered them and filled twelve baskets with the pieces of the five barley loaves left over by those who had eaten.

14After the people saw the miraculous sign that Jesus did, they began to say, "Surely this is the Prophet who is to come into the world." 15Jesus, knowing that they intended to come and make him king by force, withdrew again to a mountain by himself.

A THOUGHT: *Jesus asked Philip where they could buy a great amount of bread. Philip started assessing the probable cost. Jesus wanted to teach him that financial resources are not the most important ones. We can limit what God does in our lives by assuming what is and is not possible. Is there some impossible task you feel God wants you to do? Don't let your estimate of what can't be done keep you from taking on the task. God can do the miraculous; trust him to provide the resources.*

The Mystery of Godliness/ 1 Timothy 3:16—4:6

Beyond all question, the mystery of godliness is great:

He appeared in a body,
  was vindicated by the Spirit,
was seen by angels,
  was preached among the nations,
was believed on in the world,
  was taken up in glory.

4:1The Spirit clearly says that in later times some will abandon the faith and follow deceiving spirits and things taught by demons. 2Such teachings come through hypocritical liars, whose consciences have been seared as with a hot iron. 3They forbid people to marry and order them to abstain from certain foods, which God created to be received with thanksgiving by those who believe and who know the truth. 4For everything God created is good, and nothing is to be rejected if it is received with thanksgiving, 5because it is consecrated by the word of God and prayer.

6If you point these things out to the brothers, you will be a good minister of Christ Jesus, brought up in the truths of the faith and of the good teaching that you have followed.

A THOUGHT: *In opposition to the false teachers, Paul affirms that everything God made is good. We should ask his blessing on his created gifts that give us pleasure and we should thank him for them. This doesn't mean we should abuse what God has made (for example gluttony abuses God's gift of good food, lust abuses God's gift of love, and murder abuses God's gift of life). We should not abuse what God* has made, but enjoy these gifts by using them to serve and honor God. Have you thanked God for the good things he has made? Are you using them in a way that is pleasing to him?

Proverbs for Today/ 21:27

The sacrifice of the wicked is detestable— how much more so when brought with evil intent!

AUGUST 23

Jesus Walks on the Water/ John 6:16–21

When evening came, his disciples went down to the lake, ¹⁷where they got into a boat and set off across the lake for Capernaum. By now it was dark, and Jesus had not yet joined them. ¹⁸A strong wind was blowing and the waters grew rough. ¹⁹When they had rowed three or three and a half miles, they saw Jesus approaching the boat, walking on the water; and they were terrified. ²⁰But he said to them, "It is I; don't be afraid." ²¹Then they were willing to take him into the boat, and immediately the boat reached the shore where they were heading.

A THOUGHT: *The Sea of Galilee is 650 feet below sea level, 150 feet deep, and surrounded by hills. These physical features often lead to sudden windstorms causing extremely high waves. Such storms were part of life on this sea, but nevertheless frightening. When Jesus came to the disciples during a storm, walking on the water, he told them not to be afraid. In this difficult circumstance, Jesus displayed his great power by immediately bringing the disciples to their destination. Jesus intervened for the disciples when they really needed it. We often experience God's grace in the midst of difficult times. Jesus never leaves us to face difficulty on our own. Let us trust in God and his power when we face hard times.*

Exercise Yourself Spiritually/ 1 Timothy 4:7–11

Have nothing to do with godless myths and old wives' tales; rather, train yourself to be godly. ⁸For physical training is of some value, but godliness has value for all things, holding promise for both the present life and the life to come.

⁹This is a trustworthy saying that deserves full acceptance ¹⁰(and for this we labor and strive), that we have put

our hope in the living God, who is the Savior of all men, and especially of those who believe. ¹¹Command and teach these things.

A THOUGHT: *Are you in shape physically and spiritually? In our society, much emphasis is placed on physical fitness, but Paul declared that spiritual health is even more important than physical health. We must develop our faith through using the abilities God has given us in the service of the church.*

Proverbs for Today/ 21:28–29

A false witness will perish, and whoever listens to him will be destroyed forever. □ A wicked man puts up a bold front, but an upright man gives thought to his ways.

AUGUST 24

Jesus the Bread of Life/ John 6:22–46

The next day the crowd that had stayed on the opposite shore of the lake realized that only one boat had been there, and that Jesus had not entered it with his disciples, but that they had gone away alone. ²³Then some boats from Tiberias landed near the place where the people had eaten the bread after the Lord had given thanks. ²⁴Once the crowd realized that neither Jesus nor his disciples were there, they got into the boats and went to Capernaum in search of Jesus.

²⁵When they found him on the other side of the lake, they asked him, "Rabbi, when did you get here?"

²⁶Jesus answered, "I tell you the truth, you are looking for me, not because you saw miraculous signs but because you ate the loaves and had your fill. ²⁷Do not work for food that spoils, but for food that endures to eternal life, which the Son of Man will give you. On him God the Father has placed his seal of approval."

²⁸Then they asked him, "What must we do to do the works God requires?"

²⁹Jesus answered, "The work of God is this: to believe in the one he has sent."

³⁰So they asked him, "What miraculous sign then will you

give that we may see it and believe you? What will you do? [31]Our forefathers ate the manna in the desert; as it is written: 'He gave them bread from heaven to eat.'"

[32]Jesus said to them, "I tell you the truth, it is not Moses who has given you the bread from heaven, but it is my Father who gives you the true bread from heaven. [33]For the bread of God is he who comes down from heaven and gives life to the world."

[34]"Sir," they said, "from now on give us this bread."

[35]Then Jesus declared, "I am the bread of life. He who comes to me will never go hungry, and he who believes in me will never be thirsty. [36]But as I told you, you have seen me and still you do not believe. [37]All that the Father gives me will come to me, and whoever comes to me I will never drive away. [38]For I have come down from heaven not to do my will but to do the will of him who sent me. [39]And this is the will of him who sent me, that I shall lose none of all that he has given me, but raise them up at the last day. [40]For my Father's will is that everyone who looks to the Son and believes in him shall have eternal life, and I will raise him up at the last day."

[41]At this the Jews began to grumble about him because he said, "I am the bread that came down from heaven." [42]They said, "Is this not Jesus, the son of Joseph, whose father and mother we know? How can he now say, 'I came down from heaven'?"

[43]"Stop grumbling among yourselves," Jesus answered. [44]"No one can come to me unless the Father who sent me draws him, and I will raise him up at the last day. [45]It is written in the Prophets: 'They will all be taught by God.' Everyone who listens to the Father and learns from him comes to me. [46]No one has seen the Father except the one who is from God; only he has seen the Father."

A THOUGHT: *People eat bread to satisfy physical hunger and to sustain physical life. We can satisfy spiritual hunger and sustain spiritual life only by a right relationship with Jesus Christ. No wonder he called himself the Bread of Life. But bread must be eaten to give life, and Christ must be invited into our daily walk to give spiritual life. Jesus criticized those who followed him merely for the physical and temporal benefits they received rather than seeking after relationship with God. We should follow Christ because we need the truth. Many people use religion to gain prestige, comfort, or votes. But those are self-centered motives. True believers follow Jesus simply because they know his way is true life—eternal life.*

Role Models for God's Flock/ 1 Timothy 4:12—5:2

Don't let anyone look down on you because you are young, but set an example for the believers in speech, in life, in love, in faith and in purity. 13Until I come, devote yourself to the public reading of Scripture, to preaching and to teaching. 14Do not neglect your gift, which was given you through a prophetic message when the body of elders laid their hands on you.

15Be diligent in these matters; give yourself wholly to them, so that everyone may see your progress. 16Watch your life and doctrine closely. Persevere in them, because if you do, you will save both yourself and your hearers.

5:1Do not rebuke an older man harshly, but exhort him as if he were your father. Treat younger men as brothers, 2older women as mothers, and younger women as sisters, with absolute purity.

A THOUGHT: *Timothy was a young leader. It would be easy for older Christians to look down on him because of his youth. He had to earn the respect of his elders by setting an example in his teaching and living, of love, faith, and purity. Regardless of your age, God can use you. Whether you are young or old, don't think of your age as a handicap. Live so others can see Christ in you.*

Proverbs for Today/ 21:30–31

There is no wisdom, no insight, no plan that can succeed against the LORD. □ The horse is made ready for the day of battle, but victory rests with the LORD.

AUGUST 25

Words of Eternal Life/ John 6:47–71

"I tell you the truth, he who believes has everlasting life. 48I am the bread of life. 49Your forefathers ate the manna in the desert, yet they died. 50But here is the bread that comes down from heaven, which a man may eat and not die. 51I am the living bread that came down from heaven. If anyone eats of this bread, he will live forever. This bread is my flesh, which I will give for the life of the world."

⁵²Then the Jews began to argue sharply among themselves, "How can this man give us his flesh to eat?"

⁵³Jesus said to them, "I tell you the truth, unless you eat the flesh of the Son of Man and drink his blood, you have no life in you. ⁵⁴Whoever eats my flesh and drinks my blood has eternal life, and I will raise him up at the last day. ⁵⁵For my flesh is real food and my blood is real drink. ⁵⁶Whoever eats my flesh and drinks my blood remains in me, and I in him. ⁵⁷Just as the living Father sent me and I live because of the Father, so the one who feeds on me will live because of me. ⁵⁸This is the bread that came down from heaven. Your forefathers ate manna and died, but he who feeds on this bread will live forever." ⁵⁹He said this while teaching in the synagogue in Capernaum.

⁶⁰On hearing it, many of his disciples said, "This is a hard teaching. Who can accept it?"

⁶¹Aware that his disciples were grumbling about this, Jesus said to them, "Does this offend you? ⁶²What if you see the Son of Man ascend to where he was before! ⁶³The Spirit gives life; the flesh counts for nothing. The words I have spoken to you are spirit and they are life. ⁶⁴Yet there are some of you who do not believe." For Jesus had known from the beginning which of them did not believe and who would betray him. ⁶⁵He went on to say, "This is why I told you that no one can come to me unless the Father has enabled him."

⁶⁶From this time many of his disciples turned back and no longer followed him.

⁶⁷"You do not want to leave too, do you?" Jesus asked the Twelve.

⁶⁸Simon Peter answered him, "Lord, to whom shall we go? You have the words of eternal life. ⁶⁹We believe and know that you are the Holy One of God."

⁷⁰Then Jesus replied, "Have I not chosen you, the Twelve? Yet one of you is a devil!" ⁷¹(He meant Judas, the son of Simon Iscariot, who, though one of the Twelve, was later to betray him.)

A THOUGHT: *There is no middle ground with Jesus. When he asked the disciples if they would also leave, Jesus was showing that they could either accept or reject him. Jesus was not trying to repel people with his teachings. He was simply telling the truth. The more the people heard Jesus' real message, the more they divided into two* camps—the honest seekers who wanted to understand more, and those who rejected Jesus because they didn't like what they heard.

Helping Older Widows in the Church/
1 Timothy 5:3–10

Give proper recognition to those widows who are really in need. 4But if a widow has children or grandchildren, these should learn first of all to put their religion into practice by caring for their own family and so repaying their parents and grandparents, for this is pleasing to God. 5The widow who is really in need and left all alone puts her hope in God and continues night and day to pray and to ask God for help. 6But the widow who lives for pleasure is dead even while she lives. 7Give the people these instructions, too, so that no one may be open to blame. 8If anyone does not provide for his relatives, and especially for his immediate family, he has denied the faith and is worse than an unbeliever.

9No widow may be put on the list of widows unless she is over sixty, has been faithful to her husband, 10and is well known for her good deeds, such as bringing up children, showing hospitality, washing the feet of the saints, helping those in trouble and devoting herself to all kinds of good deeds.

A THOUGHT: *Because there were no pensions, no social security, no life insurance, and few honorable jobs for women, widows were usually unable to support themselves. If a widow had no children or other family members to support her, she was doomed to poverty. From the beginning the church took care of its widows, who in turn gave valuable service to the church.*

The responsibility for caring for the helpless naturally falls first on their families, the people whose lives are closely linked with theirs. But families cannot always provide all the necessary care. The church should support those who have no families, and it should also help others—whether elderly, young, handicapped, ill, or poverty stricken—with their emotional and spiritual needs. Often families who are caring for their own helpless members have heavy burdens. They may need extra money, a listening ear, a helping hand, or a word of encouragement. Often, those who are helped turn around and help others so that the church turns into a circle of caring.

Proverbs for Today/ 22:1

A good name is more desirable than great riches; to be esteemed is better than silver or gold.

Jesus at the Feast of Tabernacles/ John 7:1–13

After this, Jesus went around in Galilee, purposely staying away from Judea because the Jews there were waiting to take his life. 2But when the Jewish Feast of Tabernacles was near, 3Jesus' brothers said to him, "You ought to leave here and go to Judea, so that your disciples may see the miracles you do. 4No one who wants to become a public figure acts in secret. Since you are doing these things, show yourself to the world." 5For even his own brothers did not believe in him.

6Therefore Jesus told them, "The right time for me has not yet come; for you any time is right. 7The world cannot hate you, but it hates me because I testify that what it does is evil. 8You go to the Feast. I am not yet going up to this Feast, because for me the right time has not yet come." 9Having said this, he stayed in Galilee.

10However, after his brothers had left for the Feast, he went also, not publicly, but in secret. 11Now at the Feast the Jews were watching for him and asking, "Where is that man?"

12Among the crowds there was widespread whispering about him. Some said, "He is a good man."

Others replied, "No, he deceives the people." 13But no one would say anything publicly about him for fear of the Jews.

A THOUGHT: *Jesus' brothers had a difficult time believing in him. Some of these brothers would eventually become leaders in the church, but here they are still wondering if Jesus will prove once and for all his messianic claims. After Jesus died and rose again, they finally believed. Today we have every reason to believe, because we have the full record of Jesus' miracles, death, and resurrection. We also have the evidence of what the gospel has done in people's lives for hundreds of years. Don't miss this opportunity to believe in God's Son.*

Advice for Younger Widows/ 1 Timothy 5:11–16

As for younger widows, do not put them on such a list. For when their sensual desires overcome their dedication to Christ, they want to marry. 12Thus they bring judgment on themselves, because they have broken their first pledge.

13Besides, they get into the habit of being idle and going about from house to house. And not only do they become idlers, but also gossips and busybodies, saying things they ought not to. 14So I counsel younger widows to marry, to have children, to manage their homes and to give the enemy no opportunity for slander. 15Some have in fact already turned away to follow Satan.

16If any woman who is a believer has widows in her family, she should help them and not let the church be burdened with them, so that the church can help those widows who are really in need.

A THOUGHT: *Apparently older widows took a vow by which they committed themselves to work for the church in exchange for financial support. Three out of four women today eventually are widowed, and most of the older women in our churches have lost their husbands. Does your church provide an avenue of service for these women? Could you help match their gifts and abilities with your church's needs?*

Proverbs for Today/ 22:2–4

Rich and poor have this in common: The LORD is the Maker of them all. □ A prudent man sees danger and takes refuge, but the simple keep going and suffer for it. □ Humility and the fear of the LORD bring wealth and honor and life.

AUGUST 27

Jesus Preaches in the Temple/ John 7:14–36

Not until halfway through the Feast did Jesus go up to the temple courts and begin to teach. 15The Jews were amazed and asked, "How did this man get such learning without having studied?"

16Jesus answered, "My teaching is not my own. It comes from him who sent me. 17If anyone chooses to do God's will, he will find out whether my teaching comes from God or whether I speak on my own. 18He who speaks on his own does so to gain honor for himself, but he who works for the honor of the one who sent him is a man of truth; there is nothing false about him. 19Has not Moses given you the law? Yet not one of you keeps the law. Why are you trying to kill me?"

20"You are demon-possessed," the crowd answered. "Who is trying to kill you?"

21Jesus said to them, "I did one miracle, and you are all astonished. 22Yet, because Moses gave you circumcision (though actually it did not come from Moses, but from the patriarchs), you circumcise a child on the Sabbath. 23Now if a child can be circumcised on the Sabbath so that the law of Moses may not be broken, why are you angry with me for healing the whole man on the Sabbath? 24Stop judging by mere appearances, and make a right judgment."

25At that point some of the people of Jerusalem began to ask, "Isn't this the man they are trying to kill? 26Here he is, speaking publicly, and they are not saying a word to him. Have the authorities really concluded that he is the Christ? 27But we know where this man is from; when the Christ comes, no one will know where he is from."

28Then Jesus, still teaching in the temple courts, cried out, "Yes, you know me, and you know where I am from. I am not here on my own, but he who sent me is true. You do not know him, 29but I know him because I am from him and he sent me."

30At this they tried to seize him, but no one laid a hand on him, because his time had not yet come. 31Still, many in the crowd put their faith in him. They said, "When the Christ comes, will he do more miraculous signs than this man?"

32The Pharisees heard the crowd whispering such things about him. Then the chief priests and the Pharisees sent temple guards to arrest him.

33Jesus said, "I am with you for only a short time, and then I go to the one who sent me. 34You will look for me, but you will not find me; and where I am, you cannot come."

35The Jews said to one another, "Where does this man intend to go that we cannot find him? Will he go where our people live scattered among the Greeks, and teach the Greeks? 36What did he mean when he said, 'You will look for me, but you will not find me,' and 'Where I am, you cannot come'?"

A THOUGHT: *The Pharisees spent their lives trying to appear holy by keeping the meticulous rules they had added to God's Law. Jesus' accusation that they didn't keep Moses' laws stung them deeply. In spite of their pompous pride in themselves and their rules, they did not even fulfill a legalistic religion, for they were living far below what the law of Moses required. Jesus' followers should do more than the moral law requires, going beyond and beneath the mere do's and don'ts of the Law to the spirit of the Law. The spirit of God's Law is captured in love for God and one's neighbor. We must never allow rules to keep us from following the true intent of God's Law. Obedience to God must be from the heart.*

Honor Church Leaders/ 1 Timothy 5:17–25

The elders who direct the affairs of the church well are worthy of double honor, especially those whose work is preaching and teaching. 18For the Scripture says, "Do not muzzle the ox while it is treading out the grain," and "The worker deserves his wages." 19Do not entertain an accusation against an elder unless it is brought by two or three witnesses. 20Those who sin are to be rebuked publicly, so that the others may take warning.

21I charge you, in the sight of God and Christ Jesus and the elect angels, to keep these instructions without partiality, and to do nothing out of favoritism.

22Do not be hasty in the laying on of hands, and do not share in the sins of others. Keep yourself pure.

23Stop drinking only water, and use a little wine because of your stomach and your frequent illnesses.

24The sins of some men are obvious, reaching the place of judgment ahead of them; the sins of others trail behind them. 25In the same way, good deeds are obvious, and even those that are not cannot be hidden.

A THOUGHT: *Faithful, diligent church leaders should be supported and appreciated. Too often they are targets for criticism because the congregation has unrealistic expectations. How do you treat your church leaders? Do you enjoy finding fault, or do you show your appreciation? Do they receive enough financial support to allow them to live without worry and provide for the needs of their families? Jesus and Paul emphasized the importance of supporting ministers who lead and teach us.*

Proverbs for Today/ 22:5–6

In the paths of the wicked lie thorns and snares, but he who guards his soul stays far from them. □ Train a child in the way he should go, and when he is old he will not turn from it.

AUGUST 28

Rivers of Living Water/ John 7:37–53

On the last and greatest day of the Feast, Jesus stood and said in a loud voice, "If anyone is thirsty, let him come to me and drink. 38Whoever believes in me, as the Scripture has said, streams of living water will flow from within him." 39By this he meant the Spirit, whom those who believed in him were later to receive. Up to that time the Spirit had not been given, since Jesus had not yet been glorified.

40On hearing his words, some of the people said, "Surely this man is the Prophet."

41Others said, "He is the Christ."

Still others asked, "How can the Christ come from Galilee? 42Does not the Scripture say that the Christ will come from David's family and from Bethlehem, the town where David lived?" 43Thus the people were divided because of Jesus. 44Some wanted to seize him, but no one laid a hand on him.

45Finally the temple guards went back to the chief priests and Pharisees, who asked them, "Why didn't you bring him in?"

46"No one ever spoke the way this man does," the guards declared.

47"You mean he has deceived you also?" the Pharisees retorted. 48"Has any of the rulers or of the Pharisees believed in him? 49No! But this mob that knows nothing of the law—there is a curse on them."

50Nicodemus, who had gone to Jesus earlier and who was one of their own number, asked, 51"Does our law condemn anyone without first hearing him to find out what he is doing?"

52They replied, "Are you from Galilee, too? Look into it, and you will find that a prophet does not come out of Galilee."

[The earliest and most reliable manuscripts and other ancient witnesses do not have John 7:53–8:11.]

53Then each went to his own home.

A THOUGHT: *The crowd was asking questions about Jesus. As a result, some believed, others were hostile, and others disqualified Jesus as the Messiah because he was from Nazareth, not Bethlehem. (According to the prophets, the Messiah would come from Bethlehem, the city of David.) But Jesus was born in Bethlehem, although he grew up in Nazareth. We, along with the crowd, are left to decide what we believe about Jesus—is he the Son of God, the Savior of the world or not? If we claim that he is the Son of God, we are called to be completely committed to following him.*

Instructions to Masters and Slaves/ 1 Timothy 6:1–5

All who are under the yoke of slavery should consider their masters worthy of full respect, so that God's name and our teaching may not be slandered. 2Those who have believing masters are not to show less respect for them because they are brothers. Instead, they are to serve them even better, because those who benefit from their service are believers, and dear to them. These are the things you are to teach and urge on them.

3If anyone teaches false doctrines and does not agree to the sound instruction of our Lord Jesus Christ and to godly teaching, 4he is conceited and understands nothing. He has an unhealthy interest in controversies and quarrels about words that result in envy, strife, malicious talk, evil suspicions 5and constant friction between men of corrupt mind, who have been robbed of the truth and who think that godliness is a means to financial gain.

A THOUGHT: *In Paul's culture there was a great social and legal gulf separating masters and slaves. But as Christians, masters and slaves became spiritual equals, brothers or sisters in the faith. Here Paul gives guidelines for how Christian slaves and Christian masters should relate to one another. His counsel for the master/slave relationship can be applied to the employer/employee relationship today. Employees should work hard, showing respect for their employers. In turn, employers should be fair. Our work should reflect our faithfulness to and love for Christ.*

Proverbs for Today/ 22:7

The rich rule over the poor, and the borrower is servant to the lender.

AUGUST 29

Jesus Forgives an Adulterous Woman/ John 8:1–11

But Jesus went to the Mount of Olives. 2At dawn he appeared again in the temple courts, where all the people gathered around him, and he sat down to teach them. 3The teachers of the law and the Pharisees brought in a woman caught in adultery. They made her stand before the group 4and said to Jesus, "Teacher, this woman was caught in the act of adultery. 5In the Law Moses commanded us to stone such women. Now what do you say?" 6They were using this question as a trap, in order to have a basis for accusing him.

But Jesus bent down and started to write on the ground with his finger. 7When they kept on questioning him, he straightened up and said to them, "If any one of you is without sin, let him be the first to throw a stone at her." 8Again he stooped down and wrote on the ground.

9At this, those who heard began to go away one at a time, the older ones first, until only Jesus was left, with the woman still standing there. 10Jesus straightened up and asked her, "Woman, where are they? Has no one condemned you?"

11"No one, sir," she said.

"Then neither do I condemn you," Jesus declared. "Go now and leave your life of sin."

A THOUGHT: *By mentioning the throwing of stones, Jesus could not be accused of being against the Law. But by saying that only a sinless person could throw the first stone, he highlighted the importance of compassion and forgiveness. When others are caught in sin, are you quick to pass judgment? To do so is to act as though you have never sinned. It is God's role to judge, not ours. Our role is to show forgiveness and compassion.*

True Riches/ 1 Timothy 6:6–12

But godliness with contentment is great gain. 7For we brought nothing into the world, and we can take nothing out of it. 8But if we have food and clothing, we will be content with that. 9People who want to get rich fall into temptation and a trap and into many foolish and harmful desires that plunge men into ruin and destruction. 10For the love of money is a root of all kinds of evil. Some people, eager for money, have wandered from the faith and pierced themselves with many griefs.

11But you, man of God, flee from all this, and pursue righteousness, godliness, faith, love, endurance and gentleness. 12Fight the good fight of the faith. Take hold of the eternal life to which you were called when you made your good confession in the presence of many witnesses.

A THOUGHT: *Despite almost overwhelming evidence to the contrary, most people still believe that money brings happiness. Rich people craving greater riches can be caught in an endless cycle which only ends in ruin and destruction. How can you keep away from the love of money? Paul gives us some principles: (1) realize that one day riches will all be gone; (2) be content with what you have; (3) monitor what you are willing to do to get more money; (4) love people more than money; (5) love God's work more than money; (6) freely share what you have with others.*

Proverbs for Today/ 22:8–9

He who sows wickedness reaps trouble, and the rod of his fury will be destroyed. □ A generous man will himself be blessed, for he shares his food with the poor.

AUGUST 30

The Truth of Jesus' Testimony/ John 8:12–30

When Jesus spoke again to the people, he said, "I am the light of the world. Whoever follows me will never walk in darkness, but will have the light of life."

13The Pharisees challenged him, "Here you are, appearing as your own witness; your testimony is not valid."

¹⁴Jesus answered, "Even if I testify on my own behalf, my testimony is valid, for I know where I came from and where I am going. But you have no idea where I come from or where I am going. ¹⁵You judge by human standards; I pass judgment on no one. ¹⁶But if I do judge, my decisions are right, because I am not alone. I stand with the Father, who sent me. ¹⁷In your own Law it is written that the testimony of two men is valid. ¹⁸I am one who testifies for myself; my other witness is the Father, who sent me."

¹⁹Then they asked him, "Where is your father?"

"You do not know me or my Father," Jesus replied. "If you knew me, you would know my Father also." ²⁰He spoke these words while teaching in the temple area near the place where the offerings were put. Yet no one seized him, because his time had not yet come.

²¹Once more Jesus said to them, "I am going away, and you will look for me, and you will die in your sin. Where I go, you cannot come."

²²This made the Jews ask, "Will he kill himself? Is that why he says, 'Where I go, you cannot come'?"

²³But he continued, "You are from below; I am from above. You are of this world; I am not of this world. ²⁴I told you that you would die in your sins; if you do not believe that I am ˌthe one I claim to beˌ, you will indeed die in your sins."

²⁵"Who are you?" they asked.

"Just what I have been claiming all along," Jesus replied. ²⁶"I have much to say in judgment of you. But he who sent me is reliable, and what I have heard from him I tell the world."

²⁷They did not understand that he was telling them about his Father. ²⁸So Jesus said, "When you have lifted up the Son of Man, then you will know that I am ˌthe one I claim to beˌ and that I do nothing on my own but speak just what the Father has taught me. ²⁹The one who sent me is with me; he has not left me alone, for I always do what pleases him." ³⁰Even as he spoke, many put their faith in him.

A THOUGHT: *People will die in their sins if they reject Christ because they are rejecting the only way to be rescued from sin. Sadly, many are so taken up with the values of this world that they are blind to the priceless gift Christ offers. Where are you looking for meaning and value? Don't focus on this world's values and miss what is most valuable—eternal life with God.*

Fulfill Your Calling/ 1 Timothy 6:13–16

In the sight of God, who gives life to everything, and of Christ Jesus, who while testifying before Pontius Pilate made the good confession, I charge you 14to keep this command without spot or blame until the appearing of our Lord Jesus Christ, 15which God will bring about in his own time—God, the blessed and only Ruler, the King of kings and Lord of lords, 16who alone is immortal and who lives in unapproachable light, whom no one has seen or can see. To him be honor and might forever. Amen.

A THOUGHT: *God has called each Christian to a particular sphere of ministry in this life. God has called some to be plumbers, lawyers, doctors, and carpenters; others he has called to be teachers, mothers, bankers, and artists. Whatever calling in life God has given us, we must be diligent to fulfill it. True contentment in life can be found in serving others through the calling God has given each one of us. God will call us into account for the degree of faithfulness we show in our calling. Let us strive to be found faithful.*

Proverbs for Today/ 22:10–12

Drive out the mocker, and out goes strife; quarrels and insults are ended. □ He who loves a pure heart and whose speech is gracious will have the king for his friend. □ The eyes of the LORD keep watch over knowledge, but he frustrates the words of the unfaithful.

AUGUST 31

Jesus the Eternal Son of God/ John 8:31–59

To the Jews who had believed him, Jesus said, "If you hold to my teaching, you are really my disciples. 32Then you will know the truth, and the truth will set you free."

33They answered him, "We are Abraham's descendants and have never been slaves of anyone. How can you say that we shall be set free?"

34Jesus replied, "I tell you the truth, everyone who sins is a slave to sin. 35Now a slave has no permanent place in the family, but a son belongs to it forever. 36So if the Son sets you free, you will be free indeed. 37I know you are

Abraham's descendants. Yet you are ready to kill me, because you have no room for my word. 38I am telling you what I have seen in the Father's presence, and you do what you have heard from your father."

39"Abraham is our father," they answered.

"If you were Abraham's children," said Jesus, "then you would do the things Abraham did. 40As it is, you are determined to kill me, a man who has told you the truth that I heard from God. Abraham did not do such things. 41You are doing the things your own father does."

"We are not illegitimate children," they protested. "The only Father we have is God himself."

42Jesus said to them, "If God were your Father, you would love me, for I came from God and now am here. I have not come on my own; but he sent me. 43Why is my language not clear to you? Because you are unable to hear what I say. 44You belong to your father, the devil, and you want to carry out your father's desire. He was a murderer from the beginning, not holding to the truth, for there is no truth in him. When he lies, he speaks his native language, for he is a liar and the father of lies. 45Yet because I tell the truth, you do not believe me! 46Can any of you prove me guilty of sin? If I am telling the truth, why don't you believe me? 47He who belongs to God hears what God says. The reason you do not hear is that you do not belong to God."

48The Jews answered him, "Aren't we right in saying that you are a Samaritan and demon-possessed?"

49"I am not possessed by a demon," said Jesus, "but I honor my Father and you dishonor me. 50I am not seeking glory for myself; but there is one who seeks it, and he is the judge. 51I tell you the truth, if anyone keeps my word, he will never see death."

52At this the Jews exclaimed, "Now we know that you are demon-possessed! Abraham died and so did the prophets, yet you say that if anyone keeps your word, he will never taste death. 53Are you greater than our father Abraham? He died, and so did the prophets. Who do you think you are?"

54Jesus replied, "If I glorify myself, my glory means nothing. My Father, whom you claim as your God, is the one who glorifies me. 55Though you do not know him, I know him. If I said I did not, I would be a liar like you, but

I do know him and keep his word. ⁵⁶Your father Abraham rejoiced at the thought of seeing my day; he saw it and was glad."

⁵⁷"You are not yet fifty years old," the Jews said to him, "and you have seen Abraham!"

⁵⁸"I tell you the truth," Jesus answered, "before Abraham was born, I am!" ⁵⁹At this, they picked up stones to stone him, but Jesus hid himself, slipping away from the temple grounds.

A THOUGHT: *Jesus himself is the truth that sets us free. He is the source of truth, the perfect standard of what is right. He frees us from the consequences of sin, from self-deception, and from the deception of Satan. He shows us clearly the way to eternal life with God. Thus Jesus does not give us freedom to do what we want, but freedom to follow God. As we seek to live for God, Jesus' perfect truth frees us to be all that God meant us to be.*

Paul's Instructions to the Rich/ 1 Timothy 6:17–21

Command those who are rich in this present world not to be arrogant nor to put their hope in wealth, which is so uncertain, but to put their hope in God, who richly provides us with everything for our enjoyment. ¹⁸Command them to do good, to be rich in good deeds, and to be generous and willing to share. ¹⁹In this way they will lay up treasure for themselves as a firm foundation for the coming age, so that they may take hold of the life that is truly life.

²⁰Timothy, guard what has been entrusted to your care. Turn away from godless chatter and the opposing ideas of what is falsely called knowledge, ²¹which some have professed and in so doing have wandered from the faith.

Grace be with you.

A THOUGHT: *Ephesus was a wealthy city and the Ephesian church probably had many wealthy members. Paul advised Timothy to deal with that potential problem by teaching that the possession of riches carries great responsibility. Those who have money must be generous, not arrogant because they have a lot to give. They must be careful not to put their trust in money instead of in the living God for their security. Even if we don't have material wealth, we can be rich in good works toward others. No matter how poor we are, we have something to share with someone.*

Proverbs for Today/ 22:13

The sluggard says, "There is a lion outside!" or, "I will be murdered in the streets!"

SEPTEMBER 1

Jesus Heals a Blind Man/ John 9:1–12

As he [Jesus] went along, he saw a man blind from birth.
2His disciples asked him, "Rabbi, who sinned, this man or
his parents, that he was born blind?"

3"Neither this man nor his parents sinned," said Jesus,
"but this happened so that the work of God might be
displayed in his life. 4As long as it is day, we must do the
work of him who sent me. Night is coming, when no one
can work. 5While I am in the world, I am the light of the
world."

6Having said this, he spit on the ground, made some mud
with the saliva, and put it on the man's eyes. 7"Go," he told
him, "wash in the Pool of Siloam" (this word means Sent).
So the man went and washed, and came home seeing.

8His neighbors and those who had formerly seen him
begging asked, "Isn't this the same man who used to sit and
beg?" 9Some claimed that he was.

Others said, "No, he only looks like him."

But he himself insisted, "I am the man."

10"How then were your eyes opened?" they demanded.

11He replied, "The man they call Jesus made some mud
and put it on my eyes. He told me to go to Siloam and wash.
So I went and washed, and then I could see."

12"Where is this man?" they asked him.

"I don't know," he said.

A THOUGHT: *A common belief in Jewish culture was that calamity or
suffering was the result of some great sin. But Christ used this
man's suffering to teach about faith and to glorify God. We live in
a fallen world where good behavior is not always rewarded and bad
behavior not always punished. Therefore, innocent people often suffer. If God took suffering away whenever we asked, we would follow
him for comfort and convenience, not out of love and devotion.
Regardless of the reasons for our suffering, Jesus has the power to
help us deal with it. When you suffer from a disease, tragedy, or
handicap, try not to ask, "Why did this happen to me?" or "What
did I do wrong?" Instead, ask God to give you strength and offer
you a deeper perspective on what is happening.*

Encouragement to Be Faithful/ 2 Timothy 1:1–7

Paul, an apostle of Christ Jesus by the will of God, according to the promise of life that is in Christ Jesus,

2To Timothy, my dear son:

Grace, mercy and peace from God the Father and Christ Jesus our Lord.

3I thank God, whom I serve, as my forefathers did, with a clear conscience, as night and day I constantly remember you in my prayers. 4Recalling your tears, I long to see you, so that I may be filled with joy. 5I have been reminded of your sincere faith, which first lived in your grandmother Lois and in your mother Eunice and, I am persuaded, now lives in you also. 6For this reason I remind you to fan into flame the gift of God, which is in you through the laying on of my hands. 7For God did not give us a spirit of timidity, but a spirit of power, of love and of self-discipline.

A THOUGHT: *At the time of his ordination, Timothy received special gifts of the Spirit to enable him to serve the church. In telling Timothy to stir those gifts into flames, Paul was encouraging him to persevere. Timothy did not need new revelations or new gifts; he needed the courage and self-discipline to hang onto the truth and use the gifts he had already received. If he would step out boldly in faith and proclaim the gospel once again, the Holy Spirit would go with him and give him power. The power of the Holy Spirit is also available to us who believe. We too can be effective and faithful servants in the area God has called us, by relying on the power of the Spirit.*

Proverbs for Today/ 22:14

The mouth of an adulteress is a deep pit; he who is under the LORD's wrath will fall into it.

SEPTEMBER 2

A Pharisaic Investigation/ John 9:13–41

They [some people] brought to the Pharisees the man who had been blind. 14Now the day on which Jesus had made the mud and opened the man's eyes was a Sabbath. 15Therefore the Pharisees also asked him how he had received his sight. "He put mud on my eyes," the man replied, "and I washed, and now I see."

16Some of the Pharisees said, "This man is not from God, for he does not keep the Sabbath."

But others asked, "How can a sinner do such miraculous signs?" So they were divided.

17Finally they turned again to the blind man, "What have you to say about him? It was your eyes he opened."

The man replied, "He is a prophet."

18The Jews still did not believe that he had been blind and had received his sight until they sent for the man's parents. 19"Is this your son?" they asked. "Is this the one you say was born blind? How is it that now he can see?"

20"We know he is our son," the parents answered, "and we know he was born blind. 21But how he can see now, or who opened his eyes, we don't know. Ask him. He is of age; he will speak for himself." 22His parents said this because they were afraid of the Jews, for already the Jews had decided that anyone who acknowledged that Jesus was the Christ would be put out of the synagogue. 23That was why his parents said, "He is of age; ask him."

24A second time they summoned the man who had been blind. "Give glory to God," they said. "We know this man is a sinner."

25He replied, "Whether he is a sinner or not, I don't know. One thing I do know. I was blind but now I see!"

26Then they asked him, "What did he do to you? How did he open your eyes?"

27He answered, "I have told you already and you did not listen. Why do you want to hear it again? Do you want to become his disciples, too?"

28Then they hurled insults at him and said, "You are this fellow's disciple! We are disciples of Moses! 29We know that God spoke to Moses, but as for this fellow, we don't even know where he comes from."

30The man answered, "Now that is remarkable! You don't know where he comes from, yet he opened my eyes. 31We know that God does not listen to sinners. He listens to the godly man who does his will. 32Nobody has ever heard of opening the eyes of a man born blind. 33If this man were not from God, he could do nothing."

34To this they replied, "You were steeped in sin at birth; how dare you lecture us!" And they threw him out.

35Jesus heard that they had thrown him out, and when he found him, he said, "Do you believe in the Son of Man?"

36"Who is he, sir?" the man asked. "Tell me so that I may believe in him."

37Jesus said, "You have now seen him; in fact, he is the one speaking with you."

38Then the man said, "Lord, I believe," and he worshiped him.

39Jesus said, "For judgment I have come into this world, so that the blind will see and those who see will become blind."

40Some Pharisees who were with him heard him say this and asked, "What? Are we blind too?"

41Jesus said, "If you were blind, you would not be guilty of sin; but now that you claim you can see, your guilt remains."

A THOUGHT: *The Pharisees sought every angle they could think of to discredit Jesus' healing of this blind man. But the overwhelming evidence clearly showed that Jesus had healed the man. Jesus' healing ministry pointed to the fact that he was the Messiah. Faced with the same evidence—along with the rest of the New Testament—who do you say is the Messiah?*

Stand Firm for the Gospel/ 2 Timothy 1:8–14

So do not be ashamed to testify about our Lord, or ashamed of me his prisoner. But join with me in suffering for the gospel, by the power of God, 9who has saved us and called us to a holy life—not because of anything we have done but because of his own purpose and grace. This grace was given us in Christ Jesus before the beginning of time, 10but it has now been revealed through the appearing of our Savior, Christ Jesus, who has destroyed death and has brought life and immortality to light through the gospel. 11And of this gospel I was appointed a herald and an apostle and a teacher. 12That is why I am suffering as I am. Yet I am not ashamed, because I know whom I have believed, and am convinced that he is able to guard what I have entrusted to him for that day.

13What you heard from me, keep as the pattern of sound teaching, with faith and love in Christ Jesus. 14Guard the good deposit that was entrusted to you—guard it with the help of the Holy Spirit who lives in us.

A THOUGHT: *Timothy was in a time of transition. He had been Paul's bright young helper; soon he would be on his own as leader of a difficult, but critically important church. Although his responsibilities were changing, Timothy was not without help. He had everything he needed to face the future, if he would hold tightly onto it. When you are facing difficult transitions, it is good to follow Paul's advice to Timothy and look back at your experience. Who is the foundation of your faith? What gifts has the Holy Spirit given you? How can you build on the foundation that has already been laid, using the gifts you have already been given?*

Proverbs for Today/ 22:15

Folly is bound up in the heart of a child, but the rod of discipline will drive it far from him.

SEPTEMBER 3

The Good Shepherd/ John 10:1–21

"I tell you the truth, the man who does not enter the sheep pen by the gate, but climbs in by some other way, is a thief and a robber. 2The man who enters by the gate is the shepherd of his sheep. 3The watchman opens the gate for him, and the sheep listen to his voice. He calls his own sheep by name and leads them out. 4When he has brought out all his own, he goes on ahead of them, and his sheep follow him because they know his voice. 5But they will never follow a stranger; in fact, they will run away from him because they do not recognize a stranger's voice." 6Jesus used this figure of speech, but they did not understand what he was telling them.

7Therefore Jesus said again, "I tell you the truth, I am the gate for the sheep. 8All who ever came before me were thieves and robbers, but the sheep did not listen to them. 9I am the gate; whoever enters through me will be saved. He will come in and go out, and find pasture. 10The thief comes only to steal and kill and destroy; I have come that they may have life, and have it to the full.

11"I am the good shepherd. The good shepherd lays

down his life for the sheep. 12The hired hand is not the shepherd who owns the sheep. So when he sees the wolf coming, he abandons the sheep and runs away. Then the wolf attacks the flock and scatters it. 13The man runs away because he is a hired hand and cares nothing for the sheep.

14"I am the good shepherd; I know my sheep and my sheep know me— 15just as the Father knows me and I know the Father—and I lay down my life for the sheep. 16I have other sheep that are not of this sheep pen. I must bring them also. They too will listen to my voice, and there shall be one flock and one shepherd. 17The reason my Father loves me is that I lay down my life—only to take it up again. 18No one takes it from me, but I lay it down of my own accord. I have authority to lay it down and authority to take it up again. This command I received from my Father."

19At these words the Jews were again divided. 20Many of them said, "He is demon-possessed and raving mad. Why listen to him?"

21But others said, "These are not the sayings of a man possessed by a demon. Can a demon open the eyes of the blind?"

A THOUGHT: *At night, sheep were often gathered into a sheepfold to protect them from thieves, weather, or wild animals. The sheepfolds were caves, sheds, or open areas surrounded by walls made of stones or branches. The shepherd often slept in the fold to protect the sheep. Just as a shepherd cares for his sheep, Jesus, the Good Shepherd, cares for his flock (those who follow him). In speaking of himself as the Good Shepherd, Jesus was casting himself in the role of Yahweh (the special Old Testament name for God), who in Psalm 23 is pictured as a shepherd caring for his sheep.*

The Blessing of Onesiphorus/ 2 Timothy 1:15–18

You know that everyone in the province of Asia has deserted me, including Phygelus and Hermogenes.

16May the Lord show mercy to the household of Onesiphorus, because he often refreshed me and was not ashamed of my chains. 17On the contrary, when he was in Rome, he searched hard for me until he found me. 18May the Lord grant that he will find mercy from the Lord on that day! You know very well in how many ways he helped me in Ephesus.

A THOUGHT: *Onesiphorus is a model for us of Christlike living. He visited Paul in prison many times in order to encourage him. He was not ashamed to be associated with this prisoner. "'For I was hungry and you gave me something to eat, I was thirsty and you gave me something to drink, I was a stranger and you invited me in, I needed clothes and you clothed me, I was sick and you looked after me, I was in prison and you came to visit me'" (Matthew 25:35–36). We meet Christ in serving those in need. Let us be like Onesiphorus, serving with genuine love and concern those in need, without being ashamed.*

Proverbs for Today/ 22:16

He who oppresses the poor to increase his wealth and he who gives gifts to the rich—both come to poverty.

SEPTEMBER 4

Jesus Is God's Son/ John 10:22–42

Then came the Feast of Dedication at Jerusalem. It was winter, 23and Jesus was in the temple area walking in Solomon's Colonnade. 24The Jews gathered around him, saying, "How long will you keep us in suspense? If you are the Christ, tell us plainly."

25Jesus answered, "I did tell you, but you do not believe. The miracles I do in my Father's name speak for me, 26but you do not believe because you are not my sheep. 27My sheep listen to my voice; I know them, and they follow me. 28I give them eternal life, and they shall never perish; no one can snatch them out of my hand. 29My Father, who has given them to me, is greater than all; no one can snatch them out of my Father's hand. 30I and the Father are one."

31Again the Jews picked up stones to stone him, 32but Jesus said to them, "I have shown you many great miracles from the Father. For which of these do you stone me?"

33"We are not stoning you for any of these," replied the Jews, "but for blasphemy, because you, a mere man, claim to be God."

34Jesus answered them, "Is it not written in your Law, 'I have said you are gods'? 35If he called them 'gods,' to whom the word of God came—and the Scripture cannot be broken— 36what about the one whom the Father set apart as his very own and sent into the world? Why then do you accuse me of blasphemy because I said, 'I am God's Son'? 37Do not believe me unless I do what my Father does. 38But if I do it, even though you do not believe me, believe the miracles, that you may know and understand that the Father is in me, and I in the Father." 39Again they tried to seize him, but he escaped their grasp.

40Then Jesus went back across the Jordan to the place where John had been baptizing in the early days. Here he stayed 41and many people came to him. They said, "Though John never performed a miraculous sign, all that John said about this man was true." 42And in that place many believed in Jesus.

A THOUGHT: *These Jewish leaders were waiting for the signs and answers they thought would convince them of Jesus' identity. Thus they couldn't hear the truth Jesus was giving them. Jesus tried to correct their mistaken ideas, but they clung to the wrong idea of what kind of Messiah God would send. Such blindness still keeps people away from Jesus. They want him on their own terms; they do not want him if it means changing their whole lives.*

Endure As a Soldier of Christ/ 2 Timothy 2:1–7

You then, my son, be strong in the grace that is in Christ Jesus. 2And the things you have heard me say in the presence of many witnesses entrust to reliable men who will also be qualified to teach others. 3Endure hardship with us like a good soldier of Christ Jesus. 4No one serving as a soldier gets involved in civilian affairs—he wants to please his commanding officer. 5Similarly, if anyone competes as an athlete, he does not receive the victor's crown unless he competes according to the rules. 6The hardworking farmer should be the first to receive a share of the crops. 7Reflect on what I am saying, for the Lord will give you insight into all this.

A THOUGHT: *Paul directed Timothy to the lives of soldiers, athletes, and farmers as examples of ones who endure suffering for the sake of achieving a desired end. Soldiers, athletes, and farmers all must discipline themselves and be willing to sacrifice to achieve the results they want. Like soldiers, we have to give up worldly security and endure rigorous discipline. Like athletes, we must train hard and follow the rules. Like farmers, we must work extremely hard and persevere in times of difficulty. We keep going in spite of suffering because of the hope of victory, the vision of winning, and the hope of harvest, All our suffering is made worthwhile by our goal of glorifying God, winning people to Christ, and one day living eternally with him.*

Proverbs for Today/ 22:17–19

Pay attention and listen to the sayings of the wise; apply your heart to what I teach, for it is pleasing when you keep them in your heart and have all of them ready on your lips. So that your trust may be in the LORD, I teach you today, even you.

SEPTEMBER 5

The Death of Lazarus/ John 11:1–29

Now a man named Lazarus was sick. He was from Bethany, the village of Mary and her sister Martha. ²This Mary, whose brother Lazarus now lay sick, was the same one who poured perfume on the Lord and wiped his feet with her hair. ³So the sisters sent word to Jesus, "Lord, the one you love is sick."

⁴When he heard this, Jesus said, "This sickness will not end in death. No, it is for God's glory so that God's Son may be glorified through it." ⁵Jesus loved Martha and her sister and Lazarus. ⁶Yet when he heard that Lazarus was sick, he stayed where he was two more days.

⁷Then he said to his disciples, "Let us go back to Judea."

⁸"But Rabbi," they said, "a short while ago the Jews tried to stone you, and yet you are going back there?"

⁹Jesus answered, "Are there not twelve hours of daylight? A man who walks by day will not stumble, for he sees by this world's light. ¹⁰It is when he walks by night that he stumbles, for he has no light."

¹¹After he had said this, he went on to tell them, "Our friend Lazarus has fallen asleep; but I am going there to wake him up."

¹²His disciples replied, "Lord, if he sleeps, he will get better." ¹³Jesus had been speaking of his death, but his disciples thought he meant natural sleep.

¹⁴So then he told them plainly, "Lazarus is dead, ¹⁵and

for your sake I am glad I was not there, so that you may believe. But let us go to him."

16Then Thomas (called Didymus) said to the rest of the disciples, "Let us also go, that we may die with him."

17On his arrival, Jesus found that Lazarus had already been in the tomb for four days. 18Bethany was less than two miles from Jerusalem, 19and many Jews had come to Martha and Mary to comfort them in the loss of their brother. 20When Martha heard that Jesus was coming, she went out to meet him, but Mary stayed at home.

21"Lord," Martha said to Jesus, "if you had been here, my brother would not have died. 22But I know that even now God will give you whatever you ask."

23Jesus said to her, "Your brother will rise again."

24Martha answered, "I know he will rise again in the resurrection at the last day."

25Jesus said to her, "I am the resurrection and the life. He who believes in me will live, even though he dies; 26and whoever lives and believes in me will never die. Do you believe this?"

27"Yes, Lord," she told him, "I believe that you are the Christ, the Son of God, who was to come into the world."

28And after she had said this, she went back and called her sister Mary aside. "The Teacher is here," she said, "and is asking for you." 29When Mary heard this, she got up quickly and went to him.

A THOUGHT: *Jesus loved this family and often stayed with them. He knew their pain, but did not respond immediately. His delay had a specific purpose. God's timing, especially his delays, may make us think he is not answering. But though he may not be answering in the way we want, he will still meet all our needs according to his perfect schedule and purpose. Patiently await his timing.*

Suffering for Christ/ 2 Timothy 2:8–14

Remember Jesus Christ, raised from the dead, descended from David. This is my gospel, 9for which I am suffering even to the point of being chained like a criminal. But God's word is not chained. 10Therefore I endure everything for the sake of the elect, that they too may obtain the salvation that is in Christ Jesus, with eternal glory.

11Here is a trustworthy saying:

If we died with him,
   we will also live with him;
[12]if we endure,
   we will also reign with him.
If we disown him,
   he will also disown us;
[13]if we are faithless,
   he will remain faithful,
   for he cannot disown himself.

[14]Keep reminding them of these things. Warn them before God against quarreling about words; it is of no value, and only ruins those who listen.

A THOUGHT: *We are called to suffer for Christ—it is part of our identification with him. God is faithful to his children, and although we may suffer great hardships here, he promises that someday we will live eternally with him. We must remember that we are God's servants—we belong to him. We are to take up our crosses and follow him, no matter what comes our way. Living out the Good News in serving others will involve suffering. True discipleship is very costly. Are we willing to follow Christ to the point of suffering for him?*

Proverbs for Today/ 22:20–21

Have I not written thirty sayings for you, sayings of counsel and knowledge, teaching you true and reliable words, so that you can give sound answers to him who sent you?

SEPTEMBER 6

Jesus Raises Lazarus from the Dead/ John 11:30–46

Now Jesus had not yet entered the village, but was still at the place where Martha had met him. [31]When the Jews who had been with Mary in the house, comforting her, noticed how quickly she got up and went out, they followed her, supposing she was going to the tomb to mourn there.

[32]When Mary reached the place where Jesus was and saw him, she fell at his feet and said, "Lord, if you had been here, my brother would not have died."

[33]When Jesus saw her weeping, and the Jews who had come along with her also weeping, he was deeply moved

in spirit and troubled. 34"Where have you laid him?" he asked.

"Come and see, Lord," they replied.

35Jesus wept.

36Then the Jews said, "See how he loved him!"

37But some of them said, "Could not he who opened the eyes of the blind man have kept this man from dying?"

38Jesus, once more deeply moved, came to the tomb. It was a cave with a stone laid across the entrance. 39"Take away the stone," he said.

"But, Lord," said Martha, the sister of the dead man, "by this time there is a bad odor, for he has been there four days."

40Then Jesus said, "Did I not tell you that if you believed, you would see the glory of God?"

41So they took away the stone. Then Jesus looked up and said, "Father, I thank you that you have heard me. 42I knew that you always hear me, but I said this for the benefit of the people standing here, that they may believe that you sent me."

43When he had said this, Jesus called in a loud voice, "Lazarus, come out!" 44The dead man came out, his hands and feet wrapped with strips of linen, and a cloth around his face.

Jesus said to them, "Take off the grave clothes and let him go."

45Therefore many of the Jews who had come to visit Mary, and had seen what Jesus did, put their faith in him. 46But some of them went to the Pharisees and told them what Jesus had done.

A THOUGHT: *Jesus has power over life and death because he is the Creator of life. He who is Life can surely restore life. In this passage, Jesus heals Lazarus, his good friend. This demonstration of power should cause us to recognize the One sent from the Father—the Creator of life. Let us worship the Father, Son, and Spirit in wonder at such marvelous and gracious acts as this—the raising of a dead man to life. Let us also take hope in the resurrection, for Jesus here demonstrates that he holds the power of the resurrection—a power he secured by his own death and resurrection—forever conquering death.*

Be a Good Student of God's Word/
2 Timothy 2:15–21

Do your best to present yourself to God as one approved, a workman who does not need to be ashamed and who correctly handles the word of truth. 16Avoid godless chatter, because those who indulge in it will become more and more ungodly. 17Their teaching will spread like gangrene. Among them are Hymenaeus and Philetus, 18who have wandered away from the truth. They say that the resurrection has already taken place, and they destroy the faith of some. 19Nevertheless, God's solid foundation stands firm, sealed with this inscription: "The Lord knows those who are his," and, "Everyone who confesses the name of the Lord must turn away from wickedness."

20In a large house there are articles not only of gold and silver, but also of wood and clay; some are for noble purposes and some for ignoble. 21If a man cleanses himself from the latter, he will be an instrument for noble purposes, made holy, useful to the Master and prepared to do any good work.

A THOUGHT: *Life on earth is not a script which we meaninglessly act out. It is a time of deciding whether we will live for God or not and then living out what we have decided. Because God will examine what kinds of workers we have been for him, we should build our lives on his Word and build his Word into our lives. God's Word alone tells us how to live for him and serve him. Believers who ignore the Bible will certainly be ashamed at the judgment. Consistent and diligent study of God's Word is vital, or else we will be lulled into neglecting a relationship with God—our true purpose for living.*

Proverbs for Today/ 22:22–23

Do not exploit the poor because they are poor and do not crush the needy in court, for the Lord will take up their case and will plunder those who plunder them.

SEPTEMBER 7

The Prophecy of the High Priest/ John 11:47–57

Then the chief priests and the Pharisees called a meeting of the Sanhedrin.

"What are we accomplishing?" they asked. "Here is this man performing many miraculous signs. 48If we let him go on like this, everyone will believe in him, and then the Romans will come and take away both our place and our nation."

49Then one of them, named Caiaphas, who was high priest that year, spoke up, "You know nothing at all! 50You do not realize that it is better for you that one man die for the people than that the whole nation perish."

51He did not say this on his own, but as high priest that year he prophesied that Jesus would die for the Jewish nation, 52and not only for that nation but also for the scattered children of God, to bring them together and make them one. 53So from that day on they plotted to take his life.

54Therefore Jesus no longer moved about publicly among the Jews. Instead he withdrew to a region near the desert, to a village called Ephraim, where he stayed with his disciples.

55When it was almost time for the Jewish Passover, many went up from the country to Jerusalem for their ceremonial cleansing before the Passover. 56They kept looking for Jesus, and as they stood in the temple area they asked one another, "What do you think? Isn't he coming to the Feast at all?" 57But the chief priests and Pharisees had given orders that if anyone found out where Jesus was, he should report it so that they might arrest him.

A THOUGHT: *The Jewish leaders knew that if they didn't stop Jesus, the Romans would discipline them. Rome gave partial freedom to the Jews as long as they were quiet and obedient. Jesus' miracles often caused a disturbance. The leaders feared that Rome's displeasure would cause them to lose their jobs or be punished. Caiaphas had the solution for their dilemma—let Jesus be put to death on behalf of the nation. Little did he realize that he was inspired by God to predict the substitutionary effect of Jesus' death.*

Flee Evil Desires/ 2 Timothy 2:22–26

Flee the evil desires of youth, and pursue righteousness, faith, love and peace, along with those who call on the Lord out of a pure heart. 23Don't have anything to do with foolish and stupid arguments, because you know they produce quarrels. 24And the Lord's servant must not quarrel; instead, he must be kind to everyone, able to teach, not resentful. 25Those who oppose him he must gently instruct, in the hope that God will grant them repentance leading them to a knowledge of the truth, 26and that they will come to their senses and escape from the trap of the devil, who has taken them captive to do his will.

A THOUGHT: *Running away is sometimes considered cowardly. But wise people realize that removing oneself physically from temptation is often prudent. Timothy, a young man, was warned to run from anything that produced evil thoughts. Perhaps you experience a recurring temptation that is difficult to resist. Remove yourself physically from the situation. Knowing when to run is as important in spiritual battle as knowing when and how to fight.*

Proverbs for Today/ 22:24–25

Do not make friends with a hot-tempered man, do not associate with one easily angered, or you may learn his ways and get yourself ensnared.

SEPTEMBER 8

Mary Anoints Jesus' Feet/ John 12:1–11

Six days before the Passover, Jesus arrived at Bethany, where Lazarus lived, whom Jesus had raised from the dead. 2Here a dinner was given in Jesus' honor. Martha served, while Lazarus was among those reclining at the table with him. 3Then Mary took about a pint of pure nard, an expensive perfume; she poured it on Jesus' feet and wiped his feet with her hair. And the house was filled with the fragrance of the perfume.

4But one of his disciples, Judas Iscariot, who was later to betray him, objected, 5"Why wasn't this perfume sold and the money given to the poor? It was worth a year's wages." 6He did not say this because he cared about the poor but because he was a thief; as keeper of the money bag, he used to help himself to what was put into it.

7"Leave her alone," Jesus replied. "It was intended that she should save this perfume for the day of my burial. 8You will always have the poor among you, but you will not always have me."

9Meanwhile a large crowd of Jews found out that Jesus was there and came, not only because of him but also to see Lazarus, whom he had raised from the dead. 10So the chief priests made plans to kill Lazarus as well, 11for on account of him many of the Jews were going over to Jesus and putting their faith in him.

A THOUGHT: *Nard was a fragrant ointment imported from the mountains of India. Thus it was very expensive. The amount Mary used was worth a year's wages. Nard was used to anoint kings; Mary may have been anointing Jesus as her kingly Messiah. This act and Jesus' response to it do not teach us to ignore the poor so we can do extravagant things for Christ. This was a unique act for a specific occasion—an anointing for Jesus' burial and a public declaration of faith in him as Messiah. Jesus' words should have taught Judas a valuable lesson about the worth of money. Unfortunately, he did not take heed; soon he would sell his Master's life for 30 pieces of silver.*

The Character of the Last Days/ 2 Timothy 3:1–9

But mark this: There will be terrible times in the last days. 2People will be lovers of themselves, lovers of money, boastful, proud, abusive, disobedient to their parents, ungrateful, unholy, 3without love, unforgiving, slanderous, without self-control, brutal, not lovers of the good, 4treacherous, rash, conceited, lovers of pleasure rather than lovers of God— 5having a form of godliness but denying its power. Have nothing to do with them.

6They are the kind who worm their way into homes and gain control over weak-willed women, who are loaded down with sins and are swayed by all kinds of evil desires, 7always learning but never able to acknowledge the truth. 8Just as Jannes and Jambres opposed Moses, so also these men oppose the truth—men of depraved minds, who, as far as the faith is concerned, are rejected. 9But they will not get very far because, as in the case of those men, their folly will be clear to everyone.

A THOUGHT: *In many parts of the world today it does not seem especially difficult to be a Christian. No one is jailed for reading the Bible or executed for preaching Christ. But when we read Paul's descriptive list of behavior in the last days, we recognize it as a description of our society—even, unfortunately, of many Christians. There is a comfortable acceptance of a superficial Christianity that should cause us to be uncomfortable. Check your life against this list. Don't give in to society's pressures. Stand up against its evil ways by living as God would have his people live.*

Proverbs for Today/ 22:26–27

Do not be a man who strikes hands in pledge or puts up security for debts; if you lack the means to pay, your very bed will be snatched from under you.

SEPTEMBER 9

The Crowd Hails Jesus As King/ John 12:12–19

The next day the great crowd that had come for the Feast heard that Jesus was on his way to Jerusalem. 13They took palm branches and went out to meet him, shouting,

"Hosanna!"

"Blessed is he who comes in the name of the Lord!"

"Blessed is the King of Israel!"

14Jesus found a young donkey and sat upon it, as it is written,

15"Do not be afraid, O Daughter of Zion;
see, your king is coming,
seated on a donkey's colt."

16At first his disciples did not understand all this. Only after Jesus was glorified did they realize that these things had been written about him and that they had done these things to him.

17Now the crowd that was with him when he called Lazarus from the tomb and raised him from the dead continued to spread the word. 18Many people, because they had heard that he had given this miraculous sign, went out to meet him. 19So the Pharisees said to one another, "See, this is getting us nowhere. Look how the whole world has gone after him!"

A THOUGHT: *The people who were praising God for giving them a king had the wrong idea about Jesus. They were sure he would be a national leader who would restore their nation to its former glory, and thus they were deaf to the words of their prophets and blind to Jesus' real mission. When it became apparent that Jesus was not going to fulfill their hopes, many people turned against him. Loyalties change all too quickly in accordance with unfulfilled expectations. We must remain loyal to Jesus in spite of circumstances, for genuine faith goes beyond what can be seen and felt, to trust in what God has promised.*

Equipped for Every Good Work/ 2 Timothy 3:10–17

You, however, know all about my teaching, my way of life, my purpose, faith, patience, love, endurance, 11persecutions, sufferings—what kinds of things happened to me in Antioch, Iconium and Lystra, the persecutions I endured. Yet the Lord rescued me from all of them. 12In fact, everyone who wants to live a godly life in Christ Jesus will be persecuted, 13while evil men and impostors will go from bad to worse, deceiving and being deceived. 14But as for you, continue in what you have learned and have become convinced of, because you know those from whom you learned it, 15and how from infancy you have known the holy Scriptures, which are able to make you wise for salvation through faith in Christ Jesus. 16All Scripture is God-breathed and is useful for teaching, rebuking, correcting and training in righteousness, 17so that the man of God may be thoroughly equipped for every good work.

A THOUGHT: *In our zeal for the truth of Scripture, we must never forget its purpose—to equip us to do good to others. We do not study God's Word simply to increase our own knowledge or to prepare us to win arguments. We do not even study it primarily to learn how to save our own souls (most people are Christians before they begin intensively studying the Bible). We study Scripture so that we will know how to do Christ's work in the world. Our knowledge of God's Word is not useful unless we use it to do good to others.*

Proverbs for Today/ 22:28–29

Do not move an ancient boundary stone set up by your

forefathers. □ Do you see a man skilled in his work? He will serve before kings; he will not serve before obscure men.

SEPTEMBER 10

Jesus Predicts His Death/ John 12:20–36

Now there were some Greeks among those who went up to worship at the Feast. 21They came to Philip, who was from Bethsaida in Galilee, with a request. "Sir," they said, "we would like to see Jesus." 22Philip went to tell Andrew; Andrew and Philip in turn told Jesus.

23Jesus replied, "The hour has come for the Son of Man to be glorified. 24I tell you the truth, unless a kernel of wheat falls to the ground and dies, it remains only a single seed. But if it dies, it produces many seeds. 25The man who loves his life will lose it, while the man who hates his life in this world will keep it for eternal life. 26Whoever serves me must follow me; and where I am, my servant also will be. My Father will honor the one who serves me.

27"Now my heart is troubled, and what shall I say? 'Father, save me from this hour'? No, it was for this very reason I came to this hour. 28Father, glorify your name!"

Then a voice came from heaven, "I have glorified it, and will glorify it again." 29The crowd that was there and heard it said it had thundered; others said an angel had spoken to him.

30Jesus said, "This voice was for your benefit, not mine. 31Now is the time for judgment on this world; now the prince of this world will be driven out. 32But I, when I am lifted up from the earth, will draw all men to myself." 33He said this to show the kind of death he was going to die.

34The crowd spoke up, "We have heard from the Law that the Christ will remain forever, so how can you say, 'The Son of Man must be lifted up'? Who is this 'Son of Man'?"

35Then Jesus told them, "You are going to have the light just a little while longer. Walk while you have the light, before darkness overtakes you. The man who walks in the dark does not know where he is going. 36Put your trust in the light while you have it, so that you may become sons of light." When he had finished speaking, Jesus left and hid himself from them.

A THOUGHT: *Jesus knew his crucifixion lay ahead, and he dreaded it. He knew he would have to take the sins of the world on himself, and he knew this would separate him from his Father. He wanted to be delivered from this horrible death, but he knew that God sent him into the world to die for our sins, in our place. Jesus said no to his own desires in order to obey his Father and bring glory to him. Although we will never have to face such a difficult situation, we are still called to obedience. Whatever the Father asks, we should do his will and bring glory to his name.*

Paul's Charge to Timothy/ 2 Timothy 4:1–4

In the presence of God and of Christ Jesus, who will judge the living and the dead, and in view of his appearing and his kingdom, I give you this charge: 2Preach the Word; be prepared in season and out of season; correct, rebuke and encourage—with great patience and careful instruction. 3For the time will come when men will not put up with sound doctrine. Instead, to suit their own desires, they will gather around them a great number of teachers to say what their itching ears want to hear. 4They will turn their ears away from the truth and turn aside to myths.

A THOUGHT: *It was important for Timothy to preach the gospel so that the Christian faith could spread throughout the world. We believe in Christ today because people like Timothy were faithful to their mission. It is still vitally important for the church to preach the gospel. Probably half the people who have ever lived are alive today, and most of them do not know Jesus. He is coming soon, and he wants to find a faithful church waiting for him. It may be inconvenient to take a stand for Christ or to tell others about his love, but preaching the Word of God is the most important responsibility the church has been given. Be prepared, courageous, and sensitive to God-given opportunities to share the Good News.*

Proverbs for Today/ 23:1–3

When you sit to dine with a ruler, note well what is before you, and put a knife to your throat if you are given to gluttony. Do not crave his delicacies, for that food is deceptive.

The Unbelief of the Jews/ John 12:37–50

Even after Jesus had done all these miraculous signs in their presence, they still would not believe in him. 38This was to fulfill the word of Isaiah the prophet:

> "Lord, who has believed our message
>   and to whom has the arm of the Lord been
>   revealed?"

39For this reason they could not believe, because, as Isaiah says elsewhere:

> 40"He has blinded their eyes
>   and deadened their hearts,
> so they can neither see with their eyes,
>   nor understand with their hearts,
>   nor turn—and I would heal them."

41Isaiah said this because he saw Jesus' glory and spoke about him.

42Yet at the same time many even among the leaders believed in him. But because of the Pharisees they would not confess their faith for fear they would be put out of the synagogue; 43for they loved praise from men more than praise from God.

44Then Jesus cried out, "When a man believes in me, he does not believe in me only, but in the one who sent me. 45When he looks at me, he sees the one who sent me. 46I have come into the world as a light, so that no one who believes in me should stay in darkness.

47"As for the person who hears my words but does not keep them, I do not judge him. For I did not come to judge the world, but to save it. 48There is a judge for the one who rejects me and does not accept my words; that very word which I spoke will condemn him at the last day. 49For I did not speak of my own accord, but the Father who sent me commanded me what to say and how to say it. 50I know that his command leads to eternal life. So whatever I say is just what the Father has told me to say."

A THOUGHT: *Jesus had performed many miracles, but most people still didn't believe in him. Likewise, many today won't believe despite all God does. Don't be discouraged if your witness for Christ doesn't turn as many to him as you'd like. Your job is to continue as a faithful witness. You are not responsible for the decisions of others, but simply to reach out to others.*

Finishing the Race/ 2 Timothy 4:5–8

But you, keep your head in all situations, endure hardship, do the work of an evangelist, discharge all the duties of your ministry.

6For I am already being poured out like a drink offering, and the time has come for my departure. 7I have fought the good fight, I have finished the race, I have kept the faith. 8Now there is in store for me the crown of righteousness, which the Lord, the righteous Judge, will award to me on that day—and not only to me, but also to all who have longed for his appearing.

A THOUGHT: *As he neared the end of his life, Paul could confidently say that he had been faithful to his call. Thus he faced death calmly; he knew he would be rewarded at Christ's Second Coming. Is your life preparing you for death? Do you share Paul's confident expectation of meeting Christ? The Good News is that the heavenly reward is not just for giants of the faith, like Paul, but for all who have longed for Jesus' Second Coming. Paul gave these words to encourage Timothy, and us, to keep fighting no matter how difficult the fight seems. We will discover when we are with Jesus Christ that it was all worth it.*

Proverbs for Today/ 23:4–5

Do not wear yourself out to get rich; have the wisdom to show restraint. Cast but a glance at riches, and they are gone, for they will surely sprout wings and fly off to the sky like an eagle.

Jesus Washes the Disciples' Feet/ John 13:1–20

It was just before the Passover Feast. Jesus knew that the time had come for him to leave this world and go to the Father. Having loved his own who were in the world, he now showed them the full extent of his love.

2The evening meal was being served, and the devil had already prompted Judas Iscariot, son of Simon, to betray Jesus. 3Jesus knew that the Father had put all things under his power, and that he had come from God and was returning to God; 4so he got up from the meal, took off his outer clothing, and wrapped a towel around his waist. 5After that, he poured water into a basin and began to wash his disciples' feet, drying them with the towel that was wrapped around him.

6He came to Simon Peter, who said to him, "Lord, are you going to wash my feet?"

7Jesus replied, "You do not realize now what I am doing, but later you will understand."

8"No," said Peter, "you shall never wash my feet."

Jesus answered, "Unless I wash you, you have no part with me."

9"Then, Lord," Simon Peter replied, "not just my feet but my hands and my head as well!"

10Jesus answered, "A person who has had a bath needs only to wash his feet; his whole body is clean. And you are clean, though not every one of you." 11For he knew who was going to betray him, and that was why he said not every one was clean.

12When he had finished washing their feet, he put on his clothes and returned to his place. "Do you understand what I have done for you?" he asked them. 13"You call me 'Teacher' and 'Lord,' and rightly so, for that is what I am. 14Now that I, your Lord and Teacher, have washed your feet, you also should wash one another's feet. 15I have set you an example that you should do as I have done for you. 16I tell you the truth, no servant is greater than his master, nor is a messenger greater than the one who sent him.

17Now that you know these things, you will be blessed if you do them.

18"I am not referring to all of you; I know those I have chosen. But this is to fulfill the scripture: 'He who shares my bread has lifted up his heel against me.'

19"I am telling you now before it happens, so that when it does happen you will believe that I am He. 20I tell you the truth, whoever accepts anyone I send accepts me; and whoever accepts me accepts the one who sent me."

A THOUGHT: *Jesus was the model servant, and he showed this attitude to his disciples. Washing guests' feet was a job for household servants when guests arrived. But Jesus wrapped a towel around him, as the lowliest slave would do, and washed his disciples' feet. If even he, God in the flesh, is willing to serve with such humility, we, his followers, must also be servants, willing to serve in humility to bring glory to God. Are you willing to follow Christ's example of serving? Whom can you serve today?*

Paul's Final Instructions and Greetings/ 2 Timothy 4:9–22

Do your best to come to me quickly, 10for Demas, because he loved this world, has deserted me and has gone to Thessalonica. Crescens has gone to Galatia, and Titus to Dalmatia. 11Only Luke is with me. Get Mark and bring him with you, because he is helpful to me in my ministry. 12I sent Tychicus to Ephesus. 13When you come, bring the cloak that I left with Carpus at Troas, and my scrolls, especially the parchments.

14Alexander the metalworker did me a great deal of harm. The Lord will repay him for what he has done. 15You too should be on your guard against him, because he strongly opposed our message.

16At my first defense, no one came to my support, but everyone deserted me. May it not be held against them. 17But the Lord stood at my side and gave me strength, so that through me the message might be fully proclaimed and all the Gentiles might hear it. And I was delivered from the lion's mouth. 18The Lord will rescue me from every evil attack and will bring me safely to his heavenly kingdom. To him be glory for ever and ever. Amen.

19Greet Priscilla and Aquila and the household of Onesiphorus. 20Erastus stayed in Corinth, and I left Trophimus sick in Miletus. 21Do your best to get here before winter.

Eubulus greets you, and so do Pudens, Linus, Claudia and all the brothers.

²²The Lord be with your spirit. Grace be with you.

A THOUGHT: *Only Luke was with Paul at this time, and Paul was feeling lonely. Tychicus, one of his most trusted companions, had already left for Ephesus. He missed his young helpers Timothy and Mark. Mark, also called John and John Mark, had left Paul on his first missionary journey, and this had greatly angered Paul. But Mark later proved himself a worthy helper, and Paul recognized him as a good friend and trusted Christian leader. This list of Paul's co-workers should serve to remind us that Paul was not out to bring himself fame; he was a fellow servant of Christ. Paul felt the need of the body of Christ; he was not a spiritual lone ranger. We all have need of each other in the body of Christ. Let us remember that each part of the body is necessary for the building up of the whole.*

Proverbs for Today/ 23:6–8

Do not eat the food of a stingy man, do not crave his delicacies; for he is the kind of man who is always thinking about the cost. "Eat and drink," he says to you, but his heart is not with you. You will vomit up the little you have eaten and will have wasted your compliments.

SEPTEMBER 13

Judas Betrays Jesus/ John 13:21–38

After he had said this, Jesus was troubled in spirit and testified, "I tell you the truth, one of you is going to betray me."

²²His disciples stared at one another, at a loss to know which of them he meant. ²³One of them, the disciple whom Jesus loved, was reclining next to him. ²⁴Simon Peter motioned to this disciple and said, "Ask him which one he means."

²⁵Leaning back against Jesus, he asked him, "Lord, who is it?"

²⁶Jesus answered, "It is the one to whom I will give this piece of bread when I have dipped it in the dish." Then, dipping the piece of bread, he gave it to Judas Iscariot, son

of Simon. 27As soon as Judas took the bread, Satan entered into him.

"What you are about to do, do quickly," Jesus told him, 28but no one at the meal understood why Jesus said this to him. 29Since Judas had charge of the money, some thought Jesus was telling him to buy what was needed for the Feast, or to give something to the poor. 30As soon as Judas had taken the bread, he went out. And it was night.

31When he was gone, Jesus said, "Now is the Son of Man glorified and God is glorified in him. 32If God is glorified in him, God will glorify the Son in himself, and will glorify him at once.

33"My children, I will be with you only a little longer. You will look for me, and just as I told the Jews, so I tell you now: Where I am going, you cannot come.

34"A new command I give you: Love one another. As I have loved you, so you must love one another. 35By this all men will know that you are my disciples, if you love one another."

36Simon Peter asked him, "Lord, where are you going?"

Jesus replied, "Where I am going, you cannot follow now, but you will follow later."

37Peter asked, "Lord, why can't I follow you now? I will lay down my life for you."

38Then Jesus answered, "Will you really lay down your life for me? I tell you the truth, before the rooster crows, you will disown me three times!"

A THOUGHT: *Love is not simply warm feelings; it is, instead, an attitude that reveals itself in action. How can we love others as Christ loves us? We can demonstrate Christ's love by helping when it's not convenient, by giving when it hurts, by devoting energy to others' welfare rather than our own, by absorbing hurts from others without complaining or fighting back. This kind of loving is hard to do. That is why people will notice when you do it and will know you are empowered by a supernatural source—the Holy Spirit. We are called to be like Christ—a servant who came to give his life for many. Let us express this same kind of love to those around us.*

Titus Appointed to Strengthen the Churches/ Titus 1:1–5

Paul, a servant of God and an apostle of Jesus Christ for the faith of God's elect and the knowledge of the truth that leads to godliness— 2a faith and knowledge resting on the hope of eternal life, which God, who does not lie, promised before the beginning of time, ³and at his appointed season he brought his word to light through the preaching entrusted to me by the command of God our Savior,

⁴To Titus, my true son in our common faith:

Grace and peace from God the Father and Christ Jesus our Savior.

⁵The reason I left you in Crete was that you might straighten out what was left unfinished and appoint elders in every town, as I directed you.

A THOUGHT: *In one short phrase, Paul gives us insight into his reason for living. He calls himself a slave (or servant) of God—that is, he was committed to obeying God. This obedience led him to spend his life telling others about Christ. How would you describe your purpose in life? To what are you devoted?*

Proverbs for Today/ 23:9–11

Do not speak to a fool, for he will scorn the wisdom of your words. □ Do not move an ancient boundary stone or encroach on the fields of the fatherless, for their Defender is strong; he will take up their case against you.

SEPTEMBER 14

Jesus the Way to the Father/ John 14:1–14

"Do not let your hearts be troubled. Trust in God; trust also in me. ²In my Father's house are many rooms; if it were not so, I would have told you. I am going there to prepare a place for you. ³And if I go and prepare a place for you, I will come back and take you to be with me that you also may be where I am. ⁴You know the way to the place where I am going."

⁵Thomas said to him, "Lord, we don't know where you are going, so how can we know the way?"

⁶Jesus answered, "I am the way and the truth and the life. No one comes to the Father except through me. ⁷If you really knew me, you would know my Father as well. From now on, you do know him and have seen him."

8Philip said, "Lord, show us the Father and that will be enough for us."

9Jesus answered: "Don't you know me, Philip, even after I have been among you such a long time? Anyone who has seen me has seen the Father. How can you say, 'Show us the Father'? 10Don't you believe that I am in the Father, and that the Father is in me? The words I say to you are not just my own. Rather, it is the Father, living in me, who is doing his work. 11Believe me when I say that I am in the Father and the Father is in me; or at least believe on the evidence of the miracles themselves. 12I tell you the truth, anyone who has faith in me will do what I have been doing. He will do even greater things than these, because I am going to the Father. 13And I will do whatever you ask in my name, so that the Son may bring glory to the Father. 14You may ask me for anything in my name, and I will do it."

A THOUGHT: *This is one of the most basic and important passages in Scripture. It asks, "How can I find God?" and answers, "Only through Jesus." Jesus is the Way because he is both God and man. By uniting our lives with his, we are united with God. Trust Jesus to take you to the Father, and all the benefits of being God's child will be yours.*

Requirements for Church Leadership/ Titus 1:6–16

An elder must be blameless, the husband of but one wife, a man whose children believe and are not open to the charge of being wild and disobedient. 7Since an overseer is entrusted with God's work, he must be blameless—not overbearing, not quick-tempered, not given to drunkenness, not violent, not pursuing dishonest gain. 8Rather he must be hospitable, one who loves what is good, who is self-controlled, upright, holy and disciplined. 9He must hold firmly to the trustworthy message as it has been taught, so that he can encourage others by sound doctrine and refute those who oppose it.

10For there are many rebellious people, mere talkers and deceivers, especially those of the circumcision group. 11They must be silenced, because they are ruining whole households by teaching things they ought not to teach—and that for the sake of dishonest gain. 12Even one of their own prophets has said, "Cretans are always liars, evil brutes, lazy gluttons." 13This testimony is true. Therefore, rebuke them sharply, so that they will be sound in the faith [14]and will pay no attention to Jewish myths or to the commands of those who reject the truth. [15]To the pure, all things are pure, but to those who are corrupted and do not believe, nothing is pure. In fact, both their minds and consciences are corrupted. [16]They claim to know God, but by their actions they deny him. They are detestable, disobedient and unfit for doing anything good.

A THOUGHT: *Paul briefly describes some qualifications that an elder should have. He gave Timothy a similar set of instructions for the church in Ephesus. Notice that most of the qualifications involve the elder's character, not his knowledge or skill. A person's lifestyle and relationships provide a window into his or her character. Consider these qualifications as you evaluate a person for a position of leadership. While it is important to have an elder or pastor who can effectively preach God's Word, it is even more important to have one who can live out God's Word and be an example for others to follow.*

Proverbs for Today/ 23:12

Apply your heart to instruction and your ears to words of knowledge.

SEPTEMBER 15

The Promise of the Holy Spirit/ John 14:15–31

"If you love me, you will obey what I command. [16]And I will ask the Father, and he will give you another Counselor to be with you forever— [17]the Spirit of truth. The world cannot accept him, because it neither sees him nor knows him. But you know him, for he lives with you and will be in you. [18]I will not leave you as orphans; I will come to you. [19]Before long, the world will not see me anymore, but you will see me. Because I live, you also will live. [20]On that day you will realize that I am in my Father, and you are in me, and I am in you. [21]Whoever has my commands and obeys them, he is the one who loves me. He who loves me will be loved by my Father, and I too will love him and show myself to him."

[22]Then Judas (not Judas Iscariot) said, "But, Lord, why do you intend to show yourself to us and not to the world?"

[23]Jesus replied, "If anyone loves me, he will obey my

teaching. My Father will love him, and we will come to him and make our home with him. 24He who does not love me will not obey my teaching. These words you hear are not my own; they belong to the Father who sent me.

25"All this I have spoken while still with you. 26But the Counselor, the Holy Spirit, whom the Father will send in my name, will teach you all things and will remind you of everything I have said to you. 27Peace I leave with you; my peace I give you. I do not give to you as the world gives. Do not let your hearts be troubled and do not be afraid.

28"You heard me say, 'I am going away and I am coming back to you.' If you loved me, you would be glad that I am going to the Father, for the Father is greater than I. 29I have told you now before it happens, so that when it does happen you will believe. 30I will not speak with you much longer, for the prince of this world is coming. He has no hold on me, 31but the world must learn that I love the Father and that I do exactly what my Father has commanded me.

"Come now; let us leave."

A THOUGHT: *The disciples must have been perplexed, wondering how Jesus could leave them and still be with them. The Counselor—the Spirit of God himself—would come to care for and guide the disciples after Jesus was gone. This happened at Pentecost, shortly after Jesus ascended to heaven. The Holy Spirit is the very presence of God within all believers, helping us live as God wants.*

Community Life within the Church/ Titus 2:1–10

You must teach what is in accord with sound doctrine. 2Teach the older men to be temperate, worthy of respect, self-controlled, and sound in faith, in love and in endurance.

3Likewise, teach the older women to be reverent in the way they live, not to be slanderers or addicted to much wine, but to teach what is good. 4Then they can train the younger women to love their husbands and children, 5to be self-controlled and pure, to be busy at home, to be kind, and to be subject to their husbands, so that no one will malign the word of God.

6Similarly, encourage the young men to be self-controlled. 7In everything set them an example by doing what is good. In your teaching show integrity, seriousness 8and soundness of speech that cannot be condemned, so that those who oppose you may be ashamed because they have nothing bad to say about us.

⁹Teach slaves to be subject to their masters in everything, to try to please them, not to talk back to them, ¹⁰and not to steal from them, but to show that they can be fully trusted, so that in every way they will make the teaching about God our Savior attractive.

A THOUGHT: *In most churches there are people of all ages. This makes the church strong, but it also brings potential for problems. So Paul gives Titus counsel on how to help various types of people. The older people should teach the younger, by their words and by their example. Paul urged Titus to be a good example to those around him so that others might see his good deeds and imitate him. His life would give his words greater impact. If you want someone to act a certain way, be sure that you live that way yourself. Then you will earn the right to be heard.*

Proverbs for Today/ 23:13–14

Do not withhold discipline from a child; if you punish him with the rod, he will not die. Punish him with the rod and save his soul from death.

SEPTEMBER 16

The Vine and the Branches/ John 15:1–15

"I am the true vine, and my Father is the gardener. ²He cuts off every branch in me that bears no fruit, while every branch that does bear fruit he prunes so that it will be even more fruitful. ³You are already clean because of the word I have spoken to you. ⁴Remain in me, and I will remain in you. No branch can bear fruit by itself; it must remain in the vine. Neither can you bear fruit unless you remain in me.

⁵"I am the vine; you are the branches. If a man remains in me and I in him, he will bear much fruit; apart from me you can do nothing. ⁶If anyone does not remain in me, he is like a branch that is thrown away and withers; such branches are picked up, thrown into the fire and burned. ⁷If you remain in me and my words remain in you, ask whatever you wish, and it will be given you. ⁸This is to my

Father's glory, that you bear much fruit, showing yourselves to be my disciples.

9"As the Father has loved me, so have I loved you. Now remain in my love. 10If you obey my commands, you will remain in my love, just as I have obeyed my Father's commands and remain in his love. 11I have told you this so that my joy may be in you and that your joy may be complete. 12My command is this: Love each other as I have loved you. 13Greater love has no one than this, that he lay down his life for his friends. 14You are my friends if you do what I command. 15I no longer call you servants, because a servant does not know his master's business. Instead, I have called you friends, for everything that I learned from my Father I have made known to you."

A THOUGHT: *Christ is the Vine, and God is the Gardener who cares for the branches to make them fruitful. The branches are all who claim to be followers of Christ. The fruitful branches are true believers who by their living union with Christ produce much fruit. But those who become unproductive will be separated from the Vine—such are the people who have turned back from Christ after making superficial commitments. The unproductive followers are as good as dead and will be cut off and cast aside.*

Salvation Available to Everyone/ Titus 2:11-15

For the grace of God that brings salvation has appeared to all men. 12It teaches us to say "No" to ungodliness and worldly passions, and to live self-controlled, upright and godly lives in this present age, 13while we wait for the blessed hope—the glorious appearing of our great God and Savior, Jesus Christ, 14who gave himself for us to redeem us from all wickedness and to purify for himself a people that are his very own, eager to do what is good.

15These, then, are the things you should teach. Encourage and rebuke with all authority. Do not let anyone despise you.

A THOUGHT: *The power to live the Christian life comes from Jesus Christ. Because Christ died and rescued us from sin, we are free from sin's control. Jesus gives us the power and understanding to live according to God's will, to look forward to his return, and to do good. To live in accordance with God's will, we must continually submit to the control of God's Spirit. As we submit to the Spirit we will find ourselves gradually being transformed into Christlikeness.*

Proverbs for Today/ 23:15–16

My son, if your heart is wise, then my heart will be glad;
my inmost being will rejoice when your lips speak what is
right.

SEPTEMBER 17

Prepare for Persecution/ John 15:16–27

"You did not choose me, but I chose you and appointed you
to go and bear fruit—fruit that will last. Then the Father
will give you whatever you ask in my name. [17]This is my
command: Love each other.

[18]"If the world hates you, keep in mind that it hated me
first. [19]If you belonged to the world, it would love you as
its own. As it is, you do not belong to the world, but I have
chosen you out of the world. That is why the world hates
you. [20]Remember the words I spoke to you: 'No servant
is greater than his master.' If they persecuted me, they will
persecute you also. If they obeyed my teaching, they will
obey yours also. [21]They will treat you this way because of
my name, for they do not know the One who sent me. [22]If
I had not come and spoken to them, they would not be
guilty of sin. Now, however, they have no excuse for their
sin. [23]He who hates me hates my Father as well. [24]If I had
not done among them what no one else did, they would not
be guilty of sin. But now they have seen these miracles,
and yet they have hated both me and my Father. [25]But this
is to fulfill what is written in their Law: 'They hated me
without reason.'

[26]"When the Counselor comes, whom I will send to you
from the Father, the Spirit of truth who goes out from the
Father, he will testify about me. [27]And you also must
testify, for you have been with me from the beginning."

A THOUGHT: *Once again Jesus offers hope. The Holy Spirit gives
strength to endure the hatred and evil in our world and the hostility
many have toward Christ. This is especially comforting for those
facing persecution.*

Obedience to the Authorities/ Titus 3:1–8

Remind the people to be subject to rulers and authorities, to be obedient, to be ready to do whatever is good, 2to slander no one, to be peaceable and considerate, and to show true humility toward all men.

3At one time we too were foolish, disobedient, deceived and enslaved by all kinds of passions and pleasures. We lived in malice and envy, being hated and hating one another. 4But when the kindness and love of God our Savior appeared, 5he saved us, not because of righteous things we had done, but because of his mercy. He saved us through the washing of rebirth and renewal by the Holy Spirit, 6whom he poured out on us generously through Jesus Christ our Savior, 7so that, having been justified by his grace, we might become heirs having the hope of eternal life. 8This is a trustworthy saying. And I want you to stress these things, so that those who have trusted in God may be careful to devote themselves to doing what is good. These things are excellent and profitable for everyone.

A THOUGHT: *Paul summarizes what Christ does for us when he saves us. We move from a life full of sin to one led by God's Holy Spirit. All our sins, not merely some, are washed away. We gain eternal life with all its treasures. We have the fullness of the Holy Spirit, and he continually renews our hearts. None of this occurs because we earned or deserved it; it is all a gift of God's grace.*

Proverbs for Today/ 23:17–18

Do not let your heart envy sinners, but always be zealous for the fear of the LORD. There is surely a future hope for you, and your hope will not be cut off.

SEPTEMBER 18

The Promise to Send the Holy Spirit/ John 16:1–15

"All this I have told you so that you will not go astray. 2They will put you out of the synagogue; in fact, a time is coming when anyone who kills you will think he is offering a service to God. 3They will do such things because they have not known the Father or me. 4I have told you this, so that when the time comes you will remember that I warned you. I did not tell you this at first because I was with you.

5"Now I am going to him who sent me, yet none of you asks me, 'Where are you going?' 6Because I have said these things, you are filled with grief. 7But I tell you the truth: It is for your good that I am going away. Unless I go away, the Counselor will not come to you; but if I go, I will send him to you. 8When he comes, he will convict the world of guilt in regard to sin and righteousness and judgment: 9in regard to sin, because men do not believe in me; 10in regard to righteousness, because I am going to the Father, where you can see me no longer; 11and in regard to judgment, because the prince of this world now stands condemned.

12"I have much more to say to you, more than you can now bear. 13But when he, the Spirit of truth, comes, he will guide you into all truth. He will not speak on his own; he will speak only what he hears, and he will tell you what is yet to come. 14He will bring glory to me by taking from what is mine and making it known to you. 15All that belongs to the Father is mine. That is why I said the Spirit will take from what is mine and make it known to you."

A THOUGHT: *In his last moments with his disciples, Jesus (1) warned them about further persecution, (2) told them where he was going, when he was leaving, and why, and (3) assured them they would not be left alone, but that the Spirit would come. He knew what lay ahead, and he did not want their faith shaken or destroyed. God wants you to know you are not alone in the world. You have the Holy Spirit to comfort you, teach you truth, and help you.*

Avoid Foolish Arguments/ Titus 3:9–15

But avoid foolish controversies and genealogies and arguments and quarrels about the law, because these are unprofitable and useless. 10Warn a divisive person once, and then warn him a second time. After that, have nothing to do with him. 11You may be sure that such a man is warped and sinful; he is self-condemned.

12As soon as I send Artemas or Tychicus to you, do your best to come to me at Nicopolis, because I have decided to winter there. 13Do everything you can to help Zenas the lawyer and Apollos on their way and see that they have everything they need. 14Our people must learn to devote themselves to doing what is good, in order that they may provide for daily necessities and not live unproductive lives.

15Everyone with me sends you greetings. Greet those who love us in the faith.

Grace be with you all.

A THOUGHT: *Paul warns Titus, as he warned Timothy, not to get involved in arguments over unanswerable or irrelevant questions. This does not mean we should refuse to study, discuss, and examine different interpretations of difficult Bible passages. Paul is warning against petty quarrels, not honest discussion that leads to wisdom. When foolish arguments develop, it is best to turn the discussion back to a track that is going somewhere or politely excuse yourself.*

Proverbs for Today/ 23:19–21

Listen, my son, and be wise, and keep your heart on the right path. Do not join those who drink too much wine or gorge themselves on meat, for drunkards and gluttons become poor, and drowsiness clothes them in rags.

SEPTEMBER 19

Jesus Predicts His Death and Resurrection/ John 16:16–33

"In a little while you will see me no more, and then after a little while you will see me."

17Some of his disciples said to one another, "What does he mean by saying, 'In a little while you will see me no more, and then after a little while you will see me,' and 'Because I am going to the Father'?" 18They kept asking, "What does he mean by 'a little while'? We don't understand what he is saying."

19Jesus saw that they wanted to ask him about this, so he said to them, "Are you asking one another what I meant when I said, 'In a little while you will see me no more, and then after a little while you will see me'? 20I tell you the truth, you will weep and mourn while the world rejoices. You will grieve, but your grief will turn to joy. 21A woman giving birth to a child has pain because her time has come; but when her baby is born she forgets the anguish because of her joy that a child is born into the world. 22So with you: Now is your time of grief, but I will see you again and you will rejoice, and no one will take away your joy. 23In that day you will no longer ask me anything. I tell you the truth, my Father will give you whatever you ask in my name. 24Until now you have not asked for anything in my name. Ask and you will receive, and your joy will be complete.

25"Though I have been speaking figuratively, a time is coming when I will no longer use this kind of language but will tell you plainly about my Father. 26In that day you will ask in my name. I am not saying that I will ask the Father on your behalf. 27No, the Father himself loves you because you have loved me and have believed that I came from God. 28I came from the Father and entered the world; now I am leaving the world and going back to the Father."

29Then Jesus' disciples said, "Now you are speaking clearly and without figures of speech. 30Now we can see that you know all things and that you do not even need to have anyone ask you questions. This makes us believe that you came from God."

31"You believe at last!" Jesus answered. 32"But a time is coming, and has come, when you will be scattered, each to his own home. You will leave me all alone. Yet I am not alone, for my Father is with me.

33"I have told you these things, so that in me you may have peace. In this world you will have trouble. But take heart! I have overcome the world."

A THOUGHT: *The disciples did not understand Jesus' statements concerning leaving them and going to the Father. He was speaking of the fulfillment of his own mission—to redeem mankind and establish a new relationship between the believer and God. Previously, people approached God through priests. After Jesus' resurrection, any believer could approach God directly. A new day has dawned and now all believers are priests, talking with God personally and directly. We approach God, not because of our own merit, but because Jesus, our great High Priest, has made us acceptable to God.*

Paul Gives Thanks for Philemon/ Philemon 1:1–7

Paul, a prisoner of Christ Jesus, and Timothy our brother,

To Philemon our dear friend and fellow worker, 2to Apphia our sister, to Archippus our fellow soldier and to the church that meets in your home:

³Grace to you and peace from God our Father and the Lord Jesus Christ.

⁴I always thank my God as I remember you in my prayers, ⁵because I hear about your faith in the Lord Jesus and your love for all the saints. ⁶I pray that you may be active in sharing your faith, so that you will have a full understanding of every good thing we have in Christ. ⁷Your love has given me great joy and encouragement, because you, brother, have refreshed the hearts of the saints.

A THOUGHT: *Paul reflected on Philemon's kindness, love, and comfort. He had opened his heart and his home to the church. We should do likewise, opening ourselves and our homes to others, offering Christian fellowship to refresh people's spirits.*

Proverbs for Today/ 23:22

Listen to your father, who gave you life, and do not despise your mother when she is old.

SEPTEMBER 20

Jesus Prays for His Followers/ John 17:1–26

After Jesus said this, he looked toward heaven and prayed:

"Father, the time has come. Glorify your Son, that your Son may glorify you. ²For you granted him authority over all people that he might give eternal life to all those you have given him. ³Now this is eternal life: that they may know you, the only true God, and Jesus Christ, whom you have sent. ⁴I have brought you glory on earth by completing the work you gave me to do. ⁵And now, Father, glorify me in your presence with the glory I had with you before the world began.

⁶"I have revealed you to those whom you gave me out of the world. They were yours; you gave them to me and they have obeyed your word. ⁷Now they know that everything you have given me comes from you. ⁸For I gave them the words you gave me and they accepted them. They knew with certainty that

I came from you, and they believed that you sent me. 9I pray for them. I am not praying for the world, but for those you have given me, for they are yours. 10All I have is yours, and all you have is mine. And glory has come to me through them. 11I will remain in the world no longer, but they are still in the world, and I am coming to you. Holy Father, protect them by the power of your name—the name you gave me—so that they may be one as we are one. 12While I was with them, I protected them and kept them safe by that name you gave me. None has been lost except the one doomed to destruction so that Scripture would be fulfilled.

13"I am coming to you now, but I say these things while I am still in the world, so that they may have the full measure of my joy within them. 14I have given them your word and the world has hated them, for they are not of the world any more than I am of the world. 15My prayer is not that you take them out of the world but that you protect them from the evil one. 16They are not of the world, even as I am not of it. 17Sanctify them by the truth; your word is truth. 18As you sent me into the world, I have sent them into the world. 19For them I sanctify myself, that they too may be truly sanctified.

20"My prayer is not for them alone. I pray also for those who will believe in me through their message, 21that all of them may be one, Father, just as you are in me and I am in you. May they also be in us so that the world may believe that you have sent me. 22I have given them the glory that you gave me, that they may be one as we are one: 23I in them and you in me. May they be brought to complete unity to let the world know that you sent me and have loved them even as you have loved me.

24"Father, I want those you have given me to be with me where I am, and to see my glory, the glory you have given me because you loved me before the creation of the world.

25"Righteous Father, though the world does not know you, I know you, and they know that you have sent me. 26I have made you known to them, and will

continue to make you known in order that the love
you have for me may be in them and that I myself may
be in them."

A THOUGHT: *Jesus' great desire for his disciples was that they become
one. Jesus prayed for unity among the believers based on the oneness
Jesus has with the Father. Christians can know unity among themselves if they are living in union with God. Are you helping to unify
the body of Christ, the church? You can pray for other Christians,
avoid gossip, build others up, work together in humility, give your
time and money, lift up Christ, and refuse to get sidetracked by
arguing over unimportant matters that too often divide us.*

Paul's Plea for Onesimus/ Philemon 1:8–25

Therefore, although in Christ I could be bold and order you
to do what you ought to do, 9yet I appeal to you on the basis
of love. I then, as Paul—an old man and now also a prisoner
of Christ Jesus— 10I appeal to you for my son Onesimus,
who became my son while I was in chains. 11Formerly he
was useless to you, but now he has become useful both to
you and to me.

12I am sending him—who is my very heart—back to you.
13I would have liked to keep him with me so that he could
take your place in helping me while I am in chains for the
gospel. 14But I did not want to do anything without your
consent, so that any favor you do will be spontaneous and
not forced. 15Perhaps the reason he was separated from
you for a little while was that you might have him back for
good— 16no longer as a slave, but better than a slave, as
a dear brother. He is very dear to me but even dearer to
you, both as a man and as a brother in the Lord.

17So if you consider me a partner, welcome him as you
would welcome me. 18If he has done you any wrong or
owes you anything, charge it to me. 19I, Paul, am writing
this with my own hand. I will pay it back—not to mention
that you owe me your very self. 20I do wish, brother, that
I may have some benefit from you in the Lord; refresh my
heart in Christ. 21Confident of your obedience, I write to
you, knowing that you will do even more than I ask.

22And one thing more: Prepare a guest room for me,
because I hope to be restored to you in answer to your
prayers.

23Epaphras, my fellow prisoner in Christ Jesus, sends

you greetings. 24And so do Mark, Aristarchus, Demas and Luke, my fellow workers.

25The grace of the Lord Jesus Christ be with your spirit.

A THOUGHT: *What a difference Onesimus' status as a Christian made in his relationship to Philemon. He was no longer merely a servant, he was also a brother. Now both Onesimus and Philemon were members of God's family—equals in Christ. A Christian's status as a member of God's family transcends all other distinctions among believers. Do you look down on any fellow Christians? Remember, they are your brothers and sisters, your equals before Christ. How you treat your brothers and sisters in Christ's family reflects your true Christian commitment.*

Proverbs for Today/ 23:23

Buy the truth and do not sell it; get wisdom, discipline and understanding.

SEPTEMBER 21

Jesus Arrested in the Garden/ John 18:1–14

When he had finished praying, Jesus left with his disciples and crossed the Kidron Valley. On the other side there was an olive grove, and he and his disciples went into it.

2Now Judas, who betrayed him, knew the place, because Jesus had often met there with his disciples. 3So Judas came to the grove, guiding a detachment of soldiers and some officials from the chief priests and Pharisees. They were carrying torches, lanterns and weapons.

4Jesus, knowing all that was going to happen to him, went out and asked them, "Who is it you want?"

5"Jesus of Nazareth," they replied.

"I am he," Jesus said. (And Judas the traitor was standing there with them.) 6When Jesus said, "I am he," they drew back and fell to the ground.

7Again he asked them, "Who is it you want?"

And they said, "Jesus of Nazareth."

8"I told you that I am he," Jesus answered. "If you are looking for me, then let these men go." 9This happened so that the words he had spoken would be fulfilled: "I have not lost one of those you gave me."

10Then Simon Peter, who had a sword, drew it and struck the high priest's servant, cutting off his right ear. (The servant's name was Malchus.)

11Jesus commanded Peter, "Put your sword away! Shall I not drink the cup the Father has given me?"

12Then the detachment of soldiers with its commander and the Jewish officials arrested Jesus. They bound him 13and brought him first to Annas, who was the father-in-law of Caiaphas, the high priest that year. 14Caiaphas was the one who had advised the Jews that it would be good if one man died for the people.

A THOUGHT: *Trying to protect Jesus, Peter pulled a sword and wounded one of the Temple police. But Jesus told him to put away his sword and allow God's plan to unfold. At times it is tempting to take matters into our own hands, to force the issue. Instead we must trust God to work out his plan. Think of it—if Peter would have had his way, Jesus would not have gone to the cross, and God's plan of redemption would have been halted.*

God's Son Greater Than Angels/ Hebrews 1:1–14

In the past God spoke to our forefathers through the prophets at many times and in various ways, 2but in these last days he has spoken to us by his Son, whom he appointed heir of all things, and through whom he made the universe. 3The Son is the radiance of God's glory and the exact representation of his being, sustaining all things by his powerful word. After he had provided purification for sins, he sat down at the right hand of the Majesty in heaven. 4So he became as much superior to the angels as the name he has inherited is superior to theirs.

5For to which of the angels did God ever say,

"You are my Son;
today I have become your Father"?

Or again,

"I will be his Father,
and he will be my Son"?

6And again, when God brings his firstborn into the world, he says,

"Let all God's angels worship him."

7In speaking of the angels he says,

"He makes his angels winds,
his servants flames of fire."

⁸But about the Son he says,

"Your throne, O God, will last for ever and ever,
and righteousness will be the scepter of your
kingdom.
⁹You have loved righteousness and hated
wickedness;
therefore God, your God, has set you above your
companions
by anointing you with the oil of joy."

¹⁰He also says,

"In the beginning, O Lord, you laid the foundations
of the earth,
and the heavens are the work of your hands.
¹¹They will perish, but you remain;
they will all wear out like a garment.
¹²You will roll them up like a robe;
like a garment they will be changed.
But you remain the same,
and your years will never end."

¹³To which of the angels did God ever say,

"Sit at my right hand
until I make your enemies
a footstool for your feet"?

¹⁴Are not all angels ministering spirits sent to serve those
who will inherit salvation?

A THOUGHT: *God used many approaches to send his messages to people in Old Testament times. He spoke to Isaiah in visions, to Jacob in a dream, and to Abraham and Moses personally. Jewish people familiar with these stories would not have found it hard to believe that God was still revealing his will, but it was astonishing for them to think that God had revealed himself by speaking through his Son, Jesus Christ. Jesus is the fulfillment and culmination of God's many revelations through the centuries. He is the full revelation of God. You can have no clearer view of God than by looking at him. Jesus Christ is the complete embodiment of God.*

Proverbs for Today/ 23:24–25

The father of a righteous man has great joy; he who has a wise son delights in him. May your father and mother be glad; may she who gave you birth rejoice!

SEPTEMBER 22

Peter's Denials/ John 18:15–27

Simon Peter and another disciple were following Jesus. Because this disciple was known to the high priest, he went with Jesus into the high priest's courtyard, 16but Peter had to wait outside at the door. The other disciple, who was known to the high priest, came back, spoke to the girl on duty there and brought Peter in.

17"You are not one of his disciples, are you?" the girl at the door asked Peter.

He replied, "I am not."

18It was cold, and the servants and officials stood around a fire they had made to keep warm. Peter also was standing with them, warming himself.

19Meanwhile, the high priest questioned Jesus about his disciples and his teaching.

20"I have spoken openly to the world," Jesus replied. "I always taught in synagogues or at the temple, where all the Jews come together. I said nothing in secret. 21Why question me? Ask those who heard me. Surely they know what I said."

22When Jesus said this, one of the officials nearby struck him in the face. "Is this the way you answer the high priest?" he demanded.

23"If I said something wrong," Jesus replied, "testify as to what is wrong. But if I spoke the truth, why did you strike me?" 24Then Annas sent him, still bound, to Caiaphas the high priest.

25As Simon Peter stood warming himself, he was asked, "You are not one of his disciples, are you?"

He denied it, saying, "I am not."

26One of the high priest's servants, a relative of the man

whose ear Peter had cut off, challenged him, "Didn't I see you with him in the olive grove?" 27Again Peter denied it, and at that moment a rooster began to crow.

A THOUGHT: *Imagine standing outside while Jesus, your Lord and Master, is questioned. Imagine watching this man, whom you have come to believe is the long-awaited Messiah, being abused and beaten. Naturally Peter was confused and afraid. It is a serious sin to deny Christ, but Jesus later forgave Peter. No sin is too great for Jesus to forgive if we are truly repentant. He will forgive even your worst sin if you turn from it and ask his pardon.*

Do Not Drift Away from the Truth/ Hebrews 2:1–4

We must pay more careful attention, therefore, to what we have heard, so that we do not drift away. 2For if the message spoken by angels was binding, and every violation and disobedience received its just punishment, 3how shall we escape if we ignore such a great salvation? This salvation, which was first announced by the Lord, was confirmed to us by those who heard him. 4God also testified to it by signs, wonders and various miracles, and gifts of the Holy Spirit distributed according to his will.

A THOUGHT: *A central theme of Hebrews is that Christ is infinitely greater than all other proposed means to God. Your previous faith was good, the author said to his Jewish readers, but Christ is incomparably better. Just as Christ is greater than angels, so his message is more important than theirs. Don't turn your back on Christ in an attempt to escape your troubles. The only escape is to flee to him.*

Proverbs for Today/ 23:26–28

My son, give me your heart and let your eyes keep to my ways, for a prostitute is a deep pit and a wayward wife is a narrow well. Like a bandit she lies in wait, and multiplies the unfaithful among men.

SEPTEMBER 23

Jesus Before Pilate/ John 18:28–40

Then the Jews led Jesus from Caiaphas to the palace of the Roman governor. By now it was early morning, and to avoid ceremonial uncleanness the Jews did not enter the palace; they wanted to be able to eat the Passover. 29So Pilate came out to them and asked, "What charges are you bringing against this man?"

30"If he were not a criminal," they replied, "we would not have handed him over to you."

31Pilate said, "Take him yourselves and judge him by your own law."

"But we have no right to execute anyone," the Jews objected. 32This happened so that the words Jesus had spoken indicating the kind of death he was going to die would be fulfilled.

33Pilate then went back inside the palace, summoned Jesus and asked him, "Are you the king of the Jews?"

34"Is that your own idea," Jesus asked, "or did others talk to you about me?"

35"Am I a Jew?" Pilate replied. "It was your people and your chief priests who handed you over to me. What is it you have done?"

36Jesus said, "My kingdom is not of this world. If it were, my servants would fight to prevent my arrest by the Jews. But now my kingdom is from another place."

37"You are a king, then!" said Pilate.

Jesus answered, "You are right in saying I am a king. In fact, for this reason I was born, and for this I came into the world, to testify to the truth. Everyone on the side of truth listens to me."

38"What is truth?" Pilate asked. With this he went out again to the Jews and said, "I find no basis for a charge against him. 39But it is your custom for me to release to you one prisoner at the time of the Passover. Do you want me to release 'the king of the Jews'?"

40They shouted back, "No, not him! Give us Barabbas!" Now Barabbas had taken part in a rebellion.

A THOUGHT: *Pilate, the Roman governor at this time, was in charge of Judea (the region in which Jerusalem was located) from A.D. 26 to 36. Pilate was unpopular with the Jews because he had raided the Temple treasuries for money to build an aqueduct. He did not like the Jews, but when Jesus, the King of the Jews, stood before him, Pilate found him innocent. Pilate knew what was going on; he knew that the religious leaders hated Jesus, and he did not want to act as their executioner. They could not sentence Jesus to death themselves—permission had to come from a Roman leader. Jesus' life became a pawn in a political power struggle. Responding to threats from the mob, Pilate finally turned Jesus over to be crucified.*

Salvation through Jesus' Suffering/ Hebrews 2:5–10

It is not to angels that he has subjected the world to come, about which we are speaking. 6But there is a place where someone has testified:

> "What is man that you are mindful of him,
>   the son of man that you care for him?
> 7You made him a little lower than the angels;
>   you crowned him with glory and honor
> 8 and put everything under his feet."

In putting everything under him, God left nothing that is not subject to him. Yet at present we do not see everything subject to him. 9But we see Jesus, who was made a little lower than the angels, now crowned with glory and honor because he suffered death, so that by the grace of God he might taste death for everyone.

10In bringing many sons to glory, it was fitting that God, for whom and through whom everything exists, should make the author of their salvation perfect through suffering.

A THOUGHT: *God's kindness led Christ to his death—what a startling juxtaposition of ideas! Yet kindness can and often does involve sacrifice and pain. Jesus did not come into the world to gain status or political power, but to suffer and die so that we could truly live. If this is difficult to understand, perhaps it is time to evaluate our own motives. Are we more interested in power or submission, domination or service, getting or giving? If kindness, not selfishness, motivates us, we too may have to suffer.*

Proverbs for Today/ 23:29–35

Who has woe? Who has sorrow? Who has strife? Who has complaints? Who has needless bruises? Who has bloodshot eyes? Those who linger over wine, who go to sample bowls of mixed wine. Do not gaze at wine when it is red, when it sparkles in the cup, when it goes down smoothly! In the end it bites like a snake and poisons like a viper. Your eyes will see strange sights and your mind imagine confusing things. You will be like one sleeping on the high seas, lying on top of the rigging. "They hit me," you will say, "but I'm not hurt! They beat me, but I don't feel it! When will I wake up so I can find another drink?"

SEPTEMBER 24

The People Demand Jesus' Crucifixion/
John 19:1–15

Then Pilate took Jesus and had him flogged. 2The soldiers twisted together a crown of thorns and put it on his head. They clothed him in a purple robe 3and went up to him again and again, saying, "Hail, king of the Jews!" And they struck him in the face.

4Once more Pilate came out and said to the Jews, "Look, I am bringing him out to you to let you know that I find no basis for a charge against him." 5When Jesus came out wearing the crown of thorns and the purple robe, Pilate said to them, "Here is the man!"

6As soon as the chief priests and their officials saw him, they shouted, "Crucify! Crucify!"

But Pilate answered, "You take him and crucify him. As for me, I find no basis for a charge against him."

7The Jews insisted, "We have a law, and according to that law he must die, because he claimed to be the Son of God."

8When Pilate heard this, he was even more afraid, 9and he went back inside the palace. "Where do you come from?" he asked Jesus, but Jesus gave him no answer. 10"Do you refuse to speak to me?" Pilate said. "Don't you realize I have power either to free you or to crucify you?"

11Jesus answered, "You would have no power over me if it were not given to you from above. Therefore the one who handed me over to you is guilty of a greater sin."

12From then on, Pilate tried to set Jesus free, but the Jews kept shouting, "If you let this man go, you are no friend of Caesar. Anyone who claims to be a king opposes Caesar."

13When Pilate heard this, he brought Jesus out and sat down on the judge's seat at a place known as the Stone Pavement (which in Aramaic is Gabbatha). 14It was the day of Preparation of Passover Week, about the sixth hour.

"Here is your king," Pilate said to the Jews.

15But they shouted, "Take him away! Take him away! Crucify him!"

"Shall I crucify your king?" Pilate asked.

"We have no king but Caesar," the chief priests answered.

A THOUGHT: *The Jewish leaders were so desperate to get rid of Jesus that despite their intense hatred for Rome, they shouted, "We have no king but Caesar." How ironic that they feigned allegiance to Rome while rejecting their own Messiah! The priests had truly lost their reasons for being—instead of turning people to God, they claimed allegiance to Rome in order to kill their Messiah. And they encouraged the people to join them in their terrible sin.*

Christ Shared Our Humanity/ Hebrews 2:11–15

Both the one who makes men holy and those who are made holy are of the same family. So Jesus is not ashamed to call them brothers. 12He says,

> "I will declare your name to my brothers;
>   in the presence of the congregation I will sing
>   your praises."

13And again,

> "I will put my trust in him."

And again he says,

> "Here am I, and the children God has given me."

14Since the children have flesh and blood, he too shared in their humanity so that by his death he might destroy him who holds the power of death—that is, the devil— 15and free those who all their lives were held in slavery by their fear of death.

A THOUGHT: *Jesus had to be human so he could die, so he could overcome the same temptations we face, and so he could mediate between God and human beings. He identified with us so that we could identify with God. Christ's death reestablished our relationship with God. We are children of God because of what Christ did. Our hope of eternal life has been secured in Christ.*

Proverbs for Today/ 24:1–2

Do not envy wicked men, do not desire their company; for their hearts plot violence, and their lips talk about making trouble.

SEPTEMBER 25

The Crucifixion of Jesus/ John 19:16–30

Finally Pilate handed him over to them to be crucified.

So the soldiers took charge of Jesus. 17Carrying his own cross, he went out to the place of the Skull (which in Aramaic is called Golgotha). 18Here they crucified him, and with him two others—one on each side and Jesus in the middle.

19Pilate had a notice prepared and fastened to the cross. It read: JESUS OF NAZARETH, THE KING OF THE JEWS. 20Many of the Jews read this sign, for the place where Jesus was crucified was near the city, and the sign was written in Aramaic, Latin and Greek. 21The chief priests of the Jews protested to Pilate, "Do not write 'The King of the Jews,' but that this man claimed to be king of the Jews."

22Pilate answered, "What I have written, I have written."

23When the soldiers crucified Jesus, they took his clothes, dividing them into four shares, one for each of them, with the undergarment remaining. This garment was seamless, woven in one piece from top to bottom.

24"Let's not tear it," they said to one another. "Let's decide by lot who will get it."

This happened that the scripture might be fulfilled which said,

"They divided my garments among them
and cast lots for my clothing."

So this is what the soldiers did.

25Near the cross of Jesus stood his mother, his mother's sister, Mary the wife of Clopas, and Mary Magdalene. 26When Jesus saw his mother there, and the disciple whom he loved standing nearby, he said to his mother, "Dear woman, here is your son," 27and to the disciple, "Here is your mother." From that time on, this disciple took her into his home.

28Later, knowing that all was now completed, and so that the Scripture would be fulfilled, Jesus said, "I am thirsty." 29A jar of wine vinegar was there, so they soaked a sponge in it, put the sponge on a stalk of the hyssop plant, and lifted it to Jesus' lips. 30When he had received the drink, Jesus said, "It is finished." With that, he bowed his head and gave up his spirit.

A THOUGHT: *Crucifixion was a Roman form of punishment. The victim sentenced to this type of execution was forced to carry his cross along a main road to the execution site, as a warning to the people. Crosses and methods of crucifixion varied. Jesus was nailed to his cross; others were sometimes tied with ropes. Death came by suffocation, because the weight of the body made breathing difficult as the victim lost strength. Crucifixion was a hideously slow and painful death.*

Jesus was the final and ultimate sacrifice for sin. The Greek word "finished" can also mean "paid in full." Jesus came to finish God's work of salvation, to pay the full penalty for our sins. With his death, the complex sacrificial system ended because Jesus took all sin upon himself. Now we can freely approach God because of what Jesus did for us. Those who believe in Jesus' death and resurrection can live eternally with God and escape the death which comes from sin.

Jesus Our Merciful High Priest/ Hebrews 2:16—3:6

For surely it is not angels he helps, but Abraham's descendants. 17For this reason he had to be made like his brothers in every way, in order that he might become a merciful and faithful high priest in service to God, and that he might make atonement for the sins of the people. 18Because he himself suffered when he was tempted, he is able to help those who are being tempted.

3:1Therefore, holy brothers, who share in the heavenly calling, fix your thoughts on Jesus, the apostle and high priest whom we confess. 2He was faithful to the one who appointed him, just as Moses was faithful in all God's house. 3Jesus has been found worthy of greater honor than

Moses, just as the builder of a house has greater honor than the house itself. ⁴For every house is built by someone, but God is the builder of everything. ⁵Moses was faithful as a servant in all God's house, testifying to what would be said in the future. ⁶But Christ is faithful as a son over God's house. And we are his house, if we hold on to our courage and the hope of which we boast.

A THOUGHT: *In the Old Testament, the High Priest was the mediator between God and his people. His job was to regularly offer animal sacrifices according to the law and to intercede with God for the people's sins. Jesus Christ is now our High Priest. He has "once and for all" paid the penalty for all our sins by his own sacrificial death, and he continually intercedes on our behalf before God. We are released from sin's domination over us when we commit ourselves fully to Christ, trusting completely in what he has done for us.*

Proverbs for Today/ 24:3–4

By wisdom a house is built, and through understanding it is established; through knowledge its rooms are filled with rare and beautiful treasures.

SEPTEMBER 26

Jesus' Burial/ John 19:31–42

Now it was the day of Preparation, and the next day was to be a special Sabbath. Because the Jews did not want the bodies left on the crosses during the Sabbath, they asked Pilate to have the legs broken and the bodies taken down. ³²The soldiers therefore came and broke the legs of the first man who had been crucified with Jesus, and then those of the other. ³³But when they came to Jesus and found that he was already dead, they did not break his legs. ³⁴Instead, one of the soldiers pierced Jesus' side with a spear, bringing a sudden flow of blood and water. ³⁵The man who saw it has given testimony, and his testimony is true. He knows that he tells the truth, and he testifies so that you also may believe. ³⁶These things happened so that the scripture would be fulfilled: "Not one of his bones will be broken,"

37and, as another scripture says, "They will look on the one they have pierced."

38Later, Joseph of Arimathea asked Pilate for the body of Jesus. Now Joseph was a disciple of Jesus, but secretly because he feared the Jews. With Pilate's permission, he came and took the body away. 39He was accompanied by Nicodemus, the man who earlier had visited Jesus at night. Nicodemus brought a mixture of myrrh and aloes, about seventy-five pounds. 40Taking Jesus' body, the two of them wrapped it, with the spices, in strips of linen. This was in accordance with Jewish burial customs. 41At the place where Jesus was crucified, there was a garden, and in the garden a new tomb, in which no one had ever been laid. 42Because it was the Jewish day of Preparation and since the tomb was nearby, they laid Jesus there.

A THOUGHT: *Joseph of Arimathea and Nicodemus were secret followers of Jesus. They were afraid to make this known because of their positions in the Jewish community. Joseph was a leader and honored member of the Sanhedrin. Nicodemus, also a member of the Sanhedrin, had come to Jesus by night and later tried to defend him before the other religious leaders. Yet they risked their reputations to bury Jesus. Are you a secret believer? Do you hide from your friends and fellow workers? This is an appropriate time to step out of hiding and let others know of your faith.*

God's Anger against Israel/ Hebrews 3:7–14

So, as the Holy Spirit says:

"Today, if you hear his voice,
8 do not harden your hearts
as you did in the rebellion,
    during the time of testing in the desert,
9where your fathers tested and tried me
    and for forty years saw what I did.
10That is why I was angry with that generation,
    and I said, 'Their hearts are always going astray,
    and they have not known my ways.'
11So I declared on oath in my anger,
    'They shall never enter my rest.'"

12See to it, brothers, that none of you has a sinful, unbelieving heart that turns away from the living God. 13But encourage one another daily, as long as it is called Today, so that none of you may be hardened by sin's deceitfulness. 14We have come to share in Christ if we hold firmly till the end the confidence we had at first.

A THOUGHT: *Many times the Bible warns us not to harden our hearts. "Hardening our hearts" is an expression that means we have set ourselves against God to the point that we are no longer able to turn to him to be saved. Such hardheartedness begins when we refuse to obey God's revealed will. The Israelites became hardhearted when they disobeyed God's command to conquer the Promised Land. Let us be careful to obey God's Word and not allow our hearts to become hardened.*

Proverbs for Today/ 24:5

A wise man has great power, and a man of knowledge increases strength.

SEPTEMBER 27

The Resurrection of Jesus/ John 20:1–18

Early on the first day of the week, while it was still dark, Mary Magdalene went to the tomb and saw that the stone had been removed from the entrance. 2So she came running to Simon Peter and the other disciple, the one Jesus loved, and said, "They have taken the Lord out of the tomb, and we don't know where they have put him!"

3So Peter and the other disciple started for the tomb. 4Both were running, but the other disciple outran Peter and reached the tomb first. 5He bent over and looked in at the strips of linen lying there but did not go in. 6Then Simon Peter, who was behind him, arrived and went into the tomb. He saw the strips of linen lying there, 7as well as the burial cloth that had been around Jesus' head. The cloth was folded up by itself, separate from the linen. 8Finally the other disciple, who had reached the tomb first, also went inside. He saw and believed. 9(They still did not understand from Scripture that Jesus had to rise from the dead.)

10Then the disciples went back to their homes, 11but Mary stood outside the tomb crying. As she wept, she bent over to look into the tomb 12and saw two angels in white, seated where Jesus' body had been, one at the head and the other at the foot.

13They asked her, "Woman, why are you crying?"

"They have taken my Lord away," she said, "and I don't know where they have put him." 14At this, she turned around and saw Jesus standing there, but she did not realize that it was Jesus.

15"Woman," he said, "why are you crying? Who is it you are looking for?"

Thinking he was the gardener, she said, "Sir, if you have carried him away, tell me where you have put him, and I will get him."

16Jesus said to her, "Mary."

She turned toward him and cried out in Aramaic, "Rabboni!" (which means Teacher).

17Jesus said, "Do not hold on to me, for I have not yet returned to the Father. Go instead to my brothers and tell them, 'I am returning to my Father and your Father, to my God and your God.'"

18Mary Magdalene went to the disciples with the news: "I have seen the Lord!" And she told that he had said these things to her.

A THOUGHT: *Jesus' resurrection is the key to the Christian faith. Why? (1) Jesus rose from the dead, "Just as he said." We can be confident, therefore, that he will accomplish all he has promised. (2) Jesus' bodily resurrection shows us that the living Christ is the ruler of God's eternal kingdom. (3) We can be certain of our own resurrection because he was resurrected. Death is not the end—there is future life. (4) The divine power that brought Jesus back to life is now available to us to bring our spiritually dead selves back to life. (5) The resurrection is the basis for the church's witness to the world.*

Listen, Believe and Obey/ Hebrews 3:15–19

As has just been said:

> "Today, if you hear his voice,
>   do not harden your hearts
>   as you did in the rebellion."

16Who were they who heard and rebelled? Were they not all those Moses led out of Egypt? 17And with whom was he angry for forty years? Was it not with those who sinned, whose bodies fell in the desert? 18And to whom did God swear that they would never enter his rest if not to those who disobeyed? 19So we see that they were not able to enter, because of their unbelief.

A THOUGHT: *The Israelites failed to enter the Promised Land because they lacked trust in God. They did not believe God would help them conquer the land, and lacking trust, they failed. So God sent them into the wilderness to wander for 40 years, an unhappy alternative to the wonderful gift he planned for them. Lack of trust in God always prevents us from receiving his best.*

Proverbs for Today/ 24:6–7

For waging war you need guidance, and for victory many advisers. Wisdom is too high for a fool; in the assembly at the gate he has nothing to say.

SEPTEMBER 28

Resurrection Appearances/ John 20:19–31

On the evening of that first day of the week, when the disciples were together, with the doors locked for fear of the Jews, Jesus came and stood among them and said, "Peace be with you!" 20After he said this, he showed them his hands and side. The disciples were overjoyed when they saw the Lord.

21Again Jesus said, "Peace be with you! As the Father has sent me, I am sending you." 22And with that he breathed on them and said, "Receive the Holy Spirit. 23If you forgive anyone his sins, they are forgiven; if you do not forgive them, they are not forgiven."

24Now Thomas (called Didymus), one of the Twelve, was not with the disciples when Jesus came. 25So the other disciples told him, "We have seen the Lord!"

But he said to them, "Unless I see the nail marks in his hands and put my finger where the nails were, and put my hand into his side, I will not believe it."

26A week later his disciples were in the house again, and Thomas was with them. Though the doors were locked, Jesus came and stood among them and said, "Peace be with you!" 27Then he said to Thomas, "Put your finger here; see my hands. Reach out your hand and put it into my side. Stop doubting and believe."

28Thomas said to him, "My Lord and my God!"

29Then Jesus told him, "Because you have seen me, you have believed; blessed are those who have not seen and yet have believed."

30Jesus did many other miraculous signs in the presence of his disciples, which are not recorded in this book. 31But these are written that you may believe that Jesus is the Christ, the Son of God, and that by believing you may have life in his name.

A THOUGHT: *Some people think they would believe in Jesus if they could see a definite sign or miracle. But Jesus says we are blessed if we believe without seeing. We have all the proof we need in the words of the Bible and the testimony of believers. A physical appearance would not make Jesus any more real to us than the reality of his presence in the body of Christ—the church.*

Entrance into God's Rest/ Hebrews 4:1–6

Therefore, since the promise of entering his rest still stands, let us be careful that none of you be found to have fallen short of it. 2For we also have had the gospel preached to us, just as they did; but the message they heard was of no value to them, because those who heard did not combine it with faith. 3Now we who have believed enter that rest, just as God has said,

> "So I declared on oath in my anger,
> 'They shall never enter my rest.' "

And yet his work has been finished since the creation of the world. 4For somewhere he has spoken about the seventh day in these words: "And on the seventh day God rested from all his work." 5And again in the passage above he says, "They shall never enter my rest."

6It still remains that some will enter that rest, and those who formerly had the gospel preached to them did not go in, because of their disobedience.

A THOUGHT: *Some of the Jewish Christians who received this letter of Hebrews may have been on the verge of turning back from their promised rest in Christ, just as the people in Moses' day turned back from the Promised Land. In both cases, the difficulties of the present moment overshadowed the reality of God's promise, and people stopped believing that God was able to fulfill his promises. When we place our trust in our own efforts instead of in Christ, we too are in danger of turning back. Our own efforts are never adequate; only Christ can see us through.*

Proverbs for Today/ 24:8
He who plots evil will be known as a schemer.

SEPTEMBER 29

Jesus Appears in Galilee/ John 21:1–14
Afterward Jesus appeared again to his disciples, by the Sea of Tiberias. It happened this way: 2Simon Peter, Thomas (called Didymus), Nathanael from Cana in Galilee, the sons of Zebedee, and two other disciples were together. 3"I'm going out to fish," Simon Peter told them, and they said, "We'll go with you." So they went out and got into the boat, but that night they caught nothing.

4Early in the morning, Jesus stood on the shore, but the disciples did not realize that it was Jesus.

5He called out to them, "Friends, haven't you any fish?"

"No," they answered.

6He said, "Throw your net on the right side of the boat and you will find some." When they did, they were unable to haul the net in because of the large number of fish.

7Then the disciple whom Jesus loved said to Peter, "It is the Lord!" As soon as Simon Peter heard him say, "It is the Lord," he wrapped his outer garment around him (for he had taken it off) and jumped into the water. 8The other disciples followed in the boat, towing the net full of fish, for they were not far from shore, about a hundred yards. 9When they landed, they saw a fire of burning coals there with fish on it, and some bread.

10Jesus said to them, "Bring some of the fish you have just caught."

11Simon Peter climbed aboard and dragged the net ashore. It was full of large fish, 153, but even with so many the net was not torn. 12Jesus said to them, "Come and have breakfast." None of the disciples dared ask him, "Who are you?" They knew it was the Lord. 13Jesus came, took the bread and gave it to them, and did the same with the fish.

14This was now the third time Jesus appeared to his disciples after he was raised from the dead.

A THOUGHT: *These disciples had been fishing all night long. They seem to have been discouraged by the lack of fish in their nets and the sustained confusion as to Jesus' death, even after the resurrection appearances. Jesus comes to them at this time and tells them to cast their net on the "right side of the boat." When they hauled in the large catch, they were reminded of a similar incident which had occurred earlier in Jesus' ministry (recorded in Luke 5:1–10). The miracle of this great catch and its connection to the earlier event caused John to recognize Jesus as the figure on the beach. Jesus continued to appear to his disciples to comfort and encourage them. Jesus has this same kind of concern for all his followers. Let us take comfort in God's care when troubled times come.*

The Power of God's Word/ Hebrews 4:7–13

Therefore God again set a certain day, calling it Today, when a long time later he spoke through David, as was said before:

> "Today, if you hear his voice,
>   do not harden your hearts."

8For if Joshua had given them rest, God would not have spoken later about another day. 9There remains, then, a Sabbath-rest for the people of God; 10for anyone who enters God's rest also rests from his own work, just as God did from his. 11Let us, therefore, make every effort to enter that rest, so that no one will fall by following their example of disobedience.

12For the word of God is living and active. Sharper than any double-edged sword, it penetrates even to dividing soul and spirit, joints and marrow; it judges the thoughts and attitudes of the heart. 13Nothing in all creation is hidden from God's sight. Everything is uncovered and laid bare before the eyes of him to whom we must give account.

A THOUGHT: *The Word of God is not merely words from God, a vehicle for communicating ideas; it is living, life-changing, and dynamic as it works in us. With the incisiveness of a surgeon's knife, it reveals who we are and what we are not. It discerns what is within us, both good and evil. We must not only listen to the Word; we must let it shape our lives.*

Proverbs for Today/ 24:9–10

The schemes of folly are sin, and men detest a mocker. □ If you falter in times of trouble, how small is your strength!

SEPTEMBER 30

Jesus Commands Peter to Feed His Sheep/ John 21:15–25

When they had finished eating, Jesus said to Simon Peter, "Simon son of John, do you truly love me more than these?"

"Yes, Lord," he said, "you know that I love you."

Jesus said, "Feed my lambs."

16Again Jesus said, "Simon son of John, do you truly love me?"

He answered, "Yes, Lord, you know that I love you."

Jesus said, "Take care of my sheep."

17The third time he said to him, "Simon son of John, do you love me?"

Peter was hurt because Jesus asked him the third time, "Do you love me?" He said, "Lord, you know all things; you know that I love you."

Jesus said, "Feed my sheep. 18I tell you the truth, when you were younger you dressed yourself and went where you wanted; but when you are old you will stretch out your hands, and someone else will dress you and lead you where you do not want to go." 19Jesus said this to indicate the kind of death by which Peter would glorify God. Then he said to him, "Follow me!"

20Peter turned and saw that the disciple whom Jesus loved was following them. (This was the one who had leaned back against Jesus at the supper and had said, "Lord, who is going to betray you?") 21When Peter saw him, he asked, "Lord, what about him?"

22Jesus answered, "If I want him to remain alive until I return, what is that to you? You must follow me." 23Because of this, the rumor spread among the brothers that this disciple would not die. But Jesus did not say that he would not die; he only said, "If I want him to remain alive until I return, what is that to you?"

24This is the disciple who testifies to these things and who wrote them down. We know that his testimony is true.

25Jesus did many other things as well. If every one of them were written down, I suppose that even the whole world would not have room for the books that would be written.

A THOUGHT: *Jesus asked Peter three times if he loved him. The first time Jesus said, "Do you truly love [the Greek word here is* **agape**, *signifying volitional, self-sacrificial love] me more than these?" The second time, Jesus focused on Peter alone and still used the Greek word* **agape**. *The third time, Jesus used the Greek word* **phileo**, *[signifying friendship, affection, affinity, or brotherly love] and again asked, "Do you love me?" Each time Peter responded with the Greek word* **phileo**. *Jesus doesn't settle for quick, superficial answers. He has a way of getting to the heart of the matter. Peter had to face his true feelings and motives when confronted by Christ. How would you respond if Jesus asked you, "Do you love me?" Do you love Jesus in a selfless and sacrificial way? Do you even love him as a friend?*

Jesus Understands Our Weaknesses/ Hebrews 4:14—5:6

Therefore, since we have a great high priest who has gone through the heavens, Jesus the Son of God, let us hold firmly to the faith we profess. 15For we do not have a high priest who is unable to sympathize with our weaknesses, but we have one who has been tempted in every way, just as we are—yet was without sin. 16Let us then approach the throne of grace with confidence, so that we may receive mercy and find grace to help us in our time of need.

5:1Every high priest is selected from among men and is appointed to represent them in matters related to God, to offer gifts and sacrifices for sins. 2He is able to deal gently with those who are ignorant and are going astray, since he himself is subject to weakness. 3This is why he has to offer sacrifices for his own sins, as well as for the sins of the people.

4No one takes this honor upon himself; he must be called by God, just as Aaron was. 5So Christ also did not take upon himself the glory of becoming a high priest. But God said to him,

> "You are my Son;
>   today I have become your Father."

6And he says in another place,

> "You are a priest forever,
>   in the order of Melchizedek."

A THOUGHT: *Jesus is like us because he experienced every kind of temptation we experience today. But he is different because, although he was tempted, he never sinned. Jesus is the only human being who has ever lived without committing sin. Now in heaven, he completely understands our weaknesses and temptations and offers forgiveness.*

Proverbs for Today/ 24:11–12

Rescue those being led away to death; hold back those staggering toward slaughter. If you say, "But we knew nothing about this," does not he who weighs the heart perceive it? Does not he who guards your life know it? Will he not repay each person according to what he has done?

OCTOBER 1

Jesus Ascends to Heaven/ Acts 1:1–13

In my former book, Theophilus, I wrote about all that Jesus began to do and to teach 2until the day he was taken up to heaven, after giving instructions through the Holy Spirit to the apostles he had chosen. 3After his suffering, he showed himself to these men and gave many convincing proofs that he was alive. He appeared to them over a period of forty days and spoke about the kingdom of God. 4On one occasion, while he was eating with them, he gave them this command: "Do not leave Jerusalem, but wait for the gift my Father promised, which you have heard me speak about. 5For John baptized with water, but in a few days you will be baptized with the Holy Spirit."

6So when they met together, they asked him, "Lord, are you at this time going to restore the kingdom to Israel?"

7He said to them: "It is not for you to know the times or dates the Father has set by his own authority. 8But you will receive power when the Holy Spirit comes on you; and you will be my witnesses in Jerusalem, and in all Judea and Samaria, and to the ends of the earth."

9After he said this, he was taken up before their very eyes, and a cloud hid him from their sight.

10They were looking intently up into the sky as he was going, when suddenly two men dressed in white stood beside them. 11"Men of Galilee," they said, "why do you stand here looking into the sky? This same Jesus, who has been taken from you into heaven, will come back in the same way you have seen him go into heaven."

12Then they returned to Jerusalem from the hill called the Mount of Olives, a Sabbath day's walk from the city. 13When they arrived, they went upstairs to the room where they were staying. Those present were Peter, John, James and Andrew; Philip and Thomas, Bartholomew and Matthew; James son of Alphaeus and Simon the Zealot, and Judas son of James.

A THOUGHT: *After 40 days with his disciples, Jesus ascended into heaven. Two angels proclaimed to the disciples that one day Jesus would return in the same way he went—bodily and visibly. History is not haphazard; it is moving toward a specific point—the return of Jesus to judge and rule over the earth. We should be ready for his sudden return, not by standing around "looking intently up into the sky," but by working hard to share the gospel so others will be able to share in God's great blessings.*

Jesus Learned Obedience through Suffering/ Hebrews 5:7–10

During the days of Jesus' life on earth, he offered up prayers and petitions with loud cries and tears to the one who could save him from death, and he was heard because of his reverent submission. 8Although he was a son, he learned obedience from what he suffered 9and, once made perfect, he became the source of eternal salvation for all who obey him 10and was designated by God to be high priest in the order of Melchizedek.

A THOUGHT: *Jesus found no pleasure in suffering and dying, but he chose to endure pain and humiliation in order to obey his Father. At times we will choose to undergo trials, not because we want to suffer, but because we want to obey God. Let Jesus' obedience sustain you and encourage you in times of trial. You can face anything when you know Jesus Christ is with you.*

Proverbs for Today/ 24:13–14

Eat honey, my son, for it is good; honey from the comb is sweet to your taste. Know also that wisdom is sweet to your soul; if you find it, there is a future hope for you, and your hope will not be cut off.

OCTOBER 2

Matthias Chosen to Be an Apostle/ Acts 1:14–26

They all joined together constantly in prayer, along with the women and Mary the mother of Jesus, and with his brothers.

15In those days Peter stood up among the believers (a group numbering about a hundred and twenty) 16and said, "Brothers, the Scripture had to be fulfilled which the Holy Spirit spoke long ago through the mouth of David concerning Judas, who served as guide for those who arrested Jesus— 17he was one of our number and shared in this ministry."

18(With the reward he got for his wickedness, Judas bought a field; there he fell headlong, his body burst open and all his intestines spilled out. 19Everyone in Jerusalem heard about this, so they called that field in their language Akeldama, that is, Field of Blood.)

20"For," said Peter, "it is written in the book of Psalms,

" 'May his place be deserted;
let there be no one to dwell in it,'

and,

" 'May another take his place of leadership.'

21Therefore it is necessary to choose one of the men who have been with us the whole time the Lord Jesus went in and out among us, 22beginning from John's baptism to the time when Jesus was taken up from us. For one of these must become a witness with us of his resurrection."

23So they proposed two men: Joseph called Barsabbas (also known as Justus) and Matthias. 24Then they prayed,

"Lord, you know everyone's heart. Show us which of these two you have chosen ²⁵to take over this apostolic ministry, which Judas left to go where he belongs." ²⁶Then they cast lots, and the lot fell to Matthias; so he was added to the eleven apostles.

A THOUGHT: *The apostles had to choose a replacement for Judas Iscariot. They outlined specific criteria for making the choice. When the "finalists" had been chosen, the apostles prayed, asking God to guide the selection process. This gives us a good example of how to proceed when we are making important decisions. Set up criteria consistent with the Bible, examine the alternatives, and pray for wisdom and guidance to reach a wise decision.*

Maturity Versus Immaturity/ Hebrews 5:11–14

We have much to say about this, but it is hard to explain because you are slow to learn. ¹²In fact, though by this time you ought to be teachers, you need someone to teach you the elementary truths of God's word all over again. You need milk, not solid food! ¹³Anyone who lives on milk, being still an infant, is not acquainted with the teaching about righteousness. ¹⁴But solid food is for the mature, who by constant use have trained themselves to distinguish good from evil.

A THOUGHT: *In order to grow from a "baby" Christian to a "grown-up" Christian, we must learn discernment. By practice and exercise, we must train our consciences, our senses, our minds, and our bodies to distinguish right from wrong. Can you recognize temptation before it controls you? Can you tell correct uses of Scripture from mistaken or shallow uses?*

Proverbs for Today/ 24:15–16

Do not lie in wait like an outlaw against a righteous man's house, do not raid his dwelling place; for though a righteous man falls seven times, he rises again, but the wicked are brought down by calamity.

OCTOBER 3

The Coming of the Holy Spirit/ Acts 2:1–13

When the day of Pentecost came, they [the believers] were all together in one place. ²Suddenly a sound like the blowing of a violent wind came from heaven and filled the whole house where they were sitting. ³They saw what seemed to be tongues of fire that separated and came to rest on each of them. ⁴All of them were filled with the Holy Spirit and began to speak in other tongues as the Spirit enabled them.

⁵Now there were staying in Jerusalem God-fearing Jews from every nation under heaven. ⁶When they heard this sound, a crowd came together in bewilderment, because each one heard them speaking in his own language. ⁷Utterly amazed, they asked: "Are not all these men who are speaking Galileans? ⁸Then how is it that each of us hears them in his own native language? ⁹Parthians, Medes and Elamites; residents of Mesopotamia, Judea and Cappadocia, Pontus and Asia, ¹⁰Phrygia and Pamphylia, Egypt and the parts of Libya near Cyrene; visitors from Rome ¹¹(both Jews and converts to Judaism); Cretans and Arabs—we hear them declaring the wonders of God in our own tongues!" ¹²Amazed and perplexed, they asked one another, "What does this mean?"

¹³Some, however, made fun of them and said, "They have had too much wine."

A THOUGHT: *God made his presence known to this group of believers in a spectacular way—roaring wind, fire, and his Holy Spirit. Would you like God to reveal himself to you in such recognizable ways? Beware of forcing your expectations on God. Elijah, the great prophet of the Old Testament, also needed a message from God. There was a mighty wind, then an earthquake, and finally a fire. But God's message came in a gentle whisper. God may use dramatic methods to work in your life—or he may speak in gentle whispers. Wait patiently and always listen for him.*

Going Beyond Elementary Principles/ Hebrews 6:1–6

Therefore let us leave the elementary teachings about Christ and go on to maturity, not laying again the foundation of repentance from acts that lead to death, and of faith in

God, ²instruction about baptisms, the laying on of hands, the resurrection of the dead, and eternal judgment. ³And God permitting, we will do so.

⁴It is impossible for those who have once been enlightened, who have tasted the heavenly gift, who have shared in the Holy Spirit, ⁵who have tasted the goodness of the word of God and the powers of the coming age, ⁶if they fall away, to be brought back to repentance, because to their loss they are crucifying the Son of God all over again and subjecting him to public disgrace.

A THOUGHT: *Certain basics are essential for all believers. Those principles that all Christians must know include repentance, baptism, faith, etc. We need to move on to a more complete theology, to a more profound understanding of the faith. Christians should be teaching new Christians the basics, and then, acting on what they know; new Christians should be learning even more from God's Word.*

Proverbs for Today/ 24:17–20

Do not gloat when your enemy falls; when he stumbles, do not let your heart rejoice, or the LORD will see and disapprove and turn his wrath away from him. Do not fret because of evil men or be envious of the wicked, for the evil man has no future hope, and the lamp of the wicked will be snuffed out.

OCTOBER 4

Peter's Pentecost Sermon/ Acts 2:14–39

Then Peter stood up with the Eleven, raised his voice and addressed the crowd: "Fellow Jews and all of you who live in Jerusalem, let me explain this to you; listen carefully to what I say. ¹⁵These men are not drunk, as you suppose. It's only nine in the morning! ¹⁶No, this is what was spoken by the prophet Joel:

¹⁷" 'In the last days, God says,
    I will pour out my Spirit on all people.
  Your sons and daughters will prophesy,
    your young men will see visions,

your old men will dream dreams.
18Even on my servants, both men and women,
I will pour out my Spirit in those days,
and they will prophesy.
19I will show wonders in the heaven above
and signs on the earth below,
blood and fire and billows of smoke.
20The sun will be turned to darkness
and the moon to blood
before the coming of the great and glorious day of
the Lord.
21And everyone who calls
on the name of the Lord will be saved.'

22"Men of Israel, listen to this: Jesus of Nazareth was a man accredited by God to you by miracles, wonders and signs, which God did among you through him, as you yourselves know. 23This man was handed over to you by God's set purpose and foreknowledge; and you, with the help of wicked men, put him to death by nailing him to the cross. 24But God raised him from the dead, freeing him from the agony of death, because it was impossible for death to keep its hold on him. 25David said about him:

" 'I saw the Lord always before me.
Because he is at my right hand,
I will not be shaken.
26Therefore my heart is glad and my tongue rejoices;
my body also will live in hope,
27because you will not abandon me to the grave,
nor will you let your Holy One see decay.
28You have made known to me the paths of life;
you will fill me with joy in your presence.'

29"Brothers, I can tell you confidently that the patriarch David died and was buried, and his tomb is here to this day. 30But he was a prophet and knew that God had promised him on oath that he would place one of his descendants on his throne. 31Seeing what was ahead, he spoke of the resurrection of the Christ, that he was not abandoned to the grave, nor did his body see decay. 32God has raised this Jesus to life, and we are all witnesses of the fact. 33Exalted to the right hand of God, he has received from the Father the promised Holy Spirit and has poured out what you now see and hear. ³⁴For David did not ascend to heaven, and yet he said,

"'The Lord said to my Lord:
"Sit at my right hand
³⁵until I make your enemies
a footstool for your feet."'

³⁶"Therefore let all Israel be assured of this: God has made this Jesus, whom you crucified, both Lord and Christ."

³⁷When the people heard this, they were cut to the heart and said to Peter and the other apostles, "Brothers, what shall we do?"

³⁸Peter replied, "Repent and be baptized, every one of you, in the name of Jesus Christ for the forgiveness of your sins. And you will receive the gift of the Holy Spirit. ³⁹The promise is for you and your children and for all who are far off—for all whom the Lord our God will call."

A THOUGHT: *Peter had been an unstable leader during Jesus' ministry, letting his bravado be his downfall, even denying that he knew Jesus. But Christ forgave him and restored him after his denial. This is a new Peter, humble but bold. His confidence comes from the Holy Spirit, who makes him a powerful and dynamic speaker. Have you ever felt as if you've made such bad mistakes that God could never forgive and use you? No matter what sins you have committed, if you genuinely admit your sins to God and turn away from those sins, he promises to forgive them and make you useful for his kingdom. Allow him to forgive you and effectively use you in service for him.*

The Example of Abraham/ Hebrews 6:7–15

Land that drinks in the rain often falling on it and that produces a crop useful to those for whom it is farmed receives the blessing of God. ⁸But land that produces thorns and thistles is worthless and is in danger of being cursed. In the end it will be burned.

⁹Even though we speak like this, dear friends, we are confident of better things in your case—things that accompany salvation. ¹⁰God is not unjust; he will not forget your work and the love you have shown him as you have helped his people and continue to help them. ¹¹We want each of you to show this same diligence to the very end, in order to make your hope sure. ¹²We do not want you to become

lazy, but to imitate those who through faith and patience inherit what has been promised.

13When God made his promise to Abraham, since there was no one greater for him to swear by, he swore by himself, 14saying, "I will surely bless you and give you many descendants." 15And so after waiting patiently, Abraham received what was promised.

A THOUGHT: *In the midst of difficult times we must remember God's promises. Abraham serves as an example of steadfast faith. God had promised Abraham that he would be the father of a great nation. Abraham waited patiently for many years until the birth of his son Isaac. Even this great event was marked by Abraham's faith, for Abraham trusted that God would keep his promise to make him the father of a great nation even though he could only "see it" by faith. He saw in Isaac the fulfillment of the promise which was to come. Our faith in God must be based on what God has done in the past. We trust God because he has been faithful to fulfill his promises to his people.*

Proverbs for Today/ 24:21–22

Fear the LORD and the king, my son, and do not join with the rebellious, for those two will send sudden destruction upon them, and who knows what calamities they can bring?

OCTOBER 5

The Fellowship of the Jerusalem Church/
Acts 2:40–47

With many other words he [Peter] warned them; and he pleaded with them, "Save yourselves from this corrupt generation." 41Those who accepted his message were baptized, and about three thousand were added to their number that day.

42They devoted themselves to the apostles' teaching and to the fellowship, to the breaking of bread and to prayer. 43Everyone was filled with awe, and many wonders and miraculous signs were done by the apostles. 44All the believers were together and had everything in common. 45Selling their possessions and goods, they gave to anyone as he had need. 46Every day they continued to meet together in the temple courts. They broke bread in their homes and ate together with glad and sincere hearts, [47]praising God and enjoying the favor of all the people. And the Lord added to their number daily those who were being saved.

A THOUGHT: *Because they recognized other believers as brothers and sisters in the family of God, the Christians in Jerusalem shared all they had so that all could benefit from God's blessings. It is tempting—especially if we have material wealth—to cut ourselves off from one another, each taking care of his own, each providing for and enjoying his own little piece of the world. But as part of God's spiritual family, we have a responsibility to help one another in every way possible. God's family works best when its members work together.*

Assurance of God's Promises/ Hebrews 6:16–20

Men swear by someone greater than themselves, and the oath confirms what is said and puts an end to all argument. [17]Because God wanted to make the unchanging nature of his purpose very clear to the heirs of what was promised, he confirmed it with an oath. [18]God did this so that, by two unchangeable things in which it is impossible for God to lie, we who have fled to take hold of the hope offered to us may be greatly encouraged. [19]We have this hope as an anchor for the soul, firm and secure. It enters the inner sanctuary behind the curtain, [20]where Jesus, who went before us, has entered on our behalf. He has become a high priest forever, in the order of Melchizedek.

A THOUGHT: *God's promises are unchangeable and trustworthy because God is unchangeable and trustworthy. When God promised Abraham a son, he took an oath in his own name. The oath was as good as his name, and his name was as good as his divine nature. God embodies all truth, and he therefore cannot lie. Because God is truth, you can be secure in his promises; you don't need to wonder if he will change his plans. For the true seeker who comes to God in belief, God gives an unconditional promise of acceptance. When you ask God in all openness, honesty, and sincerity of heart to save you from your sins, he will do it. This assurance should give you courage and hope.*

Proverbs for Today/ 24:23–25

These also are sayings of the wise: To show partiality in judging is not good: Whoever says to the guilty, "You are innocent"—peoples will curse him and nations denounce him. But it will go well with those who convict the guilty, and rich blessing will come upon them.

OCTOBER 6

Peter Heals a Crippled Man/ Acts 3:1–26

One day Peter and John were going up to the temple at the time of prayer—at three in the afternoon. 2Now a man crippled from birth was being carried to the temple gate called Beautiful, where he was put every day to beg from those going into the temple courts. 3When he saw Peter and John about to enter, he asked them for money. 4Peter looked straight at him, as did John. Then Peter said, "Look at us!" 5So the man gave them his attention, expecting to get something from them.

6Then Peter said, "Silver or gold I do not have, but what I have I give you. In the name of Jesus Christ of Nazareth, walk." 7Taking him by the right hand, he helped him up, and instantly the man's feet and ankles became strong. 8He jumped to his feet and began to walk. Then he went with them into the temple courts, walking and jumping, and praising God. 9When all the people saw him walking and praising God, 10they recognized him as the same man who used to sit begging at the temple gate called Beautiful, and they were filled with wonder and amazement at what had happened to him.

11While the beggar held on to Peter and John, all the people were astonished and came running to them in the place called Solomon's Colonnade. 12When Peter saw this, he said to them: "Men of Israel, why does this surprise you? Why do you stare at us as if by our own power or godliness we had made this man walk? 13The God of Abraham, Isaac and Jacob, the God of our fathers, has glorified his servant Jesus. You handed him over to be killed, and you disowned him before Pilate, though he had decided to let him go. 14You disowned the Holy and Righteous One and asked that a murderer be released to you. 15You killed the author of life, but God raised him from the dead. We are witnesses of this. [16]By faith in the name of Jesus, this man whom you see and know was made strong. It is Jesus' name and the faith that comes through him that has given this complete healing to him, as you can all see.

[17]"Now, brothers, I know that you acted in ignorance, as did your leaders. [18]But this is how God fulfilled what he had foretold through all the prophets, saying that his Christ would suffer. [19]Repent, then, and turn to God, so that your sins may be wiped out, that times of refreshing may come from the Lord, [20]and that he may send the Christ, who has been appointed for you—even Jesus. [21]He must remain in heaven until the time comes for God to restore everything, as he promised long ago through his holy prophets. [22]For Moses said, 'The Lord your God will raise up for you a prophet like me from among your own people; you must listen to everything he tells you. [23]Anyone who does not listen to him will be completely cut off from among his people.'

[24]"Indeed, all the prophets from Samuel on, as many as have spoken, have foretold these days. [25]And you are heirs of the prophets and of the covenant God made with your fathers. He said to Abraham, 'Through your offspring all peoples on earth will be blessed.' [26]When God raised up his servant, he sent him first to you to bless you by turning each of you from your wicked ways."

A THOUGHT: *When we repent, God promises not only to wipe away our sin, but to bring spiritual refreshment. Repentance may at first seem painful because it is hard to give up certain sins. But if you seek God, he will give you a better way. As Hosea promised, "Let us acknowledge the LORD; let us press on to acknowledge him. As surely as the sun rises, he will appear; he will come to us like the winter rains, like the spring rains that water the earth." (Hosea 6:3). Do you feel a need to be refreshed?*

Melchizedek Greater Than the Levites/ Hebrews 7:1–11

This Melchizedek was king of Salem and priest of God Most High. He met Abraham returning from the defeat of the kings and blessed him, [2]and Abraham gave him a tenth of everything. First, his name means "king of righteousness"; then also, "king of Salem" means "king of peace." [3]Without father or mother, without genealogy, without beginning of days or end of life, like the Son of God he remains a priest forever.

4Just think how great he was: Even the patriarch Abraham gave him a tenth of the plunder! 5Now the law requires the descendants of Levi who become priests to collect a tenth from the people—that is, their brothers—even though their brothers are descended from Abraham. 6This man, however, did not trace his descent from Levi, yet he collected a tenth from Abraham and blessed him who had the promises. 7And without doubt the lesser person is blessed by the greater. 8In the one case, the tenth is collected by men who die; but in the other case, by him who is declared to be living. 9One might even say that Levi, who collects the tenth, paid the tenth through Abraham, 10because when Melchizedek met Abraham, Levi was still in the body of his ancestor.

11If perfection could have been attained through the Levitical priesthood (for on the basis of it the law was given to the people), why was there still need for another priest to come—one in the order of Melchizedek, not in the order of Aaron?

A THOUGHT: *The writer of Hebrews uses this story about Melchizedek to show that there is someone greater even than Abraham, father of the Jewish nation, and Levi (Abraham's descendant). Therefore, the Jewish priesthood (made up of Levi's descendants) was inferior to Melchizedek's priesthood (a type of Christ's priesthood). In Psalm 110:4, Melchizedek is said to be a priest forever, because his priesthood has no record of beginning or end—he was a priest of God in Salem (Jerusalem) long before the nation of Israel and the Levitical system began. Christ is the culmination of Melchizedek's priesthood—Jesus is the ultimate High Priest; there is no greater priest.*

Proverbs for Today/ 24:26

An honest answer is like a kiss on the lips.

OCTOBER 7

Peter's Defense Before the Sanhedrin/ Acts 4:1–22

The priests and the captain of the temple guard and the Sadducees came up to Peter and John while they were speaking to the people. ²They were greatly disturbed because the apostles were teaching the people and proclaiming in Jesus the resurrection of the dead. ³They seized Peter and John, and because it was evening, they put them in jail until the next day. ⁴But many who heard the message believed, and the number of men grew to about five thousand.

⁵The next day the rulers, elders and teachers of the law met in Jerusalem. ⁶Annas the high priest was there, and so were Caiaphas, John, Alexander and the other men of the high priest's family. ⁷They had Peter and John brought before them and began to question them: "By what power or what name did you do this?"

⁸Then Peter, filled with the Holy Spirit, said to them: "Rulers and elders of the people! ⁹If we are being called to account today for an act of kindness shown to a cripple and are asked how he was healed, ¹⁰then know this, you and all the people of Israel: It is by the name of Jesus Christ of Nazareth, whom you crucified but whom God raised from the dead, that this man stands before you healed. ¹¹He is

" 'the stone you builders rejected,
which has become the capstone.'

¹²Salvation is found in no one else, for there is no other name under heaven given to men by which we must be saved."

¹³When they saw the courage of Peter and John and realized that they were unschooled, ordinary men, they were astonished and they took note that these men had been with Jesus. ¹⁴But since they could see the man who had been healed standing there with them, there was nothing they could say. ¹⁵So they ordered them to withdraw from the Sanhedrin and then conferred together. ¹⁶"What are we going to do with these men?" they asked.

"Everybody living in Jerusalem knows they have done an outstanding miracle, we cannot deny it. 17But to stop this thing from spreading any further among the people, we must warn these men to speak no longer to anyone in this name."

18Then they called them in again and commanded them not to speak or teach at all in the name of Jesus. 19But Peter and John replied, "Judge for yourselves whether it is right in God's sight to obey you rather than God. 20For we cannot help speaking about what we have seen and heard."

21After further threats they let them go. They could not decide how to punish them, because all the people were praising God for what had happened. 22For the man who was miraculously healed was over forty years old.

A THOUGHT: *Not often will our witnessing send us to prison as it did Peter and John. Still, we run risks in trying to win others to Christ. We might be willing to face a night in prison if it would bring 2,000 people to Christ, but shouldn't we also be willing to suffer for even one? What do you risk in witnessing—vulnerability, rejection, persecution? We are sometimes afraid to share our faith in God because people might feel uncomfortable and disapprove. But Peter and John's zeal for the Lord was so strong that they could not keep quiet, even when threatened. If your courage to witness for God has weakened, pray that your boldness may increase. Whatever the risks, realize that nothing done for God is ever wasted. Remember Jesus' promise, "Whoever acknowledges me before men, I will also acknowledge him before my Father in heaven." (Matthew 10:32).*

Jesus a High Priest Like Melchizedek/ Hebrews 7:12–22

For when there is a change of the priesthood, there must also be a change of the law. 13He of whom these things are said belonged to a different tribe, and no one from that tribe has ever served at the altar. 14For it is clear that our Lord descended from Judah, and in regard to that tribe Moses said nothing about priests. 15And what we have said is even more clear if another priest like Melchizedek appears, 16one who has become a priest not on the basis of a regulation as to his ancestry but on the basis of the power of an indestructible life. 17For it is declared:

"You are a priest forever,
in the order of Melchizedek."

18The former regulation is set aside because it was weak

and useless [19](for the law made nothing perfect), and a better hope is introduced, by which we draw near to God.

[20]And it was not without an oath! Others became priests without any oath, [21]but he became a priest with an oath when God said to him:

> "The Lord has sworn
>   and will not change his mind:
> 'You are a priest forever.' "

[22]Because of this oath, Jesus has become the guarantee of a better covenant.

A THOUGHT: *Jesus' high-priestly role was superior to that of any priest of Levi, because the Messiah was a priest of a higher rank. The animal sacrifices under the old covenant had to be repeated, and they offered only temporary forgiveness; Christ's sacrifice was offered once, and it offers total and permanent forgiveness. Under the new covenant, the Levitical priesthood was cancelled in favor of Christ's role as High Priest.*

Proverbs for Today/ 24:27

Finish your outdoor work and get your fields ready; after that, build your house.

OCTOBER 8

The Jerusalem Believers' Prayer/ Acts 4:23–37

On their release, Peter and John went back to their own people and reported all that the chief priests and elders had said to them. [24]When they heard this, they raised their voices together in prayer to God. "Sovereign Lord," they said, "you made the heaven and the earth and the sea, and everything in them. [25]You spoke by the Holy Spirit through the mouth of your servant, our father David:

> " 'Why do the nations rage
>   and the peoples plot in vain?
> [26]The kings of the earth take their stand
>   and the rulers gather together
> against the Lord
>   and against his Anointed One. '

27Indeed Herod and Pontius Pilate met together with the Gentiles and the people of Israel in this city to conspire against your holy servant Jesus, whom you anointed. 28They did what your power and will had decided beforehand should happen. 29Now, Lord, consider their threats and enable your servants to speak your word with great boldness. 30Stretch out your hand to heal and perform miraculous signs and wonders through the name of your holy servant Jesus."

31After they prayed, the place where they were meeting was shaken. And they were all filled with the Holy Spirit and spoke the word of God boldly.

32All the believers were one in heart and mind. No one claimed that any of his possessions was his own, but they shared everything they had. 33With great power the apostles continued to testify to the resurrection of the Lord Jesus, and much grace was upon them all. 34There were no needy persons among them. For from time to time those who owned lands or houses sold them, brought the money from the sales 35and put it at the apostles' feet, and it was distributed to anyone as he had need.

36Joseph, a Levite from Cyprus, whom the apostles called Barnabas (which means Son of Encouragement), 37sold a field he owned and brought the money and put it at the apostles' feet.

A THOUGHT: *Notice how the believers prayed. First they praised God; then they told God their specific problem and asked for his help. They did not ask God to remove the problem, but to help them deal with it. This is a model for us to follow when we pray. We may ask God to remove our problems, and he may choose to do so, but we must recognize that often he will leave the problem in place and give us the grace to deal with it.*

Jesus a Priest Forever/ Hebrews 7:23–28

Now there have been many of those priests, since death prevented them from continuing in office; 24but because Jesus lives forever, he has a permanent priesthood. 25Therefore he is able to save completely those who come to God through him, because he always lives to intercede for them.

26Such a high priest meets our need—one who is holy, blameless, pure, set apart from sinners, exalted above the heavens. 27Unlike the other high priests, he does not need to offer sacrifices day after day, first for his own sins, and then for the sins of the people. He sacrificed for their sins once for all when he offered himself. 28For the law appoints as high priests men who are weak; but the oath, which came after the law, appointed the Son, who has been made perfect forever.

A THOUGHT: *What does it mean that Jesus is able to save completely? No one else can add to what Jesus did to save us; our past, present, and future sins are all forgiven. As our High Priest, Christ is our advocate, the mediator between us and God. The Old Testament High Priest went before God once a year to plead for the forgiveness of the nation's sins; Christ makes perpetual intercession before God for us. Christ's presence in heaven with the Father assures us that our sins have been paid for and forgiven. If you are a Christian, remember that Christ has paid the price for your sins once and for all.*

Proverbs for Today/ 24:28–29

Do not testify against your neighbor without cause, or use your lips to deceive. Do not say, "I'll do to him as he has done to me; I'll pay that man back for what he did."

OCTOBER 9

Ananias and Sapphira Judged/ Acts 5:1–11

Now a man named Ananias, together with his wife Sapphira, also sold a piece of property. 2With his wife's full knowledge he kept back part of the money for himself, but brought the rest and put it at the apostles' feet.

3Then Peter said, "Ananias, how is it that Satan has so filled your heart that you have lied to the Holy Spirit and have kept for yourself some of the money you received for the land? 4Didn't it belong to you before it was sold? And after it was sold, wasn't the money at your disposal? What made you think of doing such a thing? You have not lied to men but to God."

5When Ananias heard this, he fell down and died. And great fear seized all who heard what had happened. 6Then the young men came forward, wrapped up his body, and carried him out and buried him.

7About three hours later his wife came in, not knowing what had happened. 8Peter asked her, "Tell me, is this the price you and Ananias got for the land?"

"Yes," she said, "that is the price."

9Peter said to her, "How could you agree to test the Spirit of the Lord? Look! The feet of the men who buried your husband are at the door, and they will carry you out also."

10At that moment she fell down at his feet and died. Then the young men came in and, finding her dead, carried her out and buried her beside her husband. 11Great fear seized the whole church and all who heard about these events.

A THOUGHT: *The sin Ananias and Sapphira committed was not stinginess or holding back part of the money—they could choose whether or not to sell the land they owned and how much money to give. Their sin was lying to God and God's people—saying they gave the whole amount but holding back some for themselves, trying to make themselves appear more generous than they really were. This act was judged harshly because dishonesty and covetousness are destructive in a church and prevent the Holy Spirit from working effectively. When we lie to try to deceive God and his people about our relationship with him, we destroy our testimony for Christ.*

Christ, the Priest of a New Covenant/ Hebrews 8:1–6

The point of what we are saying is this: We do have such a high priest, who sat down at the right hand of the throne of the Majesty in heaven, 2and who serves in the sanctuary, the true tabernacle set up by the Lord, not by man.

3Every high priest is appointed to offer both gifts and sacrifices, and so it was necessary for this one also to have something to offer. 4If he were on earth, he would not be a priest, for there are already men who offer the gifts prescribed by the law. 5They serve at a sanctuary that is a copy and shadow of what is in heaven. This is why Moses was warned when he was about to build the tabernacle: "See to it that you make everything according to the pattern shown you on the mountain." 6But the ministry Jesus has received is as superior to theirs as the covenant of which he is mediator is superior to the old one, and it is founded on better promises.

A THOUGHT: *This new covenant or new testament is new in allowing us to go directly to God through Christ, no longer having to rely on sacrificed animals and priests to gain God's forgiveness. This new arrangement is better because, while priests died, Christ lives forever. Priests and sacrifices could not save people, but Christ truly saves.*

Proverbs for Today/ 24:30–34

I went past the field of the sluggard, past the vineyard of the man who lacks judgment; thorns had come up everywhere, the ground was covered with weeds, and the stone wall was in ruins. I applied my heart to what I observed and learned a lesson from what I saw: A little sleep, a little slumber, a little folding of the hands to rest—and poverty will come on you like a bandit and scarcity like an armed man.

OCTOBER 10

An Angel Rescues the Apostles from Jail/ Acts 5:12–25

The apostles performed many miraculous signs and wonders among the people. And all the believers used to meet together in Solomon's Colonnade. 13No one else dared join them, even though they were highly regarded by the people. 14Nevertheless, more and more men and women believed in the Lord and were added to their number. 15As a result, people brought the sick into the streets and laid them on beds and mats so that at least Peter's shadow might fall on some of them as he passed by. 16Crowds gathered also from the towns around Jerusalem, bringing their sick and those tormented by evil spirits, and all of them were healed.

17Then the high priest and all his associates, who were members of the party of the Sadducees, were filled with jealousy. 18They arrested the apostles and put them in the public jail. 19But during the night an angel of the Lord opened the doors of the jail and brought them out. 20"Go, stand in the temple courts," he said, "and tell the people the full message of this new life."

21At daybreak they entered the temple courts, as they had been told, and began to teach the people.

When the high priest and his associates arrived, they called together the Sanhedrin—the full assembly of the elders of Israel—and sent to the jail for the apostles. 22But on arriving at the jail, the officers did not find them there. So they went back and reported, 23"We found the jail securely locked, with the guards standing at the doors; but when we opened them, we found no one inside." 24On hearing this report, the captain of the temple guard and the chief priests were puzzled, wondering what would come of this.

25Then someone came and said, "Look! The men you put in jail are standing in the temple courts teaching the people."

A THOUGHT: *The apostles had power to do miracles, great boldness in preaching, and God's presence in their lives; yet they were not free from being hated and persecuted. They were arrested and put in jail, beaten with rods and whips, and slandered by community leaders. Faith in God does not make troubles disappear; it makes troubles appear less fearsome because it puts them in the right perspective. You cannot expect everyone to react favorably when you share something as dynamic as your faith in Christ. Some will be jealous of you, frightened, or threatened. Expect some negative reactions. But remember that you must be more concerned about God's reactions than the reactions of other people.*

The Old Covenant Versus the New Covenant/ Hebrews 8:7–13

For if there had been nothing wrong with that first covenant, no place would have been sought for another. 8But God found fault with the people and said:

> "The time is coming, declares the Lord,
>   when I will make a new covenant
> with the house of Israel
>   and with the house of Judah.
> 9It will not be like the covenant
>   I made with their forefathers
> when I took them by the hand
>   to lead them out of Egypt,
> because they did not remain faithful to my
>   covenant,
>   and I turned away from them,
>   declares the Lord.

¹⁰This is the covenant I will make with the house of
Israel
   after that time, declares the Lord.
 I will put my laws in their minds
   and write them on their hearts.
 I will be their God,
   and they will be my people.
¹¹No longer will a man teach his neighbor,
   or a man his brother, saying, 'Know the Lord,'
 because they will all know me,
   from the least of them to the greatest.
¹²For I will forgive their wickedness
   and will remember their sins no more."

¹³By calling this covenant "new," he has made the first
one obsolete; and what is obsolete and aging will soon
disappear.

A THOUGHT: *In this passage the writer quotes from Jeremiah 31:31–34
to compare the new covenant with the old. The old covenant was a
covenant of law between God and Israel. The new and better way
is the covenant of grace—Christ's offer to forgive our sins and bring
us to God through his sacrificial death. This covenant is new in
extent—it goes beyond Israel and Judah to all the Gentile nations.
It is new in application, since it is written in our hearts and minds.
It offers a new way to forgiveness, not through animal sacrifice but
through faith. Have you entered into this new covenant and begun
walking in the better way?*

Proverbs for Today/ 25:1–5

These are more proverbs of Solomon, copied by the men
of Hezekiah king of Judah: It is the glory of God to conceal
a matter; to search out a matter is the glory of kings. As
the heavens are high and the earth is deep, so the hearts
of kings are unsearchable. □ Remove the dross from the
silver, and out comes material for the silversmith; remove
the wicked from the king's presence, and his throne will be
established through righteousness.

OCTOBER 11

The Apostles Suffer Persecution/ Acts 5:26–42

At that, the captain went with his officers and brought the apostles. They did not use force, because they feared that the people would stone them.

27Having brought the apostles, they made them appear before the Sanhedrin to be questioned by the high priest. 28"We gave you strict orders not to teach in this name," he said. "Yet you have filled Jerusalem with your teaching and are determined to make us guilty of this man's blood."

29Peter and the other apostles replied: "We must obey God rather than men! 30The God of our fathers raised Jesus from the dead—whom you had killed by hanging him on a tree. 31God exalted him to his own right hand as Prince and Savior that he might give repentance and forgiveness of sins to Israel. 32We are witnesses of these things, and so is the Holy Spirit, whom God has given to those who obey him."

33When they heard this, they were furious and wanted to put them to death. 34But a Pharisee named Gamaliel, a teacher of the law, who was honored by all the people, stood up in the Sanhedrin and ordered that the men be put outside for a little while. 35Then he addressed them: "Men of Israel, consider carefully what you intend to do to these men. 36Some time ago Theudas appeared, claiming to be somebody, and about four hundred men rallied to him. He was killed, all his followers were dispersed, and it all came to nothing. 37After him, Judas the Galilean appeared in the days of the census and led a band of people in revolt. He too was killed, and all his followers were scattered. 38Therefore, in the present case I advise you: Leave these men alone! Let them go! For if their purpose or activity is of human origin, it will fail. 39But if it is from God, you will not be able to stop these men; you will only find yourselves fighting against God."

40His speech persuaded them. They called the apostles in and had them flogged. Then they ordered them not to speak in the name of Jesus, and let them go.

41The apostles left the Sanhedrin, rejoicing because they

had been counted worthy of suffering disgrace for the Name. 42Day after day, in the temple courts and from house to house, they never stopped teaching and proclaiming the good news that Jesus is the Christ.

A THOUGHT: *The apostles knew their priorities. While we should try to keep peace with everyone, conflict with the world and its authorities is sometimes inevitable for a Christian. There will be situations where you cannot obey both God and man. Then you must obey God and trust his Word. Let Jesus' words encourage you: "Blessed are you when men hate you, when they exclude you and insult you and reject your name as evil, because of the Son of Man. Rejoice in that day and leap for joy, because great is your reward in heaven" (Luke 6:22, 23). We should live as Christ has asked, sharing our faith no matter what the cost. We may not be beaten or thrown in jail, but we may be ridiculed, ostracized, or slandered. To what extent are you willing to suffer for the sake of sharing the gospel with others?*

The Earthly Tabernacle/ Hebrews 9:1–10

Now the first covenant had regulations for worship and also an earthly sanctuary. 2A tabernacle was set up. In its first room were the lampstand, the table and the consecrated bread; this was called the Holy Place. 3Behind the second curtain was a room called the Most Holy Place, 4which had the golden altar of incense and the gold-covered ark of the covenant. This ark contained the gold jar of manna, Aaron's staff that had budded, and the stone tablets of the covenant. 5Above the ark were the cherubim of the Glory, overshadowing the atonement cover. But we cannot discuss these things in detail now.

6When everything had been arranged like this, the priests entered regularly into the outer room to carry on their ministry. 7But only the high priest entered the inner room, and that only once a year, and never without blood, which he offered for himself and for the sins the people had committed in ignorance. 8The Holy Spirit was showing by this that the way into the Most Holy Place had not yet been disclosed as long as the first tabernacle was still standing. 9This is an illustration for the present time, indicating that the gifts and sacrifices being offered were not able to clear the conscience of the worshiper. 10They are only a matter of food and drink and various ceremonial washings— external regulations applying until the time of the new order.

A THOUGHT: *The High Priest could enter the Most Holy Place, the innermost room of the Tabernacle, one day each year to atone for the nation's sins. This was called the Day of Atonement. The Most Holy Place was a small room that contained the ark of the covenant (a gold-covered chest containing the original stone tablets on which the Ten Commandments were written, a pot of manna, and Aaron's rod). The top of the chest served as the "mercy seat" (the altar) on which the blood was sprinkled by the High Priest on the Day of Atonement. The Most Holy Place was the most sacred spot on earth for the Jews. Only the High Priest could enter—the other priests and the common people were forbidden to come into the room. Their only access to God was through the High Priest who offered a sacrifice and used its blood to atone first for his own sins and then for the people's sins.*

Proverbs for Today/ 25:6–7a

Do not exalt yourself in the king's presence, and do not claim a place among great men; it is better for him to say to you, "Come up here," than for him to humiliate you before a nobleman.

OCTOBER 12

The Church Appoints Seven Deacons/ Acts 6:1–7

In those days when the number of disciples was increasing, the Grecian Jews among them complained against the Hebraic Jews because their widows were being overlooked in the daily distribution of food. 2So the Twelve gathered all the disciples together and said, "It would not be right for us to neglect the ministry of the word of God in order to wait on tables. 3Brothers, choose seven men from among you who are known to be full of the Spirit and wisdom. We will turn this responsibility over to them 4and will give our attention to prayer and the ministry of the word."

5This proposal pleased the whole group. They chose Stephen, a man full of faith and of the Holy Spirit; also Philip, Procorus, Nicanor, Timon, Parmenas, and Nicolas from Antioch, a convert to Judaism. 6They presented these men to the apostles, who prayed and laid their hands on them.

7So the word of God spread. The number of disciples in

Jerusalem increased rapidly, and a large number of priests became obedient to the faith.

A THOUGHT: *As the early church increased in size, their needs also increased. One need was to organize the distribution of food to the needy. The apostles needed to focus on preaching, so they chose others to administer the food program. Each person has a necessary part to play in the life of the church. If you are in a position of leadership and find yourself bogged down, determine your God-given abilities and priorities and then find others to help. If you are not in leadership, you have gifts that can be used by God in various areas of the church's ministry. Offer these gifts in service to him.*

Christ the Mediator/ Hebrews 9:11–15

When Christ came as high priest of the good things that are already here, he went through the greater and more perfect tabernacle that is not man-made, that is to say, not a part of this creation. 12He did not enter by means of the blood of goats and calves; but he entered the Most Holy Place once for all by his own blood, having obtained eternal redemption. 13The blood of goats and bulls and the ashes of a heifer sprinkled on those who are ceremonially unclean sanctify them so that they are outwardly clean. 14How much more, then, will the blood of Christ, who through the eternal Spirit offered himself unblemished to God, cleanse our consciences from acts that lead to death, so that we may serve the living God!

15For this reason Christ is the mediator of a new covenant, that those who are called may receive the promised eternal inheritance—now that he has died as a ransom to set them free from the sins committed under the first covenant.

A THOUGHT: *Though you know Christ, you may still be trying to make yourself good enough for God. But rules and rituals have never cleansed people's hearts. By Jesus' blood alone (1) our consciences are cleared, (2) we are freed from death and can live to serve God, and (3) we are freed from sin's power. If you are carrying a load of guilt because you can't be good enough for God, take another look at Jesus' death and what it means for you.*

Proverbs for Today/ 25:7b–10

What you have seen with your eyes do not bring hastily to court, for what will you do in the end if your neighbor puts you to shame? If you argue your case with a neighbor, do not betray another man's confidence, or he who hears it may shame you and you will never lose your bad reputation.

OCTOBER 13

Stephen's Speech Before the Sanhedrin/ Acts 6:8—7:16

Now Stephen, a man full of God's grace and power, did great wonders and miraculous signs among the people. 9Opposition arose, however, from members of the Synagogue of the Freedmen (as it was called)—Jews of Cyrene and Alexandria as well as the provinces of Cilicia and Asia. These men began to argue with Stephen, 10but they could not stand up against his wisdom or the Spirit by whom he spoke.

11Then they secretly persuaded some men to say, "We have heard Stephen speak words of blasphemy against Moses and against God."

12So they stirred up the people and the elders and the teachers of the law. They seized Stephen and brought him before the Sanhedrin. 13They produced false witnesses, who testified, "This fellow never stops speaking against this holy place and against the law. 14For we have heard him say that this Jesus of Nazareth will destroy this place and change the customs Moses handed down to us."

15All who were sitting in the Sanhedrin looked intently at Stephen, and they saw that his face was like the face of an angel.

7:1Then the high priest asked him, "Are these charges true?"

2To this he replied: "Brothers and fathers, listen to me! The God of glory appeared to our father Abraham while he was still in Mesopotamia, before he lived in Haran. 3Leave your country and your people,' God said, 'and go to the land I will show you.'

4"So he left the land of the Chaldeans and settled in Haran. After the death of his father, God sent him to this land where you are now living. 5He gave him no inheritance here, not even a foot of ground. But God promised him that he and his descendants after him would possess the land, even though at that time Abraham had no child. 6God spoke to him in this way: 'Your descendants will be strangers in a country not their own, and they will be enslaved and mistreated four hundred years. 7But I will punish the nation they serve as slaves,' God said, 'and afterward they will come out of that country and worship me in this place.' 8Then he gave Abraham the covenant of circumcision. And Abraham became the father of Isaac and circumcised him eight days after his birth. Later Isaac became the father of Jacob, and Jacob became the father of the twelve patriarchs.

9"Because the patriarchs were jealous of Joseph, they sold him as a slave into Egypt. But God was with him 10and rescued him from all his troubles. He gave Joseph wisdom and enabled him to gain the goodwill of Pharaoh king of Egypt; so he made him ruler over Egypt and all his palace.

11"Then a famine struck all Egypt and Canaan, bringing great suffering, and our fathers could not find food. 12When Jacob heard that there was grain in Egypt, he sent our fathers on their first visit. 13On their second visit, Joseph told his brothers who he was, and Pharaoh learned about Joseph's family. 14After this, Joseph sent for his father Jacob and his whole family, seventy-five in all. 15Then Jacob went down to Egypt, where he and our fathers died. 16Their bodies were brought back to Shechem and placed in the tomb that Abraham had bought from the sons of Hamor at Shechem for a certain sum of money."

A THOUGHT: *Around the world, the gospel has most often taken root in places prepared by the blood of martyrs. Before people can give their lives for the gospel, however, they must first live for the gospel. One way God trains his servants is to place them in insignificant positions. Their desire to serve Christ is translated into the reality of serving others. Stephen was an effective administrator and messenger before becoming a martyr. Stephen's life is a continual challenge to all Christians. Because he was the first to die for the faith, his sacrifice raises questions: How many risks do we take in being Jesus' followers? Would we be willing to die for him? Are we really willing to live for him?*

Sacrifice under the Old Covenant/ Hebrews 9:16–23

In the case of a will, it is necessary to prove the death of the one who made it, 17because a will is in force only when somebody has died; it never takes effect while the one who made it is living. 18This is why even the first covenant was not put into effect without blood. 19When Moses had proclaimed every commandment of the law to all the people, he took the blood of calves, together with water, scarlet wool and branches of hyssop, and sprinkled the scroll and all the people. 20He said, "This is the blood of the covenant, which God has commanded you to keep." 21In the same way, he sprinkled with the blood both the tabernacle and everything used in its ceremonies. 22In fact, the law requires that nearly everything be cleansed with blood, and without the shedding of blood there is no forgiveness.

23It was necessary, then, for the copies of the heavenly things to be purified with these sacrifices, but the heavenly things themselves with better sacrifices than these.

A THOUGHT: *Why does forgiveness require the shedding of blood? This is no arbitrary decree on the part of a bloodthirsty God, as some have supposed. There is no greater symbol of life than blood; blood keeps us alive. Jesus shed his blood—gave his life—for our sins so that we wouldn't have to experience spiritual death, which is eternal separation from God. Jesus is the source of life, not death, and he offered his own life so that we might live. After shedding his blood for us, he rose victorious from the grave and proclaimed victory over sin and death.*

Proverbs for Today/ 25:11–14

A word aptly spoken is like apples of gold in settings of silver. Like an earring of gold or an ornament of fine gold is a wise man's rebuke to a listening ear. □ Like the coolness of snow at harvest time is a trustworthy messenger to those who send him; he refreshes the spirit of his masters. □ Like clouds and wind without rain is a man who boasts of gifts he does not give.

OCTOBER 14

Stephen's Speech—the Life of Moses/ Acts 7:17–43

"As the time drew near for God to fulfill his promise to Abraham, the number of our people in Egypt greatly increased. 18Then another king, who knew nothing about Joseph, became ruler of Egypt. 19He dealt treacherously with our people and oppressed our forefathers by forcing them to throw out their newborn babies so that they would die.

20"At that time Moses was born, and he was no ordinary child. For three months he was cared for in his father's house. 21When he was placed outside, Pharaoh's daughter took him and brought him up as her own son. 22Moses was educated in all the wisdom of the Egyptians and was powerful in speech and action.

23"When Moses was forty years old, he decided to visit his fellow Israelites. 24He saw one of them being mistreated by an Egyptian, so he went to his defense and avenged him by killing the Egyptian. 25Moses thought that his own people would realize that God was using him to rescue them, but they did not. 26The next day Moses came upon two Israelites who were fighting. He tried to reconcile them by saying, 'Men, you are brothers; why do you want to hurt each other?'

27"But the man who was mistreating the other pushed Moses aside and said, 'Who made you ruler and judge over us? 28Do you want to kill me as you killed the Egyptian yesterday?' 29When Moses heard this, he fled to Midian, where he settled as a foreigner and had two sons.

30"After forty years had passed, an angel appeared to Moses in the flames of a burning bush in the desert near Mount Sinai. 31When he saw this, he was amazed at the sight. As he went over to look more closely, he heard the Lord's voice: 32'I am the God of your fathers, the God of Abraham, Isaac and Jacob.' Moses trembled with fear and did not dare to look.

33"Then the Lord said to him, 'Take off your sandals; the place where you are standing is holy ground. 34I have indeed seen the oppression of my people in Egypt. I have heard their groaning and have come down to set them free. Now come, I will send you back to Egypt.'

35"This is the same Moses whom they had rejected with the words, 'Who made you ruler and judge?' He was sent to be their ruler and deliverer by God himself, through the angel who appeared to him in the bush. 36He led them out of Egypt and did wonders and miraculous signs in Egypt, at the Red Sea and for forty years in the desert.

37"This is that Moses who told the Israelites, 'God will send you a prophet like me from your own people.' 38He was in the assembly in the desert, with the angel who spoke to him on Mount Sinai, and with our fathers; and he received living words to pass on to us.

39"But our fathers refused to obey him. Instead, they rejected him and in their hearts turned back to Egypt. 40They told Aaron, 'Make us gods who will go before us. As for this fellow Moses who led us out of Egypt—we don't know what has happened to him!' 41That was the time they made an idol in the form of a calf. They brought sacrifices to it and held a celebration in honor of what their hands had made. 42But God turned away and gave them over to the worship of the heavenly bodies. This agrees with what is written in the book of the prophets:

" 'Did you bring me sacrifices and offerings
    forty years in the desert, O house of Israel?
43You have lifted up the shrine of Molech
    and the star of your god Rephan,
    the idols you made to worship.
Therefore I will send you into exile' beyond
    Babylon."

A THOUGHT: *Stephen's speech described Israel's relationship with God era by era. From Old Testament history he showed that the Jews had constantly rejected God's message and his prophets, and that this Council (the Sanhedrin) had rejected the Messiah, God's Son. He made three main points: (1) Israel's history is the history of God's acts in the world; (2) men worshiped God long before there was a temple, for God does not live in a temple; (3) Jesus' death was just one more example of Israel's rebellion and rejection of God. Stephen showed the religious leadership that they were just like their ancestors—they had rejected God's servant—this time, though, they had rejected God's own Son, the Messiah.*

Christ Conquered the Power of Sin/ Hebrews 9:24–28

For Christ did not enter a man-made sanctuary that was only a copy of the true one; he entered heaven itself, now to appear for us in God's presence. 25Nor did he enter heaven to offer himself again and again, the way the high priest enters the Most Holy Place every year with blood that is not his own. 26Then Christ would have had to suffer many times since the creation of the world. But now he has appeared once for all at the end of the ages to do away with sin by the sacrifice of himself. 27Just as man is destined to die once, and after that to face judgment, 28so Christ was sacrificed once to take away the sins of many people; and he will appear a second time, not to bear sin, but to bring salvation to those who are waiting for him.

A THOUGHT: *All people die physically, but Christ died so that we would not have to die spiritually. His death affects our past, present, and future. He has forgiven our past sin; he has given us the Holy Spirit to help us deal with present sin; and he promises to return and raise us to eternal life in a world from which sin is banished.*

Proverbs for Today/ 25:15

Through patience a ruler can be persuaded, and a gentle tongue can break a bone.

OCTOBER 15

The Stoning of Stephen/ Acts 7:44–60

"Our forefathers had the tabernacle of the Testimony with them in the desert. It had been made as God directed Moses, according to the pattern he had seen. 45Having received the tabernacle, our fathers under Joshua brought it with them when they took the land from the nations God drove out before them. It remained in the land until the time of David, 46who enjoyed God's favor and asked that he might provide a dwelling place for the God of Jacob. 47But it was Solomon who built the house for him.

48"However, the Most High does not live in houses made by men. As the prophet says:

⁴⁹" 'Heaven is my throne,
   and the earth is my footstool.
What kind of house will you build for me?
                                    says the Lord.
   Or where will my resting place be?
⁵⁰Has not my hand made all these things?'

⁵¹"You stiff-necked people, with uncircumcised hearts and ears! You are just like your fathers: You always resist the Holy Spirit! ⁵²Was there ever a prophet your fathers did not persecute? They even killed those who predicted the coming of the Righteous One. And now you have betrayed and murdered him— ⁵³you who have received the law that was put into effect through angels but have not obeyed it."

⁵⁴When they heard this, they were furious and gnashed their teeth at him. ⁵⁵But Stephen, full of the Holy Spirit, looked up to heaven and saw the glory of God, and Jesus standing at the right hand of God. ⁵⁶"Look," he said, "I see heaven open and the Son of Man standing at the right hand of God."

⁵⁷At this they covered their ears and, yelling at the top of their voices, they all rushed at him, ⁵⁸dragged him out of the city and began to stone him. Meanwhile, the witnesses laid their clothes at the feet of a young man named Saul.

⁵⁹While they were stoning him, Stephen prayed, "Lord Jesus, receive my spirit." ⁶⁰Then he fell on his knees and cried out, "Lord, do not hold this sin against them." When he had said this, he fell asleep.

A THOUGHT: *Stephen saw the glory of God and Jesus the Messiah standing at God's right hand. Stephen's vision supported Jesus' claim and angered the Jewish leaders who had condemned Jesus to death for blasphemy. They would not tolerate Stephen's words, so they mobbed him and killed him. Stephen was ready to suffer like Jesus, even to the point of asking forgiveness for his murderers. Such a forgiving response comes only from the Holy Spirit. The Spirit can also help us love our enemies as Stephen did. People may not kill us for witnessing about Christ, but they will let us know they don't want to hear the truth and will often try to silence us. Keep honoring God in your conduct and words; though many will turn against you and your message, some may turn to Christ.*

Christ Died Once for All/ Hebrews 10:1–10

The law is only a shadow of the good things that are coming—not the realities themselves. For this reason it can never, by the same sacrifices repeated endlessly year after year, make perfect those who draw near to worship. 2If it could, would they not have stopped being offered? For the worshipers would have been cleansed once for all, and would no longer have felt guilty for their sins. 3But those sacrifices are an annual reminder of sins, 4because it is impossible for the blood of bulls and goats to take away sins.

5Therefore, when Christ came into the world, he said:

"Sacrifice and offering you did not desire,
but a body you prepared for me;
6with burnt offerings and sin offerings
you were not pleased.
7Then I said, 'Here I am—it is written about me in
the scroll—
I have come to do your will, O God.' "

8First he said, "Sacrifices and offerings, burnt offerings and sin offerings you did not desire, nor were you pleased with them" (although the law required them to be made). 9Then he said, "Here I am, I have come to do your will." He sets aside the first to establish the second. 10And by that will, we have been made holy through the sacrifice of the body of Jesus Christ once for all.

A THOUGHT: *When people gathered for sacrifice on the Day of Atonement, they were reminded of their sins and felt guilty all over again. What they needed was forgiveness—the permanent, powerful, sin-destroying forgiveness we have from Christ. Once we have confessed a sin to him, we need never think of it again. He has forgiven it, and it no longer exists. Christ's sacrifice for sin is all sufficient—there is no sin it cannot cover.*

Proverbs for Today/ 25:16

If you find honey, eat just enough— too much of it, and you will vomit.

OCTOBER 16

Many in Samaria Become Believers/ Acts 8:1–25

And Saul was there, giving approval to his [Stephen's] death.

On that day a great persecution broke out against the church at Jerusalem, and all except the apostles were scattered throughout Judea and Samaria. 2Godly men buried Stephen and mourned deeply for him. 3But Saul began to destroy the church. Going from house to house, he dragged off men and women and put them in prison.

4Those who had been scattered preached the word wherever they went. 5Philip went down to a city in Samaria and proclaimed the Christ there. 6When the crowds heard Philip and saw the miraculous signs he did, they all paid close attention to what he said. 7With shrieks, evil spirits came out of many, and many paralytics and cripples were healed. 8So there was great joy in that city.

9Now for some time a man named Simon had practiced sorcery in the city and amazed all the people of Samaria. He boasted that he was someone great, 10and all the people, both high and low, gave him their attention and exclaimed, "This man is the divine power known as the Great Power." 11They followed him because he had amazed them for a long time with his magic. 12But when they believed Philip as he preached the good news of the kingdom of God and the name of Jesus Christ, they were baptized, both men and women. 13Simon himself believed and was baptized. And he followed Philip everywhere, astonished by the great signs and miracles he saw.

14When the apostles in Jerusalem heard that Samaria had accepted the word of God, they sent Peter and John to them. 15When they arrived, they prayed for them that they might receive the Holy Spirit, 16because the Holy Spirit had not yet come upon any of them; they had simply been baptized into the name of the Lord Jesus. 17Then Peter and John placed their hands on them, and they received the Holy Spirit.

18When Simon saw that the Spirit was given at the laying on of the apostles' hands, he offered them money 19and said, "Give me also this ability so that everyone on whom I lay my hands may receive the Holy Spirit."

20Peter answered: "May your money perish with you, because you thought you could buy the gift of God with money! 21You have no part or share in this ministry, because your heart is not right before God. 22Repent of this wickedness and pray to the Lord. Perhaps he will forgive you for having such a thought in your heart. 23For I see that you are full of bitterness and captive to sin."

24Then Simon answered, "Pray to the Lord for me so that nothing you have said may happen to me."

25When they had testified and proclaimed the word of the Lord, Peter and John returned to Jerusalem, preaching the gospel in many Samaritan villages.

A THOUGHT: *Persecution forced the believers out of their homes in Jerusalem, and with them went the gospel. Often we have to become uncomfortable before we'll move. Discomfort may be unwanted, but it is not always undesirable, for out of our hurting, God works his purposes. The next time you are tempted to complain about uncomfortable or painful circumstances, stop and ask if God may be preparing you for a special task.*

A New and Living Way/ Hebrews 10:11–22

Day after day every priest stands and performs his religious duties; again and again he offers the same sacrifices, which can never take away sins. 12But when this priest had offered for all time one sacrifice for sins, he sat down at the right hand of God. 13Since that time he waits for his enemies to be made his footstool, 14because by one sacrifice he has made perfect forever those who are being made holy.

15The Holy Spirit also testifies to us about this. First he says:

16"This is the covenant I will make with them
    after that time, says the Lord.
I will put my laws in their hearts,
    and I will write them on their minds."

17Then he adds:

"Their sins and lawless acts
    I will remember no more."

18And where these have been forgiven, there is no longer any sacrifice for sin.

19Therefore, brothers, since we have confidence to enter the Most Holy Place by the blood of Jesus, 20by a new and living way opened for us through the curtain, that is, his body, 21and since we have a great priest over the house of God, 22let us draw near to God with a sincere heart in full assurance of faith, having our hearts sprinkled to cleanse us from a guilty conscience and having our bodies washed with pure water.

A THOUGHT: *The Jewish Christians to whom this book was written were in danger of returning to the old Jewish system, which would say that Christ's sacrifice wasn't enough to forgive their sins. But adding anything to his sacrifice or taking anything from it denies its validity. We have been made perfect (complete) in Christ. Through his death and resurrection, Christ once for all made his believers perfect in God's sight. Any system to win God's approval through good works is essentially rejecting the significance of Christ's death and spurning the Holy Spirit's work. Beware of anyone who tells you that Christ's sacrifice was incomplete or that something else is needed to make you acceptable to God, because this can lead you away from right faith and right living.*

Proverbs for Today/ 25:17

Seldom set foot in your neighbor's house—too much of you, and he will hate you.

OCTOBER 17

Philip and the Ethiopian Eunuch/ Acts 8:26–40

Now an angel of the Lord said to Philip, "Go south to the road—the desert road—that goes down from Jerusalem to Gaza." 27So he started out, and on his way he met an Ethiopian eunuch, an important official in charge of all the treasury of Candace, queen of the Ethiopians. This man had gone to Jerusalem to worship, 28and on his way home was sitting in his chariot reading the book of Isaiah the prophet. 29The Spirit told Philip, "Go to that chariot and stay near it."

30Then Philip ran up to the chariot and heard the man

reading Isaiah the prophet. "Do you understand what you are reading?" Philip asked.

31"How can I," he said, "unless someone explains it to me?" So he invited Philip to come up and sit with him.

32The eunuch was reading this passage of Scripture:

"He was led like a sheep to the slaughter,
   and as a lamb before the shearer is silent,
   so he did not open his mouth.
33In his humiliation he was deprived of justice.
   Who can speak of his descendants?
   For his life was taken from the earth."

34The eunuch asked Philip, "Tell me, please, who is the prophet talking about, himself or someone else?" 35Then Philip began with that very passage of Scripture and told him the good news about Jesus.

36As they traveled along the road, they came to some water and the eunuch said, "Look, here is water. Why shouldn't I be baptized?"* 38And he gave orders to stop the chariot. Then both Philip and the eunuch went down into the water and Philip baptized him. 39When they came up out of the water, the Spirit of the Lord suddenly took Philip away, and the eunuch did not see him again, but went on his way rejoicing. 40Philip, however, appeared at Azotus and traveled about, preaching the gospel in all the towns until he reached Caesarea.

A THOUGHT: *Philip found the Ethiopian man reading the Scriptures, and he took advantage of this opportunity to explain the gospel by asking if the man understood what he was reading. Philip (1) followed the Spirit's leading, (2) began the discussion from where the man was—immersed in the prophecies of Isaiah, and (3) explained how Jesus Christ fulfilled Isaiah's prophecies. When we share the gospel, we should start where the other person's concerns are focused. Then we can bring the gospel to bear on those concerns.*

Let Us Serve One Another/ Hebrews 10:23–25

Let us hold unswervingly to the hope we profess, for he who promised is faithful. 24And let us consider how we may spur one another on toward love and good deeds. 25Let us not give up meeting together, as some are in the habit of

---

*36 Some late manuscripts *baptized?"* 37*Philip said, "If you believe with all your heart, you may." The eunuch answered, "I believe that Jesus Christ is the Son of God."*

doing, but let us encourage one another—and all the more as you see the Day approaching.

A THOUGHT: *To neglect Christian meetings is to give up the encouragement and help of other Christians. We gather together to share our faith and strengthen each other in the Lord. As we near the end of the age and as we get closer to the day when Christ will return, we may face many spiritual struggles, tribulations, and even persecution. Anti-Christian forces will grow in strength. Difficulties should never be excuses for missing church services. Rather, as difficulties arise, we should make an even greater effort to be faithful in attendance.*

Proverbs for Today/ 25:18–19

Like a club or a sword or a sharp arrow is the man who gives false testimony against his neighbor. □ Like a bad tooth or a lame foot is reliance on the unfaithful in times of trouble.

OCTOBER 18

Saul's Conversion/ Acts 9:1–19a

Meanwhile, Saul was still breathing out murderous threats against the Lord's disciples. He went to the high priest 2and asked him for letters to the synagogues in Damascus, so that if he found any there who belonged to the Way, whether men or women, he might take them as prisoners to Jerusalem. 3As he neared Damascus on his journey, suddenly a light from heaven flashed around him. 4He fell to the ground and heard a voice say to him, "Saul, Saul, why do you persecute me?"

5"Who are you, Lord?" Saul asked.

"I am Jesus, whom you are persecuting," he replied. 6"Now get up and go into the city, and you will be told what you must do."

7The men traveling with Saul stood there speechless; they heard the sound but did not see anyone. 8Saul got up from the ground, but when he opened his eyes he could see nothing. So they led him by the hand into Damascus. 9For three days he was blind, and did not eat or drink anything.

10In Damascus there was a disciple named Ananias. The Lord called to him in a vision, "Ananias!"

"Yes, Lord," he answered.

11The Lord told him, "Go to the house of Judas on Straight Street and ask for a man from Tarsus named Saul, for he is praying. 12In a vision he has seen a man named Ananias come and place his hands on him to restore his sight."

13"Lord," Ananias answered, "I have heard many reports about this man and all the harm he has done to your saints in Jerusalem. 14And he has come here with authority from the chief priests to arrest all who call on your name."

15But the Lord said to Ananias, "Go! This man is my chosen instrument to carry my name before the Gentiles and their kings and before the people of Israel. 16I will show him how much he must suffer for my name."

17Then Ananias went to the house and entered it. Placing his hands on Saul, he said, "Brother Saul, the Lord—Jesus, who appeared to you on the road as you were coming here—has sent me so that you may see again and be filled with the Holy Spirit." 18Immediately, something like scales fell from Saul's eyes, and he could see again. He got up and was baptized, 19and after taking some food, he regained his strength.

A THOUGHT: *As Saul traveled to Damascus, pursuing Christians, he was confronted by the risen Christ and brought face to face with the truth of the gospel. Sometimes God breaks into a life in a spectacular manner, and sometimes conversion is a quiet experience. Beware of people who insist you must have a particular type of conversion experience. The right way to come to faith in Jesus is whatever way God brings you.*

A Warning Against Apostasy/ Hebrews 10:26–31

If we deliberately keep on sinning after we have received the knowledge of the truth, no sacrifice for sins is left, 27but only a fearful expectation of judgment and of raging fire that will consume the enemies of God. 28Anyone who rejected the law of Moses died without mercy on the testimony of two or three witnesses. 29How much more severely do you think a man deserves to be punished who has trampled the Son of God under foot, who has treated as an unholy thing the blood of the covenant that sanctified him, and who has insulted the Spirit of grace? 30For we know him who said, "It is mine to avenge; I will repay," and again, "The Lord will judge his people." 31It is a dreadful thing to fall into the hands of the living God.

A THOUGHT: *When people deliberately reject Christ's offer of salvation, they reject God's most precious gift. They push away the work of the Holy Spirit, the one who communicates to us God's saving love. This warning was given to Jewish Christians who were tempted to reject Christ for Judaism, but it applies to anyone who rejects Christ for another religion or, having understood Christ's atoning work, deliberately turns away from it. The point is that there is no other acceptable sacrifice for sin than the death of Christ on the cross. If someone deliberately, intentionally, purposely rejects the sacrifice of Christ after clearly understanding the gospel teaching about it, then there is no other hope of salvation for that person, for God has not provided any other name under heaven by whom we could be saved.*

Proverbs for Today/ 25:20–22

Like one who takes away a garment on a cold day, or like vinegar poured on soda, is one who sings songs to a heavy heart. □ If your enemy is hungry, give him food to eat; if he is thirsty, give him water to drink. In doing this, you will heap burning coals on his head, and the LORD will reward you.

OCTOBER 19

Saul Preaches in Damascus and Jerusalem/ Acts 9:19b–31

Saul spent several days with the disciples in Damascus. 20At once he began to preach in the synagogues that Jesus is the Son of God. 21All those who heard him were astonished and asked, "Isn't he the man who raised havoc in Jerusalem among those who call on this name? And hasn't he come here to take them as prisoners to the chief priests?" 22Yet Saul grew more and more powerful and baffled the Jews living in Damascus by proving that Jesus is the Christ.

23After many days had gone by, the Jews conspired to kill him, 24but Saul learned of their plan. Day and night they kept close watch on the city gates in order to kill him. 25But his followers took him by night and lowered him in a basket through an opening in the wall.

²⁶When he came to Jerusalem, he tried to join the disciples, but they were all afraid of him, not believing that he really was a disciple. ²⁷But Barnabas took him and brought him to the apostles. He told them how Saul on his journey had seen the Lord and that the Lord had spoken to him, and how in Damascus he had preached fearlessly in the name of Jesus. ²⁸So Saul stayed with them and moved about freely in Jerusalem, speaking boldly in the name of the Lord. ²⁹He talked and debated with the Grecian Jews, but they tried to kill him. ³⁰When the brothers learned of this, they took him down to Caesarea and sent him off to Tarsus.

³¹Then the church throughout Judea, Galilee and Samaria enjoyed a time of peace. It was strengthened; and encouraged by the Holy Spirit, it grew in numbers, living in the fear of the Lord.

A THOUGHT: *Immediately after receiving his sight, Saul went to the synagogue to tell the Jews about Jesus Christ. Some Christians counsel new believers to wait until they are thoroughly grounded in their faith before attempting to share the gospel. Saul took time alone to learn about Jesus before beginning his worldwide ministry, but he did not wait to witness. Although we should not rush into a ministry unprepared, we do not need to wait before telling others what has happened to us.*

Remember Your Eternal Reward/ Hebrews 10:32–39

Remember those earlier days after you had received the light, when you stood your ground in a great contest in the face of suffering. ³³Sometimes you were publicly exposed to insult and persecution; at other times you stood side by side with those who were so treated. ³⁴You sympathized with those in prison and joyfully accepted the confiscation of your property, because you knew that you yourselves had better and lasting possessions.

³⁵So do not throw away your confidence; it will be richly rewarded. ³⁶You need to persevere so that when you have done the will of God, you will receive what he has promised. ³⁷For in just a very little while,

> "He who is coming will come and will not delay.
> 38 But my righteous one will live by faith.
> And if he shrinks back,
> I will not be pleased with him."

39But we are not of those who shrink back and are destroyed, but of those who believe and are saved.

A THOUGHT: *Hebrews encourages believers, who are in the midst of persecution, to persevere in their Christian walk. We don't usually think of suffering as good, but suffering is part of our relationship with Christ—it impresses upon us a deeper Christlikeness. During times of great stress, we can be confident that God is with us. Knowing that Jesus is with us in our suffering, we can endure the pain and realize that ultimately we will find rest in Christ.*

Proverbs for Today/ 25:23–24

As a north wind brings rain, so a sly tongue brings angry looks. □ Better to live on a corner of the roof than share a house with a quarrelsome wife.

OCTOBER 20

Peter Heals Aeneas/ Acts 9:32–35

As Peter traveled about the country, he went to visit the saints in Lydda. 33There he found a man named Aeneas, a paralytic who had been bedridden for eight years. 34"Aeneas," Peter said to him, "Jesus Christ heals you. Get up and take care of your mat." Immediately Aeneas got up. 35All those who lived in Lydda and Sharon saw him and turned to the Lord.

A THOUGHT: *Peter healed the paralyzed Aeneas by the authority of Jesus Christ. Healing in the "name" is not some magical formula, like "abracadabra," that causes healing everytime it's uttered. God cannot be manipulated! God chooses to answer the prayers of his people—and often God does heal. However, God is not obligated to heal anyone. Here God uses Peter to demonstrate his power in the healing of Aeneas in order to open opportunities for the fledgling church to share the Good News. Many "turned to the Lord" as a result of Aeneas' healing. God works in diverse ways. We must not attempt to put God in a box by saying that he has to operate according to our preconceived notions. We must let God be God.*

Faith/ Hebrews 11:1–6

Now faith is being sure of what we hope for and certain of what we do not see. ²This is what the ancients were commended for.

³By faith we understand that the universe was formed at God's command, so that what is seen was not made out of what was visible.

⁴By faith Abel offered God a better sacrifice than Cain did. By faith he was commended as a righteous man, when God spoke well of his offerings. And by faith he still speaks, even though he is dead.

⁵By faith Enoch was taken from this life, so that he did not experience death; he could not be found, because God had taken him away. For before he was taken, he was commended as one who pleased God. ⁶And without faith it is impossible to please God, because anyone who comes to him must believe that he exists and that he rewards those who earnestly seek him.

A THOUGHT: *Two words describe our faith: confidence and certainty. These two qualities need a secure beginning and ending point. The beginning point of faith is believing in God's character—he is who he says. The end point is believing in God's promises—he will do what he says. We believe that God will fulfill his promises even though we don't see those promises materializing now—this is true faith.*

Proverbs for Today/ 25:25–27

Like cold water to a weary soul is good news from a distant land. □ Like a muddied spring or a polluted well is a righteous man who gives way to the wicked. □ It is not good to eat too much honey, nor is it honorable to seek one's own honor.

OCTOBER 21

Peter Raises Dorcas from the Dead/ Acts 9:36–43

In Joppa there was a disciple named Tabitha (which, when translated, is Dorcas), who was always doing good and helping the poor. ³⁷About that time she became sick and died, and her body was washed and placed in an upstairs room. 38Lydda was near Joppa; so when the disciples heard that Peter was in Lydda, they sent two men to him and urged him, "Please come at once!"

39Peter went with them, and when he arrived he was taken upstairs to the room. All the widows stood around him, crying and showing him the robes and other clothing that Dorcas had made while she was still with them.

40Peter sent them all out of the room; then he got down on his knees and prayed. Turning toward the dead woman, he said, "Tabitha, get up." She opened her eyes, and seeing Peter she sat up. 41He took her by the hand and helped her to her feet. Then he called the believers and the widows and presented her to them alive. 42This became known all over Joppa, and many people believed in the Lord. 43Peter stayed in Joppa for some time with a tanner named Simon.

A THOUGHT: *Dorcas made an enormous impact on her community by "always doing good and helping the poor." When she died, the room was filled with mourners, people she had helped. And when she was brought back to life, the news raced through the town. God uses great preachers like Peter and Paul, but he also uses those who have gifts of kindness like Dorcas. Rather than wishing you had other gifts, make good use of the gifts God has given you.*

The Faith of Noah, Abraham, and Sarah/ Hebrews 11:7–12

By faith Noah, when warned about things not yet seen, in holy fear built an ark to save his family. By his faith he condemned the world and became heir of the righteousness that comes by faith.

8By faith Abraham, when called to go to a place he would later receive as his inheritance, obeyed and went, even though he did not know where he was going. 9By faith he made his home in the promised land like a stranger in a foreign country; he lived in tents, as did Isaac and Jacob, who were heirs with him of the same promise. 10For he was looking forward to the city with foundations, whose architect and builder is God.

11By faith Abraham, even though he was past age—and Sarah herself was barren—was enabled to become a father because he considered him faithful who had made the promise. 12And so from this one man, and he as good as dead, came descendants as numerous as the stars in the sky and as countless as the sand on the seashore.

A THOUGHT: *Noah experienced what it meant to be different from his neighbors. God commanded him to build a huge boat in the middle of dry land, and although God's command seemed foolish, Noah obeyed. Noah's obedience made him appear strange to his neighbors, just as the new beliefs of Jewish Christians made them stand out. As you obey God, don't be surprised if others consider you different. Your obedience makes their disobedience stand out. Remember, if God asks you to do something, he will give you the necessary strength to carry out that task.*

Proverbs for Today/ 25:28

Like a city whose walls are broken down is a man who lacks self-control.

OCTOBER 22

God Gives Visions to Peter and Cornelius/ Acts 10:1–23a

At Caesarea there was a man named Cornelius, a centurion in what was known as the Italian Regiment. 2He and all his family were devout and God-fearing; he gave generously to those in need and prayed to God regularly. 3One day at about three in the afternoon he had a vision. He distinctly saw an angel of God, who came to him and said, "Cornelius!"

4Cornelius stared at him in fear. "What is it, Lord?" he asked.

The angel answered, "Your prayers and gifts to the poor have come up as a memorial offering before God. 5Now send men to Joppa to bring back a man named Simon who is called Peter. 6He is staying with Simon the tanner, whose house is by the sea."

7When the angel who spoke to him had gone, Cornelius called two of his servants and a devout soldier who was one of his attendants. 8He told them everything that had happened and sent them to Joppa.

9About noon the following day as they were on their journey and approaching the city, Peter went up on the roof to pray. 10He became hungry and wanted something to eat, and while the meal was being prepared, he fell into a trance. 11He saw heaven opened and something like a large sheet being let down to earth by its four corners. 12It contained all kinds of four-footed animals, as well as reptiles of the earth and birds of the air. 13Then a voice told him, "Get up, Peter. Kill and eat."

14"Surely not, Lord!" Peter replied. "I have never eaten anything impure or unclean."

15The voice spoke to him a second time, "Do not call anything impure that God has made clean."

16This happened three times, and immediately the sheet was taken back to heaven.

17While Peter was wondering about the meaning of the vision, the men sent by Cornelius found out where Simon's house was and stopped at the gate. 18They called out, asking if Simon who was known as Peter was staying there.

19While Peter was still thinking about the vision, the Spirit said to him, "Simon, three men are looking for you. 20So get up and go downstairs. Do not hesitate to go with them, for I have sent them."

21Peter went down and said to the men, "I'm the one you're looking for. Why have you come?"

22The men replied, "We have come from Cornelius the centurion. He is a righteous and God-fearing man, who is respected by all the Jewish people. A holy angel told him to have you come to his house so that he could hear what you have to say." 23Then Peter invited the men into the house to be his guests.

A THOUGHT: *According to Jewish law, certain foods were forbidden. The food laws made it hard for Jews to eat with Gentiles without risking defilement. In fact, the Gentiles themselves were often seen as "unclean." Peter's vision meant that he was not to look upon the Gentiles as inferior people whom God would not redeem. Before having the vision, Peter would have thought a Gentile Roman officer could not accept Christ. Afterward, he understood that he should go with the messengers into a Gentile home and tell Cornelius the Good News of salvation in Jesus Christ.*

Faith in God's Promises/ Hebrews 11:13–16

All these people were still living by faith when they died. They did not receive the things promised; they only saw them and welcomed them from a distance. And they admitted that they were aliens and strangers on earth. 14People who say such things show that they are looking for a country of their own. 15If they had been thinking of the country they had left, they would have had opportunity to return. 16Instead, they were longing for a better country—a heavenly one. Therefore God is not ashamed to be called their God, for he has prepared a city for them.

A THOUGHT: *The people of faith listed here died without receiving all that God had promised, but they never lost their vision of heaven. Many Christians become frustrated and defeated because their needs, wants, expectations, and demands are not immediately met when they believe in Christ. They become impatient and want to quit. Are you discouraged because your goal seems far away? Take courage from these heroes of faith who lived and died without seeing the fruit of their faith on earth, and yet continued to believe.*

Proverbs for Today/ 26:1–2

Like snow in summer or rain in harvest, honor is not fitting for a fool. Like a fluttering sparrow or a darting swallow, an undeserved curse does not come to rest.

OCTOBER 23

Peter at the Centurion's House/ Acts 10:23b–48

The next day Peter started out with them, and some of the brothers from Joppa went along. 24The following day he arrived in Caesarea. Cornelius was expecting them and had called together his relatives and close friends. 25As Peter entered the house, Cornelius met him and fell at his feet in reverence. 26But Peter made him get up. "Stand up," he said, "I am only a man myself."

27Talking with him, Peter went inside and found a large gathering of people. 28He said to them: "You are well aware that it is against our law for a Jew to associate with a Gentile or visit him. But God has shown me that I should not call any man impure or unclean. 29So when I was sent for, I came without raising any objection. May I ask why you sent for me?"

30Cornelius answered: "Four days ago I was in my house

praying at this hour, at three in the afternoon. Suddenly a man in shining clothes stood before me 31and said, 'Cornelius, God has heard your prayer and remembered your gifts to the poor. 32Send to Joppa for Simon who is called Peter. He is a guest in the home of Simon the tanner, who lives by the sea.' 33So I sent for you immediately, and it was good of you to come. Now we are all here in the presence of God to listen to everything the Lord has commanded you to tell us."

34Then Peter began to speak: "I now realize how true it is that God does not show favoritism 35but accepts men from every nation who fear him and do what is right. 36You know the message God sent to the people of Israel, telling the good news of peace through Jesus Christ, who is Lord of all. 37You know what has happened throughout Judea, beginning in Galilee after the baptism that John preached—38how God anointed Jesus of Nazareth with the Holy Spirit and power, and how he went around doing good and healing all who were under the power of the devil, because God was with him.

39"We are witnesses of everything he did in the country of the Jews and in Jerusalem. They killed him by hanging him on a tree, 40but God raised him from the dead on the third day and caused him to be seen. 41He was not seen by all the people, but by witnesses whom God had already chosen—by us who ate and drank with him after he rose from the dead. 42He commanded us to preach to the people and to testify that he is the one whom God appointed as judge of the living and the dead. 43All the prophets testify about him that everyone who believes in him receives forgiveness of sins through his name."

44While Peter was still speaking these words, the Holy Spirit came on all who heard the message. 45The circumcised believers who had come with Peter were astonished that the gift of the Holy Spirit had been poured out even on the Gentiles. 46For they heard them speaking in tongues and praising God.

Then Peter said, 47"Can anyone keep these people from being baptized with water? They have received the Holy Spirit just as we have." 48So he ordered that they be baptized in the name of Jesus Christ. Then they asked Peter to stay with them for a few days.

A THOUGHT: *Perhaps the greatest barrier to the spread of the gospel in the first century was the Jewish-Gentile conflict. Most early believers were Jewish, and to them it was scandalous even to think of associating with Gentiles. But God told Peter to take the gospel to a Roman, and Peter obeyed despite his background and personal feelings. (Later he struggled with this again—see Galatians 2:12.) God was making it clear that the Gospel of Christ is for everyone! We cannot allow any barrier—language, culture, geography, economic class, or education—to keep us from spreading the gospel.*

God's Testing of Abraham/ Hebrews 11:17–20

By faith Abraham, when God tested him, offered Isaac as a sacrifice. He who had received the promises was about to sacrifice his one and only son, 18even though God had said to him, "It is through Isaac that your offspring will be reckoned." 19Abraham reasoned that God could raise the dead, and figuratively speaking, he did receive Isaac back from death.

20By faith Isaac blessed Jacob and Esau in regard to their future.

A THOUGHT: *Abraham was willing to give up his son when God commanded him to do so. God did not let Abraham take Isaac's life, because God gave the command to test Abraham's faith. Instead of taking Abraham's son, God gave him a whole nation of descendants through Isaac. If you are afraid to trust God with your most prized possession, dream, or person, pay attention to Abraham's example. Because Abraham was willing to give up everything for God, he received back more than he could have imagined. What we receive, however, is not always immediate, or in the form of material possessions. After all, material possessions should be among the least satisfying of rewards. Our best and greatest rewards await us in eternity.*

Proverbs for Today/ 26:3–5

A whip for the horse, a halter for the donkey, and a rod for the backs of fools! Do not answer a fool according to his folly, or you will be like him yourself. Answer a fool according to his folly, or he will be wise in his own eyes.

OCTOBER 24

Peter Defends His Preaching to the Gentiles/ Acts 11:1–18

The apostles and the brothers throughout Judea heard that the Gentiles also had received the word of God. 2So when Peter went up to Jerusalem, the circumcised believers criticized him 3and said, "You went into the house of uncircumcised men and ate with them."

4Peter began and explained everything to them precisely as it had happened: 5"I was in the city of Joppa praying, and in a trance I saw a vision. I saw something like a large sheet being let down from heaven by its four corners, and it came down to where I was. 6I looked into it and saw four-footed animals of the earth, wild beasts, reptiles, and birds of the air. 7Then I heard a voice telling me, 'Get up, Peter. Kill and eat.'

8"I replied, 'Surely not, Lord! Nothing impure or unclean has ever entered my mouth.'

9"The voice spoke from heaven a second time, 'Do not call anything impure that God has made clean.' 10This happened three times, and then it was all pulled up to heaven again.

11"Right then three men who had been sent to me from Caesarea stopped at the house where I was staying. 12The Spirit told me to have no hesitation about going with them. These six brothers also went with me, and we entered the man's house. 13He told us how he had seen an angel appear in his house and say, 'Send to Joppa for Simon who is called Peter. 14He will bring you a message through which you and all your household will be saved.'

15"As I began to speak, the Holy Spirit came on them as he had come on us at the beginning. 16Then I remembered what the Lord had said: 'John baptized with water, but you will be baptized with the Holy Spirit.' 17So if God gave them the same gift as he gave us, who believed in the Lord Jesus Christ, who was I to think that I could oppose God?"

18When they heard this, they had no further objections and praised God, saying, "So then, God has granted even the Gentiles repentance unto life."

A THOUGHT: *God had promised throughout Scripture that he would reach the Gentiles. This began with God's promise to Abraham and became very specific in Malachi's statement that God's name "will be great among the nations, from the rising to the setting of the sun"(Malachi 1:11). But this was an extremely difficult truth for Jews, even Jewish believers, to accept. The Jewish believers understood that certain prophecies were fulfilled in Christ, but they overlooked other Old Testament teachings. Too often we are inclined to accept only the parts of God's Word that appeal to us, ignoring the teachings we don't like. We must accept all of God's Word as absolute truth.*

The Faith of Jacob, Joseph, and Moses' Parents/ Hebrews 11:21–23

By faith Jacob, when he was dying, blessed each of Joseph's sons, and worshiped as he leaned on the top of his staff.

22By faith Joseph, when his end was near, spoke about the exodus of the Israelites from Egypt and gave instructions about his bones.

23By faith Moses' parents hid him for three months after he was born, because they saw he was no ordinary child, and they were not afraid of the king's edict.

A THOUGHT: *Jacob was Isaac's son and Abraham's grandson. Jacob's sons became the fathers of Israel's 12 tribes. Even when Jacob (also called "Israel") was dying in a strange land, he believed the promise that Abraham's descendants would be like the sand on the seashore and that Israel would become a great nation. True faith helps us see beyond the grave.*

Joseph, one of Jacob's sons, was sold into slavery by his jealous brothers. Eventually, Joseph was sold again, this time to an officer of the Pharaoh of Egypt. Because of his faithfulness to God, however, Joseph was given a top-ranking position in Egypt. Although Joseph could have used that position to build a personal empire, he remembered God's promise to Abraham. After he had been reconciled to his brothers, he brought his family to be near him, and requested that his bones be taken to the Promised Land when the Jews eventually left Egypt. Faith means trusting in God and doing what he wants, regardless of the circumstances.

Proverbs for Today/ 26:6–8

Like cutting off one's feet or drinking violence is the sending of a message by the hand of a fool. Like a lame man's legs that hang limp is a proverb in the mouth of a fool. Like tying a stone in a sling is the giving of honor to a fool.

OCTOBER 25

Barnabas and Saul Become Partners in Evangelism/Acts 11:19–30

Now those who had been scattered by the persecution in connection with Stephen traveled as far as Phoenicia, Cyprus and Antioch, telling the message only to Jews. 20Some of them, however, men from Cyprus and Cyrene, went to Antioch and began to speak to Greeks also, telling them the good news about the Lord Jesus. 21The Lord's hand was with them, and a great number of people believed and turned to the Lord.

22News of this reached the ears of the church at Jerusalem, and they sent Barnabas to Antioch. 23When he arrived and saw the evidence of the grace of God, he was glad and encouraged them all to remain true to the Lord with all their hearts. 24He was a good man, full of the Holy Spirit and faith, and a great number of people were brought to the Lord.

25Then Barnabas went to Tarsus to look for Saul, 26and when he found him, he brought him to Antioch. So for a whole year Barnabas and Saul met with the church and taught great numbers of people. The disciples were called Christians first at Antioch.

27During this time some prophets came down from Jerusalem to Antioch. 28One of them, named Agabus, stood up and through the Spirit predicted that a severe famine would spread over the entire Roman world. (This happened during the reign of Claudius.) 29The disciples, each according to his ability, decided to provide help for the brothers living in Judea. 30This they did, sending their gift to the elders by Barnabas and Saul.

A THOUGHT: *It was from Antioch that Christianity launched its worldwide mission and where the believers aggressively preached to the Gentiles. Philip had preached in Samaria, but the Samaritans were already partly Jewish; Peter preached to Cornelius, but he already worshiped God. Believers who scattered after the outbreak of persecution in Jerusalem, shared the gospel with other Jews in the various lands they fled to. But now the believers began actively sharing the Good News with Gentiles.*

The Faith of Moses/ Hebrews 11:24–29

By faith Moses, when he had grown up, refused to be known as the son of Pharaoh's daughter. 25He chose to be mistreated along with the people of God rather than to enjoy the pleasures of sin for a short time. 26He regarded disgrace for the sake of Christ as of greater value than the treasures of Egypt, because he was looking ahead to his reward. 27By faith he left Egypt, not fearing the king's anger; he persevered because he saw him who is invisible. 28By faith he kept the Passover and the sprinkling of blood, so that the destroyer of the firstborn would not touch the firstborn of Israel.

29By faith the people passed through the Red Sea as on dry land; but when the Egyptians tried to do so, they were drowned.

A THOUGHT: *Moses became one of Israel's greatest leaders, a prophet and a lawgiver. But when he was born, his people were slaves in Egypt and the Egyptian officials had ordered that all Hebrew baby boys were to be killed. Moses was spared, however, and Pharaoh's daughter raised Moses in Pharaoh's own household! It took faith for Moses to give up his place in the palace, but he could do it because he saw the fleeting nature of great wealth and prestige. It is easy to be deceived by the temporary benefits of wealth, popularity, status, and achievement, and to be blind to the long-range benefits of God's kingdom. Faith helps us look beyond the world's value system to see the eternal values of God's kingdom.*

Proverbs for Today/ 26:9–12

Like a thornbush in a drunkard's hand is a proverb in the mouth of a fool. □ Like an archer who wounds at random is he who hires a fool or any passer-by. □ As a dog returns to its vomit, so a fool repeats his folly. □ Do you see a man wise in his own eyes? There is more hope for a fool than for him.

OCTOBER 26

An Angel Rescues Peter from Prison/ Acts 12:1–25

It was about this time that King Herod arrested some who belonged to the church, intending to persecute them. 2He had James, the brother of John, put to death with the sword. 3When he saw that this pleased the Jews, he proceeded to seize Peter also. This happened during the Feast of Unleavened Bread. 4After arresting him, he put him in prison, handing him over to be guarded by four squads of four soldiers each. Herod intended to bring him out for public trial after the Passover.

5So Peter was kept in prison, but the church was earnestly praying to God for him.

6The night before Herod was to bring him to trial, Peter was sleeping between two soldiers, bound with two chains, and sentries stood guard at the entrance. 7Suddenly an angel of the Lord appeared and a light shone in the cell. He struck Peter on the side and woke him up. "Quick, get up!" he said, and the chains fell off Peter's wrists.

8Then the angel said to him, "Put on your clothes and sandals." And Peter did so. "Wrap your cloak around you and follow me," the angel told him. 9Peter followed him out of the prison, but he had no idea that what the angel was doing was really happening; he thought he was seeing a vision. 10They passed the first and second guards and came to the iron gate leading to the city. It opened for them by itself, and they went through it. When they had walked the length of one street, suddenly the angel left him.

11Then Peter came to himself and said, "Now I know without a doubt that the Lord sent his angel and rescued me from Herod's clutches and from everything the Jewish people were anticipating."

12When this had dawned on him, he went to the house of Mary the mother of John, also called Mark, where many people had gathered and were praying. 13Peter knocked at the outer entrance, and a servant girl named Rhoda came to answer the door. 14When she recognized Peter's voice, she was so overjoyed she ran back without opening it and exclaimed, "Peter is at the door!"

15"You're out of your mind," they told her. When she kept insisting that it was so, they said, "It must be his angel."

16But Peter kept on knocking, and when they opened the door and saw him, they were astonished. 17Peter motioned with his hand for them to be quiet and described how the Lord had brought him out of prison. "Tell James and the brothers about this," he said, and then he left for another place.

18In the morning, there was no small commotion among the soldiers as to what had become of Peter. 19After Herod had a thorough search made for him and did not find him, he cross-examined the guards and ordered that they be executed.

Then Herod went from Judea to Caesarea and stayed there a while. 20He had been quarreling with the people of Tyre and Sidon; they now joined together and sought an audience with him. Having secured the support of Blastus, a trusted personal servant of the king, they asked for peace, because they depended on the king's country for their food supply.

21On the appointed day Herod, wearing his royal robes, sat on his throne and delivered a public address to the people. 22They shouted, "This is the voice of a god, not of a man." 23Immediately, because Herod did not give praise to God, an angel of the Lord struck him down, and he was eaten by worms and died.

24But the word of God continued to increase and spread.

25When Barnabas and Saul had finished their mission, they returned from Jerusalem, taking with them John, also called Mark.

A THOUGHT: *In the midst of the plots, execution, and arrest, Luke injects the very important word "but." Herod's plan was to execute Peter, but the believers were praying for Peter's safety. The earnest prayer of the church significantly affected the outcome of these events. We know from the testimony of the Bible that prayer changes attitudes and events. So pray often and pray with confidence.*

Heroes of Faith/ Hebrews 11:30–40

By faith the walls of Jericho fell, after the people had marched around them for seven days.

31By faith the prostitute Rahab, because she welcomed the spies, was not killed with those who were disobedient.

32And what more shall I say? I do not have time to tell about Gideon, Barak, Samson, Jephthah, David, Samuel and the prophets, 33who through faith conquered kingdoms, administered justice, and gained what was promised; who shut the mouths of lions, 34quenched the fury of the flames, and escaped the edge of the sword; whose weakness was turned to strength; and who became powerful in battle and routed foreign armies. 35Women received back their dead, raised to life again. Others were tortured and refused to be released, so that they might gain a better resurrection. 36Some faced jeers and flogging, while still others were chained and put in prison. 37They were stoned; they were sawed in two; they were put to death by the sword. They went about in sheepskins and goatskins, destitute, persecuted and mistreated— 38the world was not worthy of them. They wandered in deserts and mountains, and in caves and holes in the ground.

39These were all commended for their faith, yet none of them received what had been promised. 40God had planned something better for us so that only together with us would they be made perfect.

A THOUGHT: *These verses summarize the lives of other great men and women of faith. Some experienced outstanding victories, even over death. But others were severely mistreated, tortured, and even killed. Having a steadfast faith in God does not guarantee a happy, carefree life. On the contrary, our faith almost guarantees us some form of abuse from the world. While we are on earth, we may never see the purpose of our suffering. But we know that God will keep his promises to us. Is your faith based on the assurance that God will keep his promises to you?*

Proverbs for Today/ 26:13–16

The sluggard says, "There is a lion in the road, a fierce lion roaming the streets!" As a door turns on its hinges, so a sluggard turns on his bed. The sluggard buries his hand in the dish; he is too lazy to bring it back to his mouth. The sluggard is wiser in his own eyes than seven men who answer discreetly.

OCTOBER 27

Barnabas and Paul Sent Out/ Acts 13:1–12

In the church at Antioch there were prophets and teachers: Barnabas, Simeon called Niger, Lucius of Cyrene, Manaen (who had been brought up with Herod the tetrarch) and Saul. 2While they were worshiping the Lord and fasting, the Holy Spirit said, "Set apart for me Barnabas and Saul for the work to which I have called them." 3So after they had fasted and prayed, they placed their hands on them and sent them off.

4The two of them, sent on their way by the Holy Spirit, went down to Seleucia and sailed from there to Cyprus. 5When they arrived at Salamis, they proclaimed the word of God in the Jewish synagogues. John was with them as their helper.

6They traveled through the whole island until they came to Paphos. There they met a Jewish sorcerer and false prophet named Bar-Jesus, 7who was an attendant of the proconsul, Sergius Paulus. The proconsul, an intelligent man, sent for Barnabas and Saul because he wanted to hear the word of God. 8But Elymas the sorcerer (for that is what his name means) opposed them and tried to turn the proconsul from the faith. 9Then Saul, who was also called Paul, filled with the Holy Spirit, looked straight at Elymas and said, 10"You are a child of the devil and an enemy of everything that is right! You are full of all kinds of deceit and trickery. Will you never stop perverting the right ways of the Lord? 11Now the hand of the Lord is against you. You are going to be blind, and for a time you will be unable to see the light of the sun."

Immediately mist and darkness came over him, and he groped about, seeking someone to lead him by the hand. 12When the proconsul saw what had happened, he believed, for he was amazed at the teaching about the Lord.

A THOUGHT: *This was the beginning of Paul's first missionary journey. The church was involved in sending Paul and Barnabas, but it was God's plan. Why did Paul and Barnabas go where they did? (1) The Holy Spirit led them. (2) They followed the communication routes of the Roman Empire—this made travel easier. (3) They visited key population and cultural centers to reach as many people as possible. (4) They went to cities with synagogues, speaking first to the Jews in hopes that they would see Jesus as the Messiah and help spread the Good News to everyone.*

Running the Race/ Hebrews 12:1–4

Therefore, since we are surrounded by such a great cloud of witnesses, let us throw off everything that hinders and the sin that so easily entangles, and let us run with perseverance the race marked out for us. 2Let us fix our eyes on Jesus, the author and perfecter of our faith, who for the joy set before him endured the cross, scorning its shame, and sat down at the right hand of the throne of God. 3Consider him who endured such opposition from sinful men, so that you will not grow weary and lose heart.

4In your struggle against sin, you have not yet resisted to the point of shedding your blood.

A THOUGHT: *The Christian life involves hard work. It requires us to give up whatever endangers our relationship with God, to run patiently, and to struggle against sin with the power of the Holy Spirit. To live this life effectively, we must keep our eyes on Jesus. We stumble when we look away from him and at ourselves or the circumstances surrounding us. We are running Christ's race, not our own, and we must always keep him in sight.*

Proverbs for Today/ 26:17

Like one who seizes a dog by the ears is a passer-by who meddles in a quarrel not his own.

OCTOBER 28

A Trip to Antioch of Pisidia/ Acts 13:13–23

From Paphos, Paul and his companions sailed to Perga in Pamphylia, where John left them to return to Jerusalem. 14From Perga they went on to Pisidian Antioch. On the Sabbath they entered the synagogue and sat down. 15After the reading from the Law and the Prophets, the synagogue rulers sent word to them, saying, "Brothers, if you have a message of encouragement for the people, please speak."

16Standing up, Paul motioned with his hand and said:

"Men of Israel and you Gentiles who worship God, listen to me! [17]The God of the people of Israel chose our fathers; he made the people prosper during their stay in Egypt, with mighty power he led them out of that country, [18]he endured their conduct for about forty years in the desert, [19]he overthrew seven nations in Canaan and gave their land to his people as their inheritance. [20]All this took about 450 years.

"After this, God gave them judges until the time of Samuel the prophet. [21]Then the people asked for a king, and he gave them Saul son of Kish, of the tribe of Benjamin, who ruled forty years. [22]After removing Saul, he made David their king. He testified concerning him: 'I have found David son of Jesse a man after my own heart; he will do everything I want him to do.'

[23]"From this man's descendants God has brought to Israel the Savior Jesus, as he promised."

A THOUGHT: *When they went to a new town to witness for Christ, Paul and Barnabas went first to the synagogue. The Jews who went to the synagogue believed in God and diligently studied the Scriptures. Tragically, however, many could not accept Jesus as the promised Messiah because they had the wrong idea of what kind of Messiah he would be. He was not a military king who would overthrow Rome's control, but a servant king who would overthrow sin in people's hearts. (Only later, when he returns, will he overthrow the nations of the world.) Paul and Barnabas did not separate themselves from the synagogues but tried to show clearly that the Scriptures the Jews studied pointed to Jesus.*

God Disciplines His Children/ Hebrews 12:5–11

And you have forgotten that word of encouragement that addresses you as sons:

> "My son, do not make light of the Lord's discipline,
>   and do not lose heart when he rebukes you,
> [6]because the Lord disciplines those he loves,
>   and he punishes everyone he accepts as a son."

[7]Endure hardship as discipline; God is treating you as sons. For what son is not disciplined by his father? [8]If you are not disciplined (and everyone undergoes discipline), then you are illegitimate children and not true sons. [9]Moreover, we have all had human fathers who disciplined us and we respected them for it. How much more should we submit to the Father of our spirits and live! [10]Our fathers

disciplined us for a little while as they thought best; but God disciplines us for our good, that we may share in his holiness. ¹¹No discipline seems pleasant at the time, but painful. Later on, however, it produces a harvest of righteousness and peace for those who have been trained by it.

A THOUGHT: *Who loves his child more—the father who allows the child to do what will harm him, or the one who corrects, trains, and even punishes the child to help him learn what is right? We may respond to discipline in several ways: (1) we can accept it with resignation; (2) we can accept it with self-pity, thinking we really don't deserve it; (3) we can be angry and resent God for it; or (4) we can accept it gratefully as the appropriate response towards a loving Father. It's never pleasant to be corrected and disciplined by God, but his discipline is a sign of his deep love for you. When God corrects you, see it as proof of his love and ask him what he is trying to teach you.*

Proverbs for Today/ 26:18–19

Like a madman shooting firebrands or deadly arrows is a man who deceives his neighbor and says, "I was only joking!"

OCTOBER 29

Paul Preaches to the Jews of Antioch/ Acts 13:24–44

"Before the coming of Jesus, John preached repentance and baptism to all the people of Israel. ²⁵As John was completing his work, he said: 'Who do you think I am? I am not that one. No, but he is coming after me, whose sandals I am not worthy to untie.'

²⁶"Brothers, children of Abraham, and you God-fearing Gentiles, it is to us that this message of salvation has been sent. ²⁷The people of Jerusalem and their rulers did not recognize Jesus, yet in condemning him they fulfilled the words of the prophets that are read every Sabbath. ²⁸Though they found no proper ground for a death sentence, they asked Pilate to have him executed. ²⁹When they had carried out all that was written about him, they took him down from the tree and laid him in a tomb. ³⁰But

God raised him from the dead, ³¹and for many days he was seen by those who had traveled with him from Galilee to Jerusalem. They are now his witnesses to our people.

³²"We tell you the good news: What God promised our fathers ³³he has fulfilled for us, their children, by raising up Jesus. As it is written in the second Psalm:

" 'You are my Son;
today I have become your Father.'

³⁴The fact that God raised him from the dead, never to decay, is stated in these words:

" 'I will give you the holy and sure blessings
promised to David.'

³⁵So it is stated elsewhere:

" 'You will not let your Holy One see decay.'

³⁶"For when David had served God's purpose in his own generation, he fell asleep; he was buried with his fathers and his body decayed. ³⁷But the one whom God raised from the dead did not see decay.

³⁸"Therefore, my brothers, I want you to know that through Jesus the forgiveness of sins is proclaimed to you. ³⁹Through him everyone who believes is justified from everything you could not be justified from by the law of Moses. ⁴⁰Take care that what the prophets have said does not happen to you:

⁴¹" 'Look, you scoffers,
wonder and perish,
for I am going to do something in your days
that you would never believe,
even if someone told you.'"

⁴²As Paul and Barnabas were leaving the synagogue, the people invited them to speak further about these things on the next Sabbath. ⁴³When the congregation was dismissed, many of the Jews and devout converts to Judaism followed Paul and Barnabas, who talked with them and urged them to continue in the grace of God.

⁴⁴On the next Sabbath almost the whole city gathered to hear the word of the Lord.

A THOUGHT: *Paul's message to the Jews in the synagogue in Antioch began with an emphasis on God's covenant with Israel. He began with a point of agreement, for all Jews were proud to be God's chosen people. Then Paul went on to explain how the Good News fulfilled this covenant, and some Jews found this message hard to take. This is the essence of the Good News— that forgiveness of sins and freedom from guilt are available to all people through faith in Christ— including you. Have you received this forgiveness? Are you refreshed by it each day?*

Commands for Christian Living/ Hebrews 12:12–17

Therefore, strengthen your feeble arms and weak knees. 13"Make level paths for your feet," so that the lame may not be disabled, but rather healed.

14Make every effort to live in peace with all men and to be holy; without holiness no one will see the Lord. 15See to it that no one misses the grace of God and that no bitter root grows up to cause trouble and defile many. 16See that no one is sexually immoral, or is godless like Esau, who for a single meal sold his inheritance rights as the oldest son. 17Afterward, as you know, when he wanted to inherit this blessing, he was rejected. He could bring about no change of mind, though he sought the blessing with tears.

A THOUGHT: *We must not live with only our own survival in mind. Others will follow our example, and we have a responsibility to them if we claim to live for Christ. Does your example make it easier for others to believe, follow, and mature in Christ? Or would those who follow you end up confused and misled?*

Proverbs for Today/ 26:20

Without wood a fire goes out; without gossip a quarrel dies down.

OCTOBER 30

Arguments Against Paul and Barnabas/ Acts 13:45–52

When the Jews saw the crowds, they were filled with jealousy and talked abusively against what Paul was saying.

46Then Paul and Barnabas answered them boldly: "We

had to speak the word of God to you first. Since you reject it and do not consider yourselves worthy of eternal life, we now turn to the Gentiles. 47For this is what the Lord has commanded us:

> " 'I have made you a light for the Gentiles,
>   that you may bring salvation to the ends of the
>   earth.' "

48When the Gentiles heard this, they were glad and honored the word of the Lord; and all who were appointed for eternal life believed.

49The word of the Lord spread through the whole region. 50But the Jews incited the God-fearing women of high standing and the leading men of the city. They stirred up persecution against Paul and Barnabas, and expelled them from their region. 51So they shook the dust from their feet in protest against them and went to Iconium. 52And the disciples were filled with joy and with the Holy Spirit.

A THOUGHT: *Instead of hearing the truth, these Jewish leaders ran Paul and Barnabas out of town. When confronted by a disturbing truth, people often turn away and refuse to listen. When God's Spirit points out needed changes in our lives, we must listen to him, or else we risk pushing the truth so far away that it no longer affects us.*

The Earthly and Heavenly Mount Zion/ Hebrews 12:18–24

You have not come to a mountain that can be touched and that is burning with fire; to darkness, gloom and storm; 19to a trumpet blast or to such a voice speaking words that those who heard it begged that no further word be spoken to them, 20because they could not bear what was commanded: "If even an animal touches the mountain, it must be stoned." 21The sight was so terrifying that Moses said, "I am trembling with fear."

22But you have come to Mount Zion, to the heavenly Jerusalem, the city of the living God. You have come to thousands upon thousands of angels in joyful assembly, 23to the church of the firstborn, whose names are written in heaven. You have come to God, the judge of all men, to the spirits of righteous men made perfect, 24to Jesus the mediator of a new covenant, and to the sprinkled blood that speaks a better word than the blood of Abel.

A THOUGHT: *There is a great contrast in the way people approached God under the old covenant and how people approach God under the new covenant. When God established the old covenant on Mount Sinai, the people experienced the terror of God. The Israelites saw God's awesome power demonstrated; they had to stand at a distance from the mountain. Only Moses was allowed to go up the mountain when he received the Ten Commandments. Under the new covenant, because of what Christ has done, Christians can enter directly into the presence of God without fear. Christ has made it possible to commune intimately with God the Father because he has secured the forgiveness of sin for his people. Let us come boldly before God on the basis of Christ's shed blood.*

Proverbs for Today/ 26:21–22

As charcoal to embers and as wood to fire, so is a quarrelsome man for kindling strife. □ The words of a gossip are like choice morsels; they go down to a man's inmost parts.

OCTOBER 31

The Good News Preached at Iconium/ Acts 14:1–7

At Iconium Paul and Barnabas went as usual into the Jewish synagogue. There they spoke so effectively that a great number of Jews and Gentiles believed. 2But the Jews who refused to believe stirred up the Gentiles and poisoned their minds against the brothers. 3So Paul and Barnabas spent considerable time there, speaking boldly for the Lord, who confirmed the message of his grace by enabling them to do miraculous signs and wonders. 4The people of the city were divided; some sided with the Jews, others with the apostles. 5There was a plot afoot among the Gentiles and Jews, together with their leaders, to mistreat them and stone them. 6But they found out about it and fled to the Lycaonian cities of Lystra and Derbe and to the surrounding country, 7where they continued to preach the good news.

A THOUGHT: *We may wish we could perform a miraculous act that would convince everyone once and for all that Jesus is the Lord, but we see here that even if we could, it wouldn't convince everyone. God gave these men power to do great miracles as proof, but people were still divided. Don't spend your time and energy wishing for miracles.*

Sow your seeds of Good News on the best ground you can find in the best way you can, and leave the convincing to the Holy Spirit.

Worship God with Reverence and Awe/
Hebrews 12:25–29

See to it that you do not refuse him who speaks. If they did not escape when they refused him who warned them on earth, how much less will we, if we turn away from him who warns us from heaven? 26At that time his voice shook the earth, but now he has promised, "Once more I will shake not only the earth but also the heavens." 27The words "once more" indicate the removing of what can be shaken—that is, created things—so that what cannot be shaken may remain.

28Therefore, since we are receiving a kingdom that cannot be shaken, let us be thankful, and so worship God acceptably with reverence and awe, 29for our "God is a consuming fire."

A THOUGHT: *Eventually the world will crumble, and only God's kingdom will last. Those who follow Christ are part of this kingdom, and they will withstand the shaking, sifting, and burning. When we feel unsure about the future, we can take confidence with these verses. Whatever happens here, our future is built on a solid foundation that cannot be destroyed. Don't put your confidence in that which will be destroyed; instead, build your life on Christ and his unshakable kingdom.*

Proverbs for Today/ 26:23

Like a coating of glaze over earthenware are fervent lips with an evil heart.

NOVEMBER 1

Paul Is Stoned in Lystra/ Acts 14:8–20a

In Lystra there sat a man crippled in his feet, who was lame from birth and had never walked. 9He listened to Paul as he was speaking. Paul looked directly at him, saw that he had faith to be healed 10and called out, "Stand up on your feet!" At that, the man jumped up and began to walk.

11When the crowd saw what Paul had done, they shouted

in the Lycaonian language, "The gods have come down to us in human form!" 12Barnabas they called Zeus, and Paul they called Hermes because he was the chief speaker. 13The priest of Zeus, whose temple was just outside the city, brought bulls and wreaths to the city gates because he and the crowd wanted to offer sacrifices to them.

14But when the apostles Barnabas and Paul heard of this, they tore their clothes and rushed out into the crowd, shouting: 15"Men, why are you doing this? We too are only men, human like you. We are bringing you good news, telling you to turn from these worthless things to the living God, who made heaven and earth and sea and everything in them. 16In the past, he let all nations go their own way. 17Yet he has not left himself without testimony: He has shown kindness by giving you rain from heaven and crops in their seasons; he provides you with plenty of food and fills your hearts with joy." 18Even with these words, they had difficulty keeping the crowd from sacrificing to them.

19Then some Jews came from Antioch and Iconium and won the crowd over. They stoned Paul and dragged him outside the city, thinking he was dead. 20But after the disciples had gathered around him, he got up and went back into the city.

A THOUGHT: *Paul and Barnabas were dedicated to sharing the Good News. They were not out for fame and fortune. Here they had a prime opportunity to get rich quick by capitalizing on the honor these Gentiles wanted to bestow upon them. These people considered Barnabas to be Jupiter (the Roman name for Zeus, the chief god in Greco-Roman mythology), and considered Paul to be Mercury (the Roman name for the Greek god Hermes). But Paul and Barnabas were terribly upset that these people would do such a thing. They were there to share the Good News about Jesus Christ—he alone is the way to the living God. Paul's dedication to sharing the Good News can be seen in the fact that after he was nearly stoned to death, he rose up and went back into the city to preach the gospel. We must sacrifice our own self-interests in order to share the Good News to the glory of God.*

Live Holy and Obedient Lives/ Hebrews 13:1–9

Keep on loving each other as brothers. 2Do not forget to entertain strangers, for by so doing some people have entertained angels without knowing it. 3Remember those in prison as if you were their fellow prisoners, and those who are mistreated as if you yourselves were suffering.

⁴Marriage should be honored by all, and the marriage bed kept pure, for God will judge the adulterer and all the sexually immoral. ⁵Keep your lives free from the love of money and be content with what you have, because God has said,

> "Never will I leave you;
> never will I forsake you."

⁶So we say with confidence,

> "The Lord is my helper; I will not be afraid.
> What can man do to me?"

⁷Remember your leaders, who spoke the word of God to you. Consider the outcome of their way of life and imitate their faith. ⁸Jesus Christ is the same yesterday and today and forever.

⁹Do not be carried away by all kinds of strange teachings. It is good for our hearts to be strengthened by grace, not by ceremonial foods, which are of no value to those who eat them.

A THOUGHT: *Real love toward others produces tangible actions: (1) kindness to strangers; (2) sympathy for those who are in prison and those who have been mistreated; (3) respect for one's marriage vows; and (4) satisfaction with what you have. Make sure your love runs deep enough to affect your hospitality, sympathy, fidelity, and contentment.*

Proverbs for Today/ 26:24–26

A malicious man disguises himself with his lips, but in his heart he harbors deceit. Though his speech is charming, do not believe him, for seven abominations fill his heart. His malice may be concealed by deception, but his wickedness will be exposed in the assembly.

NOVEMBER 2

Paul and Barnabas Return to Antioch/
Acts 14:20b–28

The next day he [Paul] and Barnabas left for Derbe.
21They preached the good news in that city and won a
large number of disciples. Then they returned to Lystra,
Iconium and Antioch, 22strengthening the disciples and encouraging them to remain true to the faith. "We must go
through many hardships to enter the kingdom of God,"
they said. 23Paul and Barnabas appointed elders for them
in each church and, with prayer and fasting, committed
them to the Lord, in whom they had put their trust. 24After
going through Pisidia, they came into Pamphylia, 25and
when they had preached the word in Perga, they went
down to Attalia.

26From Attalia they sailed back to Antioch, where they
had been committed to the grace of God for the work they
had now completed. 27On arriving there, they gathered the
church together and reported all that God had done through
them and how he had opened the door of faith to the
Gentiles. 28And they stayed there a long time with the
disciples.

A THOUGHT: *Paul and Barnabas returned to visit the believers in all
the cities where they had recently been threatened and physically
attacked. They knew the dangers they faced, yet they believed they had
a responsibility to encourage the new believers. No matter how inconvenient or uncomfortable the task may seem, we must never fail to
support new believers who need our help and encouragement.*

Suffering with Christ/ Hebrews 13:10–16

We have an altar from which those who minister at the
tabernacle have no right to eat.
11The high priest carries the blood of animals into the
Most Holy Place as a sin offering, but the bodies are burned
outside the camp. 12And so Jesus also suffered outside the
city gate to make the people holy through his own blood.
13Let us, then, go to him outside the camp, bearing the
disgrace he bore. 14For here we do not have an enduring
city, but we are looking for the city that is to come.
15Through Jesus, therefore, let us continually offer to

God a sacrifice of praise—the fruit of lips that confess his name. 16And do not forget to do good and to share with others, for with such sacrifices God is pleased.

A THOUGHT: *"Let us, then, go to him outside the camp, bearing the disgrace he bore." The Jewish Christians were being ridiculed and persecuted by Jews who didn't believe in Jesus the Messiah. Most of the book of Hebrews tells them how much greater Christ is than the sacrificial system. Now the writer makes the point of his lengthy argument: It may be necessary to leave the "camp" and suffer with Christ. To be outside the camp meant to be unclean. But Jesus suffered humiliation and uncleanness outside the Jerusalem gates on their behalf. The time had come for Jewish Christians to declare their loyalty to Christ above any other loyalty, to choose to follow the Messiah whatever suffering that might entail. Is there anything holding us back from complete loyalty to Jesus Christ?*

Proverbs for Today/ 26:27

If a man digs a pit, he will fall into it; if a man rolls a stone, it will roll back on him.

NOVEMBER 3

The Jerusalem Church Council/ Acts 15:1–21

Some men came down from Judea to Antioch and were teaching the brothers: "Unless you are circumcised, according to the custom taught by Moses, you cannot be saved." 2This brought Paul and Barnabas into sharp dispute and debate with them. So Paul and Barnabas were appointed, along with some other believers, to go up to Jerusalem to see the apostles and elders about this question. 3The church sent them on their way, and as they traveled through Phoenicia and Samaria, they told how the Gentiles had been converted. This news made all the brothers very glad. 4When they came to Jerusalem, they were welcomed by the church and the apostles and elders, to whom they reported everything God had done through them.

5Then some of the believers who belonged to the party of the Pharisees stood up and said, "The Gentiles must be circumcised and required to obey the law of Moses."

⁶The apostles and elders met to consider this question. ⁷After much discussion, Peter got up and addressed them: "Brothers, you know that some time ago God made a choice among you that the Gentiles might hear from my lips the message of the gospel and believe. ⁸God, who knows the heart, showed that he accepted them by giving the Holy Spirit to them, just as he did to us. ⁹He made no distinction between us and them, for he purified their hearts by faith. ¹⁰Now then, why do you try to test God by putting on the necks of the disciples a yoke that neither we nor our fathers have been able to bear? ¹¹No! We believe it is through the grace of our Lord Jesus that we are saved, just as they are."

¹²The whole assembly became silent as they listened to Barnabas and Paul telling about the miraculous signs and wonders God had done among the Gentiles through them. ¹³When they finished, James spoke up: "Brothers, listen to me. ¹⁴Simon has described to us how God at first showed his concern by taking from the Gentiles a people for himself. ¹⁵The words of the prophets are in agreement with this, as it is written:

¹⁶" 'After this I will return
　　and rebuild David's fallen tent.
　Its ruins I will rebuild,
　　and I will restore it,
¹⁷that the remnant of men may seek the Lord,
　　and all the Gentiles who bear my name,
　says the Lord, who does these things'
¹⁸　that have been known for ages.

¹⁹"It is my judgment, therefore, that we should not make it difficult for the Gentiles who are turning to God. ²⁰Instead we should write to them, telling them to abstain from food polluted by idols, from sexual immorality, from the meat of strangled animals and from blood. ²¹For Moses has been preached in every city from the earliest times and is read in the synagogues on every Sabbath."

A THOUGHT: *The real problem for the Jewish Christians was not over whether Gentiles could be saved, but whether Gentiles had to adhere to the laws of Moses. The test of whether or not the law was being followed was circumcision. The Jewish Christians were worried because soon there would be more Gentile than Jewish Christians, and the Jews were afraid of weakening moral standards among believers if they did not follow Jewish laws. Paul, Barnabas, and the other church leaders believed that the Old Testament Law was very important, but it was not a prerequisite to salvation. The Law cannot save; only faith in Jesus Christ can save.*

Final Commands and a Benediction/ Hebrews 13:17–25

Obey your leaders and submit to their authority. They keep watch over you as men who must give an account. Obey them so that their work will be a joy, not a burden, for that would be of no advantage to you.

18Pray for us. We are sure that we have a clear conscience and desire to live honorably in every way. 19I particularly urge you to pray so that I may be restored to you soon.

20May the God of peace, who through the blood of the eternal covenant brought back from the dead our Lord Jesus, that great Shepherd of the sheep, 21equip you with everything good for doing his will, and may he work in us what is pleasing to him, through Jesus Christ, to whom be glory for ever and ever. Amen.

22Brothers, I urge you to bear with my word of exhortation, for I have written you only a short letter.

23I want you to know that our brother Timothy has been released. If he arrives soon, I will come with him to see you.

24Greet all your leaders and all God's people. Those from Italy send you their greetings.

25Grace be with you all.

A THOUGHT: *The writer of Hebrews recognized the need for prayer. Christian leaders are especially vulnerable to criticism from others, pride if they succeed, depression if they fail, and Satan's constant efforts to nullify their work for God. They desperately need our prayers! For whom should you regularly pray?*

Proverbs for Today/ 26:28

A lying tongue hates those it hurts, and a flattering mouth works ruin.

NOVEMBER 4

A Letter to Gentile Believers/ Acts 15:22–41

Then the apostles and elders, with the whole church, decided to choose some of their own men and send them to Antioch with Paul and Barnabas. They chose Judas (called Barsabbas) and Silas, two men who were leaders among the brothers. 23With them they sent the following letter:

The apostles and elders, your brothers,

To the Gentile believers in Antioch, Syria and Cilicia:

Greetings.

24We have heard that some went out from us without our authorization and disturbed you, troubling your minds by what they said. 25So we all agreed to choose some men and send them to you with our dear friends Barnabas and Paul— 26men who have risked their lives for the name of our Lord Jesus Christ. 27Therefore we are sending Judas and Silas to confirm by word of mouth what we are writing. 28It seemed good to the Holy Spirit and to us not to burden you with anything beyond the following requirements: 29You are to abstain from food sacrificed to idols, from blood, from the meat of strangled animals and from sexual immorality. You will do well to avoid these things.

Farewell.

30The men were sent off and went down to Antioch, where they gathered the church together and delivered the letter. 31The people read it and were glad for its encouraging message. 32Judas and Silas, who themselves were prophets, said much to encourage and strengthen the brothers. 33After spending some time there, they were sent off by the brothers with the blessing of peace to return to those who had sent them. * 35But Paul and Barnabas remained in Antioch, where they and many others taught and preached the word of the Lord.

*33 Some manuscripts *them,* 34but Silas decided to remain there.

36Some time later Paul said to Barnabas, "Let us go back and visit the brothers in all the towns where we preached the word of the Lord and see how they are doing." 37Barnabas wanted to take John, also called Mark, with them, 38but Paul did not think it wise to take him, because he had deserted them in Pamphylia and had not continued with them in the work. 39They had such a sharp disagreement that they parted company. Barnabas took Mark and sailed for Cyprus, 40but Paul chose Silas and left, commended by the brothers to the grace of the Lord. 41He went through Syria and Cilicia, strengthening the churches.

A THOUGHT: *Gentile believers did not have to abide by the Jewish law of circumcision, but they were asked by the council to stay away from idolatry, sexual immorality (a common part of idol worship), and eating the meat of animals which have not had all the blood drained out of them (reflecting the Levitical teaching that the life of an animal is in its blood). If Gentile Christians would abstain from these three practices, they would please God and get along better with fellow Jewish Christians. Of course, there were other actions inappropriate for believers, but the Jews were especially concerned about these three. This compromise kept the church from being unnecessarily hindered by the cultural differences between Jews and Gentiles. When we share our message across cultural and economic boundaries, we must be sure that the requirements for faith we set up are God's universal requirements, not our particular cultural expressions of Christianity.*

Trials Build Character/ James 1:1–4

James, a servant of God and of the Lord Jesus Christ,

To the twelve tribes scattered among the nations:

Greetings.

2Consider it pure joy, my brothers, whenever you face trials of many kinds, 3because you know that the testing of your faith develops perseverance. 4Perseverance must finish its work so that you may be mature and complete, not lacking anything.

A THOUGHT: *We can't really know the depth of our own character until we see how we react under pressure. It is easy to be kind when everything is going well, but can we still be kind when others are treating us unfairly? Instead of complaining about our struggles, we should see them as opportunities for growth. Thank God for promising to be with you in rough times. Ask him to help you solve your problems or give you the strength to endure them. Then be patient. God will not leave you alone with your problems; he will stay close by and help you grow through the trials.*

Proverbs for Today/ 27:1–2

Do not boast about tomorrow, for you do not know what a day may bring forth. □ Let another praise you, and not your own mouth; someone else, and not your own lips.

NOVEMBER 5

Paul's Second Missionary Journey/ Acts 16:1–10

He [Paul] came to Derbe and then to Lystra, where a disciple named Timothy lived, whose mother was a Jewess and a believer, but whose father was a Greek. 2The brothers at Lystra and Iconium spoke well of him. 3Paul wanted to take him along on the journey, so he circumcised him because of the Jews who lived in the area, for they all knew that his father was a Greek. 4As they traveled from town to town, they delivered the decisions reached by the apostles and elders in Jerusalem for the people to obey. 5So the churches were strengthened in the faith and grew daily in numbers.

6Paul and his companions traveled throughout the region of Phrygia and Galatia, having been kept by the Holy Spirit from preaching the word in the province of Asia. 7When they came to the border of Mysia, they tried to enter Bithynia, but the Spirit of Jesus would not allow them to. 8So they passed by Mysia and went down to Troas. 9During the night Paul had a vision of a man of Macedonia standing and begging him, "Come over to Macedonia and help us." 10After Paul had seen the vision, we got ready at once to leave for Macedonia, concluding that God had called us to preach the gospel to them.

A THOUGHT: *We don't know how the Holy Spirit told Paul that he and his men were not to go into Asia. It may have been through a prophet, a vision, an inner conviction, or some other circumstance. To know God's will does not mean we must audibly hear his voice. He leads in different ways. When seeking God's will (1) make sure your plan is in harmony with God's Word; (2) ask mature Christians for their advice; (3) check your own motives—are you seeking to do what you want or what you believe God wants?—and (4) pray for God to open and close the doors of circumstances.*

God Supplies Wisdom to Those Who Ask/
James 1:5–8

If any of you lacks wisdom, he should ask God, who gives generously to all without finding fault, and it will be given to him. 6But when he asks, he must believe and not doubt, because he who doubts is like a wave of the sea, blown and tossed by the wind. 7That man should not think he will receive anything from the Lord; 8he is a double-minded man, unstable in all he does.

A THOUGHT: *When James speaks of wisdom, he means practical discernment. Wisdom begins with respect for God, leads to right living, and results in an increased ability to tell right from wrong. God is willing to give us this wisdom. We will be unable to receive it if our goals are self-centered instead of God-centered. To learn God's will, we need to ask him to reveal it to us, and then we must be willing to do what he tells us to do.*

Proverbs for Today/ 27:3

Stone is heavy and sand a burden, but provocation by a fool is heavier than both.

NOVEMBER 6

Lydia's Conversion/ Acts 16:11–15

From Troas we [Luke, Paul, and his companions] put out to sea and sailed straight for Samothrace, and the next day on to Neapolis. 12From there we traveled to Philippi, a Roman colony and the leading city of that district of Macedonia. And we stayed there several days.

13On the Sabbath we went outside the city gate to the river, where we expected to find a place of prayer. We sat down and began to speak to the women who had gathered there. 14One of those listening was a woman named Lydia, a dealer in purple cloth from the city of Thyatira, who was a worshiper of God. The Lord opened her heart to respond to Paul's message. 15When she and the members of her household were baptized, she invited us to her home. "If you consider me a believer in the Lord," she said, "come and stay at my house." And she persuaded us.

A THOUGHT: *After following the Holy Spirit's leading into Macedonia, Paul made his first evangelistic contact with a small group of women. Paul never allowed sexual or cultural boundaries to keep him from preaching the gospel. He preached to these women; and Lydia, an influential merchant, believed. This threw open the door for ministry in that region. In the early church God often worked in and through women. We should be careful not to exclude any group from hearing the gospel or participating in the ministry of the church.*

Enduring Temptation/ James 1:9–18

The brother in humble circumstances ought to take pride in his high position. 10But the one who is rich should take pride in his low position, because he will pass away like a wild flower. 11For the sun rises with scorching heat and withers the plant; its blossom falls and its beauty is destroyed. In the same way, the rich man will fade away even while he goes about his business.

12Blessed is the man who perseveres under trial, because when he has stood the test, he will receive the crown of life that God has promised to those who love him.

13When tempted, no one should say, "God is tempting me." For God cannot be tempted by evil, nor does he tempt anyone; 14but each one is tempted when, by his own evil desire, he is dragged away and enticed. 15Then, after desire has conceived, it gives birth to sin; and sin, when it is full-grown, gives birth to death.

16Don't be deceived, my dear brothers. 17Every good and perfect gift is from above, coming down from the Father of the heavenly lights, who does not change like shifting shadows. 18He chose to give us birth through the word of truth, that we might be a kind of firstfruits of all he created.

A THOUGHT: *The rich should be glad wealth means nothing to God, because wealth is easily lost. The poor should be glad riches mean nothing to God, otherwise they would be considered unworthy. True wealth is found in an individual's spiritual life, not his or her financial assets. God is interested in what is lasting (our souls), not in what is temporary (our money and possessions). If wealth, power, and status mean nothing to God, why do we attribute so much importance to them and honor those who possess them? Do your material possessions give you a sense of purpose and a reason for living? If they were gone, what would be left? What you have in your heart, not your bank account, matters to God and endures for eternity.*

Proverbs for Today/ 27:4–6

Anger is cruel and fury overwhelming, but who can stand before jealousy? □ Better is open rebuke than hidden love. □ Wounds from a friend can be trusted, but an enemy multiplies kisses.

NOVEMBER 7

The Conversion of the Philippian Jailer/
Acts 16:16–40

Once when we [Luke, Paul, and his companions] were going to the place of prayer, we were met by a slave girl who had a spirit by which she predicted the future. She earned a great deal of money for her owners by fortune-telling. [17]This girl followed Paul and the rest of us, shouting, "These men are servants of the Most High God, who are telling you the way to be saved." [18]She kept this up for many days. Finally Paul became so troubled that he turned around and said to the spirit, "In the name of Jesus Christ I command you to come out of her!" At that moment the spirit left her.

[19]When the owners of the slave girl realized that their hope of making money was gone, they seized Paul and Silas and dragged them into the marketplace to face the authorities. [20]They brought them before the magistrates and said, "These men are Jews, and are throwing our city into an uproar [21]by advocating customs unlawful for us Romans to accept or practice."

[22]The crowd joined in the attack against Paul and Silas, and the magistrates ordered them to be stripped and beaten. [23]After they had been severely flogged, they were thrown into prison, and the jailer was commanded to guard them carefully. [24]Upon receiving such orders, he put them in the inner cell and fastened their feet in the stocks.

[25]About midnight Paul and Silas were praying and singing hymns to God, and the other prisoners were listening to them. [26]Suddenly there was such a violent earthquake that the foundations of the prison were shaken. At once all the

prison doors flew open, and everybody's chains came loose. 27The jailer woke up, and when he saw the prison doors open, he drew his sword and was about to kill himself because he thought the prisoners had escaped. 28But Paul shouted, "Don't harm yourself! We are all here!"

29The jailer called for lights, rushed in and fell trembling before Paul and Silas. 30He then brought them out and asked, "Sirs, what must I do to be saved?"

31They replied, "Believe in the Lord Jesus, and you will be saved—you and your household." 32Then they spoke the word of the Lord to him and to all the others in his house. 33At that hour of the night the jailer took them and washed their wounds; then immediately he and all his family were baptized. 34The jailer brought them into his house and set a meal before them; he was filled with joy because he had come to believe in God—he and his whole family.

35When it was daylight, the magistrates sent their officers to the jailer with the order: "Release those men." 36The jailer told Paul, "The magistrates have ordered that you and Silas be released. Now you can leave. Go in peace."

37But Paul said to the officers: "They beat us publicly without a trial, even though we are Roman citizens, and threw us into prison. And now do they want to get rid of us quietly? No! Let them come themselves and escort us out."

38The officers reported this to the magistrates, and when they heard that Paul and Silas were Roman citizens, they were alarmed. 39They came to appease them and escorted them from the prison, requesting them to leave the city. 40After Paul and Silas came out of the prison, they went to Lydia's house, where they met with the brothers and encouraged them. Then they left.

A THOUGHT: *Paul and Silas were stripped, beaten, whipped, and placed in stocks in the inner prison dungeon. Despite this dismal situation, they praised God, praying and singing as the other prisoners listened. God caused an earthquake to occur which opened the prison doors, and all the chains fastened around the prisoners fell off. The jailer immediately drew his sword to commit suicide because Roman soldiers were usually executed if a prisoner was allowed to escape, and the Philippian jailer knew that he would be held responsible. Paul intervened to prevent the jailer from killing himself. Paul shared the gospel with the jailer and he became a Christian. We must always be open to those opportunities that God opens up to share the Good News with others.*

Hearing and Doing/ James 1:19–27

My dear brothers, take note of this: Everyone should be quick to listen, slow to speak and slow to become angry, 20for man's anger does not bring about the righteous life that God desires. 21Therefore, get rid of all moral filth and the evil that is so prevalent and humbly accept the word planted in you, which can save you.

22Do not merely listen to the word, and so deceive yourselves. Do what it says. 23Anyone who listens to the word but does not do what it says is like a man who looks at his face in a mirror 24and, after looking at himself, goes away and immediately forgets what he looks like. 25But the man who looks intently into the perfect law that gives freedom, and continues to do this, not forgetting what he has heard, but doing it—he will be blessed in what he does.

26If anyone considers himself religious and yet does not keep a tight rein on his tongue, he deceives himself and his religion is worthless. 27Religion that God our Father accepts as pure and faultless is this: to look after orphans and widows in their distress and to keep oneself from being polluted by the world.

A THOUGHT: *When we talk too much and listen too little, we communicate to others that we think our ideas are much more important than theirs. James wisely advises us to reverse this process. Put a mental stopwatch on your conversations and keep track of how much you talk and how much you listen. In your conversations, do others feel that their viewpoints and ideas have value?*

Proverbs for Today/ 27:7–9

He who is full loathes honey, but to the hungry even what is bitter tastes sweet. □ Like a bird that strays from its nest is a man who strays from his home. □ Perfume and incense bring joy to the heart, and the pleasantness of one's friend springs from his earnest counsel.

NOVEMBER 8

Paul and Silas in Thessalonica and Berea/
Acts 17:1–15

When they [Paul and Silas] had passed through Amphipolis and Apollonia, they came to Thessalonica, where there was a Jewish synagogue. 2As his custom was, Paul went into the synagogue, and on three Sabbath days he reasoned with them from the Scriptures, 3explaining and proving that the Christ had to suffer and rise from the dead. "This Jesus I am proclaiming to you is the Christ," he said. 4Some of the Jews were persuaded and joined Paul and Silas, as did a large number of God-fearing Greeks and not a few prominent women.

5But the Jews were jealous; so they rounded up some bad characters from the marketplace, formed a mob and started a riot in the city. They rushed to Jason's house in search of Paul and Silas in order to bring them out to the crowd. 6But when they did not find them, they dragged Jason and some other brothers before the city officials, shouting: "These men who have caused trouble all over the world have now come here, 7and Jason has welcomed them into his house. They are all defying Caesar's decrees, saying that there is another king, one called Jesus." 8When they heard this, the crowd and the city officials were thrown into turmoil. 9Then they made Jason and the others post bond and let them go.

10As soon as it was night, the brothers sent Paul and Silas away to Berea. On arriving there, they went to the Jewish synagogue. 11Now the Bereans were of more noble character than the Thessalonians, for they received the message with great eagerness and examined the Scriptures every day to see if what Paul said was true. 12Many of the Jews believed, as did also a number of prominent Greek women and many Greek men.

13When the Jews in Thessalonica learned that Paul was preaching the word of God at Berea, they went there too, agitating the crowds and stirring them up. 14The brothers immediately sent Paul to the coast, but Silas and Timothy stayed at Berea. 15The men who escorted Paul brought him to Athens and then left with instructions for Silas and Timothy to join him as soon as possible.

A THOUGHT: *What a reputation these early Christians had; they truly "turned the world upside down!" The power of the gospel revolutionized lives, crossed all social barriers, threw open prison doors, caused people to care deeply for one another, and stirred them to worship God. Our world needs to be turned upside down, to be transformed. The gospel is not in the business of merely improving programs and conduct, but of dynamically transforming lives.*

Do Not Favor the Rich/ James 2:1–9

My brothers, as believers in our glorious Lord Jesus Christ, don't show favoritism. 2Suppose a man comes into your meeting wearing a gold ring and fine clothes, and a poor man in shabby clothes also comes in. 3If you show special attention to the man wearing fine clothes and say, "Here's a good seat for you," but say to the poor man, "You stand there" or "Sit on the floor by my feet," 4have you not discriminated among yourselves and become judges with evil thoughts?

5Listen, my dear brothers: Has not God chosen those who are poor in the eyes of the world to be rich in faith and to inherit the kingdom he promised those who love him? 6But you have insulted the poor. Is it not the rich who are exploiting you? Are they not the ones who are dragging you into court? 7Are they not the ones who are slandering the noble name of him to whom you belong?

8If you really keep the royal law found in Scripture, "Love your neighbor as yourself," you are doing right. 9But if you show favoritism, you sin and are convicted by the law as lawbreakers.

A THOUGHT: *Often we treat a well-dressed, impressive-looking person better than someone who looks poor. We do this because we would rather identify with successful people than with apparent failures. We feel better about ourselves when we associate with people we admire. The irony, as James reminds us, is that the supposed winners may have gained their impressive lifestyle at our expense. In addition, the rich find it hard to identify with the Lord Jesus who came as a humble servant. Are you easily impressed by status, wealth, or fame? Are you partial to the "haves" while ignoring the "have nots"? This prejudice is sin. God views all people as equals, and if he favors anyone, it is the poor and the powerless. We should follow his example.*

Proverbs for Today/ 27:10

Do not forsake your friend and the friend of your father,
and do not go to your brother's house when disaster strikes
you—better a neighbor nearby than a brother far away.

NOVEMBER 9

Paul Preaches in Athens/ Acts 17:16–34

While Paul was waiting for them [Silas and Timothy] in
Athens, he was greatly distressed to see that the city was
full of idols. 17So he reasoned in the synagogue with the
Jews and the God-fearing Greeks, as well as in the marketplace day by day with those who happened to be there. 18A
group of Epicurean and Stoic philosophers began to dispute
with him. Some of them asked, "What is this babbler trying
to say?" Others remarked, "He seems to be advocating
foreign gods." They said this because Paul was preaching
the good news about Jesus and the resurrection. 19Then
they took him and brought him to a meeting of the Areopagus, where they said to him, "May we know what this new
teaching is that you are presenting? 20You are bringing
some strange ideas to our ears, and we want to know what
they mean." 21(All the Athenians and the foreigners who
lived there spent their time doing nothing but talking about
and listening to the latest ideas.)

22Paul then stood up in the meeting of the Areopagus and
said: "Men of Athens! I see that in every way you are very
religious. 23For as I walked around and looked carefully at
your objects of worship, I even found an altar with this
inscription: TO AN UNKNOWN GOD. Now what you worship as
something unknown I am going to proclaim to you.

24"The God who made the world and everything in it is
the Lord of heaven and earth and does not live in temples
built by hands. 25And he is not served by human hands, as
if he needed anything, because he himself gives all men life
and breath and everything else. 26From one man he made
every nation of men, that they should inhabit the whole
earth; and he determined the times set for them and the

exact places where they should live. 27God did this so that men would seek him and perhaps reach out for him and find him, though he is not far from each one of us. 28'For in him we live and move and have our being.' As some of your own poets have said, 'We are his offspring.'

29"Therefore since we are God's offspring, we should not think that the divine being is like gold or silver or stone—an image made by man's design and skill. 30In the past God overlooked such ignorance, but now he commands all people everywhere to repent. 31For he has set a day when he will judge the world with justice by the man he has appointed. He has given proof of this to all men by raising him from the dead."

32When they heard about the resurrection of the dead, some of them sneered, but others said, "We want to hear you again on this subject." 33At that, Paul left the Council. 34A few men became followers of Paul and believed. Among them was Dionysius, a member of the Areopagus, also a woman named Damaris, and a number of others.

A THOUGHT: *Paul was well prepared to speak to this group. He came from Tarsus, an educational center, and had the training and knowledge to present his beliefs clearly and persuasively. Paul was a rabbi, taught by the finest scholar of his day, Gamaliel, and he had spent much of his life thinking and reasoning through the Scriptures.*

It is not enough to teach or preach with conviction. Like Paul, we must be prepared. The more we know about the Bible, what it means, and how to apply it to our lives, the more convincing our words will be. This does not mean we should avoid presenting the gospel until we feel adequately prepared. We should work with what we know, but always want to know more in order to reach more people and answer their questions and arguments more effectively.

Breaking One Commandment Violates the Whole Law/ James 2:10–13

For whoever keeps the whole law and yet stumbles at just one point is guilty of breaking all of it. 11For he who said, "Do not commit adultery," also said, "Do not murder." If you do not commit adultery but do commit murder, you have become a lawbreaker.

12Speak and act as those who are going to be judged by the law that gives freedom, 13because judgment without mercy will be shown to anyone who has not been merciful. Mercy triumphs over judgment!

A THOUGHT: *It is easy to spot sins in others while we overlook or rationalize our own. James reminds us that if we've broken just one law, we are sinners. You can't break the law a little bit; if you have broken it at all, you need Christ to pay for your sin. Measure yourself, not someone else, against God's standards. Ask for forgiveness where you need it, and then renew your effort to show your faith by your actions.*

Proverbs for Today/ 27:11

Be wise, my son, and bring joy to my heart; then I can answer anyone who treats me with contempt.

NOVEMBER 10

Paul Meets Priscilla and Aquila/ Acts 18:1–8

After this, Paul left Athens and went to Corinth. 2There he met a Jew named Aquila, a native of Pontus, who had recently come from Italy with his wife Priscilla, because Claudius had ordered all the Jews to leave Rome. Paul went to see them, 3and because he was a tentmaker as they were, he stayed and worked with them. 4Every Sabbath he reasoned in the synagogue, trying to persuade Jews and Greeks.

5When Silas and Timothy came from Macedonia, Paul devoted himself exclusively to preaching, testifying to the Jews that Jesus was the Christ. 6But when the Jews opposed Paul and became abusive, he shook out his clothes in protest and said to them, "Your blood be on your own heads! I am clear of my responsibility. From now on I will go to the Gentiles."

7Then Paul left the synagogue and went next door to the house of Titius Justus, a worshiper of God. 8Crispus, the synagogue ruler, and his entire household believed in the Lord; and many of the Corinthians who heard him believed and were baptized.

A THOUGHT: *Some couples know how to make the most of life. They complement each other, utilize each other's strengths, and form an effective team. Their united efforts affect those around them. Aquila and Priscilla were such a couple. They are never mentioned separately in the Bible. In marriage and ministry, they were together.*

Priscilla and Aquila met Paul in Corinth during his second missionary journey. They had just been expelled from Rome due to Emperor Claudius' decree against the Jews. Their home was as movable as the tents they made to support themselves. They opened their home to Paul, and he joined them in tentmaking. Paul shared with them his wealth of spiritual wisdom.

Genuine Faith Produces Good Deeds/ James 2:14–26

What good is it, my brothers, if a man claims to have faith but has no deeds? Can such faith save him? 15Suppose a brother or sister is without clothes and daily food. 16If one of you says to him, "Go, I wish you well; keep warm and well fed," but does nothing about his physical needs, what good is it? 17In the same way, faith by itself, if it is not accompanied by action, is dead.

18But someone will say, "You have faith; I have deeds."

Show me your faith without deeds, and I will show you my faith by what I do. 19You believe that there is one God. Good! Even the demons believe that—and shudder.

20You foolish man, do you want evidence that faith without deeds is useless? 21Was not our ancestor Abraham considered righteous for what he did when he offered his son Isaac on the altar? 22You see that his faith and his actions were working together, and his faith was made complete by what he did. 23And the scripture was fulfilled that says, "Abraham believed God, and it was credited to him as righteousness," and he was called God's friend. 24You see that a person is justified by what he does and not by faith alone.

25In the same way, was not even Rahab the prostitute considered righteous for what she did when she gave lodging to the spies and sent them off in a different direction? 26As the body without the spirit is dead, so faith without deeds is dead.

A THOUGHT: *Intellectual assent—agreement with a set of Christian teachings—is incomplete faith. True faith transforms our lives. If our lives remain unchanged, we don't truly believe the truths we claim to believe. Living the way God wants us to live does not earn our way into heaven, but it shows that our commitment to God is real. Godly conduct is not a substitute for, but a verification of our faith in Christ.*

Proverbs for Today/ 27:12

The prudent see danger and take refuge, but the simple keep going and suffer for it.

NOVEMBER 11

Gallio Releases Paul/ Acts 18:9–23

One night the Lord spoke to Paul in a vision: "Do not be afraid; keep on speaking, do not be silent. 10For I am with you, and no one is going to attack and harm you, because I have many people in this city." 11So Paul stayed for a year and a half, teaching them the word of God.

12While Gallio was proconsul of Achaia, the Jews made a united attack on Paul and brought him into court. 13"This man," they charged, "is persuading the people to worship God in ways contrary to the law."

14Just as Paul was about to speak, Gallio said to the Jews, "If you Jews were making a complaint about some misdemeanor or serious crime, it would be reasonable for me to listen to you. 15But since it involves questions about words and names and your own law—settle the matter yourselves. I will not be a judge of such things." 16So he had them ejected from the court. 17Then they all turned on Sosthenes the synagogue ruler and beat him in front of the court. But Gallio showed no concern whatever.

18Paul stayed on in Corinth for some time. Then he left the brothers and sailed for Syria, accompanied by Priscilla and Aquila. Before he sailed, he had his hair cut off at Cenchrea because of a vow he had taken. 19They arrived at Ephesus, where Paul left Priscilla and Aquila. He himself went into the synagogue and reasoned with the Jews. 20When they asked him to spend more time with them, he declined. 21But as he left, he promised, "I will come back if it is God's will." Then he set sail from Ephesus. 22When he landed at Caesarea, he went up and greeted the church and then went down to Antioch.

23After spending some time in Antioch, Paul set out from there and traveled from place to place throughout the region of Galatia and Phrygia, strengthening all the disciples.

A THOUGHT: *The early Christians experienced persecution from every side. In this reading, the Roman governor did not want to get involved, yet he allowed the beating of Sosthenes to go on. In spite of all the disappointments and struggles, Paul and his fellow workers shared the Good News. As Christians we are called to suffer for the Good News. Let us not shrink back when those times come, but rely on the power of the Holy Spirit.*

Controlling the Tongue/ James 3:1–12

Not many of you should presume to be teachers, my brothers, because you know that we who teach will be judged more strictly. 2We all stumble in many ways. If anyone is never at fault in what he says, he is a perfect man, able to keep his whole body in check.

3When we put bits into the mouths of horses to make them obey us, we can turn the whole animal. 4Or take ships as an example. Although they are so large and are driven by strong winds, they are steered by a very small rudder wherever the pilot wants to go. 5Likewise the tongue is a small part of the body, but it makes great boasts. Consider what a great forest is set on fire by a small spark. 6The tongue also is a fire, a world of evil among the parts of the body. It corrupts the whole person, sets the whole course of his life on fire, and is itself set on fire by hell.

7All kinds of animals, birds, reptiles and creatures of the sea are being tamed and have been tamed by man, 8but no man can tame the tongue. It is a restless evil, full of deadly poison.

9With the tongue we praise our Lord and Father, and with it we curse men, who have been made in God's likeness. 10Out of the same mouth come praise and cursing. My brothers, this should not be. 11Can both fresh water and salt water flow from the same spring? 12My brothers, can a fig tree bear olives, or a grapevine bear figs? Neither can a salt spring produce fresh water.

A THOUGHT: *What you say and what you don't say are both important. Proper speech is not only saying the right words at the right time, but controlling your desire to say what you shouldn't. Examples of wrongly using the tongue include gossiping, putting others down, bragging, manipulating, false teaching, exaggerating, complaining, flattering, and lying. Before you speak, ask, "Is it true, is it necessary, and is it kind?"*

Proverbs for Today/ 27:13

Take the garment of one who puts up security for a stranger; hold it in pledge if he does it for a wayward woman.

NOVEMBER 12

Priscilla and Aquila Instruct Apollos/ Acts 18:24–28

Meanwhile a Jew named Apollos, a native of Alexandria, came to Ephesus. He was a learned man, with a thorough knowledge of the Scriptures. 25He had been instructed in the way of the Lord, and he spoke with great fervor and taught about Jesus accurately, though he knew only the baptism of John. 26He began to speak boldly in the synagogue. When Priscilla and Aquila heard him, they invited him to their home and explained to him the way of God more adequately.

27When Apollos wanted to go to Achaia, the brothers encouraged him and wrote to the disciples there to welcome him. On arriving, he was a great help to those who by grace had believed. 28For he vigorously refuted the Jews in public debate, proving from the Scriptures that Jesus was the Christ.

A THOUGHT: *Apollos had heard only what John the Baptist had said about Jesus, so his message was not the complete story. John focused on repentance from sin, the first step to faith in Christ. Apollos did not know about Jesus' life, crucifixion, and resurrection, nor did he know about the coming of the Holy Spirit. Priscilla and Aquila explained this to him.*

Heavenly Wisdom and Earthly Ambition/ James 3:13–18

Who is wise and understanding among you? Let him show it by his good life, by deeds done in the humility that comes from wisdom. 14But if you harbor bitter envy and selfish ambition in your hearts, do not boast about it or deny the truth. 15Such "wisdom" does not come down from heaven but is earthly, unspiritual, of the devil. 16For where you have envy and selfish ambition, there you find disorder and every evil practice.

17But the wisdom that comes from heaven is first of all pure; then peace-loving, considerate, submissive, full of mercy and good fruit, impartial and sincere. 18Peacemakers who sow in peace raise a harvest of righteousness.

A THOUGHT: *Have you ever known anyone who claimed to be wise but acted foolishly? True wisdom can be measured by the depth of one's character. As you can identify a tree by the type of fruit it produces, you can evaluate your wisdom by the way you act. Foolishness leads to disorder, but wisdom leads to peace and goodness.*

Proverbs for Today/ 27:14

If a man loudly blesses his neighbor early in the morning, it will be taken as a curse.

NOVEMBER 13

Paul Preaches to John the Baptist's Disciples/ Acts 19:1–10

While Apollos was at Corinth, Paul took the road through the interior and arrived at Ephesus. There he found some disciples 2and asked them, "Did you receive the Holy Spirit when you believed?"

They answered, "No, we have not even heard that there is a Holy Spirit."

3So Paul asked, "Then what baptism did you receive?"

"John's baptism," they replied.

4Paul said, "John's baptism was a baptism of repentance. He told the people to believe in the one coming after him, that is, in Jesus." 5On hearing this, they were baptized into the name of the Lord Jesus. 6When Paul placed his hands on them, the Holy Spirit came on them, and they spoke in tongues and prophesied. 7There were about twelve men in all.

8Paul entered the synagogue and spoke boldly there for three months, arguing persuasively about the kingdom of God. 9But some of them became obstinate; they refused to believe and publicly maligned the Way. So Paul left them.

He took the disciples with him and had discussions daily in the lecture hall of Tyrannus. [10]This went on for two years, so that all the Jews and Greeks who lived in the province of Asia heard the word of the Lord.

A THOUGHT: *John's baptism was a sign of repentance from sin only, not a sign of new life in Christ. Like Apollos, these Ephesian believers needed further instruction on the message and ministry of Jesus Christ. By faith they believed in Jesus as the Messiah, but they did not understand the significance of Jesus' death and resurrection or the work of the Holy Spirit. Therefore they had not experienced the presence and power of the Holy Spirit. Paul was quick to point out that salvation requires repentance and faith. People need to be confronted with their sin and their need to repent, but this is only half the story. They must also accept the Good News of forgiveness and new life through Jesus.*

God Strengthens the Humble and Opposes the Proud/ James 4:1–6

What causes fights and quarrels among you? Don't they come from your desires that battle within you? [2]You want something but don't get it. You kill and covet, but you cannot have what you want. You quarrel and fight. You do not have, because you do not ask God. [3]When you ask, you do not receive, because you ask with wrong motives, that you may spend what you get on your pleasures.

[4]You adulterous people, don't you know that friendship with the world is hatred toward God? Anyone who chooses to be a friend of the world becomes an enemy of God. [5]Or do you think Scripture says without reason that the spirit he caused to live in us envies intensely? [6]But he gives us more grace. That is why Scripture says:

> "God opposes the proud
> but gives grace to the humble."

A THOUGHT: *Quarrels among believers are always harmful. James tells us that these quarrels result from evil desires within us—we want more possessions, more money, higher status, more recognition. We fight in order to get what we want. Instead of aggressively grabbing what we want, we should ask God to help us get rid of our selfish desires and trust him to give us what we really need. The cure for evil desires is humility. Pride makes us self-centered and leads us to conclude that we deserve all we can see, touch, or imagine. It creates greedy appetites for far more than we need. The antidote to self-centered desires is to humble ourselves before God, realizing that we need nothing except his approval. When his Holy Spirit fills us, we realize that the things we have coveted are only cheap substitutes for what God has to offer.*

Proverbs for Today/ 27:15–16

A quarrelsome wife is like a constant dripping on a rainy day; restraining her is like restraining the wind or grasping oil with the hand.

NOVEMBER 14

Paul Casts Out Demons in Ephesus/ Acts 19:11–20

God did extraordinary miracles through Paul, 12so that even handkerchiefs and aprons that had touched him were taken to the sick, and their illnesses were cured and the evil spirits left them.

13Some Jews who went around driving out evil spirits tried to invoke the name of the Lord Jesus over those who were demon-possessed. They would say, "In the name of Jesus, whom Paul preaches, I command you to come out." 14Seven sons of Sceva, a Jewish chief priest, were doing this. 15One day the evil spirit answered them, "Jesus I know, and I know about Paul, but who are you?" 16Then the man who had the evil spirit jumped on them and over-powered them all. He gave them such a beating that they ran out of the house naked and bleeding.

17When this became known to the Jews and Greeks living in Ephesus, they were all seized with fear, and the name of the Lord Jesus was held in high honor. 18Many of those who believed now came and openly confessed their evil deeds. 19A number who had practiced sorcery brought their scrolls together and burned them publicly. When they calculated the value of the scrolls, the total came to fifty thousand drachmas. 20In this way the word of the Lord spread widely and grew in power.

A THOUGHT: *Ephesus was considered a center for black magic and other occult practices. The people sought spells to give them wealth, happiness, and success in marriage. Superstition and sorcery were commonplace. God clearly forbids such practices in Scripture. You cannot be a believer and hold onto the occult, black magic, or sorcery.*

Once you begin to dabble in these areas, it is extremely easy to become obsessed by them because Satan is very powerful. But God's power is even greater. If you are mixed up in the occult, learn a lesson from the Ephesians and get rid of anything that lures you into such practices.

Draw Near to God/ James 4:7–10

Submit yourselves, then, to God. Resist the devil, and he will flee from you. ⁸Come near to God and he will come near to you. Wash your hands, you sinners, and purify your hearts, you double-minded. ⁹Grieve, mourn and wail. Change your laughter to mourning and your joy to gloom. ¹⁰Humble yourselves before the Lord, and he will lift you up.

A THOUGHT: *How can you draw close to God? James gives five suggestions: (1) "Submit yourselves, then, to God." Realize that you need his forgiveness, and be willing to follow him. (2) "Resist the devil." Don't allow him to entice and tempt you. (3) "Wash your hands" (that is, lead a pure life) and "purify your hearts." Be cleansed from sin, replacing it with God's purity. (4) Let there be tears, sorrow, and sincere grief for your sins. Don't be afraid to express deep heartfelt sorrow for them. (5) Humble yourself before God, and he will lift you up.*

Proverbs for Today/ 27:17

As iron sharpens iron, so one man sharpens another.

NOVEMBER 15

A Riot Erupts at Ephesus/ Acts 19:21–41

After all this had happened, Paul decided to go to Jerusalem, passing through Macedonia and Achaia. "After I have been there," he said, "I must visit Rome also." ²²He sent two of his helpers, Timothy and Erastus, to Macedonia, while he stayed in the province of Asia a little longer.

²³About that time there arose a great disturbance about the Way. ²⁴A silversmith named Demetrius, who made silver shrines of Artemis, brought in no little business for the craftsmen. ²⁵He called them together, along with the workmen in related trades, and said: "Men, you know we

receive a good income from this business. 26And you see and hear how this fellow Paul has convinced and led astray large numbers of people here in Ephesus and in practically the whole province of Asia. He says that man-made gods are no gods at all. 27There is danger not only that our trade will lose its good name, but also that the temple of the great goddess Artemis will be discredited, and the goddess herself, who is worshiped throughout the province of Asia and the world, will be robbed of her divine majesty."

28When they heard this, they were furious and began shouting: "Great is Artemis of the Ephesians!" 29Soon the whole city was in an uproar. The people seized Gaius and Aristarchus, Paul's traveling companions from Macedonia, and rushed as one man into the theater. 30Paul wanted to appear before the crowd, but the disciples would not let him. 31Even some of the officials of the province, friends of Paul, sent him a message begging him not to venture into the theater.

32The assembly was in confusion: Some were shouting one thing, some another. Most of the people did not even know why they were there. 33The Jews pushed Alexander to the front, and some of the crowd shouted instructions to him. He motioned for silence in order to make a defense before the people. 34But when they realized he was a Jew, they all shouted in unison for about two hours: "Great is Artemis of the Ephesians!"

35The city clerk quieted the crowd and said: "Men of Ephesus, doesn't all the world know that the city of Ephesus is the guardian of the temple of the great Artemis and of her image, which fell from heaven? 36Therefore, since these facts are undeniable, you ought to be quiet and not do anything rash. 37You have brought these men here, though they have neither robbed temples nor blasphemed our goddess. 38If, then, Demetrius and his fellow craftsmen have a grievance against anybody, the courts are open and there are proconsuls. They can press charges. 39If there is anything further you want to bring up, it must be settled in a legal assembly. 40As it is, we are in danger of being charged with rioting because of today's events. In that case we would not be able to account for this commotion, since there is no reason for it." 41After he had said this, he dismissed the assembly.

A THOUGHT: *When Paul preached in Ephesus, Demetrius and his fellow shrinemakers did not quarrel with his doctrine. Their anger boiled because his preaching threatened their profits. They made statues of the goddess Diana and her temple, and if people started believing in God and discarding their idols, their livelihood would suffer. Demetrius' strategy for stirring up a riot was to appeal to the people's love of money and then hide their greed behind the mask of patriotism and religious loyalty. The rioters couldn't see the selfish motives for their rioting—instead they saw themselves as heroes for the sake of their land and beliefs.*

Don't Judge One Another/ James 4:11–12

Brothers, do not slander one another. Anyone who speaks against his brother or judges him speaks against the law and judges it. When you judge the law, you are not keeping it, but sitting in judgment on it. 12There is only one Lawgiver and Judge, the one who is able to save and destroy. But you—who are you to judge your neighbor?

A THOUGHT: *Jesus summarized the Old Testament Law as love to God and neighbor, and Paul said love demonstrated towards a neighbor fully satisfies the law. When we fail to love, we are actually breaking God's law. Examine your attitude and actions toward others. Do you build people up or tear them down? When you're ready to criticize someone, remember God's law of love and say something good about him or her instead. If you make this a habit, your tendency to find fault with others will diminish and your ability to obey God's Law will increase.*

Proverbs for Today/ 27:18–20

He who tends a fig tree will eat its fruit, and he who looks after his master will be honored. □ As water reflects a face, so a man's heart reflects the man. □ Death and Destruction are never satisfied, and neither are the eyes of man.

NOVEMBER 16

Paul Raises Eutychus from the Dead/ Acts 20:1–12

When the uproar had ended, Paul sent for the disciples and, after encouraging them, said good-by and set out for Macedonia. 2He traveled through that area, speaking many words of encouragement to the people, and finally arrived in Greece, 3where he stayed three months. Because the Jews made a plot against him just as he was about to sail for Syria, he decided to go back through Macedonia. 4He was accompanied by Sopater son of Pyrrhus from Berea, Aristarchus and Secundus from Thessalonica, Gaius from Derbe, Timothy also, and Tychicus and Trophimus from the province of Asia. 5These men went on ahead and waited for us at Troas. 6But we sailed from Philippi after the Feast of Unleavened Bread, and five days later joined the others at Troas, where we stayed seven days.

7On the first day of the week we came together to break bread. Paul spoke to the people and, because he intended to leave the next day, kept on talking until midnight. 8There were many lamps in the upstairs room where we were meeting. 9Seated in a window was a young man named Eutychus, who was sinking into a deep sleep as Paul talked on and on. When he was sound asleep, he fell to the ground from the third story and was picked up dead. 10Paul went down, threw himself on the young man and put his arms around him. "Don't be alarmed," he said. "He's alive!" 11Then he went upstairs again and broke bread and ate. After talking until daylight, he left. 12The people took the young man home alive and were greatly comforted.

A THOUGHT: *The church at Troas experienced the power of God in Paul's preaching and also in Eutychus being raised from the dead. God displayed his great power as the Christians were together to share communion and hear the preaching of Paul. Although God may not raise the dead in our midst, we may be confident that the Holy Spirit will be working among us when we are open to his ministry.*

Don't Boast about Tomorrow/ James 4:13–17

Now listen, you who say, "Today or tomorrow we will go to this or that city, spend a year there, carry on business and make money." 14Why, you do not even know what will happen tomorrow. What is your life? You are a mist that appears for a little while and then vanishes. 15Instead, you ought to say, "If it is the Lord's will, we will live and do this or that." 16As it is, you boast and brag. All such boasting is evil. 17Anyone, then, who knows the good he ought to do and doesn't do it, sins.

A THOUGHT: *It is good to have goals, but goals can disappoint us if we leave God out of them. There is no point in making plans as though God does not exist, because the future is in his hands. What would you like to be doing ten years from now? One year from now? Tomorrow? How will you react if God steps in and rearranges your plans? Plan ahead, but hang on to your plans lightly. If you put God's desires at the center of your planning, you will not be disappointed.*

Proverbs for Today/ 27:21–22

The crucible for silver and the furnace for gold, but man is tested by the praise he receives. □ Though you grind a fool in a mortar, grinding him like grain with a pestle, you will not remove his folly from him.

NOVEMBER 17

Paul's Farewell to the Ephesian Elders/
Acts 20:13–38

We went on ahead to the ship and sailed for Assos, where we were going to take Paul aboard. He had made this arrangement because he was going there on foot. 14When he met us at Assos, we took him aboard and went on to Mitylene. 15The next day we set sail from there and arrived off Kios. The day after that we crossed over to Samos, and on the following day arrived at Miletus. 16Paul had decided to sail past Ephesus to avoid spending time in the province of Asia, for he was in a hurry to reach Jerusalem, if possible, by the day of Pentecost.

17From Miletus, Paul sent to Ephesus for the elders of the church. 18When they arrived, he said to them: "You know how I lived the whole time I was with you, from the first day I came into the province of Asia. 19I served the Lord with great humility and with tears, although I was severely tested by the plots of the Jews. 20You know that I have not hesitated to preach anything that would be helpful to you but have taught you publicly and from house to house. 21I have declared to both Jews and Greeks that they must turn to God in repentance and have faith in our Lord Jesus.

²²"And now, compelled by the Spirit, I am going to Jerusalem, not knowing what will happen to me there. ²³I only know that in every city the Holy Spirit warns me that prison and hardships are facing me. ²⁴However, I consider my life worth nothing to me, if only I may finish the race and complete the task the Lord Jesus has given me—the task of testifying to the gospel of God's grace.

²⁵"Now I know that none of you among whom I have gone about preaching the kingdom will ever see me again. ²⁶Therefore, I declare to you today that I am innocent of the blood of all men. ²⁷For I have not hesitated to proclaim to you the whole will of God. ²⁸Keep watch over yourselves and all the flock of which the Holy Spirit has made you overseers. Be shepherds of the church of God, which he bought with his own blood. ²⁹I know that after I leave, savage wolves will come in among you and will not spare the flock. ³⁰Even from your own number men will arise and distort the truth in order to draw away disciples after them. ³¹So be on your guard! Remember that for three years I never stopped warning each of you night and day with tears.

³²"Now I commit you to God and to the word of his grace, which can build you up and give you an inheritance among all those who are sanctified. ³³I have not coveted anyone's silver or gold or clothing. ³⁴You yourselves know that these hands of mine have supplied my own needs and the needs of my companions. ³⁵In everything I did, I showed you that by this kind of hard work we must help the weak, remembering the words the Lord Jesus himself said: 'It is more blessed to give than to receive.' "

³⁶When he had said this, he knelt down with all of them and prayed. ³⁷They all wept as they embraced him and kissed him. ³⁸What grieved them most was his statement that they would never see his face again. Then they accompanied him to the ship.

A THOUGHT: *The Ephesian elders were told to feed the believers under their care by teaching them God's Word, and to shepherd them by being examples of God's love. All leaders of the church carry these two major responsibilities—to nourish others with God's truth and to exemplify God's truth at work in their lives. God's truth must be talked out and lived out.*

Warnings to the Rich/ James 5:1–6

Now listen, you rich people, weep and wail because of the misery that is coming upon you. ²Your wealth has rotted, and moths have eaten your clothes. ³Your gold and silver are corroded. Their corrosion will testify against you and eat your flesh like fire. You have hoarded wealth in the last days. ⁴Look! The wages you failed to pay the workmen who mowed your fields are crying out against you. The cries of the harvesters have reached the ears of the Lord Almighty. ⁵You have lived on earth in luxury and self-indulgence. You have fattened yourselves in the day of slaughter. ⁶You have condemned and murdered innocent men, who were not opposing you.

A THOUGHT: *James proclaims the worthlessness of riches, not the worthlessness of the rich. Today's money will be worthless when Christ returns, so we should spend our time accumulating treasures that will be worthwile in God's eternal kingdom. Money itself is not the problem; Christian leaders need money to live and support their families; missionaries need money to help them spread the gospel; churches need money to do their work effectively. It is the love of money that leads to evil. This is a warning to all Christians who are tempted to adopt worldly standards rather than God's standards.*

Proverbs for Today/ 27:23–27

Be sure you know the condition of your flocks, give careful attention to your herds; for riches do not endure forever, and a crown is not secure for all generations. When the hay is removed and new growth appears and the grass from the hills is gathered in, the lambs will provide you with clothing, and the goats with the price of a field. You will have plenty of goats' milk to feed you and your family and to nourish your servant girls.

NOVEMBER 18

Paul Arrives in Jerusalem/ Acts 21:1–17

After we [Luke, Paul, and his companions] had torn ourselves away from them, we put out to sea and sailed straight to Cos. The next day we went to Rhodes and from there to Patara. 2We found a ship crossing over to Phoenicia, went on board and set sail. 3After sighting Cyprus and passing to the south of it, we sailed on to Syria. We landed at Tyre, where our ship was to unload its cargo. 4Finding the disciples there, we stayed with them seven days. Through the Spirit they urged Paul not to go on to Jerusalem. 5But when our time was up, we left and continued on our way. All the disciples and their wives and children accompanied us out of the city, and there on the beach we knelt to pray. 6After saying good-by to each other, we went aboard the ship, and they returned home.

7We continued our voyage from Tyre and landed at Ptolemais, where we greeted the brothers and stayed with them for a day. 8Leaving the next day, we reached Caesarea and stayed at the house of Philip the evangelist, one of the Seven. 9He had four unmarried daughters who prophesied.

10After we had been there a number of days, a prophet named Agabus came down from Judea. 11Coming over to us, he took Paul's belt, tied his own hands and feet with it and said, "The Holy Spirit says, 'In this way the Jews of Jerusalem will bind the owner of this belt and will hand him over to the Gentiles.'"

12When we heard this, we and the people there pleaded with Paul not to go up to Jerusalem. 13Then Paul answered, "Why are you weeping and breaking my heart? I am ready not only to be bound, but also to die in Jerusalem for the name of the Lord Jesus." 14When he would not be dissuaded, we gave up and said, "The Lord's will be done."

15After this, we got ready and went up to Jerusalem. 16Some of the disciples from Caesarea accompanied us and brought us to the home of Mnason, where we were to stay. He was a man from Cyprus and one of the early disciples.

17When we arrived at Jerusalem, the brothers received us warmly.

A THOUGHT: *Paul knew he would be imprisoned in Jerusalem. His friends pleaded with him to not go there, but he knew he had to because God wanted him to. No one wants to face hardship or suffering, but a faithful disciple wants above all else to please God. Our desire to please God should overshadow our desire to avoid hardship and suffering. When we really want to do God's will, we must accept all that comes with it—even the pain. Then we can say with Paul, "The Lord's will be done."*

Perseverance in Suffering/ James 5:7–12

Be patient, then, brothers, until the Lord's coming. See how the farmer waits for the land to yield its valuable crop and how patient he is for the autumn and spring rains. 8You too, be patient and stand firm, because the Lord's coming is near. 9Don't grumble against each other, brothers, or you will be judged. The Judge is standing at the door!

10Brothers, as an example of patience in the face of suffering, take the prophets who spoke in the name of the Lord. 11As you know, we consider blessed those who have persevered. You have heard of Job's perseverance and have seen what the Lord finally brought about. The Lord is full of compassion and mercy.

12Above all, my brothers, do not swear—not by heaven or by earth or by anything else. Let your "Yes" be yes, and your "No," no, or you will be condemned.

A THOUGHT: *The farmer must wait patiently for his crops to grow, he cannot hurry the process. But he does not take the summer off and hope that all goes well in the fields. There is much work to do to ensure a good harvest. In the same way, we must wait patiently for Christ's return. We cannot make Christ return any sooner, but while we wait there is much work we can do to advance God's kingdom. Both the farmer and the Christian must live by faith, looking toward the future reward for their labors. Don't live as if Christ will never come. Work faithfully to build his kingdom, for the King will come when the time is ripe.*

Proverbs for Today/ 28:1

The wicked man flees though no one pursues, but the righteous are as bold as a lion.

NOVEMBER 19

A Riot in the Jerusalem Temple/ Acts 21:18–36

The next day Paul and the rest of us went to see James, and all the elders were present. 19Paul greeted them and reported in detail what God had done among the Gentiles through his ministry.

20When they heard this, they praised God. Then they said to Paul: "You see, brother, how many thousands of

Jews have believed, and all of them are zealous for the law. 21They have been informed that you teach all the Jews who live among the Gentiles to turn away from Moses, telling them not to circumcise their children or live according to our customs. 22What shall we do? They will certainly hear that you have come, 23so do what we tell you. There are four men with us who have made a vow. 24Take these men, join in their purification rites and pay their expenses, so that they can have their heads shaved. Then everybody will know there is no truth in these reports about you, but that you yourself are living in obedience to the law. 25As for the Gentile believers, we have written to them our decision that they should abstain from food sacrificed to idols, from blood, from the meat of strangled animals and from sexual immorality."

26The next day Paul took the men and purified himself along with them. Then he went to the temple to give notice of the date when the days of purification would end and the offering would be made for each of them.

27When the seven days were nearly over, some Jews from the province of Asia saw Paul at the temple. They stirred up the whole crowd and seized him, 28shouting, "Men of Israel, help us! This is the man who teaches all men everywhere against our people and our law and this place. And besides, he has brought Greeks into the temple area and defiled this holy place." 29(They had previously seen Trophimus the Ephesian in the city with Paul and assumed that Paul had brought him into the temple area.)

30The whole city was aroused, and the people came running from all directions. Seizing Paul, they dragged him from the temple, and immediately the gates were shut. 31While they were trying to kill him, news reached the commander of the Roman troops that the whole city of Jerusalem was in an uproar. 32He at once took some officers and soldiers and ran down to the crowd. When the rioters saw the commander and his soldiers, they stopped beating Paul.

33The commander came up and arrested him and ordered him to be bound with two chains. Then he asked who he was and what he had done. 34Some in the crowd shouted one thing and some another, and since the commander could not get at the truth because of the uproar, he ordered that Paul be taken into the barracks. 35When Paul reached the steps, the violence of the mob was so great he had to be carried by the soldiers. 36The crowd that followed kept shouting, "Away with him!"

A THOUGHT: *There are two ways to think of the Old Testament law. Paul rejects one and accepts the other. (1) Paul rejects the idea that the Old Testament law brings salvation to those who keep it. Our salvation is freely given by God's gracious act. We receive it by faith. The law is of no value for salvation except to show us our sin. (2) Paul accepts the view that the Old Testament laws prepared us for and taught us about the coming of Jesus Christ. Christ fulfilled the law and released us from its burden of guilt. But the law still teaches us many valuable principles and gives us guidelines for living. Paul was not observing the law for salvation. He was keeping the law because it served as an excellent guideline for righteous living. By keeping the law, Paul also avoided offending the Jews he wished to reach with the gospel.*

Prayer Offered in Earnest Faith/ James 5:13–20

Is any one of you in trouble? He should pray. Is anyone happy? Let him sing songs of praise. 14Is any one of you sick? He should call the elders of the church to pray over him and anoint him with oil in the name of the Lord. 15And the prayer offered in faith will make the sick person well; the Lord will raise him up. If he has sinned, he will be forgiven. 16Therefore confess your sins to each other and pray for each other so that you may be healed. The prayer of a righteous man is powerful and effective.

17Elijah was a man just like us. He prayed earnestly that it would not rain, and it did not rain on the land for three and a half years. 18Again he prayed, and the heavens gave rain, and the earth produced its crops.

19My brothers, if one of you should wander from the truth and someone should bring him back, 20remember this: Whoever turns a sinner from the error of his way will save him from death and cover over a multitude of sins.

A THOUGHT: *The Christian's most powerful resource is communion with God through prayer. The results are often greater than we thought were possible. Some people see prayer as a last resort to be tried when all else fails. This is backwards. Prayer should come first. Since God's power is infinitely greater than our own, it only makes sense to rely on it—especially because he encourages us to do so.*

Proverbs for Today/ 28:2

When a country is rebellious, it has many rulers, but a man of understanding and knowledge maintains order.

NOVEMBER 20

Paul Retells His Conversion/ Acts 21:37—22:16

As the soldiers were about to take Paul into the barracks, he asked the commander, "May I say something to you?"

"Do you speak Greek?" he replied. 38"Aren't you the Egyptian who started a revolt and led four thousand terrorists out into the desert some time ago?"

39Paul answered, "I am a Jew, from Tarsus in Cilicia, a citizen of no ordinary city. Please let me speak to the people."

40Having received the commander's permission, Paul stood on the steps and motioned to the crowd. When they were all silent, he said to them in Aramaic: 22:1"Brothers and fathers, listen now to my defense."

2When they heard him speak to them in Aramaic, they became very quiet.

Then Paul said: 3"I am a Jew, born in Tarsus of Cilicia, but brought up in this city. Under Gamaliel I was thoroughly trained in the law of our fathers and was just as zealous for God as any of you are today. 4I persecuted the followers of this Way to their death, arresting both men and women and throwing them into prison, 5as also the high priest and all the Council can testify. I even obtained letters from them to their brothers in Damascus, and went there to bring these people as prisoners to Jerusalem to be punished.

6"About noon as I came near Damascus, suddenly a bright light from heaven flashed around me. 7I fell to the ground and heard a voice say to me, 'Saul! Saul! Why do you persecute me?'

8" 'Who are you, Lord?' I asked.

" 'I am Jesus of Nazareth, whom you are persecuting,' he replied. 9My companions saw the light, but they did not understand the voice of him who was speaking to me.

10" 'What shall I do, Lord?' I asked.

" 'Get up,' the Lord said, 'and go into Damascus. There you will be told all that you have been assigned to do.' 11My companions led me by the hand into Damascus, because the brilliance of the light had blinded me.

12"A man named Ananias came to see me. He was a devout observer of the law and highly respected by all the Jews living there. 13He stood beside me and said, 'Brother Saul, receive your sight!' And at that very moment I was able to see him.

14"Then he said: 'The God of our fathers has chosen you to know his will and to see the Righteous One and to hear words from his mouth. 15You will be his witness to all men of what you have seen and heard. 16And now what are you waiting for? Get up, be baptized and wash your sins away, calling on his name.' "

A THOUGHT: *When Paul said, "I . . . was just as zealous for God as any of you are today," he acknowledged their sincere motives in trying to kill him and recognized that he would have done the same to Christian leaders some years earlier. Paul always tried to establish a common point of contact with his audience before launching into a full-scale defense of Christianity. When you witness for Christ, first identify yourself with your audience. They are much more likely to listen to you if they feel a common bond with you.*

Trials Refine Our Faith/ 1 Peter 1:1–7

Peter, an apostle of Jesus Christ,

To God's elect, strangers in the world, scattered throughout Pontus, Galatia, Cappadocia, Asia and Bithynia, 2who have been chosen according to the foreknowledge of God the Father, through the sanctifying work of the Spirit, for obedience to Jesus Christ and sprinkling by his blood:

Grace and peace be yours in abundance.

3Praise be to the God and Father of our Lord Jesus Christ! In his great mercy he has given us new birth into a living hope through the resurrection of Jesus Christ from the dead, 4and into an inheritance that can never perish, spoil or fade—kept in heaven for you, 5who through faith are shielded by God's power until the coming of the salvation that is ready to be revealed in the last time. 6In this you greatly rejoice, though now for a little while you may have had to suffer grief in all kinds of trials. 7These have come so that your faith—of greater worth than gold, which perishes even though refined by fire—may be proved genuine and may result in praise, glory and honor when Jesus Christ is revealed.

A THOUGHT: *All believers face such trials when they let their light shine into the darkness. We must accept trials as part of the refining process that burns away impurities, preparing us to meet Christ. Trials teach us patience and help us grow to be the kind of people God wants us to be. As gold is heated, impurities float to the top and can be skimmed off. Steel is tempered or strengthened by heating it in fire. Likewise, our trials, struggles, and the persecutions we face strengthen our faith and make us more like Christ.*

Proverbs for Today/ 28:3–5

A ruler who oppresses the poor is like a driving rain that leaves no crops. □ Those who forsake the law praise the wicked, but those who keep the law resist them. □ Evil men do not understand justice, but those who seek the LORD understand it fully.

NOVEMBER 21

Paul's Roman Citizenship/ Acts 22:17–29

"When I [Paul] returned to Jerusalem and was praying at the temple, I fell into a trance 18and saw the Lord speaking. 'Quick!' he said to me. 'Leave Jerusalem immediately, because they will not accept your testimony about me.'

19" 'Lord,' I replied, 'these men know that I went from one synagogue to another to imprison and beat those who believe in you. 20And when the blood of your martyr Stephen was shed, I stood there giving my approval and guarding the clothes of those who were killing him.'

21"Then the Lord said to me, 'Go; I will send you far away to the Gentiles.' "

22The crowd listened to Paul until he said this. Then they raised their voices and shouted, "Rid the earth of him! He's not fit to live!"

23As they were shouting and throwing off their cloaks

and flinging dust into the air, 24the commander ordered Paul to be taken into the barracks. He directed that he be flogged and questioned in order to find out why the people were shouting at him like this. 25As they stretched him out to flog him, Paul said to the centurion standing there, "Is it legal for you to flog a Roman citizen who hasn't even been found guilty?"

26When the centurion heard this, he went to the commander and reported it. "What are you going to do?" he asked. "This man is a Roman citizen."

27The commander went to Paul and asked, "Tell me, are you a Roman citizen?"

"Yes, I am," he answered.

28Then the commander said, "I had to pay a big price for my citizenship."

"But I was born a citizen," Paul replied.

29Those who were about to question him withdrew immediately. The commander himself was alarmed when he realized that he had put Paul, a Roman citizen, in chains.

A THOUGHT: *God used Paul's persecution as an opportunity for him to witness. Now even his enemies were creating a platform for him to address the entire Jewish Council. If we are sensitive to the Holy Spirit's leading, we will notice increased opportunities to share our faith, even in the heat of opposition.*

The Hope of Eternal Life/ 1 Peter 1:8–13

Though you have not seen him, you love him; and even though you do not see him now, you believe in him and are filled with an inexpressible and glorious joy, 9for you are receiving the goal of your faith, the salvation of your souls.

10Concerning this salvation, the prophets, who spoke of the grace that was to come to you, searched intently and with the greatest care, 11trying to find out the time and circumstances to which the Spirit of Christ in them was pointing when he predicted the sufferings of Christ and the glories that would follow. 12It was revealed to them that they were not serving themselves but you, when they spoke of the things that have now been told you by those who have preached the gospel to you by the Holy Spirit sent from heaven. Even angels long to look into these things.

13Therefore, prepare your minds for action; be self-controlled; set your hope fully on the grace to be given you when Jesus Christ is revealed.

A THOUGHT: *Although the plan of salvation was a mystery to the Old Testament prophets, they still suffered persecution and some died for God. Some Jewish Christians reading Peter's letter, by contrast, had seen Jesus for themselves and knew why he came. They based their assurance on Jesus' death and resurrection. With their firsthand knowledge and personal experience of Jesus, their faith should have been even stronger than that of the Old Testament prophets. We stand at a point in history where we have the testimony of the Old Testament and the New Testament. The nature of God's salvation in Christ has been clearly revealed in the pages of the New Testament. God kept his promise in the past—Jesus, God's Messiah, died to bring salvation to his people—and Christ will keep his promise to come again.*

Proverbs for Today/ 28:6–7

Better a poor man whose walk is blameless than a rich man whose ways are perverse. □ He who keeps the law is a discerning son, but a companion of gluttons disgraces his father.

NOVEMBER 22

Paul Before the Sanhedrin/ Acts 22:30—23:11

The next day, since the commander wanted to find out exactly why Paul was being accused by the Jews, he released him and ordered the chief priests and all the Sanhedrin to assemble. Then he brought Paul and had him stand before them.

23:1Paul looked straight at the Sanhedrin and said, "My brothers, I have fulfilled my duty to God in all good conscience to this day." 2At this the high priest Ananias ordered those standing near Paul to strike him on the mouth. 3Then Paul said to him, "God will strike you, you whitewashed wall! You sit there to judge me according to the law, yet you yourself violate the law by commanding that I be struck!"

4Those who were standing near Paul said, "You dare to insult God's high priest?"

5Paul replied, "Brothers, I did not realize that he was the

high priest; for it is written: 'Do not speak evil about the ruler of your people.'"

6Then Paul, knowing that some of them were Sadducees and the others Pharisees, called out in the Sanhedrin, "My brothers, I am a Pharisee, the son of a Pharisee. I stand on trial because of my hope in the resurrection of the dead." 7When he said this, a dispute broke out between the Pharisees and the Sadducees, and the assembly was divided. 8(The Sadducees say that there is no resurrection, and that there are neither angels nor spirits, but the Pharisees acknowledge them all.)

9There was a great uproar, and some of the teachers of the law who were Pharisees stood up and argued vigorously. "We find nothing wrong with this man," they said. "What if a spirit or an angel has spoken to him?" 10The dispute became so violent that the commander was afraid Paul would be torn to pieces by them. He ordered the troops to go down and take him away from them by force and bring him into the barracks.

11The following night the Lord stood near Paul and said, "Take courage! As you have testified about me in Jerusalem, so you must also testify in Rome."

A THOUGHT: *The Sadducees and Pharisees were both Jewish religious sects, but with strikingly different beliefs. While the Pharisees believed in a bodily resurrection, the Sadducees did not because they adhered only to the Old Testament books of Genesis through Deuteronomy, which contain no explicit teaching on resurrection. Paul's words moved the debate away from himself and toward the ongoing raging controversy between the Sadducees and Pharisees over the resurrection. The Jewish Council was split. God will help us when we are under fire for our faith. Like Paul, we should always be ready to present our testimony. The Holy Spirit will give us power to speak boldly.*

Personal Holiness/ 1 Peter 1:14–25

As obedient children, do not conform to the evil desires you had when you lived in ignorance. 15But just as he who called you is holy, so be holy in all you do; 16for it is written: "Be holy, because I am holy."

17Since you call on a Father who judges each man's work impartially, live your lives as strangers here in reverent fear. 18For you know that it was not with perishable things such as silver or gold that you were redeemed from the empty way of life handed down to you from your forefathers, [19]but with the precious blood of Christ, a lamb without blemish or defect. [20]He was chosen before the creation of the world, but was revealed in these last times for your sake. [21]Through him you believe in God, who raised him from the dead and glorified him, and so your faith and hope are in God.

[22]Now that you have purified yourselves by obeying the truth so that you have sincere love for your brothers, love one another deeply, from the heart. [23]For you have been born again, not of perishable seed, but of imperishable, through the living and enduring word of God. [24]For,

"All men are like grass,
  and all their glory is like the flowers of the field;
  the grass withers and the flowers fall,
 [25] but the word of the Lord stands forever."

And this is the word that was preached to you.

A THOUGHT: *After people commit their lives to Christ, they still feel a pull back into their old ways. Peter tells us to be like our heavenly Father—holy in everything we do. Holiness means being totally devoted or dedicated to God, set aside for his special use, and set apart from sin and its influence. We're to be set apart and different, not blending in with the crowd, yet not being different just for the sake of being different. What makes us different are God's qualities in our lives. Our focus and priorities must be his. All this is in direct contrast to our old ways. We cannot become holy on our own, but God gives us his Holy Spirit to help us obey and to give us power to overcome sin. Don't use the excuse that you can't help slipping into sin. Call on God's power to free you from sin's grip.*

Proverbs for Today/ 28:8–10

He who increases his wealth by exorbitant interest amasses it for another, who will be kind to the poor. □ If anyone turns a deaf ear to the law, even his prayers are detestable. □ He who leads the upright along an evil path will fall into his own trap, but the blameless will receive a good inheritance.

NOVEMBER 23

A Plot against Paul's Life/ Acts 23:12–35

The next morning the Jews formed a conspiracy and bound themselves with an oath not to eat or drink until they had killed Paul. 13More than forty men were involved in this plot. 14They went to the chief priests and elders and said, "We have taken a solemn oath not to eat anything until we have killed Paul. 15Now then, you and the Sanhedrin petition the commander to bring him before you on the pretext of wanting more accurate information about his case. We are ready to kill him before he gets here."

16But when the son of Paul's sister heard of this plot, he went into the barracks and told Paul.

17Then Paul called one of the centurions and said, "Take this young man to the commander; he has something to tell him." 18So he took him to the commander.

The centurion said, "Paul, the prisoner, sent for me and asked me to bring this young man to you because he has something to tell you."

19The commander took the young man by the hand, drew him aside and asked, "What is it you want to tell me?"

20He said: "The Jews have agreed to ask you to bring Paul before the Sanhedrin tomorrow on the pretext of wanting more accurate information about him. 21Don't give in to them, because more than forty of them are waiting in ambush for him. They have taken an oath not to eat or drink until they have killed him. They are ready now, waiting for your consent to their request."

22The commander dismissed the young man and cautioned him, "Don't tell anyone that you have reported this to me."

23Then he called two of his centurions and ordered them, "Get ready a detachment of two hundred soldiers, seventy horsemen and two hundred spearmen to go to Caesarea at nine tonight. 24Provide mounts for Paul so that he may be taken safely to Governor Felix."

25He wrote a letter as follows:

26Claudius Lysias,

To His Excellency, Governor Felix:

Greetings.

27This man was seized by the Jews and they were about to kill him, but I came with my troops and rescued him, for I had learned that he is a Roman citizen. 28I wanted to know why they were accusing him, so I brought him to their Sanhedrin. 29I found that the accusation had to do with questions about their law, but there was no charge against him that deserved death or imprisonment. 30When I was informed of a plot to be carried out against the man, I sent him to you at once. I also ordered his accusers to present to you their case against him.

31So the soldiers, carrying out their orders, took Paul with them during the night and brought him as far as Antipatris. 32The next day they let the cavalry go on with him, while they returned to the barracks. 33When the cavalry arrived in Caesarea, they delivered the letter to the governor and handed Paul over to him. 34The governor read the letter and asked what province he was from. Learning that he was from Cilicia, 35he said, "I will hear your case when your accusers get here." Then he ordered that Paul be kept under guard in Herod's palace.

A THOUGHT: *The Roman commander ordered Paul sent to Caesarea. Jerusalem was the seat of Jewish government, but Caesarea was the Roman headquarters for the area. God works in amazing and amusing ways. There were many possible options which God could have chosen to get Paul to Caesarea, but he chose to use the Roman army to deliver Paul from his enemies. God's ways are not our ways—ours are limited, his are not. Don't limit God by asking him to respond your way. When God intervenes, anything can happen, with much greater effectiveness than any of us could anticipate or imagine.*

Living Stones in a Spiritual House/ 1 Peter 2:1–10

Therefore, rid yourselves of all malice and all deceit, hypocrisy, envy, and slander of every kind. 2Like newborn babies, crave pure spiritual milk, so that by it you may grow up in your salvation, 3now that you have tasted that the Lord is good.

4As you come to him, the living Stone—rejected by men

but chosen by God and precious to him— 5you also, like living stones, are being built into a spiritual house to be a holy priesthood, offering spiritual sacrifices acceptable to God through Jesus Christ. 6For in Scripture it says:

> "See, I lay a stone in Zion,
>   a chosen and precious cornerstone,
> and the one who trusts in him
>   will never be put to shame."

7Now to you who believe, this stone is precious. But to those who do not believe,

> "The stone the builders rejected
>   has become the capstone,"

8and,

> "A stone that causes men to stumble
>   and a rock that makes them fall."

They stumble because they disobey the message—which is also what they were destined for.

9But you are a chosen people, a royal priesthood, a holy nation, a people belonging to God, that you may declare the praises of him who called you out of darkness into his wonderful light. 10Once you were not a people, but now you are the people of God; once you had not received mercy, but now you have received mercy.

A THOUGHT: *Peter portrays the church as a living Temple: Christ is the foundation, and each believer is a stone. Paul portrays it as a body: Christ is the head, and each believer is a member. Both pictures emphasize community. One stone is not a temple or even a wall; one bodily part is useless without the others. In our individualistic society, it is easy to imagine that we can "go it alone." But when God calls you to a task, remember that he is also calling others to work with you. Together your individual efforts can be multiplied. Look for those people and join with them to build a beautiful house for God.*

Proverbs for Today/ 28:11

A rich man may be wise in his own eyes, but a poor man who has discernment sees through him.

NOVEMBER 24

Accusations against Paul/ Acts 24:1–9

Five days later the high priest Ananias went down to Caesarea with some of the elders and a lawyer named Tertullus, and they brought their charges against Paul before the governor. [2]When Paul was called in, Tertullus presented his case before Felix: "We have enjoyed a long period of peace under you, and your foresight has brought about reforms in this nation. [3]Everywhere and in every way, most excellent Felix, we acknowledge this with profound gratitude. [4]But in order not to weary you further, I would request that you be kind enough to hear us briefly.

[5]"We have found this man to be a troublemaker, stirring up riots among the Jews all over the world. He is a ringleader of the Nazarene sect [6]and even tried to desecrate the temple; so we seized him. [8]By* examining him yourself you will be able to learn the truth about all these charges we are bringing against him."

[9]The Jews joined in the accusation, asserting that these things were true.

A THOUGHT: *The accusers arrived—Ananias, the High Priest; Tertullus, the lawyer; and several Jewish leaders. They traveled 60 miles to Caesarea, the Roman center of government, to give their false accusations against Paul. Tertullus was a special orator called to present the religious leaders' case before the Roman governor. He made three accusations against Paul: (1) he was a renegade, inciting the Jews around the world; (2) he was the ringleader of an unrecognized religious sect, which was against Roman law; and (3) he had profaned the Temple. The religious leaders hoped that these accusations would persuade Felix to execute Paul to keep the peace in Palestine.*

Life According to God's Will/ 1 Peter 2:11–16

Dear friends, I urge you, as aliens and strangers in the world, to abstain from sinful desires, which war against your soul. [12]Live such good lives among the pagans that, though they accuse you of doing wrong, they may see your good deeds and glorify God on the day he visits us.

[13]Submit yourselves for the Lord's sake to every

*6-8 Some manuscripts *him and wanted to judge him according to our law.* [7]*But the commander, Lysias, came and with the use of much force snatched him from our hands* [8]*and ordered his accusers to come before you. By* authority instituted among men: whether to the king, as the supreme authority, 14or to governors, who are sent by him to punish those who do wrong and to commend those who do right. 15For it is God's will that by doing good you should silence the ignorant talk of foolish men. 16Live as free men, but do not use your freedom as a cover-up for evil; live as servants of God.

A THOUGHT: *When Peter told his readers to respect the civil government, he was probably speaking of the Roman Empire under Nero, a notoriously cruel tyrant. Obviously he was not telling believers to compromise their consciences; as Peter had told the High Priest years before, "we must obey God rather than men" (Acts 5:29). But in most aspects of their daily lives, it was possible and desirable for Christians to live according to the law of their land. Today, some Christians live in freedom while others live under repressive governments. All are commanded to cooperate with the rulers as far as conscience will allow. We are to do this "for the Lord's sake"—so that his Good News and his people will be respected. If we are to be persecuted, it should be for standing for God and not for wantonly or selfishly breaking civil laws.*

Proverbs for Today/ 28:12–13

When the righteous triumph, there is great elation; but when the wicked rise to power, men go into hiding. □ He who conceals his sins does not prosper, but whoever confesses and renounces them finds mercy.

NOVEMBER 25

Paul's Defense Before Felix/ Acts 24:10–27

When the governor [Felix] motioned for him to speak, Paul replied: "I know that for a number of years you have been a judge over this nation; so I gladly make my defense. 11You can easily verify that no more than twelve days ago I went up to Jerusalem to worship. 12My accusers did not find me arguing with anyone at the temple, or stirring up a crowd in the synagogues or anywhere else in the city. 13And they cannot prove to you the charges they are now making against me. 14However, I admit that I worship the God of our fathers as a follower of the Way, which they call a sect.

I believe everything that agrees with the Law and that is written in the Prophets, 15and I have the same hope in God as these men, that there will be a resurrection of both the righteous and the wicked. 16So I strive always to keep my conscience clear before God and man.

17"After an absence of several years, I came to Jerusalem to bring my people gifts for the poor and to present offerings. 18I was ceremonially clean when they found me in the temple courts doing this. There was no crowd with me, nor was I involved in any disturbance. 19But there are some Jews from the province of Asia, who ought to be here before you and bring charges if they have anything against me. 20Or these who are here should state what crime they found in me when I stood before the Sanhedrin— 21unless it was this one thing I shouted as I stood in their presence: 'It is concerning the resurrection of the dead that I am on trial before you today.'"

22Then Felix, who was well acquainted with the Way, adjourned the proceedings. "When Lysias the commander comes," he said, "I will decide your case." 23He ordered the centurion to keep Paul under guard but to give him some freedom and permit his friends to take care of his needs.

24Several days later Felix came with his wife Drusilla, who was a Jewess. He sent for Paul and listened to him as he spoke about faith in Christ Jesus. 25As Paul discoursed on righteousness, self-control and the judgment to come, Felix was afraid and said, "That's enough for now! You may leave. When I find it convenient, I will send for you." 26At the same time he was hoping that Paul would offer him a bribe, so he sent for him frequently and talked with him.

27When two years had passed, Felix was succeeded by Porcius Festus, but because Felix wanted to grant a favor to the Jews, he left Paul in prison.

A THOUGHT: *Paul's talk with Felix became so personal that Felix felt convicted. Felix, like Herod Antipas, had taken another man's wife. Paul's words were interesting to Felix until they focused on righteousness and self-control and the judgment to come. Many people will be glad to discuss the gospel with you as long as it doesn't touch their lives too personally. When it does, some will resist or run away. But this is what the gospel is all about—God's power to change lives. The gospel is not effective until it moves from principles and doctrine into a life-changing dynamic.*

Following in Jesus' Steps/ 1 Peter 2:17–25

Show proper respect to everyone: Love the brotherhood of believers, fear God, honor the king.

18Slaves, submit yourselves to your masters with all respect, not only to those who are good and considerate, but also to those who are harsh. 19For it is commendable if a man bears up under the pain of unjust suffering because he is conscious of God. 20But how is it to your credit if you receive a beating for doing wrong and endure it? But if you suffer for doing good and you endure it, this is commendable before God. 21To this you were called, because Christ suffered for you, leaving you an example, that you should follow in his steps.

> 22"He committed no sin,
>   and no deceit was found in his mouth."

23When they hurled their insults at him, he did not retaliate; when he suffered, he made no threats. Instead, he entrusted himself to him who judges justly. 24He himself bore our sins in his body on the tree, so that we might die to sins and live for righteousness; by his wounds you have been healed. 25For you were like sheep going astray, but now you have returned to the Shepherd and Overseer of your souls.

A THOUGHT: *There are many reasons for human suffering. Peter writes that suffering is part of the work God has given us to do. Christ never sinned, yet he suffered so that we could be set free. When we follow Christ's example and live for others, we too may suffer. Our goal should be to live as Christ lived and to face suffering as he did—with patience, calmness, and confidence that God is in control of the future.*

Proverbs for Today/ 28:14

Blessed is the man who always fears the LORD, but he who hardens his heart falls into trouble.

NOVEMBER 26

Paul Demands a Hearing Before Caesar/
Acts 25:1–12

Three days after arriving in the province, Festus went up from Caesarea to Jerusalem, ²where the chief priests and Jewish leaders appeared before him and presented the charges against Paul. ³They urgently requested Festus, as a favor to them, to have Paul transferred to Jerusalem, for they were preparing an ambush to kill him along the way. ⁴Festus answered, "Paul is being held at Caesarea, and I myself am going there soon. ⁵Let some of your leaders come with me and press charges against the man there, if he has done anything wrong."

⁶After spending eight or ten days with them, he went down to Caesarea, and the next day he convened the court and ordered that Paul be brought before him. ⁷When Paul appeared, the Jews who had come down from Jerusalem stood around him, bringing many serious charges against him, which they could not prove.

⁸Then Paul made his defense: "I have done nothing wrong against the law of the Jews or against the temple or against Caesar."

⁹Festus, wishing to do the Jews a favor, said to Paul, "Are you willing to go up to Jerusalem and stand trial before me there on these charges?"

¹⁰Paul answered: "I am now standing before Caesar's court, where I ought to be tried. I have not done any wrong to the Jews, as you yourself know very well. ¹¹If, however, I am guilty of doing anything deserving death, I do not refuse to die. But if the charges brought against me by these Jews are not true, no one has the right to hand me over to them. I appeal to Caesar!"

¹²After Festus had conferred with his council, he declared: "You have appealed to Caesar. To Caesar you will go!"

A THOUGHT: *Paul knew he was blameless of the charges against him and could appeal to Caesar's judgment. He knew his rights as a Roman citizen and as an innocent person. Paul had met his responsibilities as a Roman, and so he had the opportunity to claim Rome's protection. The good reputation and clear conscience that result from*

*our walk with God can help us remain not only guilt-free before God,
but blame-free before the world as well.*

Instructions for Wives/ 1 Peter 3:1–6

Wives, in the same way be submissive to your husbands
so that, if any of them do not believe the word, they may
be won over without words by the behavior of their wives,
²when they see the purity and reverence of your lives.
³Your beauty should not come from outward adornment,
such as braided hair and the wearing of gold jewelry and fine
clothes. ⁴Instead, it should be that of your inner self, the
unfading beauty of a gentle and quiet spirit, which is of great
worth in God's sight. ⁵For this is the way the holy women
of the past who put their hope in God used to make themselves beautiful. They were submissive to their own husbands, ⁶like Sarah, who obeyed Abraham and called him her
master. You are her daughters if you do what is right and
do not give way to fear.

A THOUGHT: *A changed life speaks loudly and clearly, and it is often
the most effective way to influence a family member. Peter instructed
Christian wives to develop inner beauty rather than being overly
concerned about their outward appearance. Their husbands would
be won by their love rather than by their looks. Live your Christian
faith quietly and consistently in your home, and your family will see
Christ in you.*

Proverbs for Today/ 28:15–16

Like a roaring lion or a charging bear is a wicked man ruling
over a helpless people. □ A tyrannical ruler lacks judgment, but he who hates ill-gotten gain will enjoy a long life.

NOVEMBER 27

Festus Explains Paul's Case/ Acts 25:13–27

A few days later King Agrippa and Bernice arrived at
Caesarea to pay their respects to Festus. ¹⁴Since they
were spending many days there, Festus discussed Paul's
case with the king. He said: "There is a man here whom
Felix left as a prisoner. ¹⁵When I went to Jerusalem, the

chief priests and elders of the Jews brought charges against him and asked that he be condemned.

16"I told them that it is not the Roman custom to hand over any man before he has faced his accusers and has had an opportunity to defend himself against their charges. 17When they came here with me, I did not delay the case, but convened the court the next day and ordered the man to be brought in. 18When his accusers got up to speak, they did not charge him with any of the crimes I had expected. 19Instead, they had some points of dispute with him about their own religion and about a dead man named Jesus who Paul claimed was alive. 20I was at a loss how to investigate such matters; so I asked if he would be willing to go to Jerusalem and stand trial there on these charges. 21When Paul made his appeal to be held over for the Emperor's decision, I ordered him held until I could send him to Caesar."

22Then Agrippa said to Festus, "I would like to hear this man myself."

He replied, "Tomorrow you will hear him."

23The next day Agrippa and Bernice came with great pomp and entered the audience room with the high ranking officers and the leading men of the city. At the command of Festus, Paul was brought in. 24Festus said: "King Agrippa, and all who are present with us, you see this man! The whole Jewish community has petitioned me about him in Jerusalem and here in Caesarea, shouting that he ought not to live any longer. 25I found he had done nothing deserving of death, but because he made his appeal to the Emperor I decided to send him to Rome. 26But I have nothing definite to write to His Majesty about him. Therefore I have brought him before all of you, and especially before you, King Agrippa, so that as a result of this investigation I may have something to write. 27For I think it is unreasonable to send on a prisoner without specifying the charges against him."

A THOUGHT: *The fact that Paul was in prison didn't stop him from making the most of his situation. Military officers and prominent city leaders met in the palace room with Agrippa to hear this case. Paul saw this new audience as yet another opportunity to present the gospel. Rather than complain about your present situation, seek for ways to use every opportunity to serve God and share him with others. Our problems may be opportunities in disguise.*

Instructions for Husbands/ 1 Peter 3:7–9

Husbands, in the same way be considerate as you live with your wives, and treat them with respect as the weaker partner and as heirs with you of the gracious gift of life, so that nothing will hinder your prayers.

8Finally, all of you, live in harmony with one another; be sympathetic, love as brothers, be compassionate and humble. 9Do not repay evil with evil or insult with insult, but with blessing, because to this you were called so that you may inherit a blessing.

A THOUGHT: *If a man does not treat his wife kindly, his prayers become ineffective, because a living relationship with God depends on right relationships with others. Jesus said that if you have a problem with a fellow believer, you must make things right with that person before coming to worship. This principle carries over into family relationships. Our relationship with God will suffer if we do not show a respect and love for others within our family. How we relate to others within our family is part of our relationship with God.*

Proverbs for Today/ 28:17–18

A man tormented by the guilt of murder will be a fugitive till death; let no one support him. □ He whose walk is blameless is kept safe, but he whose ways are perverse will suddenly fall.

NOVEMBER 28

Paul's Defense Before King Agrippa/ Acts 26:1–32

Then Agrippa said to Paul, "You have permission to speak for yourself."

So Paul motioned with his hand and began his defense: 2"King Agrippa, I consider myself fortunate to stand before you today as I make my defense against all the accusations of the Jews, 3and especially so because you are well acquainted with all the Jewish customs and controversies. Therefore, I beg you to listen to me patiently.

4"The Jews all know the way I have lived ever since I was a child, from the beginning of my life in my own country, and also in Jerusalem. 5They have known me for a long time and can testify, if they are willing, that according to the strictest sect of our religion, I lived as a Pharisee. 6And now it is because of my hope in what God has promised our fathers that I am on trial today. 7This is the promise our twelve tribes are hoping to see fulfilled as they earnestly serve God day and night. O king, it is because of this hope that the Jews are accusing me. 8Why should any of you consider it incredible that God raises the dead?

9"I too was convinced that I ought to do all that was possible to oppose the name of Jesus of Nazareth. 10And that is just what I did in Jerusalem. On the authority of the chief priests I put many of the saints in prison, and when they were put to death, I cast my vote against them. 11Many a time I went from one synagogue to another to have them punished, and I tried to force them to blaspheme. In my obsession against them, I even went to foreign cities to persecute them.

12"On one of these journeys I was going to Damascus with the authority and commission of the chief priests. 13About noon, O king, as I was on the road, I saw a light from heaven, brighter than the sun, blazing around me and my companions. 14We all fell to the ground, and I heard a voice saying to me in Aramaic, 'Saul, Saul, why do you persecute me? It is hard for you to kick against the goads.'

15"Then I asked, 'Who are you, Lord?'

" 'I am Jesus, whom you are persecuting,' the Lord replied. 16'Now get up and stand on your feet. I have appeared to you to appoint you as a servant and as a witness of what you have seen of me and what I will show you. 17I will rescue you from your own people and from the Gentiles. I am sending you to them 18to open their eyes and turn them from darkness to light, and from the power of Satan to God, so that they may receive forgiveness of sins and a place among those who are sanctified by faith in me.'

19"So then, King Agrippa, I was not disobedient to the vision from heaven. 20First to those in Damascus, then to those in Jerusalem and in all Judea, and to the Gentiles also, I preached that they should repent and turn to God and prove their repentance by their deeds. 21That is why the Jews seized me in the temple courts and tried to kill me. 22But I have had God's help to this very day, and so I stand here and testify to small and great alike. I am saying nothing

beyond what the prophets and Moses said would happen—
23that the Christ would suffer and, as the first to rise from the dead, would proclaim light to his own people and to the Gentiles."

24At this point Festus interrupted Paul's defense. "You are out of your mind, Paul!" he shouted. "Your great learning is driving you insane."

25"I am not insane, most excellent Festus," Paul replied. "What I am saying is true and reasonable. 26The king is familiar with these things, and I can speak freely to him. I am convinced that none of this has escaped his notice, because it was not done in a corner. 27King Agrippa, do you believe the prophets? I know you do."

28Then Agrippa said to Paul, "Do you think that in such a short time you can persuade me to be a Christian?"

29Paul replied, "Short time or long—I pray God that not only you but all who are listening to me today may become what I am, except for these chains."

30The king rose, and with him the governor and Bernice and those sitting with them. 31They left the room, and while talking with one another, they said, "This man is not doing anything that deserves death or imprisonment."

32Agrippa said to Festus, "This man could have been set free if he had not appealed to Caesar."

A THOUGHT: *Agrippa answered Paul's presentation with a sarcastic remark. Paul didn't react to the brush-off, but made a personal appeal to which he hoped all his listeners would respond. Paul's response is a good example for us as we tell others about God's plan of salvation. A sincere personal appeal or personal testimony can show the depth of our concern and break through hardened hearts. Paul's heart is revealed here in his defense: he was more concerned for the salvation of these strangers than for the removal of his own bonds. Ask God to help you share Paul's burning desire to see others come to him—a desire so strong that it overshadows your problems.*

Exhortations to Holy Living/ 1 Peter 3:10–16

For,

> "Whoever would love life
>   and see good days
> must keep his tongue from evil
>   and his lips from deceitful speech.
> 11He must turn from evil and do good;
>   he must seek peace and pursue it.

12For the eyes of the Lord are on the righteous
   and his ears are attentive to their prayer,
   but the face of the Lord is against those who do
      evil."

13Who is going to harm you if you are eager to do good?
14But even if you should suffer for what is right, you are
blessed. "Do not fear what they fear; do not be frightened." 15But in your hearts set apart Christ as Lord. Always be prepared to give an answer to everyone who asks
you to give the reason for the hope that you have. But do
this with gentleness and respect, 16keeping a clear conscience, so that those who speak maliciously against your
good behavior in Christ may be ashamed of their slander.

A THOUGHT: *Some Christians believe faith is a personal matter that
should be kept to oneself. It is true that we shouldn't be boisterous
or obnoxious in sharing our faith, but we should always be ready to
answer, gently and respectfully, when asked about our faith, our
lifestyle, or our Christian perspective. Is your hope in Christ readily
observable to others? Are you prepared to tell others what Christ has
done in your life?*

Proverbs for Today/ 28:19–20

He who works his land will have abundant food, but the one
who chases fantasies will have his fill of poverty. A faithful
man will be richly blessed, but one eager to get rich will not
go unpunished.

NOVEMBER 29

Paul Begins His Voyage to Rome/ Acts 27:1–15

When it was decided that we [Luke, Paul, and his compan-
ions] would sail for Italy, Paul and some other prisoners
were handed over to a centurion named Julius, who belonged to the Imperial Regiment. 2We boarded a ship from
Adramyttium about to sail for ports along the coast of the
province of Asia, and we put out to sea. Aristarchus, a
Macedonian from Thessalonica, was with us.

3The next day we landed at Sidon; and Julius, in kindness
to Paul, allowed him to go to his friends so they might

provide for his needs. ⁴From there we put out to sea again and passed to the lee of Cyprus because the winds were against us. ⁵When we had sailed across the open sea off the coast of Cilicia and Pamphylia, we landed at Myra in Lycia. ⁶There the centurion found an Alexandrian ship sailing for Italy and put us on board. ⁷We made slow headway for many days and had difficulty arriving off Cnidus. When the wind did not allow us to hold our course, we sailed to the lee of Crete, opposite Salmone. ⁸We moved along the coast with difficulty and came to a place called Fair Havens, near the town of Lasea.

⁹Much time had been lost, and sailing had already become dangerous because by now it was after the Fast. So Paul warned them, ¹⁰"Men, I can see that our voyage is going to be disastrous and bring great loss to ship and cargo, and to our own lives also." ¹¹But the centurion, instead of listening to what Paul said, followed the advice of the pilot and of the owner of the ship. ¹²Since the harbor was unsuitable to winter in, the majority decided that we should sail on, hoping to reach Phoenix and winter there. This was a harbor in Crete, facing both southwest and northwest.

¹³When a gentle south wind began to blow, they thought they had obtained what they wanted; so they weighed anchor and sailed along the shore of Crete. ¹⁴Before very long, a wind of hurricane force, called the "northeaster," swept down from the island. ¹⁵The ship was caught by the storm and could not head into the wind; so we gave way to it and were driven along.

A THOUGHT: *Ships in ancient times had no compasses and navigated by the stars. Overcast weather made sailing almost impossible and very dangerous. Sailing was doubtful in September and impossible by November. Paul had warned the ship's officers about the possibility of trouble ahead, but they decided to follow the advice of the ship's captain instead of heeding Paul's warning. As Paul predicted, a storm overtook the ship and blew it off course. Yet in the midst of all the difficulties God was with Paul and protected all the crew as well.*

Do Good, Even When You Suffer for It/
1 Peter 3:17–22

It is better, if it is God's will, to suffer for doing good than for doing evil. ¹⁸For Christ died for sins once for all, the righteous for the unrighteous, to bring you to God. He was put to death in the body but made alive by the Spirit, [19]through whom also he went and preached to the spirits in prison [20]who disobeyed long ago when God waited patiently in the days of Noah while the ark was being built. In it only a few people, eight in all, were saved through water, [21]and this water symbolizes baptism that now saves you also—not the removal of dirt from the body but the pledge of a good conscience toward God. It saves you by the resurrection of Jesus Christ, [22]who has gone into heaven and is at God's right hand—with angels, authorities and powers in submission to him.

A THOUGHT: *You may not be able to keep people from attacking you, but you can at least stop supplying them with justification for their actions. If we suffer for wrongdoing we should humbly endure it as just punishment. When we suffer for doing what is right, then we are given the opportunity to suffer as Christ suffered. Since Jesus suffered injustice, his followers should expect to suffer injustice as well. It is a privilege to suffer for Christ, even though it is not at all a pleasant experience. Let us keep our conduct above criticism, so that when we do suffer, our suffering can be a testimony to those around us.*

Proverbs for Today/ 28:21–22

To show partiality is not good—yet a man will do wrong for a piece of bread. □ A stingy man is eager to get rich and is unaware that poverty awaits him.

NOVEMBER 30

The Shipwreck on the Way to Rome/ Acts 27:16–44

As we [Luke, Paul, and his companions] passed to the lee of a small island called Cauda, we were hardly able to make the lifeboat secure. [17]When the men had hoisted it aboard, they passed ropes under the ship itself to hold it together. Fearing that they would run aground on the sandbars of Syrtis, they lowered the sea anchor and let the ship be driven along. [18]We took such a violent battering from the storm that the next day they began to throw the cargo overboard. [19]On the third day, they threw the ship's tackle overboard with their own hands. 20When neither sun nor stars appeared for many days and the storm continued raging, we finally gave up all hope of being saved.

21After the men had gone a long time without food, Paul stood up before them and said: "Men, you should have taken my advice not to sail from Crete; then you would have spared yourselves this damage and loss. 22But now I urge you to keep up your courage, because not one of you will be lost; only the ship will be destroyed. 23Last night an angel of the God whose I am and whom I serve stood beside me 24and said, 'Do not be afraid, Paul. You must stand trial before Caesar; and God has graciously given you the lives of all who sail with you.' 25So keep up your courage, men, for I have faith in God that it will happen just as he told me. 26Nevertheless, we must run aground on some island."

27On the fourteenth night we were still being driven across the Adriatic Sea, when about midnight the sailors sensed they were approaching land. 28They took soundings and found that the water was a hundred and twenty feet deep. A short time later they took soundings again and found it was ninety feet deep. 29Fearing that we would be dashed against the rocks, they dropped four anchors from the stern and prayed for daylight. 30In an attempt to escape from the ship, the sailors let the lifeboat down into the sea, pretending they were going to lower some anchors from the bow. 31Then Paul said to the centurion and the soldiers, "Unless these men stay with the ship, you cannot be saved." 32So the soldiers cut the ropes that held the lifeboat and let it fall away.

33Just before dawn Paul urged them all to eat. "For the last fourteen days," he said, "you have been in constant suspense and have gone without food—you haven't eaten anything. 34Now I urge you to take some food. You need it to survive. Not one of you will lose a single hair from his head." 35After he said this, he took some bread and gave thanks to God in front of them all. Then he broke it and began to eat. 36They were all encouraged and ate some food themselves. 37Altogether there were 276 of us on board. 38When they had eaten as much as they wanted, they lightened the ship by throwing the grain into the sea.

39When daylight came, they did not recognize the land, but they saw a bay with a sandy beach, where they decided to run the ship aground if they could. ⁴⁰Cutting loose the anchors, they left them in the sea and at the same time untied the ropes that held the rudders. Then they hoisted the foresail to the wind and made for the beach. ⁴¹But the ship struck a sandbar and ran aground. The bow stuck fast and would not move, and the stern was broken to pieces by the pounding of the surf.

⁴²The soldiers planned to kill the prisoners to prevent any of them from swimming away and escaping. ⁴³But the centurion wanted to spare Paul's life and kept them from carrying out their plan. He ordered those who could swim to jump overboard first and get to land. ⁴⁴The rest were to get there on planks or on pieces of the ship. In this way everyone reached land in safety.

A THOUGHT: *God was faithful to the promise he had made to Paul by way of the angel—everyone arrived safely on shore. God is sovereign over all the affairs of nature and people. We can take comfort in the promises of God even when the circumstances do not seem to indicate that God will fulfill his promises. We must remember that the story is never over until the final chapter is closed. Difficult times will come, but they are not the ultimate end for Christians, for we have the hope of the resurrection and life eternal ahead of us. The next time you find yourself in difficult circumstances, trust God to bring you through them—he is faithful.*

Life According to God's Will/ 1 Peter 4:1–6

Therefore, since Christ suffered in his body, arm yourselves also with the same attitude, because he who has suffered in his body is done with sin. ²As a result, he does not live the rest of his earthly life for evil human desires, but rather for the will of God. ³For you have spent enough time in the past doing what pagans choose to do—living in debauchery, lust, drunkenness, orgies, carousing and detestable idolatry. ⁴They think it strange that you do not plunge with them into the same flood of dissipation, and they heap abuse on you. ⁵But they will have to give account to him who is ready to judge the living and the dead. ⁶For this is the reason the gospel was preached even to those who are now dead, so that they might be judged according to men in regard to the body, but live according to God in regard to the spirit.

A THOUGHT: *Some people will do anything to avoid pain. As followers of Christ, however, we should be willing and prepared to do God's will and to suffer for it if necessary. Sin loses its power when we suffer*

*if we focus on Christ and what he wants us to do. When our bodies
are in pain or our lives in jeopardy, our real values show up clearly,
and sinful pleasures seem less important.*

Proverbs for Today/ 28:23–24

He who rebukes a man will in the end gain more favor than
he who has a flattering tongue. □ He who robs his father
or mother and says, "It's not wrong"—he is partner to him
who destroys.

DECEMBER 1

On the Island of Malta/ Acts 28:1–10

Once safely on shore, we [Luke, Paul, and his companions]
found out that the island was called Malta. ²The islanders
showed us unusual kindness. They built a fire and welcomed us all because it was raining and cold. ³Paul gathered
a pile of brushwood and, as he put it on the fire, a viper,
driven out by the heat, fastened itself on his hand. ⁴When
the islanders saw the snake hanging from his hand, they
said to each other, "This man must be a murderer; for
though he escaped from the sea, Justice has not allowed
him to live." ⁵But Paul shook the snake off into the fire and
suffered no ill effects. ⁶The people expected him to swell
up or suddenly fall dead, but after waiting a long time and
seeing nothing unusual happen to him, they changed their
minds and said he was a god.

⁷There was an estate nearby that belonged to Publius,
the chief official of the island. He welcomed us to his home
and for three days entertained us hospitably. ⁸His father
was sick in bed, suffering from fever and dysentery. Paul
went in to see him and, after prayer, placed his hands on
him and healed him. ⁹When this had happened, the rest of
the sick on the island came and were cured. ¹⁰They honored us in many ways and when we were ready to sail, they
furnished us with the supplies we needed.

A THOUGHT: *God had promised safe passage to Paul, and he allowed
neither sea nor serpent to stop his servant. The snake that bit Paul,
though poisonous, was unable to harm him. God still had work for*

Paul to do. Our lives are in God's hands, to continue or to end according to his good timing.

Use Your Gifts for Service/ 1 Peter 4:7–11

The end of all things is near. Therefore be clear minded and self-controlled so that you can pray. 8Above all, love each other deeply, because love covers over a multitude of sins. 9Offer hospitality to one another without grumbling. 10Each one should use whatever gift he has received to serve others, faithfully administering God's grace in its various forms. 11If anyone speaks, he should do it as one speaking the very words of God. If anyone serves, he should do it with the strength God provides, so that in all things God may be praised through Jesus Christ. To him be the glory and the power for ever and ever. Amen.

A THOUGHT: *Some people, well aware of their abilities, believe they have the right to use them as they please. Others feel they have no special talents at all. To both groups Peter addresses these verses. Peter says, everyone has some abilities; find yours and use them. All our abilities should be dedicated to others, he points out; none are for our own exclusive enjoyment. We must use the gifts which God has given to us to serve others.*

Proverbs for Today/ 28:25–26

A greedy man stirs up dissension, but he who trusts in the Lord will prosper. ☐ He who trusts in himself is a fool, but he who walks in wisdom is kept safe.

DECEMBER 2

Paul Lives under Guard in Rome/ Acts 28:11–31

After three months we [Luke, Paul, and his companions] put out to sea in a ship that had wintered in the island. It was an Alexandrian ship with the figurehead of the twin gods Castor and Pollux. 12We put in at Syracuse and stayed there three days. 13From there we set sail and arrived at Rhegium. The next day the south wind came up, and on the following day we reached Puteoli. 14There we found some brothers who invited us to spend a week with them. And so we came to Rome. 15The brothers there had heard that we were coming, and they traveled as far as the Forum of Appius and the Three Taverns to meet us. At the sight of these men Paul thanked God and was encouraged. 16When we got to Rome, Paul was allowed to live by himself, with a soldier to guard him.

17Three days later he called together the leaders of the Jews. When they had assembled, Paul said to them: "My brothers, although I have done nothing against our people or against the customs of our ancestors, I was arrested in Jerusalem and handed over to the Romans. 18They examined me and wanted to release me, because I was not guilty of any crime deserving death. 19But when the Jews objected, I was compelled to appeal to Caesar—not that I had any charge to bring against my own people. 20For this reason I have asked to see you and talk with you. It is because of the hope of Israel that I am bound with this chain."

21They replied, "We have not received any letters from Judea concerning you, and none of the brothers who have come from there has reported or said anything bad about you. 22But we want to hear what your views are, for we know that people everywhere are talking against this sect."

23They arranged to meet Paul on a certain day, and came in even larger numbers to the place where he was staying. From morning till evening he explained and declared to them the kingdom of God and tried to convince them about Jesus from the Law of Moses and from the Prophets. 24Some were convinced by what he said, but others would not believe. 25They disagreed among themselves and began to leave after Paul had made this final statement: "The Holy Spirit spoke the truth to your forefathers when he said through Isaiah the prophet:

26" 'Go to this people and say,
    "You will be ever hearing but never understanding;
       you will be ever seeing but never perceiving."
27For this people's heart has become calloused;
       they hardly hear with their ears,
       and they have closed their eyes.
    Otherwise they might see with their eyes,
       hear with their ears,

understand with their hearts
and turn, and I would heal them.'

28"Therefore I want you to know that God's salvation has been sent to the Gentiles, and they will listen!"*

30For two whole years Paul stayed there in his own rented house and welcomed all who came to see him. 31Boldly and without hindrance he preached the kingdom of God and taught about the Lord Jesus Christ.

A THOUGHT: *Paul wanted to preach the gospel in Rome, and he eventually got there—in chains, through shipwreck, and after many trials. Although he may have wished for an easier passage, he knew that God had blessed him greatly in allowing him to meet the believers in Rome and preach the message to both Jews and Gentiles in that great city. God "worked all things for good" (Romans 8:28) for Paul, and you can trust him to do the same for you. God may not make you comfortable or secure, but he will provide the opportunity to do his work.*

Suffering with Christ/ 1 Peter 4:12–19

Dear friends, do not be surprised at the painful trial you are suffering, as though something strange were happening to you. 13But rejoice that you participate in the sufferings of Christ, so that you may be overjoyed when his glory is revealed. 14If you are insulted because of the name of Christ, you are blessed, for the Spirit of glory and of God rests on you. 15If you suffer, it should not be as a murderer or thief or any other kind of criminal, or even as a meddler. 16However, if you suffer as a Christian, do not be ashamed, but praise God that you bear that name. 17For it is time for judgment to begin with the family of God; and if it begins with us, what will the outcome be for those who do not obey the gospel of God? 18And,

"If it is hard for the righteous to be saved,
what will become of the ungodly and the sinner?"

19So then, those who suffer according to God's will should commit themselves to their faithful Creator and continue to do good.

A THOUGHT: *Again Peter brings to mind Jesus' words: "Blessed are you when people insult you, persecute you and falsely say all kinds of evil against you because of me" (Matthew 5:11). It is never*

*28 Some manuscripts listen!" 29After he said this, the Jews left, arguing vigorously among themselves.

shameful to suffer for Christ, and he will send his Spirit to strengthen those who are persecuted for their faith. This does not mean that all suffering is good, however. Sometimes a person will grumble, "he's just picking on me because I'm a Christian," when it's obvious to everyone else that it is the person's own unpleasant behavior that is the cause of his problems. It may take careful thought or wise counsel to determine the real cause of our suffering. We can be assured, however, that whenever we suffer because of our loyalty to Christ, he will be with us all the way.

Proverbs for Today/ 28:27–28

He who gives to the poor will lack nothing, but he who closes his eyes to them receives many curses. □ When the wicked rise to power, people go into hiding; but when the wicked perish, the righteous thrive.

DECEMBER 3

A Greeting and a Doxology/ Revelation 1:1–8

The revelation of Jesus Christ, which God gave him to show his servants what must soon take place. He made it known by sending his angel to his servant John, 2who testifies to everything he saw—that is, the word of God and the testimony of Jesus Christ. 3Blessed is the one who reads the words of this prophecy, and blessed are those who hear it and take to heart what is written in it, because the time is near.

4John,

To the seven churches in the province of Asia:

Grace and peace to you from him who is, and who was, and who is to come, and from the seven spirits before his throne, 5and from Jesus Christ, who is the faithful witness, the firstborn from the dead, and the ruler of the kings of the earth.

To him who loves us and has freed us from our sins by his blood, 6and has made us to be a kingdom and priests to serve his God and Father—to him be glory and power for ever and ever! Amen.

7Look, he is coming with the clouds,
　　and every eye will see him,
　　even those who pierced him;
　　and all the peoples of the earth will mourn
　　　　because ot him.

So shall it be! Amen.

8"I am the Alpha and the Omega," says the Lord God, "who is, and who was, and who is to come, the Almighty."

A THOUGHT: *Jesus gave his message to John in a vision, allowing him to see and record certain future events so they could be an encouragement to all believers. The vision includes many signs and symbols, because they well convey the essence of what is to happen. What John saw, in most cases, was indescribable, so he used illustrations to show what it was like. When reading this symbolic language, don't think you have to understand every detail—John didn't. Instead, realize that John's imagery is used to show us that Christ is indeed the glorious and victorious Lord of all.*

Exhortations Concerning Church Leadership/ 1 Peter 5:1–7

To the elders among you, I appeal as a fellow elder, a witness of Christ's sufferings and one who also will share in the glory to be revealed: 2Be shepherds of God's flock that is under your care, serving as overseers—not because you must, but because you are willing, as God wants you to be; not greedy for money, but eager to serve; 3not lording it over those entrusted to you, but being examples to the flock. 4And when the Chief Shepherd appears, you will receive the crown of glory that will never fade away.

5Young men, in the same way be submissive to those who are older. All of you, clothe yourselves with humility toward one another, because,

　　"God opposes the proud
　　　　but gives grace to the humble."

6Humble yourselves, therefore, under God's mighty hand, that he may lift you up in due time. 7Cast all your anxiety on him because he cares for you.

A THOUGHT: *Peter describes several characteristics of good leaders in the church: (1) they realize they are caring for God's flock, not their own; (2) they lead out of eagerness to serve, not out of obligation; (3) they are concerned for what they can give, not for what they can get; (4) they lead by example, not force. All of us lead others in some way. Whatever your role, your leadership should be in line with these characteristics.*

Proverbs for Today/ 29:1

A man who remains stiff-necked after many rebukes will suddenly be destroyed—without remedy.

DECEMBER 4

John's Vision on the Lord's Day/ Revelation 1:9–20

I, John, your brother and companion in the suffering and kingdom and patient endurance that are ours in Jesus, was on the island of Patmos because of the word of God and the testimony of Jesus. 10On the Lord's Day I was in the Spirit, and I heard behind me a loud voice like a trumpet, 11which said: "Write on a scroll what you see and send it to the seven churches: to Ephesus, Smyrna, Pergamum, Thyatira, Sardis, Philadelphia and Laodicea."

12I turned around to see the voice that was speaking to me. And when I turned I saw seven golden lampstands, 13and among the lampstands was someone "like a son of man," dressed in a robe reaching down to his feet and with a golden sash around his chest. 14His head and hair were white like wool, as white as snow, and his eyes were like blazing fire. 15His feet were like bronze glowing in a furnace, and his voice was like the sound of rushing waters. 16In his right hand he held seven stars, and out of his mouth came a sharp double-edged sword. His face was like the sun shining in all its brilliance.

17When I saw him, I fell at his feet as though dead. Then he placed his right hand on me and said: "Do not be afraid. I am the First and the Last. 18I am the Living One; I was dead, and behold I am alive for ever and ever! And I hold the keys of death and Hades.

19"Write, therefore, what you have seen, what is now and what will take place later. 20The mystery of the seven stars that you saw in my right hand and of the seven golden lampstands is this: The seven stars are the angels of the seven churches, and the seven lampstands are the seven churches."

A THOUGHT: *John describes himself as a "companion in the suffering and kingdom . . . that are ours in Jesus," indicating that the church was undergoing intense persecution as he was writing this letter. The whole church, as the body of Christ, should experience joy and suffering together. Follow John's example in your relationships with other Christians: identify with them, encourage them to be steadfast and faithful, and remind them of their future reward with God.*

Standing Firm in Suffering/ 1 Peter 5:8–14

Be self-controlled and alert. Your enemy the devil prowls around like a roaring lion looking for someone to devour. 9Resist him, standing firm in the faith, because you know that your brothers throughout the world are undergoing the same kind of sufferings.

10And the God of all grace, who called you to his eternal glory in Christ, after you have suffered a little while, will himself restore you and make you strong, firm and steadfast. 11To him be the power for ever and ever. Amen.

12With the help of Silas, whom I regard as a faithful brother, I have written to you briefly, encouraging you and testifying that this is the true grace of God. Stand fast in it.

13She who is in Babylon, chosen together with you, sends you her greetings, and so does my son Mark. 14Greet one another with a kiss of love.

Peace to all of you who are in Christ.

A THOUGHT: *When we are suffering, we feel as though our pain will never end. Peter shows these faithful Christians the wider perspective. In comparison with eternity, their suffering would last only "a little while." Some of Peter's readers would be picked up, set in place, and strengthened in their own lifetimes. Others would be released from their suffering through death. All of God's faithful followers, however, are assured of Christ's eternal glory—endless, joyful life in which suffering plays no part at all.*

Proverbs for Today/ 29:2–4

When the righteous thrive, the people rejoice; when the wicked rule, the people groan. □ A man who loves wisdom brings joy to his father, but a companion of prostitutes squanders his wealth. □ By justice a king gives a country stability, but one who is greedy for bribes tears it down.

DECEMBER 5

The Letter to the Church in Ephesus/ Revelation 2:1–7

"To the angel of the church in Ephesus write:

These are the words of him who holds the seven stars in his right hand and walks among the seven golden lampstands: 2I know your deeds, your hard work and your perseverance. I know that you cannot tolerate wicked men, that you have tested those who claim to be apostles but are not, and have found them false. 3You have persevered and have endured hardships for my name, and have not grown weary.

4Yet I hold this against you: You have forsaken your first love. 5Remember the height from which you have fallen! Repent and do the things you did at first. If you do not repent, I will come to you and remove your lampstand from its place. 6But you have this in your favor: You hate the practices of the Nicolaitans, which I also hate.

7He who has an ear, let him hear what the Spirit says to the churches. To him who overcomes, I will give the right to eat from the tree of life, which is in the paradise of God.

A THOUGHT: *The church at Ephesus is commended for (1) working hard, (2) being patient, (3) resisting sin, (4) critically examining the claims of false apostles, and (5) suffering patiently without quitting. Every church should have these characteristics. But these good things should spring from our love for Jesus Christ. The Ephesians had lost their first love, and they may have been in danger of falling into legalism. Work for God is not lasting unless it is based on love for God and others.*

Knowing God and His Will/ 2 Peter 1:1–11

Simon Peter, a servant and apostle of Jesus Christ,

To those who through the righteousness of our God and Savior Jesus Christ have received a faith as precious as ours:

2Grace and peace be yours in abundance through the knowledge of God and of Jesus our Lord.

³His divine power has given us everything we need for life and godliness through our knowledge of him who called us by his own glory and goodness. ⁴Through these he has given us his very great and precious promises, so that through them you may participate in the divine nature and escape the corruption in the world caused by evil desires.

⁵For this very reason, make every effort to add to your faith goodness; and to goodness, knowledge; ⁶and to knowledge, self-control; and to self-control, perseverance; and to perseverance, godliness; ⁷and to godliness, brotherly kindness; and to brotherly kindness, love. ⁸For if you possess these qualities in increasing measure, they will keep you from being ineffective and unproductive in your knowledge of our Lord Jesus Christ. ⁹But if anyone does not have them, he is nearsighted and blind, and has forgotten that he has been cleansed from his past sins.

¹⁰Therefore, my brothers, be all the more eager to make your calling and election sure. For if you do these things, you will never fall, ¹¹and you will receive a rich welcome into the eternal kingdom of our Lord and Savior Jesus Christ.

A THOUGHT: *Many believers want more of God's kindness and peace, but they are unwilling to put forth the effort to get to know him better. To enjoy the privileges God offers us freely, we have to combine hard work with complete trust. In order to get to know God's will for our lives, we must faithfully obey what he has already revealed as his will in the Scriptures. As we internalize the Scriptures, the Holy Spirit transforms us into greater and greater Christlikeness—God's kindness and peace are then made realities in our lives.*

Proverbs for Today/ 29:5–8

Whoever flatters his neighbor is spreading a net for his feet. □ An evil man is snared by his own sin, but a righteous one can sing and be glad. □ The righteous care about justice for the poor, but the wicked have no such concern. □ Mockers stir up a city, but wise men turn away anger.

DECEMBER 6

The Letter to the Church in Smyrna/ Revelation 2:8–11

"To the angel of the church in Smyrna write:

These are the words of him who is the First and the Last, who died and came to life again. 9I know your afflictions and your poverty—yet you are rich! I know the slander of those who say they are Jews and are not, but are a synagogue of Satan. 10Do not be afraid of what you are about to suffer. I tell you, the devil will put some of you in prison to test you, and you will suffer persecution for ten days. Be faithful, even to the point of death, and I will give you the crown of life.

11He who has an ear, let him hear what the Spirit says to the churches. He who overcomes will not be hurt at all by the second death.

A THOUGHT: *Everyone would like to feel good and live comfortably, but pain is part of life—and it is not easy to suffer, no matter what the cause. Jesus commended the church at Smyrna for their faith in the midst of suffering. He then encouraged them that they need not fear the future if they remained faithful. If you are experiencing difficult times, don't let them turn you away from God. Instead let them draw you toward greater faithfulness. Trust him and remember your heavenly reward.*

Peter an Eyewitness of Christ/ 2 Peter 1:12–18

So I will always remind you of these things, even though you know them and are firmly established in the truth you have. 13I think it is right to refresh your memory as long as I live in the tent of this body, 14because I know that I will soon put it aside, as our Lord Jesus Christ has made clear to me. 15And I will make every effort to see that after my departure you will always be able to remember these things.

16We did not follow cleverly invented stories when we told you about the power and coming of our Lord Jesus Christ, but we were eyewitnesses of his majesty. 17For he received honor and glory from God the Father when the voice came to him from the Majestic Glory, saying, "This is my Son, whom I love; with him I am well pleased." [18]We ourselves heard this voice that came from heaven when we were with him on the sacred mountain.

A THOUGHT: *Outstanding coaches constantly review the basics of the sport with their teams, and good athletes can execute the fundamentals consistently well. In our spiritual lives we must not neglect the basics of our faith when we go on to study deeper truths. Just as an athlete needs constant practice, we need constant reminders of the fundamentals of our faith and of how we came to believe in the first place. Don't allow yourself to be bored or impatient with messages on the basics of the Christian life. Instead, take the attitude of an athlete who continues to practice and refine the basics even as he learns more advanced skills.*

Proverbs for Today/ 29:9–11

If a wise man goes to court with a fool, the fool rages and scoffs, and there is no peace. □ Bloodthirsty men hate a man of integrity and seek to kill the upright. □ A fool gives full vent to his anger, but a wise man keeps himself under control.

DECEMBER 7

The Letter to the Church in Pergamum/ Revelation 2:12–17

"To the angel of the church in Pergamum write:

These are the words of him who has the sharp, double-edged sword. [13]I know where you live—where Satan has his throne. Yet you remain true to my name. You did not renouce your faith in me, even in the days of Antipas, my faithful witness, who was put to death in your city—where Satan lives.

[14]Nevertheless, I have a few things against you: You have people there who hold to the teaching of Balaam, who taught Balak to entice the Israelites to sin by eating food sacrificed to idols and by committing sexual immorality. [15]Likewise you also have those who hold to the teaching of the Nicolaitans. [16]Repent

therefore! Otherwise, I will soon come to you and will fight against them with the sword of my mouth.

17He who has an ear, let him hear what the Spirit says to the churches. To him who overcomes, I will give some of the hidden manna. I will also give him a white stone with a new name written on it, known only to him who receives it.

A THOUGHT: *As the center for four idolatrous cults, Pergamum is called the city "where Satan has his throne." Surrounded by Satanic worship, the church at Pergamum refused to deny Christ even when Satan's worshipers martyred one of their members. There is no room for heresy and moral impurity among Christians. Your town may not participate in idol feasts, but it probably has pornography, sexual sin, cheating, gossiping, and lying. Don't tolerate sin under the pressure to be open-minded. Standing firm against Satan's attractive temptations is never easy, but the alternative is deadly.*

True and False Prophets/ 2 Peter 1:19—2:11

And we have the word of the prophets made more certain, and you will do well to pay attention to it, as to a light shining in a dark place, until the day dawns and the morning star rises in your hearts. 20Above all, you must understand that no prophecy of Scripture came about by the prophet's own interpretation. 21For prophecy never had its origin in the will of man, but men spoke from God as they were carried along by the Holy Spirit.

2:1But there were also false prophets among the people, just as there will be false teachers among you. They will secretly introduce destructive heresies, even denying the sovereign Lord who bought them—bringing swift destruction on themselves. 2Many will follow their shameful ways and will bring the way of truth into disrepute. 3In their greed these teachers will exploit you with stories they have made up. Their condemnation has long been hanging over them, and their destruction has not been sleeping.

4For if God did not spare angels when they sinned, but sent them to hell, putting them into gloomy dungeons to be held for judgment; 5if he did not spare the ancient world when he brought the flood on its ungodly people, but protected Noah, a preacher of righteousness, and seven others; 6if he condemned the cities of Sodom and Gomorrah by burning them to ashes, and made them an example of what is going to happen to the ungodly; 7and if he rescued

Lot, a righteous man, who was distressed by the filthy lives of lawless men [8](for that righteous man, living among them day after day, was tormented in his righteous soul by the lawless deeds he saw and heard)— [9]if this is so, then the Lord knows how to rescue godly men from trials and to hold the unrighteous for the day of judgment, while continuing their punishment. [10]This is especially true of those who follow the corrupt desire of the sinful nature and despise authority.

Bold and arrogant, these men are not afraid to slander celestial beings; [11]yet even angels, although they are stronger and more powerful, do not bring slanderous accusations against such beings in the presence of the Lord.

A THOUGHT: *Jesus had told the disciples that false teachers would come. Peter had heard these words, and now he was seeing them come true. Just as false prophets had contradicted the true prophets in Old Testament times, telling people only what they wanted to hear, so false teachers twisted Christ's teachings and the words of his apostles. These teachers belittled the significance of Jesus' life, death, and resurrection. Some claimed he couldn't be God; others claimed he couldn't have been a real man. They allowed and even encouraged all kinds of wrong and immoral acts, especially sexual sin. Though these false teachers were popular, Peter warned that they would be destroyed. We should beware of those who make such claims against God's Word today. Let us avoid those who seek their own profit, their own glory, cause divisions within the church, and deny the truths of God's inspired Word.*

Proverbs for Today/ 29:12–14

If a ruler listens to lies, all his officials become wicked. □ The poor man and the oppressor have this in common: The LORD gives sight to the eyes of both. □ If a king judges the poor with fairness, his throne will always be secure.

DECEMBER 8

The Letter to the Church in Thyatira/
Revelation 2:18–29

"To the angel of the church in Thyatira write:

These are the words of the Son of God, whose eyes are like blazing fire and whose feet are like burnished bronze. 19I know your deeds, your love and faith, your service and perseverance, and that you are now doing more than you did at first.

20Nevertheless, I have this against you: You tolerate that woman Jezebel, who calls herself a prophetess. By her teaching she misleads my servants into sexual immorality and the eating of food sacrificed to idols. 21I have given her time to repent of her immorality, but she is unwilling. 22So I will cast her on a bed of suffering, and I will make those who commit adultery with her suffer intensely, unless they repent of her ways. 23I will strike her children dead. Then all the churches will know that I am he who searches hearts and minds, and I will repay each of you according to your deeds. 24Now I say to the rest of you in Thyatira, to you who do not hold to her teaching and have not learned Satan's so-called deep secrets (I will not impose any other burden on you): 25Only hold on to what you have until I come.

26To him who overcomes and does my will to the end, I will give authority over the nations—

27'He will rule them with an iron scepter;
　　he will dash them to pieces like
　　　　pottery'—

just as I have received authority from my Father. 28I will also give him the morning star. 29He who has an ear, let him hear what the Spirit says to the churches.

A THOUGHT: *Obedience to Christ always involves a change of attitude. When we are converted, a battle begins inside us as Satan tries to keep us from changing. John records this example from Jezebel's life to show the importance of changes in attitude. Our attitudes powerfully influence our behavior. Which of your attitudes would Jesus highlight as needing change? If you're having trouble doing right in an area of your life, perhaps you need a change of attitude.*

The Danger of False Teachers/ 2 Peter 2:12–22

But these men blaspheme in matters they do not understand. They are like brute beasts, creatures of instinct, born only to be caught and destroyed, and like beasts they too will perish.

13They will be paid back with harm for the harm they have done. Their idea of pleasure is to carouse in broad daylight. They are blots and blemishes, reveling in their pleasures while they feast with you. 14With eyes full of adultery, they never stop sinning; they seduce the unstable; they are experts in greed—an accursed brood! 15They have left the straight way and wandered off to follow the way of Balaam son of Beor, who loved the wages of wickedness. 16But he was rebuked for his wrongdoing by a donkey—a beast without speech—who spoke with a man's voice and restrained the prophet's madness.

17These men are springs without water and mists driven by a storm. Blackest darkness is reserved for them. 18For they mouth empty, boastful words and, by appealing to the lustful desires of sinful human nature, they entice people who are just escaping from those who live in error. 19They promise them freedom, while they themselves are slaves of depravity—for a man is a slave to whatever has mastered him. 20If they have escaped the corruption of the world by knowing our Lord and Savior Jesus Christ and are again entangled in it and overcome, they are worse off at the end than they were at the beginning. 21It would have been better for them not to have known the way of righteousness, than to have known it and then to turn their backs on the sacred command that was passed on to them. 22Of them the proverbs are true: "A dog returns to its vomit," and, "A sow that is washed goes back to her wallowing in the mud."

A THOUGHT: *Many believe freedom means doing anything you want. But no one is ever completely free in that sense. If we refuse to follow God, we will follow our own sinful desires and become enslaved to what our bodies want. If we submit our lives to Christ, he will free us from slavery to sin. Christ frees us to serve him, which always results in our ultimate good.*

Proverbs for Today/ 29:15–17

The rod of correction imparts wisdom, but a child left to himself disgraces his mother. □ When the wicked thrive, so does sin, but the righteous will see their downfall. □ Discipline your son, and he will give you peace; he will bring delight to your soul.

DECEMBER 9

The Letter to the Church in Sardis/ Revelation 3:1–6

"To the angel of the church in Sardis write:

These are the words of him who holds the seven spirits of God and the seven stars. I know your deeds; you have a reputation of being alive, but you are dead. 2Wake up! Strengthen what remains and is about to die, for I have not found your deeds complete in the sight of my God. 3Remember, therefore, what you have received and heard; obey it, and repent. But if you do not wake up, I will come like a thief, and you will not know at what time I will come to you.

4Yet you have a few people in Sardis who have not soiled their clothes. They will walk with me, dressed in white, for they are worthy. 5He who overcomes will, like them, be dressed in white. I will never blot out his name from the book of life, but will acknowledge his name before my Father and his angels. 6He who has an ear, let him hear what the Spirit says to the churches.

A THOUGHT: *The church at Sardis was urged to hold on to the Christian truth they had heard when they first believed in Christ, to get back to the basics of the faith. It is important to grow in our knowledge of the Lord, to deepen our understanding through careful study. But no matter how much we learn, we must never abandon the basic truths about Jesus. Jesus will always be God's Son, and his sacrifice for our sins is permanent. No new truth from God will ever contradict these biblical teachings.*

Scoffers in the Last Days/ 2 Peter 3:1–7

Dear friends, this is now my second letter to you. I have written both of them as reminders to stimulate you to wholesome thinking. 2I want you to recall the words spoken in the past by the holy prophets and the command given by our Lord and Savior through your apostles.

3First of all, you must understand that in the last days scoffers will come, scoffing and following their own evil desires. 4They will say, "Where is this 'coming' he promised? Ever since our fathers died, everything goes on as it has since the beginning of creation." 5But they deliberately forget that long ago by God's word the heavens existed and the earth was formed out of water and by water. 6By these waters also the world of that time was deluged and destroyed. 7By the same word the present heavens and earth are reserved for fire, being kept for the day of judgment and destruction of ungodly men.

A THOUGHT: *Scoffers in the last days would say Jesus was never coming back, but Peter refutes their argument by explaining God's mastery over time. The "last days" are the time between Christ's first and second comings; thus we, like Peter, live in the last days. We must do the work to which God has called us and believe he will return as he promised. God is not on man's time schedule, but man is bound within God's schedule.*

Proverbs for Today/ 29:18

Where there is no revelation, the people cast off restraint; but blessed is he who keeps the law.

DECEMBER 10

The Letter to the Church in Philadelphia/ Revelation 3:7–13

"To the angel of the church in Philadelphia write:

These are the words of him who is holy and true, who holds the key of David. What he opens no one can shut, and what he shuts no one can open. 8I know your deeds. See, I have placed before you an open door that no one can shut. I know that you have little strength, yet you have kept my word and have not denied my name. 9I will make those who are of the synagogue of Satan, who claim to be Jews though they are not, but are liars—I will make them come and fall down at your feet and acknowledge that I have loved you. 10Since you have kept my command to endure patiently, I will also keep you from the hour of trial that is going to come upon the whole world to test those who live on the earth.

11I am coming soon. Hold on to what you have, so that no one will take your crown. 12Him who overcomes I will make a pillar in the temple of my God. Never again will he leave it. I will write on him the name of my God and the name of the city of my God, the new Jerusalem, which is coming down out of heaven from my God; and I will also write on him my new name. 13He who has an ear, let him hear what the Spirit says to the churches.

A THOUGHT: *Christians have differing gifts, abilities, experience, and maturity. God doesn't expect us all to be the same, but he does expect us to persevere in using our assets for him. The Philadelphians are commended for their effort to obey and encouraged to hold tightly to whatever strength they have. You may be a new believer and feel that your faith and spiritual strength are small. Use what you have to live for Christ, and God will commend you.*

The Day of the Lord/ 2 Peter 3:8–13

But do not forget this one thing, dear friends: With the Lord a day is like a thousand years, and a thousand years are like a day. 9The Lord is not slow in keeping his promise, as some understand slowness. He is patient with you, not wanting anyone to perish, but everyone to come to repentance.

10But the day of the Lord will come like a thief. The heavens will disappear with a roar; the elements will be destroyed by fire, and the earth and everything in it will be laid bare.

11Since everything will be destroyed in this way, what kind of people ought you to be? You ought to live holy and godly lives 12as you look forward to the day of God and speed its coming. That day will bring about the destruction of the heavens by fire, and the elements will melt in the heat. 13But in keeping with his promise we are looking forward to a new heaven and a new earth, the home of righteousness.

A THOUGHT: *God may have seemed slow in keeping his promise of return to these believers as they faced persecution every day and longed to be delivered. But God is not slow; he just is not on our timetable. Jesus is waiting so that more sinners will repent and turn to him. We must not sit and wait for him, but live with the realization that time is short and we have important work to do. Be ready to meet him any time, even today; yet plan your course of service as if he may not return for many years.*

Proverbs for Today/ 29:19–20

A servant cannot be corrected by mere words; though he understands, he will not respond. ☐ Do you see a man who speaks in haste? There is more hope for a fool than for him.

DECEMBER 11

The Letter to the Church in Laodicea/ Revelation 3:14–22

"To the angel of the church in Laodicea write:

These are the words of the Amen, the faithful and true witness, the ruler of God's creation. 15I know your deeds, that you are neither cold nor hot. I wish you were either one or the other! 16So, because you are lukewarm—neither hot nor cold—I am about to spit you out of my mouth. 17You say, 'I am rich; I have acquired wealth and do not need a thing.' But you do not realize that you are wretched, pitiful, poor, blind and naked. 18I counsel you to buy from me gold refined in the fire, so you can become rich; and white clothes to wear, so you can cover your shameful nakedness; and salve to put on your eyes, so you can see.

19Those whom I love I rebuke and discipline. So be earnest, and repent. 20Here I am! I stand at the door and knock. If anyone hears my voice and opens the door, I will come in and eat with him, and he with me. 21To him who overcomes, I will give the right to sit with me on my throne, just as I overcame and sat down with my Father on his throne. 22He who has an ear, let him hear what the Spirit says to the churches."

A THOUGHT: *Some believers falsely assume that an abundance of material possessions is a sign of God's spiritual blessing. Laodicea was a wealthy city, and the church was also wealthy. But what the Laodiceans could see and buy had become more valuable to them than what is unseen and eternal. Wealth, luxury, and ease can make people feel confident, satisfied, and complacent. But no matter how much you possess or how much money you make, you have nothing if you don't have a vital relationship with Christ. How does your current level of wealth affect your spiritual desire? Instead of centering your life primarily on comfort and luxury, find your true riches in Christ.*

Prepare for Christ's Return/ 2 Peter 3:14–18

So then, dear friends, since you are looking forward to this, make every effort to be found spotless, blameless and at peace with him. 15Bear in mind that our Lord's patience means salvation, just as our dear brother Paul also wrote you with the wisdom that God gave him. 16He writes the same way in all his letters, speaking in them of these matters. His letters contain some things that are hard to understand, which ignorant and unstable people distort, as they do the other Scriptures, to their own destruction.

17Therefore, dear friends, since you already know this, be on your guard so that you may not be carried away by the error of lawless men and fall from your secure position. 18But grow in the grace and knowledge of our Lord and Savior Jesus Christ. To him be glory both now and forever! Amen.

A THOUGHT: *We should not become lazy and complacent because Christ has not yet returned. Instead, our lives should express our eager expectation of his coming. What would you like to be doing when Christ returns? Is that the way you are living each day?*

Proverbs for Today/ 29:21–22

If a man pampers his servant from youth, he will bring grief in the end. □ An angry man stirs up dissension, and a hot-tempered one commits many sins.

A Vision of God's Throne/ Revelation 4:1–11

After this I looked, and there before me was a door standing open in heaven. And the voice I had first heard speaking to me like a trumpet said, "Come up here, and I will show you what must take place after this." ²At once I was in the Spirit, and there before me was a throne in heaven with someone sitting on it. ³And the one who sat there had the appearance of jasper and carnelian. A rainbow, resembling an emerald, encircled the throne. ⁴Surrounding the throne were twenty-four other thrones, and seated on them were twenty-four elders. They were dressed in white and had crowns of gold on their heads. ⁵From the throne came flashes of lightning, rumblings and peals of thunder. Before the throne, seven lamps were blazing. These are the seven spirits of God. ⁶Also before the throne there was what looked like a sea of glass, clear as crystal.

In the center, around the throne, were four living creatures, and they were covered with eyes, in front and in back. ⁷The first living creature was like a lion, the second was like an ox, the third had a face like a man, the fourth was like a flying eagle. ⁸Each of the four living creatures had six wings and was covered with eyes all around, even under his wings. Day and night they never stop saying:

"Holy, holy, holy
is the Lord God Almighty,
who was, and is, and is to come."

⁹Whenever the living creatures give glory, honor and thanks to him who sits on the throne and who lives for ever and ever, ¹⁰the twenty-four elders fall down before him who sits on the throne, and worship him who lives for ever and ever. They lay their crowns before the throne and say:

¹¹"You are worthy, our Lord and God,
to receive glory and honor and power,
for you created all things,
and by your will they were created
and have their being."

A THOUGHT: *Who are these 24 elders? Since there were 12 tribes of Israel in the Old Testament and 12 apostles in the New Testament, the 24 elders in this vision probably represent all the redeemed of God for all time (both before and after Christ's death and resurrection). They symbolize all those—both Jews and Gentiles—who are now part of God's family. The 24 elders show us that all the redeemed of the Lord are worshiping him—all beings in heaven and earth will praise and honor God because he is the Creator and Sustainer of everything.*

An Eyewitness of the Incarnate Christ/ 1 John 1:1–4

That which was from the beginning, which we have heard, which we have seen with our eyes, which we have looked at and our hands have touched—this we proclaim concerning the Word of life. 2The life appeared; we have seen it and testify to it, and we proclaim to you the eternal life, which was with the Father and has appeared to us. 3We proclaim to you what we have seen and heard, so that you also may have fellowship with us. And our fellowship is with the Father and with his Son, Jesus Christ. 4We write this to make our joy complete.

A THOUGHT: *As an eyewitness to Jesus' ministry, John was qualified to teach the truth about him. The readers of this letter had not seen and heard Jesus themselves, but they could trust that what John wrote was accurate. We are like those second and third-generation Christians. Though we have not personally seen, heard, or touched Jesus, we have the New Testament record of his eyewitnesses, and we can trust that they spoke the truth about him.*

Proverbs for Today/ 29:23

A man's pride brings him low, but a man of lowly spirit gains honor.

DECEMBER 13

The Scroll and the Lamb/ Revelation 5:1–14

Then I saw in the right hand of him who sat on the throne a scroll with writing on both sides and sealed with seven seals. 2And I saw a mighty angel proclaiming in a loud voice, "Who is worthy to break the seals and open the scroll?" 3But no one in heaven or on earth or under the earth could open the scroll or even look inside it. 4I wept and wept because no one was found who was worthy to open the scroll or look inside. 5Then one of the elders said to me, "Do not weep! See, the Lion of the tribe of Judah, the Root of David, has triumphed. He is able to open the scroll and its seven seals."

6Then I saw a Lamb, looking as if it had been slain, standing in the center of the throne, encircled by the four living creatures and the elders. He had seven horns and seven eyes, which are the seven spirits of God sent out into all the earth. 7He came and took the scroll from the right hand of him who sat on the throne. 8And when he had taken it, the four living creatures and the twenty-four elders fell down before the Lamb. Each one had a harp and they were holding golden bowls full of incense, which are the prayers of the saints. 9And they sang a new song:

> "You are worthy to take the scroll
>   and to open its seals,
> because you were slain,
>   and with your blood you purchased men for God
>   from every tribe and language and people and
>   nation.
> 10You have made them to be a kingdom and priests
>   to serve our God,
>   and they will reign on the earth."

11Then I looked and heard the voice of many angels, numbering thousands upon thousands, and ten thousand times ten thousand. They encircled the throne and the living creatures and the elders. 12In a loud voice they sang:

> "Worthy is the Lamb, who was slain,
> to receive power and wealth and wisdom and
>   strength
> and honor and glory and praise!"

13Then I heard every creature in heaven and on earth and under the earth and on the sea, and all that is in them, singing:

> "To him who sits on the throne and to the Lamb
> be praise and honor and glory and power,
>   for ever and ever!"

14The four living creatures said, "Amen," and the elders fell down and worshiped.

A THOUGHT: *Jesus Christ is pictured as both a Lion (symbolizing his authority and power) and a Lamb (symbolizing his humble submission to God's will). One of the Elders calls John to look at the Lion, but when John looks he sees a Lamb. It is the Lamb, not the Lion, that becomes the focus in this vision. Christ the Lamb was the perfect sacrifice for the sins of all mankind; therefore, only he can save us from the terrible events revealed by the scroll. Christ the Lamb won the greatest battle of all—defeating all the forces of evil and death by submitting humbly to God's will and dying on the cross, the perfect sacrifice for sin. Christ the Lion will be victorious because of what Christ the Lamb has already done. We will enjoy the rewards of victory not because of our power and might, but because we belong to God.*

Forgiveness through the Blood of Jesus/ 1 John 1:5–10

This is the message we have heard from him and declare to you: God is light; in him there is no darkness at all. 6If we claim to have fellowship with him yet walk in the darkness, we lie and do not live by the truth. 7But if we walk in the light, as he is in the light, we have fellowship with one another, and the blood of Jesus, his Son, purifies us from all sin.

8If we claim to be without sin, we deceive ourselves and the truth is not in us. 9If we confess our sins, he is faithful and just and will forgive us our sins and purify us from all unrighteousness. 10If we claim we have not sinned, we make him out to be a liar and his word has no place in our lives.

A THOUGHT: *Confession is supposed to free us to enjoy fellowship with Christ. It should ease our consciences and lighten our cares. But some Christians do not understand how it works. They feel so guilty that they confess the same sins over and over, and then wonder if they might have forgotten something. Other Christians believe God forgives them when they confess their sins, but if they died with unconfessed sins, they would be forever lost. These Christians do not understand that God wants to forgive us. He allowed his beloved Son to die just so he could pardon us. When we come to Christ, he forgives all the sins we have committed or will ever commit. We don't need to confess the same sins all over again, and we don't need to fear that he will cast us out if we don't keep our slate perfectly clear at all moments. Of course, we want to continue to confess our sins, but not because we think failure to do so will make us lose our salvation.*

Our hope in Christ is secure. Instead, we confess our sins so that we can enjoy maximum fellowship and joy with him.

True confession also involves a commitment not to continue in sin. We are not genuinely confessing our sins before God if we plan to commit the sin again and just want temporary forgiveness. We must pray for strength to defeat the temptation the next time it appears.

Proverbs for Today/ 29:24–25

The accomplice of a thief is his own enemy; he is put under oath and dare not testify. □ Fear of man will prove to be a snare, but whoever trusts in the LORD is kept safe.

DECEMBER 14

The Lamb Opens the Seals/ Revelation 6:1–17

I watched as the Lamb opened the first of the seven seals. Then I heard one of the four living creatures say in a voice like thunder, "Come!" 2I looked, and there before me was a white horse! Its rider held a bow, and he was given a crown, and he rode out as a conqueror bent on conquest.

3When the Lamb opened the second seal, I heard the second living creature say, "Come!" 4Then another horse came out, a fiery red one. Its rider was given power to take peace from the earth and to make men slay each other. To him was given a large sword.

5When the Lamb opened the third seal, I heard the third living creature say, "Come!" I looked, and there before me was a black horse! Its rider was holding a pair of scales in his hand. 6Then I heard what sounded like a voice among the four living creatures, saying, "A quart of wheat for a day's wages, and three quarts of barley for a day's wages, and do not damage the oil and the wine!"

7When the Lamb opened the fourth seal, I heard the voice of the fourth living creature say, "Come!" 8I looked, and there before me was a pale horse! Its rider was named Death, and Hades was following close behind him. They were given power over a fourth of the earth to kill by sword, famine and plague, and by the wild beasts of the earth.

9When he opened the fifth seal, I saw under the altar the souls of those who had been slain because of the word of God and the testimony they had maintained. 10They called out in a loud voice, "How long, Sovereign Lord, holy and true, until you judge the inhabitants of the earth and avenge our blood?" 11Then each of them was given a white robe, and they were told to wait a little longer, until the number of their fellow servants and brothers who were to be killed as they had been was completed.

12I watched as he opened the sixth seal. There was a great earthquake. The sun turned black like sackcloth made of goat hair, the whole moon turned blood red, 13and the stars in the sky fell to earth, as late figs drop from a fig tree when shaken by a strong wind. 14The sky receded like a scroll, rolling up, and every mountain and island was removed from its place.

15Then the kings of the earth, the princes, the generals, the rich, the mighty, and every slave and every free man hid in caves and among the rocks of the mountains. 16They called to the mountains and the rocks, "Fall on us and hide us from the face of him who sits on the throne and from the wrath of the Lamb! 17For the great day of their wrath has come, and who can stand?"

A THOUGHT: *Four horses appear as the first four seals are broken. The horses represent God's judgment of mankind's sin and rebellion. God is directing human history—even using his enemies to unknowingly accomplish his purposes. The four horsemen are given control of one-fourth of the earth, indicating that God is still limiting his judgment—it is not yet complete. With these judgments there is still time for people to turn to Christ and away from their sin. In this case, the limited punishment not only demonstrates God's wrath toward sin, but also his merciful love in giving people yet another opportunity to turn to him before he brings final judgment.*

Our Advocate Before the Father/ 1 John 2:1–6

My dear children, I write this to you so that you will not sin. But if anybody does sin, we have one who speaks to the Father in our defense—Jesus Christ, the Righteous One. 2He is the atoning sacrifice for our sins, and not only for ours but also for the sins of the whole world.

3We know that we have come to know him if we obey his commands. 4The man who says, "I know him," but does not do what he commands is a liar, and the truth is not in him. 5But if anyone obeys his word, God's love is truly made complete in him. This is how we know we are in him: 6Whoever claims to live in him must walk as Jesus did.

A THOUGHT: *To people who are feeling guilty and condemned, John offers reassurance. They know they have sinned, and Satan (called "the Accuser of our brothers" in Revelation 12:10) is demanding the death penalty. When you feel this way, don't give up hope—the best defense attorney in the universe is pleading your case. Jesus Christ, your advocate, is the Judge's Son. He has already suffered the Judge's penalty in your place. You can't be tried again for a case that is no longer on the docket. United with Jesus, you are as safe as he is. Don't be afraid to ask him to plead your case—he has already won it.*

Proverbs for Today/ 29:26–27

Many seek an audience with a ruler, but it is from the LORD that man gets justice. □ The righteous detest the dishonest; the wicked detest the upright.

DECEMBER 15

144,000 Marked by God/ Revelation 7:1–17

After this I saw four angels standing at the four corners of the earth, holding back the four winds of the earth to prevent any wind from blowing on the land or on the sea or on any tree. 2Then I saw another angel coming up from the east, having the seal of the living God. He called out in a loud voice to the four angels who had been given power to harm the land and the sea: 3"Do not harm the land or the sea or the trees until we put a seal on the foreheads of the servants of our God." 4Then I heard the number of those who were sealed: 144,000 from all the tribes of Israel.

5From the tribe of Judah 12,000 were sealed,
  from the tribe of Reuben 12,000,
  from the tribe of Gad 12,000,
6from the tribe of Asher 12,000,
  from the tribe of Naphtali 12,000,
  from the tribe of Manasseh 12,000,

⁷from the tribe of Simeon 12,000,
from the tribe of Levi 12,000,
from the tribe of Issachar 12,000,
⁸from the tribe of Zebulun 12,000,
from the tribe of Joseph 12,000,
from the tribe of Benjamin 12,000.

⁹After this I looked and there before me was a great multitude that no one could count, from every nation, tribe, people and language, standing before the throne and in front of the Lamb. They were wearing white robes and were holding palm branches in their hands. ¹⁰And they cried out in a loud voice:

"Salvation belongs to our God,
who sits on the throne,
and to the Lamb."

¹¹All the angels were standing around the throne and around the elders and the four living creatures. They fell down on their faces before the throne and worshiped God, ¹²saying:

"Amen!
Praise and glory
and wisdom and thanks and honor
and power and strength
be to our God for ever and ever.
Amen!"

¹³Then one of the elders asked me, "These in white robes—who are they, and where did they come from?"
¹⁴I answered, "Sir, you know."
And he said, "These are they who have come out of the great tribulation; they have washed their robes and made them white in the blood of the Lamb. ¹⁵Therefore,

"they are before the throne of God
and serve him day and night in his temple;
and he who sits on the throne will spread his tent
over them.
¹⁶Never again will they hunger;
never again will they thirst.
The sun will not beat upon them,
nor any scorching heat.

17For the Lamb at the center of the throne will be
their shepherd;
he will lead them to springs of living water.
And God will wipe away every tear from their
eyes."

A THOUGHT: *People try many methods to remove the guilt of sin—good works, intellectual pursuits, and even casting blame. The crowd in heaven, however, praises God, saying, "Salvation belongs to our God, who sits on the throne, and to the Lamb." Salvation from sin's penalty can come only through Jesus Christ. Have you had the guilt of sin removed in the only way possible?*

Love One Another/ 1 John 2:7–11

Dear friends, I am not writing you a new command but an old one, which you have had since the beginning. This old command is the message you have heard. 8Yet I am writing you a new command; its truth is seen in him and you, because the darkness is passing and the true light is already shining.

9Anyone who claims to be in the light but hates his brother is still in the darkness. 10Whoever loves his brother lives in the light, and there is nothing in him to make him stumble. 11But whoever hates his brother is in the darkness and walks around in the darkness; he does not know where he is going, because the darkness has blinded him.

A THOUGHT: *The commandment to love is both old and new. It is old because it comes from the Old Testament, but it is new because Jesus interpreted it in a radically new way. In the Christian Church, love goes beyond respect to self-sacrifice and servanthood. In fact, it can be defined as "selfless giving." It reaches beyond friends to enemies and persecutors. Love should be the unifying force and the identifying mark of the Christian community. It is the key to walking in the light, because we cannot grow spiritually while we hate others. A growing relationship with God results in growing relationships with others.*

Proverbs for Today/ 30:1–4

The sayings of Agur son of Jakeh—an oracle: This man declared to Ithiel, to Ithiel and to Ucal: "I am the most ignorant of men; I do not have a man's understanding. I have not learned wisdom, nor have I knowledge of the Holy One. Who has gone up to heaven and come down? Who has gathered up the wind in the hollow of his hands? Who has wrapped up the waters in his cloak? Who has established all the ends of the earth? What is his name, and the name of his son? Tell me if you know!"

DECEMBER 16

The Seventh Seal and the Trumpets/
Revelation 8:1–13

When he opened the seventh seal, there was silence in heaven for about half an hour.

2And I saw the seven angels who stand before God, and to them were given seven trumpets.

3Another angel, who had a golden censer, came and stood at the altar. He was given much incense to offer, with the prayers of all the saints, on the golden altar before the throne. 4The smoke of the incense, together with the prayers of the saints, went up before God from the angel's hand. 5Then the angel took the censer, filled it with fire from the altar, and hurled it on the earth; and there came peals of thunder, rumblings, flashes of lightning and an earthquake.

6Then the seven angels who had the seven trumpets prepared to sound them.

7The first angel sounded his trumpet, and there came hail and fire mixed with blood, and it was hurled down upon the earth. A third of the earth was burned up, a third of the trees were burned up, and all the green grass was burned up.

8The second angel sounded his trumpet, and something like a huge mountain, all ablaze, was thrown into the sea. A third of the sea turned into blood, 9a third of the living creatures in the sea died, and a third of the ships were destroyed.

10The third angel sounded his trumpet, and a great star, blazing like a torch, fell from the sky on a third of the rivers and on the springs of water— 11the name of the star is Wormwood. A third of the waters turned bitter, and many people died from the waters that had become bitter.

12The fourth angel sounded his trumpet, and a third of

the sun was struck, a third of the moon, and a third of the stars, so that a third of them turned dark. A third of the day was without light, and also a third of the night.

13As I watched, I heard an eagle that was flying in midair call out in a loud voice: "Woe! Woe! Woe to the inhabitants of the earth, because of the trumpet blasts about to be sounded by the other three angels!"

A THOUGHT: *When the seventh seal is opened, the seven trumpet judgments are revealed. The trumpet judgments, like the seal judgments, are only partial. God's final and complete judgment has not yet come. In God's mercy, he is drawing out his judgment in order that there will be sufficient time for people to repent and turn to him for salvation. If justice seems to be long in coming, we must learn to be patient; it is God's mercy that brings delay. Judgment is coming— be sure of that. We should thank God for the time he gives us to turn from sin, and work to help others turn as well.*

Do Not Love This Evil World/ 1 John 2:12–17

I write to you, dear children,
> because your sins have been forgiven on account of his name.
13I write to you, fathers,
> because you have known him who is from the beginning.
I write to you, young men,
> because you have overcome the evil one.
I write to you, dear children,
> because you have known the Father.
14I write to you, fathers,
> because you have known him who is from the beginning.
I write to you, young men,
> because you are strong,
> and the word of God lives in you,
> and you have overcome the evil one.

15Do not love the world or anything in the world. If anyone loves the world, the love of the Father is not in him. 16For everything in the world—the cravings of sinful man, the lust of his eyes and the boasting of what he has and does—comes not from the Father but from the world. 17The world and its desires pass away, but the man who does the will of God lives forever.

A THOUGHT: *Some people think worldliness has to do with external behavior—the people we associate with, the places we go, the activities in which we participate. This is not entirely accurate, for worldliness begins in the heart. It is characterized by three attitudes: (1) lust—preoccupation with gratifying physical desires; (2) materialism—craving and accumulating things, and (3) pride—obsession with one's status or importance. When the serpent tempted Eve, he tempted her in these areas. Also, when the devil tempted Jesus in the wilderness, these were his three areas of attack. By contrast, God values self-control, a spirit of generosity, and humble service. It is possible to avoid "worldly pleasures" while still harboring worldly attitudes in one's heart. It is also possible, like Jesus, to love sinners and spend time with them while maintaining the values of God's kingdom. What values are most important to you? Do your actions reflect the world's values or God's values?*

Proverbs for Today/ 30:5–6

"Every word of God is flawless; he is a shield to those who take refuge in him. Do not add to his words, or he will rebuke you and prove you a liar."

DECEMBER 17

Trumpets Announce God's Judgment/ Revelation 9:1–21

The fifth angel sounded his trumpet, and I saw a star that had fallen from the sky to the earth. The star was given the key to the shaft of the Abyss. ²When he opened the Abyss, smoke rose from it like the smoke from a gigantic furnace. The sun and sky were darkened by the smoke from the Abyss. ³And out of the smoke locusts came down upon the earth and were given power like that of scorpions of the earth. ⁴They were told not to harm the grass of the earth or any plant or tree, but only those people who did not have the seal of God on their foreheads. ⁵They were not given power to kill them, but only to torture them for five months. And the agony they suffered was like that of the sting of a scorpion when it strikes a man. ⁶During those days men will seek death, but will not find it; they will long to die, but death will elude them.

⁷The locusts looked like horses prepared for battle. On

their heads they wore something like crowns of gold, and their faces resembled human faces. 8Their hair was like women's hair, and their teeth were like lions' teeth. 9They had breastplates like breastplates of iron, and the sound of their wings was like the thundering of many horses and chariots rushing into battle. 10They had tails and stings like scorpions, and in their tails they had power to torment people for five months. 11They had as king over them the angel of the Abyss, whose name in Hebrew is Abaddon, and in Greek, Apollyon.

12The first woe is past; two other woes are yet to come.

13The sixth angel sounded his trumpet, and I heard a voice coming from the horns of the golden altar that is before God. 14It said to the sixth angel who had the trumpet, "Release the four angels who are bound at the great river Euphrates." 15And the four angels who had been kept ready for this very hour and day and month and year were released to kill a third of mankind. 16The number of the mounted troops was two hundred million. I heard their number.

17The horses and riders I saw in my vision looked like this: Their breastplates were fiery red, dark blue, and yellow as sulfur. The heads of the horses resembled the heads of lions, and out of their mouths came fire, smoke and sulfur. 18A third of mankind was killed by the three plagues of fire, smoke and sulfur that came out of their mouths. 19The power of the horses was in their mouths and in their tails; for their tails were like snakes, having heads with which they inflict injury.

20The rest of mankind that were not killed by these plagues still did not repent of the work of their hands; they did not stop worshiping demons, and idols of gold, silver, bronze, stone and wood—idols that cannot see or hear or walk. 21Nor did they repent of their murders, their magic arts, their sexual immorality or their thefts.

A THOUGHT: *All the judgments God had sent to the earth were not enough to bring these people to repentance. People don't usually fall into immorality and evil suddenly—they slip into it a little at a time until, hardly realizing what has happened, they are irrevocably mired in their wicked ways. Those who allow sin to take root in their lives can find themselves in this predicament. Temptation entertained today becomes sin tomorrow, then a habit the next day, then separation from God. To think you could never become evil is the first step toward becoming hard hearted.*

The Coming of Antichrists/ 1 John 2:18–27

Dear children, this is the last hour; and as you have heard that the antichrist is coming, even now many antichrists have come. This is how we know it is the last hour. 19They went out from us, but they did not really belong to us. For if they had belonged to us, they would have remained with us; but their going showed that none of them belonged to us.

20But you have an anointing from the Holy One, and all of you know the truth. 21I do not write to you because you do not know the truth, but because you do know it and because no lie comes from the truth. 22Who is the liar? It is the man who denies that Jesus is the Christ. Such a man is the antichrist—he denies the Father and the Son. 23No one who denies the Son has the Father; whoever acknowledges the Son has the Father also.

24See that what you have heard from the beginning remains in you. If it does, you also will remain in the Son and in the Father. 25And this is what he promised us—even eternal life.

26I am writing these things to you about those who are trying to lead you astray. 27As for you, the anointing you received from him remains in you, and you do not need anyone to teach you. But as his anointing teaches you about all things and as that anointing is real, not counterfeit—just as it has taught you, remain in him.

A THOUGHT: *John is talking about the "last days," the time between Christ's first and second comings. The first-century readers of 1 John lived in the last days, and so do we. During this time, "antichrists" (false teachers who pretend to be Christians and lure weak members away from Christ) will appear. Finally, just before the world ends, one great Antichrist will arise. We do not need to fear these evil people, however. The Holy Spirit shows us their errors, so we are not deceived. However, we must teach the Word of God clearly and carefully to the peripheral, weak members among us so they won't fall prey to these teachers who "come to you in sheep's clothing, but inwardly they are ferocious wolves"(Matthew 7:15).*

Proverbs for Today/ 30:7–9

"Two things I ask of you, O LORD; do not refuse me before I die: Keep falsehood and lies far from me; give me neither poverty nor riches, but give me only my daily bread. Otherwise, I may have too much and disown you and say, 'Who is the LORD?' Or I may become poor and steal, and so dishonor the name of my God."

DECEMBER 18

A Little Scroll/ Revelation 10:1–11

Then I saw another mighty angel coming down from heaven. He was robed in a cloud, with a rainbow above his head; his face was like the sun, and his legs were like fiery pillars. 2He was holding a little scroll, which lay open in his hand. He planted his right foot on the sea and his left foot on the land, 3and he gave a loud shout like the roar of a lion. When he shouted, the voices of the seven thunders spoke. 4And when the seven thunders spoke, I was about to write; but I heard a voice from heaven say, "Seal up what the seven thunders have said and do not write it down."

5Then the angel I had seen standing on the sea and on the land raised his right hand to heaven. 6And he swore by him who lives for ever and ever, who created the heavens and all that is in them, the earth and all that is in it, and the sea and all that is in it, and said, "There will be no more delay! 7But in the days when the seventh angel is about to sound his trumpet, the mystery of God will be accomplished, just as he announced to his servants the prophets."

8Then the voice that I had heard from heaven spoke to me once more: "Go, take the scroll that lies open in the hand of the angel who is standing on the sea and on the land."

9So I went to the angel and asked him to give me the little scroll. He said to me, "Take it and eat it. It will turn your stomach sour, but in your mouth it will be as sweet as honey." 10I took the little scroll from the angel's hand and ate it. It tasted as sweet as honey in my mouth, but when I had eaten it, my stomach turned sour. 11Then I was told, "You must prophesy again about many peoples, nations, languages and kings."

A THOUGHT: *Throughout history people have wanted to know what would happen in the future, and God reveals some of it in this book. But John was stopped from revealing certain parts of his vision. An angel also told the prophet Daniel that some things he saw were not to be revealed yet to everyone, and Jesus told his disciples that the time of the end is known by no one but God. God has revealed all we need to know to live for him now. In our desire to be ready for the end, we must live holy lives before God, and avoid speculation about the details and timing of the last days.*

The Children of God/ 1 John 2:28—3:6

And now, dear children, continue in him, so that when he appears we may be confident and unashamed before him at his coming.

29If you know that he is righteous, you know that everyone who does what is right has been born of him.

3:1How great is the love the Father has lavished on us, that we should be called children of God! And that is what we are! The reason the world does not know us is that it did not know him. 2Dear friends, now we are children of God, and what we will be has not yet been made known. But we know that when he appears, we shall be like him, for we shall see him as he is. 3Everyone who has this hope in him purifies himself, just as he is pure.

4Everyone who sins breaks the law; in fact, sin is lawlessness. 5But you know that he appeared so that he might take away our sins. And in him is no sin. 6No one who lives in him keeps on sinning. No one who continues to sin has either seen him or known him.

A THOUGHT: *The visible proof of being a Christian is right behavior. Many people do good things but don't have faith in Jesus Christ. Others claim to have faith but rarely produce good works. A deficit in either faith or right behavior is cause for shame when Christ returns. Because true faith always results in good works, those who claim to have faith and who consistently live rightly are true believers. Good works cannot produce salvation, but they are necessary proof that true faith has actually occurred.*

Proverbs for Today/ 30:10

"Do not slander a servant to his master, or he will curse you, and you will pay for it."

Two Witnesses/ Revelation 11:1–19

I was given a reed like a measuring rod and was told, "Go and measure the temple of God and the altar, and count the worshipers there. 2But exclude the outer court; do not measure it, because it has been given to the Gentiles. They will trample on the holy city for 42 months. 3And I will give power to my two witnesses, and they will prophesy for 1,260 days, clothed in sackcloth." 4These are the two olive trees and the two lampstands that stand before the Lord of the earth. 5If anyone tries to harm them, fire comes from their mouths and devours their enemies. This is how anyone who wants to harm them must die. 6These men have power to shut up the sky so that it will not rain during the time they are prophesying; and they have power to turn the waters into blood and to strike the earth with every kind of plague as often as they want.

7Now when they have finished their testimony, the beast that comes up from the Abyss will attack them, and overpower and kill them. 8Their bodies will lie in the street of the great city, which is figuratively called Sodom and Egypt, where also their Lord was crucified. 9For three and a half days men from every people, tribe, language and nation will gaze on their bodies and refuse them burial. 10The inhabitants of the earth will gloat over them and will celebrate by sending each other gifts, because these two prophets had tormented those who live on the earth.

11But after the three and a half days a breath of life from God entered them, and they stood on their feet, and terror struck those who saw them. 12Then they heard a loud voice from heaven saying to them, "Come up here." And they went up to heaven in a cloud, while their enemies looked on.

13At that very hour there was a severe earthquake and a tenth of the city collapsed. Seven thousand people were killed in the earthquake, and the survivors were terrified and gave glory to the God of heaven.

14The second woe has passed; the third woe is coming soon.

15The seventh angel sounded his trumpet, and there were loud voices in heaven, which said:

"The kingdom of the world has become the
kingdom of our Lord and of his Christ,
and he will reign for ever and ever."

16And the twenty-four elders, who were seated on their thrones before God, fell on their faces and worshiped God, 17saying:

"We give thanks to you, Lord God Almighty,
the One who is and who was,
because you have taken your great power
and have begun to reign.
18The nations were angry;
and your wrath has come.
The time has come for judging the dead,
and for rewarding your servants the prophets
and your saints and those who reverence your
name,
both small and great—
and for destroying those who destroy the earth."

19Then God's temple in heaven was opened, and within his temple was seen the ark of his covenant. And there came flashes of lightning, rumblings, peals of thunder, an earthquake and a great hailstorm.

A THOUGHT: *The whole world rejoices at the deaths of these two prophets, who have caused trouble by saying what the people didn't want to hear—words about their sin, their need for repentance, and the coming punishment. Sinful people hate those who call attention to their sin and who urge them to repent. They hated Christ, and they hate his followers. When you obey Christ and take a stand against sin, be prepared to draw the world's hatred. But remember that the great reward awaiting you in heaven far outweighs any suffering you face now.*

God's Children Do Not Continue in Sin/
1 John 3:7–11

Dear children, do not let anyone lead you astray. He who does what is right is righteous, just as he is righteous. 8He who does what is sinful is of the devil, because the devil has been sinning from the beginning. The reason the Son of God appeared was to destroy the devil's work. 9No one who is born of God will continue to sin, because God's seed remains in him; he cannot go on sinning, because he has been born of God. ¹⁰This is how we know who the children of God are and who the children of the devil are: Anyone who does not do what is right is not a child of God; nor is anyone who does not love his brother.

¹¹This is the message you heard from the beginning: We should love one another.

A THOUGHT: *There is a difference between committing a sin and remaining in sin. We all have areas where temptation is strong and habits are hard to conquer. We all struggle with particular sins; however, these verses are not directed at us, even if for a time we seem to "keep on sinning." John is not talking about people whose victories are still incomplete; he is talking about people who make a practice of sinning and look for ways to justify it.*

Three steps are necessary to find victory over prevailing sin: (1) one must seek the power of the Holy Spirit and the Word of God; (2) one must flee lustful desires; and (3) one must seek support from the body of Christ by being accountable to others and receiving their prayer support.

Proverbs for Today/ 30:11–14

"There are those who curse their fathers and do not bless their mothers; those who are pure in their own eyes and yet are not cleansed of their filth; those whose eyes are ever so haughty, whose glances are so disdainful; those whose teeth are swords and whose jaws are set with knives to devour the poor from the earth, the needy from among mankind."

DECEMBER 20

The Woman and the Dragon/ Revelation 12:1–13:1a

A great and wondrous sign appeared in heaven: a woman clothed with the sun, with the moon under her feet and a crown of twelve stars on her head. ²She was pregnant and cried out in pain as she was about to give birth. ³Then another sign appeared in heaven: an enormous red dragon with seven heads and ten horns and seven crowns on his heads. ⁴His tail swept a third of the stars out of the sky and flung them to the earth. The dragon stood in front of the woman who was about to give birth, so that he might devour her child the moment it was born. 5She gave birth to a son, a male child, who will rule all the nations with an iron scepter. And her child was snatched up to God and to his throne. 6The woman fled into the desert to a place prepared for her by God, where she might be taken care of for 1,260 days.

7And there was war in heaven. Michael and his angels fought against the dragon, and the dragon and his angels fought back. 8But he was not strong enough, and they lost their place in heaven. 9The great dragon was hurled down—that ancient serpent called the devil, or Satan, who leads the whole world astray. He was hurled to the earth, and his angels with him.

10Then I heard a loud voice in heaven say:

"Now have come the salvation and the power and
        the kingdom of our God,
    and the authority of his Christ.
For the accuser of our brothers,
    who accuses them before our God day and night,
    has been hurled down.
11They overcame him
    by the blood of the Lamb
    and by the word of their testimony;
they did not love their lives so much
    as to shrink from death.
12Therefore rejoice, you heavens
    and you who dwell in them!
But woe to the earth and the sea,
    because the devil has gone down to you!
He is filled with fury,
    because he knows that his time is short."

13When the dragon saw that he had been hurled to the earth, he pursued the woman who had given birth to the male child. 14The woman was given the two wings of a great eagle, so that she might fly to the place prepared for her in the desert, where she would be taken care of for a time, times and half a time, out of the serpent's reach. 15Then from his mouth the serpent spewed water like a river, to overtake the woman and sweep her away with the torrent. 16But the earth helped the woman by opening its mouth and swallowing the river that the dragon had spewed out of his mouth. 17Then the dragon was enraged at the woman and went off to make war against the rest of her offspring—those who obey God's commandments and hold to the testimony of Jesus. 13:1And the dragon stood on the shore of the sea.

A THOUGHT: *The critical blow to Satan came when the Lamb, Jesus Christ, shed his blood for our sins. John says the war is still being waged, but the outcome is already determined. Satan and his followers have been defeated and will be destroyed. Nevertheless, Satan is battling daily to bring more into his ranks and to keep his own from defecting to God's side. Those who belong to Christ have gone into battle on God's side, and he has guaranteed them victory. God will not lose the war, but we must make certain not to lose the battle for our own souls. Don't waver in your commitment to Christ. A great spiritual battle is being fought, and there is no time for indecision.*

Effective Love/ 1 John 3:12–24

Do not be like Cain, who belonged to the evil one and murdered his brother. And why did he murder him? Because his own actions were evil and his brother's were righteous. 13Do not be surprised, my brothers, if the world hates you. 14We know that we have passed from death to life, because we love our brothers. Anyone who does not love remains in death. 15Anyone who hates his brother is a murderer, and you know that no murderer has eternal life in him.

16This is how we know what love is: Jesus Christ laid down his life for us. And we ought to lay down our lives for our brothers. 17If anyone has material possessions and sees his brother in need but has no pity on him, how can the love of God be in him? 18Dear children, let us not love with words or tongue but with actions and in truth. 19This then is how we know that we belong to the truth, and how we set our hearts at rest in his presence 20whenever our hearts condemn us. For God is greater than our hearts, and he knows everything.

21Dear friends, if our hearts do not condemn us, we have confidence before God 22and receive from him anything we ask, because we obey his commands and do what pleases him. 23And this is his command: to believe in the name of his Son, Jesus Christ, and to love one another as he commanded us. 24Those who obey his commands live in him, and he in them. And this is how we know that he lives in us: We know it by the Spirit he gave us.

A THOUGHT: *Real love is an action, not a feeling. It produces selfless, sacrificial giving. The greatest act of love anyone can do is to give himself or herself for others. How can we lay down our lives? Sometimes it is easier to say we'll die for others than to truly live for them, which involves putting others' desires first. These verses give an example of how to lay down our lives for others—provide money to help meet others' needs. How clearly do your actions say you really love others? Are you as generous as you should be with your money, possessions, and time?*

Proverbs for Today/ 30:15–16

"The leech has two daughters. 'Give! Give!' they cry.
"There are three things that are never satisfied, four that never say, 'Enough!': the grave, the barren womb, land, which is never satisfied with water, and fire, which never says, 'Enough!' "

DECEMBER 21

A Beast from the Sea/ Revelation 13:1b–18

And I saw a beast coming out of the sea. He had ten horns and seven heads, with ten crowns on his horns, and on each head a blasphemous name. 2The beast I saw resembled a leopard, but had feet like those of a bear and a mouth like that of a lion. The dragon gave the beast his power and his throne and great authority. 3One of the heads of the beast seemed to have had a fatal wound, but the fatal wound had been healed. The whole world was astonished and followed the beast. 4Men worshiped the dragon because he had given authority to the beast, and they also worshiped the beast and asked, "Who is like the beast? Who can make war against him?"

5The beast was given a mouth to utter proud words and

blasphemies and to exercise his authority for forty-two months. 6He opened his mouth to blaspheme God, and to slander his name and his dwelling place and those who live in heaven. 7He was given power to make war against the saints and to conquer them. And he was given authority over every tribe, people, language and nation. 8All inhabitants of the earth will worship the beast—all whose names have not been written in the book of life belonging to the Lamb that was slain from the creation of the world.

9He who has an ear, let him hear.

10If anyone is to go into captivity,
   into captivity he will go.
If anyone is to be killed with the sword,
   with the sword he will be killed.

This calls for patient endurance and faithfulness on the part of the saints.

11Then I saw another beast, coming out of the earth. He had two horns like a lamb, but he spoke like a dragon. 12He exercised all the authority of the first beast on his behalf, and made the earth and its inhabitants worship the first beast, whose fatal wound had been healed. 13And he performed great and miraculous signs, even causing fire to come down from heaven to earth in full view of men. 14Because of the signs he was given power to do on behalf of the first beast, he deceived the inhabitants of the earth. He ordered them to set up an image in honor of the beast who was wounded by the sword and yet lived. 15He was given power to give breath to the image of the first beast, so that it could speak and cause all who refused to worship the image to be killed. 16He also forced everyone, small and great, rich and poor, free and slave, to receive a mark on his right hand or on his forehead, 17so that no one could buy or sell unless he had the mark, which is the name of the beast or the number of his name.

18This calls for wisdom. If anyone has insight, let him calculate the number of the beast, for it is man's number. His number is 666.

A THOUGHT: *Throughout the Bible we see miracles performed as proofs of God's power, love, and authority. But here we see counterfeit miracles performed to deceive. This is a reminder of Pharaoh's magicians, who duplicated Moses' signs in Egypt. True signs and miracles point us to Jesus Christ, but miracles alone can be deceptive. That is why we must ask of each miracle we see, "Is this consistent with what God says in the Bible?" The Creature here gains influence through the signs and then orders the people to worship a statue—a direct flouting of the second commandment. Allowing the Scriptures to guide our faith and practice will keep us from being deceived by false signs, however convincing they may appear. Any teaching that contradicts God's Word is false.*

The Incarnation—A Test for Truth/ 1 John 4:1–6

Dear friends, do not believe every spirit, but test the spirits to see whether they are from God, because many false prophets have gone out into the world. ²This is how you can recognize the Spirit of God: Every spirit that acknowledges that Jesus Christ has come in the flesh is from God, ³but every spirit that does not acknowledge Jesus is not from God. This is the spirit of the antichrist, which you have heard is coming and even now is already in the world.

⁴You, dear children, are from God and have overcome them, because the one who is in you is greater than the one who is in the world. ⁵They are from the world and therefore speak from the viewpoint of the world, and the world listens to them. ⁶We are from God, and whoever knows God listens to us; but whoever is not from God does not listen to us. This is how we recognize the Spirit of truth and the spirit of falsehood.

A THOUGHT: *Some people believe everything they read or hear. Unfortunately, many things printed and taught are not true. Christians should not be gullible. Verify every message you hear, even if the person who brings it says it's from God. If the message is truly from God, it will be consistent with Christ's teachings.*

Proverbs for Today/ 30:17

"The eye that mocks a father, that scorns obedience to a mother, will be pecked out by the ravens of the valley, will be eaten by the vultures."

The Lamb Stands on Mount Zion/ Revelation 14:1–7

Then I looked, and there before me was the Lamb, standing on Mount Zion, and with him 144,000 who had his name and his Father's name written on their foreheads. 2And I heard a sound from heaven like the roar of rushing waters and like a loud peal of thunder. The sound I heard was like that of harpists playing their harps. 3And they sang a new song before the throne and before the four living creatures and the elders. No one could learn the song except the 144,000 who had been redeemed from the earth. 4These are those who did not defile themselves with women, for they kept themselves pure. They follow the Lamb wherever he goes. They were purchased from among men and offered as firstfruits to God and the Lamb. 5No lie was found in their mouths; they are blameless.

6Then I saw another angel flying in midair, and he had the eternal gospel to proclaim to those who live on the earth—to every nation, tribe, language and people. 7He said in a loud voice, "Fear God and give him glory, because the hour of his judgment has come. Worship him who made the heavens, the earth, the sea and the springs of water."

A THOUGHT: *Some believe these angels are offering a final, worldwide appeal for all people to recognize the one true God. No one will have the excuse of never hearing God's truth. Others, however, see this as an announcement of judgment rather than an appeal. The people of the world have had their chance to proclaim their allegiance to God, and now God's great judgment is about to begin. If you are reading this, you have already heard God's truth. You know that God's final judgment will not be put off forever. Have you joyfully received the everlasting Good News? Have you confessed your sins and trusted in Christ to save you? If so, you have nothing to fear from God's judgment. The Judge of all the earth is your Savior!*

Let Us Love One Another/ 1 John 4:7–15

Dear friends, let us love one another, for love comes from God. Everyone who loves has been born of God and knows God. 8Whoever does not love does not know God, because God is love. 9This is how God showed his love among us: He sent his one and only Son into the world that we might live through him. 10This is love: not that we loved God, but that he loved us and sent his Son as an atoning sacrifice for our sins. 11Dear friends, since God so loved us, we also ought to love one another. 12No one has ever seen God; but if we love one another, God lives in us and his love is made complete in us.

13We know that we live in him and he in us, because he has given us of his Spirit. 14And we have seen and testify that the Father has sent his Son to be the Savior of the world. 15If anyone acknowledges that Jesus is the Son of God, God lives in him and he in God.

A THOUGHT: *Everyone believes love is important, but we usually think of it as a feeling. In reality, love is a choice and an action. God is the source of our love: he loved us enough to sacrifice his Son for us. Jesus is our example of what it means to love; everything he did in life and death was supremely loving. The Holy Spirit gives us the power to love; he lives in our hearts and makes us more and more like Jesus. God's love always involves a choice and an action, and our love should be like his. How well is your love for God displayed in the choices you make and the actions you take?*

Proverbs for Today/ 30:18–20

"There are three things that are too amazing for me, four that I do not understand: the way of an eagle in the sky, the way of a snake on a rock, the way of a ship on the high seas, and the way of a man with a maiden. □ "This is the way of an adulteress: She eats and wipes her mouth and says, 'I've done nothing wrong.' "

DECEMBER 23

Angels Announce the Judgment to Come/ Revelation 14:8–20

A second angel followed and said, "Fallen! Fallen is Babylon the Great, which made all the nations drink the maddening wine of her adulteries."

9A third angel followed them and said in a loud voice: "If anyone worships the beast and his image and receives his mark on the forehead or on the hand, 10he, too, will drink of the wine of God's fury, which has been poured full strength into the cup of his wrath. He will be tormented with burning sulfur in the presence of the holy angels and of the Lamb. 11And the smoke of their torment rises for ever and ever. There is no rest day or night for those who worship the beast and his image, or for anyone who receives the mark of his name." 12This calls for patient endurance on the part of the saints who obey God's commandments and remain faithful to Jesus.

13Then I heard a voice from heaven say, "Write: Blessed are the dead who die in the Lord from now on."

"Yes," says the Spirit, "they will rest from their labor, for their deeds will follow them."

14I looked, and there before me was a white cloud, and seated on the cloud was one "like a son of man" with a crown of gold on his head and a sharp sickle in his hand. 15Then another angel came out of the temple and called in a loud voice to him who was sitting on the cloud, "Take your sickle and reap, for the time to reap has come, for the harvest of the earth is ripe." 16So he who was seated on the cloud swung his sickle over the earth, and the earth was harvested.

17Another angel came out of the temple in heaven, and he too had a sharp sickle. 18Still another angel, who had charge of the fire, came from the altar and called in a loud voice to him who had the sharp sickle, "Take your sharp sickle and gather the clusters of grapes from the earth's vine, because its grapes are ripe." 19The angel swung his sickle on the earth, gathered its grapes and threw them into the great winepress of God's wrath. 20They were trampled in the winepress outside the city, and blood flowed out of the press, rising as high as the horses' bridles for a distance of 1,600 stadia.

A THOUGHT: *This news about God's ultimate triumph should encourage God's people to remain firm through every trial and persecution. They can do this, God promises, by trusting in Jesus and obeying the commands in his Word. The secret to enduring, therefore, is trust and obedience. Trust God to give you patience to endure even the small trials you face daily; obey him, even when obedience is unattractive or dangerous.*

Living in God's Love/ 1 John 4:16–21

And so we know and rely on the love God has for us.

God is love. Whoever lives in love lives in God, and God in him. 17In this way, love is made complete among us so that we will have confidence on the day of judgment, because in this world we are like him. [18]There is no fear in love. But perfect love drives out fear, because fear has to do with punishment. The one who fears is not made perfect in love.

[19]We love because he first loved us. [20]If anyone says, "I love God," yet hates his brother, he is a liar. For anyone who does not love his brother, whom he has seen, cannot love God, whom he has not seen. [21]And he has given us this command: Whoever loves God must also love his brother.

A THOUGHT: *It is easy to say we love God when it doesn't cost us anything more than weekly attendance at religious services. But the real test of our love for God is how we treat the people right in front of us—our family members and fellow believers. We cannot truly love God while neglecting to love those who are created in his image.*

Proverbs for Today/ 30:21–23

"Under three things the earth trembles, under four it cannot bear up: a servant who becomes king, a fool who is full of food, an unloved woman who is married, and a maidservant who displaces her mistress."

DECEMBER 24

Seven Angels and Seven Plagues/ Revelation 15:1–8

I saw in heaven another great and marvelous sign: seven angels with the seven last plagues—last, because with them God's wrath is completed. [2]And I saw what looked like a sea of glass mixed with fire and, standing beside the sea, those who had been victorious over the beast and his image and over the number of his name. They held harps given them by God [3]and sang the song of Moses the servant of God and the song of the Lamb:

"Great and marvelous are your deeds,
  Lord God Almighty.
Just and true are your ways,

King of the ages.

⁴Who will not fear you, O Lord,
and bring glory to your name?
For you alone are holy.
All nations will come
and worship before you,
for your righteous acts have been revealed."

⁵After this I looked and in heaven the temple, that is, the tabernacle of the Testimony, was opened. ⁶Out of the temple came the seven angels with the seven plagues. They were dressed in clean, shining linen and wore golden sashes around their chests. ⁷Then one of the four living creatures gave to the seven angels seven golden bowls filled with the wrath of God, who lives for ever and ever. ⁸And the temple was filled with smoke from the glory of God and from his power, and no one could enter the temple until the seven plagues of the seven angels were completed.

A THOUGHT: *The song of Moses celebrated Israel's deliverance from Egypt. The song of the Lamb celebrates the ultimate deliverance of God's people from the power of Satan.*

The Most Holy Place was the innermost room in the Temple, where the ark of the covenant resided—a symbol of God's presence among his people. This room was closed off from view by a great curtain. Only the High Priest could enter there, and only once a year on the Day of Atonement. The Most Holy Place was thrown open once before—at Christ's crucifixion, when the curtain was ripped from top to bottom. The wide open entrance into the Most Holy Place symbolizes the open access to God's very presence which Christians have on the basis of Jesus' shed blood. Those of us who are united with the sinless Christ, our High Priest, can approach God boldly, but unrepentant sinners will be unable to come into his presence.

Eternal Life in God's Son/ 1 John 5:1–15

Everyone who believes that Jesus is the Christ is born of God, and everyone who loves the father loves his child as well. ²This is how we know that we love the children of God: by loving God and carrying out his commands. ³This is love for God: to obey his commands. And his commands are not burdensome, ⁴for everyone born of God overcomes the world. This is the victory that has overcome the world, even our faith. ⁵Who is it that overcomes the world? Only he who believes that Jesus is the Son of God.

⁶This is the one who came by water and blood—Jesus

Christ. He did not come by water only, but by water and blood. And it is the Spirit who testifies, because the Spirit is the truth. 7For there are three that testify: 8the Spirit, the water and the blood; and the three are in agreement. 9We accept man's testimony, but God's testimony is greater because it is the testimony of God, which he has given about his Son. 10Anyone who believes in the Son of God has this testimony in his heart. Anyone who does not believe God has made him out to be a liar, because he has not believed the testimony God has given about his Son. 11And this is the testimony: God has given us eternal life, and this life is in his Son. 12He who has the Son has life; he who does not have the Son of God does not have life.

13I write these things to you who believe in the name of the Son of God so that you may know that you have eternal life. 14This is the confidence we have in approaching God: that if we ask anything according to his will, he hears us. 15And if we know that he hears us—whatever we ask—we know that we have what we asked of him.

A THOUGHT: *Some people hope they will be given eternal life. John says we can know we have it. Our certainty is based on God's promise that he has given us eternal life through his Son. This is true whether you feel close to God or distant from him. Eternal life is not based on feelings, but on facts. You can know you have eternal life if you believe God's truth. If you lack assurance as to whether you are a Christian, ask yourself if you have honestly committed your life to him as your Savior and Lord. If so, you know by faith that you are indeed a child of God.*

Proverbs for Today/ 30:24–28

"Four things on earth are small, yet they are extremely wise: Ants are creatures of little strength, yet they store up their food in the summer; coneys are creatures of little power, yet they make their home in the crags; locusts have no king, yet they advance together in ranks; a lizard can be caught with the hand, yet it is found in kings' palaces."

Angels Pour Out Plagues upon the Earth/ Revelation 16:1–21

Then I heard a loud voice from the temple saying to the seven angels, "Go, pour out the seven bowls of God's wrath on the earth."

2The first angel went and poured out his bowl on the land, and ugly and painful sores broke out on the people who had the mark of the beast and worshiped his image.

3The second angel poured out his bowl on the sea, and it turned into blood like that of a dead man, and every living thing in the sea died.

4The third angel poured out his bowl on the rivers and springs of water, and they became blood. 5Then I heard the angel in charge of the waters say:

"You are just in these judgments,
    you who are and who were, the Holy One,
    because you have so judged;
6for they have shed the blood of your saints and
        prophets,
    and you have given them blood to drink as they
        deserve."

7And I heard the altar respond:

"Yes, Lord God Almighty,
    true and just are your judgments."

8The fourth angel poured out his bowl on the sun, and the sun was given power to scorch people with fire. 9They were seared by the intense heat and they cursed the name of God, who had control over these plagues, but they refused to repent and glorify him.

10The fifth angel poured out his bowl on the throne of the beast, and his kingdom was plunged into darkness. Men gnawed their tongues in agony 11and cursed the God of heaven because of their pains and their sores, but they refused to repent of what they had done.

12The sixth angel poured out his bowl on the great river Euphrates, and its water was dried up to prepare the way for the kings from the East. 13Then I saw three evil spirits that looked like frogs; they came out of the mouth of the dragon, out of the mouth of the beast and out of the mouth of the false prophet. 14They are spirits of demons performing miraculous signs, and they go out to the kings of the whole world, to gather them for the battle on the great day of God Almighty.

15"Behold, I come like a thief! Blessed is he who stays awake and keeps his clothes with him, so that he may not go naked and be shamefully exposed."

16Then they gathered the kings together to the place that in Hebrew is called Armageddon.

17The seventh angel poured out his bowl into the air, and out of the temple came a loud voice from the throne, saying, "It is done!" 18Then there came flashes of lightning, rumblings, peals of thunder and a severe earthquake. No earthquake like it has ever occurred since man has been on earth, so tremendous was the quake. 19The great city split into three parts, and the cities of the nations collapsed. God remembered Babylon the Great and gave her the cup filled with the wine of the fury of his wrath. 20Every island fled away and the mountains could not be found. 21From the sky huge hailstones of about a hundred pounds each fell upon men. And they cursed God on account of the plague of hail, because the plague was so terrible.

A THOUGHT: *Sinful men will unite to fight against God in a final display of rebellion. Many are already united against the people of Christ and everything they stand for—truth, peace, justice, and morality. Your personal battle with evil foreshadows the great battle pictured here, where God will meet evil and destroy it once and for all. Be strong and courageous as you battle against sin and evil; you are fighting on the winning side.*

God's Children Do Not Continue in Sin/
1 John 5:16–21

If anyone sees his brother commit a sin that does not lead to death, he should pray and God will give him life. I refer to those whose sin does not lead to death. There is a sin that leads to death. I am not saying that he should pray about that. 17All wrongdoing is sin, and there is sin that does not lead to death.

18We know that anyone born of God does not continue to sin; the one who was born of God keeps him safe, and the evil one cannot harm him. ¹⁹We know that we are children of God, and that the whole world is under the control of the evil one. ²⁰We know also that the Son of God has come and has given us understanding, so that we may know him who is true. And we are in him who is true—even in his Son Jesus Christ. He is the true God and eternal life.

²¹Dear children, keep yourselves from idols.

A THOUGHT: *Christians commit sins, of course, but they ask God to forgive them and then they continue serving him. God has freed them from their slavery to Satan, and he keeps them safe from Satan's continued attacks. The rest of the world does not have the Christian's freedom to obey God. Unless they come to Christ in faith, they have no choice but to obey Satan. There is no middle ground; people either belong to God and obey him, or they live under Satan's control.*

Proverbs for Today/ 30:29–31

"There are three things that are stately in their stride, four that move with stately bearing: a lion, mighty among beasts, who retreats before nothing; a strutting rooster, a he-goat, and a king with his army around him."

DECEMBER 26

The Woman, A Symbol of Babylon/ Revelation 17:1–18

One of the seven angels who had the seven bowls came and said to me, "Come, I will show you the punishment of the great prostitute, who sits on many waters. ²With her the kings of the earth committed adultery and the inhabitants of the earth were intoxicated with the wine of her adulteries."

³Then the angel carried me away in the Spirit into a desert. There I saw a woman sitting on a scarlet beast that was covered with blasphemous names and had seven heads and ten horns. ⁴The woman was dressed in purple and scarlet, and was glittering with gold, precious stones and pearls. She held a golden cup in her hand, filled with abominable things and the filth of her adulteries. ⁵This title was written on her forehead:

MYSTERY

BABYLON THE GREAT

THE MOTHER OF PROSTITUTES

AND OF THE ABOMINATIONS OF THE EARTH.

⁶I saw that the woman was drunk with the blood of the saints, the blood of those who bore testimony to Jesus.

When I saw her, I was greatly astonished. ⁷Then the angel said to me: "Why are you astonished? I will explain to you the mystery of the woman and of the beast she rides, which has the seven heads and ten horns. ⁸The beast, which you saw, once was, now is not, and will come up out of the Abyss and go to his destruction. The inhabitants of the earth whose names have not been written in the book of life from the creation of the world will be astonished when they see the beast, because he once was, now is not, and yet will come.

⁹"This calls for a mind with wisdom. The seven heads are seven hills on which the woman sits. ¹⁰They are also seven kings. Five have fallen, one is, the other has not yet come; but when he does come, he must remain for a little while. ¹¹The beast who once was, and now is not, is an eighth king. He belongs to the seven and is going to his destruction.

¹²"The ten horns you saw are ten kings who have not yet received a kingdom, but who for one hour will receive authority as kings along with the beast. ¹³They have one purpose and will give their power and authority to the beast. ¹⁴They will make war against the Lamb, but the Lamb will overcome them because he is Lord of lords and King of kings—and with him will be his called, chosen and faithful followers."

¹⁵Then the angel said to me, "The waters you saw, where the prostitute sits, are peoples, multitudes, nations and languages. ¹⁶The beast and the ten horns you saw will hate the prostitute. They will bring her to ruin and leave her naked; they will eat her flesh and burn her with fire. ¹⁷For God has put it into their hearts to accomplish his purpose by agreeing to give the beast their power to rule, until God's words are fulfilled. ¹⁸The woman you saw is the great city that rules over the kings of the earth."

A THOUGHT: *Throughout history people have been killed for their faith. Over the last century, millions have been killed by oppressive govern-*

*ments, and many of these were believers. The woman's drunkenness
shows her pleasure in her evil accomplishments and her false feeling
of triumph over the church. But every martyr who fell before her
sword only strengthened the church. No matter what happens, we
must trust that God is still in charge, and his plans will happen just
as he says. He even uses people opposed to him to execute his will.
Although he allows evil to permeate this present world, the new earth
will never know sin.*

Loving others Is Obeying God/ 2 John 1:1–6

The elder,

To the chosen lady and her children, whom I love in the
truth—and not I only, but also all who know the truth—
2because of the truth, which lives in us and will be with us
forever:

3Grace, mercy and peace from God the Father and from
Jesus Christ, the Father's Son, will be with us in truth and
love.

4It has given me great joy to find some of your children
walking in the truth, just as the Father commanded us.
5And now, dear lady, I am not writing you a new command
but one we have had from the beginning. I ask that we love
one another. 6And this is love: that we walk in obedience
to his commands. As you have heard from the beginning,
his command is that you walk in love.

A THOUGHT: *The love Christians should have for one another is a
recurrent New Testament theme. Love is not an option for Christians, it is a command. True obedience to God is measured by our
love for others. We can show love in many ways: by accepting people
regardless of their differences from us, by listening, helping, giving,
serving, and refusing to judge. But just knowing God's command
is not enough. We must put it into practice.*

Proverbs for Today/ 30:32

"If you have played the fool and exalted yourself, or if you
have planned evil, clap your hand over your mouth!"

DECEMBER 27

The Fall of Babylon/ Revelation 18:1–24

After this I saw another angel coming down from heaven. He had great authority, and the earth was illuminated by his splendor. ²With a mighty voice he shouted:

> "Fallen! Fallen is Babylon the Great!
>   She has become a home for demons
> and a haunt for every evil spirit,
>   a haunt for every unclean and detestable bird.
> ³For all the nations have drunk
>   the maddening wine of her adulteries.
> The kings of the earth committed adultery with
>   her,
>   and the merchants of the earth grew rich from
>   her excessive luxuries."

⁴Then I heard another voice from heaven say:

> "Come out of her, my people,
>   so that you will not share in her sins,
>   so that you will not receive any of her plagues;
> ⁵for her sins are piled up to heaven,
>   and God has remembered her crimes.
> ⁶Give back to her as she has given;
>   pay her back double for what she has done.
>   Mix her a double portion from her own cup.
> ⁷Give her as much torture and grief
>   as the glory and luxury she gave herself.
> In her heart she boasts,
>   'I sit as queen; I am not a widow,
>   and I will never mourn.'
> ⁸Therefore in one day her plagues will overtake her:
>   death, mourning and famine.
> She will be consumed by fire,
>   for mighty is the Lord God who judges her.

⁹"When the kings of the earth who committed adultery with her and shared her luxury see the smoke of her burning, they will weep and mourn over her. ¹⁰Terrified at her torment, they will stand far off and cry:

" 'Woe! Woe, O great city,
　O Babylon, city of power!
In one hour your doom has come!'

11"The merchants of the earth will weep and mourn over
her because no one buys their cargoes any more— 12cargoes of gold, silver, precious stones and pearls; fine linen,
purple, silk and scarlet cloth; every sort of citron wood, and
articles of every kind made of ivory, costly wood, bronze,
iron and marble; 13cargoes of cinnamon and spice, of incense, myrrh and frankincense, of wine and olive oil, of fine
flour and wheat; cattle and sheep; horses and carriages;
and bodies and souls of men.

14"They will say, 'The fruit you longed for is gone from
you. All your riches and splendor have vanished, never to
be recovered.' 15The merchants who sold these things and
gained their wealth from her will stand far off, terrified at
her torment. They will weep and mourn 16and cry out:

" 'Woe! Woe, O great city,
　dressed in fine linen, purple and scarlet,
　and glittering with gold, precious stones and
　　　pearls!
17In one hour such great wealth has been brought to
　　ruin!'

"Every sea captain, and all who travel by ship, the sailors, and all who earn their living from the sea, will stand
far off. 18When they see the smoke of her burning, they will
exclaim, 'Was there ever a city like this great city?' 19They
will throw dust on their heads, and with weeping and
mourning cry out:

" 'Woe! Woe, O great city,
　where all who had ships on the sea
　became rich through her wealth!
In one hour she has been brought to ruin!
20Rejoice over her, O heaven!
　Rejoice, saints and apostles and prophets!
God has judged her for the way she treated you.' "

21Then a mighty angel picked up a boulder the size of a
large millstone and threw it into the sea, and said:

"With such violence
the great city of Babylon will be thrown down,
never to be found again.
22The music of harpists and musicians, flute players
and trumpeters,
will never be heard in you again.
No workman of any trade
will ever be found in you again.
The sound of a millstone
will never be heard in you again.
23The light of a lamp
will never shine in you again.
The voice of bridegroom and bride
will never be heard in you again.
Your merchants were the world's great men.
By your magic spell all the nations were led
astray.
24In her was found the blood of prophets and of the
saints,
and of all who have been killed on the earth."

A THOUGHT: *Babylon lived in "glory and luxury." She boasted, "I sit as queen; . . . I will never mourn." The powerful, wealthy people of this world are susceptible to this same attitude. A person who is financially comfortable often feels invulnerable, secure, and in control, not in need of God or anyone else. This kind of attitude defies God, and his judgment against it is harsh. We are told to avoid her sins. If you are financially secure, don't become complacent and deluded by the myth of self-sufficiency. Christians are warned to stay free from the enchantment of money, status, and the "good life." We are to live according to the values Christ lived by: service, giving, self-sacrifice, obedience, and truth. Use your resources to help others and advance God's kingdom.*

Beware of False Teachers/ 2 John 1:7–13

Many deceivers, who do not acknowledge Jesus Christ as coming in the flesh, have gone out into the world. Any such person is the deceiver and the antichrist. 8Watch out that you do not lose what you have worked for, but that you may be rewarded fully. 9Anyone who runs ahead and does not continue in the teaching of Christ does not have God; whoever continues in the teaching has both the Father and the Son. 10If anyone comes to you and does not bring this teaching, do not take him into your house or welcome him. 11Anyone who welcomes him shares in his wicked work.

¹²I have much to write to you, but I do not want to use paper and ink. Instead, I hope to visit you and talk with you face to face, so that our joy may be complete.

¹³The children of your chosen sister send their greetings.

A THOUGHT: *In John's day, many false teachers taught that spirit was good and matter was evil; therefore, they reasoned that Jesus could not have been both God and man. In strong terms, John warned against this kind of teaching. There are still many false teachers who promote an understanding of Jesus that is not biblical. They are dangerous because they twist the truth and undermine the foundations of Christian faith. They may use the right words but change the meanings. The way your teachers live shows a lot about what they believe about Christ.*

Proverbs for Today/ 30:33

"For as churning the milk produces butter, and as twisting the nose produces blood, so stirring up anger produces strife."

DECEMBER 28

A Vast Crowd in Heaven Praises God/ Revelation 19:1–21

After this I heard what sounded like the roar of a great multitude in heaven shouting:

"Hallelujah!
Salvation and glory and power belong to our God,
² for true and just are his judgments.
He has condemned the great prostitute
who corrupted the earth by her adulteries.
He has avenged on her the blood of his servants."

³And again they shouted:

"Hallelujah!
The smoke from her goes up for ever and ever."

⁴The twenty-four elders and the four living creatures fell down and worshiped God, who was seated on the throne. And they cried:

"Amen, Hallelujah!"

⁵Then a voice came from the throne, saying:

"Praise our God,
all you his servants,
you who fear him,
both small and great!"

⁶Then I heard what sounded like a great multitude, like the roar of rushing waters and like loud peals of thunder, shouting:

"Hallelujah!
For our Lord God Almighty reigns.
⁷Let us rejoice and be glad
and give him glory!
For the wedding of the Lamb has come,
and his bride has made herself ready.
⁸Fine linen, bright and clean,
was given her to wear."

(Fine linen stands for the righteous acts of the saints.)

⁹Then the angel said to me, "Write: 'Blessed are those who are invited to the wedding supper of the Lamb!' " And he added, "These are the true words of God."

¹⁰At this I fell at his feet to worship him. But he said to me, "Do not do it! I am a fellow servant with you and with your brothers who hold to the testimony of Jesus. Worship God! For the testimony of Jesus is the spirit of prophecy."

¹¹I saw heaven standing open and there before me was a white horse, whose rider is called Faithful and True. With justice he judges and makes war. ¹²His eyes are like blazing fire, and on his head are many crowns. He has a name written on him that no one knows but he himself. ¹³He is dressed in a robe dipped in blood, and his name is the Word of God. ¹⁴The armies of heaven were following him, riding on white horses and dressed in fine linen, white and clean. ¹⁵Out of his mouth comes a sharp sword with which to strike down the nations. "He will rule them with an iron scepter." He treads the winepress of the fury of the wrath of God Almighty. ¹⁶On his robe and on his thigh he has this name written:

KING OF KINGS AND LORD OF LORDS.

17And I saw an angel standing in the sun, who cried in a loud voice to all the birds flying in midair, "Come, gather together for the great supper of God, 18so that you may eat the flesh of kings, generals, and mighty men, of horses and their riders, and the flesh of all people, free and slave, small and great."

19Then I saw the beast and the kings of the earth and their armies gathered together to make war against the rider on the horse and his army. 20But the beast was captured, and with him the false prophet who had performed the miraculous signs on his behalf. With these signs he had deluded those who had received the mark of the beast and worshiped his image. The two of them were thrown alive into the fiery lake of burning sulfur. 21The rest of them were killed with the sword that came out of the mouth of the rider on the horse, and all the birds gorged themselves on their flesh.

A THOUGHT: *Praise is the heartfelt response to God by those who love him. The more you get to know him and realize what he has done, the more you will respond with praise. Praise is at the heart of true worship. Let your praise of God flow out of your realization of who he is and how much he loves you.*

Imitate What Is Good/ 3 John 1:1–15

The elder,

To my dear friend Gaius, whom I love in the truth.

2Dear friend, I pray that you may enjoy good health and that all may go well with you, even as your soul is getting along well. 3It gave me great joy to have some brothers come and tell about your faithfulness to the truth and how you continue to walk in the truth. 4I have no greater joy than to hear that my children are walking in the truth.

5Dear friend, you are faithful in what you are doing for the brothers, even though they are strangers to you. 6They have told the church about your love. You will do well to send them on their way in a manner worthy of God. 7It was for the sake of the Name that they went out, receiving no help from the pagans. 8We ought therefore to show hospitality to such men so that we may work together for the truth.

⁹I wrote to the church, but Diotrephes, who loves to be first, will have nothing to do with us. ¹⁰So if I come, I will call attention to what he is doing, gossiping maliciously about us. Not satisfied with that, he refuses to welcome the brothers. He also stops those who want to do so and puts them out of the church.

¹¹Dear friend, do not imitate what is evil but what is good. Anyone who does what is good is from God. Anyone who does what is evil has not seen God. ¹²Demetrius is well spoken of by everyone—and even by the truth itself. We also speak well of him, and you know that our testimony is true.

¹³I have much to write you, but I do not want to do so with pen and ink. ¹⁴I hope to see you soon, and we will talk face to face.

Peace to you. The friends here send their greetings. Greet the friends there by name.

A THOUGHT: *In the early days of the church, traveling prophets, evangelists, and teachers were helped on their way by people like Gaius who housed and fed them. Hospitality is a lost art in many churches today. We would do well to invite more people for meals—fellow church members, young people, traveling missionaries, those in need, visitors. This is an active and much appreciated way to show your love. In fact it is probably more important today. Because of our individualistic, self-centered society, there are many lonely people who wonder if anyone cares whether they live or die. If you find such a lonely person, show him or her that you care!*

Proverbs for Today/ 31:1–7

The sayings of King Lemuel—an oracle his mother taught him: "O my son, O son of my womb, O son of my vows, do not spend your strength on women, your vigor on those who ruin kings. □ "It is not for kings, O Lemuel—not for kings to drink wine, not for rulers to crave beer, lest they drink and forget what the law decrees, and deprive all the oppressed of their rights. Give beer to those who are perishing, wine to those who are in anguish; let them drink and forget their poverty and remember their misery no more."

Satan Bound for a Thousand Years/
Revelation 20:1–15

And I saw an angel coming down out of heaven, having the key to the Abyss and holding in his hand a great chain. 2He seized the dragon, that ancient serpent, who is the devil, or Satan, and bound him for a thousand years. 3He threw him into the Abyss, and locked and sealed it over him, to keep him from deceiving the nations anymore until the thousand years were ended. After that, he must be set free for a short time.

4I saw thrones on which were seated those who had been given authority to judge. And I saw the souls of those who had been beheaded because of their testimony for Jesus and because of the word of God. They had not worshiped the beast or his image and had not received his mark on their foreheads or their hands. They came to life and reigned with Christ a thousand years. 5(The rest of the dead did not come to life until the thousand years were ended.) This is the first resurrection. 6Blessed and holy are those who have part in the first resurrection. The second death has no power over them, but they will be priests of God and of Christ and will reign with him for a thousand years.

7When the thousand years are over, Satan will be released from his prison 8and will go out to deceive the nations in the four corners of the earth—Gog and Magog—to gather them for battle. In number they are like the sand on the seashore. 9They marched across the breadth of the earth and surrounded the camp of God's people, the city he loves. But fire came down from heaven and devoured them. 10And the devil, who deceived them, was thrown into the lake of burning sulfur, where the beast and the false prophet had been thrown. They will be tormented day and night for ever and ever.

11Then I saw a great white throne and him who was seated on it. Earth and sky fled from his presence, and there was no place for them. 12And I saw the dead, great and small, standing before the throne, and books were opened. Another book was opened, which is the book of life. The dead were judged according to what they had done as recorded in the books. 13The sea gave up the dead that were in it, and death and Hades gave up the dead that were in them, and each person was judged according to what he had done. 14Then death and Hades were thrown into the lake of fire. The lake of fire is the second death. 15If anyone's name was not found written in the book of life, he was thrown into the lake of fire.

A THOUGHT: *Satan's power is not eternal—he will meet his end. He began his evil work in mankind at the beginning and continues it today, but he will be destroyed when he is thrown into the Lake of Fire. Satan will be released from the bottomless pit for a time, but he will never be released from the Lake of Fire. He will never be a threat to anyone again—his doom is sure.*

Contend for the Faith/ Jude 1:1–7

Jude, a servant of Jesus Christ and a brother of James,

To those who have been called, who are loved by God the Father and kept by Jesus Christ:

2Mercy, peace and love be yours in abundance.

3Dear friends, although I was very eager to write to you about the salvation we share, I felt I had to write and urge you to contend for the faith that was once for all entrusted to the saints. 4For certain men whose condemnation was written about long ago have secretly slipped in among you. They are godless men, who change the grace of our God into a license for immorality and deny Jesus Christ our only Sovereign and Lord.

5Though you already know all this, I want to remind you that the Lord delivered his people out of Egypt, but later destroyed those who did not believe. 6And the angels who did not keep their positions of authority but abandoned their own home—these he has kept in darkness, bound with everlasting chains for judgment on the great Day. 7In a similar way, Sodom and Gomorrah and the surrounding towns gave themselves up to sexual immorality and per-version. They serve as an example of those who suffer the punishment of eternal fire.

A THOUGHT: *Many first-century false teachers taught that Christians could do whatever they liked without fear of God's punishment. They took a light view of God's holiness and his justice. Even today, some*

Christians minimize the "sinfulness" of sin, believing that how they live has little to do with their faith. They may do well to ask, "Does the way I live show that I am sincere about my faith?" Those who truly have faith will show it by their deep respect for God and their sincere desire to live according to the principles in his Word.

Proverbs for Today/ 31:8–9

"Speak up for those who cannot speak for themselves, for the rights of all who are destitute. Speak up and judge fairly; defend the rights of the poor and needy."

DECEMBER 30

The New Jerusalem/ Revelation 21:1—22:6

Then I saw a new heaven and a new earth, for the first heaven and the first earth had passed away, and there was no longer any sea. 2I saw the Holy City, the new Jerusalem, coming down out of heaven from God, prepared as a bride beautifully dressed for her husband. 3And I heard a loud voice from the throne saying, "Now the dwelling of God is with men, and he will live with them. They will be his people, and God himself will be with them and be their God. 4He will wipe every tear from their eyes. There will be no more death or mourning or crying or pain, for the old order of things has passed away."

5He who was seated on the throne said, "I am making everything new!" Then he said, "Write this down, for these words are trustworthy and true."

6He said to me: "It is done. I am the Alpha and the Omega, the Beginning and the End. To him who is thirsty I will give to drink without cost from the spring of the water of life. 7He who overcomes will inherit all this, and I will be his God and he will be my son. 8But the cowardly, the unbelieving, the vile, the murderers, the sexually immoral, those who practice magic arts, the idolaters and all liars—their place will be in the fiery lake of burning sulfur. This is the second death."

9One of the seven angels who had the seven bowls full of the seven last plagues came and said to me, "Come, I will show you the bride, the wife of the Lamb." 10And he carried me away in the Spirit to a mountain great and high, and showed me the Holy City, Jerusalem, coming down out of heaven from God. 11It shone with the glory of God, and its brilliance was like that of a very precious jewel, like a jasper, clear as crystal. 12It had a great, high wall with twelve gates, and with twelve angels at the gates. On the gates were written the names of the twelve tribes of Israel. 13There were three gates on the east, three on the north, three on the south and three on the west. 14The wall of the city had twelve foundations, and on them were the names of the twelve apostles of the Lamb.

15The angel who talked with me had a measuring rod of gold to measure the city, its gates and its walls. 16The city was laid out like a square, as long as it was wide. He measured the city with the rod and found it to be 12,000 stadia in length, and as wide and high as it is long. 17He measured its wall and it was 144 cubits thick, by man's measurement, which the angel was using. 18The wall was made of jasper, and the city of pure gold, as pure as glass. 19The foundations of the city walls were decorated with every kind of precious stone. The first foundation was jasper, the second sapphire, the third chalcedony, the fourth emerald, 20the fifth sardonyx, the sixth carnelian, the seventh chrysolite, the eighth beryl, the ninth topaz, the tenth chrysoprase, the eleventh jacinth, and the twelfth amethyst. 21The twelve gates were twelve pearls, each gate made of a single pearl. The great street of the city was of pure gold, like transparent glass.

22I did not see a temple in the city, because the Lord God Almighty and the Lamb are its temple. 23The city does not need the sun or the moon to shine on it, for the glory of God gives it light, and the Lamb is its lamp. 24The nations will walk by its light, and the kings of the earth will bring their splendor into it. 25On no day will its gates ever be shut, for there will be no night there. 26The glory and honor of the nations will be brought into it. 27Nothing impure will ever enter it, nor will anyone who does what is shameful or deceitful, but only those whose names are written in the Lamb's book of life.

22:1Then the angel showed me the river of the water of life, as clear as crystal, flowing from the throne of God and of the Lamb 2down the middle of the great street of the city. On each side of the river stood the tree of life, bearing twelve crops of fruit, yielding its fruit every month. And the leaves of the tree are for the healing of the nations. 3No longer will there be any curse. The throne of God and of the Lamb will be in the city, and his servants will serve him. 4They will see his face, and his name will be on their foreheads. 5There will be no more night. They will not need the light of a lamp or the light of the sun, for the Lord God will give them light. And they will reign for ever and ever.

6The angel said to me, "These words are trustworthy and true. The Lord, the God of the spirits of the prophets, sent his angel to show his servants the things that must soon take place."

A THOUGHT: *Have you ever wondered what eternity will be like? The "Holy City, the new Jerusalem" is described as the place where God "will wipe every tear from their eyes." Forevermore, there will be no death, pain, sorrow, or crying. What a wonderful truth! No matter what you are going through, it's not the last word—God has written the final chapter, and it is about true fulfillment and eternal joy for those who love him. We do not know as much as we would like, but it is enough to know that eternity with God will be more wonderful than we can imagine.*

The Punishment of False Teachers/ Jude 1:8–16

In the very same way, these dreamers pollute their own bodies, reject authority and slander celestial beings. 9But even the archangel Michael, when he was disputing with the devil about the body of Moses, did not dare to bring a slanderous accusation against him, but said, "The Lord rebuke you!" 10Yet these men speak abusively against whatever they do not understand; and what things they do understand by instinct, like unreasoning animals—these are the very things that destroy them.

11Woe to them! They have taken the way of Cain; they have rushed for profit into Balaam's error; they have been destroyed in Korah's rebellion.

12These men are blemishes at your love feasts, eating with you without the slightest qualm—shepherds who feed only themselves. They are clouds without rain, blown along by the wind; autumn trees, without fruit and uprooted—twice dead. 13They are wild waves of the sea, foaming up their shame; wandering stars, for whom blackest darkness has been reserved forever.

14Enoch, the seventh from Adam, prophesied about these men: "See, the Lord is coming with thousands upon thousands of his holy ones 15to judge everyone, and to convict all the ungodly of all the ungodly acts they have done in the ungodly way, and of all the harsh words ungodly sinners have spoken against him." 16These men are grumblers and faultfinders; they follow their own evil desires; they boast about themselves and flatter others for their own advantage.

A THOUGHT: *False teachers claimed that they possessed secret knowledge which gave them authority. Their "knowledge" of God was esoteric—mystical and beyond human understanding. In reality, the nature of God is beyond our understanding. But God, in his grace, has chosen to reveal himself to us—in his Word, and supremely in Jesus Christ. Therefore, we must seek to know all we can about what he has revealed, even though we cannot fully comprehend God with our finite human minds. Beware of those who claim to have all the answers and who belittle what they do not understand.*

Proverbs for Today/ 31:10–24

A wife of noble character who can find? She is worth far more than rubies. Her husband has full confidence in her and lacks nothing of value. She brings him good, not harm, all the days of her life. She selects wool and flax and works with eager hands. She is like the merchant ships, bringing her food from afar. She gets up while it is still dark; she provides food for her family and portions for her servant girls. She considers a field and buys it; out of her earnings she plants a vineyard. She sets about her work vigorously; her arms are strong for her tasks. She sees that her trading is profitable, and her lamp does not go out at night. In her hand she holds the distaff and grasps the spindle with her fingers. She opens her arms to the poor and extends her hands to the needy. When it snows, she has no fear for her household; for all of them are clothed in scarlet. She makes coverings for her bed; she is clothed in fine linen and purple. Her husband is respected at the city gate, where he takes his seat among the elders of the land. She makes linen garments and sells them, and supplies the merchants with sashes.

The Promise of Jesus' Return/ Revelation 22:7–21

"Behold, I am coming soon! Blessed is he who keeps the words of the prophecy in this book."

⁸I, John, am the one who heard and saw these things. And when I had heard and seen them, I fell down to worship at the feet of the angel who had been showing them to me. ⁹But he said to me, "Do not do it! I am a fellow servant with you and with your brothers the prophets and of all who keep the words of this book. Worship God!"

¹⁰Then he told me, "Do not seal up the words of the prophecy of this book, because the time is near. ¹¹Let him who does wrong continue to do wrong; let him who is vile continue to be vile; let him who does right continue to do right; and let him who is holy continue to be holy."

¹²"Behold, I am coming soon! My reward is with me, and I will give to everyone according to what he has done. ¹³I am the Alpha and the Omega, the First and the Last, the Beginning and the End.

¹⁴"Blessed are those who wash their robes, that they may have the right to the tree of life and may go through the gates into the city. ¹⁵Outside are the dogs, those who practice magic arts, the sexually immoral, the murderers, the idolaters and everyone who loves and practices false-hood.

¹⁶"I, Jesus, have sent my angel to give you this testimony for the churches. I am the Root and the Offspring of David, and the bright Morning Star."

¹⁷The Spirit and the bride say, "Come!" And let him who hears say, "Come!" Whoever is thirsty, let him come; and whoever wishes, let him take the free gift of the water of life.

¹⁸I warn everyone who hears the words of the prophecy of this book: If anyone adds anything to them, God will add to him the plagues described in this book. ¹⁹And if anyone takes words away from this book of prophecy, God will

take away from him his share in the tree of life and in the holy city, which are described in this book.

20He who testifies to these things says, "Yes, I am coming soon."

Amen. Come, Lord Jesus.

21The grace of the Lord Jesus be with God's people. Amen.

A THOUGHT: *The first of the Ten Commandments is "You shall have no other gods before me" (Exodus 20:3). Jesus said that the greatest command of Moses' laws was "Love the Lord your God will all your heart and with all your soul and with all your mind" (Matthew 22:37). Here, at the end of the Bible, this truth is reiterated. The angel instructs John not to bow down before him, but to "Worship God!" God alone is worthy of our worship and adoration. He is above all creation, even the angels. Are there people, ideas, goals, or possessions that occupy the central place in your life, crowding God out? Worship only God by allowing nothing to distract you from your devotion to him.*

Exhortations to Holy Living/ Jude 1:17–25

But, dear friends, remember what the apostles of our Lord Jesus Christ foretold. 18They said to you, "In the last times there will be scoffers who will follow their own ungodly desires." 19These are the men who divide you, who follow mere natural instincts and do not have the Spirit.

20But you, dear friends, build yourselves up in your most holy faith and pray in the Holy Spirit. 21Keep yourselves in God's love as you wait for the mercy of our Lord Jesus Christ to bring you to eternal life.

22Be merciful to those who doubt; 23snatch others from the fire and save them; to others show mercy, mixed with fear—hating even the clothing stained by corrupted flesh.

24To him who is able to keep you from falling and to present you before his glorious presence without fault and with great joy— 25to the only God our Savior be glory, majesty, power and authority, through Jesus Christ our Lord, before all ages, now and forevermore! Amen.

A THOUGHT: *In trying to find common ground with those to whom we witness, we must be careful not to fall into the quicksand of compromise. When reaching out to others, we must be sure our own footing is safe and secure. Be careful not to become so much like non-Christians that no one can tell who you are or what you believe. Influence them for Christ—don't allow them to influence you to sin!*

Proverbs for Today/ 31:25–31

She [a wife of noble character] is clothed in strength and dignity; she can laugh at the days to come. She speaks with wisdom, and faithful instruction is on her tongue. She watches over the affairs of her household and does not eat the bread of idleness. Her children arise and call her blessed; her husband also, and he praises her: "Many women do noble things, but you surpass them all." Charm is deceptive, and beauty is fleeting; but a woman who fears the LORD is to be praised. Give her the reward she has earned, and let her works bring her praise at the city gate.

Where Can I Find It?

Great Chapters from the New Testament

Great Stories from the New Testament